EVERY JOURNEY MATTERS

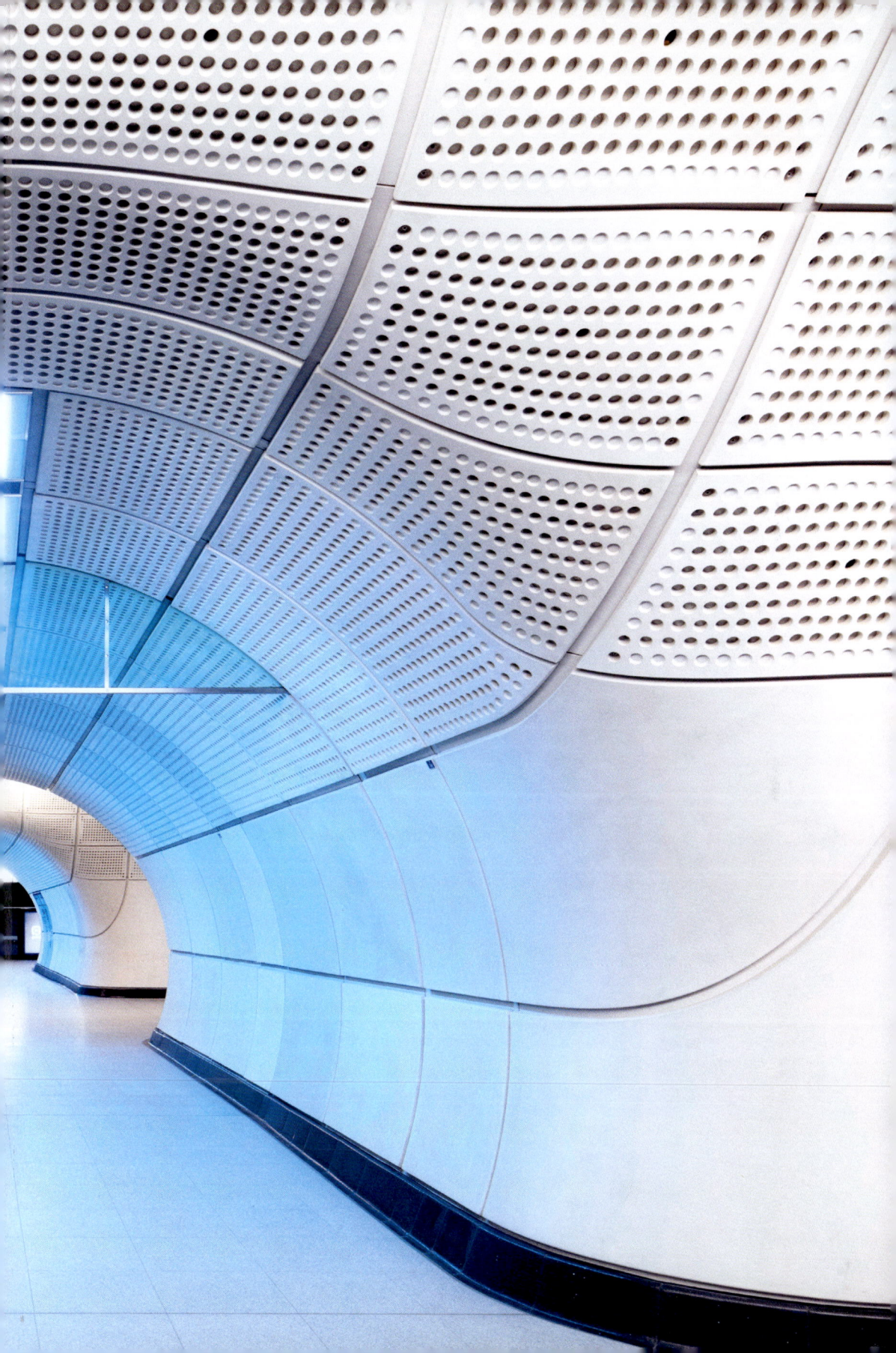

EVERY JOURNEY MATTERS

MOVING LONDON INTO THE 21ST CENTURY

Sam Mullins

PAUL HOLBERTON PUBLISHING

Published in partnership with London Transport Museum, and with thanks to Cubic Transportation Systems for their support

First published in 2025
Text © copyright Sam Mullins and London Transport Museum

ISBN 978-1-917976-02-2
British Library Cataloguing in Publication Data
A catalogue record for this book is available from the British Library

Produced by Paul Holberton Publishing
www.paulholberton.com

Designed by Paul Sloman
Printed by Gomer, Llandysul

Distributed by Yale University Press, New Haven and London
Authorized Representative in the EU: Easy Access System Europe,
Mustamäe tee 50, 10621 Tallinn, Estonia, gpsr.requests@easproject.com

MIX
Paper | Supporting
responsible forestry
FSC
www.fsc.org   FSC® C114687

CONTENTS

FOREWORD

As we mark 25 years since the formation of Transport for London, it is a moment to reflect with pride on the extraordinary journey we have taken together. Since 2000, TfL has been at the heart of London's transformation – supporting jobs, homes, tourism and economic growth, and connecting Londoners to education, employment and leisure.

Our transport network, and the thousands of dedicated colleagues who keep it running every day, are woven into the very fabric of this great city. It is an important point to reaffirm our commitment to delivering a world-leading transport network for the capital.

Over the past 25 years, we have delivered momentous change. From the expansion of the bus network and the introduction of the Oyster card, to the opening of the Elizabeth line and the transformation of cycling infrastructure, TfL has consistently risen to the challenge of a growing and evolving capital.

Millions of Londoners and visitors rely on our services every day, and our achievements have improved how everyone travels, but they have also enhanced lives socially, culturally, economically and environmentally. Transport investment can bring transformative economic and social impact.

While we celebrate the past, we are equally focused on what lies ahead. The next 25 years will bring new challenges and opportunities, and we are committed to delivering the projects that will shape the London of tomorrow. From the introduction of new DLR and Piccadilly line trains to the opening of the Silvertown Tunnel, we are investing in a network that is more sustainable, more accessible, and more resilient.

Our vision is clear: a transport system that supports a thriving, inclusive London and contributes to the prosperity of the UK as a whole. We are excited to continue this journey with you – our passengers, partners and communities – as we build a future that works for everyone and strive to become the strong, green heartbeat for the city.

Thank you for being part of our story.

Andy Lord
Commissioner, Transport for London

INTRODUCTION

"The work to the Underground was a significant part of civilizing the city. If things are well designed, people feel happier and more engaged with them."
– Frank Pick (1878–1941), vice chair and CEO, London Transport

In 2025, Transport for London (TfL) passed its 25th birthday, the longest-lasting of the capital's transport authorities since the creation of London Transport in 1933. Looking back, it is already hard to put ourselves on public transport in the London of the 1990s, before the changes of the past three decades. Transport journeys in the capital then involved the friction of cash transactions and coin-operated machines to purchase pasteboard tickets and travelcards, printed timetables for buses and trains, queues for season ticket renewals, the uncertainty of when the next bus or tube train might arrive, when bicycles were essentially for leisure and when passengers bought and read daily and evening newspapers on their commute. In other words, a transport world without smartphones, real-time information or contactless payments – an entirely analogue system. There was also no Overground, no Elizabeth or Jubilee extension lines, no electric or hybrid buses. Public transport in London at TfL's inception in 2000 was crowded, poorly regarded, unreliable, a necessary discomfort for its citizens and desperately in need of advocacy and accountability, investment and upgrade. So, how has the 'London model' worked since 2000?

TfL was brought into being in a world where traffic congestion, passenger numbers and consumer expectations had risen inexorably year on year since the mid-1980s. The omens were not good in July 2000 as the Greater London Authority (GLA) and its transport arm TfL were brought into existence: Tube investment was to be funded through a public–private partnership (PPP) which would take a further three years to negotiate to contract; Crossrail had been mothballed; the bus fleet was still dependent in central London on the open-platform Routemaster, the Jubilee line extension had opened on New Year's Eve having overrun its budget; the new mayor was a left-wing radical and the mayoralty itself an entirely unknown quantity.

London is an old city. Its plumbing, sewers, water and gas pipes and its arteries, roads, railways and waterways, were all laid down during the city's rise to world city status as the metropolitan centre of the British Empire in the second half of the 19th century. London was the first city to take advantage of the innovations of the industrial age, and to access the benefits of concentrating services and infrastructure together in what we now call agglomeration. During the century to 1914, in response to the economic benefits of such proximity, the population of London grew six times. By the first decade of the 20th century, this old city had developed many of the features we now associate with the modern city, notably an urban transport network with red buses and trams criss-crossing its streets, electric underground tube railways, commuter railways which prompted suburban expansion, even the roundel brand, network maps and colourful posters. London is a city whose personality continues to be formed by its transport; the Underground roundel, Johnston typeface, red buses, Harry Beck's map, Tube stations and Mind the Gap announcements. Through the 20th century transport continued to be the engine and the enabler of London's growth and prosperity, both the city's brand and its barometer.

The government and funding of transport was in a state of regular governance flux, from the private companies of the Victorian and Edwardian years to a public corporation, London Transport, in 1933, nationalization after the war, devolution to the Greater London Council in 1963 and back into central government control in 1984. In 2000, with the creation of the new GLA and an elected mayor, transport was to be devolved to a London-wide body once more. A small group of visionary civil servants and the minister for London, Nick Raynsford, designed the new authority for London, taking evidence and lessons from elected mayoralties in Europe and the United States. They laid out a model with two critical London-wide functions: integrated transport and strategic planning. Where London Transport had responsibility for Underground and buses, the new TfL also embraced the strategic road network, trams and Docklands Light Railway, taxis and private hire, walking, cycling and river services and the powers to operate an integrated public transport network.

Since its creation in 2000, TfL has had responsibility for delivering day-to-day transport operations as well as supporting the big picture painted by the London Plan for the capital's future. Against the rapid pace of societal and digital changes, much has been achieved since, despite the challenges of an old city, by respecting its personality, by going with its grain, its historical legacy.

Now, as we emerge into the changed and changing post-Covid world, the 25th anniversary of the founding of TfL occasions reflection on the central role of transport in the health, success and resilience of a world city and of the transport leaders who have pursued service and technical innovation for the city since 2000.

While it is too soon for a full-scale history, my experience of the power of oral history, of first-person human stories, suggested that an initial history of TfL could be made through the testimony and insights of those who had been instrumental in its creation and leadership. TfL is highly regarded among city and transport executives worldwide for the integration of all modes of transport and strategic planning to support living and working in London. There is an interest in cities across the world in TfL's city leadership and management, in its innovation in service delivery and the application of technology. How did TfL take the opportunity its integrated model offered, and how and why were decisions taken, risks assessed, and innovations made at particular moments in time?

This method also reveals the human dimension of leadership in a major public institution such as TfL. From the outside, this organization might appear to be a behemoth, a large and faceless bureaucracy without personality, feelings or values. From within TfL, I have always been struck by the high degree of personal commitment to public service I encountered. The men and women I worked alongside and was privileged to interview are deeply committed to the purpose of keeping London on the move and facilitating Londoners' pursuit of work, leisure and education. The seven-day-week operational imperative means constant accountability to Londoners and to the mayor. Transport leaders are perennially presented with myriad daily challenges: extreme weather, major events management, technical failure, accidents, the political tide. There is no hiding place when a Tube line falls over, a cyclist loses their life or gridlock brings the city to a halt. Transport executives carry an hourly responsibility to those who pay for their services. Such a challenge renders being a transport leader the toughest and most accountable of leadership roles, and this industry is a meritocracy from top to bottom. At a time when Post Office and water company executives, to name but two, are being exposed as having lost sight of those they serve, this is a study in commitment and accountability to the transport system's customers and stakeholders, and to building a culture which promotes and sustains that commitment.

In explaining my purpose to those I interviewed and with whom I discussed this project, I typically cited how little we really know about those two titans of London Transport, Lord Ashfield and Frank Pick, who created the Underground Combine before 1914 and carried their vision for an urban transport system into the creation of London Transport in 1933 – a vision of much more than mere mobility, a civilizing agenda for London. Just fancy, if we had recorded interviews on a crackling wax cylinder or a vinyl disc with them and their colleagues in the 1920s and 1930s about how they worked together, their decisions and leadership styles, their contacts with the politicians of the day, their motives and values; but alas, for Ashfield and Pick, two hugely influential figures in the shaping of the capital, we have to rely upon official documents, newspaper accounts and occasional published articles. This project will provide the historians of the future a ringside seat at the TfL table at moments of crisis, of pressure, of innovation, of strategy, amidst the daily challenge of keeping London on the move.

The legacy of Ashfield and Pick is not heritage in aspic but a philosophy for the power of design that is not merely decorative but fit for purpose, manifested in TfL's commitment to design – the roundel, the Johnston font, station architecture from

Leslie Green to the Elizabeth line, the Routemaster, the new Routemaster, from the 1938 Tube stock to new trains for the Piccadilly line. TfL is supported in this mission by the world's leading museum of urban transport, the London Transport Museum, which in its collections and exhibitions demonstrates how the past has shaped the present, and how we in the present day are shaping the future city.

Consequently, in an era of boundless digital and ephemeral output, we have taken the opportunity to record the leaders and innovators, to encourage them to reflect on their time and experiences within TfL, an organization that as a transport network in a city of nine million people obliges them to live very much in the moment, in the day-to-day of getting people in and out, across and through the metropolis. How was this decision taken, from where or whom did the initiative come, how did this moment feel at the time and would they do it differently if they had their time again?

This book is the first word and not the last on TfL's story. The chapters are both chronological and thematic in their approach, narrating to a timeline and diving deeper into key themes and moments in the story. As we approach the present day, my interviewees step back, less willing to make a judgement, less able to evaluate what still feels contemporary rather than history.

Others will follow to research and write the definitive history of TfL. It is my hope that the verbatim transcripts of interviews conducted for this project, quarried and edited for clarity to form the narrative of this book, will preserve the personal motivations, the reflections and regrets, the triumphs and tribulations, within TfL's organizational frame of those who have kept London on the move as the dynamo of the UK economy and have enabled it to remain a rich and varied place in which to live and work in the early 21st century.

ACKNOWLEDGEMENTS

The experts on TfL's first 25 years are my interviewees. I have a historical perspective as the London Transport Museum director, a witness of these years and with a mission to collect the recent past in the interests of posterity, but I am a well-placed historian not a transport executive. This is the opportunity, as an observer of LT and TfL from the inside, for the movers and shakers of London's transport to tell me their story and to tell it while it is fresh in their memories, in their own words and from their own perspectives. Most have enjoyed the opportunity to reflect on their careers and the big moments they have faced; some even likened it to being on the therapist's couch.

My profound thanks go to the interviewees who have indulged me with their time and trusted me with their memories and insights for deployment in this book as well as in the record for posterity. There were moments when there was a request for confidentiality or for the recording to be paused. The limitation of near-contemporary histories is inevitably the loyalty and responsibility my respondents have to colleagues, politicians and predecessors, particularly as we approach contemporary issues and times. They have been consulted on being directly quoted, and have had an opportunity to see how their testimony has been rendered as part of the TfL story.

The interviewees, in alphabetical order, are: Heidi Alexander, Steve Allen, Jennette Arnold, Harry Barlow, Andy Barr, Prof. David Begg, Maggie Boepple, Nick Bowes, Andrew Braddock, David Brown, Ian Brown, Mike Brown, Richard Brown, Andy Byford, Neale Coleman, Leon Daniels, Isabel Dedring, Michèle Dix, Rob Easterby, Vernon Everitt, Mark Evers, Jeremy Fraser, Prof.Stephen Glaister, Baroness Tanni Grey-Thompson, Peter Lord Hendy, John Hill, David Hampson-Ghani, Geoff Hobbs, Jon Hunter, Alexander Jan, Kat Jennings, Boris Johnson, Ken Livingstone, Andy Lord, Martyn Loukes, Chris MacLeod, Anthony Mayer, Anne McMeel, Liz Meek, Charles Monheim, Daniel (Lord) Moylan, Malcolm Murray-Clark, Andy Neather, Vincent Nolan, Will Norman, Patricia Obinna, Tim O'Toole, Richard Parry, Caroline Pidgeon, Ben Plowden, Gareth Powell, Ian Pring, Nick Raynsford, Bridget Rosewell, Richard Rowlands, Lauren Sager Weinstein, Rikesh Shah, Steve Shewmaker, Howard Smith, Hugh Sumner, Valerie Todd, Roger Torode, Prof. Tony Travers, Denis (Lord) Tunnicliffe, Genie Turton, Shashi Verma, Mike Weston, Alex Williams.

The kernel of this project emerged from conversations in 2018 with Shashi Verma, TfL's head of strategy and chief technology officer, who typically brings a historical perspective to his thinking. We were encouraged down this track by Vernon Everitt, then TfL MD for Customers, Communication and Technology and a trustee of the London Transport Museum, with ready support from the former TfL commissioner Peter (Lord) Hendy and his successors Mike Brown, Andy Byford and Andy Lord.

The early commitment of Simon Banks and David Wear at Cubic Transportation Systems has been crucial to the writing and publication of this book. As TfL's long-term ticketing partners since 1998, the role of Cubic in the development of the Oyster card and contactless payments is a key part of TfL's story. Cubic's corporate support of the London Transport Museum since 1984 and our book for the Underground's 150th anniversary in 2013 has been followed with a long-term commitment through the Covid years to this history of TfL, for which I am personally most grateful.

Tony Travers, director of LSE London, has consistently encouraged me to make a book and not just an archive. He has generously contributed a counterfactual Afterword, which draws on his long experience of London government. Most historians do not have their principal sources looking over their shoulder, so the advice and comments on 'their' chapters by Leon Daniels, Vernon Everitt, Stephen Glaister, Peter Hendy, Alexander Jan, Chris Macleod, Charles Monheim, Will Norman, Roger Torode, Tony Travers, Shashi Verma, Andy Lord and Alex Williams have given me essential feedback and helpful promptings. My colleagues at the LT Museum have been endlessly supportive: notably Claire Williamson, Simon Murphy, Chris Nix, Wesley Salton, Molly Jackson and Caterina Tiezzi, with support from Emma, Caroline, Emma and Katy, and notably my successor as director Elizabeth McKay. Errors and misjudgements are of course entirely my responsibility as author.

Finally, in shaping the final edit, Candida Hunt has been a wise and measured deployer of the editorial red pen and scalpel, which I have much appreciated; she has made this a much better book. I would also like to acknowledge Paul Sloman, who designed the book, Jo Walton for her picture research, and my publisher Paul Holberton for his timely encouragement.

David Bownes, Michael Day, Stephen Feber, Diane Lees, Steph Mastoris and Finbarr Whooley have been good and critical friends, encouraging my balancing of museum director and historian. Manifestly, none of this would have happened without the support of my wife Meg Andrews, who urged me to apply to be director of London Transport Museum in 1994, and of my sternest critics and greatest fans, Edward and Kate Mullins.

Sam Mullins
Dalston, London, July 2025

1.

SHAPING LONDON'S GOVERNMENT FOR THE 21ST CENTURY

"You don't have to be very fanciful to see that Mrs Thatcher created the office of mayor of London … If the GLC hadn't been abolished, there'd be no mayor of London. So Mrs Thatcher is the accidental grandparent of Ken Livingstone as mayor of London."

– Professor Tony Travers, 2020[1]

Providing an effective and sustainable transport network for a world city demands political support and funding as much as high-order transport management. After the abolition of the Greater London Council in 1986 by Prime Minister Margaret Thatcher, London was left without control over its own government or accountability for London Transport; this was to be remedied by the creation of the Greater London Authority, led by an elected mayoralty and with all modes of transport devolved to its direction. Devolved governance for London created a new agency, Transport for London, integrating functions from 15 previous agencies including London Transport. The key design work for this was done within the Government Office for London in the late 1990s. In May 2000, London elected Ken Livingstone as its first mayor with key manifesto commitments for a congestion charge, an improved bus network and public ownership of the Tube.

From GLC to GLA via GOL

London-wide governance had first been instituted in 1855 when the Metropolitan Board of Works (MBW) was set up to bring together some one hundred parish vestries and boroughs, purposed to upgrade infrastructure across the city. The board's most notable works included Joseph Bazelgette's sewer system, the building of the Embankment, and slum clearance for new streets such as

Engraving of section through the Embankment at Cannon Street, 1867, showing the sub-surface Metropolitan District railway alongside Bazelgette's sewer

the Aldwych. Mired in accusations of corrupt procurement, some proven, the 'Metropolitan Board of Perks' was replaced by the London County Council (LCC) in 1889, the largest UK local authority of its day, with powers that extended across education, city planning and public housing.

The third London-wide authority, the Greater London Council (GLC), succeeded the LCC in 1965. This new strategic authority had been designed following the Royal Commission Report of 1960, which recommended expanding the boundaries of Greater London better to embrace the capital's spread into Essex, Hertfordshire and Kent and to amalgamate the capital's hundred-plus local authorities – the county, municipal and metropolitan boroughs, and urban districts. From 1965 the GLC was responsible for London Transport (LT), transferred to the GLC from the nationalized British Transport Commission in 1970 while other public service delivery remained the responsibility of the newly grouped 32 boroughs, alongside the City of London. London Transport was then lost back to central government control in 1984, in anticipation of the abolition of the GLC.

The abolition of the GLC in 1986 was the response of a partisan Conservative prime minister, Margaret Thatcher, who held a deep mistrust of local authorities, to the provocations of a GLC Labour leader in Ken Livingstone. From his election as leader in 1981 Livingstone had "declared his intention of using the GLC as a platform to oppose the government more effectively than the Party was able to do in Parliament".[2] The GLC may not have been perfect – it was certainly at odds with the

Thatcher government's view of the world – "but abolishing it was a short-sighted act of political spite" her biographer John Campbell suggests, "which left behind worse problems than it solved".[3]

It is now difficult to conceive of London without an elected mayor and with its transport network directed from Whitehall. Yet London in the 1990s was just such a world. LT operated the Tube and buses as the delivery arm of the Department for Transport; other agencies were tasked with planning, strategic roads, streets, police, ambulances, walking, the river, cycling and taxis. In the 1990s LT was an organization in recovery from the low point of the King's Cross fire of 1987, further challenged by a rapid growth in public transport ridership from the mid-1980s. LT's leadership was hobbled by short-term funding, financial annuality, deference to national and ministerial politics, and ultimate accountability to civil servants. Thanks to the financial overrun of the Jubilee line extension (JLE), which opened on Millennium Night, 31 December 1999, its successor TfL was also to be saddled with the Treasury's and Chancellor Gordon Brown's implacable pursuit of the public–private partnership (PPP) model to finance and deliver the comprehensive upgrade urgently needed by the Underground.

The abolition of the GLC in 1986 had been an especially high tide for the centralizing tendency of Whitehall government, the dominant feature of UK governance through the 20th and into the present century. Although replaced by a raft of joint committees and boards nominated by the London boroughs, the strategic direction of the capital, including that of LT, was determined by central government. In the only Western capital without elected city-wide government, borough collaborations were difficult and rare; across transport and London's economic development, planning, policing and the environment, the city lacked co-ordinated strategic direction and advocacy. This gap was partially filled from 1994 by the creation of a Government Office for London (GOL) headed by a minister for London. Initially this was John Gummer, the secretary of state for the environment. After the 1997 general election brought in Tony Blair's New Labour, Nick Raynsford, a London councillor, MP and front-bench spokesman for London, became minister for London with responsibility for restoring democratic city-wide government to the capital – in his words, "replacing not replicating the GLC".[4]

Since the mid-1980s and the Big Bang, the deregulation of the City's finance sector in 1986, London's inner-city population had begun to grow once more after decades of decline since the war, from 8.6 million in 1939 to 6.8 million in 1981. This was driven by the performance of the capital's economy and a renewed interest in urban living. After the recession of the early 1990s, the financial and services sectors – administration, retail, professional, legal, accountancy, consultancy and scientific, information, communication and culture – boomed through the decade. From some 670 million a year in the 1950s, passenger numbers had declined on

Packed Northern line at Tottenham Court Road station, June 1990

A low point for London: the ticket hall and top of the escalators at King's Cross in the aftermath of the 1987 fire

the Underground to a low point of 498 million in 1982, but then saw strong year-on-year growth to 970 million by 2001–01.[5] The absence of a strategic framework for the capital, and of a controlling mind to respond to the pressures of growth across all modes of transport, was especially evident for the long-term horizons demanded by major transport investments such as the Overground and Crossrail, let alone supporting a credible bid to host the Olympic Games.

Minding the strategic gap

"… the London agenda [for devolution] was to a very large degree a blank sheet of paper … the structure of the new authority, how it would be elected, what powers it would have, and how these were to be exercised, all had to be determined."

– Nick Raynsford, Minister for London 1997–996

Genie Turton, as director of the GOL from 1997, was the senior civil servant responsible for designing the Greater London Authority (GLA). Turton remembers how the abolition of the GLC had left a vacuum in the capital. "London needed leadership … the absence of any leadership in London and the ridiculous situation where London was represented by 33 squabbling boroughs, rather than any coherence of policy … however good the minister for London was and however caring and however dedicated, they had no London democratic mandate."[7]

Liz Meek worked with Turton in the GOL on the design of the GLA Act; as a civil servant she had already lived through the lean years when "boroughs didn't talk to each other in the seven years or so after the abolition of GLC."[8] The arrival of John Gummer[9] as the first minister for London in 1993 was designed to placate the increasingly effective lobbying of London business for government planning and strategy for the capital. "London First, Alan Sheppard and business were fed up with government. It's why the Conservatives had a minister for London."[10] This led to GOL initiatives in which "boroughs were obliged to work together, on the Hungerford Bridge or London Pride … getting local authorities to talk to each other and work together and getting them to talk to businesses, because they had retreated into their shells." Gummer cared about London, had the instincts of a mayor and acted as a figurehead. "He went about tossing pancakes on theatre stages and opening bridges. He was also very good with London Pride[11] and London First, substituting for the strategic authority we didn't have at the time."[12]

The creation of a London-wide authority to replace the loss of the GLC had been advocated increasingly persuasively by the business community, and notably articulated by Alan Sheppard and London First (established in 1992, now BusinessLDN) on their behalf "to make London the best city in the world". Back in the 1990s, London's prospects looked bleak. Business leaders came together to lead when others would not; "with the capital's population reaching a historic low for modern times, London was at risk of being overshadowed by other European cities".[13] World city was not a description used of 1990s London; public transport was lagging behind the capital's growth and was a potential brake on London's position in a rapidly globalizing world.

For better London-wide public transport, a single body empowered to take a strategic approach joining up all modes of transport into an integrated plan was needed. The future mayor's ownership of both the London Plan and transport would enable a key lock-up between London's economic development and the transport infrastructure and services needed to deliver. Devolution for London and the creation of TfL was to prove crucial to the city's economic performance. TfL would be able to target investment to support growth and regeneration, take a joined-up approach to seamless journeys from home to destination, and above all be accountable to the mayor and the London electorate. Transport was to prove the most powerful delivery agency in the new mayoralty's armoury.

The question of devolution for London

At the *Evening Standard* London Debate on 28 April 1998, broadcast that evening on BBC's *Newsnight*, Prime Minister Tony Blair put the case for the devolution of London government and an elected mayor as the mayoral referendum on 28 May 1998 approached:

I believe having a directly elected mayor can help make London a city that we can really be proud of, a city that is economically prosperous, a city where we tackle crime and poverty properly, a city with a transport system that operates effectively and one that our citizens are proud to use ... Why, therefore, is it important that we alter the structure of government in London? ... Whether it's on transport or crime or jobs or the environment, the mayor will have the power to make a difference and will be expected by Londoners to do so. It's also the right innovation. We have taken the steps to give you the chance to make it happen. Use that chance.[14]

Devolution had entered the national political discourse in the 1990s, largely in response to the growing influence of nationalism in Scotland and Wales, rather than as a strategic solution for the revival of London-wide governance. For New Labour from 1997 the deputy prime minister, John Prescott, was a powerful advocate for devolution to regional assemblies. His Department for the Environment, Transport and the Regions (DETR) brought together and integrated key parts of Whitehall, which eased the creation of a new London authority.

Tony Travers, director of LSE London and London governance specialist, recalls that devolution had been a growing theme for Labour in opposition "It was seen as a way of warding off nationalism, because nationalism in parallel had been growing [during]18 years of Conservative government, the sense of alienation, the Scottish National Party (SNP) definitely growing ... Blair is explicit about it in his autobiography, it was seen as a way of killing nationalism."[15]

"By the end of the 20th century the levers of power were overwhelmingly held in London and Westminster," reflected Nick Raynsford, the minister responsible for creating devolved government for London; and whereas much thinking had been done on devolved government for Scotland, "the London agenda was largely a blank sheet of paper" due to a fundamental disagreement in New Labour about which model to follow.[16]

Simon Jenkins, journalist and editor of the *Evening Standard* from 1976 to 1978 and of *The Times* from 1990 to 1992, believes Blair was converted to devolution in 1995; Jenkins had chaired a commission on local democracy, and the one thing that came up repeatedly was mayoralty as a dominant force – in France, in Germany, in the US. He had worked for John Lindsay (mayor of New York 1966–73); "he was very impressive, far ahead of anything we had in England". Jenkins wanted to know why London couldn't have one of these people.

But when I met with Blair he was quite hostile to the idea ... he was worried about local parties and local leaders and Labour-led councils who didn't like him and he didn't like. I remember saying that the whole point about local mayors is that in a sense they supplant local politics. He said, 'What do you mean?' I said, 'Well, anyone can stand for mayor. You normally stand with a party's support, but anyone can stand, including independents. And either way, because it's a direct election, if you decide to stand as a mayor, you're going to have to be reasonably plausible and charismatic in your own right.' And Blair almost leapt out of his chair; he bought it lock, stock and barrel."[17]

At the 1997 general election, the Labour manifesto included for the first time a commitment to devolution for London:

London is the only Western capital without an elected city government. Following a referendum to confirm popular demand, there will be a new deal for London, with a strategic authority and a mayor, each directly elected. Both will speak up for the needs of the city and plan its future. They will not duplicate the work of the boroughs, but take responsibility for London-wide issues – economic regeneration, planning, policing, transport and environmental protection. London-wide responsibility for its own government is urgently required. We will make it happen.[18]

Devolution for London was realized following the 1997 election through Blair's support and the vision for regional government of John Prescott. An influential advocate of devolution for the English regions, Prescott had commissioned work on the case for regional authorities in England after the 1997 election victory, based on the tiering of authorities in Germany that had been put in place by Britain after the Second World War to counter the re-emergence of an over-mighty central state. Old Labour in instinct, Prescott was not keen on elected executive mayors, favouring the municipal model, but loyalty to Blair overcame his preference. For Prescott, not being able to set up regional assemblies in England was the biggest disappointment in his political career.[19]

Professor Stephen Glaister, transport economist and later a board member of TfL, recognized that in the devolution debate, London was a secondary consideration:

Blair was talking about a devolution agenda for Scotland and Wales, as well as London. It was all in the same breath, creating sovereign bodies of some kind, crucially with their own income. The part that never happened, but I think was originally conceived by Blair, was a much more autonomous London, from a money point of view. The only bit that survived Brown and the Treasury, once they got going, was the congestion charge as the one source of income of which the mayor eventually got full control. But as soon as the Labour government got into power and started to draft that legislation, the Treasury got very active in stopping all the financial independence of the body as it was being formed.[20]

Nick Raynsford, as minister for London from 1997 to 1999, worked up a detailed model for London's governance and then delivering it in the GLA Act. The redesign of the government of a world city was an intriguing and challenging opportunity.

Raynsford's view, informed by experience as a Greenwich borough councillor, London MP and shadow minister for London, was that centralized governance after 1986 was not working well for the capital; that the "spaghetti of different bodies" was unsustainable and without democratic oversight, but he also recognized that the old GLC had been bureaucratic and "seen as over-mighty by the boroughs".[21]

John Prescott's advocacy of the mayoralty was part of his broader vision for enhanced public transport. Turton believes that this "has been obscured because he didn't cultivate journalists. I used to say to him that he was very much like Michael Heseltine, because he had some real long-term vision beyond tomorrow … He really cared about transport. I think he was just misguided about pushing a central government-driven PPP rather than letting the new mayor decide … he didn't see that it did not fit with having an executive mayor of London who is going to be accountable."[22]

By contrast with devolution for Scotland, very little work had been undertaken on the design of devolution for London before the general election, not least because Labour itself was divided between the municipal and executive mayoral models. In the event, proponents of the municipal model of governance, such as Frank Dobson, were swept aside by Blair's enthusiasm for a directly elected mayor and strategic authority, supported by Prescott's vision of devolution for the English regions. As the new minister for London in 1997, Raynsford found he "had a blank sheet of paper. There was a commitment to the creation of a democratically elected city-wide authority and a presumption this would be a streamlined strategic body authority and not a large bureaucracy as had the former GLC, for all its virtues, been widely perceived. But as to the structure of the new authority, how it would be elected, what powers it would have and how these were to be exercised, all this had to be determined."[23]

Designing government for London

"It was a remarkable opportunity that I seized with great enthusiasm … the work needed to be completed to an incredibly tight timetable."

– Nick Raynsford, minister for London from 1997[24]

A high-calibre civil service team moved quickly, initially under the head of the GOL, Robin Young, and then his successor Genie Turton. The decision to have the elections in May 2000 posed a significant deadline:

> In fact it was quite unusual for central government to have an immoveable deadline. We brought in Ernst & Young to run a programme office for us. We had something like twenty-seven key projects, all of which had to happen by May 2000, one of which was setting up an interim organization for TfL and procuring

a building. There were some really big decisions and we had to run the [mayoral] election, which we'd never done before, so there were a whole series of things to deliver to a tight timetable with no get-out.[25]

Turton herself was an enthusiast for better London government.

Liz [Meek] and I were both involved in London in the nineties ... We all got to know London First and Alan Sheppard and co., and saw actually that London needed leadership ... Nick [Raynsford] himself, he cared with a passion ... I'd met and worked with him on housing before, there was a lot of sympathy. I also think, because of the relatively dismissive attitude within central government, when London Transport needed a new chair people said, 'Oh, it's not important, there are many more important things.' Actually, London is important.[26]

With solid political support, and with transport and the regions being within Prescott's portfolio, the design of a new authority for London proceeded at a rapid pace towards the target date of May 2000 for the first mayoral election. Liz Meek headed the GOL team whose job, starting three months before the general election, was to flesh out the 1997 election commitment into a proposal. "We took that paragraph in the manifesto as absolute gospel ... that was the Bible as far as we were concerned. We very quickly moved to a green paper referendum on that basis."[27]

When she became director of GOL, Turton found that Liz Meek, knowing it was tight, was already on the case to get the thing legislated and up and running by 2000 ... "We knew that we had to do things that were taking power away from Whitehall departments. The only time you can possibly do that is in the first flush of an election victory and before secretaries of state become totally captured by their departments and defend their patches." Turton regarded this as probably the best job in Whitehall at the time:

There's nothing like inventing or working with good ministers, with a prime minister who cared and who was accessible, and with a policy that was popular. Liz and I were reinventing the governance of the city that I lived in and loved ... If we had a question, Liz would ring Pat McFadden, who was Tony Blair's advisor, and it was almost as if he opened the door to Tony Blair's office and said, 'Tony, that woman's asking, what do we do about the Queen?' We'd get an answer back saying 'Don't touch the Queen' or whatever the issue was; we had fantastic access.[28]

For Liz Meek, Raynsford's intellectual skills and his powers to be reasonable and persuade were just what were needed:

Nick Raynsford was a stunningly competent minister, intellectually all there, he knew his subject and he was tenacious. He reported to John Prescott, who in his bones didn't like this mayor business, and certainly didn't like fancy forms of suffrage, didn't like the single transferable vote we had in mind. He kind of writhed a bit internally when we had to put submissions to him about which voting system shall we go for and what are the pros and cons. But I became a great admirer of him because he was fantastic, with really [sound] political instincts.[29]

Meek and the team worked through all the options in a short time. "We were going to have a mayoralty, a strong mayor – that was in the manifesto; it was going to be strategic, and it wasn't going to be running things … So the territory it could occupy was quite thin and quite high up. It was doing top-level stuff, strategic planning. Transport was a bit odd because it's both top level and also bottom level, so it doesn't quite work. But the idea was that it shouldn't ever duplicate anything boroughs did if that could be avoided." [30]

Meek recollects meeting Raynsford on his first day as minister. "On day one we had a sort of quiz; we said, 'Okay, Assembly, what size?' I think he said 25 or he may have said between 25 and 30, or something like that. We got [his] instinctive judgement on 63 questions and actually that's what we factored into the green paper. He answered those and we pretty much stuck to them."[31]

Because of the paramount need for strategic leadership for London, running schools, housing and homelessness, public health and waste management were dropped in this high-level model for the mayoralty. "We were different … we wanted leadership for London, above all else, and a plan for London," Meek said. This led to a model in which there was deliberately a very strong mayor and a very weak Assembly. "I did make myself very unpopular by saying that it was quite deliberate to have an Assembly that really couldn't overturn the will of the mayor, unless the mayor was barking mad, basically." London ended up with a model that is both weak and strong; it doesn't run a wide range of services, which were largely left to the boroughs, but it is strong because the mayor really could do what he wanted. "There was a cunning provision in the Act that gave the mayor the power to do anything that he wasn't prohibited by some other statute from doing. That allowed him to meddle and do things as long as he absolutely wasn't prevented from doing so. To advocate on the Olympics came out of that thought, [of]a leadership role for London."[32]

The team at GOL reviewed other mayoral models as part of its research on all the moving parts needed for constructing the new London authority. Visits were made to cities in Europe and North America, interviewing powerful figureheads in Rome, New Orleans, Washington and Toronto, as Genie Turton recalled:

I remember meeting the very charismatic mayor of Rome, Francesco Rutelli. 'I have no powers at all,' he said, 'but people believe that I have.' The example of the Washington mayor's jail sentence did lead to the London mayor's budget requiring a two-thirds majority. The MP for Brent East and future mayor of London, Ken Livingstone, was a sceptic at this point, dismissing it as 'just another example of New

Labour's obsession with all things American'; I pointed out that over fifty American mayors were in prison for fraud ... I was totally opposed to a mayoral system.[33]

Meek knew they were making history as they created a mayoral model for London. "The local government, traditional local government [people] did not like it, for the reason that we don't do single powerful people, [we select] the leader from the majority party ... Nick Raynsford and I did a tour, we went to Cologne, and Paris, and then Washington, which was interesting, and Boston, and New York... one of the key issues was how powerful should the mayor be and how weak should the Assembly be?"[34]

Travers was amazed by the speed at which the mayoral proposal was worked up. "The general election took place in May [1997]. In mid-July, just over eight weeks later, they published the green paper [which] proved to be an accurate reflection of the legislation and what eventually emerged. That was a remarkable piece of work ... that Labour government had managed to produce this green paper and separately equivalent ones about Scotland and Wales within two months. Remarkable ... Raynsford was 99 per cent of the ministerial effort."[35]

Turton recollects that by no means all they had envisioned was eventually realized. The Treasury was always nervous about money, and securing the hypothecation for congestion charging proved quite a victory; "our defence always was, we want a genuine accountability. That's the comparison with the GLC, because the GLC did have a lot of power, but where was the accountability? ... By having a single person who is elected who is held to account by an Assembly, in a very real sense, was a very important check on powers." What the designers of the GLA did not anticipate was that the Assembly would be partisan and would divide on party lines. Perhaps most significantly of all, they did not anticipate party politicians as mayor: "We thought we might get politicians as mayor, but we didn't think that there would be a party. We didn't really plan for party candidates in the same way. I suppose we were a bit naive in that respect. The idea was to get a collective group of people who really cared about London, and who have some interests and expertise on London who would hold the mayor to account."[36]

Turton remembers drafting the bill being a battle. "We enthusiasts, Nick and his civil servants, wanted a powerful mayor. It was a question of getting what we could get and fighting every bit of ground. We tried to get suburban railways in, for example, and failed ... You're trying to work to a timetable, trying to get the important things. Transport was the important battle and you could say in a way we lost that because of the PPP. Some of that we lost, but at least we got the control, we got TfL."[37]

Undoubtedly the key power wrung from a reluctant Treasury for the future TfL was the ability to retain the income from a congestion charge, which was to be a flagship project for the first mayor. Prescott's pioneering environmental vision for UK cities included, among other things, British cities adopting road charging. "It was part of a much bigger picture that was all being developed at the same time. He really wanted to get [national] congestion charging in and he tried to get a transport bill – it must have been in 1997 to 1998 – he was turned down … and he was very upset. We were having a meeting with him, and I said, 'Why don't we put it in the London bill?' 'Oh,' he said, 'all right, let's do that' … so it went into the London bill and if it hadn't, it would not have happened."[38] Turton is clear that it was John Prescott who convinced Gordon Brown of the need for hypothecation – that proceeds from a congestion charge could be spent only on public transport. Despite Blair's last-minute message for Prescott not to promise it "ten minutes before I was to make a statement in the House … I ignored the message and went ahead," Prescott later recalled.[39]

Just as the GOL team was bringing the draft GLA bill together to its tight timeline, the PPP for the Underground was imposed upon them, and came in as an amendment. For Meek,

> It was a shocking thing because it was completely counter to the philosophy of a strong organization for transport controlled by the mayor, as well as being a very bad idea from all sorts of practical and financial perspectives … I hope somebody somewhere has worked out how many billions were wasted on it and what one might have bought with it … It was nine filing cabinets full of contractual documents that added up to such a mess nobody could operate it at all.[40]

PPP for the Underground

Labour had been in opposition for a long time, and had spent years developing policies on a whole series of things. Turton perceived that this had been done in pockets, with ideas such as regional development agencies, devolution and the PPP "being developed entirely without the fact that we're going to have a mayor".[41]

"There was a sort of time bomb tucked away in the manifesto," which Meek and the team ignored for some time, "because Ken Livingstone was not going to win. I remember being told that by Pat McFadden.[42] They were quite relaxed and then suddenly, when it became more clear how the cookie was going to crumble and as Gordon Brown started looking for the things that he'd wanted to do that hadn't been done, up popped this thing, and we were told we had to amend everything and allow for a PPP."[43]

Travers recalls, "The PPP add-on required a massive amount of amendment put down in the Commons in the committee stage … it was definitely tacked on to the bill so as to allow, effectively, the government to limit what the mayor could do with transport, even though they were handing the mayor power over this."[44]

Despite pushbacks on housing and suburban rail, Travers maintains that "the GLA and its transport arm TfL ended up with a more comprehensive portfolio of responsibilities for London's transport than any of its predecessor bodies – LT,

London Regional Transport (LRT) – who were limited to bus and Tube, with no control over the roads, bus lanes, river services, taxis or private hire". Travers sees this as very much the spirit of the age, reunifying London Transport with city-wide government, filling the vacuum between 1986 and the late 1990s. "Against that backdrop, it was reverting to the GLC LT model from 1970 to 1984, in a sense undoing the Thatcher dismantling which had first taken LRT out of the GLC and then abolished the GLC and then the ILEA [Inner London Education Authority]."[45]

"The mayor has got really quite extraordinary [powers]" was the judgement of transport economist Stephen Glaister. "There are lots of things he doesn't have power over, but there are some things he has personal power over: setting fares is one and setting the congestion charge is another; it's the mayor that makes that decision. [Blair] was persuaded by Prescott – that was one of the really good things Prescott did, he became convinced in the very early days of the government in 1997 that if you're going to resolve the transport problems of big cities in the UK you have to have road pricing: [that is] step one, correct by the way; step two, you can't introduce it unless the money's ring-fenced … Because it's just politically [toxic], if the money goes into the Exchequer, forget it. You had a really vicious battle with the Treasury over that ring-fencing and won it. That's why the legislation in the GLA Act says the money raised from congestion charging must be spent on transport in the London area … that money is hypothecated and that's very, very unusual in our system."[46]

"It wasn't quite making it up as you go along," reflected Liz Meek, "but it was certainly [fast moving], because the privatization stuff [PPP] was in itself complicated. And then to put the congestion charging on top of all the other things, what powers, exactly how are you going to develop the policy?"[47] Perhaps it is no wonder that the GLA Act ended up as the longest since the Government of India Act of 1935, with 425 sections across twelve chapters.

Raynsford has described this as "a ground-breaking prospectus, very different to the traditional structures of local government and light years away from the GLC … the mayor would have one of the largest mandates in any European country, second only to the president of France, and the opportunity to exercise a powerful influence on the future of our capital city."[48]

Glaister and Travers discussed the GLA as a hybrid of British and American models. "The part of the American model which didn't actually get done properly in my view was the feeble scrutiny of TfL and the mayor by the GLA. I think I'm right, in an America model where it works well, there's much more sharp and effective scrutiny by the Assembly. The mayor is just the executive, and operates with laws passed by the legislature. With this system [i.e. London] the mayor is both the executive and the legislature, and the Assembly was given the powers of a select committee at best."[49]

Although it was a radical new government structure, there were limits to the powers of the mayor, notes Stephen Glaister. "He had very little power over what the boroughs did … I think the point Tony [Travers] makes – I've heard him say this about Bloomberg and New York mayors – is that they achieve an enormous amount more than their statutory powers would, on the face of it, allow them to do, through power and influence and persuasion."[50]

Referendum, May 1998

The green paper of July 1997 was followed by the white paper, the GLA bill, in March 1998 which proposed the referendum for May that year, which asked just this single question: "Are you in favour of the Government's proposals for a Greater London Authority, made up of an elected mayor and a separately elected Assembly?" The Yes vote was 72.01 per cent, the No vote was 27.99 per cent, with a majority for Yes in every London borough, despite a disappointingly low turnout of just 34 per cent.

The London mayoral referendum voted by more than two to one, and strongly and widely across the city's boroughs and political colours, in favour of setting up an elected mayoralty. The GLC had been abolished by Parliament as a political act by the Thatcher government, with no opportunity for Londoners to approve or reject. By seeking approval for the new authority through a referendum, the new GLA was potentially protected from abolition – "given the legitimacy of clear public support" – without at least a further referendum. Until the referendum result in May 1998, the GLA proposals were still opposed by the Conservatives. Subsequently, after such a convincing result they dropped their opposition.

There was to be an executive mayor with oversight by a 25-member Assembly, elected by a single transferable vote. The GLA's remit extended across transport, economic development, strategic planning, police and fire services.[51] Funding powers were limited to a council tax precept and the congestion charge. After 14 years of no regional government, the GLA had wider responsibilities than the old GLC, though less than the Scottish Parliament and Welsh Assembly.[52]

How will a London mayoralty work?

As the GLA bill was being worked up, Turton and the team had tested their homework with a simulation day in the life of the mayor, hosted by Olympia and York on the top floor at Canary Wharf:

> John Snow played the mayor; he would probably be an ideal candidate in some respects. All the key London players came and played their parts – borough leaders, Alan Sheppard and London First; Ian Johnson, a deputy assistant

commissioner of the Yard. We had a narrative that everyone had to play through. Shaun Ley and a guy from the FT did the journalists' commentary throughout, and interviewed people at different stages. There was one [scenario] when Alan Sheppard nearly came to blows with one of the borough leaders – it actually was quite real. We were testing out how the dynamics would work.[53]

The mayoral system was a new system of government, with a single, high-profile individual with the potential to change attitudes and to take decisions that would affect people in different ways. The relationship with the boroughs would be crucial, but was untested. Turton remembers "having a big meeting with some of the local authorities in the wider south-east, and saying, 'What do you want out of a mayor?' They said, 'We want somebody who's going to provide some leadership for the wider south-east, because it's not just London; London is the south-east sometimes'." [54]

This was a period of excitement about the new arrangements for London government. There had been frustration among business leaders about central government not delivering for London. "It wasn't just us pushing for a powerful mayor," Turton reflected. "London First and the borough leaders were quite interesting because there were quite a few borough leaders at the time who were coming to the end of their terms, so they weren't fighting for the boroughs in the way you might have done; they even said, The right thing to do would be, once we've got the mayor, to collapse the 33 boroughs into four. And I said, 'Oh good, are you going to argue that?' 'We are not going to stick our necks out on that.' But again, they were interested in getting it to work."[55]

Within London Transport, planning was in hand for the orderly transition to mayoral government after May 2000. As the PPP came into the picture, LT was divided, the Underground moved to a structure to manage three PPP contracts, two deep tube and one sub-surface. There was uncertainty about the change, particularly among senior executives, about whom the leading candidate Ken Livingstone had been disparaging, describing them as "dullards" whom he would sack if he was elected. In the event it was no surprise that there was to be no continuity between the senior leadership of London Transport and that of Transport for London.

First mayoral campaign, 2000

"I'd rather vote for Jeffrey Archer or even Sadam Hussein than Ken Livingstone."
– Gerald Kauffman, Labour MP, 1998[56]

As there were no precedents for the election of a London mayor, who was best suited to the role – a national politician, a borough leader, a captain of industry or a celebrity? As London had moved from referendum to election campaign, the

GLC transport committee chair Dave Wetzel and leader Ken Livingstone launching their campaign in 1981 at City Hall to promote the use of public transport by reducing fares, following it being ruled illegal by the Law Lords

media proposed and canvassed a broad spectrum of potential candidates, ranging from industry figures such as Richard Branson, British Airways' Bob Ayling and broadcaster Trevor Phillips, to a large cast of Westminster veterans such as Tony Banks, Margaret Hodge, Chris Patten and Simon Hughes. Eventually a list of smaller parties and independents, including briefly Malcolm McLaren, former manager of the Sex Pistols, put their names in the ring. High-profile media-friendly characters such as Livingstone and, for the Conservatives, wealthy author and MP Jeffrey Archer, appealed to the public pollsters as being from outside the party-political mainstream.

Genie Turton recollects hearing people say, "'We don't want to create the GLA as the GLC all over again'. I used to say, 'Oh, don't be silly, you won't see Ken Livingstone within a mile of this!' I had to eat my words over the years. At that stage, of course, Ken was going around saying, 'I'm not going to touch this with a bargepole'."[57] Turton recalls going to "meetings and occasionally Ken would appear and he would always say nothing – you know, just a load of rubbish sort of thing, you won't catch me anywhere near this."[58] Early on, Jeffrey Archer appeared to be the natural candidate for the Conservatives.

The Labour Party machine had scanned far afield and wide within to find an alternative credible candidate. None of the star names from the business world Blair had in mind wanted to stand, nor could Mo Mowlam be persuaded. New Labour's Blairites were desperate to identify an alternative to Ken Livingstone, whose reputation as Red Ken from his GLC days and his unfashionable endorsement of radical left-wing causes had led him to be dubbed by *The Sun* as "the most odious man in Britain" in 1981.[59]

From the GLC and within Parliament, Livingstone had consistently opposed Neil Kinnock, John Smith and now Blair's New Labour centrist policies, and very publicly espoused causes seen then as being 'loony left' – Irish republicanism, LGBT rights, nuclear disarmament, anti-racism. He was seen by Blair as an uncontrollable throwback to the bad old days of Labour, to strife and division. Alastair Campbell's diary for January 2000 records Blair being in a real state about Livingstone; it was the worst of both worlds: "We had a candidate in the ring who can't win [Dobson] and a candidate outside the ring who would probably walk it [Livingstone]."[60]

Eventually, three candidates stood for the Labour nomination in a two-stage race: Livingstone, Frank Dobson and Glenda Jackson. Dobson narrowly won the first ballot, and became the Labour nominee. Livingstone was obliged to run as the independent candidate against Dobson in the run-off, which he also lost. By March 2000, Livingstone had chosen to stand as an independent candidate; Campbell records what a good press he got. "There was a sense running through it that we had really fucked it up. He was running rings around us. The press and TV were doing Livingstone's job for him, using him to kick us."[61]

Peter Hendy, second TfL commissioner (from 2006 to 2015), remains amazed at the mess New Labour got into over their nomination for the mayoralty. "How did they manage to establish the mayoralty without knowing who was going to be the mayor? That must be one of the most outstanding political failures of modern times. Why would you define that job without thinking who might do it? ... Whatever the question was, Frank Dobson wasn't the answer."[62] It demonstrates that for New Labour devolution was above all a response to the Scottish nationalists, not to the urgent need to fill the vacuum in London government.

As time went by, the passage of the GLA bill and the prospect of a mayoral election effected a transformation in Livingstone's view of the mayoralty. This was to be an unusual election. It would share few of the traditional characteristics of borough elections; instead, it would have a franchise of more than eight million, a transferable voting system, electronic counting, with a carefully crafted strategic remit and powers, all as yet untried – the first page of an intriguingly blank book. Prior to the referendum, Livingstone had argued for a choice between an elected mayor and a council. New Labour thought otherwise, and proposed Blair's choice of an elected mayor. As the campaign gathered momentum for a simple 'Yes' or 'No' for an elected mayor, Livingstone became a regular commentator and speaker, and a prominent proponent for the 'Yes' vote. As he recalls:

> The media had fun with Labour's inability to find a suitable candidate. The first television debate in the autumn of 1997 was chaired by Trevor Phillips, with Archer and myself joined by Darcus Howe and the leader of the City of London Corporation, Michael Cassady. As we waited for the audience to vote I realized I actually wanted to win. From that point on, although I expected to be vetoed by Blair, I fought to win. When John Prescott presented his White Paper to the Commons in March 1998, Speaker Betty Boothroyd couldn't contain herself as I said, 'Let me be the first to congratulate the deputy prime minister for placing before us Londoners this radical and exciting new job opportunity'; Prescott's initial smile faded.[63]

Ultimately, "Blair's attempt to martyr Ken Livingstone, like those of Margaret Thatcher," mused Tony Travers, "proved wholly counter-productive. 'Ken' as he was universally known, was seen as an underdog and a London populist. He was also strangely glamorous."[64]

Ken Livingstone's background was as the radical leader of the abolished GLC, a traditional municipal council model. He was out of favour with New Labour, reflecting the Old Labour past Blair was working hard to replace. Unlike more acceptable candidates, Livingstone was a known figure, recognized as a fighter and an advocate for London. "There was massive pressure from the public for me to stand. I couldn't walk down the street without people saying 'Won't you stand?' I also thought, as we've got it, it's coming, at least if I'm there, I'll set it up properly."[65] As the mayoral role emerged, he was first canvassed for his opinions, then became a candidate.

The first mayoral election

On the eve of the election, the editorial in the *Evening Standard* urged voters to vote for Steve Norris and avoid 'the disaster in the making' that was folk hero Ken Livingstone:

> Barring an extraordinary upset, Londoners seem determined to make Mr Ken Livingstone the capital's first directly elected mayor. Rather than a vote for regional government, this will be a vote for defiance of New Labour's manipulation of democracy and show of affection for the most plausible Londoner in the contest. Mr Livingstone is fluent, funny, cheeky, the archetypal loner. Every punch thrown at him by the government's heavyweights, up to and including Mr Gordon Brown's barrage last week, has served only to enhance his popularity.[66]

London Against Racism rally, July 1984; as a GLC member, Livingstone campaigned for many causes, such as anti-racism, then seen as radical, acquiring the media soubriquet 'Red Ken'

At the election on 4 May, in the first round Livingstone polled 39 per cent of the votes to Dobson's 13 per cent, which was only 1.2 per cent ahead of Susan Kramer's for the Liberal Democrats. In the second round, Livingstone ran off against Steve Norris, the former Conservative transport minister, who had been adopted as the Conservative candidate after Jeffrey Archer had been obliged to stand down after being indicted for perjury in February. In the second ballot, Livingstone won by a clear 58 per cent to 42 per cent majority over Norris, and was elected as the first London mayor.

The elected mayoralty was to be a second chance for Livingstone, which he took with vigour and a fresh appreciation of economics and the needs of business, with a long-established appreciation of London, a regular user of its public transport and disillusioned with the "least productive years of my life" in Parliament. "It's much more centralized than any of the other European democracies. I mean, being in Parliament's just a rubber stamp ... Everyone in Parliament's just sitting there hoping they'll get a job one day so they don't undermine the prime minister ... I mean, Blair just basically shut down the Labour Party. Everything was run among his little core of advisors. So I was quite happy to give up Parliament and become mayor."[67]

Tony Travers had noted the change in Livingstone during his wilderness years as an MP. The GLC had not been very interested in business and had stifled London First; however,

That was one of the huge changes in Ken; like lots of politicians on the far left he went from having an active disdain for business in its conventional form to reading *The London Industrial Strategy* as mayor ... same world, different planet, Ken in the City. Everybody moves on of course, everybody changes, but the abolition of the GLC cleared the decks for all sorts of things which can be seen, with the benefit of hindsight, to have created not only the lobby for London's transport but also a single lobbyist for the money.[68]

City Hall

The novel scheme of London government was to be expressed tangibly in the choice of the site and design for the new City Hall – not the grandiose Edwardian symbol of municipal pride of the erstwhile GLC County Hall, but a small, unmistakably modern building commissioned from Ken Shuttleworth of Foster & Partners by the GOL team in advance of the first election, and sited not in Westminster but in Southwark across the Thames from the Tower of London. City Hall was completed in 2002, the centrepiece of More London or London Bridge City, a development to regenerate the South Bank to the southwest of Tower Bridge.

The task of finding the GLA a home had fallen to Turton and the GOL team. "We chose that site, opposite the oldest grandest building in London, the Tower of London, next to the most iconic symbol of London [Tower Bridge] deliberately, and a Norman Foster design, which is not to everyone's taste, but that was all part of saying it's got to be something that is recognized. It's not the GLC, this is a small building – and no doubt subsequent mayors cursed us for using a small building– it was going to be quality, and really in an iconic position to show this is New London, this is different … and it worked. We weren't allowed to have our own building, we had to do a leasing arrangement because we weren't given enough money, unlike the Welsh and the Scots, who were given their own, which was curious] when you think that London has a larger population."[69]

"There were people who made fun of the mayor's building, not least Ken himself, who called it a 'glass testicle'," Turton recalls. Livingstone later sent a note of thanks to Raynsford for having provided him with a fitting home for the mayoralty. "His only complaint was that it was too small." Raynsford responded by pointing out that "this was deliberate, to discourage empire building!"[70]

The first mayor arrives in power

One commentator suggested that the new mayor would be powerless: "Coffee without caffeine is still coffee, but politics without power is just public relations. Ken Livingstone's new London cabinet met round its oval table for the first time yesterday, but it doesn't have any power just now. After Ken is officially installed in the office of London mayor on the third of July, it still won't have any power, and it never will."[71] Turton believed this to be wrong, "as the mayor of Rome had suggested: 'People believe I have the power, and that makes me powerful'. That journalist is wrong because the mayor was given powers. Even if he hadn't had powers, just having somebody who was elected as a single person, people believe it. You can say what's wrong ... have a minister for London until you're blue in the face. But the minister of London can be appointed by the prime minister and dismissed and the next person can come along. This is somebody who was actually there for four years, by the will of the people. He wasn't just a figurehead."[72]

The creation of GLA/TfL and of the shape it took was down to key individuals: Blair, Prescott, Raynsford, Turton, Meek and the GOL team, and then Livingstone and the new leadership of TfL, who defined it. For Turton, "It was not the GLC, where they'd spend hours making decisions, and caucus meetings, the mayor could just make the decisions – that's the difference. I can remember going out with Ken in 2001 or 2002. We did a tour of the street homeless ... everybody, all these people on the street said, 'Oh, hello Ken' – that level of recognition. You can take a minister around, which I often did, 'Who is he?' ... I think it's intriguing to look at the Ken who finished with the GLC in the mid 1980s and the Ken who winds up as mayor as pretty different individuals."[73]

There were benefits to the government of no longer being responsible for the troublesome everyday of problems on the Northern line, traffic at a halt in the Blackwall Tunnel or queues of buses on Oxford Street, let alone the megaprojects. Stephen Glaister recalls that as congestion charging was approaching implementation, back benchers in the Commons would ask the government to intervene on their behalf. "The answer was always, this was the responsibility of the mayor of London and the government had no powers to intervene. The clear expectation was that [congestion charging] would fail spectacularly and it would all be Ken Livingstone's fault." [74]

The creation of the GLA and of TfL had been brought about by Margaret Thatcher's abolition of the GLC, so it is appropriate to end with Thatcher herself. How did the former PM and bitter opponent of Livingstone view the new mayoralty? Turton attended a dinner at London Zoo:

> ... the guest of honour was Mrs Thatcher and the main speaker was Ken Livingstone. The organizers had this carefully orchestrated, making sure the two didn't meet beforehand. There must have been an exhibition there and they were both taken around, separately. Then we had the dinner, and Mrs Thatcher was at a table over here and I was sitting at her table, so I was next to Denis Thatcher and Ken was right over there. Ken gave a brilliant speech, and at the end, he said, 'I really have to say, I've got to thank you, Mrs Thatcher, because if it hadn't been for you, the GLC would still be there. And you know, that's not much of a job. As a result of you, I've got the best job in the world.' He came over to her, walked across the room and everyone's going, 'Oh, God, what's going to happen?' She beamed at him, fantastic![75]

Ken Livingstone was a non-driver and habitual user of public transport, seen here on his way to the Labour mayoral selection panel, 18 November 1999

Livingstone himself records meeting Thatcher at the Queen Mother's one-hundredth birthday lunch at the Guildhall in June 2000, when Thatcher "made her way through the crowd to say, 'Stick to your guns. Everyone will be trying to tell you to do something else, but you must keep your resolve. You're now the leader of the equivalent of a small nation. Resolute, that's what you must be, resolute.'" Livingstone reflected how times had changed from her greeting his election as GLC leader in 1981 by comparing him to a communist dictator.[76]

Meanwhile, back at London Transport, the transition into the new body of all functions, except the Underground as it headed out to PPP, was taken forward by an interim Transitional TfL organization. Transport would prove the key to the success of the new mayoralty in terms of flagship projects such as congestion charging, and by delivering improved day-to-day services across what was now potentially the most integrated city transport network in the world. The first challenge was to create the new transport executive, which brought together functions from 15 different agencies – strategic roads, taxis and private hire, cycling, the river and walking – including the Tube and the buses. The second challenge would be for TfL to respond to the political agenda of the first mayor.

2.

THE FORMATIVE FIRST TERM

"We were starting from scratch. No modern British politician had ever had the opportunity I was now presented with to create a new body, recruiting staff and drawing up planning, transport and environmental strategies. Future mayors would inherit the machine I created."

– Ken Livingstone, 2011[1]

The first mayor, Ken Livingstone, put his mark on the new scheme of London government. Transport was the mayor's most significant power to influence the life of capital. The appointment of American Bob Kiley as the first TfL commissioner shaped and galvanized the mayor's influential transport agency. A series of transport major initiatives, of which congestion charging was the most innovative and instrumental, established the credibility for renewed London-wide government. Despite reasoned and combative attempts to reverse it, the public–private partnership (PPP) for the Underground was eventually signed and only then, in 2003, did the management of the Underground pass to TfL This first mayoral term had a lasting influence on the shape of London government and the strategic purpose of TfL.

The shaping of the GLA

At a large and raucously enthusiastic gathering in July 2000 at Tate Modern of the public servants who made London move and work every day – transport workers, firemen, nurses, civil servants – the newly elected mayor began his address from a prepared speech. He spoke for a few minutes and then, putting his papers to one side, paused, and resorted to a much more engaging appeal. "I'd been sitting on the Tube and a guy leant over and said, 'When you get elected you should say this: Now, where were we before I was so rudely interrupted?'"[2] It brought the house down, much as it had done following his victory at the election count the previous day. "Our Ken" was back at the helm. London had an elected mayor and assembly after a 14-year gap in government since the abolition of the GLC, of which Livingstone had been the final and most controversial leader.

Ken Livingstone had learned much in those 14 wilderness years, without losing his tendency to speak his mind. He had become more of a public figure and less of a pariah through newspaper and media work; weekly restaurant reviews for the *Evening Standard* and *Esquire*, a column in *The Sun*, appearances on the BBC's *Have I Got News For You* show, and even TV ads for cheese and coal. This suggested a 'cuddlier' Ken than the firebrand of his GLC days, though he still maintained a strong streak of 'Red Ken' in his instinctive opposition as MP for Brent East to the New Labour line under Tony Blair. He had remained a gift for headline writers, cartoonists and the tabloid press. Although Blair and most of his colleagues in 1998 believed Livingstone would be "a financial disaster, a disaster in terms of crime, police and business,"[3] Blair later had to concede that it had been wrong to try and centrally control a devolved authority. "After the race we settled down to a proper relationship with remarkable ease, something [Ken] deserved real credit for."[4]

Here was the first elected mayor of the capital, himself a Londoner, a non-driver and habitual user of public transport, eager to take this second chance to shape the future of his city for the better "... because I just love London. I mean, all my life I've lived in London and, born at the end of the war, I just grew up in London where everything got better all the time. And it's now become the most diverse city on the planet."[5] It was a momentous occasion for Livingstone and his well-established group of trusted advisors when they arrived at their temporary home at Romney House, Marsham Street[6] in July 2000 to start the GLA from scratch and to define the role of the country's first executive mayor. Most of the team had worked with Livingstone through the wilderness years, and formed his campaign team when he had decided to run as an independent following Labour's bungled attempt to fix candidate selection and exclude him. Within weeks of his election, Ken had advertised posts as policy advisors, and most of these were filled by familiar faces from within his trusted circle.

Like many others who had dreamed and planned for the return of London-wide government, Alexander Jan, then in the GLA transitional team, remembers well the first day at Romney House and Livingstone's arrival. "It was a sunny day, and we were all standing outside and we clapped him in – like you do with the new prime minister – and it was one of those moments when for anybody who's interested or believes in London, believes in devolution of power, giving London its authority back ... we were all caught up in it. There was a tremendous sense of achievement: this thing had been done."[7]

Despite the length of the GLA bill and the thoughtful design that lay behind it, the new mayoral advisors, the transitional teams at the GLA, the GLA Assembly and TfL now needed to test the model and establish working relationships between its

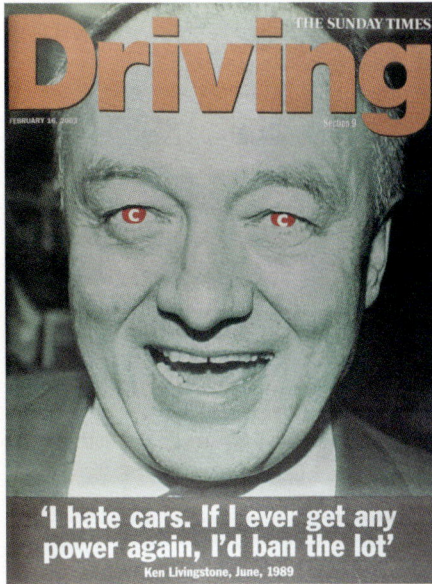

component parts. These relationships were to prove formative and make a lasting impression on the shape of mayoral government and transport in the city.

For TfL, the new and much-expanded transport authority, organizational building blocks had been manoeuvred into position in the months before the mayoral election. A proto-TfL had been established when Anthony Mayer was appointed in February 2000 as its first employee and interim CEO. It was a mammoth task to form a single organization out of London Transport (even without the Underground at that stage) and functions drawn from 14 other organizations, covering the strategic road network in London, taxis and private hire, cycling and walking, the DLR, Victoria Coach Station, river services and city planning.

Livingstone and Mayer had not met before the elections, but the latter's directness and hail-fellow-well-met qualities meant they soon hit it off. Mayer was considered an unconventional appointment, seen as flamboyant, even exotic, by civil service standards, having worked for N.M. Rothschild and the Housing Corporation."A certain barrow-boy quality saw him nicknamed Sid in his early days in the civil service."[8] It reinforced the GLA's reputation as something apart from other local authorities, and perhaps as a precursor of where other councils might follow with devolution to elected mayors. "Mr Mayer will help the mayor to act and the Assembly to scrutinize."[9]

Mayer led Transitional TfL and smoothed the arrival of Livingstone and his team. He was a fan of Livingstone, and observed that there were two sides to the mayor.

"There were two Kens. There was the serious managerial politician who never got the credit, in my view, for his genuine achievements as a managerial politician ... I saw him overwhelmingly in the work experience. We'd have a bottle of wine every week for eight years. It's one of the Ken myths, he did used to get a bit pissed and did used to sound off. I always thought that was the theatre. The real Ken was the geezer who turned up having read all the papers."[10]

The key role of the minister for London, Nick Raynsford, in designing and setting up the GLA was recognized by Mayer. "I think it was very fortuitous that you had Raynsford, who was essentially a political technocrat, and he got the arrangement set up in a way that hardly any other politician would have been able to do ... Ken was a political leader, and basically came in with an agenda, which he wanted to lead, and I think that was a perfect combination."[11]

The new teams take to the field

TfL's relations with the mayor were to be managed day-to-day through his chief of staff and his advisors, principally the director or deputy mayor for transport but also for communications, finance, housing, and other close lieutenants. The relationship with the individuals within this group was crucial to the delivery of the mayor's agenda. This is the knuckle where politics meets transport, where manifesto and other political commitments are driven hard for delivery within four-year electoral terms, and where transport executives are held accountable for the delivery of both the major initiatives and the day-to-day network across the capital.

In designing the GLA, Raynsford had limited the mayor's powers of appointment to two political advisors and 10 expert advisors, other appointments being in the gift of the assembly. Once in office, Livingstone did a deal with Labour Assembly leader Len Duvall on appointments: if the Assembly gave him a free hand on appointing his advisors, he would fund the Assembly for individual and party group support. Securing the appointment of all Livingstone's advisors, this was "one of the most important deals in shaping how the GLA would operate" suggests Richard Brown, then working in the mayor's office.

The mayor's long-standing and loyal team were all from the political left, albeit from different denominations. Simon Fletcher, Livingstone's chief of staff, was a former parliamentary researcher; John Ross was a brilliant Marxist economist, who had been wooing business in the City and Canary Wharf. The mayor used to describe his advisors – Redmond O'Neill, Neale Coleman, John Ross, Mark Watts, Jude Woodward and Lee Jasper – as being like ministers, with full authority to represent his views.[12] Neale Coleman had joined the team for the election campaign, and went on to be the key advisor for the successful Olympic bid and its delivery under Johnson. The team was consistent through Ken's two terms, with the mayor showing deep loyalty when advisors became embroiled in newspaper allegations of cronyism. Such loyalty was to be notably extended to TfL's commissioner, Bob Kiley, as his health deteriorated in Livingstone's second term.[13]

Redmond O'Neill was director of Transport and Livingstone's deputy chief of staff. He was a lifelong revolutionary socialist and an Irish republican, but despite not having held any such role before he proved a highly effective manager of the relationship between TfL and Livingstone's office for eight years, as Peter Hendy recognized. "He did so with honesty, conviction and a strong commitment to excellent public services, equality and inclusion. He worked hard, and encouraged others to do the same, by example."[14] Coleman recalls Redmond "as very bright, very detailed, you'd see him, he had a propelling pencil and you'd see him going through a document, making little notes in his pencil". O'Neill, always known as Redmond, was firm and direct with TfL as Livingstone's transport fixer. "They didn't mess about if they thought people weren't doing what the mayor wanted or weren't doing what they wanted. They were quite firm in their approach, he was quite acerbic in some of his dealings."[15]

John Ross[16] as director of Economic and Business Policy had a major influence in the group. "Ross had an agenda, which was to build up the City of London and contain London's growth within the boundaries of London, rather than what happened in the 1960s and 1970s – export London's growth out to these new towns and expanding towns. [Livingstone] was more than aware of the fact that in London you had to respect the markets. He was as much a business-friendly mayor as any politician I know of," Mayer recalled. "I think it was down to John Ross to put him on the straight and narrow."[17] He was not easy to deal with, Coleman relates: "He had no sense of how to behave with people or to persuade. It was more, you tell them what to do. He was there doing economics, but basically interfered in everything ... I remember John being on the phone during the campaign to the guys at Canary Wharf, talking business with them, in particular about the campaign to get Crossrail to go to Canary Wharf, which at that stage was by no means certain, but which John regarded rightly as important 'from an economic point of view'."[18]

Anyone from outside that coterie of advisors found Ken being protected very carefully from speaking to anybody, remembered Stephen Glaister, a TfL board member from 2000, who had that access himself. "I think a lot of people felt very resentful of not being able to get to Ken because they always got stopped by Ross and people."[19] Livingstone's loyalty extended to the executive team: "Anne McMeel, the director of Finance, Jeff Jacobs, the director of Policy, and Manny Lewis, the director of Corporate Services [to whom] he was immensely loyal – he hates all bureaucrats until he loves you, and once he loves you you're indispensable. That fate did not apply to Turner and to a lesser extent Tunnicliffe [the last chair and CEO of London Underground]," Anthony Mayer reflected, "but he was pretty suspicious of the TfL team I'd inherited."[20] Indeed, each mayor was to be suspicious of the loyalty of his inherited team at TfL, and in due course the change of regime to Boris Johnson and Sadiq Khan was to prove equally difficult.

Harry Barlow[21] had been Livingstone's campaign advisor and continued into mayoral communications.

> Once you established a trust with him and he liked what you were doing … he said to me, 'Oh, you know, just do your best', which is obvious … It's a hell of a responsibility. But you really tried and he'd back you up if something went wrong, but there was an incredible loyalty among that staff. He didn't get any leaks of stuff. Not that there was anything that was untoward anyway, it was so straight and principled. He gave you the responsibility so you made damn sure you got it right or do the best you could possibly do. Which freed him up to do what he was really good at … Redmond [O'Neill] was very good … I had terrible arguments regularly with Redmond but they were funny, you know.[22]

A member of the GLA transitional team recalls in the early days that "some of the advisors were absolutely lethal. Not only were they fiercely protective of the mayor but they were paranoid in a manner after Trotsky. I remember appointments being made with people by Ken in Romney House and by the time you got back to Windsor House [TfL HQ, 10 minutes' walk away], the advisors had found out and got the mayor to reverse his decision. You could go from having a close relationship with the mayor one day to being totally frozen out by his people."[23]

The first TfL commissioner

"Livingstone didn't want a local government chief executive [for TfL]," Tony Travers reflected.

> He evidently wanted somebody who signalled, 'This is different and I am going to run this place … by not bringing in a traditional British transport operator' … it had the effect of making the mayoralty seem more special, something that isn't classic British local government. It is a hybrid, it's partly constitutionally devolution and partly part of local government. Transport for London is a local authority; on the other hand, TfL is nothing like any other part of local government and the GLA group has more in common in some ways with Wales and Scotland than it does with a county. It was exploiting that hybridity, that signalling, through the appointment of Kiley and Anthony Mayer, that this was all going to be very different and serious, not local government as it was known.[24]

The mayor, his appointments committee and their advisors were clear that the search for the commissioner should be aimed well beyond the civil service to candidates who would understand the concept of a powerful mayor with executive power and political authority. From the start they had both UK and international candidates in their sights; by undertaking a worldwide search Livingstone was seeking somebody who would be his own person, rather than someone whose familiarity with Whitehall would limit them to working within the limits usually expected in local or central government.

PricewaterhouseCoopers (PWC) was appointed to undertake the international search for a TfL commissioner and for the five top team roles – the directors of Bus, Taxi and River; Integration; Performance and Finance; Communications and Public Affairs; and Corporate Services. Candidates were invited to "be one of London's movers and shakers ... to solve the crisis of London's transport system ... a unique opportunity to get London moving again". Livingstone's foreword to the briefing pack stressed the need to modernize and integrate the system and deliver real and meaningful change to the everyday experience of getting around London. "My priority is to make the Tube, buses, trains, cycling and walking more attractive and safer in order to persuade some drivers to leave their cars at home and use public transport." Consultation within two years on the introduction of a congestion charge in central London was announced.[25]

A key departure from the past was signalled in the method and targeting for the appointment of the CEO or commissioner of TfL. "What Ken did do was something that would have been considered fairly unusual at the time," recollected Jay Walder, TfL's first MD of Finance and Planning, "which was to undertake an international search for someone."[26] Stephen Glaister remembers Ken saying, "We're not having this job advertised in *The Guardian* or some lefty rag, we want it in the *Sunday Times* and *The Economist* where we'll get serious candidates."[27] The appointment board for the new head of TfL included Livingstone, board members Rob Lane, Steve Norris and Stephen Glaister, with Tony Travers, LSE expert on London and local government, as an advisor, credited with casting the top job as 'commissioner', a title familiar in the United States. The successful candidate would be pulling levers on the transport system, the one area where in the London mayoral model there was real power to deliver on the scale of London as a world city. Livingstone's oft-stated low opinion of London Transport executives and comments about dullards ensured that there were no internal candidates from the old London Regional Transport. Livingstone made it "... absolutely clear in the election I'll be getting rid of all of them, pension them all off. I think, basically, most senior people took their own voluntary retirement just before I took control. I didn't have to sack any of them, they'd all gone."[28]

The future maestro of the congestion charge, Derek Turner, remembers conversations with various people about whom to seek as commissioner. He thought the American model had that powerful role in it, which was then, and to certain extent now, not native. "To really hammer and take the government through the courts is, apart from Brexit, something which is not normal, spending millions and millions opposing the PPP. That needed, if it was to be successful, somebody with that type of experience and that type of personality ... I just don't think that it is in the nature of the British public sector to oppose government to that degree."[29]

Peter Hendy, who was to become Kiley's successor as the second commissioner in 2006, recognized that Livingstone "wanted to show that they'd searched the world for the best chief executive.

> In the process ... they'd rung up Kiley, who was then running the equivalent of London First in New York, and said, effectively, 'Bob, do you know anybody who might do this job?' He said, 'Well, I don't really know anybody', but then had a think about it, and they'd spoken to him again, and he said he might be interested. Bob was quite a big character in New York, he'd ... been the deputy mayor in Boston, which is a political job. He had run the MTA [Metropolitan Transport Authority] for long enough to stop all its hopeless attempts at expansion and actually concentrate the management and the money on doing up what was then a very dilapidated and antiquated system which was very unreliable, and he'd got a reputation for it, so Redmond O'Neill, who then worked for Ken, and Simon Fletcher, and Ken himself, became enormously animated at the prospect of getting somebody from somewhere else, who they could claim as an international figure – which Bob was – and they set about courting him, and they courted him by offering him a very large salary [up to £500,000 per annum for four years] ... they insisted that they were going to come and live in London in style, so a house was bought for them, a Georgian house, it wasn't actually quite as nice as it looked, because it was round the back of Victoria Coach Station, and the District Line ran virtually underneath, so all the cups rattled in the basement kitchen![30]

The terms and conditions were way beyond anything conventionally offered to a UK public servant. Livingstone announced Kiley's appointment in October 2000. "I was elected to tackle London's transport crisis. In making the appointment of commissioner of Transport for London I have therefore carried out a search for the best in the world. I have offered the job to Robert Kiley, who turned New York's transport system from one of the most crisis-ridden in the world into one of the best."[31] Kiley was also familiar with an alternative funding model for the Tube, the issuing of bonds which he and Livingstone would advocate for London in preference to the government's plans for a public–private partnership (PPP).

Jay Walder had worked with Kiley in New York in the 1980s, and would be appointed by him in 2001 as TfL's MD for Finance and Planning. "The fact is that Bob was great at setting up an organization and setting up a thought process, moving this forward with a logic and a set of things to happen, terrific with the press, and creating presence. He had always relied on other people to be able to be the operations gurus in doing it … I don't know that that was really known at that time to Ken and his team; I think the fact is, Bob would have come across very credibly in speaking to this, but, in Bob's mind, he thought David Gunn[32] was going to join."[33] Gunn had effected the turnaround of the New York subway as president of the Transit Authority during Kiley's tenure at the MTA in the late 1980s and was a consummate rail operator.

Arriving with Bob Kiley from the tough school of New York's transit politics, lobbyist and now personal advisor Maggie Boepple was in the midst of the creation of mayoral government and TfL. Boepple was born in the UK and educated at Oxford, but had made a distinguished career in New York as a communications specialist and lobbyist. Boepple had worked for Kiley previously and was drawn back to London by Kiley's brilliance. "I've worked for pretty great people, but Bob was the best in taking a complicated problem, reading it out, and then figuring out, 'I need to understand this and this and this'. He was just brilliant. We hit it off really very quickly. Because I actually had to be good for him to succeed because he had no idea coming from Boston. New York City is tough, tough, tough. This whole [TfL] project was tough, tough, tough."[34]

Kiley called Boepple early in 2001, asking:

'Could I come over?' and I said, 'To do what?' He said, 'I can't understand a word anyone's saying to me.' I was translator for a week and then he said, 'You've got to stay, I need you here' and a week became five years. They were the most exciting five years of my professional life. It was unbelievably difficult. My office was down the corridor from Bob's and as you know, he had a tendency to be very tough on his team. He frequently asked me to come into a meeting, and then ask my opinion [afterwards], and I said, 'Well, you were absolutely horrible to this person.'[35]

As Kiley's special advisor, Boepple became the velvet glove to Kiley's steely fist, and helped the commissioner and the Livingstone administration find their mayoral feet. As Boepple described:

I had worked for a mayor, for Ed Koch, very closely; I was the head of Intergovernmental Relations, which meant our relationship with Washington, and Albany, the state capiital, and the New York City politicians … I'd frequently get calls from Redmond [O'Neill], 'Please come over, can you? Can you let us know what you would do in this situation?' It wasn't just in transport, they were trying to understand what a mayor meant, as opposed to the head of the GLC, and they worked hard at that.[36] … The problem was [the mayor] had been screwed by Gordon Brown in the writing of the bill. They wanted to give him as little real power as possible. I think he did a great job with the power that he had. But it was not like New York City or an American mayor that has huge power in running the city ... I'd suddenly get a phone call from Kiley: 'What would Ed Koch[37] do in this situation?'[38]

Tony Travers recalls the appointment of Bob Kiley.

[It] completely threw everybody because he was terribly expensive and he was going to be given a house in Belgravia. He was a former CIA spy with lots of friends in the British political establishment, we all discovered later. Nobody quite knew how to handle it really. When he came to London, he had a better network in London than any of us, dinner parties with all sorts of High Court judges and spies and God knows [who]. I found I went to a dinner there at the house once, found myself sitting next to a member of the House of Lords who'd clearly been a spy and that's how she knew him. I'm not making this up! Rona [Kiley's second wife] was a big social animal, so we mustn't forget Rona, they brought a kind of salon to London, in addition to being the transport commissioner.[39]

There had been considerable interest in the employment by London's radical mayor of a former CIA operative with the grand American title of commissioner. However, Kiley and Livingstone got along from the off. "From the moment I spoke to Kiley over the internet, I just thought, he seems brilliant. He transformed the Boston underground, the New York underground. He immediately flew out within about twenty-four hours with his wife. We met up, we went out, had a brilliant meal at my favourite restaurant. That was it, I just thought, this guy is going to be brilliant, and he was. He said, 'I'll take the job, but you've got to leave me free to assemble the team I want,' and we brought the best people in America for running public transport, got them all running London ..."[40]

Livingstone maintained that he was "employing the best transport professional in the world"; the *Evening Standard* headline was 'New York Tough Guy to Run the Tube', while the *New York Times* led on 'Ex-Transit Chief Takes on London's Ailing Subway'[41]. Kiley's expertise in the governance of city transport, as well as his experience of politics, was to be formative for the new mayoralty and for the mayor himself. Isabel Dedring was Kiley's chief of staff from 2002, another American by birth but living in London. "We had a lot of really interesting perspectives on large organizations and leadership. The other thing that's interesting about Bob was his long-standing engagement and interest in politics. That was one of the things I think that made him successful, especially in that early period, where being a real thought partner with Ken was critical. Somebody who wasn't political, let's say, or didn't grasp politics would not have done well in that set-up."[42]

Stephen Glaister also recognized Kiley's significance in forming TfL. "The first thing Ken did was to say, 'I want the best transport commissioner in the world', and he eventually managed to recruit Bob Kiley ... He was the greatest guy, he really was, it all went wrong subsequently, but I sat in meetings where Bob was where we'd get off the agenda and he'd start talking in really inspirational terms about how you plan cities, what you had to do to make cities work, and it was all about getting decent infrastructure and a decent long-term funding plan."[43]

Professor David Begg was a board member of TfL from 2001.

> What Kiley brought with him was experience of working with some top mayors in US cities. Kiley had this inflated US perception of what a mayor should do, whereas, in Britain, we never had [elected] mayors. Kiley was aiming high and he actually taught Ken, even though Ken had been leader of the GLC, which is a different role ... how to be a really effective mayor. In that sense, Kiley was invaluable and then he got a lot of other people ... Tim O'Toole was a top exec running a huge rail freight company in America; Jay Walder was an intellectual heavyweight ... Peter Hendy in at Surface Transport ... These were top executives.[44]

Neale Coleman, one of the close circle of Livingstone's advisors, takes the contrary view that Ken knew full well what being an executive mayor was about. "He'd run the GLC as an executive leader ... he was a terrific administrator ... his political judgement, and his general judgement on issues was very strong ... having a team around him who he trusted completely, rightly or wrongly, was a huge advantage."[45]

Bob Kiley had a quietly commanding presence, but in his dark suits and tortoiseshell glasses he blended easily into the rows of executives bent over their briefing papers on the Heathrow–Kennedy shuttle. At first he was even able to ride the Tube without being recognized. Kiley was an inspiring communicator but hated public speaking, shunning the limelight, leaving that to Livingstone, but his calm media work did much to bring the British press and broadcasters around to questioning the PPP.[46]

People were frightened of Kiley, and with good reason as his default mode typically was belligerent, as Maggie Boepple related. "Bob did go overboard a bit. There were times when I'd walk in – and I wasn't the only one – and I'd say, 'I think I'll come back tomorrow'. I'd say that to him. Or I've got calls from his front office: 'Come talk to him'."[47] Tim O'Toole was struck by how often Kiley was angry. "I'd learned very early on that I needed to deal with Bob, and I didn't allow the LU people to deal with him. I told everyone, I handle everything, and I would just try to force Bob to deal with me and look at me, because he was so scary to those people, they would shut down and perform poorly, they would misrepresent what they were capable of and so I had to control the conversation at all times."[48]

"[Bob] had extraordinary instincts," Maggie Boepple recalls, "and he asked questions. He'd read a lot and then pull in some people. The thing that made him angry was when he pulled in people, and they were trying to say what they thought he wanted. That's why he felt so strongly about having a few of the people he'd had around him at the MTA. You know, we weren't particular friends, we'd worked together. He said, 'I've worked with you for many years and I trust you'."[49]

Then in came these Americans

"Bob [Kiley[felt he had an awful lot to do very quickly and he only had a certain amount of time to do it in before the press turns or the politicians turn."

– Maggie Boepple[50]

Liz Meek was seconded from Government Office for London (GOL) to smooth the transition from London Transport to TfL, and recalls the moment when Kiley and the team arrived.

> In came these Americans. I think it was a bit like the Americans [in] the Second World War. Most of them, not Bob particularly, had fantastic teeth. They were tall and fine-looking men and they walked with an air of the cavalry coming in. I think there were three or four of them – Jay Walder was obviously one – very sharp, clever people, some of whom survived in the London scene and went on to do other things. They swept into this open-plan space ... There was huge suspicion among the regulars, a lot of whom had been a long time in London Transport and were London Transport people. They were very, very wary and suspicious. Then to add to insult to injury for the old timers, Redmond O'Neill and John Ross were scathing about the abilities of the inherited tribe of London Transport people.[51]

There was the inevitable collision between the TfL transitional team led by Mike Swiggs, director of Corporate Services and acting deputy commissioner, seeking to affect a smooth handover, and the incoming American commissioner and his trusted advisors and consultants. Kiley was in a hurry, and often came across as abrasive and aloof and untrusting of the LT old guard. The American takeover was to be formative for TfL, but in the early days it felt as if an American colony had been established on the 14th floor of Windsor House, "watching CNN and Bloomberg TV over coffee, gossiping about baseball, discussing old times together in the CIA and FBI and their operations in the 1960s, 1970s and 1980s, reading specially delivered copies of *The Wall Street Journal*, *Washington Post* and *The New York Times* and planning their next first-class trip back to the Big Apple."[52]

Kiley was a highly competent, experienced and strategic chief executive but perhaps crucially, unlike the commissioners who were to follow him, not a transport operator and certainly not a public servant in the mould with which Whitehall was used to dealing. Kiley was concerned about the influence of Whitehall, and before taking the job asked Professor David Begg about this. "How much autonomy did

Mayor Livingstone and TfL's first commissioner, Bob Kiley, at St James's Park station in November 2001

he have? They used to keep him away from Whitehall because he used to be such a bruiser. Civil servants weren't used to any of this ... I think he [Livingstone] thought that he was getting a transport operator; Bob is not a transport operator. No ... he brought a private-sector culture, a hire-and-fire culture, to Transport for London."[53]

Jay Walder had been tasked with convincing a former New York colleague, David Gunn, to come to London. Gunn had been instrumental in turning round the New York subway in the 1980s. "He came over, he spent time trying to understand the PPP. Gunn found it an anathema, he liked control, he liked to know he was going to do this" – and he saw all of the ways in which the day-to-day operations would struggle to deal with the conflicts within the PPP. Jay Walder recalled that Gunn predicted the outcome of the PPP: "David saw all of that and basically would not come if the PPP was going to be there."[54] Gunn told Walder, "You'll need a lawyer, not a train man."[55]

Maggie Boepple recalls the early days in London as being pretty traumatic for both the Americans and the Londoners. "I heard a lot of that [unhappiness] because they knew I had Bob's ear ... I'm not sure you ever had to deal with the black Irish moods that he would have, but it was pretty tough. We were getting to know Ken and Ken's team. We had to pay attention to them, obviously. But there's an American expression – we rolled Ken's team from time to time. I mean, we just went 'No, no.' They weren't experts in transportation."[56]

Meek saw in Kiley "a kind of distain almost for what he found ... nobody was brave enough, including me, to say anything at the time; it wouldn't have been very sensible to challenge it … I suppose he did frighten people, because he had Ken and John Ross and Redmond [O'Neill] behind him. Everyone knew that they were on trial, and they were going to be booted out."[57]

"I think that Bob was in many ways removed from politics," recalled Jay Walder, his first major appointment. "He was politically getting cues from Ken, but he wasn't steeped in London politics … Maybe that made it easier to be able to say, 'Okay, well, I can't actually run this organization by pretending that I'm going to have a deep knowledge of London per se and the transport issues and other things of that nature. What I'm really gonna have to concentrate on is creating a professionalism in this organization that's going to allow me to really succeed in doing that.'"[58]

Bringing together functions from 15 predecessor organizations to create TfL was a huge task. Kiley engaged consultants McKinsey late in 2001 to advise on the shape of TfL. Jay Walder observed that Kiley appreciated that people had brought things together, but had not thought it all the way through. "He thought of it as mouldable clay. McKinsey had a number of teams looking at different areas. It led to reorganizing the organization, the creation of certain functions within the organization. That then built up into this professionalism that I think people began to really respect about TfL."[59]

Maggie Beopple recalled that despite the length of the GLA Act, not much thought had been given to how this huge entity of TfL was going to function. "I think we interviewed five or six of the big companies, all the big companies essentially came in, and I was there, Jay was there, Bob was there towards the end, and they did presentations … It was especially hard for the people at the Underground because there was no trust. I'd have people come over to my office, I'd see anyone who wanted to talk about it … They would cry, and I couldn't promise that they'd have a job, but I could promise that they'd have plenty of opportunity to show how good they were. But it was uncomfortable, I can't pretend it wasn't; some people took early leave."[60]

In retrospect, the most significant impact of the McKinsey work may have been the recruitment from them of Shashi Verma and Will Judge to deliver Oyster and then contactless payment. Conversely, the two principal achievements of the first term, the congestion charge and a revolution in the bus service, were not touched by the McKinsey work.

Jeroen Weimar was Kiley's first chief of staff. "Kiley brought with him a small group of trusted advisors, all Americans, all of whom he had worked with before: Drew Hyde, Maggie Boepple, Steve Polan, a lawyer … Bob had a retinue of about five or six people who were all advisors… most of them had no job in the bureaucracy, in the organization, apart from Jay [Walder] …The others were very much the commissioner's retinue of people to come in and burrow into various things … Steve Polan came in to sort out the PPP, because that was the burning platform that Bob was associated with. He made it pretty clear he didn't want anybody from the existing organization ... dear old Mike Swiggs set up some other people to fill the vacuum, and Bob said, 'Oh no, I want my own person'."[61]

An economist and transport planner, Jeroen Weimar had joined the GLA transition team before the first mayoral election, and was there as the search for the TfL commissioner was undertaken. Weimar had met Kiley on one of his prior visits to London in November 2000. "Kiley said, 'Look, I just want you to ... help me work stuff out, help me work out what's going on, what the issues are that are important, and we'll work it out as we go along.' And we hit it off pretty quickly on the first interview." Weimar stepped "straight into a TfL transition team that he [Kiley] had no real understanding of, and part of it was just about keeping some of those people away from him so he can get on with the stuff that he saw as important. It was a difficult role, no question, but it was obviously fascinating to be there at that point where there was that collision ... It was a role without a job description and little structure initially, which Kiley needed to control but not be distracted by, as the major issues to be addressed in his mind were unseating the PPP and finding a better funding model, such as bond finance, for the new organization."[62]

London Transport's legacy to TfL

The new regime's judgement on London Transport's record in the 1990s was a tough one. Despite stop–start Whitehall funding, significant progress had been made on the leadership, managerial competence and service delivery of the organization since the dark days of 1987 and the King's Cross Fire.

After the trauma of the fire, the Tube had made notable progress in the 1990s under Denis Tunnicliffe's[63] leadership. Under the banner of the 'decently modern metro', a pragmatic ambition argued for regular investment in upgrade and maintenance, recognizing that government funding remained an uphill task. Tunnicliffe was responsible for a management revolution on the Tube within

Denis Tunnicliffe, chair and CEO of LT when the Jubilee line extension was opened in May 1999

Foster & Partners' Tube cathedral, Canary Wharf station booking hall, November 2005

the limits of annual financial settlements and lack of capital investment, which aimed to make the Tube safer, better led and carrying a rapidly growing number of passengers. The Jubilee line extension (JLE) expanded the network and created a series of outstanding new stations. Its financial overrun was a product of the government deadline imposed to open the Millennium Dome at North Greenwich on New Year's Eve, 1999, the delay caused by the collapse of a tunnel being built to Heathrow by an innovative spray concrete method (NATM), by optimistic budgeting to get funding approval, and by contractors being unable to deliver a moving block signalling system and being obliged to return to traditional block signals.

The Tube was made safe by removing all flammable materials from trains and stations, "a gargantuan task", as Tunnicliffe's successor as Underground MD Tim O'Toole notes. "I used to feel overwhelmed by having 20 escalators out of service; he had four-fifths of the system out at a time. Denis could take special pride in knowing that when the bombs went off on 7/7 nothing burned, and if that had happened a lot of people would have died in that tunnel from the smoke and instead we had explosions in the darkness, but we had no fire ... because the Underground is a remarkably safe place. That was because of that generation of management. I had tremendous respect for that."[64]

In the 1990s improvements had struggled to make an impact against a long backlog of work and rising passenger numbers. At the 1997 general election, the Conservatives had pledged to privatize the Tube, while Labour argued for investment through a PPP. This was the only game in town available in the 1990s for funding the Tube upgrade; Tunnicliffe and his team had of necessity become advocates for the PPP after bitterly opposing it, which divided them from Livingstone and Kiley after 2000. Their successors, once the PPP contracts were signed in 2003, were to benefit from devolution, an integrated transport strategy, and better and longer-term funding under the devolved mayoralty. The need to spend a billion pounds a year on maintaining the Tube was, ironically, made crystal clear by the process of specifying and concluding the PPP contracts.

Tony Travers acknowledges:

> By the time we got to 2000 the buses in London were running without a subsidy. It did look a bit battered and threadbare, and some of the buses were a bit old, but actually it was an extraordinary achievement ... and the Tube was breaking even on operations, that's what convinces me that Denis was good at what he did, that he was precisely delivering what the British sort of want, which is something that looks like the Paris metro and bus system that doesn't cost anything like it in taxes ... quite a lot was delivered during Denis's watch. The Thatcher government, though affecting not to like railways, actually delivered extensions to the Heathrow Tube, the Croydon tram link, Heathrow Express; there's more railway activity than you'd expect, certainly from the Thatcher–Major government added together.[65]

The new TfL team takes shape

Interim appointments had been made by the mayor's office before Kiley arrived as commissioner. Peter Hendy was appointed as the head of Bus, Taxi and River Services, Derek Turner as the head of Street Management. Liz Meek was seconded to set up the organization, having been deeply involved in writing the GLA Act at the GOL. On his arrival at TfL in 2001, Jay Walder felt very much an outsider compared to those already there. "I come as an outsider, Bob is obviously an outsider. Bob now sets out to create this professionalism and to re-create the organization through the work that's taking place with McKinsey. I think that was also really, really important in doing that … We actually picked up probably half a dozen people from that McKinsey team to come to TfL: Shashi [Verma], Isabel Dedring, Will Judge."[66]

The fresh perspective and expertise of the new appointments steadily took root in TfL. "This company is now beginning to feel a lot different, because you're starting to bring in people, they're not coming through the ranks of government, through the ranks of LRT, through GOL. They're coming in a different way, they're bringing a different experience, and they're challenging things," Jay Walder recalled. "I started to bring some people in: Steve Allen, who comes in to run the corporate finance department; Tom Amenta, of course, who had joined with me, right from the beginning; Eric Rothman, who comes in to run the strategic planning organization; Lauren Sager-Weinstein, who came shortly after that, became my chief of staff."[67]

Jeroen Weimar was moved across into leading TfL transport policing and enforcement, an important Kiley initiative. In New York he had been used to a closer relationship between policing and transport. Once in London he judged the Met leadership as useless and uninterested in transport concerns. His combative manner did not inspire the Met, so Kiley was obliged to put £70m into transport policing and enhance the presence on the system of British Transport Police (BTP) and their liaison with the Met and emergency services.

Isabel Dedring became Kiley's second chief of staff early in 2003, and saw the relationship between mayor and commissioner at close hand. "I think that Bob certainly wanted to play that role [of guiding the new mayoralty]. He sought to play that role, and he would definitely give Ken advice. Ken completely accepted that as well, which was interesting in itself. You know, Bob was older, he was more experienced in many of these matters, and so they were certainly almost like peers."[68]

Charles Monheim was another American recruit, brought in to apply his experience of city transport operations to the ticketing project that led to the Oyster card. He reflected:

> Ken and the mayoralty started to establish a presence, again, separate and apart from the GLA, from the Assembly. One of the early signs of that was the mayor starting to have a weekly press conference, which was something that Bob had actually suggested and said, 'This is the way the mayor of New York would do this. You should make yourself available, control the agenda, make yourself available for questions by doing that.' It was a sort of learning process that everybody was going through. The other part of the learning process was that Ken was the chairman of the TfL board. That's a place where I think there was maybe a disconnect in communication. I think Bob always thought that Ken would turn over the chairmanship of TfL to Bob. Again, that would follow the model from the MTA in New York: the MTA is led by the chairman and chief executive officer. But Ken actually found that it was useful to him, and beneficial to him, to be chairing the

TfL board meetings. It created this sense, and I think this was absolutely right, this sense of responsibility and accountability for the outcomes of the transit system that people had long felt was missing.[69]

Walder recollects this too.

This idea of accountability, responsibility, the fiduciary trust that was being placed in the mayor and with Bob and with TfL became that much more visible because of the way the structure was taking shape … TfL needed to establish itself as an organization that was not, in quotes, a political function, but was a professional function with a fiduciary responsibility toward the use of public funds in the way in which it was going to do things. [This] was something that people I don't think would have articulated. But it flowed out of all this. When I came in the role of managing director of Finance, that was falling very directly to me in the way that that was taking place. But it flowed up, that's the point, it flowed up. It wasn't just staying with me, it wasn't somebody in the bowels, who was trying to do this, it flowed straight through to the commissioner and the mayor in doing it. And decisions that were being taken were now being taken in the lens against that fiduciary responsibility. Again, if you think about the history of Ken and the transit system, that's 180 degrees different from the way that people perceived Red Ken and the way in which the old issues of the fare structure and other things like that were being done.[70]

The new mayor and his team were also very able to use the news agenda to extend their influence beyond the limited powers of the GLA. Livingstone instituted a weekly press conference, which enabled him to make the news. "This keeping in front of them, rather than fleeing the press … reciting the agenda constantly – it allowed him to control the agenda. He was making more headlines than the national figures that were trying to control him."[71] The government wanted to prove that its new creation, the mayor and the Assembly, had worked, and so had an incentive to help the GLA. "Livingstone negotiated hard with his arch-enemy Gordon Brown for money, and low and behold, huge sums of money were forthcoming," noted Tony Travers.

That in many ways is the single most important legacy of the mayoralty, having the one powerful individual able to go into Gordon Brown and then George Osborne, Philip Hammond and … going in at the highest level and pushing hard and convincing the government it's not in their best interests to have the Tube dropping to bits. The Johnson settlement, given the rest of the public spending settlement, was extremely good; the Livingstone settlement, compared with the rest of the country, was extraordinarily good.[72]

With the Underground, the new mayor and his commissioner had inherited a singularly rich mix: a poor reputation from growing passenger numbers on the Tube and a long-term investment backlog in maintaining and upgrading track, trains, signals and stations; the Treasury's belief, post-Jubilee line extension, that only the private sector could deliver big infrastructure upgrade projects to time and budget; the New Labour commitment to harnessing the private sector through a 'third way' of partnership in public service delivery; and the financial hair shirt of New Labour's commitment to their Conservative predecessors' borrowing targets.

This situation was brought to a head by the personalities of the newly elected and independent Mayor Livingstone and Commissioner Kiley, who inevitably exposed the fault lines within New Labour that divided Blair, Brown and Prescott, and the power of the Treasury and Chancellor Gordon Brown. The ensuing debacle over the PPP was to see Brown and the Treasury dictate the funding model for upgrading the London Underground against all advice, and directly contrary to Blair and Prescott's devolved elected governance for London. Liz Meek, a key architect at GOL of the GLA Act, reflected that "it was just an affront to logic that you could set up a strong mayor with a particular design and then go and ruin it in such a ridiculous kind of cack-handed way" by imposing the PPP.[73] "Quite frankly, I thought they had been written on the other side of Venus" commented Bob Kiley on the 2800-page PPP contracts.[74]

The first mayoral transport strategy

The GLA was statutorily required to produce a London Plan, a strategic framework for planning the city's future. This was a major piece of work, the first strategic plan for London's development in two decades. The plan was developed in 2002, consulted upon and published in February 2004. Meanwhile, the transport elements of Livingstone's manifesto were quickly developed into the first published Mayor's Transport Strategy in July 2001. This was the transport vision and blueprint for the first term and beyond, following the pledges of the manifesto: a flat rate 70p bus fare, safer streets, and disabled access to more stations. The two big-ticket items were public-sector management of the Tube and innovative commitment to address central London traffic congestion by introducing a congestion charge within two years. This was to be the most public and visible flagship of the new TfL, to which a whole chapter has been devoted (see chapter 4), while the revolution of the bus service, Trafalgar Square and other flagships can be found in the next chapter.

The public–private partnership

"The three London Underground public–private partnership [LU PPP] agreements were contracts between private sector infrastructure companies and the Greater London Authority," explains Professor Stephen Glaister. "They were signed in 2003 at the insistence of Tony Blair's 1997 New Labour government but they were one of the most expensive and wasteful failures in UK government history."[75]

The Underground was to arrive late to the TfL party, having been diverted around the loop line represented by the PPP. Chancellor Gordon Brown's remorseless advocacy of private sector solutions to public infrastructure investment had dictated that the Underground would only rejoin the mayoral main line after PPP contracts had been signed, sealed and delivered. As the elements of TfL were being assembled from its predecessor organizations – including London Transport, the Public Carriage Office, the residual bodies, borough partnerships, etc. – the largest and most politically charged element, the blue riband London Underground, was withheld from mayoral control until the PPP was contractually welded into place. Originally envisaged as being finalized before the mayoral elections of May 2000, it would not be until 2003, and following a bonanza of lucrative work for transport lawyers and consultants, that the Underground would join the new mayor's TfL team. They would then be obliged to work in partnership with the Metronet and Tube Lines consortia for the upgrade and maintenance of track, signals and stations across the network over the next 30 years.

The longer the negotiations for the PPP contracts went on, the more any real transfer of risk receded, the scale and complexity of the contracts growing and the cost ballooning from nothing to a billion pounds a year. Kiley did pose an alternative, which had worked to finance the turnaround in the New York transit system during his tenure: the issuing of government bonds funded by the Tube's revenue stream. Liz Meek was not alone in seeing Kiley's arrival at TfL as having the potential to reverse the PPP. "I was saying to everybody that I could get hold of while I was in Whitehall, and the legislation was being mangled … I did have a one-to one-with [minister] Stephen Byers[76] and David Rowlands in which I said, 'Look, this is not sensible. We have here a man who could run a good, integrated operation for us and we have to do it'."[77]

It was the JLE and its cost overruns that convinced the Treasury that London Underground should never again be allowed to run a project, believes Tony Travers.

Well, they were hopping out of the frying pan and into the fire; it's hard to believe that London Underground could have wasted money on quite the scale that the PPP eventually did, though we'll never know how much was lost. We're now back, in effect, with London Underground managing what was the PPP, and they have managed the Overground upgrades and improvements very, very efficiently and very effectively one has to say, largely of course by conventional contracting and contracting out; even Livingstone has … contracted out the operation of the Overground, so Ken by the time he was at City Hall was completely reformed in many political ways … We will even look back on the PPP as having done good, the one good thing it has done is substantially to raise the money going into rebuilding the Tube, because it's largely still there even though the PPP isn't.[78]

The long-term funding agreement that followed in the wake of signing the the PPP contracts was in itself a major innovation.

"The PPP was a big moment," Maggie Boepple recalled, "and then we knew we'd lost, essentially because we'd come in too late. For Bob, that was a big moment, we were all discouraged. Bob decided, 'Okay, we're going to be proved right at some point, let's keep going and try to make it work and be quite public where the roadblocks are or where the cost is'."[79] Kiley himself felt from the beginning he had arrived two years late."[80] Tim O'Toole was recruited in 2003 from Conrail in Philadelphia to make the PPP work, or take it over if it failed. For either outcome, his legal and railroad funding background would be essential.

Charles Monheim was brought into TfL to lead another public–private partnership already in being, the ticketing public finance initiative (PFI), known as Prestige,[81] which would lead to the Oyster card. Monheim contends "that the whole notion of PPPs was a broader topic that the government had an attachment to for reasons completely unrelated to the transport system and without very much knowledge. It had to do with the way in which they felt that the finances needed to look for a Labour government to be a credible steward of UK finances."[82]

Jay Walder offered several reasons why he thought there were times when the PPP fight could have been won, as it was clear that the idea was flawed.

> It requires you to be prescient for about 30 years, amazingly difficult to do; the numbers didn't stack up so finance was difficult and needed government shelter; and TfL was increasingly being recognized as a strong and professional organization. You've got these three things going on, and I thought there was a lot of reason why you might be able to believe that. On the flip side of that, you had a deep, deep distrust of Ken and Bob by the Gordon Brown wing of the Labour Party, hugely distrustful … holding onto the philosophy that we still believe in PFIs and PPPs as a way to be able to do this.[83]

Stephen Glaister recalls that there was a moment when the PPP train did seem to have been halted.

> Kiley was rung up, so the story goes, at five o'clock on a Friday evening; would he go down to Chequers? … Of course you don't say no, he cancels his Saturday dinner party and goes down to Chequers and finds Blair with all the contracts laid out. I mean there's this room full of contracts … Being a lawyer, and a contract lawyer at that, he thought, 'Well, I'd better have a look at these contracts' – and in fact by all accounts of course he was completely mystified, because I don't think there's any living soul who is capable of understanding how these contracts work,

they were just far too big and complicated … You could spend a lifetime getting to grips with this monster.[84]

In an apparently stunning volte face, Blair asked Kiley to negotiate for central government with the consortia that had bid on the contracts, and to hammer out a version that Kiley could live with. Kiley told Glaister that "he felt obliged to try, if only because the prime minister had asked him to. And so, while remaining transport commissioner of London, he became chairman of London Regional Transport."[85]

Blair's hiring of Kiley was a bombshell, and was widely seen as a direct rebuff to Gordon Brown. The immediate effect was to remove the controversy from the news, as Kiley disappeared into lengthy negotiating sessions and any fear about Livingstone campaigning against Labour candidates in the 2002 election were allayed. "There were handshakes between Kiley and Prescott in Number Ten before the election, it's all been resolved, we finally got it off the agenda, then when they won the election, on day one Kiley was out. They did not honour any of those promises … but Blair had realised this [the PPP] was an electoral problem for him … it was absolutely disgraceful."[86]

Tony Travers described Blair's move as "heroic cynicism … breathtaking". For Simon Jenkins, "It was heartbreaking, to invite him to Chequers, to appoint him to that job, to let yourself be photographed with him, to let it be known that you had faced down Gordon Brown and gone with Bob Kiley, and then to sack him straight after the election. I told Bob, 'Anything you can do in American politics we can do worse'."[87] Blair had not only fired Kiley; his government immediately obtained a gagging order from the courts to prevent him from releasing two publicly financed consultants' reports on the safety implications and financial outlook of the PPP contracts. In the High Court, Kiley won permission to release the consultants' reports, and polls showed that he and Livingstone had the support of almost ninety per cent of Londoners.

Jay Walder recognized that momentum in the case against the PPP "had been built up when Bob came. He spoke very well to this … [that the PPP] created a separation between track and train, for example, in terms of responsibility and accountability … Bob and I, and Maggie, probably all underestimated the powerful forces on the other side of this and how … the PPP fight got set up so it was a win or lose for the government and there was almost no way to give them a way back. There was no way that one could find grounds for something other than that which continued to make people dig in the other way."[88]

Kiley had brought his New York bond-funded experience and was a great advocate of it. When he spoke to London Labour MPs "he was a wow. He just said, 'I have no political axe to grind, but here's my record, and I can give you private-sector procurement, delivery, the money, and so on,' and the meeting just roared with approval. We came out thinking, we have seen the future and it is called Bob Kiley."[89]

Once Kiley appreciated that all PPP roads actually led to Gordon Brown, he sought to negotiate a compromise so that the government could back off and let TfL do what it was set up to do. A senior civil servant with access to Whitehall sought to facilitate reconsideration of the PPP: "I remember going and talking to, at least to Stephen Byers[90] and with David Rowlands[91] present, as the senior civil servant." There was even a "secret meeting with Shriti Vadera[92] which took place in Bob Kiley's flat overlooking Hyde Park early on a Sunday morning, going in a back entrance, at which I have to say, Bob Kiley completely demolished Shriti to the point that she was sort of agreeing with him and said, 'Well, yeah, but I'm afraid Gordon wants it and it's got to happen', which was a little phrase that I had heard from at least three different people. I was always trying, at that point, naively really, to bring about some sort of deal because the PPP seemed like such a bad idea."[93]

All roads may have led to Gordon Brown, but Brown simply refused ever to talk to Kiley. Brown would get it, Kiley believed, if only they could meet. After all, Brown was an Americanophile who spent holidays on Cape Cod and often expressed admiration for American ingenuity. "Kiley had a house on Martha's Vineyard, asked to see him. Brown did not reply. Kiley asked again. Brown did not reply. Kiley, exasperated, went public with his desire to speak to the chancellor. Brown did not respond. Kiley, flabbergasted, began to ask, publicly, whether Brown even existed. He called him the Wizard of Oz on *Breakfast with Frost*. No response from Brown." Theories abound at Brown's stance – a hatred of Livingstone, a Scotsman's hostility to London – but most people saw Brown's stubborn public silence in terms of the Treasury's great power and self-regard. The chancellor of the exchequer almost never meets with a local government functionary. When the Treasury sends someone to a meeting with another government department, it tends to send a representative of a lower rank than that of the person being met, simply to underline the Treasury's institutional superiority. "An elite brains trust at the Treasury made policy, and the department expected implementers like Kiley to carry that policy out, without discussion or complaint."[94]

Tony Travers reflects, "I think Blair and the core of Downing Street, 10 Downing Street, who after all we now know were not very fond of Gordon Brown, for that reason alone were pretty suspicious of this thing that was causing all this brouhaha in the papers, and there was a very wide range of people opposing the PPP including the *Standard* which, under Max Hastings, threw itself very hard against it, but, you know, this is Britain and majority governments can do what they want. This, as Lord Hailsham memorably said, is an elective dictatorship, and they did what they wanted to."[95] Meek remembers a conversation with Ed Balls, then a

Cartoon by Martin Rowson in 2003, the broken train set a present for investment in the Tube from Chancellor Gordon Brown's public–private partnership

Treasury junior minister under Brown, "in which, really early on, I said, this [PPP] is a bad idea. He was another one who basically said, 'Yes, but Gordon wants it, he's got to have it'."[96]

Chancellor Brown got his way, the contracts were eventually signed and the Underground joined TfL in early 2003. Metronet held two contracts, managing nine of the Underground's lines (the Sub-Surface and Bakerloo, Central and Victoria line contracts), Tube Lines the other three (Jubilee, Northern and Piccadilly lines). Progress in the early years by both contractors was uneven and sharply recognized in a report to the London Assembly in 2007: "Live or work along the District, Piccadilly and Jubilee lines and the Tube service you are provided with is more reliable and/ or has greater capacity than when the PPP started. Live or work along the Northern, Bakerloo and Victoria lines and the Tube service has been blighted by persistent delay, and inconsistent performance."[97]

When Kiley was first introduced to his job, Livingstone had said, "'The best way to think about Britain is to think East Germany at the height of the Cold War, with a required election every four or five years that is more or less democratic.' [Kiley] kind of laughed. But, after a year of bureaucratic battles, he said to Livingstone, as they came out of a meeting with representatives of the Treasury, 'You were wrong about this East German model. North Korea is a better example.'"[98] It is perhaps remarkable that the prolonged wrangling over the PPP did not destabilize the new mayoralty. It was certainly not the best use of Bob Kiley's vision and experience.

It consumed his drive and well-being when his contribution could have been most influential. "We shouldn't underestimate the distraction, aggravation, rage associated with the PPP" suggests Bridget Rosewell, then economics advisor to Livingstone.[99]

Into the future – the PPP unravels

Any rationale the PPP might have once had steadily unwound during three years of protracted contract negotiations, as risk and costs were steadily returned to the government and ultimately to its balance sheet. The PPP delivery of the Tube upgrade was delayed, and even after 2003 real improvements proceeded unevenly. "These companies come together with the government to create the most complex contracted structure that the world of public procurement has ever seen, and then they say, 'Boy, there's a lot of bureaucracy here, this is very confusing, this is outrageous'." LU MD Tim O'Toole likened this in 2006 to "Claude Rains in *Casablanca* saying, 'I'm shocked to see gambling going on here' just before he takes his winnings."[100]

Kiley and O'Toole went to work on fixing the Tube through the PPP contracts. "The chalice is definitely poisoned," Kiley conceded in 2004. "The question is whether you can detoxify the contents." The Treasury never publicly recognized the calamitous course it had set for the Tube, but by 2005 it came around to empowering local authorities to borrow, including granting TfL access to public-bond financing for improvements on the Tube. In 2004, in the wake of the success of congestion charging and before the second mayoral election, Livingstone was readmitted to the Labour Party, with Tony Blair publicly admitting that he had been wrong about his old antagonist.[101]

Arriving in TfL, Lauren Sager-Weinstein recognized the dynamics of the PPP: on the one hand, Underground people, starved of investment, desperate to fund the

Tim O'Toole and Bob Kiley at Westminster station control room on O'Toole's arrival as MD London Underground, July 2003

upgrades; on the other hand, many people able to see how cumbersome this was, how it was a "cottage industry of measurement, and penalizing things that weren't done and lost customer hours. It was not a model that made you think about customers. It was a model that made you think about managing your infracos" – the infrastructure contractors.[102]

King and Crewe estimated that "although the figures are open to dispute ... the PPP blunder certainly cost UK taxpayers not less than £2.5 billion and probably far, far more, possibly in the region of £20–£30 billion."[103] This was an expensive and inflexible funding model for the upgrade of the system. Letting the private sector loose was not, after all, the panacea for reviving tired public sector assets. "Looking back, the whole episode looks like a triumph of dogma and personal prejudice over common sense."[104] What the long and sorry PPP story did demonstrate was the need for at least a billion pounds a year to be invested in the Underground to keep the infrastructure in a good and reliable state, and for such funding to be planned across several years and not be subject to wasteful stop–start annual funding.

To complete the PPP story, TfL bought out the remaining Tube Lines contract in 2007. Ironically, it was on the watch of the second mayor, Boris Johnson, a Conservative, that the Underground was in effect renationalized. Johnson's deputy mayor, Daniel Moylan, gave TfL the political support such a move demanded:

> It was problematic because Boris kept running out on the other side. Boris didn't quite believe [the buyout] was going to deliver and he kept wanting assurances that this would work. Unfortunately, it wasn't possible to give him those assurances. He kept coming up with other ideas which wouldn't have worked at all, like bringing Tim O'Toole back to run Tube Lines. Why would you bring back somebody you rated in order to work for the other side? We had to put a stop to that. Boris was operating under a deadline because Bechtel was about to start work on the Northern line, having failed to deliver on the Jubilee line. Having learned some of the lessons from the Jubilee line, [Tube Lines] had announced that they were going to close the Northern line every evening at eight o'clock and they had to be stopped from doing that. Boris was understandably very, very anxious to find a way out of this. We had to work very hard to keep him on the right track. What I said was, 'This is the only thing that will work, because no other way will work. You have to get them out, you have to be able to destroy the contracts. This is the only way that will work but you've got to stick with it and be really difficult and keep shaking the trees. Eventually, if you shake the trees hard enough and stamp your feet, something will fall into your lap, so to speak. You've got to believe this, you know, you've just got to understand this is going to happen – and he didn't really'.[105]

Transport for London
Street Management

Trafalgar Square is changing for the better

Trafalgar Square is being transformed. From 1 September the north side of the square will be pedestrianised. Lifts will be installed and a new, grand central staircase will lead from the fountains to the National Gallery. There will be changes to traffic flows and bus stop locations plus new bus lanes and improved access for people with disabilities. This scheme will create a space that all Londoners can enjoy and be proud of.

For more information and for details of traffic diversions, please visit www.worldsquares.com call London Travel Information on 020 7222 1234 or textphone 020 7918 3015.

MAYOR OF LONDON   Getting London moving   STREETS

3.

THE FIRST MAYOR'S FLAGSHIPS

"No modern British politician had ever had the opportunity I was now presented with, to create a new body, recruiting staff and drawing up planning, transport and environmental strategies. Future mayors would inherit the machine I created."[1]

– Ken Livingstone, *Just Say No*, 2000

Transport was the new mayor's principal means of making a major beneficial impact on the capital, and TfL was his delivery agency. First there was a litmus test project, the long-debated pedestrianization of Trafalgar Square. The Mayor's Transport Strategy then placed emphasis on the rollout of two linked first-term initiatives: the controversial congestion charge to reduce central London traffic by moving car use onto an enhanced public transport offer through a revived bus service. Contesting the public–private partnership for the Underground consumed time and energy, but the objections ultimately failed and the contracts were signed in 2003. Meanwhile, passenger numbers continued to rise and to challenge the operation of the Tube within the PPP upgrade regime. The terrorist attacks of 7 July 2005 were a terrible test for TfL, but suggested that the organization had come a long way in public esteem and confidence since the low point of the King's Cross Fire in 1987. Innovative government funding and powers to borrow offered the longer-term investment horizons the transport strategy needed as the constraints and cost of the PPP grew ever more evident.

Livingstone gets to work

"Transport is the single most important priority for the mayor and the Greater London Authority."

– Livingstone's mayoral manifesto, 2000

Fully aware that the new mayoralty would be judged at the end of its first term on the three flagship projects, Ken Livingstone and his advisory team set TfL to work immediately. Livingstone relished the opportunity to be "running something again"[2] but as the new mayor he was under scrutiny from the off to show results.

His prior reputation as the controversial GLC firebrand Red Ken was an easy and welcome target for his opponents and the press. Yet time and energy were needed to set up the new GLA from scratch and to manage the transition of functions from 15 agencies to combine within the new Transport for London. Despite this, 'so what is the point of Ken?' was very much the media tone, not least of the *Evening Standard*, as it reviewed the first two years of the mayoralty, describing him as a "finger-pointing, snarling snapping brute ... facing the awful truth that what he promised he would do for London simply wasn't happening".[3]

The first flagship: a world square for all

"It is the world-famous square that no longer looks world-class. Blighted by traffic and pigeons, Trafalgar Square has become a shadow of the 'grand piazza' envisaged when it opened in 1840. But yesterday a grand redesign of the square took a step forward when traffic was banned from its northern side."

– *Evening Standard*, 2 September 2002[4]

The transformation of one of London's iconic locations, Trafalgar Square – Nelson's Column, Landseer's lions, the fountains, the National Gallery, the country's venue for political demonstrations by the Chartists, suffragettes, CND, anti-apartheid, oppression in Chile and China, and Thatcher's poll tax – from what had declined to a traffic roundabout into a square worthy of iconic status was a knotty problem. Multiple stakeholders, pigeon lovers, heavy traffic, seven access roads, tourist crowds all competed for attention. In microcosm, this wicked challenge (which Westminster council had dropped) was well suited to London's new figurehead, a test of the new mayor's ability to integrate and solve thorny planning and traffic issues.

On the day after the election, the mayor had already asked Derek Turner to take over as interim director of Streets, to introduce both the pedestrianization of Trafalgar Square and the congestion charge. "We had a conversation of several hours," Turner recalled, "before being taken down to what effectively was an ongoing party after the winning of the election. It was a very interesting stage, as I reflect on it over the many years that have passed, how we went from what was a very conventional government organization to a very personal organization for London."[5]

Despite the dire warnings of the traffic congestion that pedestrianization of the square would bring to central London, the media helpfully focused attention on the removal of the pigeons as the "ultimate test of the mayoral mettle".[6] Tony Banks MP led a mass pigeon feed-in, veteran campaigner Pat Arrowsmith was willing to go to jail for the 11th time in their cause, while pigeon dieticians were marshalled behind the mayor reassuring that this would not lead to mass pigeon starvation. Simon Jenkins suggested that the pigeons needed only to waddle north to Leicester Square for a tasty morsel of Kentucky Fried Chicken and Haagen-Daz.[7] "As a pastime it has thrilled Britons and tourists for more than a century, but feeding pigeons in London's famous Trafalgar Square is now illegal – a move that has angered bird lovers but delighted the capital's controversial mayor. Mayor Ken Livingstone's new by-law came into effect on Monday after he had already banned sellers of bird food from the square and introduced Harris hawks and megaphones to the area – measures that helped reduce the number of pigeons from 4000 to about 200."[8] This also involved paying off Bernie Rayner, whose family had sold bird seed on the Square for 50 years; "Livingstone sows the seed for exodus of Trafalgar Square pigeons" reported *The Guardian*.[9]

Work on such a high-profile and heavily used space was not without its difficulties. "Lorries and buses queue for hundreds of yards in all directions. Tourists grimace as they pose for their souvenir photographs to the sound of pneumatic drilling … the plethora of temporary traffic lights, dug-up pavements and new traffic islands."[10] Cabbies and delivery drivers bemoaned the congestion. Trafalgar Square was a microcosm of the necessary rebalancing of space in central London, reducing space for cars by a third to accommodate more public space. The daily battle of Trafalgar Square was to be repeated throughout the next two decades as all three mayors sought to move Londoners towards active travel – walking, cycling and public transport – by shifting the balance away from the car.

TfL reported that "to heighten the enjoyment and make use of one of London's most historic locations, construction work has been completed at Trafalgar Square for phase one of the World Squares for All scheme. Unfortunately, this meant major road layout changes, but the north side of Trafalgar Square is now pedestrianized and links to the National Gallery via a grand central staircase."[11] Trafalgar Square proved to be a first and significant milestone for the new mayoralty. It is telling that Derek Turner, the godfather of the congestion charge, regards it as a career high. "The pedestrianization of Trafalgar Square has had enormous benefits in terms of creating a true centre for London. It was an exciting period, and we were given huge opportunities … he [Livingstone] wanted change, he wanted it to be a success."[12]

Livingstone reopened the square in July 2003, giving it "back to Londoners. Trafalgar Square was originally dedicated to the public for their free and unfettered use. Today it meets that objective more than at any other time since it was first built."[13] For Livingstone "the seal was set on the turnaround when I reopened Trafalgar Square after 18 months of work. Lord Foster's team had paved over the racetrack that used to be the street outside the National Gallery and installed a grand flight of steps down to a piazza worthy of a great world city. Some evenings on the way home I stopped to savour the atmosphere in the new square as it became a meeting point for Londoners."[14]

The second flagship: momentum on the buses

The workhorse of public transport, the red London bus and its network of 675 routes and 19,000 stops was by 2000 in urgent need of updating and investment. The privatization of the bus service since 1985 had been completed in 1994, continuing the regulated model (unlike everywhere else in the UK) with fares set by London Transport (LT) and bus services tendered route by route to private-sector bus contractors. Escape from the rigid bureaucracy of LT and competition for contracts among the private companies had delivered significant cuts in cost. LT's last director of Buses, Clive Hodson, had driven down the costs of the tendered operation sufficiently to achieve (briefly) breakeven on bus operating costs in 1997–98. But staff shortages, wage inflation and traffic congestion rendered this a false position. Hodson successfully trialled Quality Incentive Contracts (QICs), which rewarded or penalized the companies across a range of customer- and service-focused indicators. New-style contracts of up to seven years were introduced, switching the emphasis from growing passenger numbers to increasing the reliability and quality of the service. By 2006 all bus contracts had moved to the QICs.

The regulated approach in London over the two decades from 1981 to 2001 had seen bus passenger journeys rise by 33 per cent, while in the deregulated world beyond they had fallen by 37 per cent. Privatization of the bus companies and route tendering within London had crucially led to the "shuffling and weeding of supervisory and management responsibilities right down to garage and local area level. This process permitted the dead wood to retire with some honour and gave the brighter shoots the scope to make themselves a name," commented one of the LT managers who had seized the opportunity to buy out their company in the sale of the bus companies in 1994.[15]

The issue of accessibility, service quality, faster boarding, bus lane enforcement, bus staff recruitment and environmental performance remained key issues on arrival for the new mayor and for Peter Hendy, appointed as TfL's first MD for Buses in 2001. He would demonstrate that the bus service had significantly more capacity than was being delivered, especially when latent demand was unlocked by moving from single- to double-deck buses.

The regeneration of the bus service had been a manifesto commitment of Livingstone, with specific pledges to freeze fares for four years, a 70p flat fare, camera enforcement of bus lanes and conductors on buses. Dave Wetzel, the mayor's deputy chair of TfL, was a stern advocate, having himself been a conductor, bus driver and union official in the 1960s, a leading figure in the GLC Fares Fair campaign in the 1970s and chair of the GLC Transport Committee. Livingstone and Wetzel had on arrival been keen to unpick the route tendering system and bring the bus service back in-house, but a major review persuaded them that the tendering system had been a success and they left it alone. It has survived to this day, and for Stephen Glaister is "one of the great, and little-noticed, success stories in public authority procurement".[16] Wetzel sought a direct hand in the improvement of the bus service and the remuneration of its crew, as he had done in GLC days, until his wings were clipped with the arrival of Bob Kiley as the first TfL commissioner.

Peter Hendy, busman and later TfL's second commissioner, recalls that on his arrival at TfL from First Bus in 2000, the bus service was "on the edge of starting to crumble again". Bus companies were experiencing up to 40 per cent a year turnover in bus drivers, a symptom of wages falling behind the market; the recruitment and training of drivers became a major cost and preoccupation for the bus contractors. £30 per driver per week worked was offered by TfL to the bus companies to address the staff pay and recruitment issue.

As Peter Hendy recalls,

> Wages had got way out of sync with the prevailing market. That was the origin of the mayor's supplement – 30 quid a week. It was quite evident that you needed to do something substantial with wages ... it didn't alter the contracts with the operators, you didn't let them make any money on it. You just paid them back the [extra] money that they paid to the staff and that solved the staff shortage and enabled us to expand the service to deal with the increase in levels of service for congestion charging ... we were also in the course of rolling out Countdown real-time information.[17]

In the era before digital apps and open data, the provision of Countdown dot matrix signs at 2500 stops was a revolution in itself, helping passengers to know for the first time exactly when the next bus was coming and making public transport an easier and more attractive option.

The service and the bus fleet were in need of attention, with central London routes still reliant on 550 open-platform Routemasters first introduced in the late 1950s. The social context of the bus service in London had changed since the Routemaster was in its heyday as the London bus. Ticketing developments had speeded up boarding by moving cash transactions off the bus to Oyster, corner shops and ticket machines. Hendy explains:

> On the Routemasters conductors were wasting their time because there were no fares to collect. The service was faster for doored buses than it had ever been because of the speed of boarding; the doored buses were all accessible. So why were you running Routemasters? We persuaded Ken to get rid of them, and we

introduced artics for capacity reasons. That all seemed to be a virtuous circle except for the public outcry about the Routemasters, and the fact that there was a section of society that didn't like articulated buses which became politicized.[18]

Despite nostalgia for the freedom of the open platform, which was to emerge as a populist issue in the 2008 mayoral election, there was a significant safety issue with people falling off open platforms. In 2003–04 there were 287 reported injuries as a result of falls from Routemaster buses, and one fatality.[19] Early in the new mayoralty, Livingstone supported retaining the iconic bus and its conductors, and indeed bought back and refurbished 49 Routemasters. Hendy has judged this as a necessary political gesture but conceded that it was "symptomatic of a wish to enhance the bus network".[20]

Although low-floor buses had been introduced in contracts from 1998, the bus fleet's age and size needed investment. In March 2003 Hendy was reported saying that the implementation of a low-floor, accessible bus fleet was a higher priority than keeping the historic Routemaster buses.[21] Despite criticism from the media and the public, the remaining crewed Routemaster services were consequently replaced from August 2003 onwards by low-floor double-deck or articulated buses, as existing bus contracts were retendered. The last day in regular service in 2005 saw nostalgic crowds of bus enthusiasts mourning on Streatham Hill as overloaded Routemasters laboured to the garage, accompanied by an open-top TfL press bus full of celebrating accessibility campaigners.

The introduction of a central London congestion charge was the third flagship commitment of the mayor for his first term. Such a momentous innovation merits a chapter to itself (see Chapter 4). The charge made a significant demand on the bus service. To shift the reputation of the buses as the last resort in public transport and encourage drivers out of their cars, the quality, frequency and reliability of London's buses needed urgent attention and investment.

The carrying capacity of the bus network was addressed by the specification of new and more buses, notably articulated buses on the busiest routes. In 2002, TfL launched Mercedes Citaro articulated buses on two bus routes, the Red Arrow services 527 and 501, as "the speediest bus boarding system in the UK; at 18 metres long, the bendy and cashless bus services are able to carry up to 140 people, at least 60 more than a double-deck bus and 76 more than the vehicles currently serving the routes. They will make journeys more reliable and quicker as passengers must have a ticket before boarding and can board or alight from all three doors like in many cities on the continent." [22]

Mayor Livingstone said:

London is leading the way in innovative bus services. I've made them cheaper, more reliable and brought them nearer to more people than ever before. These

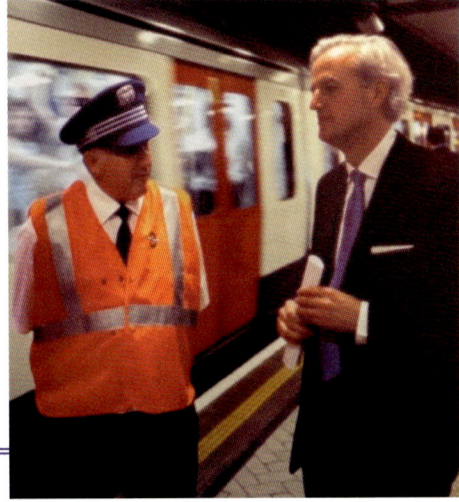

Peter Hendy, second TfL commissioner, on steam loco Met 1 at Tube150 anniversary, January 2013

Tim O'Toole, Underground MD from 2002 to 2009, spent his first five months on the network meeting staff while waiting for the PPP to be signed

two new bendy-bus services are just one of many bus improvements for London before congestion charging is introduced. Just like on the Continent, all the doors can be used for getting on or off the bus, providing hassle-free, comfortable and reliable travel for everyone.[23]

Other routes followed, with 390 articulated buses eventually being introduced and the last Routemasters withdrawn by 2005 except on two heritage routes, the 9 and the 15. By 2006 all London buses were low-floor and accessible. The size of the London bus fleet grew from 5446 in 1999 to 7037 in 2006 and to 8145 in 2016. Alongside the bus driver premium, this wide range of measures led to the subsidy of the bus network rising to £600 million a year.

Powers were obtained to fit cameras to buses to support enforcement of no parking in bus lanes. This, together with bus priority measures at key junctions and the reduction of central London traffic congestion from 2003, sped up the service. Bus usage had grown in the 1990s, and increased by a further 40 per cent between 2000 and 2006, while falling elsewhere in England by another 7 per cent. In 2006, Hendy commented:

What we have seen in London in recent years shows what effective regulation, political will, prudent investment and, crucially, listening to what the public want and then delivering it to them can achieve. With some 8000 buses on 700 routes, the London bus network is now the most comprehensive public transport operation in Europe. Couple this with the Tube and other public transport networks, and a picture emerges of a city which is delivering a real alternative to the private car for millions of Londoners and visitors.[24]

Hendy described the regeneration of London's bus service as a virtuous circle. "If you're the proprietor of the bus network, there's only one way to enhance the revenue – to get it performing properly. Congestion charging made a huge difference to traffic speeds and sped the bus service up. We got a virtuous circle, we got more miles from existing vehicles and we put on more mileage and it was all more reliable … the more mileage you put in, the higher the frequencies are, the more likely it is to be reliable because there's more buses so there are less likely be gaps. A virtuous circle as long as you're not bothered about how much it costs. At the same time we were taking cash off the bus …by incrementally increasing the cash fare and making every alternative more attractive, including carnets of tickets and ticket machines by the bus stops."[25]

Managing the Underground

"The government must recognize the fundamental flaws inherent in this PPP and, in accordance with the wishes of Londoners, hand TfL the power to raise the necessary investment, and provide for unified management. Only then can we think about returning the Tube to its former glory."

– Bob Kiley, TfL commissioner, in 2001[26]

Devolution to the elected mayor and the GLA had given the capital the opportunity to shape its transport. However, TfL was still dependent on central government funding, "unable to raise its own finance as LPTB [London Passenger Transport Board] once was", as Kiley had rued in 2001. "This is untenable. It is time the government recognized the devolution agenda must be completed if we are to make a real difference to transport in London. It is ironic the government is pledging a Railtrack Mark II for London Underground, while introducing a system similar to that which I am proposing for the Tube to replace Railtrack."

The London Underground PPP contracts were nevertheless finally signed in 2003, and the shadow regime within the Underground, which had separated the private sector infrastructure upgrade contracts from the public sector operation of stations and trains, became a reality. From then on, the maintenance and upgrade of the track, signals and stations of the Underground were vested in three PPP contracts over a life of 30 years for work worth £17 billion in total; two contracts were held by the Metronet consortium,[27] the infrastructure companies BCV–Bakerloo, Central and Victoria lines, and Sub-Surface line (SSL) – the Circle, District, East London,

Articulated or 'bendy' buses at Victoria bus station, December 2005

Hammersmith & City and Metropolitan lines. The third contract, for InfraCo[28] JNP (Jubilee, Northern Piccadilly lines) was awarded to the Tube Lines[29] consortium. After years of negotiation and extended shadow running of the separate infrastructure companies and the operations that remained with the Underground, Tube Lines took over responsibility on 31 December 2002, Metronet the rest of the network on 4 April 2003.

A new London Underground MD, Tim O'Toole, had been appointed five months before the prolonged contractual negotiations had been signed off. From Philadelphia, O'Toole had not met or worked with Kiley before. He came with a legal and financial background from the American freight railroad Conrail, and had experience of taking a rundown railway, rebuilding it and fashioning it into something else. "That's what I was schooled in. In that respect, my coming to this arcane PPP financial structure from basically a similar story in the US, was something that Jay Walder I know focused on right away."[30]

O'Toole had a remarkable induction to London: he spent his first five months riding the network and talking to controllers, signallers, drivers and station staff while waiting for the Tube and the PPP contracts to be signed and their management vested in TfL. "That was enormously valuable to me. In fact, I really despair thinking how I would have performed in the early time if I hadn't had that delay, because I just spent all my time out on the railway and I got to meet a lot of people."[31] O'Toole had been taught that as a manager you had to go out into the field. "Executives on my railroad were assigned as safety officers of different districts. Mine was Indianapolis, and I spent my time going in and out of engine houses and drivers' depots, and that was fairly intimidating stuff for me in the beginning because there was a lot of hard bark on some of those guys; you get used to it and really learn about the railway. I remember a friend of mine said, 'You have to understand what it is we make'."[32]

Despite the to and fro of the PPP question, O'Toole was aware that the Underground still required daily direction and operational leadership.

> While Bob and Ken could attack, I actually had to run this place, and you can't run something by attacking your own people, so I quickly started to spread this story even in Kiley's presence and Ken's presence – 'terrible structure but I am here to make it work' – and truth be told they wanted me to make it work. I think they liked the sound of that, maybe because they were a bit tired of the battle, all the court cases and all the rest, they never challenged me on it, and anyway the Tube was a very intimidating thing for a politician. They didn't want to be too close to it because things happen. Kiley and Ken were perfectly happy just to let me run it.[33]

O'Toole grasped that his problem wasn't so much the PPP itself as the broken relationships and uncertainty it had brought in its wake. "I had all these people who'd been called names and were told they were worthless, I had a senior management that thought it was on its way out, I had stakeholders who were insisting on more war, more blood, and I'm thinking to myself, 'I've got to run this!' And my greatest danger is that LU would go passive-aggressive on me. That they would just say, 'All right, you're so clever, pal, you figure it out. You tell us what to do'."[34] Since the announcement of the PPP, the leadership of the Underground had been sidetracked by creating shadow companies, moving jobs, the PPP negotiations and writing the contracts.

O'Toole distanced himself from the PPP and from the political dogfight between Kiley and the government. "I remember going hat in hand with Bob to see [Alistair] Darling, who was the secretary of state for transport. Bob kept challenging him, 'When are you gonna give it to us, when are you gonna to give it to us?' I can remember Darling turning to me and saying, 'What are you going to do with it when I do?' and then having to try to come across as some dynamic new leader."[35]

O'Toole very quickly decided that the legal, finance side of this, "the fighting the PPP battles and all the stuff that got the headlines was all a sideshow, and I did as much as I needed to keep my stakeholders at bay. The real job was running the railway and rebuilding it and bringing the employees back into the story."[36] He couldn't just wait on the PPP to deliver or to implode, it was important to get on with what needed to be done on the Underground that was within his grasp and outside the PPP. "If the PPP is what this is all about, I'm going to spend the next five years of my life with lawyers in courtrooms … I thought I had to create a narrative here, and the holding … position was, 'Forget about the PPP. Nobody is to think about it. In fact, you're not to think about anything in terms of any grand design.' I even used to discourage the world-class metro talk, and I said, 'All we need, right now, is a safe, reliable, clean railway. Just give me that'."[37]

For O'Toole, the PPP upgrades were only part of the story and a distraction from the real work that needed to be done.

> I used to tell people, 'It's not your business, don't worry about it. We've just gonna run this railway'. But it was tough because we kept having signal failures, and [with] all the finger pointing at the infracos and all the time spent working with them, those early periods were very, very difficult … The only way to get through this was that we also needed a steady drumbeat of improvements, even little improvements, just constant … We did make a lot of improvements, some of them I think people have recalibrated and people don't notice them any more. I am very proud of the fact that we painted out the whole network. We removed all the graffiti. There used to be graffiti from Earl's Court to Hatton Cross on every single wall. It has all gone, the only time you see graffiti on the Underground is when you are actually looking at a Network Rail wall.[38]

The provision of so-called rainbow boards at each station, updated with the state of play on each line, was an O'Toole initiative. Along with station announcements that stated, "There is good service on all LU lines", messaging was moved from what was wrong – delays, signal failures, failed trains – to what was right, the good service. "I'm delighted, tickled by, the fact they're all over the world now," says O'Toole. "I was in Australia, where they had them; I went into the station in Melbourne and I thought, these things are everywhere!"[39]

In 2007 a poster campaign, 'We Are Transforming Your Tube', was mounted, asking for passengers' patience with disruption from closures. This was part of a wider communications strategy to explain the disruption caused by the massive upgrade programme in the context of the long-term plans for an improved Tube. As O'Toole explained, "It's simply easier to tolerate the Victoria line being shut early every evening if passengers understand the long-term benefits."[40] This would grow from posters and press announcements to omnichannel campaigns including emails, text messaging and posters in stations, which became line specific, to the growing database of customers.

O'Toole believed the real story around the PPP was that the Underground had been starved of cash and investment, not management capability. "Look at Metronet. It was an organizational mess but still its lines were getting better because of the vast volume of cash being thrown at the system. If they had given us the money directly, I think we would have delivered the same improvements faster and cheaper."[41] Two other failing PFIs – Connect for train radios, a major safety improvement in terms of communication underground, and EDF Energywork – were turned around as well as major station work such as Wembley Park where, unusually, Tube Lines was hired to do the work in an LU-led project, rather than within the PPP.

Initially there was inevitable scepticism about the appointment to head the Tube of another American. But O'Toole became the flag waver for the London Underground culture.[42] He may not have been an Anglophile on arrival, but once in London he immersed himself in the Underground and came rapidly to an appreciation of its pedigree, which he felt had been lost in recent years. It was easy to regard the Underground's heritage as backward-looking and resistant to change. O'Toole recognized, as perhaps only an outsider could do, pride in the Tube's story, in its history of moving London, and in good design as a narrative that had positive power to motivate and address current issues. "We had to rebuild it for the employee; you had to make the brand consistent again, you had promote it, you had to support the art programme, you had to do it all. You couldn't just rebuild Victoria station, that was not enough. That is the narrative that I created, which I think encapsulates more of what I was attempting to do than any other – and we rolled that out after 7/7." [43]

Terror comes to the Tube

The greatest test to date for the mayor and TfL was to come on 7 July 2005, the morning after the incredible high of securing the 2012 London Olympics. The four bombs, the first such attacks on public transport since the 19th century, saw 56 people killed and more than eight hundred seriously injured. A detailed account of 7/7 and its aftermath (see Chapter 5) tells us much about the quality and resilience of TfL, both the operational staff on the front line and the senior leadership.

It's time to talk

"Time to Talk," according to Tim O'Toole, was the kind of thing that not only breaks through to your line employees but causes your managers to think, 'Hey, I could do that, this positive communication works, I'm empowered by this' ... A lot of people can't communicate. When you give them that skill, you really make them a better executive."[44]

The perennial issue with trade union relations is the expectation of the Underground leadership that they should face down the unions, be the tough guy, until "strikes happen and then everybody wants you after about twenty-four hours to get out of them". O'Toole had formed the belief that the only way to deal with this was to go around the unions through a comprehensive communication programme. He maintained that most managers are unwilling or afraid to talk to their employees, worried about walking into mess rooms in case they said the wrong thing, even preferring the rules and structures of the disciplinary process. Once empowered, managers found the benefit of going out and talking. It also addressed the fact that employees are hungry for information: they need to hear the big picture from the bridge, whereas too often they heard it only though trade union sources. "It is a big beast to communicate with, the Underground, and it is very distributed, and how you talk to the guys who are running the trains – it is hard to get to them." [45]

For O'Toole, the unsupportive agendas of the trade unions at the 7/7 terrorist attacks also needed a leadership response. "They did some really bad things that we never talked about, only because it wouldn't have done society any good to create a fight about that subject in public. But they did things that I would consider very unpatriotic, you know, as an American would call it." [46]

Time to Talk was delivered live more than thirty times by O'Toole and Underground COO Mike Brown, with top-quality video material, even deploying

A packed hall at one of the Time to Talk conferences

We are transforming your Tube

River Thames

MAYOR OF LONDON

Transport for London UNDERGROUND

The LU 'rainbow boards' changed the tone of customer messaging, displaying line by line good service not just service interruptions

a hologram of O'Toole in a later iteration at Victoria House for the sessions he was obliged to miss. They hired a tented party venue at Waterloo … "We had it all set up as our stage," Brown recalls. "It was a very slick, very well-managed event … they were exceptionally nerve racking – to be in front of about two hundred people all the time, and then there were all the questions … I'd never done anything, any show of that size before and it was really like theatre … and getting the message consistently communicated across was really good."[47]

Time to Talk did cause many employees to view the leadership differently. There was initial resistance; they were seeking to communicate directly with employees, working around the trade unions, who put out flyers urging employees not to go to the 'Tim O'Toole Scientology lectures', and some drivers would come in and turn their chairs so their backs were to the presentation.

> I remember the first time we showed the 7/7 films in it, we had people who cried, and we had people who complained afterwards … then it just grew and grew and grew. People forget that in the last four years there were no strikes, because I think they [the unions] really couldn't take them out. The employees were proud of themselves – and don't get me wrong, if we had hit them with extreme wage demands, they

facing: TfL's Transforming the Tube campaign suggested that short-term disruption for upgrades would lead to a more reliable network for passengers

would go out, people always go out for money. But they weren't going to go out just because Bob Crow told them to any more. They were proud of themselves and they thought, 'I get what is going on here'. What you get out of programmes like this is, you don't eliminate issues, you still have issues with your employees but you make it impossible for unions to demonize you and make their job simple. I think the average employee thought, 'There are other ways and I want to be part of that railway', because the employees felt we understand what they're doing.[48]

When the Underground looked back in 2008 on three years of Time to Talk and associated communications initiatives, they found a clear upward trend since 2005 in staff response rates to the Speak Up surveys, and that clear direction, company leadership and staff motivation scores had risen by some 20 per cent. Even more significantly, there was also a clear upward trend in 'soft' attributes experienced by customers at the operational sharp end – driver announcements, station staff helpfulness and visibility.[49]

As part of his narrative for the Tube, O'Toole re-established a design committee to oversee the application of principles of good design, which were such a significant aspect of London Transport's brand DNA but had been diluted in the face of funding and operational constraints. "One of the little things I just was so thrilled to see the other day was something that our design committee produced. Central line stations on Oxford Street used to have hideous dirty red canopies, and our team replaced them with modest but distinctive canopies, all lit Underground blue with the name of the station and the script and it is all so clean; [Frank] Pick would have put it there, and paying attention to stuff like that matters."[50]

The PPP starts to unravel

The PPP took seven years to unwind, pretty much as Bob Kiley had predicted to Tim O'Toole in 2003 when first in London to run the Underground. "He was an amazingly prescient guy. He said to me, 'Tube Lines will rob us blind, but they'll do a good job', because he had unwavering faith in Bechtel; and he said, 'Metronet will never work. It's a disaster and you watch, they'll go bankrupt'."[51]

Metronet was already behind the contract programme on all major station upgrades by early 2005. Affordability constraints had already meant that many major improvements under the PPP regime had been deferred until after the first seven-and-a-half years of the contract period. There had been improvements to the ambience of the system with deep cleaning on stations and graffiti removal, but train performance in terms of lost customer hours as a result of engineering overruns and signalling failures remained below contract benchmarks, which were themselves based on lower than pre-PPP performance.

The Metronet contracts had continued to underperform when, in November 2006, the PPP Arbiter reported that the consortium was responsible for an estimated £750 million cost overrun due to mismanagement of its contracts. Metronet was criticized for its tied supply chain approach, in which contracts were awarded only within the consortium, which led to high costs. The PPP Arbiter Chris Bolt promised to apportion costs in January, but concluded "that neither of the two Metronet infracos has performed in line with the required standard over the period as a whole".[52]

As Metronet's financial position worsened, the PPP Arbiter did not agree an increase in monthly payments by the Underground, and, after a major derailment at Mile End, in July 2007 Metronet went into administration. The government defended its position, blaming the corporate failure of Metronet rather than the PPP. Stephen Glaister, then a TfL board member, disagreed: "The objective was to deliver public services with economy and efficiency," he said. "The PPP was proposed as a method of doing that, and it has failed."[53]

Tube Lines was, meanwhile, judged to be delivering on time and on budget, using competitive tendering rather than Metronet's closed shop to minimize costs as it approached negotiations for the next seven-and-a-half years' tranche of the contract in 2008. Ultimately and ironically, it would prove to be a Conservative mayor who bought out the final PPP contract and renationalized the Tube.

Funding and prudential borrowing

In Livingstone's manifesto, the first line was no Tube sell-off; "maintain the Tube in public ownership and raise finance for modernization by the cheapest method – bonds". On his arrival as TfL commissioner, Bob Kiley had sought to overturn the PPP, proposing that funding for the upgrade of the Tube and other infrastructure investment would be far better raised through bonds, through prudential borrowing in the financial markets, the usual funding model for infrastructure projects in the United States. Kiley argued that this offered a simpler capital funding route than the increasingly complex PPP contracts and the shrinking transfer of risk to the private sector contractors that had been necessary to keep the bidding consortia interested.

In the same year that the immensely cumbersome PPP contracts had finally been signed, by a bizarre government sleight of hand the bond funding route that Kiley had been advocating was made available to all local authorities. Under the prudential borrowing regime,[54] major local authorities such as TfL were free to finance capital works by borrowing, provided that they could afford to service those debts from revenues. This would have precluded the complexity and cost (at least £1 billion) of the set up and management of the PPP contracts. However, for the Treasury proponents of PPP, in the wake of their experience with the Jubilee line extension, the bond finance route did not bring private sector expertise to the Tube upgrade, nor did it take the expenditure off the government's books, both of which had been the alleged benefit of the PPP. In the event, the leadership of TfL did succeed in securing funds through prudential borrowing, bypassing government restrictions and substituting the credit agencies as the indicator of reputational success. The Office for National Statistics was to rule in 2006 that PPP investment was to remain stated as government expenditure; PPP was not 'off the books' after all.

Jay Walder, TfL's MD of Finance and Strategy, recalled:

> When we began to have these discussions about prudential borrowing and the way in which we could put together a transport package, the reality was that the Labour government would not work with Ken or Bob. Alistair Darling [now chancellor of the exchequer] literally said he would not work with Ken or Bob to do this. In this strange, bizarre way the party that everybody agreed would be in the middle of this was me. These were huge decisions for TfL and for the government. We were in the midst of negotiating this, involving Tony McNulty, who was the transport minister, Jeremy Heywood, Blair's principal private secretary at that point in time … There were a lot of people who were really intrigued by this, because they felt that it was actually creating a new way, it was prescribing certain things for TfL that TfL would have to agree to explicitly in what it was doing, most prominently raising fares [to service the debt].[55]

Walder remembered being at the final stages of agreeing the prudential borrowing deal when Livingstone was on holiday.

> I called his office; Redmond O'Neill, John Ross, Simon Fletcher – all of them, they said, 'This is too big, you have to talk to Ken directly, we can't make this decision without Ken.' I called Ken, and said to him, 'Here's the deal, it's going to give us billions of dollars of funding to be able to invest. Part of it is that we have to agree to a fare increase.' I said, 'Let me be clear, if we agree to this, you can't back away, it has to be real, because we're gonna have to go to the rating agencies, we're gonna have to be able to do this in a way that is not just [tokenistic].' We talked about it for a while and he said, 'Okay, I agree to that.' My joke is that the next day, I called Ken again and we went through everything again. He finally said to me, 'Jay, we talked about this yesterday.' I said, 'Yeah, but I didn't believe you, so I want to go through it again and make sure that you really meant it.' He came back from his holiday, and in his first press conference he stood up and said, 'We've made this agreement and we're going to raise fares, and I stand behind that,' and he held to that in every way in being able to do it. You know, when I said to him that the rating agencies were going to want to

meet with the mayor, he asked, 'Why would they want to meet with me?' I said, 'Because you ultimately have the powers.' And so, again, in a funny way, these are all reinforcing mechanisms of that [TfL reputation for] professionalism and accountability.[56]

For Walder, prudential borrowing against future revenues, from local taxes and fare revenue, was the means to make the TfL funding model work. "The mayoral model was only half baked because the model effectively said, 'You're the mayor, you can do this, but you don't have any ability to raise funds, you don't have the ability to borrow, you don't have an ability to tax, you're gonna come back to us, cap in hand, and ask for whatever we're going to give you'.

> We were now moving this forward in a fundamentally different way than we did before. It's not just TfL that's looking at this, it's actually government that is seeing it very positively from that perspective, as well. The only thing that was this amazing distrust that was there [evidenced] when I say that we were working with Number Ten, because working with the Treasury was virtually impossible. It had to be brokered by Number Ten rather than the Treasury, working with people within the Department for Transport who would work with me and the permanent secretary, Tony McNulty,[57] and try to keep it out of the people who have long-standing political animosity.[58]

The other hugely significant change of the Livingstone terms was the willingness of the government to move to multi-year operational funding agreements. Charles Monheim was developing the Oyster payments revolution.

> There was quite generous funding of the transit system initially, and then there was an agreement, quite an unusual agreement, on a multi-year funding plan that crossed spending review boundaries to enable TfL and its agencies to plan what they were going to do over a more reasonable timeframe. That required a certain level of co-operation, which to everybody's credit the PPP fight didn't disrupt. So when you're talking about the personalities, you have Ken ... and the permanent secretary in the Department for Transport; Jay and he had a productive relationship. Those personalities were important – Jay, Bob, Ken, Robert. But at the same time, none of that works if you don't have the financial wherewithal to do things that are going to impress the public. To their credit, they gave people like Malcolm and Michèle[59] and me, and Mike Brown and Peter Hendy, the latitude to do stuff. [They] made sure that they chose well, and then gave those people the latitude to do things that met or exceeded their standard.[60]

Steve Allen was brought into Walder's team in 2003 to lead on the investment programme. Allen brought experience as a civil servant to prudential borrowing,

Crossrail funding and later to restructuring the PPP. Although investment in the Tube was being delivered by the PPP, borrowing powers enabled TfL's plans for development of other parts of the transport system to be realized: extensions to the Docklands Light Railway, further powers over suburban rail in London – which led to the creation of London Overground – and investment in roads.

> We quickly seized on the opportunity of prudential borrowing ... the Treasury's expectation with prudential borrowing was that authorities would exclusively borrow from the Public Works Loans Board [PWLB], a source the Treasury controlled ... we saw a particular value in TfL having a public rating to its creditworthiness, rated by external agencies. One part of that was to put some discipline, around the mayor in particular and the board more generally, to be prudent ...The government was charging us more to borrow from the PWLB than we could go and borrow in the markets, so we were able to say we weren't borrowing more expensively just out of some sort of perverse view of wanting to be independent of government. We were actually saving cash for TfL by borrowing from private investors.[61]

Crucially, TfL was obliged to write a prospectus, described by Stephen Glaister as "a fantastically detailed account, lawyered word by word, stating to the markets the financial health of TfL and saying what the borrowed money would be spent on; no mayor has ever had to set this out in such detail".[62]

Introducing a Low Emissions Zone

Air quality monitoring in London had demonstrated that the capital's air quality had been worsening since the 1990s. On 9 May 2007 the mayor confirmed that he would proceed with a low emission zone (LEZ) for London focused on vehicle emissions, with plans to reduce emissions overall by 16 per cent by 2012. The strategy for creating an LEZ took time to deliver, as decision-making within TfL had become more developed. As TfL's director of Planning, Michèle Dix, recalls: "That took slightly longer to do in some ways than the original congestion charge because more of a system was in place for TfL. With the ultra low emission zone [ULEZ from 2019], we did most of the work in terms of devising the scheme under the mayoralty of Boris ... we spent a lot of time talking to all the groups who might be affected by a scheme such as ULEZ. We talked to them about different things that we could do, who should be exempt and what time frame it should be introduced over so that they all bought into it. So not only did the public vote – 'Do you support it or not?' – but all the different user groups, because of the timing of it and the advance warning of it, bought into it coming in. It was one of those schemes that we did take a lot of time over, but it did get the buy-in".[63]

Londoners move on

"I can honestly say that it was an absolute privilege to be on the board of Transport for London for five years, when it was at the cutting edge of radical transport policies worldwide. It was a roller coaster exciting ride."

– Professor David Begg, 2019[64]

The Livingstone years had seen a revolution in the bus service and the successful introduction of the congestion charge. They also saw significant spadework done on two initiatives that would have been inconceivable in the pre-mayoral era: the Oyster card was introduced and developed as a revolution in payments and ticketings from June 2003, and the heavy lifting was done on organizing London's bid for the 2012 Olympic Games, secured in July 2005. The digital revolution of fares and ticketing and the challenge of mounting a public transport Games were huge and demanding projects for TfL and for public transport in London, and have both been accorded their own chapters in this book (see Chapter 6 and Chapter 11).

Bob Kiley left TfL in January 2006 after emergency surgery in London, and for health reasons retired to Massachusetts. Kiley was delighted with the appointment of Peter Hendy as the second commissioner.[65]

Despite the achievements and innovation of his two terms in office, Livingstone lost the 2008 mayoral election. His campaign was lacklustre, perhaps hubristic after eight years; he did not appear on top of his game; he lost outer London; and he was distracted by a relentless personal campaign against him by the *Evening Standard*. He was his own worst enemy, feeding the *Standard*'s campaign with remarks about sending the Reuben brothers back to Iran or likening journalists to concentration camp guards, from which he never backed down despite the damage. He was not helped by the Labour chancellor raising the lowest rate of income tax, causing their ratings to slump massively.

Looking back more than a decade later in 2019, Livingstone's view was that "Boris is this charismatic character. I think people [regard] Boris based on his being on *Have I Got News For You*, and I used to watch and laugh at him. That's why he's had this landslide this time [2019 General Election] … That was one big factor … Just a month before the [mayoral] election, Brown had changed the tax system. So for the five and a half million people on the lowest rate of tax, he replaced the 10 per cent with 20 per cent. And pollsters came to me and said, 'Labour's support and yours has just slumped'. So, it was Brown's economic strategy and Boris's charisma."[66] While the national context may have been unfavourable, Johnson was uniquely suited to take on Livingstone. He was a fresh face to the now familiar Livingstone, was backed by a remorseless campaign of support from the *Evening Standard*, and was an irreverent, amusing crowd-pleasing campaigner with equally sharp political and populist instincts.

4.

THE CONGESTION CHARGE

"The whole of the British media and I think probably most politicians, bar Ken, thought it would fail. When it worked, it was like a huge relief, rather than a surprise."

– Michèle Dix, *TfL co-director, congestion charging, 2000-07*[1]

The GLA Act gave the mayor powers to reduce traffic levels in central London by introducing a congestion charge, with the income from the charge to be spent on public transport. Thanks to work commissioned in advance, a blueprint for the charge was available when Ken Livingstone was elected on a pledge of introducing it in his first term. Despite widespread anxiety, the charge was successfully introduced in 2003, the first such in any major European city, and traffic congestion in the central charge zone was substantially reduced. TfL's reputation was enhanced and given confidence to continue as an innovator in world city management. Livingstone was readmitted to the Labour party, and re-elected as mayor in 2004.

The prehistory of road charging

"Traffic expands to meet the available road space or jam yesterday, jam today and jam tomorrow?"

– Lewis–Mogridge position on traffic in towns, 1990[2]

Congestion and delay on London's roads had been a perennial issue arising from the organic growth of its dense street network and sustained population increases from 1800 to the Second World War. This had long fostered transport innovation: the building of new streets; the world's first Underground, the Metropolitan Railway from Paddington to Farringdon in 1863; the first traffic light in 1868; the deep Tube network from 1890; the North Circular and Great West Road in the 1920s; and the

Ringway scheme and the Westway in 1970. Traffic nonetheless continued to expand to fit the road space available – now an accepted maxim of transport planning but originally propounded in 1990 by David Lewis and Martin Mogridge.

The potential of a payment to constrain traffic and reduce congestion was surprisingly first proposed in 1951 by free market economist Milton Friedman, who envisaged a future of nuclear-powered vehicles, equipped with Geiger counters to measure road use from radioactive road markings.[3] The Smeed Report of 1964, *Road Pricing: The Economic and Technical Possibilities*,[4] was commissioned by the Ministry of Transport from the Roads Research Laboratory.[5] This radical report suggested that speeding up congested traffic would benefit the country's economy by between £100 million and £150 million a year. "It would be possible and feasible to impose car user restraint strategies by charging through the metering of road usage, if the government had the will to do so."[6] The Conservative government of Harold Macmillan lacked such will to proceed, viewing charging as a restraint on the motorist rather than valuing its wider economic benefit.

The political baton was next taken up by Barbara Castle as the Labour minister of transport in Harold Wilson's government from 1964, but, in the face of the dominant road-building lobby, congestion charging was not a priority. In 1967 the Road Safety Act introduced a national speed limit of 70 mph, and the breathalyzer to measure alcohol levels in drivers. In the late 1960s the Greater London Council (GLC) had considered an area toll around central London served by toll booths, but by 1970 congestion charging had been all but forgotten.[7]

This was the last era when planners sought to solve congestion by proposing more roads. The London Ringways, four concentric motorway rings including miles of Westway-style elevated motorways around the capital, had been proposed in 1966-67 as the solution to London's growing traffic problem. The Ringways have been described as "the most astonishing and destructive thing never to happen to London".[8] The first elements of the Ringways, the East Cross Route to the Blackwall Tunnel (today's A12) and the elevated Westway on the A40, had been built by 1970. At its opening the Westway, part of the London Motorway Box, the inner ring, was the largest continuous concrete structure in Britain. The extensive demolition of property in North Kensington and East London to build the Westway had provoked sustained community protest and political opposition to such intrusive urban road

top: The proposed London Ringways included an elevated motorway over the North London line, accessed by large clover-leaf interchanges such as this one at Dalston

bottom: Four concentric motorways, some elevated like the Westway, were proposed in 1966 as the solution to traffic congestion in London but required extensive housing demolition and ultimately an unacceptably high cost

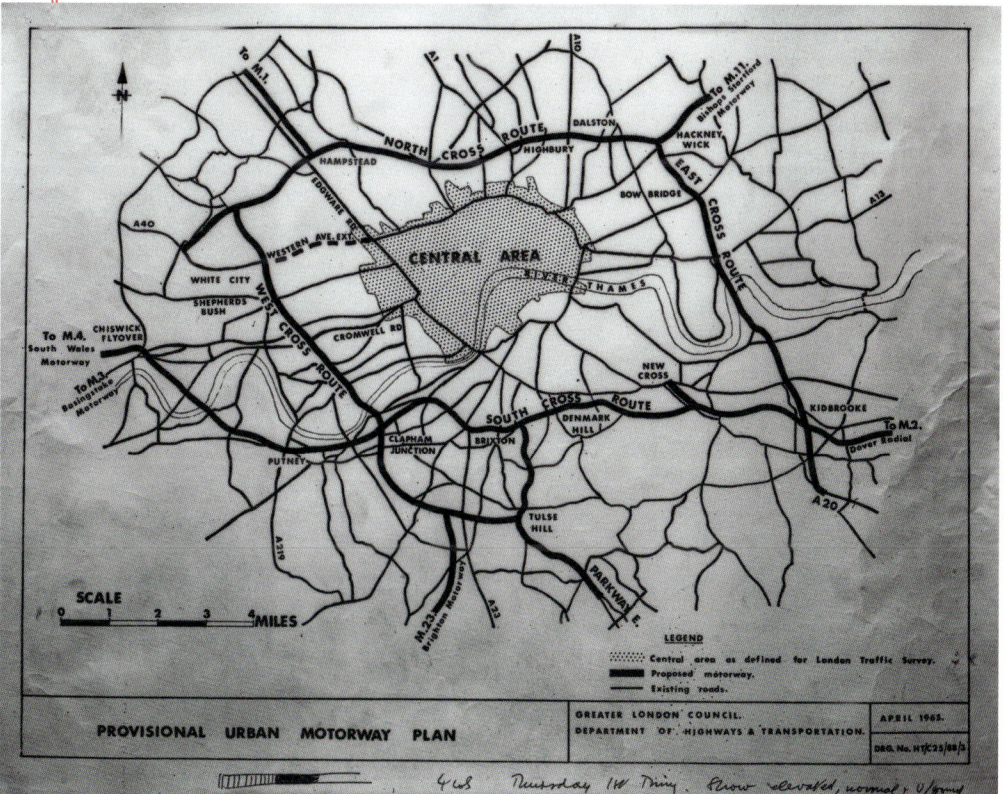

PROVISIONAL URBAN MOTORWAY PLAN

GREATER LONDON COUNCIL.
DEPARTMENT OF HIGHWAYS & TRANSPORTATION.

APRIL 1965.

DRG. No. HT/C23/88/3

LEGEND

Central area as defined for London Traffic Survey.
Proposed motorway.
Existing roads.

building. The six-lane Ringway One was to be elevated on concrete piers, like the Westway. Connections with arterial roads bringing traffic out of central London demanded space-hungry clover-leaf junctions with ramped access roads. Ringway One alone was at the time expected to cost £480 million, including £144 million for property purchases, requiring 424 ha (1048 acres) of land and the demolition of 7585 houses,[9] a cost that had risen to £2 billion when, despite the GLC's plan being subject to a highly contested two-year planning inquiry, it was approved in 1973. In response, The *Sunday Times* ran a two-page spread, under the headline *The Motor Car Wins its Biggest Victory.*

The Ringways finally fell foul of a significant sea change in thinking about cities, influenced from 1961 by Jane Jacobs's *The Death and Life of Great American Cities*,[10] which argued that contemporary enthusiasm for urban renewal and slum clearance did not respect the needs of city dwellers. Jacobs and a grassroots protest – 'Downtown is for People' – led to the cancellation of the Lower Manhattan Expressway, which would have cut through SoHo, Little Italy and Chinatown in New York. Jacobs's argument against the dominant trends in town planning, specifically in New York and then Toronto, became widely influential and crystallized a reappraisal of town planning and transport policy. In the UK, Colin Buchanan's *Traffic in Towns* report for the Department for Transport (DfT) in 1963 advanced similar arguments, daring to suggest that building ever more roads was not the solution to traffic congestion in cities. Buchanan signalled that a fundamental change was needed in attitudes to roads and the primacy of the motor car if towns were to be attractive places in which to live. (An abridged version of the report, published by Penguin in 1964, proved popular and sold 18,000 copies.) Buchanan maintained that "our British cities are not only packed with buildings, they are also packed with history, and to drive motorways through them on the American scale would inevitably destroy much that ought to be preserved".[11] He also suggested that limiting access to city centres was inevitable. "When everything that it is possible to do by way of building new roads and expanding public transport has been done, there would still be, in the absence of deliberate limitation, more cars trying to move into or within our cities than could possibly be accommodated."[12]

> Traffic congestion has already placed in jeopardy the well-being of many people in towns and the efficiency of many activities. The potential increase in the number of vehicles is so great that unless something is done ... the utility of vehicles in towns will decline rapidly or the pleasantness and safety of surroundings will deteriorate catastrophically – in all probability both will happen together.[13]

While building the Westway had provoked strong community protest, the Ringways were to meet their Waterloo at Archway. The six-lane Archway Road had been built from 1968 to 1971 as an element of the Ringway plan, sweeping up the hill from

the Holloway Road at Archway to narrow and end abruptly at the former London County Council (LCC) boundary beneath the Archway Bridge. The road's planned route northward attracted organized resistance, reflecting a new public appetite for protest at the impact of the planners' schemes. Four prolonged planning inquiries were severely disrupted by well-informed protest and the scheme was abandoned, initially in 1978 and altogether in 1990. Archway Road was the first successful UK road protest and contributed to the Conservative administration being defeated at the 1973 GLC elections, in which the Ringway proposals were a key factor and Labour, having pledged to scrap the Ringways, won a convincing majority. In the event, the outer elements of the Ringway scheme were later combined to form the M25, fully opened by 1986. The Westway and the A12 East Cross Route to the Blackwall Tunnel represent the high tide of the private car's domination of transport policy in London.

At the Archway Public Enquiry in the early 1970s, a young, relatively unknown activist and Camden councillor cut his transport teeth. Ken Livingstone, for it was he, recalled: "Ted Knight and I supported the opponents of the scheme. The enquiry regularly collapsed into chaos, and on one occasion the chairman climbed out of the window to escape local residents. I followed, trying to persuade him to come back, when Michael Howard [later leader of the Tory party], who was presenting the pro-motorway case, appeared on the roof crying, 'Don't throw him off!'."[14] The pro-roads tide was decidedly on the ebb, to be replaced by an emphasis on public transport and traffic management. A congestion charge study was given consideration in 1974 by the GLC – which by then included Ken Livingstone as a newly elected councillor.[15] Livingstone remembers:

> When I was leader of the Greater London Council two decades ago, we published the GLC's work on this subject but the manifesto on which we were elected had specifically rejected road pricing. There was significant spare capacity on public transport at the time, so making public transport more attractive, and fares cheaper, encouraged a shift from car to public transport, and reduced traffic and congestion and the consequent air pollution and accidents.[16]

By the 1990s, the average speed of road trips across London had fallen below that prevailing in the horse-drawn era a century before. Traffic speeds in central London had fallen more than 20 per cent since the 1960s, from an average 12.7 mph for the morning peak period in 1968 to 10 mph in 1998. Even in inner London, drivers in 1998 spent some 30 per cent of their time stationary during peak periods, and more than half their time travelling at speeds of less than 10 mph. By 2002, the all-day average travel speed in central London was just 8.6 mph, compared to an uncongested (night-time or free flow) average speed of around 20 mph. Congestion, measured in terms of minutes of delay per mile compared to uncongested conditions, averaged 3.7 minutes per mile. With more than one million people entering central London between 7.00 and 11.00 a.m. on an average workday, and more than a quarter of those by road, the cost of congestion and delay was clearly considerable.[17]

Public and business concerns over levels of traffic congestion were high. An independent survey in 1999 identified public transport and congestion as the two most important problems requiring action – selected by 46 and 33 per cent of London residents respectively, compared to 20 per cent for crime or law and order. Ninety per cent of London residents said, "There is too much traffic in London."[18] The moment for a congestion charge had arrived. In the mid-1990s, London First began promoting the need for a charge to resolve the business disbenefit of unpredictable journeys through congestion in central London. The future TfL co-director of congestion charging, Michèle Dix, worked as project director on both this study and the ROCOL (Review of Charging Options for London)[19] working group.

Planning for a congestion charge

"In 1997 ... big changes for London were clearly in the air. It was decided that there ought to be something to offer a new mayor on roads, because they had always been a big issue in London, and congestion was the big issue for Londoners and the business community."

– Derek Turner, TfL MD Streets and creator of the congestion charge[20]

Significant work had been done on what was to become congestion charging in London before the mayoral election of 2000, enabling its inclusion in Livingstone's manifesto. The Department for Transport had set up the London Congestion Charging Research Programme in the 1990s, reporting in 1995 that a congestion charge of £4 a day would reduce congestion, offer rapid payback of the initial set-up costs, and generate net revenues as well as broader net economic benefits. While formulating the Greater London Authority (GLA) Act, Genie Turton, director of the Government Office for London (GOL), understood that charging powers would be helpful in addressing the major concern of traffic congestion. Turton set up ROCOL, and its report in 2000 gave the new mayor cost and benefit options and the blueprint for a charge.

The congestion charge had been the joker in the GLA pack since powers were included in the GLA Act (see Chapter 1). Livingstone had been advised against putting it in his manifesto. "All my political advisors in the run-up to the 2000 election were saying, 'Don't make a commitment to the congestion charge, it might cost us the election.' They were worried, and then in the run-up to it coming in they were saying, 'Put it off till after your re-election in 2004, just in case it doesn't work'."[21]

Michèle Dix recalled that survey results showed people agreed that more public transport was the answer to congestion, and that it should be paid for by charging the vehicles that caused congestion:

> When we were doing ROCOL ... all the surveys showed that people would support a congestion charging scheme, because London was grinding to a halt on a regular basis, because it was just overcrowded. Some incident would happen at one end of town and then the rest of the town would become blocked ... huge demand to do something about it, so there was huge support for congestion charging.[22]

The powers to charge

"Putting congestion in really threw a cat among the pigeons," Turton recalls. "I was told by the team, 'You can't do that ... the bill is complicated enough' – but anyway, we did it. It is the longest piece [of legislation] since the Government of India Act [1935]."[23]

Even though options for congestion charging for London had been developed, powers for the new mayor to act came later. Genie Turton, the architect of the GLA bill, recalled that this was the initiative of John Prescott, whose national transport bill was turned down due to lack of parliamentary time. "Congestion charging was John Prescott's national congestion charge, it was John Prescott's flagship idea. Alongside PFI, he really wanted to get congestion charging in ... We were having a meeting with him, and I said, 'Well, why don't we put it in the London bill?' 'Oh,' he said, 'all right, let's do that'."[24]

The great triumph for Turton had been to convince the Treasury to include hypothecation for the income from the charge. "Treasury was always nervous about money, which is why congestion charging hypothecation was quite a victory with them. In terms of the powers, I think, for what we wanted, and I suppose and what our defence always was, was we want a genuine accountability, that's the comparison with the GLC in a way, because the GLC did have a lot of power, but where was the accountability?"[25]

Turton is convinced that if it had not gone into the GLA bill, congestion charging would not have happened. "We didn't at that stage know who was going to be the mayor ... it will be a controversial policy. But if it's going to happen, it has to be the first mayor, the first mayor will have the momentum to do it. But the first mayor won't be able to do it unless there's a scheme that the first mayor can do. We employed consultants and we set up a working group to develop the scheme."[26]

The work on road charging in the 1990s gave the first mayor a ready-to-roll scheme. Derek Turner, then traffic director for London, and the future godfather of the charge, was a member of the group.

> We brainstormed a number of possibilities, and a firm of consultants, Halcrow Fox, were appointed to help us. We focused on two options; one was a road pricing/charging type option and the other was charging for all (non-residential) off-street parking. They were both run through various models, and while both proved to achieve the objective of reducing congestion in central London, practicality ... led to congestion charging showing up better. The report recommended congestion charging, showing that, overall, it was a better option. All the mayoral candidates supported the report, and most of them said that they would introduce congestion charging but not during their first term of office. It was only Ken [Livingstone] who said he would introduce it during his first term and then included it in his manifesto.[27]

Livingstone was to apply a tight timetable for the introduction of a charge by 2003, giving sufficient time before he would be held to account at the mayoral election in 2004. The go-live date of 17 February 2003 was set in stone in the scheme order that enabled the charge, and was a good year earlier than the team would have wished.

The introduction of a congestion charge, Dix maintains, could only have happened in the empowered culture of the new mayor and TfL in their first term.

> The thing I thought was marvellous was that, having had 15 years without a London government and being part of that world, post the GLC and pre-TfL, when no one really had a grip on London, and not a lot happened … as soon as you brought TfL into being with powers for the strategic road network, for the buses, for the Tube, for congestion charging, you were able to create a strategy that had meaning. Up until then, all those things were done by different people, and they weren't joined up. Congestion charging was a scheme that enabled you to join those dots together in detail, you were planning public transport improvements, parking controls, and bus routes and cycle routes, car shares as well as the congestion charging scheme all at the same time."[28]

Designing the congestion charge

"This was going to be [Ken's] signature; he wanted to be absolutely clear about the risk … But his strong message was, 'I am not doing this for dollars or pounds. I'm doing this to create the transport outcome'."

– Jay Walder, TfL MD Finance & Planning, 2001–07[29]

Of significance to the delivery of congestion charging, Turner was used to having the traffic director's autonomy to deliver the red routes, and had built an encyclopaedic knowledge of London and its traffic patterns and road network. The day after the 2000 election, Livingstone gave Turner two years to design and deliver the congestion charge, "with a third to withdraw it and Ken to rebuild his image if it was a failure; it gave him two years to adjust it to make it work the way it needed to before the election, which gave him the confidence to say, 'I'm prepared to take the risk'."[30]

Turner describes implementing the charge as "very, very exciting and very liberating, but complicated and stressful … It was a very, very interesting period because the relationship between Ken and myself was quite clear. He was surrounded by various acolytes and I was surrounded by the American TfL team, which had its own managerial tensions. I came with the recent experience of running my own little non-departmental public body [NDPB], which reported directly to the minister for transport for London and was accountable to Parliament. All my powers were effectively absorbed into TfL; that change was not particularly different. In reality, because of the nature of Ken, it was much more empowering."[31]

Turner's knowledge of London's traffic management and his personal style equipped him ideally for the delivery of congestion charging. Peter Hendy, then his TfL colleague as MD of Buses, recalled:

> Before TfL existed, Derek had been tasked with doing something about London's traffic. It was a pretty shrewd idea actually; if you manage the highway properly on a foot-by-foot basis, then you will produce better traffic flow, better arrangements, fewer violations and it will work better ... Ken said, 'I want that Derek Turner'... Derek could be both absolutely charming and completely dogmatic, he was actually a lone ranger; Derek's team worked for Derek, but it was Derek who did things and he had experience of being the traffic director and setting things up his own way ... then he had to come into the organization. He didn't much enjoy that and he certainly didn't accept direction comfortably."
>
> He did know what he was doing, though, and Ken was right to get him appointed, because of all the people who could have done congestion charging he, together with Malcolm [Murray-Clark] and Michèle [Dix], co-directors of congestion charging, who he also appointed, would get it done. They lanced every boil on the way and managed to do it ... the [mayoral] advisors actually got cold feet at various stages; on more than one occasion, they told Ken it was never going to work and he should give it up and he said, 'No, I've said I'm doing it so I'm doing it'. Derek was proved absolutely right ... But also he's the sort of bloke who never had any doubts about his own competence. I think that what they devised for congestion charging, they knew it would work. That's why there was quite a lot of politics and anger about it because they just ploughed on, knowing it would work – and it did work.[32]

Livingstone had recognized Turner's qualities as a "workaholic whose obsessive attention to detail made him the ideal person to operate the congestion charge with its complex IT system".[33] Turner got under way quickly.

> Because of the timetable that Ken wanted, the congestion charging scheme needed to be introduced in the first term of office. I was building upon ROCOL work with Genie, Michèle and Malcolm[34] and the DfT's congestion charging research programme. I was set up and well under way before Bob [Kiley] arrived. At Bob's arrival, because he was a very, very strong character, Ken took me to one side and said, 'Whatever Bob wants to do in TfL and the management of Streets, Bob and I are in charge. However, there's one exception: whatever you want to do, or feel we need to do, with congestion charging, you and I are in charge. You have to persuade me and I will back you' – and he did. He backed me against Kiley on a number of occasions, much to the annoyance of some of the advisors ... We had a very interesting dynamic, Ken and I ... an unspoken agreement that he would deal with the politics and the top-line media and I would deal with the

(left) Derek Turner, MD Streets Management 2000–03 for the implementation of the congestion charge by *(right)* co-director Michèle Dix, who later led the western extension and ULEZ implementations

technocrats … yet if you look back through some of the media from the time, it was almost like that; he would brush off an issue and say, 'Well that's for Derek'. That is how it would appear in the *Standard*, and the following edition, or the following day, there I was trying to explain it all.[35]

Murray-Clark and Dix became the midwives of the new charging scheme. Dix recalls, "I wanted that job to put the charge in. It was a very full-on job and, because I had previously worked part time, I didn't want to go back to 24/7 working, I persuaded Malcolm that he'd want to do it with me as a job share, so we were there from the beginning."[36] Murray-Clark recalled, "We often joked that we were the worst advert for job shares as we both regularly worked 60 hours a week!"[37] The ROCOL study had suggested that it would take four years to implement; the team did it in two-and-a-half years. "The speed at which we did it was pretty amazing … We were there from the beginning, our job was get it up and running, to make sure it could operate properly, that the traffic management systems were in place, communication systems were in place, and then to operate it, very successfully."[38]

Stephen Glaister recognized the significance of the ROCOL work, which was "a very big piece of research, it was almost word for word what Ken adopted … The £5 charge was [proposed], I remember it happening at a session of that committee, which drafted both the design and the charges and the estimates of how traffic would change. The whole thing, Ken took over lock, stock and barrel, which is why he survived two judicial reviews once he was in power. He'd said he would adopt those proposals in his manifesto and he did, so there was absolutely no doubt that they had a mandate."[39] "Without that foresight [from ROCOL], Livingstone would have found [it] exceedingly difficult to implement an effective scheme ahead of the 2004 election."[40]

In TfL's early days and with a clear political mandate, though the details were complex, decision-making for this major initiative was simple. Dix's recollections are vivid:

> We were taking decisions to the mayor. It would be a meeting with Bob [Kiley] about what we're going to do and then you'd take that to Redmond [O'Neill] who was the mayor's key advisor, and then to a meeting with the mayor to get a decision. He was totally informed, really, really good at asking the right questions about what needed to happen. Redmond was on the ball in terms of challenging all that we'd done to make sure that he had the same confidence that we had about how it would work ... that section of the Mayor's Transport Strategy was written specifically to set out the congestion charging scheme ... We got the powers through a scheme order, we designed the charging scheme, we designed the traffic management around it. We worked with the boroughs on a major budget for complementary measures to ensure that the scheme would work, putting in new parking controls – car share schemes and bike schemes, and supporting the new buses that would be needed because we don't have time to do anything about the Tube ... We did all the publicity, the campaign to explain to everybody what was going to happen. We were even involved in picking the actors who would play key roles on television, because there was going to be a major television and radio campaign across the nation. So many people come into London on an infrequent basis, they needed to know that this scheme was in place. Then the procurement of the scheme itself, major procurement, really big complicated IT and traffic engineering solutions and bringing those things together. That really gave someone like me a huge variety of tasks to do during that period. I would say it was one of the most exciting things that I've worked on during my career ... [It was] very tight ... we did it in just over two-and-a-half years.

Setting the strategy for the whole of London, and all the things that you'd have to have in place to support the policy and make it work, that in itself was a key challenge. Then all the legal side and getting the scheme order through, the work that was required with all the different groups to explain how they would be affected. Challenges about whether people would have discounts or exemptions. Working with different groups like shift workers, market workers, residents, on the different ways in which they might be able to use the scheme. Helping different companies in understanding what different methods, approaches they could take with the scheme in place. Then collecting all the data about what happened before the scheme came in and regularly reporting on its impacts. We did do an annual report for about six years on the congestion charging. Thereafter, it's very difficult to determine its effects because of everything else that's going on around it. But pre- and post-regular monitoring allowed us to say what was happening. Later on, people said the scheme was not having an impact any more, because congestion started to come back. That's not because there was an increase in traffic, it's because deliberate decisions were made to use the space that was created to help address some of the issues about making walking and cycling much more pleasant within the central area – the reallocation of space to walking and cycling and buses.[41]

Peter Hendy recalls: "Derek, however histrionic, was good at delivering things like that. We improved the bus service with a bit of money. Putting the drivers' wages up and a plan to paint all the buses red, for which I got a round of applause in the chamber at City Hall …You can't diminish the fact that we delivered Ken in his first term far more than he ever bargained for … PPP was intellectually dead before the contracts were signed, the government were determined to do it. Ken and Kiley had won the political and economic battle, they just hadn't won it with the government … then congestion charging happened and it was a huge success."[42]

Michèle Dix recalls how they had studied it in a huge amount of detail.

> We made projections using different modelling approaches, which all gave a similar answer, which gave you confidence in that answer. We had a lot of research in terms of monitoring the situation beforehand, not just the traffic but wider factors, and then testing scenarios for the situation afterwards and over time monitoring the outcomes. We did a lot of work in preparing for the opening of the scheme, all the things that could go wrong. Then planning activities we'd have to have in place to mitigate against them. A huge amount of planning was done and it paid off. The whole of the British media and I think probably most politicians, bar Ken, thought it would fail. When it worked, it was like a huge relief, rather than a surprise.[43]

Despite the meticulous planning, in the days before introduction Turner remained cautious, "concerned at the public's and politicians' reaction because it will take weeks, possibly months, to operate as designed, and it is asking a lot of people to bear that in mind. The nightmare is whether they are patient. I'm not a patient person, so people have my sympathy."[44]

Delivering the congestion charge

There was an ironic contrast in these early TfL days between Turner delivering the congestion charge strictly within the GLA legislation, not least anticipating being buffeted by a potential judicial review, while at the same time Kiley was seeking to break the PPP part of the GLA Act. As Turner explains:

The whole system had to work within the GLA Act. I promised Ken I would build a congestion-charging machine that would work; how he adjusted the machine, the levers and the knobs was up to him. I would have to work within the established legal framework. Then we were challenged on the legal framework, we were taken to the High Court and to a judicial review. But on the PPP side we – TfL, Bob and Ken – were the challengers of the government. The congestion charging was trying to work within the legal framework, whereas he [Bob] was trying to break it. We had huge problems on my side and on their side as a consequence of the two different approaches. I had difficulty, for instance, in getting the necessary co-operation for the secondary legislation which was needed. Secondary legislation could only be granted by Parliament, but that required civil servants to draft [it]. There were difficulties with that because of political ramifications. The political animosity between Ken and Gordon Brown and Blair was very great indeed.[45]

There were differences between the two strong personalities of Kiley and Turner, exposed by the technology of congestion charging; Turner argued for existing proven technology and Kiley for more innovative solutions. "Bob had an American view – there was a thing called Easy Pass, which was an electronic tag system for a number of the bridges in New York. He felt that was the model that should be used. Ken was very, very low tech – 'Let's make it flexible, let's make sure we have time to change it, we want to get it in very quickly' – so we still had two years to adjust the knobs and levers and get it the way he wanted it or get it so that he would be re-elected."[46]

ROCOL had done work to suggest the robust technical and IT solutions available to deliver a congestion charge system. Turner was not interested in systems innovation: "What I'm about is getting something in on time that is going to work and enable the mayor to be a success. That was a clear approach that we adopted … It wasn't completely low tech, but it wasn't as high tech as being totally innovative and cutting edge. It was using established technology and pushing it to the limits, not to let aiming for the best defeat the good. The main thing that was worrying was the number plate recognition and the cameras." Turner recalled, "The back-office side of the whole system was a huge procurement, and we were careful about [not] actually specifying the type of cameras and number plate recognition systems. If we specified it, we would become responsible for it, and I didn't want to do that, for obvious reasons."

With support from Deloitte's, brought in to sit alongside the congestion charge team, the procurement process broke the system required into its component parts and picked the tried-and-tested, best-in-class bids. At the time this was one of the largest IT public procurements: cameras, number plate recognition technology, a payments database."[47] Given the time limit, a clear scope and effective procurement strategy was vital. "This felt like a tall order, particularly given that the record of delivering such projects in the public realm was not good," recalled Murray-Clark.[48]

Selecting the contractors was only the start; such a complex implementation required proactive project and contractor management, internally across TfL and with the mayor's office, and externally as an intelligent but demanding client with the suppliers. While the contract was robust enough for TfL to say 'tough' to the contractor, it was TfL's reputation on the line and it became clear that the "users' experience of paying the charge and disputing unpaid charges could easily become difficult, be highlighted by a still-hostile press and cause reputational and operational damage to the scheme and the mayor". Indeed, it was necessary to renegotiate parts of the operational contracts and increase the payment to Capita to ensure that the "transport benefits of the scheme were not undermined by day-to-day difficulties for drivers engaging with the scheme".[49]

"One of the cries that was often heard before all this started back in the nineties was, 'Why can't London be like it is during the school holidays?'." Turner recalled. "That became almost one of our objectives and a sound bite we could use. We knew how much the traffic levels dropped, it gave us a tangible measure to actually work on, it's about 14 per cent and in the end, when it settled down, it turned out at about 14 to 20 per cent down ... But it also gave us a reason for introducing it in the February school holidays. The traffic levels were down then anyway, so that we had time for them to accustomize because people were, understandably, initially frightened."[50]

The media had piled into the congestion charge since Livingstone's election, especially in the weeks leading up to its introduction on 17 February 2003. An extraordinary range of scare stories reached a crescendo as 'C-Day' approached. The *Evening Standard* accused the mayor of rigging traffic lights so that drivers would face a sea of red lights, then to make congestion worse to improve the impact of the charge: "Ken Livingstone is refusing to come clean on secret plans to rig London's traffic lights".[51] "Livingstone's great plan will drive London mad," stormed the *Sunday Telegraph*.[52] A legal challenge was made, unsuccessfully, by Westminster City Council in 2002 on grounds of inadequate consultation and the charge breaching planning law. "Road toll threatens to overwhelm our rail system" the paper thundered in the week before the charge was introduced.[53]

As C-Day approached, Dix saw "support was dwindling, because people thought, 'This is real, this might affect me, I might be asked to pay to make the journey I normally make', so opposition to it was increasing. People around Ken were getting very nervous, the government was getting nervous about it. But Ken was totally supportive of it going ahead, he didn't feel he had many friends but, as mayor, he was leading from the front and wanting this to happen."[54]

Turner needed the cover given him by Livingstone: "'Go-Live' [i.e. 17 February 2003] was the one point when I had to call in the promise; Bob [Kiley] wanted to delay and Ken didn't want to delay the introduction. Ken would say, siding with me, that it should be introduced on the due date. Ken did back my recommendation and his own judgement, much against the advisors and against the American team. It was literally just the two of us, but, obviously, I had my team with me. It was quite exciting!"[55] A change of date would have led not only to delay but also to a further round of consultation. The congestion charge team modelling had given them confidence through various scenarios that the scheme would work, so they were confident in advising the mayor to proceed.[56]

This might have been the moment for a fainter-hearted politician than Livingstone to reconsider. His principal advisors, John Ross and Redmond O'Neill, were advising him against it; they "thought it was a bad policy", Neale Coleman, one of Livingstone's close advisors, recalls. "To be fair, particularly to Redmond, his advisors always took the view that they would argue about it, but, if Ken wanted it done, it was their job to try and make sure it was done as best as it could be."[57] Jay Walder remembers:

> Bob and I get called to a meeting at Romney House with Ken, and it's just the three of us, there's nobody else in the room. Ken looks at us, and he says, 'All of my advisors – and these are my closest advisors, these are the people who've worked with me for me to get elected – are advising me that I should delay implementing congestion pricing until after my first term. My instinct is not to do that, but I want to hear from you about whether you are confident that congestion pricing can be delivered and be delivered successfully' ... I don't remember exactly the date of this meeting, but we told Ken at that point that we believed that it could be delivered. Ultimately Ken made the decision and said, 'I'm going to go forward with this ... it's in my manifesto, I said I was going to do this in my first term'.[58]

The mayor's unwavering commitment to the charge gave Turner and TfL the cover to work up all the fine details and complex planning of the scheme's rollout, and to resist endless calls for exemptions and the remorseless media carping. Isabel Dedring, then Kiley's chief of staff, remembers, "We got all these crazy letters, like the animal ambulance people who pick up the injured pigeons in Trafalgar Square, [who were] based outside the congestion charging zone but would come into the zone to help the injured pigeons and wanted an exemption from the charge. No exemptions, that was the rule. Then the meat market guys at Smithfield. I mean, there were a few pretty hot, tiny but hot, topics. But that's politics."[59] Meat traders at Smithfield did indeed threaten to refuse to pay,[60] while exemptions were sought by a broad spectrum of groups, from the US Embassy and its 700 staff, to Madonna

Martin Rowson, "Well I suppose it worked," 2003

who refused to register and share her address[61] and Miss Moneypenny, Bond actress Samantha Bond, who led an Equity campaign to exempt theatre workers.[62]

Livingstone might have come from hard-left politics, but as mayor he proved to be an effective manager of the high-quality experts he appointed to advise him. Peter Hendy maintains that Livingstone could have run a major multinational company. "There aren't many people with a political mind who understand how to run a team … He understood, dividing out responsibility, and he understood taking responsibility for what had been done, and he was deeply loyal."[63]

Livingstone said he "approached everything like I did when I was a research technician. That's why I don't think anything went wrong in my years … everything was checked out. I had a brilliant team of people from the old Socialist Action group who just focused on it, and I think I do occasionally hear that people at TfL got sometimes quite battered around by some of my staff making sure everything's going to work … [Derek Turner] came out of one meeting with Redmond O'Neill, saying, 'I'm resigning, I can't stand any more of this', because Redmond was really pressing hard to make sure [the congestion charge] bloody worked."[64]

Isabel Dedring had become Kiley's chief of staff in 2002, when the congestion charge was at the top of the TfL agenda.

It was endless, Redmond pouring over every single one of those posters. We had to do a poster of London, the map of London and then the congestion charge, teeny tiny in the middle – 3 per cent of London will be covered by the congestion charge. We were trying to make it as big as possible, so people could see where it was. He was saying that politically it looked like it's the whole city, and the zone is actually sort of the same shape as London. So just the instant reaction will be – what?! We had these weekly meetings, what will happen when you call the call centre, he wanted to see the script from the call centre. I mean, Redmond was all over it. But he was right, because it was really significant politically and a big gamble for Ken – it had to work and be seen to be a success.[65]

C-Day arrives

The congestion charge finally arrived on 17 February 2003, the first-ever implementation of such a measure in a major European city, the only other being Singapore's Area Licensing Scheme in 1975. The charge of £5 per vehicle was initially levied between 7 a.m. and 6.30 p.m. on Mondays to Fridays within the charge zone, eight square miles of central London, just 1.3 per cent of the capital's area. Seven hundred cameras at the zone's boundary and at key places within it took images of vehicle number plates and sent them to a number recognition computer system. The numbers were checked against lists of payments for registered vehicles – online, by text, phone or purchased at local shops – and unpaid use was subject to a penalty notice after midnight; £80, reduced to £40 if paid within 14 days, increased to £120 if not paid within 28 days. The charge system was outsourced to Capita, which established a call centre in Coventry.

On C- Day the *Daily Telegraph* described the congestion charge apocalyptically as Livingstone's doodlebug: "The congestion charge comes crashing down among us today and great clouds of smoke will go billowing into the sky, choking long-suffering Londoners as they struggle to work."[66] The *Telegraph*'s Sean O'Neill eagerly doorstepped Livingstone early that morning:

This was Ken's big idea, the one that will distinguish or destroy his political career, the first initiative to have a real impact on real lives … the mayor stepped out of the front door of his house in Cricklewood at 6.01 a.m. 'It's going to be a long day,' he announced wearily … By 6.19 a.m. the mayor was at Willesden Green Tube station, and a minute later caught a southbound Jubilee line train. Early-morning commuters – many reading newspapers that foretold gridlock on the roads – paid little heed to his presence until at Finchley Road a man leaving the train turned and spat, 'What you're doing is ridiculous, it's stupid'. The mayor glanced up from his planning papers and sighed, 'Obviously not a supporter'. Arriving at the Metropolitan Police traffic control centre at Victoria minutes before the first cars incurred the £5 charge, 'Mr Livingstone watched a bank of screens as everything went so much better than predicted ... it was traffic bliss ... then on to TfL offices. Recognizing him, a female pedestrian beamed, 'Ken, the buses are being told to slow down because they are getting too far ahead of schedule'. 'Really? That's wonderful,' smiled the mayor, the first crack in his deliberately gloomy façade ... As if knowing he had won the public relations battle, Mr Livingstone stopped to treat himself to a large cappuccino with a shot of vanilla syrup ... Then he was off again, whisking along Victoria Street. At TfL he had a briefing with senior staff: traffic flowing easily, calls being answered within 20 seconds, payments being processed within three minutes. It was all going terribly well and there was no need for the mayor to hang around. By 9.30 a.m. he was behind his desk at City Hall.[67]

Dix recalls well the horror stories in the weeks leading up to 17 February:

They thought there'd be major congestion with queues and queues of people at the boundary waiting for the hours to change in some way, that it would crucify London's economy, that it wouldn't be successful. What did happen was on day one, there was tumbleweed because people didn't come in because they weren't quite sure what to do. Then slowly after that, people did come in, the systems worked. The predicted level of traffic reduction and increase in speed was as we had said, which was probably a first for these major projects. It worked and it works and gave us the results that we expected it to get. It was very exciting to be part of.[68]

Turner and his team had wisely planned to introduce the scheme during the school half-term break.

We knew that the traffic levels would be down anyway, so that gave us time for them to genuinely adjust because the people were frightened by Ken's statements of stay away, etc., but also to ensure we got the technology up and running during that fortnight ... but I must admit, the first day, I can remember walking down Victoria Street in the evening, and feeling, 'Have we overdone it?' Because on that first day we'd reduced traffic, clearly, much more than school holidays' 14 per cent. Fortunately, once people began to realize what was going on, they started to return, and you know, we settled down at about 20 per cent, which proved to be very successful in terms of reducing congestion, just as we had predicted. Now, of course subsequently, Ken and Boris decided to take away a lot of the capacity we released within the road system, and congestion has risen, but we've had probably 15 years of relatively efficient operation of the central London road network.[69]

Evening Standard

LONDON, MONDAY, 17 FEBRUARY 2003   www.thisislondon.co.uk   Incorporating THE EVENING NEWS   **40p**

Sadie makes a surprise show at Fashion Week
See Page 7

Beckham and the amazing saga of Fergie's flying boot
See Page 9

C DAY

- ● It's official ... car charging is in force
- ● 30,000 drivers pay £5 in advance
- ● Commuters set off hours early to get in
- ● Half-term helps ease chaos on Day 1
- ● Hundreds stage demos in protest
- ● Fears call centre will fail to cope

Full reports: Pages 2 to 6

C for costly: traffic passes into the £5 congestion charging zone on Vauxhall Bridge this morning, the first day of the new scheme

The front page of the *Evening Standard* on 17 February 2003, the day the first congestion charge in Europe was implemented

By the following day, the media story had gone into reverse. The *Daily Telegraph*, having railed that the charge would tip London into recession and overload the rail system, sounded decidedly disappointed in its editorial. "What if the wretched thing works after all? The evidence of the first 24 hours seems to be that the congestion charge is functioning as planned, that it's reducing congestion."[70] Even *The Guardian* asked, "Whatever has happened to the rush hour?"[71] Showing remarkable prescience, the *Standard* called for more teleworking to ease the strain on the transport network.[72] Simon Jenkins, himself a central London driver, was similarly wrong-footed: "Road users are certainly driving around the capital in a delighted daze. For once a British transport reform has actually worked. It is eerie. The buses are having to be rescheduled because they keep crossing London too fast."[73]

The atmosphere at TfL headquarters was euphoric, even with the inevitable occasional teething problem as the technical systems were tested for real. Anomalies and glitches were delighted in by the media – an 1898 Daimler in Bristol Museum, which had not been on the road since 1947, was fined for dodging the congestion charge – but the system bedded down and rapidly became the day-to-day norm.[74]

On Go-Live Day, as C-Day was also known, mayoral advisors and GLA staff went up to the top of City Hall, to London's Living Room, where you could see out across the city and the charge boundary on Tower Bridge. "It looked like we'd killed London, it was so quiet," recalled mayoral advisor Neale Coleman. "It was that first day, and I think for a few days, it was unbelievable, there was just no traffic."[75] Underground MD Tim O'Toole joined them. "I got to sit there the night the congestion charge came in, and broke open a bottle of wine in Ken's offices. We watched Tower Bridge not turn into a traffic nightmare. It was very exciting to see all that. The whole place was very exciting back then … there was absolutely no fear of change, quite the opposite, people were desperate to change and so there was none of the calcification you get in a bureaucracy."[76]

Significance of the congestion charge

"We both knew the scheme would work…[it] won me the next election, but a year too soon."

– Ken Livingstone, 2011[77]

The immediate success of the charge was to limit the traffic entering the zone during the original weekday charging hours by 18 per cent and congestion within the zone by 30 per cent. It contributed to a 33 per cent increase in central London bus travel, and enabled 10 per cent of journeys to switch to walking, cycling and public transport.

This was an innovation to which Livingstone, as a lifelong public transport user and non-driver, was personally attached. Charles Monheim, responsible for that other great innovation, the Oyster card, recognized the significance of the first mayor's vision. "One has to give Ken an awful lot of credit for implementing congestion charging against the wishes of his circle, and his continuing his thinking about things like the travel card into this new world of a whole different fare collection technology."[78]

The success of the congestion charge proved decisive for Livingstone's mayoralty and to his readmittance to the Labour Party for the 2004 mayoral election. The charge "had worked, and it was fairly remarkable to do something that quickly," mayoral advisor Neale Coleman judged, "and it was entirely due to Ken's political acumen and determination; it would never have happened without that."[79] Of course it worked perfectly from day one, Livingstone was proud to recall, but not least because a careful, well-funded, analytical study had been commissioned by the GOL before the advent of the GLA.[80]

"The success of the congestion charge was a big moment for TfL. The delivery of its first major project comprehensively silenced the media pessimism of the preceding months, as Isabel Dedring recalled. "It was on a dime, it all turned around. Brilliant, well done TfL, well done Ken. I think it had a really interesting impact on London more widely, people [said] the UK can't deliver a big project. This was a big project that had been delivered flawlessly … Just from talking to friends at the time, wow, we did that, hey, look at that, we can do stuff which was beyond TfL, and actually about the relationship between TfL and the city." As Dedring suggests, early success was crucial for TfL in building trust, which prepared the ground for major innovations such as Oyster and contactless. "People now have this immense trust for the TfL logo and TfL, and what it embodies, and therefore are prepared to give up their data in a different way than they would with many other public agencies. That's because of these seminal moments where TfL has delivered and has responded, and so trust has been built up; it doesn't exist with other public agencies."[81]

This was the first of a series of big successes: the Oyster card, DLR, Overground, the new bus for London, the Olympics, contactless payments. For TfL the successful introduction of the congestion charge was to breed confidence in being innovative and taking risks. Such a significant innovation had been well planned over time and would later be extended and serve as the low emission zone (LEZ).

After 2003, many other cities were looking at similar systems to alleviate traffic congestion. "It was the first scheme of its type in the world," Dix recalls. "We had the eyes of the world on us in terms of wanting to understand what we had done and what the key measures were in making it work so successfully."[82] The triumph of 2003 was all the more impressive as cities worldwide struggled in the years that followed to win a mandate for road charging. While Stockholm introduced a cordon tax in 2006 and Milan in 2008, Manchester, Hong Kong, Edinburgh and the West

Midlands failed to convince their citizens of the wider benefits when the idea was put to a referendum.

Derek Turner left TfL shortly after the success of the congestion charge, ostensibly to set up a consultancy to advise other cities on the introduction of a charge but actually as a result of a restructuring of the TfL leadership team by Commissioner Bob Kiley. Peter Hendy was by then TfL MD Surface Transport, and inherited the congestion charge and its onward leadership by Dix and Murray-Clark. Hendy's understanding was that "Kiley and Jay [Walder] conspired to torpedo Derek because he was quite difficult to deal with on a personal basis and he didn't like being part of a bigger organization ... Jay and Kiley between them had made his life so difficult that he couldn't carry on. He accepted a proposition to become a consultant to advance the cause of congestion charging elsewhere ... he was deeply unhappy about it and, probably, quite rightly so ... But whatever you say about Derek, he not only did the red route network as the traffic director, but he also managed to get congestion charging in, and he did a lot of other good things as well in Streets. It was his design that took out the traffic space on the north side of Trafalgar Square. I remember standing on the north side after it been taken out, thinking, 'Thank you – we have done something here'."[83]

Derek Turner reflected in 2020 that there are still few city leaders prepared to take what they perceive as the risk with congestion charging. "If I was to start again today, I would be exploring the use of mobile phone technology to provide an option for a distance- or time- based charging system. Decades ago, that technology was not available to us. We did look at GPS – it had various problems, coverage was a real issue in the city canyons ... but today I would almost guarantee that nobody who drives in central London doesn't carry a mobile phone."[84]

The successful implementation of such a major innovation in city management was the first test of the mettle of Livingstone and his transport team at TfL. The delivery of this controversial and first innovative major project surprised many who were used to the Red Ken soubriquet and the financial overrun of the Jubilee line extension. It established the mayoralty and TfL as capable of delivering a major project. London's extensive public transport network proved well suited to a congestion charge, thanks to the availability of public transport alternatives to the private car. The congestion charge set a pattern for future innovation in city management: a determined mayor willing to take calculated risks, backed by public consultation, effective design, project management and delivery by TfL, and relentless communications to drown out the media naysayers.[85]

LONDON UNITED

5.

TESTING TIMES

"We have to be lucky all the time; they have to be lucky only once."

– Senior spy, quoted in *The Economist*, 2005[1]

Transport is tested every day by events beyond its control – weather, equipment faults, accidents, overcrowding – and also by the complexity of planning investment, service design and operational delivery for the future. July 2005 was to test severely both the mayor and TfL twice within 24 hours: a successful Olympic bid was secured against the odds in Singapore on 6 July; the day after, the terrorist attacks in London pushed TfL and London to the limit, not least when they recurred two weeks later. Leading the capital's recovery saw TfL's reputation enhanced as an organization that could both deliver an Olympic transport strategy and cope in the worst of crises. Londoners' esteem for the transport network, and especially for those who operated it, reached a new high.[2]

From the euphoria of success ...

A bid to host the 2012 Olympic Games in London had gained Ken Livingstone's support in 2001. For the delegates of the International Olympic Committee (IOC), it was the only UK location worthy of consideration for their Games. The scale and complexity of a bid based in the Lower Lea Valley, on a brownfield site across four London boroughs, demanded a coalition between public and private, national, regional and local government, parks, water, power and transport agencies, united by the IOC's remorseless timetable and arguably uniquely coalescing by the strategic potential of an elected mayor.[3] In truth, even mounting the bid was a triumph, as it was widely suggested that London's transport could not and would not cope.[4]

Ken Livingstone was far from being an enthusiast for sport, but he had been convinced early in his mayoralty that the regenerative benefits for East London were well worth pursuing, whether or not the bid was successful. As his second term began, the transport case for hosting the Games was being supported by the building of the Channel Tunnel link via Stratford International to St Pancras. Approval had been given for the Overground to revive the former East London line to Stratford: the DLR was to be extended to Stratford International. Tessa Jowell, as secretary of state for culture, media and sport, had worked hard and persuasively to bring the Blair government onside despite Chancellor Gordon Brown's scepticism. A coalition of local authorities and agencies had been brought together, initially united arguably more by the prospect of regeneration than by hosting an international sporting event. Indeed, there had been widespread scepticism about the prospects for a successful bid, but satisfaction that the bid was pulling investment into the Lower Lea Valley and East London.

The London Development Agency's CEO, Tony Winterbotham, recalled seeing Livingstone in 2002, three years before the bid proved successful. "I said, 'Ken, we've won. As far as I'm concerned, we've got all these things funded, we've achieved it with great teamwork, we've got a vision for the Lea Valley and the Thames Gateway.' ... But Ken said to me, 'Tony, I want the Olympics now'."[5]

And he got them: on 6 July the IOC announced its choice of London for the 2012 Olympics at a meeting in Singapore. As IOC President Jacques Rogge declared: "The Games of the thirtieth Olympiad are awarded to the city of [slight pause] London", British Olympians on the base of Nelson's Column and the crowd in Trafalgar Square jumped for joy, while Parisians slumped in disbelief. Livingstone, who was in Singapore with Sebastian Coe, Tony Blair and Tessa Jowell supporting the bid team, declared 6 July to be "one of the best days London has ever had – and one of the proudest days for Britain and for British sport"[6]. Tube drivers made special announcements; commuters went home with the day's euphoric copy of the *Evening Standard*, with its pictures of unbridled celebration and ticker tape in Trafalgar Square, under their arms; the Wembley Arch was lit up at sunset; and householders in East London took their houses off the market in expectation of their enhanced value.[7] We all felt good: London was back as a world city. (The full Olympic Games transport story is told in Chapter 11.)

... to the horror of terrorist attacks

"We saw the very best of humankind and the very worst of humankind on the same day."

– Tim O'Toole and Mike Brown, Time to Talk staff briefings, autumn 2005[8]

The very next day, the morning commute had started badly on the Underground with three lines experiencing serious delays because of technical faults: at 6.29 a.m. the Northern line had been suspended due to a train failing with a defective axle box causing locked wheels at Balham; at 7.27 a traction motor had flashed on a Piccadilly train at Caledonian Road; and a main line air hose on a Bakerloo train had burst as air under 100 psi pressure escaped.[9] Each fault had been heralded by a loud bang

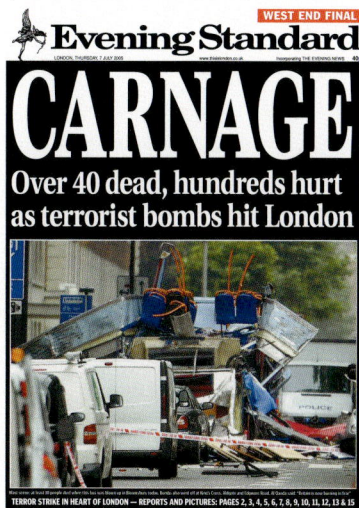

The *Evening Standard*'s sharply contrasting front pages
over the two days of 6 and 7 July 2005

and clouds of smoke, as reported to the Underground's Network Control Centre (NCC) at 55 Broadway.[10] At 8.49 the service was well on the way to recovery as some 250,000 people travelled into central London – standing, sitting, reading a book, doing their makeup, worrying about being late for work, reading the newspaper, relieved to find a seat, in their usual car on the train, scanning the Metro, listening to music on their iPods, seeing but trying not to look at each other[11] – a normal day on the Underground network, if more crowded than usual on the Piccadilly line where there had been 15-minute gaps in the service between trains after the fault at Caledonian Road.

The NCC co-ordinated the recovery of the system. Gold Control (the highest level of incident command) was taken by Andy Barr, an operational veteran. "Well, you get this flashback of what was going on in the control room. Although I wasn't [on duty] in the control room, I was at 55 Broadway and got a phone message to come down because, quote, we're in the shit, unquote. I went in; at that point I wasn't the Gold Control, because the guy who was [Kevin Bootle], it was his first week as a new duty officer and I was monitoring him." Barr, with the agreement of his less experienced colleague, took over Gold Control for the next twelve hours. Andy Barr recalls of that fateful morning that "any one of the failures that had occurred on the day on its own would have been quite a significant issue".[12]

From 8.50 a.m. the NCC and emergency services began to receive a fresh and initially confusing stream of calls. "We'd got about fourteen stations that had lost power, we'd got significant amounts of the traction current network that had lost power, we'd got loads of trains stalled. As soon as you finished with one call, you didn't even have time to put the call back down, you immediately pressed the 'receive' button or a 'shift over' button, and it was incessant."[13] Calls described an explosion and loss of power at Liverpool Street and Edgware Road, someone under a train, an explosion on a train at Aldgate, loss of power on the Moorgate to Aldgate sections, loud bangs at both Edgware and Aldgate. The station supervisor at Aldgate reported smoke coming up the tunnels, called the Fire Brigade and evacuated the station. A policeman on the scene at Aldgate reported, "Looks like a Tube collision". Smoke was coming out of the westbound Piccadilly tunnels at King's Cross, and then large numbers of people began to be reported walking, wounded, out of the tunnels onto the platform.

"The huge number of calls reaching the NCC and the adjoining Metropolitan Police incident control room meant that a clear picture of what had happened and where across six sites was initially difficult to discern. At first it was thought that a serious power outage had brought the system to a standstill, as had happened in August 2003. Then three major incidents involving six stations emerged from the communications traffic. A major incident was declared by the police at 9.06, and a report made at 9.17 stated, "Clear bomb damage to one carriage", with passengers dead, severely wounded and trapped.

At the NCC the focus was on the quick and safe halting of trains at platforms, and on bringing 250,000 passengers to the surface from 275 stations on 10 lines over 250 miles of track. The NCC broadcast Code Amber (the second-highest alert level), and the calm evacuation of every station and every train began at 9.20. "Even after we said it was a bomb, it was under control," Barr recalls. "The way it was announced, the way that information was put out, was in a cohesive, intelligent way" to avoid panic.[14] Meanwhile, the emergency services concentrated on bringing paramedics, fire appliances and ambulances to the incidents, and activating well-rehearsed plans for the dispersal of casualties to hospitals. Above ground, sirens and blue lights proliferated, roads were progressively closed, traffic ground to a halt, and the city held its collective breath as the message changed from a loss of power to a co-ordinated series of terrorist explosions below ground. The city clogged up as people emerged from Tube stations, a cloud hung over it, everyone was urged to stay put in case of further attacks. Those manning the NCC fielded and logged the calls; by 9.40 a.m. the reality of a multi-site terrorist attack had become all too clear to the leadership at TfL.

At 8.50 a.m. four young British Muslims, radicalized Islamists, had carried improvised explosive devices onto the Underground at King's Cross in identical backpacks. The suicide bombers exploded their devices on three trains between stations – Circle line train 204 between Aldgate and Liverpool Street, Circle line train

216 between Edgware Road and Paddington, and Piccadilly line train 331, which had just left King's Cross for Russell Square. A fourth bomb, intended for the Northern line, had failed to explode; the bearer backtracked to buy a new battery from WHSmith at King's Cross. This fourth device was exploded at 9.47 a.m. on the top deck of a route 30 bus in Tavistock Square. The effect inside packed morning rush-hour trains in the confined spaces of the Tube and the bus was devastating.

Bombing on the Underground

For three trains and their passengers, the routine of the morning commute had been literally torn asunder; only survivors close to the explosions can adequately describe the experience, and their words from the coroner's inquest have been used here to describe what happened.

On Circle line train 204, driven by Timothy Batkin, as it pulled westwards out of Aldgate station for Liverpool Street at about 8.49, "It felt and sounded like a loud thud ... through the body of the train ... and through my body ... It didn't appear to me at the time to be particularly loud."[15]

About a hundred metres west of Aldgate station, Tim Batkin's Circle line train had come to a halt. "Passengers on the train I could hear crying for help, it was a chilling, haunting cry for help, something that, you know, still makes my blood run cold when I think about hearing it, and it just made me think that a problem with the train is not necessarily my priority, I should maybe start thinking about what's happening to the people who need help on the train."[16] He walked back at track level towards the rear of the train. "I remember calling to the people inside the carriages as I went down past each set of doors that we were going to detrain everybody into the tunnel, and that they should walk towards the rear of the train as soon as they could." About five hundred passengers were taken off the train at Aldgate.

A British Transport Police (BTP) sergeant, Tony Silvestro, ran down the tunnel. "As I got round the bend, you could actually see the train, and by this time my eyes were focusing a bit more and I could see there was a carriage full of debris, the doors had been blown out, and people milling around ... They were dishevelled, they were dazed. People were shouting 'Help!' It was pretty much chaotic, really." He told the Underground staff to go and get help. "I got to the bombed-out carriage, I got close to it, the door was hanging, there was still people milling around, there was lots of people screaming for help. I looked into the carriage itself. At this stage, as I've climbed in, the guy is still trying to get up, so I've sat him back down, told him to 'Stay there, mate', and the doctor then started saying 'This girl needs urgent assistance'."[17]

Further west, two trains were passing in the tunnel between Edgware Road and Paddington, one of them Circle line train 216. The driver of the train going the opposite way, Jeffrey Porter, reported:

I saw the driver pass me, and I was gazing, as I was slowing down, gazing idly into the carriages of the other train because it was the only real source of light in the area and of entertainment, and in the second ... car, it looked like an orange bubble, and it seemed to go into slow motion, there was an orange ball in that car which gradually seemed to expand and get bigger and bigger ... and at the moment it seemed to reach its largest extent ... suddenly went completely dark and ... the slow motion of time seemed to stop, and time speeded up to real-time again. Everything went completely dark and I heard a noise that sound like a huge whooshing of wind and screaming [like] in the film *Raiders of the Lost Ark* and all the terrible things fly out – that was exactly the sound it made in that film, a rushing of wind and screaming.[18]

A passenger in the second car remembered, "The train was just pulling out of Edgware Road station ... I was thinking about the half-day's leave from work I had scheduled and that I should really be in work by now to get everything done before I left at lunchtime. Then there was a loud bang and a ball of fire appeared from my left-hand side and seemed to go right round me and then quickly retracted."[19]

Leaving Edgware Road with train 216, train operator Ray Whitehurst had "felt the front of the carriage raise and it was as if I'd hit a brick wall ... the train just stopped dead in the air and came down with a thump, and I hit my head on the windscreen, I was then thrown back, hit the back of my head and jarred my back, and I thought, 'This is going to hurt', and the next thing I saw was all this dust just go past me very, very fast ... I informed the signalman that a bomb had gone off on my train, and he said, 'No, it's all right, don't worry about it, it's only a power surge'... I walked to the signal phone and again phoned the signalman, who put me through to Bryan Corbin who is line standards manager. Bryan said, 'I hear you've got a compressor gone'. I said, 'No, it's a bomb. The second car is vanished.' I again requested emergency help."

A group of staff and drivers awaiting their duty turns in the mess room at Edgware Road heard the bang and met at the tunnel entrance. "It was clear that something very serious had just happened in the tunnel. I could just see the end lights of the westbound train in the tunnel and by now there was a mass of dust and smoke billowing out of the tunnel. There was a strong smell like an electrical fire."[20] The traction current was shorted and several of this group set off down the tunnel 50 yards [46 metres] to the train, which they worked their way through calling out, "We're evacuating from the rear of the train, please make way", all the way to the crater where the bomb had been in the second car. They formed a chain to help passengers up the track onto the platform and then into the booking hall to await paramedics.

Trevor Rodgers, duty trains manager at Edgware Road, heard the bang and ran to the signal cabin, where he took a call from Whitehurst, "who said, 'Oh, you've

Camera phone image of passengers walking down the tunnel from
the bombed Piccadilly line train 331 near Russell Square

Circle line train 204 halted by a bomb between Liverpool Street and Aldgate

Members of the emergency services with a casualty at Edgware Road on 7 July 2005

got to come down to me, the trains, the doors have been blown open, there's people lying dead, you've got to come down and help me ... something's exploded.' The first thing I actually said to Ray was, 'Sorry, Ray, thanks for that, but I must ask you, was the explosion trackside or train side, Ray, in your opinion?' and he said, 'Trevor, it's definitely train side, I felt the train lift.'"[21]

Rodgers made his way down the tunnel where the drivers were evacuating the train, and covered up a casualty in the 'six-foot' between the rails. On the blast car, "it was dark, there was no emergency lighting at all ... it was only the light that was reflected through from the tunnel wall lights and from the train and the emergency lighting from the train on the opposite side."[22] Staff and passengers assisted the wounded in the gloom. The train doors were opened and the generous space of the sub-surface railway enabled casualties to be taken off the train on stretchers by the Fire Brigade.

Michael Cooney, instructor operator: "The train was very stuffy and smoky with a strong smell of burning flesh. I was unable to open the train doors in the second-from-front car. I could see that the centre doors on both sides of the train had been blown out. There was a hole in the train floor. I could hear screaming. There was a man who appeared to be on the track screaming. I saw a woman lying motionless in the aisle door where the second and third cars meet. She was covered in dust. There were body parts in the vicinity of the hole in the floor. Paramedics had arrived and were treating injured people. I made my way to the front car, where I found that there were still passengers on board. I did not want to lead these past the site of the explosion, so I assisted them in detraining through the driver's cab. I did this with the assistance of the driver, Ray Whitehurst. I led the passengers along the side of the train by the tunnel wall and placed a ladder so that they could reboard the train once clear of the damaged section and be evacuated by walking through the train."[23]

Just before Piccadilly line train 331 had pulled out of King's Cross for Russell Square, all the lights in the station went off and then on again (later understood to be the result of a power surge after the Aldgate bomb damaged the high-tension power cable). Train operator Tom Nairn left King's Cross westbound. "I was the first train through in passenger service by about fifteen minutes, and I was completely full at Turnpike Lane, and each platform was full as I went through it. We drew out of the platform and went over the crossover and there was an almighty bang, a large, really loud, metallic bang".[24] "The whole train shook, the lights went out instantaneously, and the train ground to a halt … The train was completely dead."[25] "There was an extremely loud pop and a very bright yellow light, and I was thrown to the ground with such force that I can't actually recall the moments in between standing and being on the floor."[26] "I remember the double doors trying to close several times, people were just stuck in the doors, they just kept trying to close … and eventually they did close … there was a loud bang and a pop and I thought it might have been part of the music that I was listening to," recalled Paul Mitchell. "Then I thought, 'What's wrong with my earphones? Something's just gone in my ear' … then all of a sudden just being blown backwards."[27]

Below ground, for a few moments all was eerily quiet, the air thick with smoke and brake dust from the trains, the blasted cars in darkness, the emergency lights further down the train flickering into life. In the Piccadilly train, "at first it was very, very quiet, just nothing," and Julie Gruen remembers "looking to my right and … where there had been so many people, it was just empty, and I remember just sort of making out forms on the floor and thinking it was just out of some kind of horror film … then I would say after, maybe, five or six seconds, very slow gradual moaning started from the injured people, and that moaning continued and then I think more people started to get hysterical."[28]

It was the Underground train operators and station staff who were first to reach the confused, terrible scenes. "I have tremendous respect for what they did. They could have gone off and saved themselves, but they acted in the best interests of everyone," recalled one of the survivors.[29] On the Piccadilly line train, the train operator Tom Nairn and his colleague Raymond Wright, travelling with him in the cab, were in the dark; Nairn's train had lost all power, including that to the driver's radio and the PA. "Tom opened the M door [train cab central door] at the very end of the train, and I handed him the SCD, the short-circuiting device [device to stop traction current being recharged]. He jumped down onto the track … and took the emergency telephone handset with him and tried to communicate with the line controller via the tunnel telephone wires." They opened the door between the driver's cab and the first carriage, where the bomb had exploded, and shone a torch. "What confronted us was a sea of faces, blackened, bloodied, in a state of panic, naturally, and we tried to communicate with them and the only way we could do that was by shouting … because we had to make ourselves heard … it was imperative that we told them there were staff at the front of the train." "I started shouting, I was aware that there was a problem, I was going to sort it out, and there was a couple of women right beside the door. I spoke to them and they seemed to kind of take control of the situation and calm people down to a certain extent." The ladder was deployed from the M door on the front of the train down onto the track. "The first passengers out were more blackened and with kind of frizzy hair. As those passengers came out, it got progressively worse, the kind of state of the people that were leaving the train … burns, splattered with blood, hair standing on end, clothes blackened."[30]

Some 700 yards (640 metres) up the track at Russell Square station, staff saw the traction current go off and sensed that something was wrong. David Boyce, station supervisor, was looking down the tunnel and could see "a dim torch coming round the bend and what looked like light reflecting off a high visibility jacket. After I saw that, I said to Gary Stephens [duty station manager at Russell Square], 'Something's not right'. I jumped down onto the track … I could see someone who I knew was Ray Wright at the time … He said that he believed something was wrong with a motor or something along those lines, but he never mentioned any words of an explosion of the magnitude that we now know it was. I told him that Russell Square station was very close by and that he could see the platform, and that we were going to get help on the way." Boyce recalled, "The smoke was very, very heavy. At one point, it was difficult to see that far in front of me. The smoke began to dissipate when I got to the train, but before that, it was quite bad. I went past him towards the train and there was quite a few walking wounded behind him. I would say somewhere in the range of fifty to seventy [people], possibly more."

Boyce and Stephens reached the train and found Nairn with a badly injured passenger, Paul Glennerster, "at the front, on the track, in front of the emergency ladder, propped up against the wall; I believe the gentleman had lost part of his leg". Nairn had improvised a tourniquet; "I put my hi-vis [jacket] over them quite tightly to try and help in any way I can, but also to raise his legs above the level of his heart … I said to him that help was on the way."[31]

Wright recalls, "We made our mind up to take the walking wounded on to Russell Square and Tom stayed with his train … We made an announcement through the J door to the passengers that one of the drivers was going to stay on the train and one was going to walk through with passengers to Russell Square station." This proved difficult and slow in the dark with injured passengers. "There are obstructions, there's always obstructions in the tunnels, like check rails and other bits of engineering, so you have to stop and say to people, 'You're going to have to cross over the centre rail, the negative rail, to get round this obstruction'."

Five hundred yards (457 metres) away, staff were helping passengers onto the platform. Stretchers were improvised with blankets and sheets from the Russell Hotel. Casualties unable to walk were carried to the platform by Stephens, Boyce, Burne and other staff from Russell Square, two British Transport policemen and the first paramedics: "We'd hold one corner of a blanket or a sheet each, and then, as fast as we could we'd walk down the tunnel, and drop them off at the platform, then go back and do it again. It was a ten-minute walk each way and very hot down there as well." Finally, all the casualties who had survived reached Russell Square. The ticket hall had become a clearing station manned by doctors and nurses who had come from "nearby hospitals, University College and Great Ormond Street, and they were trying to treat the dying and the mortally injured and we just assisted with putting drips in, reassuring people, carrying them out to the ambulances outside".[32]

First on to the rear of the train was Simon Cook, a trainee station manager. Working in the control room at the top of the King's Cross escalators, he had felt them stop, investigated, and ordered the evacuation of the station to avoid overcrowding at platform level. On the platform a colleague, Lee Merritt, reported smoke; he called the NCC, who by 8.56 a.m. had called for Fire Brigade support at King's Cross. Cook radioed the control room to check if the power was off. "I was looking around the platform trying to establish what was causing the smoke, and I think at that point I heard some noise – it sounded like voices – up that tunnel, so I went down onto the track and started walking towards the noise to see what was happening … It was very dark … after some distance, I came across a couple of people who were obviously customers off their train. They were near panic. They were reassured to see me, I think, and carried on. I wanted to keep going up to find out what had actually happened." Cook could see the rear of the train ahead of him, straddling the crossover tracks. "I saw the side of the train and one set of double doors, there were people struggling to get through and get down onto the track in front of me … I tried to walk forward along the side of the train. There were an awful lot of people trying desperately to get off the train … I still wasn't sure what the actual problem was with the train and why the people were so desperate to get off."[33]

He worked his way through the train and kicked open the interconnecting doors into the first car. "I couldn't go very far through at all. I remember seeing … on that first set of seats that I came to, there were obviously severely injured people, and in the area between the double doors there seemed to be really a pile of people and I couldn't tell out of that pile – some I think were dead and some were obviously very severely injured, and because of the way that people had fallen and were piled up, I couldn't even get past them for fear of treading on people and causing them a lot worse injuries."[34]

The bus in Tavistock Square

Bus driver George Psaradakis, with five years' experience, had set out at 5.30 a.m. on route 30 from Hackney Wick to Marble Arch and back to Hackney. Leaving Marble Arch on his third round trip, he began to hear from CentreComm about disruption on the Underground instructing drivers to take care and assist the public emerging from Tube stations. As he turned right at Baker Street into the Euston Road at about 9.15 there were crowds evacuated from the station at the stand who almost filled his bus. "As I was approaching Euston station," recalled Psaradakis, "I could see, especially from Euston Square Tube station in front of me, many people, thousands of people, on the pavement and even on the road, and I could hear the sirens of the emergency service vehicles."[35] The bus was soon packed tight, and he refused to move off until the front was cleared and he could see his mirrors.

At least two of the passengers had been evacuated from the Edgware Road bomb and had joined the crowds making their way to work on foot. One of the people who boarded the bus was the fourth bomber, the one whose device had not exploded on the Northern line as intended. He had tried to phone his colleagues, who were by then dead on the three trains they had attacked. He took his seat near the back on the top deck.

The bus moved off but only crawled forward through traffic by now at a near standstill. Police cordoned off the Euston Road, his usual route, so Psaradakis drove across to the junction into Upper Woburn Place, stopped at the bus stop, and announced that the bus was diverting, he was seeking guidance from his control and that passengers might wish to get off and continue their journey on foot. More than thirty passengers left the bus at this point. He asked a passing traffic warden, "What is this place? They said to me, 'It's Tavistock Square'. I thanked them, and then, as I tried to press to call my garage – bang!"[36]

Three BTP officers were making their way in a car down the Euston Road to the rendezvous point at King's Cross. "We were using the blue light and the siren," PC Sims remembered. "We were on the wrong side of the road in Upper Woburn Place, which puts us on the same side of the road as the bus, the bus is coming towards us. As we approached the junction at Upper Woburn Place where you would turn right into Tavistock Place, just on that junction there was a very, very loud booming

The bus on route 30 bombed at Tavistock Square, 7 July 2005

sound … and, at the same time, there was a large cloud of debris – it was a very dark grey-white smoke cloud which went possibly a hundred to two hundred feet [30–60 metres] up in the air, and, as that went up, there was a lot of debris and there were unfortunately parts of people in that."[37]

The first police officers on this awful scene of carnage, anxious about the possibility of a secondary device, tried to stop the bus engine and clear and cordon around the bus to keep people at a distance. PC Sims was telling people to get back into the building, the British Medical Association (BMA) offices. "They then came back out and one of them tapped me on the shoulder and said, 'Excuse me, officer, I'm a doctor, can I help?' and I said 'Yes', and at that point that group of people basically starburst round me and went to wherever there were casualties who were clearly alive."[38] Triage of the worst casualties took place at the BMA itself, while walking wounded were helped to the County Hotel nearby.

At the inquest Psaradakis described the loud, blunt noise of the explosion. "I thought, 'What did I hit?' … then I saw the windscreen blow away, debris is falling all over me. I was stunned, shocked, and I remember I touched my head and I could only feel dust. So, shocked as I was, I got out of the bus, out of my cabin. I thought, 'What happened to my passengers?' On the wall opposite [the BMA], I've seen a leg stuck on that wall, a leg or an arm, but I think it was a leg, a whole leg, I was so shocked … a few minutes before … people talking, even laughing, you know, the normal chatting the passengers have on their mobiles, and then seeing my passengers in such a state … I was overwhelmed."[39]

TfL moves into crisis management mode

"It was a bit like where you were when you first heard that Kennedy had been assassinated," recalls Peter Hendy, then MD of Buses, "because everybody can remember. I'd just arrived at Paddington on the train from Bath, and Tim [O'Toole, MD Underground] rang me up and he said, 'We've got some major problems, I'm not quite sure what they are but we've got some major problems and the bus service is going to have to do some heavy lifting' … I went out in the street and I got a bus to the office and I passed Edgware Road, not long before the whole place filled up with ambulances and wounded, but I didn't even know of a bomb at Edgware Road at that time."[40]

O'Toole himself was in the lift lobby on the seventh floor of 55 Broadway, Underground HQ, when he received a message.

I get a text if anything happens on the railway; this one said that there was a major power outage on the northern side of the Circle. I get 50 to 70 of these things a day and read them, and it allows me to follow the rhythm of the place … it was probably because of that power outage in August 2003 and the trauma of dealing with that, that without even going back to my office, I spun on my heel and I ran downstairs. I walked into the NCC, the Network Control Centre, around nine o'clock … so about ten minutes into the situation, and I walked in and there was a lot of activity, although people were very calm and professional. One of the guys on the desk turned to me and said, 'Mr O'Toole, this is a bad one'. I got their initial reports, and by that time the story had morphed into, 'We might have had a derailment at Edgware Road'. There's reports of a body on the track, there was a report of a train hitting the side wall and maybe that's what kicked off the power. Now none of these things happened. It's just the kind of confusing reports you get in. I hear 'derailment potential' and my first call is to Peter Hendy because, remember, this is an hour before the bus bomb, and I said, 'We have a bad situation going on here. We're going to be pushing a lot of people at you. Get ready.' I called Bob [Kiley] and told him … by that time we had gotten much more clarity about multiple incidents. Things are going on while I'm doing this. Now it's maybe ten minutes past and Geoff Dunmore, the security manager on call,[41] said, 'This is terrorism. We have to get a Code Amber, we need to get everybody off this network and check it.' Andy agreed and he turned to me and he said, 'We're going to Code Amber[42] on the railway. Are you comfortable with that?' and I said, 'Yes'.[43]

Hendy soon reached the TfL HQ at Windsor House, where it was immediately apparent that something was badly wrong. "What happens when the Underground stops for any significant purpose is that the control arrangements just flick into action, and they ask London Buses to take Underground passengers. You don't have to do anything, but clearly it's worrying when large parts of the system come to a stop and nobody's quite sure why. My memory is that work became overtaken by events because then the bomb on the bus went off and we saw that on the television, at about the same time as we were told it, and then it became apparent that this was a big, big, big, issue. CentreComm, the bus control centre, in communication with all buses on the road, rang me up and said, 'We're going to withdraw out of Zone 1 [central London], not because we don't want to operate but because many of the roads are so full of fire engines and ambulances and police vehicles that it's becoming impractical'."[44]

The crisis management of a major incident on the Underground follows the UK emergency services hierarchy of a three-tier structure of Gold, Silver, and Bronze control: single individuals identified and trained as having respectively strategic, tactical and operational control. The Underground's response was to inform the emergency services – police, fire, ambulance – for them to do their jobs, and then to do their own by bringing all the passengers on the system safely to the surface. On 7 July the NCC took control of incident management across the Underground system as Gold Control, with the duty officer (Andy Barr) in charge in conjunction with the security manager (Geoff Dunmore). The response of the emergency services that day was indeed heroic. The earlier response of operational staff on the Underground, however, has been obscured and also needs to be told.[45]

"We went to Code Amber and over the next hour or so, that's when we made our reputation," O'Toole recalls, "because all those people did such a magnificent job of moving about a quarter of a million people off this railway without a single injury, if you can imagine the madness of doing that. These are all commuters and you're dumping them in places they don't even know where they are, and you can imagine the resistance and all the rest of it, but they did a fantastic job."[46]

The truth of that terrible day was that everyone involved was not only in new territory in terms of the scale and severity of the bombings but also fearful of further attacks. PM Tony Blair was in Scotland, at Gleneagles for the G8 summit; he was immediately informed and, like everyone in positions of responsibility in London, had no certainty about what had happened or what might still happen.[47]

That morning, COO Mike Brown and the Underground's leadership team were at Canary Wharf for an awayday. "We got a text message to say there'd been this power surge, and then it became obvious it wasn't and that something else had happened and I said, 'We've got to get back'. We tried to get to the Jubilee line and it was clear the Jubilee line wasn't working, the network was now being suspended, and so we got in a car … but the traffic was just solid. I remember talking to Ian Johnston, the chief constable of the BTP, and Ian said, 'Mike, Bob Crow was on the radio in the car saying this is lack of investment in the Tube and it's typical of London Underground not spending money on the power supply system … we should bring it all back in to state ownership' … he obviously had been talked to before he knew anything."[48]

Brown then took a call from the group station manager at Edgware Road, Steve Goszka, who was only on his fourth day in the role there but who had NCC and Resilience Group experience.

'Mike, I just want to let you know, I've just been down the tunnel, this is not a train crash or a power issue, this is something much worse and I think it's terrorism.' He was the first one that had planted that thought in my mind – I can still feel the shivers going down my spine as I recount this tale … so we were in a car with this phone call going on, eventually we got to Wapping, where the traffic was so solid we couldn't move but we saw a police station … We piled out of the car, I walked into the police station and this Met police officer from behind the desk said, 'Hello Mike'. This guy had been my home beat officer when he was in the British Transport Police when I was a group station manager of Liverpool Street in 1990. I said, 'Look, any chance of a blue-light car? We need to get back to St James's Park to our network operations centre,' and he said, 'Well, hang on, give me five minutes, I'll get you in a boat, that's the best way to get back'. The river was just closed at that point to river traffic, but of course the police didn't have that problem. We got on a river boat and he ferried us up to Westminster pier, and a combination of walking briskly and running [got us] back to the Network Control Centre where Tim and Andy Barr were already installed.[49]

Andy Barr's personal memories "aren't so much about bombs going off and casualties because I wasn't really engaged in that aspect of it. It's about the whole command-and-control stuff. About the fact that all the senior management were at Canary Wharf, not in the building. I had to deal with that, with the lack of information from Metropolitan Police, lack of communication; this is a terrorist activity, we will get on with it. We weren't called to the very first Gold meeting at New Scotland Yard. That became an issue because we were seen as civilian agents. It had happened to us, but they were responsible. Then for the rest of the day it was formulating a response and working through it."[50]

Barr had to be certain about the incident being a bomb. "I only gave the instruction to send that information out once I was absolutely stone certain. Other agencies had the level of information which I wasn't privy to."[51] As the day progressed, Barr's task "was moving out of the shock issue into, how do we get things restored? Who is coming to relieve me so that I can come back next morning and start the process all over again? We had a series of network emergency plans, which I was the custodian of anyway, and so it was about invoking those and fairly rapidly I was moved off the incident."[52]

Mike Brown and the team joined Tim O'Toole an hour and a half into the incident, after they had sprinted up to the NCC from the Thames. Brown knew within hours that the three Tube attacks had all happened at the same time, within a minute of each other.

> The Met Police didn't know that, and in fact they kept talking about the sequence of attacks, they were talking publicly about it and I kept saying, 'Hang on, this isn't right. I know because I've seen the power logs and I've seen when current was lost and where signals were lost.' We just knew, I mean we have the piece of paper, the printout, that showed this. Eventually I got Ian Johnston, who was just a fantastic guy to work alongside as the chief constable of the BTP because he was the railway's policeman. I got him in the office and I put up on my big screen the Tracker Net train tracker which was the replica of the signalling system which you could replay, and I showed him the timelines and I showed him line by line the two bits of the Circle line and the Piccadilly line where it happened, and the timer was in the corner, and it was all 08.50.[53]

It was this simultaneity above all that had posed the Underground its greatest challenge.

Brown ensured that the operational plan was put in place, with separate leadership teams for incident management and another for recovery, "and some people to be completely separate to start to work with the engineers to think about how we return the sites to operation, because we knew they were going to be scenes of crime and would not be available to us right away."[54] Some staff were sent home so they were available both later in the day and for the subsequent days.[55]

The first group continued to work with the station staff on site, and with the Ambulance Service and Fire Brigade. Already attention was turning to getting the service started again. The second group was in hourly conference calls with line general managers. Despite the uncertainty, O'Toole is clear that "in those earliest conversations we [were saying], 'We must bring this place back as soon as possible, because it's going to be important to the country'. We actually said things like that, because we thought we're kind of the show and what we do will determine how people feel about this day."[56]

Once back at HQ, the Underground leadership team faced three tasks: continuing to deal with the incidents, returning the three sites to operation, and the operational plan to bring back the service across the network. Barr recalls that for starting the service the next day they had to give all the staff briefings on what had happened and the ongoing arrangements for security.[57]

The TfL leadership encountered resistance to bringing the network back on the following day, particularly from Commissioner Bob Kiley. "Bob called me, I was in the Operations Room. He said, 'This is out of control, send everyone home, close the Underground and send everyone home.' I thought, 'Hmm, well, I'm not doing that.' I said, 'Okay, Bob, let me look at that and I'll get back to you' … Can you imagine how history would have looked at us?"[58]

At the NCC, O'Toole was getting a stream of calls from people needing updates, not least from Ken Livingstone, in Singapore with the successful Olympic bid team, from mayoral transport advisor Redmond O'Neill, and from Jonathan Powell, with the prime minister at Gleneagles.

Bob Kiley held a series of meetings through the day at TfL's Windsor House offices, "but I didn't really want to leave here [NCC]," O'Toole recalled, "so I sent Nigel Holness over and he handled all those, and then we just kept doing this through the day".[59] After lunch Peter Hendy, whose bus service would be the first means of recovery, went to see Kiley to tell him they needed to restart the bus service. "We've got millions of people in central London that are not going to get home and I think we should restart the bus service … It transpired that there were people in government who thought that you couldn't do that unless the home secretary said so, and I said, 'I'm not sure I agree with that'."[60]

Called in from the NCC at short notice at about 3 p.m. to face the press at the QEII Conference Centre opposite Westminster Abbey, where a media centre had been established, O'Toole and Hendy brought clarity to the proceedings, the first explanation of what was really happening. O'Toole recollects "sitting there thinking 'What shall I say, what shall I say?' I remember then, when I ran out of the NCC, some of the guys said 'Don't forget the employees'," which stuck with him throughout an intense day. "That was part of my message, completely off the cuff, thank God I did that because that paid enormous dividends later and that message was not missed by anyone." Hendy recalls saying to himself, "If nobody from government agreed with restarting the bus service I'd restart it on my own. I wasn't going to go to a press conference and be asked when the bus service was going to restart and not be able to say. If you didn't restart by four o'clock in the afternoon you'd never take people home. Actually, just as we left to go we got a message saying it's okay. Still to this day I have no idea on what basis they made that judgement, because actually there is no judgement that you can make that it's all safe. I went to the press conference and we all said what we knew and I said that the Tube wasn't going to restart that day and we'd take everybody home if people are patient, and they were patient and we did take everybody home. Of course, it was all very emotional and traumatic but the fact is that actually most people in London worked a full day's work and they did all get home, and the following morning the Tube did largely restart and the transport systems worked as normal."[61] "There were further media briefings explaining how we knew when the bombs went off and all that," O'Toole recalls. "I did a Tracker Net explanation on Saturday. It just went on and on."[62]

O'Toole reflects with the benefit of hindsight that they should have decided earlier on to bring back the Tube service first thing in the morning, rather than just some time the next day. But after evacuating passengers, all 500 trains were returned to their depots, where they were subject to thorough security checks including under the seats. This process went on all night and into the following day, which disrupted the restart in the morning. It was also important to brief all the drivers on what had happened and what action had been taken before they felt safe to take their trains out once more.[63]

"We lost all that first batch of drivers," O'Toole recalled. "That's when all these people out on the network showed amazing ingenuity. I mean, it was people grabbing vans and putting drivers in them and driving them around the city and getting them [to their trains] … having to get through police cordons, which was a big problem for us in certain isolated cases." [64]

O'Toole's story about the pride and professionalism of his staff and Hendy's commitment to getting everyone home chimed closely with Londoners' reawakened respect for *their* Underground and buses. Customer satisfaction scores peaked, Underground staff in particular were regarded with renewed respect, and the reputation of the organization reached a new high, from being seen as always on strike to being "incredibly well-trained professionals who did the right thing when it was called upon. That had an enormous effect on the staff themselves, because for the first time in their lives when they went to work the next day and people came to the system, people thanked them, it was remarkable. That was the most powerful lasting effect about 7/7, because the passengers came back within three months."[65]

Hendy recalls:

It was all a bit eerie that evening, it was all very quiet. One of the things we proved is that actually the city doesn't function well without any public transport at all. It's not good for the city not to have public transport, and the right thing to do is to run. We proved that the whole thing is incredibly resilient. The bus service is fantastically resilient because it runs out of nearly a hundred garages, so unless you burn them all down you've still got buses and you ought to be able to run them. Even the Tube proved to be pretty resilient because it restarted

Floral tributes left by well-wishers outside King's Cross station, later viewed by Mayor Ken Livingstone and Underground MD Tim O'Toole

the following morning, except for the damaged sections, and the staff were magnificent because they were all frightened out of their skins but they all turned up for work, and that's the great thing.[66]

The bus workforce were worried, but they still came to work. Their trade union, then the TGWU, had been in touch with Hendy, so he decided that the day after the attacks he would go and see them at their London District Office at Woodberry, Green Lanes. "To my knowledge no senior officer of LT/TfL had ever gone to see them; they came to see us, as the employer. They were pretty astonished, but I said that in extraordinary circumstances we should all do extraordinary things. I wanted to show them some respect – the London Bus Committee were serving bus drivers themselves and I thought they deserved some. I found it a tough meeting; they wanted reassurance, which I couldn't of course give – there was none to be had from anywhere. So I just said, 'We're an essential public service to London and Londoners, there's no information that suggests any reason to change what we do, so we carry on.' And, to their enormous credit, they accepted that. I think maybe my going there helped too."[67]

Back in Singapore, seven hours ahead of the UK, the Olympic bid team switched from euphoric hangovers to despair as the terrible news arrived from London. Neale Coleman recalls that Livingstone went for a swim. Then, composed but visibly shaken, he delivered his memorable speech to the Press in the lobby of the Swissotel.

This is a cowardly attack … our thoughts are with everyone who has been injured or lost loved ones … This was not a terrorist attack against the mighty and powerful … It was aimed at ordinary working-class Londoners, black and white, Muslim and Christian, Hindu and Jew, young and old … They seek to divide Londoners … I said yesterday to the International Olympic Committee that the city of London is the greatest in the world, because everyone lives side by side in harmony. Londoners will not be divided by this cowardly attack. They will stand together in solidarity around those who have been injured, those who have been bereaved, and that is why I'm proud to be the mayor of that city. Finally, I wish to speak through you directly to those who came to London today to take life. I know that you personally do not fear to give your own life in exchange for taking others. It is why you are so dangerous. But I know you do fear that you may fail in your long-term objective to destroy our free society, and I can show you why you would fail in the days that follow. Look at our airports, look at our seaports and look at our railway stations, and even after your cowardly attack, you will see that people from the rest of Britain, people from around the world, will arrive in London to become Londoners and to fulfil their dreams and achieve their potential. They choose to come to London as so many have come before because they come to be free. They come to live the life they choose. They come to be able to be themselves. They flee you because you tell them how they should live. They don't want that, and nothing you do, however many of us you kill, will stop that flight to our cities where freedom is strong and where people can live in harmony with one another. Whatever you do, however many you kill, you will fail.[68]

This was civic leadership of a high order, and perhaps Livingstone's finest speech as London mayor.

Copycat attacks

Just two weeks later, on 21 July, the unthinkable happened again, with London rocked by four copycat attacks, when all four bombs were detonated but mercifully failed to explode.[69] Andy Barr remembered the level of disbelief, "when it went off again … almost an incredulity that this was going on again. Luckily, they didn't pick a Tube railway, they picked the City and Hammersmith (line), and because it was in the open it was easier to manage."[70]

Three of the attacks were made on the Underground – at Shepherd's Bush, Warren Street and the Oval – and one on a number 26 bus at Shoreditch. A fifth bomber dumped his device without attempting to set it off. Although detonators were exploded on the trains, in each case the main charge did not explode and the bombers fled the scene. A huge manhunt followed across the country to arrest the bombers, driven by the fear that they might have the means to strike again. By the end of the month the principal suspects had been arrested, together with their

London United, the vigil for those lost in the 7 July terrorist attacks,
held in Trafalgar Square a week later on 14 July

accomplices. In July 2007 the four copycat bombers were found guilty of conspiracy to murder, and received life sentences.

"We were still, when the second lot of bombs went off," Barr recalls, "in recovery mode. We hadn't got the Piccadilly line back, we hadn't got the trains back from Aldgate, Edgware Road, I can't remember when we craned it out … We were trying to learn what was going on and recover."[71] For Underground MD O'Toole, 21/7 was almost worse than 7/7 itself. "I thought to myself, 'Oh Christ! I'm going to be doing this for the rest of my life! This is just going to keep happening. How the hell do you hold this together?'"[72] The Met Police commissioner made a TV broadcast for everyone to stay where they were. "This time some drivers just wouldn't drive – 'No, no, he didn't mean you,' O'Toole protested. 'We need to keep the place running! – and we lost the Bakerloo for part of the day." The next day in the fevered atmosphere of the police manhunt for the bombers, a Brazilian electrician, Jean Charles de Menezes, was misidentified and shot dead on a train at Stockwell station. "I was sitting in a staff meeting with Bob Kiley, and all of a sudden a report [came in] of a bomber shot … that just … solidified the fears of the prior day, that this is just going to keep going on and on and on and on."[73]

The verdict

"I think it is stunning that employees were so well trained in dealing with emergencies that they did go to the sound of the guns; they ran into those tunnels, they didn't raise questions about the their own safety and they did respond immediately, bringing relief to hundreds of people on those trains."

– Tim O'Toole, Underground MD[74]

O'Toole, Hendy and Kiley appeared at the GLA in the aftermath of 7/7 to report on what happened. At that time, the *Evening Standard* had started a story about the missing 20 minutes after the bombs were exploded when no one did anything. O'Toole was quick to counter this; "Remember those stories which we killed by saying, 'No, no, people did stuff immediately'? The 20 minutes was the delayed call on what had happened, and that wasn't for us to do. Anyhow, we got that message out and one of the ways was at that GLA meeting when I recited what happened during the day. Coming into that meeting I met with Bob, who said, 'This is gonna be really bad, I don't know what we're gonna do,' and I remember saying to him, 'Bob, let me do this, just let me do it,' because I had to handle it. He said, 'Fine, that's good. You do it.' When I presented that day, I remember Ken was crying a little bit. Bob just said, 'That was brilliant, that was brilliant.' I think he was so afraid of people coming in doing a big exposé and he saw the *Evening Standard* as starting that … I think he was really scared – not physically scared, I think he thought, 'This is bad. There will be a review of this and I know how these things go and you know, we'll be blamed.'"[75]

The coroner's inquest took evidence from survivors, transport workers and the emergency services to establish what had happened and what lessons should be learned. Lady Justice Hallett's report in May 2011, following an exhaustive review of the evidence and testimony, offered a detailed narrative of the terrorist attack on London. The inquest filled a gap occupied since 2005 by conspiracy theories and personal memories, and offered closure both organizationally and individually for those who had been involved. What emerged were many individual acts of heroism on the part of Underground staff, passengers, policemen, firemen and medics. The inquest vividly related how Underground staff were first on the scene, first to experience the carnage, and for 20 minutes or more did their best to make sense of what they saw and to bring comfort to the victims. "At each of the Underground stations, the LU staff demonstrated great courage in assisting passengers in the tunnels. Their efforts were invaluable. The evidence showed that the rigorous training undertaken by LU employees paid dividends. The train drivers of each of the bombed trains attempted to make Mayday calls, staff at the stations as well as train drivers sought to ensure the traction current was discharged, and in the station control rooms swift steps were taken to ensure the emergency services attended promptly."[76]

Lady Hallett was reminded of this during Andy Barr's evidence. "We've heard much evidence over the course of the last few months about how superbly well individual members of your staff performed on that day and, if there was insufficient credit given to them at the time, I hope very much that that's been corrected."[77] Her thanks to Edgware Road train operator Dave Matthews stands in for them all. "For those of us who travel by Tube, it's very reassuring to know there are people like you prepared to go down into a tunnel, not knowing what to expect, but to do your best to help, and you obviously did do your best to help, and you stayed to the bitter end until there was nothing more you could do. I'm sorry we've had to ask you to relive it, and I hope you haven't found it too distressing."[78]

The 7/7 bombings demonstrated just how far the Underground had come since the King's Cross Fire in 1987 and the damning conclusions of the Fennell Report that had followed. The improved management of safety had created clear ownership and roles and responsibilities. Plans that had been put in place for major incidents, tested and exercised, worked well. Roles and responsibilities were well understood, despite the shock of a multi-site attack, and the emergency services collaborated effectively. The inquest concluded that none of the dead could have been saved by a more rapid response. London and its public services proved to be remarkably resilient in July 2005; the bus service was back in place from around 4 p.m. to take Londoners home, and the Tube was in operation the next morning, albeit without the three crime scenes still under investigation. The London bombings were the biggest terrorist attack in the UK since Lockerbie in 1988, but the capital had proved its resilience. A severely injured passenger summed it up, "London is my home and I continue to use the Tube every day".[79]

O'Toole reflected on the challenge his staff had faced. "You have to deal with all those contrary flows, contrary emotions and yet they did that and that was just breathtaking. They pulled it off, and they were able to do it because we do drill all the time, because we do emergency planning, but the real reason why, I think, goes back to Denis Tunnicliffe's days. After the King's Cross fire they put fire equipment throughout this whole network which goes off all the time, sometimes you have these false alarms so everybody on the Underground knows how to take people off the network, they have been trained just because of the frailties of the place." O'Toole also reflected on how Tunnicliffe could also take special pride, "[as] when the bombs went off on 7/7 nothing burned ... we had explosions in the darkness, we had no fire." [80]

Tested and passed

Emergency planning moved to embrace the experience of 7 July. Barr reflected that "the big gap was more that our plans were always formulated for single incidents, perhaps at two locations being either side of an incident. But in this case, it was actually three quite separate sites. And that's what our plans didn't legislate for ... should have done, I guess. The plans we have now deal with that."[81] TfL learned many lessons from this incident. Over the following years, the command-and-control structure was modernized to make it more resilient, not relying on individual managers being on call outside their normal office hours. When 55 Broadway was vacated, the NCC was relocated to TfL's Palestra House at Southwark, with the police, buses and engineering centres located in the same building to facilitate direct contact.

Peter Hendy reflects that "one of the marks of the seventh of July is that it did actually make the place very confident. People sat back afterwards and said, 'Christ, we did that' – and we did do it, it was fantastic. We carried on, and there's a great, huge glow out of that, tinged with an enormous sadness because lots of people lost their lives, but actually we did all right ... and the people of London recognize that we did all right and I think that's fantastic actually. You don't want that sort of terrible occasion to have to provoke it, but actually it's a good reminder that actually it all matters".[82] O'Toole is convinced that the way the staff reacted at 7/7 "turned many Londoners' heads, and the heads of many of our employees, who told me that they had passengers thank them over the next few days, and that was the silver lining of this awful day, the rediscovery of the dignity of these positions."[83]

The events of 7/7 and its aftermath brought Hendy and O'Toole to the attention of the public, and earned them both CBEs for the performance of bus and Tube staff,

A Bakerloo line train leaves Charing Cross station, past
a London Stands United poster, September 2005

a rare honour for an American such as O'Toole. He deserved it not just for his calm
approach when addressing the press and the public on the day, but in managing to
bring the system back in use with amazing speed. He resisted pressure from some
line managers not to restart any lines that day, took the operational staff with him,
restored the whole system the next day, with shuttles around the bomb sites, which
remained crime scenes. Even more remarkably, the damage was repaired and a full
service restored within four weeks, a singular achievement for his under-appreciated
organization and its leadership.[84]

> We ... got all the people who were involved that day and we had made for them
> these very high-quality medals and had a formal ceremony down at the Painted
> Hall in Greenwich with their spouses ... They loved being treated with that level
> of seriousness; we knew they weren't all going to get gongs so we wanted them to
> feel like they had.[85]

O'Toole believed that any delay in bringing the system back could have been unduly
prolonged by government or the trade unions. He quoted research on restoring a
public transit system that suggests you make decisions based on fear for the first
week, and then you make decisions based on risk after that. "That's a transition
everyone goes through, and commuters are the first ones to make the change,
tourists are the last. What would have happened is the unions would have exploited
all of that and we would have been shut down between them and the government,
having to make changes before any of this can happen again. There would have been

a bureaucracy to decision-making that would have paralysed us for a while."[86] Having restored the service, O'Toole took the opportunity of high staff morale and public esteem to embark on a massive staff communications and engagement programme, 'Time to Talk'. (See Chapter 3 for more information on this initiative.)

For the Underground COO, Mike Brown, there was a tremendous pride in what had been achieved by Underground staff who had responded in the moment before the emergency services arrived. "One of my abiding memories was the driver on the Jubilee line who sat in his train for something like 18 hours before he could be moved back into the depot. But he wouldn't leave his train, even though the passengers were off it … There were all the feelings of humility, meeting that supervisor at Russell Square who'd held onto a woman at the top of the station, who he'd brought up as she died, and then meeting her parents as he did and was able to relay to them her last words … I mean, I was hugely proud, had a real sense of pride in the place and the people."[87]

After the upheavals of the PPP, O'Toole and Brown had reinstated a management system based on the individual lines, bringing back accountability for the state of the service and ownership of the stations, encouraging a pride in the individual lines. For Brown this was emphasized by their response to the bombings. Mike Challis was the general manager of the Piccadilly line, who had led from the front. Brown recalls saying to him, "I'm really, really impressed by your leadership, and what you're doing with your people here is really impressive stuff," and Challis said, "Yeah, but it's what they've done to my Piccadilly line."[88]

Four weeks after the attacks had taken place, on 3 August the first train ran through the tunnel from Russell Square to King's Cross; it was a difficult moment. Managers were lined up to accompany drivers in the cab as they went through the site of the bombing. Brown recalls, "When the Piccadilly line started running through again … going through with the first driver, and actually I do remember feeling personally a bit anxious. And I thought, gosh, these drivers are doing this and they were anxious and nobody was speaking and it was just such a human thing, you were looking at this cabling along the track that wasn't covered in dust and it was, it was really quite emotional at the time."[89]

Two months later, George Psaradakis climbed back into a number 30 bus to drive across London again, itself an act of defiance against terrorism. And he said: "You will not defeat us, you will not break us."

Conclusion

There were 129 passengers packed into the front car of 331 as it left King's Cross, of whom 27 were killed, including the suicide bomber. Six died at Edgware Road and seven passengers were killed at Aldgate. The fourth bomb on the bus at Tavistock

The 52 people who lost their lives on 7 July 2005

Square, killed a further 13. In all, 52 passengers were killed and nearly eight hundred wounded. The 7/7 bombings were the worst incidence of peacetime loss of life in London; by comparison, during the Second World War the greatest loss of life was the Nazi bomb that penetrated the Northern line at Bank, killing 68 people sheltering from the Blitz, while in peacetime the Moorgate disaster in 1975 saw 43 lives lost and 74 people injured.

The GLA Assembly 7 July Review Committee reported a year later. "What happened in London on 7 July 2005 could happen in any country, in any city, at any time. Ordinary people, going about their everyday lives, were suddenly swept up in a maelstrom of extraordinary events over which they had no control. What is clear is that the humanitarian response to these events was astounding, from the passengers who helped and supported each other, to the Underground workers, blue light response teams, shop staff, office workers, hotel employees and passers-by who offered what help they could. The individual acts of bravery and courage are too numerous to list. Often the heroes have been reticent to come forward and have stayed silent about the role they played, known only to those that they helped. We are all in their debt; in the face of terror, they restored our faith in the strength and dignity of the human spirit."[90]

6.

THE PAYMENTS REVOLUTION

"A concept that changed the face of mass transit like nothing else in the last forty years."

– Steve Norris, former minister of transport, on Oyster's 20th anniversary in 2023[1]

"What now looks like this obvious and really very comprehensive system was really a series of small steps."

– Charles Monheim, TfL director of fares and ticketing, 2001–06[2]

Delivering a successful congestion charge scheme and investing in the bus network were key challenges for Ken Livingstone's first term as mayor, and their success helped him, now as the official Labour candidate, to win the second mayoral election in 2004, with 55 per cent of the vote to Steve Norris's 45 per cent. The second term was to change the face of urban transport through the development of the Oyster card, which revolutionized ticketing and payment transactions. To develop and deliver the ticketing revolution, TfL needed to recruit fresh and visionary leaders and to foster a close partnership with Cubic Transportation Systems. In tandem with innovation in customer insight and communications, Oyster proved to be essential to the success of the 2012 London Olympics, and both continue to be influential tools for city management in London today.

The origins of Oyster

Since the earliest days of the railways, travel was paid for and the contract recognized by a paper or card ticket. In the contemporary world of frictionless movement through card and mobile readers on ticket gates, buses and trams, it is now an effort to recall the traditional ways in which London Transport services and sales were still transacted in the 1990s. The revolution since the introduction of Oyster cards in 2006, from cash and cheques to contactless and cashless payment

transactions, has utterly changed passengers' experience, from Tube passengers buying paper tickets at banks of machines for a variety of fares and destinations in station booking halls, magnetic striped season tickets, weekly passes and Travelcards pushed through ticket gate slots or shown to staff at ungated stations, to weekly and season ticket renewals inflicting long queues for commuters on Monday mornings at station ticket windows.

It was equally cumbersome for bus passengers, who struggled aboard with small change amid exhortations to have the right fare ready. For the bus network, fare collection was also a challenge. "The employment of conductors ... inspectors to check on passengers and conductors, garage staff to count the cash, security in the garage and for transit to the bank and the associated bank charges were an immense cost." The sheer scale of a cash-based system is recalled by Roger Torode. "When decimalization came in 1971, it was estimated LT handled 80 per cent of the coins circulating in London every week, and 68 tons of sixpences were stockpiled to enable a smooth transition to the new currency with all fares in units of sixpence."[3]

Staff shortages gave LT the impetus to seek greater automation of ticketing and payments. Automatic fare collection, using stored value cards, was being pioneered in American and Asian cities. As the transport network in London grew busier and more congested from the late 1980s, the time taken to negotiate ticketing transactions became more critical, and the hidden cost of collecting cash grew higher. Ticketing solutions were sought separately by the Tube and Bus arms of London Transport.

LT board member Antony Bull visited the United States in 1962 to see the emerging fare collection systems, which Cubic Transportation Systems later installed for the opening of the San Francisco BART network in 1974. When London's Victoria line was authorized in 1962, Robert Dell, LU chief signals engineer, a keen advocate of automation, committed the project to a gated and automatic system.

Automatic ticketing and gates were introduced on the new Victoria line when it opened in 1969. This was hampered by reliability issues with the equipment and by being the only gated line in an open London-wide network. It did, however, prove the financial benefits of gating the system in terms of revenue protection. Robert Dell retired in 1969, and his successors and their GLC masters pursued potential gating increments across the central area, albeit without his zeal. The original gates on the Victoria line had been removed by 1972. The technology did not yet match the vision for an automated ticketing system.

A radical shake-up of thinking on fares in London had been provoked by the introduction of the Fares Fair policy in 1981 by Ken Livingstone, then leader of the GLC. He fell out with the Thatcher government over this and other radical causes, which led to the abolition of the GLC in 1984. But Fares Fair opened the way for the

Passengers queueing to purchase tickets *(top)* at Morden Underground station, February 1982 and *(bottom)* at Highbury & Islington

We're not impressed by big money.

Please have your exact fare ready.
Please.

London's Transport

replacement of point-to-point or stage fares for a trip from A to B. Flat fares within inner and outer zones were introduced in 1981,and changed the LT mindset in favour of zonal ticketing. The Travelcard was introduced in London 1983, based on the Carte Orange in Paris. This innovation reduced the need to queue for a ticket for each Tube and bus journey, encouraged unlimited Tube and bus travel, made transactions fewer and easier and put a ceiling on travel costs, all of which promoted greater use of public transport. Travelcard was the essential precursor to Oyster and the payments revolution that was to come from 2003[4].

Cubic Transportation Systems was a technical and data company established in Santiago in 1966. Cubic had made an innovative move into transport ticketing by supplying an automatic fare collection (AFC) system for Chicago's Illinois Central Gulf Railroad, followed by applications in Hong Kong, Sydney, the BART in San Francisco and Washington DC. The company had maintained an interest in London from the early 1970s thanks to its visionary president, Ray de Kozan. Steve Shewmaker, later de Kozan's successor as Cubic's president, was appointed in 2006 to realize "the vision that London could become the biggest thing that the company had ever undertaken. We bought the Western Data Products Company, they had this brand-new technology called magnetic ticketing and files on opportunities including London."[5]

Shewmaker remembers:

> The gating contract was coming up in London in the late 1970s; de Kozan knew he had to have a base of operations in the UK, so he bought a company called Tiltman Langley, a small gate manufacturer with offices in the aerodrome down in Redhill [Surrey] … he felt he needed to have a bigger partner … so he formed this joint venture, Westinghouse Cubic Limited. Westinghouse Brake and Signal had half, Cubic had the other half, and he leveraged the strong relationship [with LT] to get that gating contract. At some point [1997], at Ray's suggestion Cubic bought out the Westinghouse portion, because there really wasn't much in it for them … I'll tell you what kind of a strategist he was, he was talking about this concept of what he called an AFC, automatic fare collection utility company, where you bought all of your transportation needs through a private supplier, such as Cubic; like any public utility company, you paid your water bill, your electric bill and you paid your transit bill … [Ray] had this idea back in the 1980s, and the customers weren't ready for it back then.[6]

In 1979 Westinghouse Cubic won a two-stage tender, first to develop a new LU ticketing system. This led to the installation of the Universal Ticketing System (UTS) in all stations with ticket gates across busy central area stations. Banks of multi-

facing: A London Transport poster from 1983 urging passengers to have the right change and speed up bus boarding

fare and ten-fare push-button ticket machines taking cash and notes were installed across the network, linked via local computers to a central London computer centre at Baker Street.

A visit to Westinghouse Cubic headquarters in San Diego in 1989 introduced LU to the G-Card system, and was the start of what would prove to be a long and highly significant commercial partnership; ticket gates on the Underground have ever since been installed by Cubic. A renewed search for an automated solution resulted in the 'touch and pass' project, a smartcard trial on three stations in London in 1990 and 1991. The cards relied on battery power to transfer data to the card reader and were bulky; credit-card size, 86 × 54mm, but 5mm thick. Cubic veteran Rob Easterby recalled, "It was the very early days of seeing what could be done with self-powered tags. It was all bespoke that came out from Cubic in the States ... which ultimately led to a trial, which was reasonably successful, but [the card] was far too chunky for normal passengers to put in their wallets."[7]

Meanwhile in another part of the LT forest, London Buses was in pursuit of the cost benefits of one-person operation (OPO). Buses had pursued the introduction of electronic ticketing machines since 1984, resulting in the introduction of Wayfarer machines across the bus fleet in 1985. This was followed by tests of various types of ticket readers as well as adaptations to buses to speed up boarding. It was important to put a system in place that would work with the imminent move to privatization of the London bus companies. The appointment as London Regional Transport (LRT) chair and chief executive Sir Wilfrid Newton in 1989 from the Hong Kong Mass Transit Railway Company, pioneer developers of a smartcard-based system, gave impetus to ticketing innovation.

London Buses evaluated an alternative smartcard ticketing technology, Buscom from Finland, originally a contactless system for ski lifts, enabling the cardholder to keep the credit-card sized, stored value ticket inside their ski gloves.[8] The system was tested in the demanding everyday London bus environment by project manager Roger Torode in 1992 on a single route, the 212 between Chingford and Walthamstow. The stored value Buscom card was loaded with 10 journeys; when it was placed on the reader next to the driver a green light flashed, and a beep indicated that it was a valid pass. There was no connection to the driver's ticket machine, but the trial was deemed promising. This led to a full-scale trial in 1994–95 on 21 routes in the relatively self-contained Harrow bus network, costing £2 million, with 18,000 cards issued and covering 700 drivers, 235 buses of various types and five operators. The Harrow Smartcard Trial was the largest in the world, and confirmed the benefits of smartcards for boarding times, ease of use, journey data collection, fare calculation, and above all the efficiency of extending one-person operation.

Passenger numbers rose rapidly in the 1990s. London Transport was in urgent need of investment to tackle the backlog of maintenance on ageing infrastructure, to

Experimental automatic ticket gates on the Victoria line at Seven Sisters, 1970

source new rolling stock and invest in future technology to smooth payments and reduce fare evasion. Life-expired systems on the buses had to be replaced, and the gating of the Underground needed to be completed as significant revenue was being lost through fare evasion. The various strands of ticketing and fare collection across Tube and bus were brought together when investment became available from central government. In the 1990s, both the Major and then the Blair governments had adopted public–private finance initiatives (PFIs), which were intended to harness private-sector managerial skills and funding capacity to complete and manage major investment projects and to take such projects off the government's balance sheet.

With the Blair/Brown government expanding the scope of PFIs, this was the only route for significant public investment in the Tube; a PFI with Alstom was signed for new trains for the Northern (Misery) line in 1995, for DLR extensions, power supply, transport police accommodation and significantly smart ticketing, known as the Prestige[9] project. When London Transport morphed into TfL in 2000, the new organization inherited no fewer than 13 PFIs[10], with the largest of all still being formulated, the public–private partnership (PPP) for the Underground. Meanwhile, as John Hill of Cubic recalls, "TfL were about to enter probably the biggest change programme, with regards to the ticketing system, they had ever gone through."[11]

A Metroline bus driver operates the new Smartcard ticketing system for a boarding passenger during the trial at Harrow in 1994–95

Charles Monheim was brought in by Bob Kiley and Jay Walder in July 2001 to lead for TfL on fares and ticketing, including the Prestige ticketing PFI. Monheim was a Stanford Business School graduate with significant operational experience on both rail and bus in the turnaround of the New York MTA, where he had first worked for Kiley and Walder. Monheim brought a vision for fares and ticketing innovation that was to extend far beyond what was contracted within the Prestige project. The many small steps taken to date had been bundled together into the Prestige PFI project from 1998. Monheim was to transform a simple fare collection project into a vision for frictionless travel in London.

The Prestige project

Investment in developing and rolling out a smartcard-based ticketing system for London was secured through the Prestige project, a PFI between London Transport and the TranSys (Transactional Systems Ltd) consortium: Cubic and EDS (Electronic Data Systems[12]), Fujitsu and WS Atkins. TranSys was responsible for developing, installing, managing and maintaining an automatic fare-collection system for London, including the Oyster card system, on behalf of London Transport. The

PFI contract was to last for a term of 17 years, with unusually – and significantly – a break clause in 2010, to provide for the first time an integrated ticketing system for London across the Underground, buses, trams and the DLR.

Cubic and EDS were the principal shareholders in the PFI, Cubic as the developers, installers and maintainers of the hardware – the ticket gates across the whole network – while EDS managed and operated the system.

John Hill worked for Cubic as senior programme director during the Prestige years when Oyster was being developed.

> LU had things it wanted to do ... the primary business case was based around gating. The buses needed to upgrade their [ticketing] equipment ... The government was basically saying, 'If you want the money to do these upgrades, you're going to have to pull it all together as one project and go get private financing for it.' The way of pulling it all together was with this smartcard system, layered over the top of the primary business case around gating. Zone 1 had been gated previously, so LU knew the benefits you could get from gating from a fraud reduction perspective, and they wanted gates across the system.[13]

Initially the Prestige project's focus was simply to replicate on a smartcard the ticketing that existed on paper tickets. "The smartcard system as originally specified had two elements to it. One was season tickets. So, converting those currently on paper in terms of weekly or monthly annual passes on to smart. Then there was pay as you go. It wasn't called pay as you go at the time [stored value], but we'll refer to it as that." From the conversations Hill and Richard Rowlands, Cubic software engineer and programme manager in the 1990s, had with people at TfL at the time, "pay as you go was an incidental add-on to the contract that someone figured would be a good thing to have".[14] "The turning point in the whole thing was the point at which TfL recognized that pay as you go is actually a tool that they could use to transform how they collect revenue, that goes back to the days ... of Charlie Monheim."[15]

Hill and Rowlands recalled the turning point for ticketing and Prestige, which became evident at a momentous workshop that Monheim ran on 'stored value'. Prestige was a complex proposition, by the nature of the contract specification and the way it had evolved in the first few years of the contract. "It wasn't until Charlie convened a workshop, which I think was at the Cubic office [at Redhill] ... There was a breakthrough moment ... He had the foresight to recognize the value that [pay-as-you-go] could add ... If he could say to people 'Use Oyster, pay as you go, and you're guaranteed best value' then that opened the door for him to start introducing price differentials between magnetic tickets and Oyster."[16] Through this insight, the smart ticket was transformed from merely a replacement for the paper ticket to the key to the city. Hill suggests that up to that moment,

I don't think any of us understood how transformative Oyster would prove to be. Pay as you go was viewed by many as a 'nice to have' in the contract, but credit for it has to go to Charlie Monheim and Jay Walder, who saw the opportunity to heavily promote it and forever change the way Londoners would pay for public transport.[17]

From ticket to payment

"My job was to keep the project focused on a flawless, timely, staged rollout of ticketing features that would tame the complexity of London's transport ticketing system. Anything that could get in the way of that – messy interfaces with third parties, rigid interpretations of contract terms, public impatience – had to be cleared away or assuaged."

– Charles Monheim

Monheim was engaged by Walder to bring a dedicated focus on the PFI contract to deliver an integrated transport ticketing and payments system for London. Monheim brought both a fresh vision and an operational perspective to the restrictions of the PFI contract management, seeing the potential early on to "establish this as a real TfL project, not as a collection of agency projects ... a much more centralized control of the progress of the project, rather than a loose monitoring of ticketing on buses, ticketing on the Underground".[18] He assembled a team led by Shashi Verma to develop what over time became a transport-led societal revolution in payments from cash to card.

John Hill from Cubic recalls how the project progressively accumulated cost benefits by reducing the number of times a ticket needed to be purchased.

> People would buy weeklies and monthlies, so that would increase the average, but it came out about a four-to-one ratio between the two. By the time Oyster pay as you go was fully implemented, that had gone to about eight to one. There were half as many ticket purchase events as the number of journeys. Every one of those events has a cost associated with it. Whether it be a commission fee that you're paying through an agent, or a transaction fee to the banks, or paying someone to sit in a ticket office, or you're buying more ticket machines – whatever, there is a cost associated with doing that. If you can cut the number of those events in half there's a significant cost saving to be had. If you look at it going forward, contactless is like Oyster pay as you go on steroids, because there are no ticket selling events associated with the use of contactless. So now, that ratio is about 12 to one. Had TfL not done what they did with pay as you go, then today or pre-Covid, you would have three times as many people queueing in ticket halls. It's been absolutely transformative.[19]

Monheim stressed the political imperative that drove Prestige. "He [Livingstone] came into his role already with a very well-formed and very strong view about what transport in London should look like. In particular, he had to have projects that were going to make or break his chances to be re-elected as mayor in 2004. Those two projects were congestion charging and the Prestige project. Prestige was the implementation of smartcard ticketing, and the Oyster card is the most visible sign of that project." Monheim was able to use this when standing up to DfT pressure to make Prestige compliant with the "half-baked ITSO[20] standard for public transport ticketing."[21]

Monheim was clear about his debt to "the people in the 1990s, who conceived the Prestige project, and entered into the contract; [they] deserve a lot of credit for what came after. They understood that there was a lot more that one could do with an electronic ticket, both in terms of new fare products and in terms of the way those fare products would enable one to transform the whole fare structure of London, particularly with regard to things like multiple trips. London's fare structure is incredibly complicated." He valued the work he inherited from those who in pre-TfL days had framed the Prestige project, such as Richard Parry, Adam Goulcher, Paul London and Richard Smith.[22, 23]

"Why we don't see real integrated ticketing [across most cities] is because you don't have integrated transit. An integrated ticketing system needs that." John Hill remembers "a session with Charlie Monheim; we're sitting in, he was telling different parts of the TfL organization at the time, 'This is what you're getting, you get ready for it. It's coming, it's going live, you get your training done, you need to be ready'. How many other jurisdictions around the world have that authority to be able to say that to operators?"[24]

"The project was not an easy project," but Monheim never felt that there was a "point where I think there was any doubt that it was going to happen ... TfL was a very unusual organization. This is as much a credit to Ken as to Bob [Kiley] and Jay [Walder], there was an appreciation which you do not often find in projects that have a large information technology component ... They were very good about not committing to dates for delivery. We knew when we wanted to deliver, but it's death to these projects to put a date over the quality of the product that's being inflicted on the public. And so, the attitude was very much that this will only be turned on when it is ready, when we're positive it's going to work properly."[25]

Hill was also clear about how important it was to win trust. "They had to establish people's trust that this system is going to work. We had to provide all this capability for people to look at their balance, look at their journeys, satisfy themselves that they had been charged properly. But after things had been out there for about two weeks, nobody looked at it any more. They realized that it worked, and they just used it."[26]

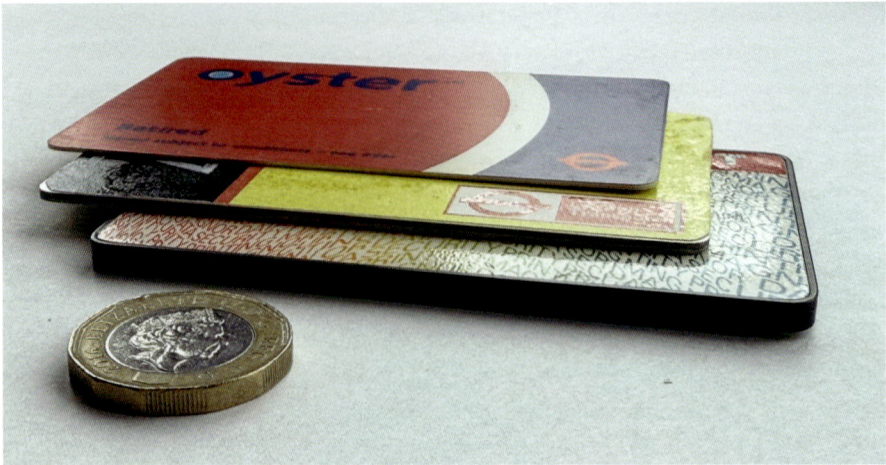

The evolution of the smart card from the 5mm thick 'touch and pass' card in 1990–91, through the Harrow trial card in 1994–95 to the Oyster card from 2003

As a new customer product, the new card needed a name, a brand. The brief from TranSys to the agency Saatchi & Saatchi had been to find a name that best embodied the criteria of travel, stored currency, security, modernity and a London theme. Oyster was conceived, mainly because of the metaphorical implications of security and value in the hard bivalve shell and the concealed pearl. Its associations with London through the Thames estuary oyster beds, and the major relevance of the popular idiom 'the world is your oyster' were also significant factors in its selection. Saatchi had worked with Andrew McCrum of Blue Sky Enterprise to draw up potential brand names.[27]

The dynamics of the TranSys consortium were illustrated by the process to choose the name for the new card in 1998–99. The presentation of six potential names to a meeting was remembered by Richard Parry, then taking the lead on Prestige for the Underground, who suggests that the decision-making process at the time was less focused:

> I recall there being a shortlist of six that had come through an agency-led process …
> a series of prior discussions that culminated in us all to make a choice. I remember
> two of the alternative names: one was Amigo, a friendly sort of thing, and then,
> slightly more oddly, more technology-based, Cube was a name that had a place on
> the shortlist, and Oyster … I remember quite a long day backwards and forwards
> about which of them … with hindsight it seems obvious it should have been
> Oyster. I know it was very influenced by, of course, Hong Kong and their Octopus
> card. The connection with London was emphasized with the pearly kings and

queens. There was tension with TranSys thinking it was their decision [rather than] London Transport's. Ian Coucher, TranSys chief executive, had a view that they were much more in the driving seat on policy than we really thought they could be; this was fundamental to everything about ticketing, for Underground and buses in London. It couldn't be entirely surrendered to a contractor … No one really disliked it and so it became the favourite almost by a process of elimination.[28]

Monheim recalls the significance of a Far East tour.

We went to Singapore, Hong Kong and Japan, where smartcard ticketing was most developed. We were looking to learn from their experience … Your fare collection system has to be the handmaiden of your ticketing system. If you go to places like Hong Kong, they have a relatively simple ticketing system, which means their fare collection system doesn't have to do that much. Here zones and modes all had to be put together into something quite elegant[29]… In Hong Kong in particular, Octopus Card Limited[30] was very, very helpful in suggesting how we should think about the whole implementation process. In fact, we hired Octopus Card to provide a certain amount of peer review of the implementation process. They reinforced and strengthened our commitment not to play schedule over performance.[31]

Monheim recalled that "certainly, Ken's advisors were often looking at things through that lens, but Ken was looking at things through the lens of what is going to make the transport system successful."[32]

Monheim recognized that for TfL and the mayor the credibility of Oyster was going to be vital to public acceptance; essential for this was the integrity of the payments system and the security of usage data. A crucial decision was making finite the time to hold the data. Monheim had asked, "Tell me the least amount of time that we need the data in order for the system to work. It really came down to how short a period of time can we keep the data and still respond to customer needs, for one reason or another. [It is actually eight weeks.] But number one, we made it perfectly clear that you could hold your card anonymously, in which case you would not be able to get your money back if you lost it. And second, that we were only keeping the data so long as it was necessary to deal with things like miss-taps."[33]

"We got remarkably little pushback on that policy," recalls Monheim. "It really put to rest one of the things that would have been a major cause for resistance to using it. Once we did start having large quantities of data, which we could anonymize, the question was, how can we use it to understand travel behaviour better?" The move from smoothing ticketing and revenue collection to harvesting data to better

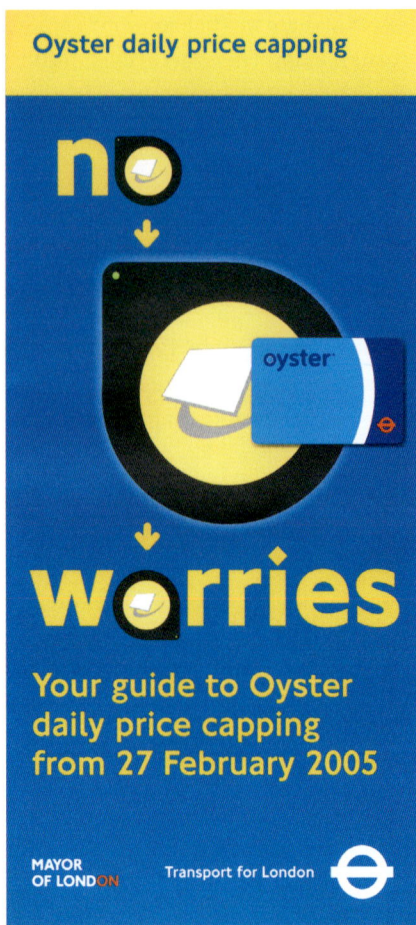

Leaflets promoting the introduction of the Oyster card in June 2003
and the innovation of price capping in February 2005

understand customer behaviour on the system was to be of major significance. For Monheim, "That's really when MIT[34] came into the picture. What you need is open-minded people who were data-fluent to use that data to pull out key trends. Through an arrangement with MIT, we had a number of graduate students who began looking at that data and pointing out ways in which that data itself was superior to any number of other things we were spending money on, to figure out how people behaved on the system."[35]

There had to be the expectation that the technology itself was going to be flawless, but the real notion of better came once Oyster was implemented and you started to be able to improve the whole ticketing experience. Most notably through best value

... but the first real improvement was stored value [pay as you go], which had two benefits: number one, you could have cash on your card, and you could take multiple rides without having to go to a ticket machine every ride; but second, it made the whole transfer process easier because you didn't get to the end of a trip and then have to add value if you were doing something different. That was taken care of automatically, so there was an immediate benefit for people.[36]

Taking the lead on contactless payments

"Those were interesting days," the Cubic team remembered.

There was a lot of doubt as to whether contactless would ever work. I certainly did at one point ... it was a lot more difficult to get everything to work and integrate than we had thought ... Probably the single biggest challenge was that, all of a sudden, you were introduced to this whole new industry, this payments industry ... When we were doing Oyster, we had complete control over that card; we specified the cards, we knew how they performed, what data was on them. Now we're entering a world where we're not issuing the cards any more. There's thousands of banks around the world issuing them and they're all different to a certain degree. You've got Visa, you've got MasterCard, you've got Amex. You've got different chips inside the cards, different configurations, everything. Having to design a system that would work with that sort of variety and get certified to work was a big step change, a big challenge ... the big card schemes, Mastercard and Visa, hadn't really thought through how their cards were going to work in transit as opposed to in retail.[37]

Richard Rowlands on the Cubic team remembers a big moment with the banks.

There was an event that Shashi [Verma] and Will [Judge] organized at the [LT] Museum, briefing the issuing banks, saying, 'This is what we're going to do, we've got Amex, MasterCard and Visa on board, and you're going to have to issue your cards in a particular way with, for example, counters on the card in terms of how many times you can use it in an offline fashion.' They needed to set higher than would normally or previously have been done. 'There's a huge prize out there, this is what we want to do and we need your support to make it happen. We need you to use the best possible chips in the card.' We no longer had control over what chips are actually used in the plastic cards and the payment industry allows a wide variety. They're all specified and certified, but there's a range of different performance characteristics. The banks had to be encouraged to spend a little bit more, a few pennies more per card to get the best possible chips, rather than go with the cheapest.[38]

From Prestige to partnership

Shashi Verma had joined TfL from McKinsey in 2002, initially to innovate in making the case to secure Crossrail funding, and was appointed director for Fares and Ticketing at TfL in late 2006. "In my very first week," Verma related, "I started looking at this job that I'd taken up, given that the delivery of Oyster was, by and large, complete. Take-up had improved, we were still running at about 10 or 15 per cent of journeys on Oyster, the other 85 to 90 per cent was still on paper. Clearly, there was a job to increase take-up. But beyond that, I wasn't content with the idea that I'm just going to come and run a system that already has been rolled out".

Verma went around and talked to everybody involved in the world of fare collection in the Underground and in Buses, but did not find clarity about what they wanted. There were very immediate pain points on Oyster, but they were to recede. Beyond that, there was no clarity about whether the business wanted anything new. "In fact, it's clear that the business had no particular demands of us, other than just running the system properly. But one discussion that I've had with Charlie and Jay, and Charlie had done work on this, was on how much money you're spending and collecting in revenue. Instinctively, we all knew that it was a big number. And so, at the end of my first week in the job, I decided that if I was going to make an impact as a director of Oyster card, then the way to do it was by going after this one single metric, the cost of revenue collection.[39]

Verma explained what they did next.

> We got a bright kid from MIT working with us for six months and we let him loose on this problem. He produced a fantastic report by the end of 2006 that collated all the costs, which lay in disparate cost centres across the entire business. He did some fantastic analysis on breaking that cost down, how much were we spending on infrastructure, people, commissions ... the big buckets of costs ... and while we were doing this, I'd been doing blue-sky thinking about how to make that number smaller. It was very clear that the Prestige contract, which had been incredibly successful until then, had reached the end of its life. It's important to be nuanced in the critique: the Prestige contract was actually incredibly successful, up to a point. When you think of all the deliverables that were laid out in the beginning of the Prestige contract, it had achieved every single one of them.[40]

Verma's analysis was that in 2005–06 the cost of revenue collection was £348 million, or 14.7 per cent of all Tube, tram, bus and DLR revenue. With Oyster and contactless, by 2019–20 that cost had fallen to 6.6 per cent or about £330 million, while inflation, traffic growth and fare increases had increased the revenue pot from £2.4 to £5 billion since 2005–06.[41]

Six months into the job, Verma had realized that the £100 million PFI Prestige contract was hobbling his ambitious and visionary agenda to innovate, to smooth the customer experience and cut the cost of ticketing and payments for TfL through new technology. The Oyster project with TfL, with EDS and Cubic as TranSys in the PFI contract lasting until 2015, was going well, winning industry awards, but the expansion into using Oyster on the bus network and for small cash retail purchases was met with contractual stances that threatened the project and hindered its potential.

Verma recollects that there was a fundamental problem with TfL's model of fare collection: as long as you have a forced exchange of money, there is a cost associated with every transaction. "Oyster had clearly made a big dent, by reducing the number of ticketing transactions that were needed quite substantially. But despite its enormous success, it was still the same business model. It just meant that you interact with the system less frequently … But we started thinking, how do we enable people to travel without this money exchange problem at all?"

Jay Walder had previously led the delegation to Hong Kong, where they had looked at the Octopus card system. Walder and Monheim had come back with the idea of converting Oyster into an Octopus-like card where it could be used not just for transport but also for small payments. Will Judge moved from corporate finance to work for Monheim to run what they called the e-money project. As Verma reflected:

> The more we looked at e-money, the clearer it became that the conditions between Hong Kong and London were very different. First, Hong Kong was a cash-dominated economy with very few bank cards; London had a very high penetration of bank cards to start off with, and much lower cash penetration. There was a very big ecosystem of Visa and MasterCard in existence in London, which was not true in Hong Kong.
>
> The second way is that we were stuck in this PFI where making any change to it was difficult and the cost of implementing an Octopus-like system in London was going to be horrendous. All the equipment was expensive, the contract was inflexible. The third is that the financial regulations are very different as well. There was the e-money directive in the EU, not so dissimilar to UK. That meant that to set ourselves up to be an Octopus-like card in London, we would have had to get a banking licence and that comes with all of its compliance costs. Whereas in Hong Kong, they were exempt. So, when you add all three of those factors together, it just made the idea of making an Oyster as an open-value card unimplementable, so when I took charge of Oyster, this e-money project was already in its death throes, and so I decided to kill it.

Verma understood that the essential innovation was to get rid of the money exchange step in ticketing. "How about we allow people to travel with a product that's already in their pocket? The two things that people carry in their pockets are bank cards

The pioneers of the ticketing revolution, TfL directors of Ticketing and Fares:
(left) Charles Monheim, 2001–06, *(right)* Shashi Verma, 2007–11,
later director of Customer Experience and chief technology officer

and mobile phones, and we started investigating both in earnest. The mobile phone industry was more mature and more open to these kinds of things. We ran two trials with mobile phones in 2007 with a large number of partners – Barclays, Visa, Nokia and O2 – at Imperial College, and the product was a runaway hit. Had we been able to launch that commercially, it would have been a huge success. It wouldn't get rid of the money exchange problem entirely. But because the product will be sitting in a phone, it will make the money exchange problem purely one of a banking transaction where you could push a few buttons on your phone. The money would move from the bank into your Oyster card, rather than have to go through a ticket machine. You could go to a ticket machine and top up, but that wasn't essential. The problem is that at about the same time, there was this almighty battle going on between handset manufacturers and mobile network operators as to who controlled this new near-field communication [NFC][42] technology. The industry went into this complete tailspin from which it didn't recover until Apple came out with NFC in 2014."[43]

The TfL team had tried very hard to make the mobile technology work, but was obliged to give up on it.

Alongside mobiles, bank cards were also being considered. Verma and Judge found there was much less openness from the banking industry people at that point – no openness from Visa, some openness from MasterCard. The first discussion Verma had with MasterCard started with them saying that if they wanted NFC payments they would have to pay a fee.

We've never paid a fee, but that was where the banking industry was at that point. They didn't see the potential of contactless payment. In fact, the whole micropayments world was invisible to the banking industry, they didn't care about it, they didn't think there was any money in it. We, on the other hand, had seen the potential of loyalty that comes with micropayments. At that point, back in 2006, if you had a bank card, you would use it maybe once a day, often less frequently than that. Whereas people were using their Oyster card three, four or five times a day. We saw the value in that, that being front of wallet actually had some real value ... Transys had approached Barclays with the idea of embedding an Oyster card into bank cards. We had done a deal with TranSys and Barclays and Dundee, where we created this thing called the One Pulse card, with an Oyster card embedded into a credit card. Very bad timing on that one, because that card got launched the weeks after Northern Rock went under ... people just didn't want credit cards at that point.

We had done that deal in December of 2006. Even as we were signing the deal in Canary Wharf I was thinking, it looks elegant to put an Oyster card inside a bank card, but it is a complicated product. None of this embedding business, let's just get rid of that problem. How could the bank card work like an Oyster card? Now, it's one of those crazy ideas, where if you look at it, it would have been very easy to get daunted by the scale of the challenge. To an extent innovation comes out of being naive. I started pursuing the idea with Will, very much my comrade in arms, but within a month or so we had figured out the broad outlines of how a bank card needed to work for it to be accepted on our system.

For Shashi Verma, the £348 million cost of revenue collection was his prime objective. "Figuring out that the contract was getting in the way, figuring out that we needed a different system of collection, and bringing it all together – because we wouldn't get to a contactless card without doing something to the PFI ... All of these things had to come together. I have to say, even at that point I could see the threads between all of them. They all were enabling each other, and to crack it I had to crack the whole lot ... All of this looks very easy in hindsight but we didn't know in any detail what we were trying to build."[44]

Verma had rapidly come to believe that: "The consortium that constituted TranSys was basically dysfunctional, a marriage made in hell, and we were acting as marriage counsellors all the time. That manifested itself very clearly in the first big deal that I tried to do with TranSys, which was to expand the retail network [tickets sold through third party shops]. The reason was to reduce cash on buses, and to start mandating Oyster on to buses and eventually to fulfil the aim of buses going cashless, we needed to have a much denser retail network than the one that we ran at that time. We had a network of about two thousand agents, and the aspiration was to go up to about four thousand agents. That requires a completely different way of running the retail network, and there was absolutely zero openness with anyone to figure out a way we could do this. Eventually, we got to a point where I thought we had done a deal, a handshake deal on the basis that certain basic principles were accepted. Then [EDS] just completely went back on it. For me, that was a very significant test of trustworthiness."[45]

Verma had also taken stock of his relationship with Cubic, testing the ability of their new man in London in 2006, Steve Shewmaker, to bring positive change, as Shewmaker remembers.

> It was almost like clockwork. I would get home on a Friday night, seven-ish, I'd be out to dinner with my wife, nice little Italian restaurant around the place that we lived and then the phone would ring, it'd be Shashi, telling me that there was an array of gates down in some station somewhere, and what was I going to do about it? So, instead of telling him 'I'm not going to do anything about it, it's Friday night', I would start my meal, get hold of the right people, we'd get a crew sent out to that particular station, they'd fix the problem, and I'd report back to Shashi. This happened not just once, not just twice, not just three times. I think he was testing me to see about how responsive I was going to be to what they thought was important. So, I must have passed the test at some point![46]

Shewmaker, Cubic Transportation's new CEO, had arrived in London in 2006, brought back from Thales[47] by Cubic president Ray de Kozan. The Prestige contract was Cubic's biggest and most important project, whereas for the much larger EDS it was of far less significance. In the summer of 2006 Shewmaker saw at first hand that the relationship with TfL was not all that good, very strained. "I knew that what needed to happen was to get the company more customer-focused and get out of this constant exchange of claims that went back and forth between London and Cubic. Cubic would make a claim to London for some breach of contract, and London would come back and blame Cubic; they stacked up on top of each other. We were spending our time answering their claims and they were spending their time answering our claims." As he then explained,

> We all worked, both the TfL ticketing people and the Cubic team, at Pelham Street. I think the TfL people had floor two and we had floor three. There was really no communication, you'd pass each other going up or down the stairs, and that was it. The first thing I did was, I took this pile of claims, a fair-sized stack on our side, and I said, 'Okay, how do we get through this? How do we just put them to bed?' and I worked with Andy Barrie and company, I told my team, 'We're not going to be claiming [against] this client for everything, you know, we're going to sit there, we're going to negotiate a deal that settles all these claims, and we're gonna put them away'.[48]

Shewmaker had quickly realized that delivering in London for TfL was the best way to secure Cubic's future. He instinctively understood that this now demanded a new style of relationship, more of a creative partnership and less of a contractual tussle, moving the tone with TfL from argumentative to accommodating. The tipping point was around the expansion of the retail network, held up by EDS despite making a verbal agreement. Outside the meeting Shewmaker told Verma, "We're not going to let you fail for a half a million pounds, don't worry about it, we'll cover it. That's the point, in my mind, when the relationship really started to drift more towards Cubic and away from EDS … and EDS being so tone deaf, they couldn't pick up on it."[49]

Shewmaker restructured Cubic soon after his arrival, John Hill at Cubic recalls. "It was a very contractual relationship until, at some point, Steve got it that this was going to be big. This was going to be the future of the company, a really interesting moment … he created the environment that allowed Rob and Richard and I and the hundreds of other people in Cubic to do what we did. There's no question about that … That was when TfL ended up making the decision to take on the back-office development themselves. We worked with them to flesh that out into a three-tier system; you've got the equipment in the stations, you've got the middle office, which we've provided, and the TfL back office."[50]

By early 2007, and after prolonged persuasion, Verma had reached a verbal agreement with Cubic and EDS on the expansion of the retail network for bus ticket sales, but then in April received a new set of financial demands from EDS. This solidified Verma's view:

> There was something fundamental that has to be done to this contract. Fortuitously, we had this termination provision in the contract, which was very unusual among PFI contracts, there was a very simple and cheap way of getting out of the contract at its twelfth anniversary, so in a 17-year contract, five years before the end of contract we could get out without paying penalties. I looked at that, it's like a financial option. One of the things about a financial option is that its value declines as time goes on, the closer you come to the strike date, after which you can't exercise the option, the value keeps diminishing. With my financial training, I was very clear that to maximize value on this option we had to act early. Even though I had no intention, as such, to terminate the contract, I wanted to extract good value out of this option. The only way to do it was to make the threat of a termination absolutely credible. A lot of effort went into making that threat credible. Eventually, Cubic understood the game, and they changed their behaviour radically; EDS did not.[51]

Verma persuaded TfL to take the risk of breaking the Prestige contract and to sign a Future Ticketing Agreement with Cubic alone. This was a difficult moment, as after the May 2008 elections he needed to convince the new mayor, Boris Johnson, and the new finance committee of the TfL board. EDS lobbied frantically, "trying to paint me as an upstart who didn't understand the technology", and took out a high court injunction, but eventually settled on relatively modest terms. Oyster and its brand moved into TfL's ownership for £1 million, and Verma's vision for the frictionless facility and financial efficiencies of contactless payment was back in view.

In November 2008, TfL announced the agreement of a new contract for the future management and development of the Oyster card system and other ticketing services. Verma said at the time, "This new deal will see Oyster in the pockets of Londoners for years to come, and will save significant money that TfL will invest in improving transport in the capital. Transport for London is delighted that its successful partnership with Cubic and EDS will now continue for the next five years. The new contracts will deliver better value for money and improvements to Oyster for passengers across London."[52]

"The PFI was finally terminated in 2010," recollected Cubic's Hill and Rowlands. "That's the point at which Cubic took on the replacement contract as the prime contractor. But terminating the PFI and entering into the direct agreement with Cubic was an essential part of implementing contactless payment. Because they [TfL] did not believe that the PFI contract gave them the flexibility to be able to do that ... the PFI structure was very complex, just on the Cubic/EDS logistics side [alone], it was very unwieldy. [TfL] made sure the contract that they entered into with Cubic had all the flexibility built into it, so they were going to be able to do what they wanted to do."[53]

"The other missing piece," Verma noted, "was that the whole national rail industry was outside Oyster. That had to be cracked, because that was a very serious source of complaint. Frankly, it was a reason for a very large number of Londoners to stick with their paper tickets. The rail industry has been incredibly difficult on this whole issue. It took real effort to get them on board."[54]

"By 2008," he continued, "we had a reasonably clear idea of what we wanted to do with contactless and the ideas were looking better by the day, and we kept up the volume after that. By 2008, we had a decent buy-in from MasterCard and more tentative from Visa. But, you know, I was prepared to work with MasterCard, and even at Visa the lines of communication were open. What we didn't have was any buy-in from the banks ... When the financial crisis happened in 2008, it became very difficult to engage with banks. Their attention was focused entirely elsewhere, the idea of looking for new ideas and investment was clearly not where they were. It took us longer to implement contactless for that reason."[55]

"Meanwhile, we were engaging with MasterCard and with Visa, looking at all the different technical requirements. Visa and MasterCard can't 'talk' to each other, there's no standard for everybody. We were laying out very clear requirements for both of them as to what needed to happen, we were setting global standards. There are three types of standards that we were instrumental in setting; some of this we wrote, some of this we got Visa and MasterCard to write." The first of these, explained Verma, were "technical standards about how the card had to work. A lot of the customer experience around how contactless works worldwide came out of that. We were pedantic in saying that the customer experience had to be absolutely top notch. Both Visa and MasterCard had to give the same customer experience. That ended up completely rewriting all the contractor standards we had been working on until then."

The second were security standards, which were "very overbearing. One of the consequences of the security standards being the way they were is that transactions were too slow. That's a very critical part of the customer experience, so you've got to get the industry to change that." And the third were commercial standards. "The challenge we had was that with the Oyster card, when the card is presented at the reader, you know what value is on the card, and therefore you know whether to accept or not accept the card. You don't have that luxury with bank cards. There is a whole commercial model that has to be developed about how you consider the card to be acceptable, who takes the risk, and how the risk gets shared between us and the banking industry. Eventually, what got implemented was slightly different between Visa and MasterCard, but as a customer you will be completely oblivious to all of this, which was important … A lot of work had to be done with Visa and MasterCard to make all this happen."[56]

"Then of course, we have to build the technology," Verma continued, "a multi-application reader, which had never been done until that stage, a reader that could do Oyster and contactless bank cards. Because we are working with the government, it also has to do ITSO.[57] There was this whole ITSO saga running in the background, which essentially has been a complete waste of time and a diversion and resulted in nothing. But you can't ignore the fact that we had to deal with that, as we were going through all this. So, the whole question of the card reader, the whole question of the back office; all of this looks very easy in hindsight, but you look at the chart and say, I'm not sure we can do this. We didn't know in any detail what we were trying to build … We took a very bold step and said we would build the technology ourselves, and with very little experience of doing things of this kind before. In fact, TfL had no experience of building software until then. I had initiated something for Oyster on National Rail and that was like a little tiny project with three developers, but in that process we had developed a methodology for delivering software. I was confident that we could scale it up. In 2009, we decided to take those three people, hire a few more, about a dozen people, and said, 'Let's build a prototype for the contactless back office.' That's what we did, starting in 2009, and by 2010 we were able to demonstrate to the organization that this is something we could do."[58]

It was in late 2010 that they were finally ready to move to the next stage, which Verma explains was the process of "fighting the big organizational battles to get the investment to get the go-ahead, and that final authority came in early 2011. By that time, we'd spent very little money; our total expenditure on contactless at that point was two or two and a half million pounds. We had done all the globally pathbreaking things with practically no money, a huge testament to the fact that we had some very clever people working on it. I had Will [Judge], who was running around making alliances in the industry and pushing them hard; Tim Carman, who had come to do the software with Sebastian Losq, our head of technology back then. In early 2011, once we had had approval internally to do this, then came the crunch time to take the financial industry on."[59]

"We finally managed to get Visa to the point by saying, 'Look, there is a huge opportunity here for your constituent banks. Why is it that you don't get it?' They finally, very reluctantly, came on board," Verma explained. "Visa invited us to their board meeting in April of 2011, and Peter Hendy and I went along. Peter asked me on the way to Visa, 'What do you think I should say to them?' I said, 'Peter, there's a very simple message you need to give them, which is that, look, whether you like it or not, we're going to implement this. If all of you together in Visa, all of the member banks have either decided they don't want this, we'll do this with MasterCard, because they're ready. If some of you decide to issue cards and others don't, well that's fine. I have no problem with that, but just remember one thing: the ones who issue cards will have their cards used five times a day. You can decide whether you want to be a bank whose cards are being used five time a day or not.' So, Peter very calmly delivered that message and we walked away. It was very clear: that message landed with a big thump on all the banks." For Verma, this proved to be a turning point. "About two months after this, HSBC became the first bank after Barclays to say that they will start issuing cards – and remember, Barclays had committed to doing this in 2006. We're talking about something that's happening four to five years later. HSBC decided to start issuing cards and then, one by one, the dominoes fell. At the end of 2012, we launched contactless on buses in London. If you look back at the statistics on the usage of contactless outside TfL in the retail environment, you see the first kink in the curve when we launched on buses because suddenly contactless became a thing in people's imagination."[60]

"Barclays had been issuing cards, but frankly, apart from a few aficionados, nobody was using them. And then two years later, in September 2014, we started accepting contactless across the entire network, with weekly capping and everything else. That's the point at which you see a second kink in the use of contactless in the retail world. I could draw the story today, the stats are that 86 per cent of all retail transactions that involve a card are contactless."[61]

Verma reflected on Monheim's view of the whole process of Oyster as a series of small steps rather than a grand design.

> I think he's right about that for Oyster, discovering our way as we went along. But I think contactless was different. Contactless started with the grand design. It was very clear to me from day one that what we were trying to do was radical,

The ticketing revolution enables a range of frictionless payment methods for transport

that it involves us changing the way we work, the banking industry changing the way they work. There will be numerous challenges, many of which looked daunting, and perhaps insurmountable. But I was convinced that we would find a way through them. I wasn't willing to give up. I think this is really important; there are many points, perhaps even dozens of points at which we could have compromised on the customer offering, the customer proposition, and made the delivery much easier. I wasn't keen on doing that, and I have to say my team were not keen on doing that either. We were reinforcing each other's views, strongly, that we should not compromise on what we were doing, we were absolutely there to build a high-quality product ... There was never a doubt in my mind that it was going to happen. The only doubt going through all this pain, was there a way, for example, of integrating Oyster better with auto top-up? ... That thought kept knocking at my head, every time we tried doing something to make life easier on that front, we realized it wasn't easy. The clunkiness of trying to join up an Oyster card with the banking system, and the number of points at which you could fail, was just very high ... I didn't have any doubts about whether this thing will work and I had no doubts about whether it would get accepted. You know, there's always a question of what level of acceptance would we get? And we'd done some market research on it. That was sufficiently comfortable.

But to relay a debate I used to have with Vernon [Everitt], Vernon was very much into customer research: 'Let's talk to customers, let's see what they're telling us. We should do what they ask and want us to do.' I was taking the opposite view – that there are times when customers don't know what they want us to do, because it's very difficult for customers to imagine something that they've never seen before.[62]

The conditions in London in TfL's first decade were well aligned in terms of both the elected mayoralty and Livingstone as the mayor, as Monheim, the godfather of Oyster, reflects. "[In London] we had the luxury of doing things right. There's so many other places you go, where the politician is so anxious to tout what is going to happen, that it ends up putting undue pressure on the organization that has to deliver."[63]

Charles Monheim considered the achievement:

The beauty of TfL when it came to transport was that it was essentially a benign dictatorship. The power rested with Ken. He got to decide what the fares were, he decided what happened in these projects. The GLA could provide a certain amount of scrutiny but they were not involved in making the decisions. In different hands … that power can be destructive. But certainly, in Ken's hands that power was incredibly important in allowing to happen things that just scared the daylights out of any number of people, particularly congestion charging and changes to the fare structure, such as raising cash fares to drive people to Oyster that were, in retrospect, fundamental to the whole thing working. All that completely underpinned the ultimate elimination of cash on buses, the overall adoption of Oyster card and ultimately, the move to contactless. Because without the success of Oyster as the fare medium, people don't get the natural transition to contactless. My mantra always was that the Oyster card was not the killer application. People were always saying that in order for contactless to be adopted, you needed a killer application. We have to keep in mind that it ended up taking fifteen years to get from Oyster to contactless. At the end of the day, what did turn out to be the killer application was the adoption of contactless here. That was certainly the tipping point for what has become the ubiquity of contactless.[64]

Cubic's veterans recognized Verma's crucial role.

The driving force and vision behind the payments revolution was Shashi Verma and, of course, an organization that gave him the rope to be able to do that. He had a contract [after 2010] with Cubic that was flexible enough to allow him to do it. Cubic worked with TfL. He didn't have to specify everything that he needed from Cubic up front then spend the next two, three, four years arguing over every change, we had a very flexible working relationship that meant we were sort of in it together. It was almost a risk-sharing approach. But there were many, many times, particularly in the early years, when ... we'd hit some technical barrier, we'd hit some commercial barrier with the payments industry or we'd hit something and it would have been very easy to say, 'Oh, this is all too hard'. Shashi was having none of that. He just kept ploughing and ploughing and ploughing until he got what he needed ... Shashi had a great team working for him and it was a very different way of working for us ... to take software that TfL has developed and integrate it and then deploy it and support it, was completely foreign to us. Now, it's the normal way of working; back then it was strange, but everybody was focused on the ultimate objective.[65]

On 13 December 2012 TfL became the first public transport provider in the world to accept contactless payment cards. The take-up of this facility was rapid, and indeed has proved to be Monheim's "killer application", with half of all journeys on the TfL network by 2017, and 71 per cent by 2022, made using contactless payments on cards or mobile devices. In 2014 the bus network went cashless, and from 2015 the Underground closed all but a handful of ticket offices.[66]

Using contactless for transport has brought major advantages for passengers. TfL's contactless ticketing system automatically calculates the best-value fare based on the customer's specific journey history, and then charges them at the end of the day – ensuring that customers always pay the cheapest fare in the easiest and most convenient way. Customers save money compared to buying a one-day Travelcard, helping them to travel more affordably. The ease of the transactions and the clear customer benefits drove more general societal adoption of contactless payment, further accelerated by concerns about physical contact spreading Covid at the onset of the pandemic in 2020.

Taking cash payments off the buses from 2014 was a major event. "Removing cash from our bus network not only offers customers a quicker and more efficient bus service but it enables us to make savings of £24 million a year, which will be reinvested to further improve London's transport network." By 2014 less than 1 per cent of bus journeys were paid for by cash; it had been 25 per cent a decade before. The removal of cash fares was estimated to deliver £130 million in savings to bus operations alone in the years to 2022–23.[67] Taking cash out of the Underground stations enabled similar efficiency, with only 4 per cent of tickets being bought across the counter at the 256 ticket offices when they were closed in 2015.

Outside London, by agreement with TfL, Cubic went on to provide smartcard ticketing technology to world cities, including Sydney, Brisbane, Miami, Boston, Vancouver and Chicago. This new non-exclusive agreement enabled them to combine the best features from the London and other Cubic systems and make these available to other cities across the globe. Shashi Verma, in 2016 then chief technology officer and director of Customer Experience at TfL, said, "We're delighted to have agreed this licensing deal with Cubic Transportation Systems to introduce our contactless payment system to other world cities. Contactless payments have completely transformed the way people pay for travel in London, and this deal will allow other world cities to benefit from the hard work we put into making the system work for our customers."

Matthew Cole, president of Cubic, said of the licensing deal: "The challenges of mobility in 21st-century cities – including access for all, inclusion, environmental concerns and the pressure of ever-growing populations – can only be met through co-operation and partnership. No single entity has all the answers, and this agreement between Cubic and TfL sets a new standard in public–private partnerships for addressing these issues, and acknowledges the success of account-based payment for transit for which there is clear interest from many cities across the world."[68]

The pace of innovation may now make the Oyster card itself redundant, with contactless and mobile payments eliminating the need both to top up and to queue. However, TfL has no current plans to phase out the Oyster card. "This is because there will always be customers, such as children or those who need to manage their finances more carefully, who will benefit from the card," says TfL head of Customer Payments, Mike Tuckett. "However, as the system is now more than fifteen years old, and it is clear that more people are switching to using pay as you go with contactless bank cards or mobile devices, we are no longer extending Oyster to other stations outside London." Tuckett says TfL is working closely with mobile payment providers such as Apple Pay, Google Pay and Samsung Pay, to see how they can make further improvements to the customer experience and support the uptake of mobile payments. Perhaps it is only a matter of time before TfL again moves to new cutting-edge payment systems, and the future phasing out of bank cards will need to be considered. Smartphones, wearables and facial recognition are how Tuckett sees the payment landscape of the future.[69]

On the national network, the payments revolution was much discussed and hampered by the fragmentation of the industry into multiple train-operating companies. It has indeed taken so long that National Rail never adopted the smartcard and will leap straight to contactless. Investment in contactless over three years was announced by the transport secretary, Grant Shapps, in November 2021. TfL was awarded the contract, with Cubic as its subcontractor in 2022, for the first phase of the expansion to the Home Counties and south-east England. Oyster readers at 233 stations in a ring around London had contactless technology by 2024.

Conclusions

Twenty years after its launch, and perhaps twenty-five after it was designed, the Oyster card and the frictionless travel environment it enabled continues to work well, is loved by people who use it and provides an essential service for many.

Despite being outrun on some fronts by contactless payments – also a TfL creation – the Oyster card remains iconic in its brand and what it does. Cubic programme director John Hill reflected that "it was by far the most challenging project that I had been involved with at that point in my career (only to be surpassed 10 years later with the launch of contactless!)".[70] For Steve Shewmaker, Cubic president, "working on Oyster was the highlight of my career … people get things done, particularly when their vision is aligned. There were great people on both sides of the client–provider relationship who weren't afraid to disrupt an industry."[71]

The first 25 years of TfL were the story of the progressive moulding of the modes – Underground, Buses, Overground, DLR, cycling, walking – into an integrated transport network. Unlike in other UK cities, mayoral powers over both fares and operations across all modes of transport enable a holistic approach. The ticketing initiatives, starting with the Harrow smartcard and Oyster, smoothed the access to and payments for the system, promoting greater use of London's public transport network. In turn the data set derived from Oyster enabled third-party development of apps that brought mobility, leisure and shopping together as real-time data, the digital doorway to all London has to offer. The GLA's London Data Store from 2010 released the data to app developers, who equipped users of the network with the real-time tools to facilitate mobility and access to the capital's rich tapestry of opportunity.

By the 2012 Olympic Games, thanks to Oyster TfL had better data on customer behaviours than just a few years earlier, and enhanced techniques to manage transport demand. These were driven not only by the great international event at Stratford, but also the need to manage the network through planned closures, industrial action, security incidents, demonstrations, state events and congestion. These were significant innovations in which TfL led the world's urban transport management playbook. Perhaps the best measure of their influence is just how rapidly they became baked into day-to-day life in London, and how soon they became the norm in large cities worldwide.

Reflecting on the significance of the payments and ticketing revolution for TfL itself, Verma is clear about the lessons learned in taking risks to drive such innovative service design. "The client needs to be intelligent … no amount of clever contracting substitutes for an intelligent client willing to take bold decisions and manage risk."[72]

Twenty years after the introduction of the first Oyster card, Verma reflected on the enormity of the change that its introduction had brought about. "Gone are the queues for tickets, snaking out of stations often into the street. Gone are the bits of paper littering the system, the ticket touts willing to buy your used but still useful One Day Travelcards to sell on. Gone is the hassle of coins and change, and much else. The impact of the Oyster card has been transformational in the way people use transport. It remains the strongest symbol of the integrated transport system for which Transport for London was created."[73]

7.

NOT THE UNDERGROUND

"If I had made a speech then about what we were planning to do about London's Docklands, predicting everything that has happened there – Canary Wharf, the Dome, the Exhibition Centre, the Olympics, the high-speed rail link, London City airport – they would have sent the men in white coats and had me locked up."

– Michael Heseltine in 2021[1]

The key obligation placed on the new Greater London Authority (GLA) and the elected mayor had been for a statutory plan, the London Plan, a strategic planning framework for all 610 square miles of Greater London. The plan covered of necessity more than a single mayoral term, and framed strategic planning and transport developments across London. This would be particularly evident for the regeneration of the Docklands and East London, given impetus by hosting the Olympic Games at Stratford in 2012. TfL had inherited the Docklands Light Railway (DLR), which proved an agile response to this regeneration, and was joined in 1999 by the extended Jubilee line connecting Canary Wharf to central London. The challenge of the Olympics was met by major investment in the bus network and DLR, and from 2008 brought the Overground into existence. When the Crossrail project was approved, it was to be integrated with the Underground network but operated by a third-party concessionaire, as had been successful on the DLR and Overground.

Docklands and the DLR

The post-war decline of the working docks in London – the last working docks, the Royal Docks, closed in 1981 – provided the space and opportunity to revive late 20th-century London as a world city and draw the city's focus eastwards. The regeneration of eight-and-a-half square miles of former docks and warehousing

Canary Wharf emerges from its foundations with the DLR already in place, 1988

four miles from the City of London's Square Mile morphed from an initially modest and pragmatic low-rise vision to the steel and glass towers of Canary Wharf. The regeneration of Docklands demanded innovation and agility from public transport to secure the development of a new quarter for London.

The London docks had been built and progressively expanded to secure London's position as the trading hub of a worldwide empire from the 18th century until the 1960s. As ships became larger, the docks moved downstream from the Port of London to the Royal Docks. From the mid-19th century an extensive network of railways was built to serve the maze of docks on both sides of the Thames. Port traffic continued to increase in the inter-war period, facilitated by the newly nationalized Port of London Authority's (PLA) investment in docks further downriver. After the Second World War the decline of the older riverside wharves and docks was

Canary Wharf, as built and still building, 2006

accelerated by the growth of secure containerized cargoes and the ever-larger vessels that carried them. Maritime traffic moved 25 miles downstream to new docks with access to deep water, such as the PLA's container port at Tilbury, opened in 1967. The older docks from St Katharine's eastwards closed from 1968. The London Docklands, a closely knit area just four miles from the City but with poor transport connections to it, had shed 150,000 jobs in 25 years. Architectural commentator Deyan Sudjic, then a Docklands resident, remembered that "there was now a full seven miles of continuous dereliction all the way from Tower Bridge to Beckton".[2]

Jon Willis, then the GLC's transport planner (later London Transport's head of Strategy and Planning) was involved with the development of transport in Docklands from 1974, and in planning all four stages of the DLR and the Jubilee line extension. "Until this time Docklands was not seen as an area requiring better public transport, in particular better passenger rail access. Traditionally, the majority of people who worked there lived locally, and walked, cycled or used the bus, and before that, the tram ... There was little long-distance commuting and certainly no need to provide better connections to central London. The area was self-contained and there was little reason for anyone not associated with the port activities to travel to the area – indeed, they were positively discouraged by high walls and heavy security."[3]

Planning for the redevelopment of Docklands was initially articulated by the Docklands Joint Committee (DJC), comprising the GLC and five East London boroughs, in the Docklands Strategic Plan of 1976. The DJC's consultation paper *Setting the Scene* in 1975 recognized that Docklands was "the largest area to become available in London since the Great Fire [in 1666], the largest area for urban development available in Europe today, and will encompass a large proportion of any changes in London between now and the end of the century".[4] The DJC set out to see the Docklands redeveloped quickly and to solve the employment and housing problems of East London. The plan of 1976 envisaged filling in most of the docks, the retention of as much as possible of traditional employment and river-based activity, the attraction of new employment, and large-scale new, mostly social, housing. Even though this was intended to double the population and increase employment by 20 per cent by 1990, this was insufficient justification to extend the Tube network. Improvements in transport provision with a cost much lower than extending the Fleet (later Jubilee) line – express busways, street tramways, automatic light rail – were being envisaged when, at Michael Heseltine's initiative as environment secretary in Margaret Thatcher's 1979 government, the London Docklands Development Corporation (LDDC) was created in 1981.

This was a radical new approach to cut through existing planning regulations and work around opposition from the GLC and the five boroughs. Modelled on the New Towns Commission, Heseltine's advocacy of the LDDC was the response to "a multitude of studies and plans prepared by local and transport authorities, but with no concrete way forward".[5] The corporation had a 10-year remit to redevelop Docklands and facilitate development through exemption from business rates, tax breaks and a simplified planning process, initially within an Enterprise Zone on the Isle of Dogs. By comparison with what came later, the LDDC vision was for modest low-rise regeneration – low-rise housing and business parks – and up to 25,000 jobs on the Isle of Dogs.

The initial DLR has been described by one of its planners, Jon Willis, as "an act of faith, thought up as a simple and cheap solution to an identified access problem, seized by the inspirational politician Michael Heseltine to stimulate redevelopment ... I am sure that he ... had absolutely no inkling of what the railway might trigger in the area".[6] Designed to a tight turn-out budget of £77 million, running on former railway viaducts and steel and concrete viaducts to avoid impact on the road network

DLR train captain at Canary Wharf station, 1993

below, accessed by stairs rather than escalators, with one-car articulated trains, short platform canopies and tight 38-metre radius curves, the DLR reached from Docklands into the City at Tower Gateway, north on a former railway alignment to a vacant platform at Stratford, and south to the Thames at Island Gardens. Significantly, the design and build of the railway, to London Transport's specification, was put out to tender, the first private-sector construction of a railway in the UK since the Great Central Railway in late 19th century. A consortium of GEC and Mowlem won the contract in 1984, and the DLR opened in 1987.

The first UK driverless automatic railway, the DLR was designed for 23,000 passengers a day. 'Train captains' on board checked tickets, made announcements, controlled the doors and took over driving when the signalling system crashed. Reliability proved a major problem in the early years; it could take over an hour to reset the system and get it working again. Nevertheless, it offered a direct way in to work for construction and office workers and was surprisingly popular with tourists, who enjoyed the elevated view over this new London locale and the luxury of a driver's eye view from the front seat of the cars. The 11 single cars carried 18,000 passengers a day in the opening weeks in 1987.

Low-rise construction within Docklands and of the first stage of the DLR to provide access to the new developments was already well under way when the Canary Wharf development was first proposed in 1987, and enthusiastically endorsed by the LDDC's visionary chief executive Reg Ward. Indeed, the DLR's daily passenger numbers of 27,000 had soon exceeded the expected 22,000 to 24,000, and by 1997 would rise past 60,000.

The rise of Canary Wharf

The restructuring and liberalization of world financial markets, encapsulated in the Big Bang of 27 October 1986, underpinned London's centrality in the globalization of those markets and reversed the city's fortunes. On that day the restrictive practices within the London Stock Exchange were swept away and opened to takeover by the world's major banks, shouted bargains were replaced with digital screens, and the bowler-hatted city stockbroker morphed into a sharp-suited international financier. This demanded cultural and spatial changes in the old Square Mile of the City. Instead of small, corridor- and office-based buildings co-located within the financial district, the need now was for large floor-plate, open-plan spaces for trading floors. International banks such as Credit Suisse First Boston (CSFB) had spent years trying without success to locate suitable space close to the financial heart of London. The Corporation of the City of London was unwilling to loosen planning constraints within the Square Mile, and many British chief executives were reluctant to sever their attachment to the City and all it represented in terms of friends, colleagues, restaurants, bars and clubs.

In 1984, Shed 31, a two-storey former banana warehouse on Canary Wharf,[7] received visitors. At lunch on the *Res Nova* moored alongside were Reg Ward, visionary CEO of the LDDC, and the American Michael von Clemm, chairman of CSFB, investment banker, restaurateur and anthropologist. In 1967, von Clemm had borrowed $900 to help two young French brothers, Michel and Albert Roux, to start a restaurant business in London.[8] Le Gavroche, in London's Mayfair, flourished, winning first one, then two, and finally three Michelin stars, the first restaurant in the UK so to do. Von Clemm was now looking for a site for a processing facility for a cook-in-the-bag venture by the Roux brothers. During lunch it crossed von Clemm's mind that there might be an even better use for the old wharf for his bank's support operations. Ward recalled von Clemm suddenly leaning back and saying, "I don't know why we don't go for a shed like 31 as a 200,000 square-foot [18,580 square-metre] back office." The view from Shed 31 reminded him of warehouses in Boston that had been converted into back offices and small business premises.[9]

The original Canary Wharf banana warehouse shortly before demolition in 1986

The lunch set off a chain of events that would change the face of the Docklands and of London itself. When von Clemm presented his idea to the board of CSFB, board member and property developer Gooch Ware Travelstead from Kentucky – who had been conducting painful negotiations to acquire office space for the bank in the City of London – said they were asking themselves the wrong question: instead of asking whether they could convert Shed 31 as a back office, they should be asking, "Can we move our front office to the Isle of Dogs?" In other words, was it a suitable location for the bank's main London operations, not just for its support?[10]

Travelstead thought big; his father had been a subcontractor for the World Trade Center in New York and for Cape Kennedy, and he himself would be behind the redevelopment of the docks in Barcelona as Porto Olimpico for the 1992 Barcelona Games. The LDDC vision had been for light industry and low-level housing. Instead, Travelstead convinced Reg Ward and the LDDC to consider the site as a location for top-quality corporate offices and computerized trading systems. LDDC was willing to option and sell the land at low industrial prices, but the project required such large land servicing and construction costs that Travelstead was unable to raise interim financing from banks. In July 1987 the project was taken over by Olympia and York Developments (O&Y) led by the Reichmann brothers.

The sheer scale of the development now envisaged by O&Y, a Manhattan-on-Thames with Britain's tallest office block at its centre creating 65,000 jobs, blew

The 'yuppies', young upwardly mobile professionals, seen here at the London Metals Exchange in 1985, were a driver of inner London's economy after the Big Bang

the previous transport plans out of the water and rendered the "toy town"[11] DLR hopelessly underpowered even before it carried its first paying passenger in 1987. Far greater capacity on public transport into Canary Wharf was an urgent necessity, and with the Fleet line Tube extension at least a decade away, the extension of the DLR was vigorously pursued. When the DLR City branch opened in 1991, it represented a major upgrade, not only giving interchange with five[12] Underground lines at Bank but also upgrading signalling and lengthening all the station platforms for two-car trains. It had cost £276 million, a huge sum by comparison with the original DLR budget of just £77 million. With O&Y meeting about 40 per cent of its cost, the Bank extension was realized in five years from planning to opening to match the developers' building programme.

O&Y had become leading office developers worldwide, led by the redevelopment of Toronto and then the World Finance Centre at Battery Park, New York. They were attracted by the shortage of space in the City, but Canary Wharf proved a much greater risk than their previous ventures. The flagship 244-metre tower, One Canada Square, the tallest building in London for 20 years, neared completion in August 1991. The Reichmanns' unusual financing arrangements, borrowing against their property portfolio's cash flow, faltered in the property recession of the early 1990s. With only 14 per cent occupation at Canary Wharf and surplus space in the City itself, O&Y defaulted on a series of bond and mortgage payments in 1992. Their

Canary Wharf DLR station, 2000

entire real-estate empire in Canada and Britain slid into bankruptcy. A consortium of banks administered the project from 1993 to 1995, but made little progress in leasing space during the recession. Eventually, with new backers, as Canary Wharf PLC the Reichmanns were able to buy back Canary Wharf in 1995 at a discount, and reap the benefit of an upturning property market in the late 1990s to achieve 100 per cent rental and make a start on 10 more buildings, including two 42-storey towers.[13]

Meanwhile, the DLR had been struggling to cope and the LDDC recruited Ian Brown from British Rail to make it work. "It was futuristic, automatic, 11 little cars; the problem was it didn't work … the signalling wouldn't work, it was gloriously unreliable and the whole of Canary Wharf was dependent on having some other transport. At the same time the government wanted to privatize it." Brown, then working on the privatization of BR Rail Freight Distribution, was asked in 1996 to join Docklands Light Railway as CEO, who would report to the LDDC to put some operational, signalling and control systems in to make it work.

> What I found was that the Docklands Light Railway was a bit like the PPP, it was at war with its suppliers, working through lawyers, trying to get compensation and of course, none of that made the system work .... so instead of the lawyers, you get a partnership with Alcatel who provided the automatic signalling system. We realized that a supplier, rather than just losing money, if it saw a system in a city like London really working in a place like Canary Wharf, they've got every interest in being part of that. So, we made friends, a bit like trying to make a go of the PPP. The Docklands Light Railway started to show [improvement].[14]

In the newly globalized financial world, London's position in the 24-hour market between New York and the Far East was underpinned by this revolution in the business culture of the City of London. The consolidation of banking and stockbroking, and the competition for talent within the deregulated City, brought new wealth to young brokers and bankers, dubbed 'yuppies' (young upwardly mobile professionals) and promoted a new enthusiasm and the resources for living an inner-city life. They were attracted to previously run-down residential quarters close to the City, such as Spitalfields and Islington, and to warehouse conversions and new builds alongside the river. Museum of London curator Alex Werner characterized the 1980s as being about "the individual and money ... For London it was about financial deregulation – driven young traders who seemed to have incredible amounts of money. The 'never had it so good' feel was a reflection of that. There was a massive privatization of utilities and it was a cultural shift – the end of the old way."[15]

Having hit a post-war low point in the mid-1980s, passenger numbers increased rapidly on the Tube, driven by a boom in London financial services and facilitated by the Travelcard. The new MD of London Underground, Tony Ridley, found by the mid-1980s that his job had changed abruptly from "'Stop the decline' to 'How are we going to going to cope with this enormous growth in traffic?'"[16] The colossal step change in ambition envisaged by the Canary Wharf development, from back office and warehousing to global financial centre with 50,000+ jobs, had put the extension of the Jubilee line, opened in 1979 only as far as Charing Cross, back on the agenda. In 1993 the confirmation of government funding for the Jubilee line extension (JLE) was instrumental in bringing Canary Wharf Ltd out of administration. Meanwhile, it was the DLR that took the strain for nearly a decade until the JLE opened on 1 January 2000.

The creation of the DLR had established an innovative alternative model for public transport in London, with the agility of a light rail system, the capacity to connect to the City and Underground network, with its maintenance and operation outsourced, and its ability to deliver relatively quickly for a modest outlay – a model

Bob Kiley and Ian Brown at Poplar DLR station

very different from that of the London Underground. Ian Brown had commissioned a visionary *Horizon* report in 1998 from consultants Steer David Gleave on the options for future DLR extensions to a 15- to 20-year timescale. He cultivated borough leaders, the Canary Wharf Group and community groups to build support for the extensions outlined in the report. The DLR vision exploited former railway viaducts and rights of way left from the high tide of the extensive Docklands freight rail network, which proved to be amenable to successive extensions (to Bank 1991, Royal Docks and Beckton 1994, Greenwich and Lewisham 1999, City Airport 2005, Woolwich 2009, Stratford International 2011), and increasing capacity to two- and then three-car trains and extending platforms.

Howard Smith, an LSE economics graduate, started in transport as an operations graduate at Network Rail. He gained hands-on operational experience as the Balham station manager, walking the track, managing staff, handling incidents. Having worked with Ian Brown in British Rail, he was recruited in 1998 as planning director of the DLR, just the seventh member of the DLR team. Brown and Smith flourished in the wild west of the east:

> Things could be tried in Docklands … growth came back and there was this feeling that this was the place that you could draw a line on a map, which was really, really exciting. I still obviously get quite energized about it. You could draw a line on a map and then go out and do it. You couldn't do that anywhere else in London or in the UK in the same way. Ian built on that, a genius in terms of drawing in stakeholders, so very attentive – we weren't in TfL at the start of

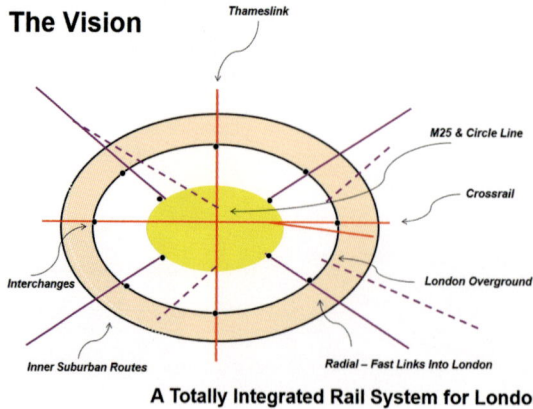

The Vision

Thameslink

M25 & Circle Line

Crossrail

London Overground

Radial – Fast Links Into London

Inner Suburban Routes

Interchanges

A Totally Integrated Rail System for London

this – very attentive to DETR[17] as they were then. To a massive government mega department, throwing a few hundred million at the only railway that they had actually felt like spending money on.[18]

Outsourcing specialist Serco was contracted to operate the DLR, including taking revenue risk, but when the JLE was delayed by two years Serco did well out of the delay, with good revenue from increasingly packed trains. "In an urban environment people have to use the train," Smith explained. "Revenue largely comes from central London employment, activity, housing. Therefore, the incentive on you to give a good service commercially is very low indeed. It's an inelastic market, and basically, that's where the TFL concession model developed … the incentive should effectively be driven by the public sector, which then collects the money, and concessionaires should be paid on performance. Their job is to make the trains run on time. They shouldn't be either betting on or rewarded by the ups and downs of employment and economic activity. That followed through to all the activities that we did."[19] This would influence the operating contract for the next ambitious phase of the 'electron diagram', the creation of the Overground.

London Rail

"The little dinosaur generally escapes because it can run faster; that was the DLR."

– Ian Brown, CEO of DLR, 1996–2001, TfL MD London Rail, 2001–11[20]

When TfL was created in 2000 the DLR was included, and its visionary MD Ian Brown was recruited in 2001 by the TfL commissioner, Bob Kiley, to run the new London Rail directorate of TfL, the DLR and Crossrail.

Bob said to me, I want you to come and join TfL as something a bit bigger than the Docklands Light Rail ... Bob had sat in New York when various suburban railways around New York went bankrupt and the MTA, which he ran, the TfL equivalent to New York, absorbed control ... basically they got the suburban railway for nothing. Bob could not understand why in London the national rail is just run completely differently, with no respect for what London needs as far as he was concerned.[21]

As discussions to transfer the Silverlink Metro franchise to TfL proceeded in 2005, Kiley stated that London virtually stands alone among major cities in the world with an extensive rail configuration both in and around the city that does not control its own destiny with respect to the nature of that service. "I believe that has to change and I believe this is the necessary, but hardly sufficient, first step on the road to getting much more influence, not to say control, over the entire commuter rail system."[22]

Brown saw how frustrated Kiley was by having no control over suburban rail in London.

He knew that I'd been a managing director of one of the sections for British Railways. He knew that we had a model with the DLR that the government liked, and he knew that we had a track record of delivery in that context. So he then said, 'Look, we need to form a rail division, we don't want London Underground in that, that's bad enough to manage as it is,' and Tim O'Toole came to manage the Underground very capably – a great leader.[23]

Ian Brown had a vision of London Rail filling in the gaps in the capital's network, much as the successive extensions of the DLR had done in Docklands, working to a shorter timetable, using under-used or disused railway infrastructure and operated by a concessionaire.

Brown had a vision for orbital rail in London that he called the 'electron diagram' ... with the Underground in the middle, Thameslink running north to south, Crossrail east to west and the Overground running around the outside. "That orbital diagram was sold to every stakeholder in the land ... You've got an integrated transport system for the city which is rail-based rather than just the Underground, which is lovely as long as you live on it." O'Toole argued for the Underground, but Brown's experience on the DLR showed that it would be cheaper and quicker to create the Overground from the under-used existing national rail infrastructure. [24]

Significantly, for the development of the Overground and later the Elizabeth line, the DLR had pioneered the concession model, outsourcing many aspects of construction, maintenance and operations. Brown had overseen the privatization in 1997 of DLR operations and maintenance to Serco after the LDDC was wound

A 1906 postcard view of the North London Railway's grand Italianate Highbury & Islington station of 1872, designed by Edwin Henry Horne, damaged in the Second World War and demolished in the 1960s

The East London line platform at Whitechapel, c.1975

up. "When it [DLR operations] was privatized, which we did, they had to have a model which was based on operational quality rather than commercial risk. It's a good model ... it did mean with the DLR that the management team were focused on technical and operational, which is good. DLR prospered as part of the Travelcard situation with fares and it prospered even more when we went into Oyster."[25]

As the mayor in London sets the fares, the franchise model as deployed on national rail was inappropriate. "We went for the concession model, which is what we had done with the DLR."[26] The concessionary model puts the responsibility for investment and service development squarely back with the public authority, with TfL. "It was very obvious that the decisions that needed to be made about more rolling stock or changing the layout were going to fall back on the public authority. It wasn't as if the contract was either structured to cope with or actually offered any sensible incentive, the incentive under the contract was actually to do nothing and just let people queue up and join your services."[27]

As DLR representative, Howard Smith joined the Transport Integration Group set up by the GOL in 1999 to bring together the Underground, the Public Carriage Office and the Traffic Directorate to anticipate their incorporation into TfL. Smith reflected that stretching ahead and risk-taking was part of the spirit of London Rail:

> If the DLR or the City Airport extension had crashed and burned maybe history would have been different, but the DLR, the City Airport extension sort of begat Woolwich which in turn set us thinking about Stratford International, which in turn led to the possibility of taking over the North London line and Silverlink Metro, as it was called. We could show that we'd done something ... we were the people who were capable of making things happen very, very quickly.[28]

The Overground

"Ian Brown had the vision of how to bring that little lot together, branding it as London Overground and making it something greater than the sum of the parts ... the Olympics gave it a compelling reason to be taken seriously."

– Geoff Hobbs, head of London Rail Strategy, 2005–13[29]

"It's one of the greatest changes in our time. I'm very proud of the work done on the Underground and I think it was vital, but the Overground as an innovation stands up there with Oyster."

– Tim O'Toole, MD Underground, 2002–09

As TfL began to contemplate an Olympic Games in Stratford with a bid to the IOC in 2003–04, the agile model of the ever-expanding DLR and the executive team that had created and animated the light rail network stepped up for the creation of the Overground, again mostly from under-used or disused railway infrastructure. Built from the 1840s, the North London line had been the busy rail link between the national rail network around the north of the city to connect to the old London Docks. The stations of the North London Railway were ambitious, Victorian Gothic confections in brick and stone. Highbury & Islington was a turreted brick palace with stone facings, spaciously laid out with long platforms, valances, waiting rooms and signal boxes. The now-lost city terminus at Broad Street was sumptuous, and in 1890 was the third busiest London terminus, serving more passengers than all but Liverpool Street and Victoria, with 800 arrivals and departures each day. The line was electrified from Watford to Broad Street by 1922.[30]

Passenger services around this inner suburban arc from Richmond in the west, through Highbury & Islington to Broad Street and North Woolwich in the east had long been in decline. There had been significant damage during the Second World War, and freight had ebbed with the closure of the Docks. Despite modernization in the 1950s, the stations around the northern edge of Victorian London had fallen into near-dereliction by the 1970s. Under threat of closure as railway rationalization proceeded, station architecture was replaced by bus shelters, and in the era of the cuts following the Beeching Report[31] in the 1960s and 1970s it was saved only by the remaining freight traffic to the new docks at Tilbury.

Proposals for the upgrade of this near-derelict line as an orbital railway had first been advanced as Ringrail in the 1970s and incorporated in the London Rail Study of 1974, the Barran Report. This suggested consideration of a North London Network of orbital services, based on a suggestion by the Ringrail Group, which involved using existing rail routes rather than new construction. As commuter passenger numbers increased, the real pressure was felt by the Underground at main-line termini where passengers poured onto the Tube, so an orbital approach appeared to be a lower priority. First steps were made in 1979, when the GLC sponsored an improved service from Camden Road through Dalston to Stratford, the Crosstown Linkline. When Broad Street station was closed and demolished for the Broadgate development in 1986, the increasingly overcrowded Silverlink services around North London were diverted to Liverpool Street. Rail campaigners continued to argue for the revival of lines on the under-used Outer Circle.

Livingstone's first Mayoral Transport Strategy in 2001 proposed to reverse the lack of investment in rail in the capital, increase its capacity and take pressure off the Underground through better partnerships with Network Rail within London for metro-style services, better cross-London and orbital connections, and new rail schemes such as Thameslink, Crossrail and the East London line. It proposed in the medium term to "raise standards sufficiently to create a London Metro with 'turn up and go' [10-minute] frequencies, that is, fully integrated with the London

Underground. This will include development of high-frequency orbital rail services – OrbiRail",[32] and the extension of the East London line north to Hackney and southwards was regarded as an early priority.[33]

With the creation of TfL, a strategic approach to all of London's rail assets could be adopted. A first attempt to run inner suburban rail was the South London Metro in 2003, a pilot in South London which brought several National Rail local services, operated by Connex South Eastern, Southern and South West Trains under the ON – Overground Network – brand. TfL introduced consistent information displays, station signage and maps on the selected routes in South London. This pilot was primarily an exercise in branding, although some service improvements were introduced but with no fares integration. It was the first instance of TfL having a visible influence over the National Rail network in Greater London. It was not a success but a stepping-stone which presaged the more significant Overground development

By the early 2000s, the Silverlink Metro franchise run by National Express since 1997 on the North London line had become unreliable and unloved, its trains neglected and grubby. The Office of Passenger Rail Franchising (OPRAF) ranked it in the bottom tier of franchises, with 20 per cent of services delayed and 3 per cent cancelled. The DfT regarded the line as an expensive, subsidy-hungry irrelevance that carried next to no one.[34] Silverlink covered a network of metro services in North and West London: the North London line from Richmond to North Woolwich, Gospel Oak to Barking, Euston to Watford Junction, Clapham Junction to Willesden Junction. In 2006 it was announced that the Silverlink franchise would be broken up and the metro lines would be transferred to TfL; the East London line would be transferred from the Underground and reinstated north of Shoreditch to Dalston on the viaduct which had once carried the line into Broad Street. Ian Brown worked with the Rail Group at the DfT on the transfer of franchises to TfL. "They had a series of really astonishing conversations which changed the scope of what we could do," recalled Geoff Hobbs, head of London Rail Strategy.[35]

Brown himself recalls:

All the modelling suggested that orbital railways wouldn't work. The only solution in London is buses, except for radial journeys. Anyway, for the North London line quality was the key, to have a concession where the only way to make money out of it was to run the trains properly. That didn't half focus the mind and we bought the trains, we invested in the stations, the other way around from the [national] railway model … and it paid off. The next little job that came along for that pre-Crossrail was the East London line.[36]

As the bid for the 2012 Olympic Games gained momentum from 2001, the urgent need to address the demands of hosting a public transport Games at Stratford saw investment in rail infrastructure such as the DLR extension to Stratford International, and brought the Overground into being. "London Rail suddenly got pushed into being by the Olympics," Brown recalled. "These jigsaw pieces that Richard de Cani, Rob Niven, Jon Fox and myself had been working on … all of a sudden the money was there and not only the money but the massive urgency to transform a bit of wasteland in East London."[37] Brown and Hugh Sumner at the Olympic Delivery Authority [ODA] cooked up getting the future Overground written into the Olympic Transport Strategy, without which it would never have happened.[38]

The North London line was a major project costing £326 million, which restored a half-derelict network of lines with refurbished stations and new platforms at Stratford for the Overground. DLR was extended to Stratford International to connect to the Javelin service from St Pancras International. The former Silverlink stations were transformed by being cleaned up, given a coat of paint, re-signed with the orange Overground brand and enamel line diagrams, and staffed for the first time in years.

The Overground was added to the Underground map in 2007, wrapping a growing orange network in an outer circle around central London. Mayor Livingstone launched the new Overground network at Hampstead Heath station in 2007; posters proclaimed London's New Train Set. Since then, the Overground has had a profound influence on the capital, raising the bar for commuter rail, moving the capital's centre of gravity significantly eastwards and bringing Hackney, Tower Hamlets and the Olympic boroughs into a closer relationship with the centre. It has had a transformative effect on some of the places which were previously poorly served by rail. Convenient travel options were now available from some of East London's most deprived neighbourhoods to employment hotspots, including financial districts and major hospitals. It opened new career prospects for unskilled and semi-skilled workers, and provided the support staff necessary to stimulate the creation of high-value jobs. "No other UK railway has seen such dramatic growth or catered for it so effectively."[39]

Having launched the initial Overground service on the North and West London lines, it soon became apparent that extending the East London line was the key to unlocking access to the South London line and completing the circle at Clapham Junction. The Overground's second development was opened in May 2010 at a cost of £800 million; it ran down the viaduct from Dalston Junction across a new 'bow string' bridge over Shoreditch High Street and through the former East London line tunnel to New Cross/New Cross Gate. Not only did this bring disused and under-used railway viaduct and tunnels back to life, it also used the world's first tunnel under a navigable river, Marc Brunel's Thames Tunnel, which had opened in 1843 and been converted to railway use in 1869. The line was extended to Crystal Palace and Croydon later in 2010. The following year Highbury & Islington joined the Overground family, and in 2012

An Overground train approaching Hoxton station on the refurbished Victorian viaduct, 2010

the circle around London was completed at a cost of £140 million when Surrey Quays was connected with Clapham Junction, the South London line, using an alignment to Queen's Road Peckham that had lain unused since 1911.

By 2010 TfL had replaced all the legacy rolling stock on the Overground with new Class 378s. Shiny, reliable trains, safer staffed and refurbished stations, a doubled frequency of services and an additional fifth car in 2016 contributed to a dramatic rise in passenger numbers from 28.8 million journeys a year in 2007–08 to 189.8 million by 2017–18. Mayor Johnson and TfL argued for further devolution of commuter rail within London in 2012, pointing out the success of the Overground by contrast with a confusing mix of franchised ticket products, fare levels, service quality standards and information provision for customers. These also act as a barrier to integrated planning and operational management, and to service innovation. "The current franchise model is ill-suited to inner-suburban rail management. It is both more expensive and less efficient than other alternative models that have been tested successfully on TfL's Overground network."[40]

Johnson advocated in 2012 that "responsibility for London's inner suburban rail services should be devolved to the mayoralty. In that way a single coherent vision for the city's railways can be made real. A single investment strategy, a single fares policy, consistently high levels of customer service and safety," and a network fully integrated across all of London's communities.[41] In 2015 Greater Anglia services out of Liverpool Street to Enfield Town, Cheshunt and Chingford as well as Romford to Upminster were devolved to TfL, and equipped with new trains by 2020. Further devolution had been announced in the Rail Prospectus for London in 2016 by Mayor

Johnson and Transport Minister Patrick McLoughlin, with the South Eastern and Southern franchises the likely next steps. This was put on hold by his post-Brexit successor Chris Grayling on cost grounds – before he was revealed to have written to Johnson in 2013 that he wished to "keep suburban rail out of the clutches of any future Labour mayor".[42] Further rail devolution fell badly out of political fashion. Passengers in London in 2024 expressed far higher satisfaction with both London Overground and the Elizabeth line, which consistently out-perform Whitehall-managed train operating companies (TOCs). Currently, these are the only two services in England to register user satisfaction at or above 90 per cent.[43]

London's rail travellers have continued to suffer from having two separate public transport networks: an integrated network run by TfL – including buses, the Tube, TfL's Overground network, DLR and trams – and different TOCs providing commuter rail services under commercial franchise agreements with central government. This results in a fractured approach to rail service provision, and existing assets are not exploited to their full capacity.

The success of the Overground exemplified the benefits of rail devolution in London. By 2012, customer satisfaction had reached 92 per cent and reliability at a UK record of 96 per cent, against a TOC average of 91 per cent. Demand had trebled since TfL took over Silverlink, one of the poorest-performing franchises.[44] Renewed arguments for resuming rail devolution as franchises come to an end have been made in 2024, for the Great Northern, Southern, South West and South Eastern services. Mayor Khan has argued that Londoners rely on train services to be fast, frequent and affordable every day, and that services on the rail network should meet the same high standards achieved by the rest of London's transport network. Rail devolution would also lead to economic benefits within communities. The biggest impact would be in South London, where house-building rates are less than half of the rest of London because of poor connections. Meeting new PM Sir Keir Starmer after the May 2024 election Khan said, "Watch this space on rail devolution".[45] In mid-2025 it is unclear what shape this might take as the London franchises are taken back in-house by the future Great British Railway.

Crossrail

Crossrail, the future Elizabeth line (see Chapter 13 for a detailed account), had been a mark on the planners' maps since the Abercrombie Plan for London in 1944. The name Crossrail was first applied to an east–west, large-diameter tunnelled line in the 1974 London Rail Study. With government support, Crossrail was developed jointly by LU and Network Rail in the early 1990s. The project had made a start with a parliamentary bill, supported by studies, architectural models and even a Network Rail-style train mock-up. The bill was rejected in 1994, the victim of recession,

Treasury opposition and the critique of Jim Steer of Tower Hamlets' consultants Steer Davies Gleave. The project was mothballed to just four members of staff, but significantly the route from Paddington to Liverpool Street was safeguarded, protecting it from developments that might compromise a future revived scheme.[46]

As passenger numbers and population began to boom once more, Crossrail's primary purpose of relieving congestion on the transport network in central London came back into favour.

Ian Brown recalls:

> It started because Alison Munro [projects director at the DfT] asked me to go and see her for a quiet chat. 'Ken wants Crossrail, what he called Crossrail 2. The government are quite keen on doing the original Crossrail 1. Could you persuade Ken to go with Crossrail 1 rather than 2? If so, we'll set up some seed corn money – £157 million to the penny, not a penny more – to set up a joint organization to develop Crossrail.' They didn't want Network Rail involved, they didn't want London Underground involved. They [DfT] wanted to be involved but not to deliver it because their model was the DLR model and the Overground model, which is the concessionary model. So what was agreed was that it should be a joint venture project between the government [DfT], with two sponsors, and TfL, also with two sponsors – me and the commissioner … So that took out the confrontation for going ahead with getting the parliamentary bill through, which was led by the Crossrail team … I know it ran over budget by a couple of billion towards the end but it's so fabulous in the round of things, this is success, a big, big success.[47]

Brown makes the case for transport being the key to London growing and competing, as Livingstone had gone for.

> So did the government, they wanted to know what is the cheapest way of achieving these economic objectives. Building a £17- or £18-billion-pound project was the least costly way of achieving those objectives, provided it could be built on time and on budget. I went to the Treasury … [it's] a bit like selling a used car, 'This is the cheapest, you can't resist this, and this will save you so much money to achieve growth for London.' Their concerns were, 'Can this be done effectively?' … We had people from TfL on the board, we had DfT on the board, Treasury, an independent engineer, everything double-guessed but it did build the project." Brown was clear on how best to operate Crossrail. "You want a concession, a private sector operator, and you need a good strong client side. We've learned with London railways, right from DLR to the Overground, the client that doesn't know what they're doing is taken for a ride or they just go berserk. Getting a strong client side at TfL on the rail side paid off in spades. Crossrail, of course, did open – and it's been phenomenally successful.[48]

Lift 👫 ♿
to Platforms 3 to 17 and exit

8.

ACTIVE AND ACCESSIBLE TRAVEL

"The work to the Underground was a significant part of civilizing the city. If things are well designed, people feel happier and more engaged with them."

– Frank Pick, as MD of London Transport in the 1930s[1]

Over 25 years, by radically improving the city's public transport environment – Tube, bus, tram, river and taxi – TfL has become increasingly influential in support of London's wider health, civic ambience and sustainability. Being the principal delivery arm for mayoral policies, under all three mayors TfL has shaped the transport network to deliver wider outcomes that make living and working better for Londoners: housing, accessibility, air quality, the public realm, low traffic neighbourhoods, and walking and cycling. Pick's vision for city transport as not just mobility but a civilizing force remains at the heart of TfL's public service and civic values, not least in its commitment to accessible, equitable and active transport.

Making transport accessible

"I realized then that buses should be for everyone, including us. Up to that point, I just thought it was my fault I couldn't walk and couldn't get on."

– Wheelchair warrior at Campaign for Accessible Transport, bus protest in Oxford Street, 1990[2]

Giving access to public transport for everyone remains a live issue in London today, despite the progress made on the accessibility of Tube, bus and rail. The age and design of much of London's transport infrastructure makes retrofitting for accessibility expensive, but access for all is now accepted as both a principle and a right, obligated by legislation, incorporated in the Mayor's Transport Strategy, and advanced by the recognition that mobility is essential for access to education, employment, leisure and an independent life.

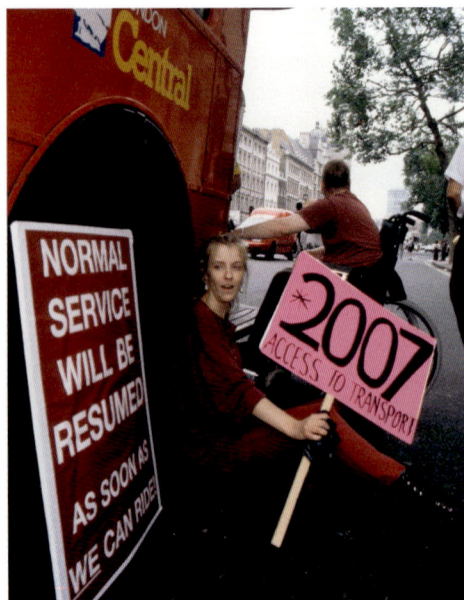

Wheelchair users from Disabled Action Network protest on Westminster Bridge in 1995 *(left)*, and *(right)* again chain themselves to a bus in Whitehall in 1997; 'Normal service will be resumed as soon as we can ride'

The Greater London Assembly Act of 1999 required the GLA to promote equality of opportunity for all Londoners. Until at least the 1980s, public transport in London had lagged behind other cities, notably in the United States, in terms of providing access to its network for the million or so Londoners coping with a physical or mental impairment. Indeed, until 1959 London Transport had required blind or disabled passengers wishing to travel independently to sign an indemnity accepting financial liability for any accident. Wheelchair users were banned from all deep Tube lines until 1993. By contrast, the new Bay Area Rapid Transit in San Francisco was opened with lift access in 1972; in the UK, the Tyne and Wear Metro had followed suit in 1980. No lifts were provided when London's Victoria line was designed and built in the 1960s, and fully opened by 1971. There was no obligation placed on public transport to provide disabled access until 1984.

Change for access within London Transport had initially been slow and piecemeal. The GLC first offered concessionary bus fares for pensioners in 1973; a new guidebook, *Access to the Underground*, was produced in 1982 with the assistance of the Cloudesley School for the Disabled; and the Dial-a-Ride door-to-door bus service, first tried in the 1970s, was re-established and made London-wide in 1985. The LT Unit for Disabled Passengers was established in 1984 to co-ordinate initiatives within LT to make stations, buses and trains more accessible to people with disabilities. These included adaptations to buses such as wider doors, more and brighter handrails, illuminated stopping signs and priority seating.

In 1986 a report by the Greater London Association for Disabled People (GLAD) argued for a "radical reappraisal of accessible transport with a new co-ordinated strategy to meet the needs of transport handicapped people" as "over 450,000 Londoners are unable to use buses, Tubes or trains at all, or if they can, only with considerable difficulty".[3] The running continued to be made by disability rights groups pressing and protesting loudly in the early 1990s for better access to public transport, with buses a particular target as they were predominantly high floor and non-accessible. Direct action was taken by protestors across the country, chaining themselves to trains and buses, most noticeably in Oxford Street and outside the Palace of Westminster in 1994 as the issue was debated in Parliament and the Disability Discrimination Act (DDA) passed in 1995.

In 1993 the first 'kneeling' single-deck buses were trialled in London, and introduced the following year on route 88. At stops, the bus lowered its front entrance closer to the kerb to reduce the height of the step from street to bus. In 1994, route 120 was the first UK route to use solely low-floor buses. In 1998 the first low-floor double-decker route was introduced, on the 242 route, and high-floor buses were steadily replaced, notably the platformed Routemaster, by 2005. As enthusiasts mourned their departure, disability campaigners waved banners declaring 'Routemaster Good Riddance'; Transport for All said, "Yes, the old bus was a London icon, but it was an icon of an inaccessible London – where disabled people and especially wheelchair users were barred from bus travel."[4] With the departure of the Routemaster, by the end of 2005 the entire London bus fleet was low floor and wheelchair accessible. Simple issues such as the kerb height at bus stops varying from the ideal of 125mm were also steadily addressed.

Planning guidelines and standards in transport were obliged to respond both to the 1995 Act and to changing social attitudes and standards. The Docklands Light Railway was built in the 1980s with lifts from street to platform at all its stations; "the lifts will be slow running to discourage people from using them all the time. They are primarily for the disabled, people with shopping and children and the elderly",[5] while the Jubilee line extension opened in 1999 with 11 new step-free stations. When it was introduced in 1987, the MCW Metrocab was the first London wheelchair-accessible taxi. New cabs were required to be accessible for wheelchair passengers from 1989, and the whole cab fleet to be compliant by 2000.

Bryan Heiser became the first special advisor on disability to the TfL board in 2000, determined to make London's public transport a model of accessibility. Heiser had launched the first Dial-a-Ride service in Camden in 1982, with GLC support expanded the scheme across London, and with government funding across the UK. He brought energy and personal experience as a wheelchair passenger to TfL's

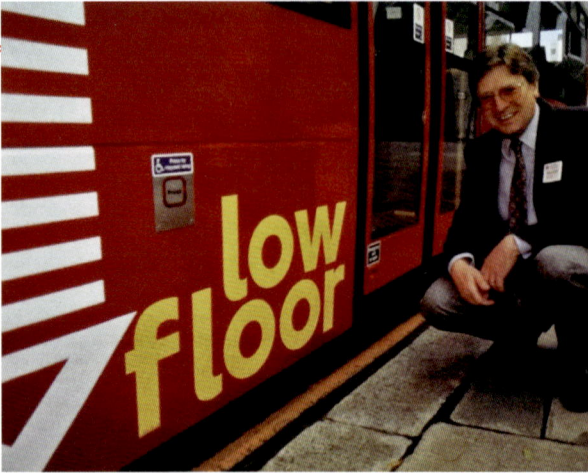

access strategy and delivery. With Andrew Braddock as head of Access and Mobility, the LT Disabled Passenger Unit joined TfL and they brought forward a strategy for all people who were mobility impaired, whether through physical disabilities, sensory impairments or learning difficulties. As well as addressing access to the transport network, this identified improvements needed to door-to-door service, service accessibility on buses, more regular dialogue with users through the new Independent Disability Advisory Group (IDAG) set up in 2007, and through TfL itself becoming an exemplary employer.

The Equality Act replaced the DDA in 2010 and rolled together discrimination legislation into the single concept of equality, including laws around disability, gender, sexual harassment, race and sexual orientation. During these years, it was recognized that to serve London in all its diversity demanded a strategy founded on equality. London was one of the most diverse world cities, with 40 per cent of its population identifying as Black, Asian or minority ethnic (BAME[6]) and likely to rise to nearly 50 per cent by 2040. The city's population was expected to grow, and, despite a relatively youthful population, by 2020 12 per cent of Londoners would be over the age of 65, so there would be more disabled and mobility-impaired Londoners to cater for in the future city.[7]

In response to the Equality Act, TfL's Single Equality Scheme, 2012–15, made progress on a broad spectrum of equality issues, including the bus drivers' All Aboard training, developed with disabled and older people's organizations, real-time information at every bus stop available on smartphones or text, the Legible London pedestrian maps across half of the boroughs, working with the Metropolitan Police on Project Guardian to encourage women to report unwanted sexual behaviour on the transport network, increasing accessible stations on the Overground to 56 out of 112 (50 per cent) and increasing bus stop accessibility to 85 per cent of all stops. This included internal initiatives that increased the proportion of women and BAME employees at senior levels and staff networks.

It was increasingly recognized as important for TfL to have a workforce that represented the diversity of the capital's population. Within TfL there was a distinct difference in the profile of back office and operational staff – station staff, train drivers, revenue inspectors, network controllers – who made up some 57 per cent of the TfL workforce; this was a lower proportion of women but a higher proportion of BAME than the representation within TfL as a whole.[8]

Equality and inclusion

"Our vision for Equality and Inclusion is that 'every person matters in keeping London moving, working and growing'"

– Michèle Dix, chair of TfL's Equality & Inclusion Leadership Group, 2016

The first mayor, Ken Livingstone, had long been a campaigner on social issues such as gay and women's rights, so when the GLA was established significant pressure was applied on TfL to adopt best practice in terms of employment and culture, not least because of a number of discrimination cases with the Commission for Racial Equality (CRE), station facilities informally divided on racial lines, and poor facilities for front-line female staff. Employment lawyer Valerie Todd, appointed to develop the TfL equality, diversity and inclusion (EDI) brief, recollects that mayoral advisor Lee Jasper "used to challenge me and say, 'TfL has got a snowy peak', and what he meant was that at the more junior levels what you have is front-line staff, particularly gate-line staff, buses, bus drivers, being well represented in ethnic diversity, while in the office, the back office staff, often the routes to higher promotion, etc., it's very much white British".[9]

"Commissioner Bob Kiley brought the commitment to improving equality and inclusion then being strongly pursued in the United States. It was he who appointed Valerie Todd, who reported directly to him and worked with Livingstone's advisors at City Hall. "I ended up working for Bob. He was an amazing guy, an amazing intellect, great experience, but he was pretty tough, and he made it very clear to me that I had to make a difference on EDI across the organization, or it would be a long walk off a short pier!" With such leadership, progress was made in the formative years of TfL, with Todd sitting at the top table. "I was in the room when we had debates around what should our approach to EDI be? How did we want to set it up? What do we want to deliver? How do we want to report on it? There was a high degree of commitment at that point, and we used to produce an annual report saying everything that we had done to improve equality and inclusion, which included

A bus, taxi and DLR train in their Pride rainbow livery in 2015

recruitment practices, apprenticeship, a trade union forum, a disability forum [IDAG] and celebration of the diversity of the transport industry."[10]

In 2006 TfL established staff network groups (employee resource groups today) to give their staff an opportunity to share their experiences with like-minded colleagues, and to act as consultative bodies for annual surveys, and policy and strategy development. TfL was then ahead of the corporate game in establishing network groups for BAME staff, carers, disability, faith and well-being, women and LBGT+ people, and rose to fifth in the 2007 Stonewall workplace index for best places for LBGT+ people to work. But as diversity progressed across workplaces elsewhere, and EDI became less of a priority after the mayoral election of 2008, TfL fell behind, becoming more reactive and less proactive.

Good practice did remain, especially through the staff network groups. Martyn Loukes was an active member of the LGBT+ staff network group and chair from 2012, when he renamed it OUTbound. "What's good in one year is not necessarily good in the next year, you can't keep doing the same thing. You have to keep doing different things."[11] Loukes recognized the need to raise the group and its members' profile, and to get TfL senior staff to demonstrate their support and approval. His breakthrough initiative was Mike Freer's idea for a 'rainbow crossing', using

facing: TfL's 2015 poster celebrating Pride

ACTIVE AND ACCESSIBLE TRAVEL   203

the colours of the LBGT+ community's rainbow flag, first pioneered in Sydney in 2013. With Vernon Everitt's leadership support, they created a temporary rainbow covering for an existing zebra crossing in Trafalgar Square, at the junction of Pall Mall East and Suffolk Street, on the route of the London Pride parade in June 2014. The event was sponsored by the mayor, with TfL staff participating by heading the parade in an open-top bus. In the following years, the rainbow crossing was requested by other Pride events, while Loukes secured rainbow wraps for taxis, a new bus and a DLR train to raise the profile of diversity within TfL. OUTbound won the Inclusive Networks 'Awesome Network' award in 2015.

Loukes is proud that TfL invented the rainbow bus.

> No one had done it anywhere else in the world, and I invented the first rainbow train ... to show people that London is open for everybody, TfL is open for everybody. Membership of our network group grew by 300 per cent over that period of time. It made people feel more inclusive, more included. I had a more representative leadership team. I had a trans person, I had black people on my team, it was an absolute marvel ... At TfL, we influence a culture, and that's very, very important ... I defy you to find anybody that had a logo in rainbow colours before 2015.[12]

An awareness of diversity in all its forms, including hidden disabilities, informed TfL's accessibility agenda, advanced through equality training for staff delivered in collaboration with disabled people's organizations, bus driver training, and the turn up and go assistance on the Underground and Overground.[13]

The current TfL director of Diversity and Inclusion, Patricia Obinna, is clear about the benefits of diversity:

> Especially at the most senior level of an organization, it leads to better decision-making, greater productivity and more creative problem-solving, which in turn leads to increased profits. Inclusion results in a more motivated and engaged workforce and is better for the mental health of employees. On a personal level, having an inclusive workplace is important because a workplace where everyone feels respected and valued, somewhere where they feel like they belong and can have the career that they want, strikes me as the only fair and just approach to working life.[14]

The challenge for a public body like TfL is to be more than just reactive or performative to the issues of the day; "So there's 'Me Too', we need to do something about women, there's George Floyd's murder, so we need to do something around race or anti-racism. But actually, what we genuinely need to do is to make sure that all of our people feel valued and respected and able to do their best work. That's where we need to be."[15]

For TfL the challenge of being at the cutting edge of diversity practice remains a continuous imperative, effecting cultural change across a range of dynamics. "It's very difficult to put your finger on," Todd reflected. "I would never simply characterize it as we don't take EDI seriously. I just think we haven't found the right combination of levers to pull to actually change the way the organization looks."[16]

In 2024, after extensive consultation with their own six staff network groups, TfL published a customer inclusion strategy and plan, Equity in Motion,[17] moving its emphasis in equality from treating everyone the same to equity focusing on "the unfair and avoidable differences some customers experience when travelling in London".[18] Progress was noted on more step-free stations, cleaner air from expanding the ULEZ, and the 20 mph limit on the TFL road network, with further improvements to come by mitigating health inequalities and improving safety on the network. For Obinna and TfL, "our aim is to serve London's population in all its diversity"[19] with actions across all modes of operation and communications, as well as for its own workforce, and engaging schools to encourage students to consider a career in the transport industry.

TfL, and transport as a sector, has always been welcoming to a range of backgrounds, whereas the trickier challenge has been how it gets those people into leadership roles. As Todd points out, "Whilst there have been one or two unicorns – myself, Patricia [Obinna], Shashi [Verma] – it's not managed to reflect in its most senior levels and in its corporate levels the wonderful talent it has on the front line, and that's still the prize to play for, because there is talent there that would make it even better; that's the aim for a 21st-century TfL."[20]

The leap forward for 2012

British Olympian Baroness Tanni Grey-Thompson met Peter Hendy and David Brown at a launch event for the Olympic Transport Strategy in the German Gymnasium[21] at King's Cross in 2006. They were talking about accessibility and buses, and "I said, 'Well, I can't really get on buses.' Peter and David said, 'Well, you can in London!' I said, 'Are you sure?' 'Yes you can.' At the end of the meeting, Peter said, 'Where are you going next?' I said, 'I'm going to Westminster'. Peter said, 'Oh, right, we'll get on the bus'. We got on, and it's like, oh wow, bus transport is accessible. For me it was a real eye-opening moment." The last time she had been on the Tube was in 1977, when her parents had carried her wheelchair up and down the steps.[22]

Grey-Thompson knew disabled people's concerns about poor access to public transport, and successfully applied to join the TfL board in 2008, to improve transport accessibility and as an ex-athlete to promote the public transport Olympic Games. She was struck by the genuine commitment by TfL people to improve accessibility.

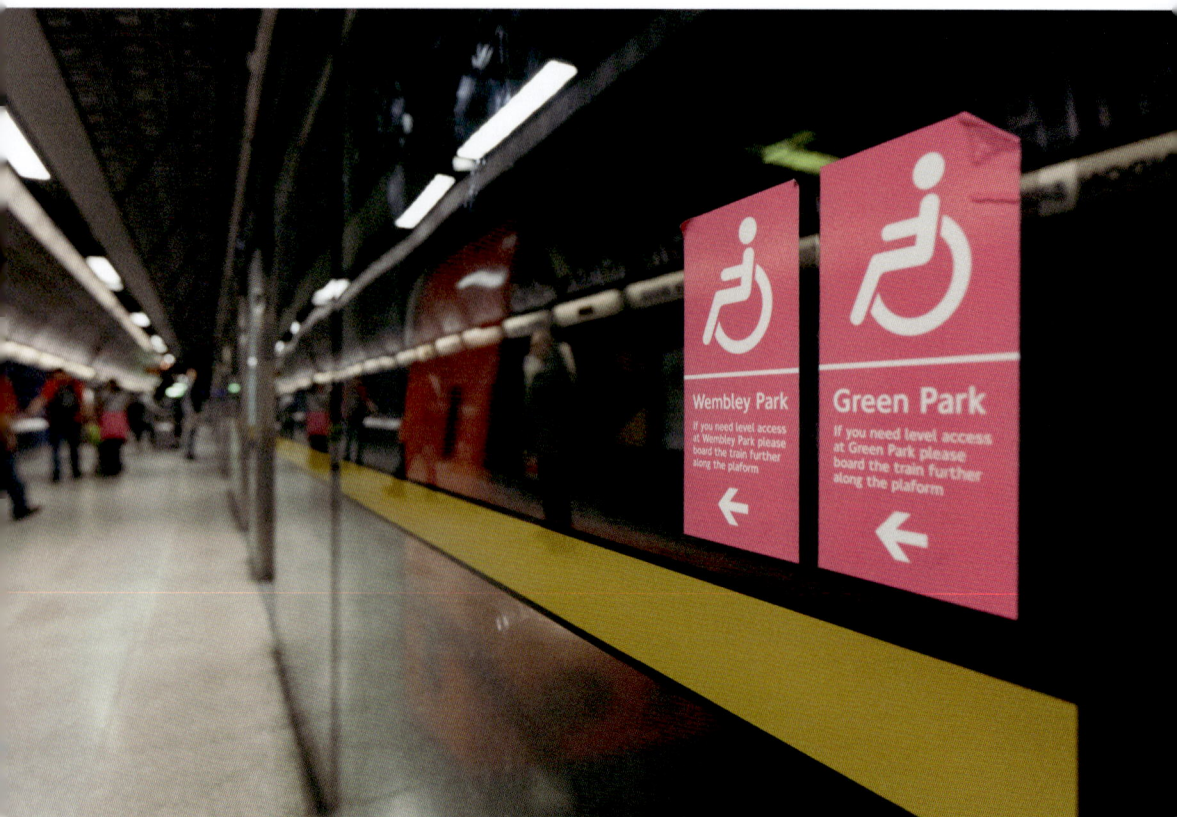

The magenta Olympic signage for wheelchair access to venues on the Jubilee line

> One of the big changes I saw while I was on the board, rather than talking about
> accessibility as a separate issue when they were doing any upgrades or looking at
> work, it was actually just having it as part of the budget. It was about changing the
> mindset of the people who were working on this, that accessibility wasn't thought
> about right at the end.[23]

The long planning and investment road from 2005 to the Games in 2012 gave
impetus to accessibility across the TfL network. Integral to the Games Transport
Strategy was a commitment to invest in a range of measures to make the most
accessible ever Olympics and Paralympics. Lifts and step-free access were installed
at key stations such as Stratford, Green Park and Greenwich, with manual boarding
ramps deployed at 16 Tube stations. Accessibility assistants were put in place at key
stations, and magenta signage included wheelchair users. This was supported by the
accessible Journey Planner, an Accessibility Desk at the Transport Co-ordination
Centre, accessible shuttle buses on 37 routes from station to venue, lift marshals

and bookable accessible parking. During the Games, there were more than 10,000 journeys on the accessible shuttle buses, carrying more than 60,000 passengers, with as many as 1700 passengers a day being taken to the Olympic Park itself. During the Paralympics there were fewer venues, with 11 routes operating, but the demand for the accessible shuttles was much higher, with some 2500 passengers on the Olympic Park route on a single day.[24] The Olympic Delivery Authority (ODA) transport director, Hugh Sumner, commented:

> These accessible shuttle buses have been a big hit, bridging the gap between public transport and venues for people who cannot walk at all, or those who cannot manage long distances, to get easily, speedily and conveniently to their Olympic and Paralympic events ... This has been an important step forward in the provision of transport to big sports and other major events – and has given real practical experience and new skills not just to the London 2012 team, but to the community businesses that have been providing the buses and the drivers. This is another powerful legacy benefit from London and the UK hosting the world's biggest sporting events.[25]

The 2012 Games marked a major leap forward in disabled access to public transport. Through a combination of controlled traffic management, communication with Londoners and collaboration with industry and community partners, TfL was able to develop practical and efficient transport solutions for all who visited the Games. These fulfilled the transport requirements for the Olympic and Paralympic Games, and left TfL with a legacy for further progress in the years that followed.

Since the Games

"Mass transit is all about providing for the average and actually, we're not here to provide for the average, we're here to provide for everybody."

– Mark Evers, TfL chief customer officer, 2025

Independent travel is the key to an independent life. The RNIB maintains that one in three hearing- or vision-impaired people rarely or never use public transport.[26] Assisting passengers who have movement or sight impairment to access the platform and make interchanges as needed was a major step forward for TfL. When it was introduced, the turn up and go service had required 24 hours' notice to be given. By 2014 the service was on-demand, extended across the Tube, DLR and Overground, offering staff assistance from ticket hall to train with information on disruptions and step-free routes, using boarding ramps where available, making interchanges and at the final destination back to the ticket hall. This was welcomed by Tanni Grey-Thompson at the extension of the service to the Overground:

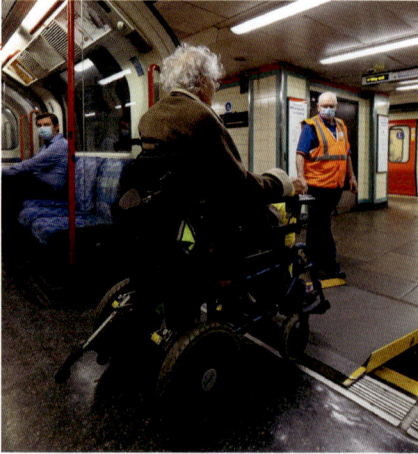

Supporting disabled passengers: a wheelchair user negotiates the ramp at Mile End station; an LU staff member communicates with other stations about the turn up and go service

> TfL really are now leading the way in accessible transport. While it isn't perfect, and many stations were built in an era when accessibility wasn't even considered, all London buses, taxis, the whole DLR and large parts of the Tube and now London Overground networks are accessible to disabled customers, including wheelchair users. As of today, the entire London Overground network is turn up and go, which has long been an issue for me. For me, TfL have another brilliant asset, which is their staff, who will be visible and available to help and advise all customers.[27]

During 2022, about 27,000 'turn up and go' journeys were recorded on the London Underground network, and 7121 journeys recorded on the Elizabeth line.[28]

Equity in Motion

The Equity In Motion initiative was outlined in the 2023 Mayor's Transport Strategy to underpin all the individual modal plans by setting out actions designed to address inequality on the TfL network, to put TfL on the "path to making London socially and economically inclusive and environmentally sustainable".[29] The plan demonstrated that there were still significant barriers to travel and to accessing the opportunities offered by London: the cost of fares, security from harassment for women, gaps in provision (closed by the Superloop bus services), step-free access (to be increased from a third to a half of all stations), accessible toilet facilities, and consistency of customer experience promoted by staff disability and equality training.

By the time new trains were introduced on the Overground, on the Victoria and sub-surface lines and the Elizabeth line in 2022, a wide range of accessibility features – including wheelchair spaces, priority seats, wide doorways, audio-visual announcements and colour contrasts between surfaces, walls, seats and grab poles – had become the normal design standard. Access at older stations proved to be difficult and expensive, but 68 stations were identified at the right shopping and tourist locations that could be made accessible. The Elizabeth line had lift access to platform level, with technical difficulties solved by innovative sloping lifts at Liverpool Street and at Farringdon's Barbican exit. The varying platform heights at stations were also addressed by adding humps to get wheelchairs onto trains.

TfL has moved beyond the legal or moral obligation to cater for all to an awareness that the use of public transport has barriers for many people: the safety issue for young women and girls after dark, the elderly struggling to change between services, as well as the less abled groups typically addressed by the access agenda. A good customer proposition for all Londoners is both a political and a financial imperative in post-pandemic London.

The rise of active travel

Walking is the necessary component of every London journey, to access, transfer between and exit Tube, bus, boat, cab or tram. Even in the Victorian and Edwardian decades of significant innovation in transport – horse buses, Underground railways, the electric tram, the Tube and the motor bus – Londoners other than the middle classes still walked to work and to the markets, shops and entertainments of the high streets and town centres in the metropolis.

When TfL was created in 2000 walking was thought of as a recreational activity and not as a mode of transport. But the overcrowded capacity of rail, Tube and bus, and an integrated approach to moving around the city, its streets and public spaces, suggested that walking should also be considered part of a city-wide transport strategy.

Ben Plowden had been chief executive of the non-profit organization Living Streets, which campaigned for better provision for walking in the city. He had written to the candidates before the 2000 mayoral election asking for something about walking to be included in the manifesto. "The London Walking Charter that we wrote and sent to them, some of which was then included in Livingstone's election manifesto, had the aim of making London one of the world's most walkable cities," he explained. Still with Living Streets, Plowden met Kiley and spent a very enjoyable half day with him walking around a number of pedestrian spaces: "Strutton Ground opposite Windsor House, and some less nice pedestrian spaces; we started off in Parliament Square and then went up to Camden High Street to show what good looked like and what less good looked like."[30] Plowden was to be a key figure in the creation of what became known as TfL's active travel strategy, bringing together planning and delivery of the non-transport modes of travel in London – walking, cycling and the public realm. [31]

Plowden recalls that Kiley's experience in New York with the crime and policing agenda on the Subway was a significant influence, as was his relationship with William Bratton, the commissioner of the Transit Police, and the experience of dealing with the "small things like fare evasion and graffiti on trains as a way of making people feel safe and looked after and not inclined to commit their own offences … he kind of intuitively understood this point".[32]

Plowden was appointed in 2002 to be TfL's first director of Borough Partnerships, a new role created to improve TfL's "quite challenging" relationship with the boroughs. The boroughs were sceptical about the creation of TfL as a layer of government between them and the DfT or the GOL. TfL rapidly started to recruit some of the key talent from the boroughs at salaries that the boroughs at that stage could not match. "We introduced some conditionality around the Annual Funding Settlement for the boroughs, which had previously basically been given out without many conditions attached to it. I was responsible for that process. I arrived in TfL from a campaigning background, particularly around walking and road safety in the public realm, to do a stakeholder management and funding programme role."[33]

TfL had brought together a wide of range of city functions from its predecessor organizations, but in 2000 it was still massed around the public transport modes of Underground, Buses and Streets, focused on traffic management but soon to introduce the congestion charge. Plowden recalls that there really was no discernible interest in, understanding of or desire to support non-motorized modes such as walking and cycling.

> TfL in its early days was essentially a public transport organization, pretty pure and simple. The sums of money in the annual budget for walking and cycling were, from memory, in the high single millions, and at best in the low double millions of pounds. The bulk of that money was given to the boroughs for schemes for their roads to be what was then called the borough spending plan process, which I presided over. The notion that TfL really had any business thinking about walking or cycling was very far from the organization's core beliefs and principles … That was true of pretty much every other transport organization in the country at that stage.[34]

There was a growing realization, and not just in London, Plowden recalled, that economically attractive, environmentally sustainable, socially equitable world cities promote moving around predominantly by public transport, particularly for high-volume movements of people. Many cities still have large numbers of walking trips and cycling, and whether you are interested in the climate emergency, public health, air pollution, road danger, social cohesion, cities will have all those characteristics. "There is a broader direction of travel going on, certainly in large parts of Europe, some parts of the US, parts of Australasia, and some Asian cities."[35]

Plowden believed, "since walking often accounted for somewhere between a quarter and a third of journeys in London, that as a minimum pedestrians ought to be given some care and attention, because if they weren't, they would probably start driving". Closely allied to this was the potential of cycling, "which at that point was very, very small, in terms of mode share, I think it was one per cent at the time, and had huge potential to unlock, particularly suburban car journeys. This made the case internally in a variety of ways for TfL to pay more attention to those two modes in particular."[36]

Plowden had noted London Buses' annual survey of spend by mode of arrival in suburban town centres.

> The press release that went with it said, 'Buses just the ticket for suburban town centres, says TfL survey'. It showed that bus passengers spent significantly more than car drivers every week on average, because they spent less per trip but made more trips per week than car drivers did. What the press release didn't say was what the survey also showed, which was that pedestrians spent twice as much as bus passengers for exactly the same reason: you walked to and from the town centre every day and spent a bit. I sent an email to Peter Hendy, then TfL MD for Bus and River Services, and said, 'Why didn't the press release mention pedestrians?' He emailed back and said, 'Because it was a London Bus press release!'[37]

The survey made a very strong case for buses and also for supporting pedestrian journeys. Plowden worked with the commissioner's policy unit, looking at journey times in minutes door-to-door from the southern end of the Northern line into central London by bike and by Tube. At that point the Northern line was under severe pressure in terms of capacity, overcrowding and unreliability. "What that showed was that you had to go as far out, from memory, as Tooting Bec before it was quicker by Tube door to door, if you took into account the walk at either end, than it was to go by bike."[38]

The seeds of the transport demand management (TDM) programme that were to be applied so successfully to the Olympic Games were sown in Livingstone's second term, with school travel planning and personal travel planning. "I don't think that Ken took much persuading that this was a useful thing, because the people who would vote for him were the people who were interested in those things, the alignment between policy and politics. However, the sums of money involved were still at that point tiny in relative terms."[39]

Plowden also observed that, in that second term, "the Greens on the London Assembly had the casting vote on the mayor's budget, which was a critical change of circumstances; they 'forced' the mayor – or 'persuaded' the mayor – to significantly increase, relatively speaking, the amount of money for walking and cycling, particularly for travel demand management, which I also managed."[40]

Active travel grew from modest beginnings by 2016 to forming one of the pillars of an integrated transport strategy for London. "Because if you'd asked someone in 2003, what's our overarching goal, the answer depended on who you'd asked. Now, it's 80 per cent in the service of sustainable world city and sustainable growth."[41] An 80 per cent mode share from public transport, walking and cycling, for Plowden "that seems to me to be a big change".[42]

Get on a bike

"Imagine if we could invent something that cut road and rail crowding, cut noise, cut pollution and ill-health – something that improved life for everyone, quite quickly, without the cost and disruption of new roads and railways. Well, we invented it 200 years ago: the bicycle."

– Mayor Boris Johnson, 2010[43]

Mayor Johnson's vision was for cycling to be a normal part of everyday life, something you feel comfortable doing in your ordinary clothes. "I want more women cycling, more older people cycling, more black and minority ethnic Londoners cycling, more cyclists of all social backgrounds – without which truly mass participation can never come. As well as the admirable Lycra-wearers, and the enviable East Londoners on their fixed-gear bikes, I want more of the kind of cyclists you see in Holland, going at a leisurely pace on often clunky steeds. I will do all this by creating a variety of routes for the variety of cyclists I seek."[44]

Cycling, cycle hire and cycle safety measures were a significant component of the active travel strategy, promoted through investment in cycling infrastructure, notably the Cycle Superhighways, cycle commuter routes in and out of central London, the first of which opened in 2010.

As a former campaigner himself, Plowden recognized the effectiveness of the London Cycling Campaign "as a really clever and timely piece of campaigning, because all three candidates [in 2008] signed up to Love London, Go Dutch, which was about Dutch design standards. We worked on what that might mean in terms of the level of investment, design standards, traffic priority, and £913 million was in the business plan the following year. We went from not really knowing what 'Love London, Go Dutch' meant to saying, 'Well, it's something just shy of a billion quid's worth of investment over five years'."[45]

Plowden recalls securing that "unimaginably large" cycling budget of £913 million from 2009, spread across four programmes of work: the Cycle Superhighways, fast, high-capacity commuter routes on arterial corridors in and out of central London; the Quietways, a network of smaller routes, predominantly in outer London, connecting neighbourhoods in town centres; the mini-Hollands, significant packages of investment in three boroughs to improve infrastructure throughout the borough – Enfield, Kingston and Walthamstow receiving £30 million to £35 million each; and safety campaigns. The final thing was the Central London Grid, the Quietways network in central London connecting up the Cycle Superhighways.

Johnson's second term saw a deepening of the commitment to cycling, most notably through the appointment of journalist Andrew Gilligan as cycling commissioner. Gilligan controversially delivered the brief far beyond what Johnson had envisaged, enraging the road lobby with the works for cycle infrastructure in central London, notably on the Embankment. (For more on cycling investment during Johnson's second term as mayor, between 2012 and 2016, see Chapter 12.)

Healthy streets

Following the election of Sadiq Khan as the third London mayor in 2016, work that had been done around public health and transport, published in Johnson's health strategy in his second term, evolved into the Healthy Streets agenda, championed for Khan by Val Shawcross, deputy mayor for transport.[46] Walking, cycling and public transport was dealt with systematically and with substantial investment; Plowden rued that this was "a sum of money that you simply could not have imagined in 2002, when I first arrived, and remains probably one of the largest budgets for non-motorized transport in the world ... Over the twenty-ish years that TfL's been in existence, we've gone from virtually no money at all, no interest, no attention, no knowledge about walking and cycling [just some road safety] to a substantial programme of investment and institutional and decision-making changes that sort of allow that money to be spent in a structured, in a sensible and explicable way."[47]

The capacity of the highway network in London has become noticeably finite. With the 80 per cent mode shift target in the Mayor's Transport Strategy, general traffic, in the sense of private car vehicles, is not now seen as a priority – it is about walking, cycling, road safety, air quality, and buses. For TfL the challenge really is – whether in allocating space on the carriageway or at junctions, or time at junctions – how to get the best possible outcomes on the road network for moving a large number of people in the most efficient and safe way. For Plowden, the Healthy Streets debate is "how you maintain the reliability of the bus network and bus journey times and bus speeds at the same time as trying to allocate more highway capacity to walking and cycling".[48]

Congestion, traffic delay compared to free flow, has crept up gently over the period since 2002 because the capacity of the network has been deliberately and explicitly reallocated towards walking, cycling, and public transport. Plowden suggests that what TfL has needed to become good at is active traffic management in real time: managing traffic on the key corridors, keeping the network operating in a way that service standards for all road users are broadly maintained.

> At the margin, you're constantly trading off: if I give this group greater time or more space or more safety, how is that going to affect people who are already there? The debate about the East–West Cycle Superhighway along the Embankment was a really good example of that. The Cycle Superhighways are very visible reallocations of space and time in favour of both pedestrians and cyclists actually, because a lot of them offer pedestrian improvements. If you're a current user in a car or a van or a lorry, you look at the road and think, I've got less space than I used to have.[49]

The trend towards active travel has become the direction of travel for transport strategy, putting resources into changing how the city looks and feels. This was initially promoted by the Greens having the casting vote on Livingstone's second-term budget. As a cyclist, Boris Johnson gave Gilligan his head in the second term, signed up for Love London, Go Dutch, "and suddenly," observed Plowden, "you're into completely different territory in terms of investment – in this case, in cycling. Then in Sadiq's first term, the Healthy Streets agenda linking transport to public health very explicitly."[50]

The different modes within Surface Transport were once focused on traffic flow, reflected Plowden:

> But that is not true any more ... They're doing some really sophisticated stuff around support for cycles, SCOOT[51] – how you account for demand for pedestrians and cyclists, buses at junctions, automatically through radar ... the whole setup, infrastructure, design, data gathering, traffic management priorities, that is now organized, to a much greater extent, around a common set of goals ... 80 per cent mode share, public transport, walk and cycle ... There's Vision Zero for road deaths and buses, and there's air quality targets and 2030 for carbon reduction, which are all consistent with that as our overarching goal. Now, it's 80 per cent in the service of sustainable world city and sustainable growth."[52]

Johnson's first term, in juxtaposition to Livingstone, sought to be less 'anti-car' for the motorist, whom he judged had suffered under Ken and congestion charging. The Roads Task Force proposed smoothing traffic flow, maintaining reliability for cars along key arterial routes. "Our intelligence about the road network was born out of needing to understand it in terms of how it performed generally in Boris's first term."[53]

For Plowden this was a really good example of how the organization had to develop a new way of thinking, planning and investing in response to a mayoral, political, electoral commitment. "The fact that Boris was a commuter cyclist is not incidental, because he did it in the same way that Ken went on the bus and the Tube … if the mayor cycles, it's what senior successful people do, it suddenly becomes a different sort of proposition. He did it in his regular suit, not in Lycra, then he hired Gilligan, and Gilligan said, 'We've just got to crack on with this'. The combination of the money, the mayor being a cyclist, being held to account for Love London, Go Dutch, and appointing someone whose job in City Hall was to push this agenda together meant the level of activity significantly increased. And then that morphed into Healthy Streets, which is a broader version of the same agenda."[54]

Cycling post-2016

"Because active travel, walking and cycling, has not been built into the city historically in terms of the way the city is designed, or the way that this organization works, it does require somebody to champion it."

– Will Norman, 2024[55]

Will Norman was appointed Walking and Cycling commissioner by Mayor Khan early in 2017. He was following in the footsteps of Andrew Gilligan, who had ruthlessly taken the cycling agenda forward in Johnson's second term. "Andrew was fearless in taking people on. I think he defined success in most things, in my experience, if he wasn't pissing someone off, he didn't feel like he was doing his job properly, so that got stuff done. The Embankment and Blackfriars, in terms of two bike lanes, were exceptionally bold statements of ambition and intent. I inherited a situation where there was bold intent and there was ambition."[56]

In reflecting on active travel, Norman recalls:

It was championed by deputy mayor Val Shawcross, setting a brave, bold direction with everything hinging off from that mayoral policy. I'm not sure that would have happened without Val in terms of setting that ambition, and that then gave us the embedded Healthy Streets approach of designing streets for people rather than for cars, not just in the policy around transport, but also in the environment strategy, in the London Plan, in the health strategy … particularly the environment plan, which was really important when you come on to the ULEZ and the air quality agenda, a co-ordinated policy for changing the city for the better. If you want to dial up the transport outcomes, it's reducing congestion, getting more ridership. If you want to dial up health outcomes, it's less chronic disease, less air pollution, a graphic equalizer of outcome that flowed through every piece of the policy landscape.[57]

Cycling to Covid and after

The TfL Cycle Hire scheme had promoted cycling in central London since its introduction in 2010. This was further promoted with the arrival of independent and unregulated electric bike operators – Uber from San Francisco in 2017 and Lime in 2018 – which disrupted the market with their offer of electric bikes by app and without fixed bays. Active in 230 cities worldwide, Lime have come to dominate the 'free-floating' cycle market in London. In response the TfL cycle scheme, sponsored by Santander since 2015 with 20,000 bikes and 1400 stations across inner London, in 2022 introduced e-bikes to the docked scheme. The appearance of Lime bikes on pavements, at stations and in huge discarded shoals at big central London events has again raised questions about whether this is a convenient and sustainable addition to the transport mix in London or a menace that clogs up pavements.[58]

In 2010 the Cycling Vision had also noted the distinct culture of cycling in London. "Those most likely to cycle are white men aged 25 to 44. Current cyclists have a higher than average income and are more likely to be resident in inner London."[59] Chris Macleod, TfL director of Customer and Revenue up to 2021, reflected that "cycling is very heavily white male, and if you worked for *The Times* or *The Telegraph* or the *Evening Standard* there'd usually be a Brompton in the corner".[60] The demographics of cycling have, however, not moved significantly in recent years, despite the belief that if TfL builds segregated and safer cycle infrastructure cycling will flourish and grow in numbers and diversity. Not surprisingly, London has a different culture from that of the Netherlands; even in 1911 the Dutch owned more cycles per capita than any other country in Europe. Despite the rise of the private car in the Netherlands, cycling was still the transport choice for millions, and was accommodated in the expansion of cycle lanes and segregation from the 1970s, with cycle path length nationally doubling in the 1980s to 11,800 miles as part of a national Bicycle Master Plan.[61]

In response to the potential for electric e-scooters to boost sustainable and active travel, TfL instituted a trial rental scheme in 2021 with Lime and Voi in 11 boroughs, extended to run until September 2025. With 4000 vehicles available and larger wheels, speed is limited to 12.5 mph and the lights are always on. After fires were caused by defective lithium batteries, e-scooters were banned from TfL stations, premises and services. Since launch, more than five million journeys have been made on rental scooters, replacing 7 per cent of car journeys, TfL reported in May 2025.[62]

In the years since 2010, cycling infrastructure has seen major investment from TfL in both its quality and extent, being expanded from a 55-mile network in 2016 to 250 miles by 2024. In the years to Covid, the annual growth in cycling from 580,000 daily journeys in 2010 had slackened despite significant investment in infrastructure. The pandemic once more prompted a net increase in cycling: by 2024, 1.33 million

A mini-Holland low-traffic neighbourhood in Orford Road, Walthamstow, 2020

journeys were being made by bike each day, a 26 per cent increase since pre-Covid of 1.05 million in 2019.[63] In April 2025 the City of London Corporation reported that cycling within the City had increased by some 50 per cent in the past two years. October 2024 saw a record 139,000 people a day cycling across 30 locations – up from 89,000 in 2022. According to the Corporation, people cycling now make up 56 per cent of all traffic in the peak commuting hours, and dockless bicycles account for one in six bikes on City streets.[64] Lime bikes – dockless, app-enabled and electric, in 200 cities worldwide, with 16 million journeys in London in 2024 – have apparently broadened the demographics of cycling, as the London Cycling Campaign's CEO Tom Fyans said when announcing a £20 million investment in London in January 2025: "Lime bikes are changing the face of cycling in London, bringing joy to a huge and diverse audience new to cycling in London … With this new investment, Lime is helping to ensure new riders cycle and park more responsibly." Nearly half of Londoners aged 18 to 34 now use Lime bikes weekly, and journey numbers rose too.[65]

UPGRADE UNDER WAY

148. That's how old the Tube is. It was the very first underground railway in the world. Last year alone our trains carried over a billion passengers across London, and covered over 200 million miles. That's a heavy workload, and it's taken its toll. But we have a plan. We're upgrading the Underground so that we can meet growing demand, and keep London moving now and in the future. It's a huge task. Our plan is already well under way, but there's a lot more to do. Please bear with us. We're doing everything we can to keep disruptions to a minimum.

Keep up with the upgrade plan and how it might affect you at tfl.gov.uk

MAYOR OF LONDON

Transport for London

UNDERGROUND

9.

REDISCOVERING A CUSTOMER SERVICE MENTALITY

"TfL had, and has, no divine right to exist. It cannot therefore act like a monopoly – its biggest competitor today is the car – and must respond to customers. The founding fathers of London Transport understood this, and I think all my team and I did was help rediscover it."

– Vernon Everitt, TfL MD for Customers, Communication and Technology, 2007–22[1]

Most of TfL's potential customers are Londoners and voters. TfL is responsible to the mayor of London, who is elected by winning those Londoners' votes. Political accountability for TfL demanded a better understanding of the customers' view of TfL's services and communications, as well as upgrades to stations, lines, trains and buses. TfL recognized the opportunity to innovate within the digital revolution. Enabled by the smartphone, GPS location tracking, the data mine provided by Oyster ticketing, new customer service tools for its staff and fresh insights from customer research, TfL made innovative strides to deliver for the customer daily on the crowded network and also in response to major events, notably the challenge of the 2012 Olympic Games. They raised the bar of customer service for the Games, which enhanced TfL's reputation in the years that followed. During the Covid pandemic, these methods were stood on their head first to urge Londoners to stay off the network and then to encourage them back to fuel the capital's recovery.

Customers are voters

"If you make your customers happy, they vote for the mayor."

– Max Weston[2]

The story of a city's transport network is typically dominated by the headline infrastructure projects, the heroic construction of new lines, tunnels, bridges and roads across the challenging grain of a dense metropolis, or the introduction of new vehicles, roads, trains and trams, and of ever-changing service patterns to respond to changing demand. In the UK, transport is set the additional challenges of securing long-term funding from politicians who operate under short-term political cycles, managing press criticism and public consultation, and the perennial challenge of delivering to time and budget.

Alongside the triumphs of S-stock trains and the greening of the bus fleet, introducing the congestion charge and ULEZ, the Tube extension to Battersea and the new Elizabeth line, the most significant developments for city management in TfL's first 25 years were arguably in the back office, in transport's adoption of and response to the digital revolution: the payment revolution of the Oyster card and contactless ticketing, the sharing of big data sets with third-party apps and the application of cutting-edge customer insight to the creation of a customer service mentality. Taken together, these innovations enabled TfL to be more genuinely customer-focused, a transport authority that recognized the importance of being trusted by its customers and that applies customer insight and research to investment decisions, service design and development. Being at the cutting edge of innovation revolutionized Londoners' relationship with their transport provider TfL.

If the 1990s had been the final analogue decade, by 2010 Londoners' lives were substantially digitally enabled. In 2002 TfL made its online Journey Planner available, while in July 2003 the Oyster card was introduced (see Chapter 6). Through the decade the mobile phone was transformed into a digital device, an assistant that combined the Filofax organizer, the iPod, navigation systems, the landline and the digital camera. Rapid advances in network coverage, mobile processing power and storage technologies enabled this convergence and fostered a broad spectrum of applications including mobile gaming, video streaming, mobile banking and image exchange.

TfL's integrated city-wide mayoral model was well equipped to respond to the opportunities of this digital new world. As a major mover of people, TfL was the single mind accountable for formulating and delivering an integrated digital strategy for services, ticketing, payment and customer information across the capital. It is hard to overestimate the significance of local democratic accountability in TfL developing an innovative approach to customers and their needs. Transport was the headline issue in every mayoral election and candidate manifesto from 2000 to 2016. A democratically accountable mayor equates customers with voters. In the 1960s and 1970s transport executives were often at loggerheads with the GLC and national politicians because they believed they knew better than the politicians and, by implication, than their customers and voters. Peter Hendy recalls: "London Transport went to astonishing lengths to be independent when it should have done no such thing, it should have said, 'We can do this for you if that's what you want'."[3]

From the formative years of mayoral governance, TfL's leadership was clear about their responsibility to deliver the elected mayor's mandate. Its predecessor organization, London Transport, had maintained that it was customer-focused and had appointed senior executives for marketing and customer care. From the rock bottom of the King's Cross fire of 1987, LT stations and services had been steadily refurbished, initially in response to disaster and then through investment in response to London's booming economy in the years following the Big Bang of 1986. Within the world of their customers, however, public transport was playing catch-up in a fast-moving market, TfL's proposition notoriously once described by a customer as "Waitrose prices for an Aldi service".[4] Vincent Nolan, founder of TfL's research contractors 2CV, remembers that this "was a quote weeded out of many quotes and delivered and then picked up on and became a sort of a big stick to wave around the organization".[5]

From 2000, mayoral governance made the performance of public transport accountable, against a background of the relentless rise in passenger numbers. The network was increasingly self-funded and less centrally subsidized. Benefiting from a decade of PPP-funded improvement, the Underground was more reliable, better maintained and cleaner than it had been for many years.

In the white heat of preparation for the challenge on the horizon of the first public transport Olympic Games in 2012, the modal silos – Underground, Streets, Buses – were disrupted by the imperative of an integrated plan for service delivery and public information. Fortunately, fresh means of insight into customers and their behaviours had been recognized and had already achieved some measurable successes. TfL began to win advertising industry awards for its campaigns.

The key insight of the new leadership at TfL was that public transport should be judged by the same criteria as the other services used by its customers. The reality of its unreliable and second-rate recent past was being steadily reversed through infrastructure investment and upgrade. But a dose of 'outsider-in' was needed to work across the operational silos of such a large and not well-integrated organization. The client for this was the second TfL commissioner, Peter Hendy, and its advocates were the MD for Marketing and Communications, Vernon Everitt, and director of Customer and Revenue, Chris Macleod.

Vernon Everitt was appointed in 2007 by Peter Hendy and Redmond O'Neill, mayoral advisor. Everitt's brief, and his personal commitment, was to hold the mirror of customer perception up to the organization. His background was financial services and regulation at the Bank of England, not the transport industry. Hendy recalls: "The panel was me and Redmond O'Neill ... it's one of the best appointments of any job I've ever made ... it's really interesting that somebody who isn't from transport gets the relationship of transport organizations with customers a lot better than most of the people who are from transport."[6]

Having a democratically elected mayor whose job is to look after London – housing, economy, jobs – with transport as the core enabler, changed and democratized everything, asserts Everitt.

> People could have a view; people could vote at the ballot box as to who they thought would be best positioned to make their life in the city better. A lock-up between that and the mayoralty, a spatial plan for London, an economic plan for London and a transport plan for London – that is absolute genius. It drove this organization to be much more outcome-based, rather than input-based; if you're a transport operator, you're more inclined, frankly, to be interested in inputs rather than on outcomes. The way in which London was now governed changed all that.[7]

This insight, equating a monopoly's customers with voters, was internally dubbed 'Vernonomics'.[8] Coming from outside the transport industry, Everitt and Macleod, a veteran of the advertising industry, brought customer perspectives from the wider world, and Tesco's 'Every Little Helps' slogan was later to find its TfL equivalent in 'Every Journey Matters'. They were good at raising the customer profile within TfL. They instinctively understood that the mayoral lever makes TfL very sensitive to its public reputation, the mayor's support is needed to secure funding, and an upward reputation wins votes.

Peter Hendy was very clear on TfL being granted its licence by the mayor.

> Though the commissioner's job has been demonstrated not to be a job dependent on one mayor or another, the fact is – and I will defend it to the hilt – if you're going to be the commissioner of Transport, you'd better work out who the boss is, because the mayor's elected by four or five million people, and you'd better do what he wants. That doesn't mean that you shouldn't do what London needs and the right transport thing is, but if – as some of my predecessors did, they sort of looked down their noses and said, 'Well, we don't want any of this political interference' – you can, frankly, expect to be fired, and you can certainly expect not to get any money, because if you're the mayor, why would you put up with that?[9]

Hendy had started his career as a graduate trainee in London Transport, TfL's predecessor, before rejoining as TfL MD for Bus and River Services (later renamed Surface Transport) from 2001. "I think the thing that the organization [LT] hadn't really worked out is that they were working for an elected politician. That politician was put into office on a mandate to do certain things and this organization's job, therefore, was to deliver that, not what it itself fancied delivering."[10] Hendy also reflected:

> Every single mayor that we've had has carried forward this notion that transport is not an end in itself. It's a means to an end. It enables social justice, allows all

Vernon Everitt,
MD Customers,
Communication
and Technology,
2007–22, presenting
TfL's In Bloom
Awards in 2019

citizens to participate in life in London on equal terms. The progressive things –
like trying to make all of our stations in due course fully accessible – it's only right
and proper, and I think the mayor, the mayoralty and its range of objectives was
core to that. No longer transport operators, we're enablers of people living and
working in a city.[11]

At this time there was a big focus on advertising, which had produced a succession
of highly creative campaigns, culminating in TfL being made National Advertiser
of the Year in 2008. It was evident to Everitt from his first days in TfL that if they
were going to stand a chance of delivering the wider objectives from the transport
strategy, then the internal wiring had to be changed.[12] He soon appreciated that he
simply could not do his job,

> if I'm having to have separate sets of conversations with lots of different people
> about the same thing. The whole purpose of my job was to encourage more people
> on to public transport. The wider context for all of this was that London was
> growing very rapidly; there was demand and that demand needed to be managed
> effectively. We needed to hit the mode shift targets that were in the Mayor's
> Transport Strategy, which meant further reductions in use of cars in London, so
> that set the strategic context for it all. I had to have a wider brief to fix that.[13]

Ultimately this led to a change in role for Everitt, to MD for Customers,
Communication and Technology, and for TfL from an advertising- to a
customer-focused approach.

Turning pain into gain

In driving the creation of a customer service mentality, Everitt also believed it was really helpful that he didn't come from a transport background.

> The things that were obvious to me didn't appear obvious to people that have been here for a long time. I was able to point out some simple, straightforward things. Even now I don't feel like I'm part of this industry, but rather a user of it. I'm not a transport professional. I'm interested in the outcomes that are achieved … through transportation. If you look at the world through that lens, it drives you in quite a different direction than it would do if you looked at it in a modal, transport-provider way. I remember the first meeting, must have been in early 2008, where I got everybody involved in marketing and communications and customer-related issues in a room at Centre Point. I was introducing people who had worked in the same organization for 10, 20 or 30 years, but some who'd never spoken to each other about what we were collectively trying to achieve. It was a really odd and awkward meeting and people sort of thought, 'What on earth are we all doing here?' But that was the start of trying to turn the organization to being driven more by insight, much of which already resided in the organization, to help us make some progress, rather than which mode of transport we represented.[14]

Everitt established a monthly Customer Group meeting to bring together practice and to promote a customer-led approach across the TfL family. "The truth I tried to tell the barons," reflected Everitt, "was that it's not all about you, it's about the people who use us. Not quite in those words, but using evidence and measurement. Some liked it, like Peter [Hendy], while others didn't."[15]

Everitt discovered the Customer Research Unit soon after his arrival.

> I was looking around thinking, who knows stuff about this thing I've joined, because I was bewildered when I first turned up. The head of research said, 'Here's everything we know about buses, here's everything we know about the Underground' … They knew stuff about what made people want to use us, but that had been under-exploited. We rejuvenated the research function, encouraging them to get insight out of the numbers. Rather than just say the numbers this month were this, this and this, what we really wanted to do was say, 'Why are those numbers like they are, and what could we do in order to improve them? What is it that would connect with people and make them want to use us more to move around London?'[16]

The team were tasked with burrowing into what they held. "What is the complaints data telling us, and the compliments data, the stakeholders' sentiment from business, politicians, journalists and the third sector?' We just took all of that and put that into the marketing machine. The marketing team under Chris ground that down into some basic truths. That's when Every Journey Matters arrived, from that sideboard load of data."[17]

"We're not a business apart, we're a business that other people compare with" was the starting point for a fresh approach to customers. Chris Macleod was the key architect of this as TfL's head of Marketing Communications from January 2009, and later as Customer and Revenue director; he explains: "So our customer experience, our customer service, our customer information, our products, our advertising, have to be as good as everyone else's".[18]

Macleod also believes that he and Everitt had impact because "we presented ourselves as being independent, and not personality driven, if you like – more about what was the right thing. Vernon isn't particularly a baron, because he says, 'Well, what does the data say? What does the insight say? What are the customers saying? Have we thought about this?'"[19] Macleod brought into TfL the concept of the 'pain points' in the customers' journey, the moments revealed by research that led to friction on the journey and customer dissatisfaction, such as a lack of driver announcements or interactions with staff. Concentrating communications or investment on these issues turned the pain into 'gain points'.

Macleod and Everitt rapidly formed a new axis for the customer. As Everitt recalled:

I distinctly remember an early discussion with Chris [Macleod], where we said, 'This organization is a sleeping giant and it does the most wonderful things for the city. Now we've got to plan for its future 10, 20, 30, 40, 50 years hence.' But we were not in that game of trying to identify what customers really needed from us ... That was the moment when it became evident to me that it was a big job to be done, that you could win that investment case if you combined an understanding that not only did you have to replace a lot of things that were clapped out, you had to do that for a purpose and that purpose was to keep London moving, working and growing. The more London continued to be successful as an engine of growth, the more the country would be successful.[20]

In his first two years Everitt dug into the organization. "The penny suddenly dropped. We knew that we needed a much more customer-focused view of the world if we were going to be successful".[21] Chris Macleod talks in similar terms of the virtuous circle.

The customers needed to feel that we were on their side; it would be very easy for people to think we weren't. The way the virtuous circle went was, if people thought we were doing a good job that informed their stakeholders, the media, politicians, local politicians, everybody to talk well and think well of TfL, then when we're looking for money and looking for support for projects – because we can't fund everything ourselves – people will say, 'I'll give it to TfL, because they're a bunch of good people who think about customers and do a good job'. The virtuous circle is obviously, if we're perceived to do that, then we get more money, more support, on we go, and the wheel turns. So that's really where that customer focus won.[22]

This was much more than a change in strategy. It demanded a radical change in research methods away from testing proposals with customers to solving problems by an improved understanding of customer motivation and sentiment. This demanded a cultural shift within TfL's decision-making towards being led by customer insights rather than by the operators' instincts. New methods and tools were being suggested by the research world, as nudge theory became popular with politicians following Thaler and Sunstein's publication in 2008.[23]

One of the key tools that enabled a fresh approach to being genuinely customer-led was the ethnographic method, based on observing what people actually do rather than what they say they do in a survey. Vincent Nolan, founder and chair of 2CV, TfL's contracted customer research agency since 2005, characterized observational research or ethnography as "a disarmingly simple technique. It involves hanging around and watching people".[24] For the work with TfL, Nolan noted that typically

we'd started from the wrong end of the telescope, with the bus route, which I can understand because that's where the question emanated within the business. But actually, as a researcher, I'd say maybe you could start with the people, we can start to come round on a different route. It took a while for that to percolate through. So it was actually quite a backward step that we were talking about: people being recruited on the basis of how they behave or on a particular thing, rather than any attitude or demographic.[25]

The potential of this fresh and revolutionary approach was recognized by Ian Pring, then a research manager in Underground, today a TfL behaviour change manager. Pring joined in 2003, and found that Underground had a huge body of very good research. It was mostly customer satisfaction research that was quantitative, mystery travel research, which was really to manage staff and suppliers, and ad hoc projects that were again predominantly quantitative. As he explained, "They did their job; they were there to solve the business problems that we saw in front of us." Pring continued:

I'd love to be able to say that I thought ... we need to use different methodologies, but the fact of the matter was, I went to a presentation by a guy called Mark Ritson[26] who was quite a bigwig in the marketing world. He'd done a massive ethnographic project which involved dozens of people watching TV ads ... about how much notice do people take of TV ads ... it was quite a revelation really, because I'd never seen ethnography before, the kind of research which doesn't involve talking to people necessarily but involves observing what they do and what they're saying. What it showed was that people don't take anywhere near as much notice of TV ads as a lot of people think. A lot of the advertising agencies there were not very happy! I thought, this is a really interesting method, we could apply it to TfL. I didn't really know what we might get out of it at the time. I thought it was a hell of a lot better than just playing a numbers game and asking people what boxes they wanted to tick.[27]

We did a similar project that was looking at customer focus in LU which used semiotics, which is a study of what organizational signals are given out by marketing, and what that indicated was a lack of customer focus. I moved over to the TfL team at a time when its marketing and communications research ... needed greater insights because we weren't getting as much in the way of marketing insight as we could have done. We were doing quite a lot of very straightforward qualitative research which sometimes was not going deep enough. So we started to think, right, let's actually have more rigour applied to qualitative techniques. This has taken us to around 2007, and the Teenage Road Safety and Sustainable Travel campaigns.[28]

Managing behaviour change

The partnership with research agency 2CV, re-engaged by TfL from 2005, was to prove of lasting significance and engendered this fresh approach to the agency relationship, as Ian Pring endorses. "You've got to have a way of working together with your agency–client relationship that works in a challenging environment and we've done it ... You know, 2CV have been thought leaders for us, introducing concepts that I hadn't thought about before. TfL have challenged them with organizational problems which have been really difficult and have often said, 'Okay, well, that's brilliant, now you've got to tell me in five minutes, so I can tell somebody else, that whole elevator pitch thing'.[29]

As 2CV's lead researcher, Kat Jennings recognized that the TfL relationship was "very different compared to how most other organizations buy research and insight services. I think it pays off for TfL in terms of this long-term understanding of your customers. You know, we've got a team who know what customers were thinking and feeling five years, ten years ago, and can build and join the dots between projects."[30]

TfL and 2CV have worked together for two decades and developed a partnership mode of working. "We challenge ourselves, we challenge each other ... when things haven't gone down as well [we ask] 'What was it that didn't work, how can we change our systems, our processes?' When things do go well, 'How can we replicate that?'" This extended relationship, not unlike that with Cubic in the fares and ticketing revolution, has a commitment to transparency and improvement that keeps the partnership at the leading edge. "TfL will come to us and say, 'We've heard about this, can we integrate that into our work?' We'll push back on briefs and say, 'We're not sure if that's quite the right way' ... We know that for TfL to be a success ... what we're doing continuously needs to improve."[31]

Jennings also recognized that "we often talk about the behaviour change of customers, but, actually, you're also trying to change the habits and beliefs *within* the organization as well".[32] "How do you get people to genuinely understand and empathize with people outside the organization? Because once you are within an organization, very quickly, within the machinery and the knowledge that TfL holds ... you can understand why the ticketing system is as it is, or the system works the way it does. You forget what customers are having to battle with or experience on a day-to-day basis."[33]

> The experience, for instance, of ticketing and paying for the service was one of those where I suddenly had this blinding flash of realization that nobody watching these people complaining bitterly about the price of travel around London had ever paid for travel. They had no idea how much it cost to get from Zone 5 to Zone 1, in peak time or whatever. Their experience was a completely different one; just on that one basis alone they were immediately removed from the rest of the population.[34]

On getting to grips with his new role at TfL, Vernon Everitt found himself amazed by the siloed nature of the organization.

> There was this front end on it, which had a blue roundel and was called Transport for London, but it didn't operate internally like that at all. There were very, very strong, independent fiefdoms around the place, it felt very siloed. My job in essence was to find common cause and purpose across those siloes and gradually erode them. The internal workings of TfL could not stand in the way of delivering more for London. We put a front end on that so that it came across to the public, to politicians, to other stakeholders as an integrated and unified operation, because that's what we needed in order to secure the investment that was necessary to improve transport.[35]

Describing how this approach to the customer would enable better operational outcomes gradually persuaded the fiefdoms to come alongside Everitt's approach.

As Customers MD, Everitt was in a position to make the link between emerging research techniques and securing investment in public transport.

> It seemed to me that in order to win the argument for multiple millions of pounds of public money to keep improving the service, you also had to demonstrate to customers what we were doing for them, how we were making their life easier, why we were charging the fares that we were charging, what they were getting in

return for all of that. Although I was brought in with a communications brief ... I started to be given jobs that went beyond my job title towards more fundamental elements of our relationship with customers. It's probably also the reason why, much later, I was asked to stand in as MD London Underground. I could see the relationship between safe and reliable operations, investment, and what was necessary to improve the experience of customers.[36]

It was soon evident to Everitt that TfL was sitting on an enormous cache of insight about London, and about what could be done to make London a city in which people wanted to come and live and work. It was all there, it just wasn't visible to anyone.

> Research had been commissioned in silos and there was stuff on what did people think about the Tube, what did people think about the buses, but there was no real insight generated from it, with a view to working out what the pain points, the gain points were that we could then improve which would then feed into that investment case. So that was the revelation, when the penny dropped for me that we were sitting on top of a whole bunch of insight that could really drive and help develop the city. We hadn't really exposed or shared it.[37]

Having recognized that "this is an interesting methodology to pursue", TfL Marketing looked for a problem it could solve. Ian Pring found one.

> Our customer satisfaction scores were quite high, but our reputational scores were terrible. There's going to be all sorts of things that might be happening that could be causing those. One of the things we didn't expect was the sort of halo effect on how people feel about the Underground, caused by the Underground environment, and this was one of those customer insights which, along with the best insights, are blindingly obvious in retrospect, but are not there until you get them.[38]

An example of how this ethnographic approach might give a better insight into customer behaviours and motivation was provided by the Teenage Road Safety campaign in 2007. "We were fortunate to have a researcher at 2CV at the time who'd done a PhD on teenage graffiti and risk-taking, Nancy McDonald." This enabled a shift towards a much deeper understanding and a much deeper empathy with people, customers, teenagers. As Jennings explained:

> We looked at teenagers, we did ethnography, going out and doing trips on the road with individual teens, groups of teens, understanding their world. But also we started to incorporate behavioural science and psychology ... from a brain development and psychological perspective. What are the things that might be driving their impulses? One of the things that threw up was the role of social

and peers in risk-taking. From a cultural perspective, we knew that belonging and getting respect was for teens a big part of driving that risk-taking. We also knew that from a neuroscience perspective, teenagers have higher rewards for risk-taking behaviour, and they're more likely to pursue higher risks when the approval of their peers is at stake, which is where that campaign shifted.[39]

Teen friendships was the key emotional lever that made the Teenage Road Safety campaign hit home, "genuinely trying to see the world from the perspective of the [teenage] customer".[40] The campaign message through radio adverts and hard-hitting posters – 'Don't let your friendship die on the road' – concentrated on safer behaviour, and on the consequences of the distractions of a mobile phone and a moment's inattention. "The insights for that, which changed the advertising campaign, were so well regarded in the research and advertising industry that the research won three industry awards in one year, the insights were regarded as ground-breaking, we came at them from a different angle than you would normally do."[41] Injuries to teenagers declined in the year following the campaign.

'Going Underground' was the project that really launched this fresh approach. The Tube upgrade campaign was proving disruptive of the service and stakeholders were starting to be concerned, especially on the Jubilee line. TfL Marketing was asked to devise a campaign for the Underground investment programme in 2010 to help customers understand why the work needed to be done and what they could expect at the end of it. Regarding customers as stakeholders laid the foundations for measuring TfL's reputation model.[42]

The fact that customers wanted to be treated in exactly the same way as the media, the politicians and the government was a lightbulb moment for Pring and Jennings. At a customer focus group they had decided at the last minute to share the packs of information on Tube upgrades that had been produced for business and political stakeholders.

> Customers kind of grabbed on to them. 'This is what we want, why haven't we been given this information?' … They were just waving [the pack] around and saying, 'Why don't you give us this?' It would have shown that TfL cared. They also said, 'We are stakeholders, we pay for it.' … TfL can demonstrate that this is about a return on investment, this is about how we are using your money to fund an investment.[43]

Macleod and Pring recollect that this innovative approach took time to be accepted. "We'd done some work on buses, for example. The Buses teams simply couldn't understand why some people stop using the bus … We said, 'You've spent a long

TfL's second hard-hitting teenage road safety campaign poster from 2010

Don't let your friendship die on the road

THINK. Look out for your mates

MAYOR OF LONDON

Transport for London

time looking at quantitative data, which has given you flatline ratings, you haven't done any qualitative research and you haven't done any cultural analysis ... The elevator pitch basically is the bus is not the mode of the zeitgeist; it's old-fashioned, its customer service ethos is virtually non-existent, and people use it if they have to.' We sat and did a debrief with Vernon and senior London Bus managers, and the penny dropped."[44] The managers in Buses then became big converts to the customer-led approach, recognizing that as well as improving bus frequency and journey times, they had to improve customer service dramatically to match rising expectations. This resulted in the award-winning Hello London bus driver training programme from 2015, when all 25,000 London bus drivers participated in two days of customer service training. This was designed to help drivers understand the importance of their role in the customer experience and to provide them with the tools and skills they need to deliver excellent service.[45]

Chris Macleod recalls the period from 2007 onwards.

> A really intense period for what I call executional campaign marketing, and very good ... a lot of the themes that were developed then have been maintained – considerate travel, promoting a range of services, upgrade programmes. In 2008 we were awarded Advertiser of the Year by the ad industry and were runners-up in 2010, major achievements for a local transport authority. But we were also aware that you needed to do more to be an effective customer service organization ... With Vernon joining, we had a better representation at executive level, and someone who recognized that the ads are great but that we also needed to try and put this into some sort of strategic framework. That's when we did a lot of work around what our purpose was ... It wasn't until some years later that we launched Every Journey Matters; it didn't come until 2012, but we had been thinking about it.[46]

But the major insight that came out of it was the importance of trust ... not just practical trust – 'Will the bus come?' – but more emotional trust – 'Do these people care about me?' and 'What do you stand for?' The idea that people wanted to sense that we had a purpose, and that we had the customers' interests at heart. Which was interesting, because of course we were a public body, that's how we were set up. Customers didn't necessarily think that; in fact, quite a lot of them didn't even know that TfL was a public body, and they lumped us in with the train companies, then perceived as being run by fat cats. That was quite an eye opener. You can get too close to your own product. A lot of people thought we were a private sector operation, particularly with fares going up, which they did quite consistently under Boris, for good reason. We even ran a campaign talking about how we reinvested customers' fares in the network.[47]

As Everitt remembers,

There came a point in the first couple of years when we were able to start writing this down. The core thing was establishing a clear sense of purpose for the whole organization. Without that it was almost impossible to align our activity to best effect ... We decided that the purpose of the organization was to keep London working and growing, and to make life in the city better. That simple articulation of what we were here for unified everybody. Regardless of where you worked in the organization, you could look at that statement and see how that relates to your job. That clear rearticulation, or first articulation, of TfL's core purpose was crucial. We went through agony writing it, there were lots of workshops and engagement round the organization, but we got there.[48]

Hanging down from the purpose were a set of priorities, and an articulation of what our customers wanted. We were sitting on all this insight. I asked for that work to be reviewed, so that we could draw out the core, the eternal verities that people who use public transport networks would always want to see. From this pile of really, really crucial insight, Chris and the team constructed what we called the 'customer model', a picture of the world that is very straightforward. Our customers wanted safety and reliability, value for money, and they wanted to see progress and innovation. Those three things are almost timeless expressions of what organizations like us have to deliver ... It was also vitally important to use 'care' as a measure, given that trust in us is such an important element for our customers.[49]

TfL's customer model

To achieve the purpose, "to keep London working and growing and to make life in the city better", the 'customer model' posed the need to address five key areas to secure customer support:

Care		
Show us you care		
Know what you stand for		
Customer experience	**Value for money**	**Progress and innovation**
Run a safe and reliable service, get the basics right	Make sure we get what we pay for	Reinvest our fares to improve your service
Trust		
Get us from A to B		
Make us feel we can trust you		

"The real added value was that we came to understand that, in order to deliver things under those three big headings, people had to know who we are and what we do," confirmed Everitt.

> Trust in bigger organizations is at a premium. We've been through banking crises, political crises, when trust in government and in authority has been brought into question and challenged. We knew that TfL needed to be a trusted brand, in the same way as you would trust people from whom you buy your food. Moreover, from a technological and customer service perspective, customers were expecting us to behave in ways which were similar to the way in which the other companies that they do business with behaved – like Amazon and Google.

For Marketing's customer-led approach, the five-box model was a great tool for getting the internal message across. "Vernon really took that on because it was such an easy thing to talk about, a really good way of creating memorable insights that got around the fact that customers are very complex. The complexities in human psychology are not concepts which are very easy to get across within organizations. It was important to brand it in such a way as to say, right, okay, there's a gap [which we need to fill]."[50]

Pring maintains:

> The customer strategy is the pinnacle of what I would now call a sort of second phase of customer insight, the first one being 2004 to 2011, the next one being really kicked off by the reputation work in 2012 to now, with this emphasis on consistency, and knowing the Mayor's Transport Strategy work and the work among car drivers that we've done has made it abundantly clear to ourselves and to some senior managers that, if we're going to get anywhere near the mayor's transport aims, we've got to make public transport much, much better – and we're going to make it better than the car.[51]

Everitt believed:

> Most people were completely indifferent as to whether we were a public- or private-sector body. They just wanted to do business with us in a simple and straightforward way. Hence the development of the Oyster card, and contactless payment and open data. All of this worked, and reached a crescendo when we were able to assemble that model; starting from a clear sense of purpose, we were able to construct the intellectual model for it, and then we were able to populate, under each of those headings, things we would actually do to improve customer experience, and then start putting money alongside it in order to get that done. We integrated that approach into business planning rounds, because prior to that, it was all done in a fairly random, siloed way. But given that we could coalesce the story, we were able to

articulate in a joined-up way what we wanted to do, and then the organization could make investment decisions against that and integrate it into the business plan. That was an enormous change.[52]

I suppose it started to gain purchase when we were able to articulate the model and how that would benefit the organization, and how that in turn would benefit the mayor, and how that in turn would enable us to secure the resources to keep going. It was just visibility around the boardroom and executive table to give voice to. Ian Pring and his semiotics, they'd always been there, it just hadn't risen to the surface as a business imperative. That's what I was able to do with the team, hugely supported by Peter Hendy, who just got it from day one. He was probably already there. But I at least gave him the evidence.[53]

It was tough, because you take a few steps forward, then a few back. People still wanted to have an argument about whether the advertising should be blue or orange, because the fragmented and siloed way in which we were working as an organization gave rise to the friction of bureaucracy. People used to look at it and say, 'Well, why should I do it, I'm not measured on care, I'm measured on kilometres of the bus service or Tube reliability'. We managed to persuade them that if people got more emotional connection … that would make operations more successful. Even things like open data … were, in some people's eyes, heresy. I didn't have the evidence for that either. We just had to take a leap of faith, and fortunately Peter [Hendy] gave me the backing for that too … without his support I doubt if any of it would have happened.[54]

"You're working towards the wider objectives for the city and for the country, and that demands a really sophisticated and open outlook on the world, which I think this organization has been able to exhibit," Everitt reflected. "I think it's a great opportunity to work with others to deliver the basic things that the mayor wants for the city … we've learned how to work with start-ups and with other people seeking to get into the marketplace for transport, and the future's going to demand ever more of that."[55]

Every Journey Matters

One of the most lasting innovations of this period was the formulation of a core purpose statement for TfL every bit as persuasive as Tesco's 'Every Little Helps' (created in 1993 and still in use). 'Every Journey Matters' was part of M&C Saatchi's pitch when TfL re-tendered their advertising agency contract in 2011. Chris Macleod remembers that the phrase "sat around for a while. Vernon, who's naturally quite cautious on some things until he's sure he can make them work with the politicians and stakeholders, was sort of staring at it … We didn't do a big launch … Every

Journey Matters was seen as useful and helpful on the internal comms piece as well. That swung it, and I'd say now it's become a fixture … we always saw it as more than a slogan – it was a general summation of the purpose."[56]

The declaration has become a mantra for the organization, as much a guiding light for staff as it is a commitment to customers. "It was something we debated long and hard. Research will tell you only so much but we thought it was important … that we made a strong public statement about our relentless customer focus. It has served the organization well, becoming as familiar as 'Mind the Gap'."[57] Everitt remembers being "thoughtful about the way we did Every Journey Matters because it could have been, 'Here they go, rebranding themselves out of a problem', and I didn't want that. We didn't launch Every Journey Matters, we just let it seep out. I started putting it on stuff because we felt that it would connect with how people felt about us. The real massive leverage it gave us was internally: we said, we now have a single guiding purpose."[58]

The statement remains in use today, and has proved consistently strong as a summary of TfL's purpose – that getting people safely and efficiently from A to B is at the heart of all TfL does.

Real-time information and open data

"Through strategic digital and data partnerships with technology partnerships ranging from world leading technology companies and 17,000 developers using TfL's open data, we changed how people accessed transport information across the world."

– Rikesh Shah, TfL head of Open Innovation 2017–22[59]

As TfL became rich in passenger data harvested from Oyster and in real-time GPS data on train and bus location, in the years before 2010 there was a major internal and GLA debate, mirroring the national debate, about whether to keep, sell or share publicly created data. This resulted in the open data approach, which recognized that there was more value to be won by sharing this data hoard. "Open data was a metaphor for the wider liberalization and opening up of what we did," remembers Everitt, "and an acknowledgement that we didn't have the monopoly of wisdom on how the city and its transport system should develop."[60]

Rikesh Shah, then in TfL Marketing and Communications, recalls TfL's approach originally being inspired by the BBC sharing its programme listings, with a code to record it on your video. "The BBC were sharing all the listings data and people were publishing it on websites and other channels, and we thought 'Why can't we do that with some of our timetable data?'" In 2007 TfL started with live travel news, maps and a journey planner made available online. "We started with static data, and we found people were scraping a lot of our data and getting it wrong and then I'd get complaints. It's a statutory requirement for us to publish timetable data. Why don't we make it available in a format that's machine-readable?"[61]

At the time, many in TfL were challenged by the notion of sharing data, especially as companies were going to profit financially from using it. For years TfL had been an organization that had been seen by developers as something of a black box; as one person put it: "You pour money in at one end and you get transport out at the other, but you're not allowed to see inside it."[62]

TfL Marketing and Communications was at the centre of TfL's response to the challenge and the opportunity presented by data sharing as a key element of the organization's customer service mentality. As demands for a more open approach to data grew, a Cabinet Office report in 2009 proposed that the presumption should be in favour of information created by public bodies being available for reuse, albeit through clear and consistent copyright and licensing rules.[63] Mayor Johnson pushed for the opening up of GLA and TfL data, resulting in the creation of the London Datastore in January 2010.

The London Datastore released a wide range of live and static transport data sets from 2010, including TfL station and pier locations, live traffic cameras, Oyster ticket stop locations, cycle hire locations, bus stops and routes. At the launch, TfL's lifting of all restrictions on commercial reuse of its data was described as a huge boost for London's software developer community and SMEs. TfL's then marketing director, Chris Macleod, described it as just a beginning: "I hope that our announcement will result in new relationships between the open data community and TfL/London's Datastore. We know from international experience that the majority of smartphone apps built on public data are focused around the reuse of public transport data."[64]

This open approach was not without its hitches, not least creating a huge demand for the data. Newly introduced API[65] feeds saw an unexpectedly huge growth in demand and crashed the system. 'Live Tube map halted as TfL hit by 50-fold growth in web calls', as *The Guardian* declared.[66] This was a key moment, as over a period of years TfL began to appreciate the value of opening its data to a wide range of third parties. Its value was felt immediately in the transport portal launched for the 2012 Olympics and Paralympics, which included live bus arrivals for the first time.

To inform its digital strategy TfL had run a long-term partnership with the Massachusetts Institute of Technology (MIT) to focus on how to exploit data and create predictive systems. By 2015, TfL's chief technology officer, Shashi Verma, could reflect on the growth of smartphone usage and the success of releasing data to developers. By then a data use ecology had been created, in which about 500 developers had signed up to the TfL website and there were about 360 apps on the iOS App store using its data – the most notable being the route planning app CityMapper, which derives some 70 per cent of its data from TfL. Verma says.

"The growth of apps meant making data available online was the most efficient way to exploit it. We can put it on our website for others to use, and that offsets our expenditure."[67]

Rikesh Shah shaped and ran the team responsible for the innovative open data and digital partnerships work at TfL. Through strategic digital and data partnerships with technology partnerships, from world-leading technology companies to 17,000 developers using TfL's open data, "we changed how people accessed transport information across the world. Building on the 700 customer-facing apps powered by TfL data and used by 42 per cent of Londoners, a series of innovative world-class outputs with start-ups such as established app developers CityMapper shaped the transport features of world-leading platforms such as Twitter, Google and Apple. The value of this activity was over 130 million pounds per annum."[68]

Key to this was building and structuring relations with each tier of data users as partners. From 2014 Shah created a hierarchy of relationship managers to work at the top level with the big tech platforms, then the app providers such as CityMapper, Waze and Bus Checker, thirdly the academic institutions, and finally the hobbyists.

> We had a team that were directly facing off with them. If it was a strike day, I would say to the team, 'Right, the relationship manager for the tier one platforms, and the transport developers, let's focus on them'. They'll be in the control room, they'll be working closely with them. Eventually we had Google in our control room. I remember Pride London, and we're working closely hand-in-hand with Google. This is the power of virtual tools like these. Google were closing open roads, they were virtually closing the roads for us to manage traffic flow. People were changing their behaviour according to what Google was saying. This is the power that we have.
>
> I was worried about rat runs, but we designed algorithms and said to Waze and Google, 'We do not want you to send people down side streets. This is about creating shared value.' Google wants something out of it, they want access to an audience; we want to make sure our traffic is flowing smoothly and people are using sustainable forms of transport. TfL offers its brand, its data and its problems, and in return we get the market through these relationships to come up with innovative solutions, and the sweet spot can be found.[69]

Time for open innovation

The opening up of TfL to a wide range of data-sharing partnerships at different levels led to this approach being increasingly adopted across the organization. TfL had valued its pragmatic partnership with Cubic, which had enabled them to step together through the fares and ticketing revolution, and the horizon-scanning potential of the MIT partnership in supporting the development of contactless payment. Rikesh Shah was tasked with setting up the open innovation function in 2017, to introduce a new approach for public- and private-sector collaboration to solve problems, deliver cost savings, and to increase revenue and improve public policy outcomes to achieve London's goals.

This was a big change for TfL, from command and control to partnership. TfL could be inclined, when it came to innovation, to believe that "we have to do everything ourselves, we know best, we're different", as Shah had observed. "London is different. TfL is different. We can't trust anyone on the outside to do it for us, so we'll do it ourselves … which is very command and control."[70] Open innovation applied the lessons from the outcomes of data sharing to problem solving on a wider scale. Shah's team worked with start-ups, scale-ups, venture capitalists, investment banks, corporates, academia and not-for-profit entities to focus on how cities can drive more value by transforming the approach to procurement, outcome-led problem statements, co-development, setting a culture of controlled risk-taking and failing fast.

Shah recalls another occasion.

> The problem statement was, 'How do we get more people to walk?' I remember I sat in a meeting with Will [Norman, Cycling commissioner]. 'Rikesh, what's the solution?' And I said, 'Well, I don't know'. They said, 'What do you mean, you don't know? You're about to run an innovation challenge, and don't know what the answer is?' I said, 'That's just the point, we're going to go out to the market with a very clear problem statement, and we're going to let the market come up with the answers.' We met a company called Go Jauntly [that was] crowdsourcing walking routes. When we first worked with them, they had 5000 users in total; we gave them £20,000 and a bit of PR, they now have 450,000 users … But the point is, if we define the problem really well, we're able to work with the market completely differently, and build different relationships.[71]

The whole ecosystem of TfL's suppliers has changed since the 1970s and 1980s. Computing power is such that a one-woman band can do as much as a whole office once did. As Shah observed:

> We also have start-ups that are incredible, we have scale-ups that are incredible, we have large corporates that are looking at open innovation, we have academic spinouts, so the whole supply chain has changed. With open innovation my job was, how do we unlock value from that supply chain that can do things for us? So how can we be more vulnerable? How can we be better at sharing our problems, and spending more time on defining the problems rather than defining the solution?[72]

Open innovation is changing the way that the public sector works with the private sector. In 2018 TfL was awarded for being the best public-sector authority in Europe for open innovation.

> In the culture that we created we took badges off, we want a matrix organization. If you've got a particular problem, you'd have the HR, the engineering, the IT, everyone around the table, and we'd say, 'Are we all up for this?' ... We started to create a new way of working where we created agile teams, we looked at problem statements. We took them to Mike Brown [the TfL commissioner], who said at ExCo, 'Right, these are my 10 problem statements.' Gareth [Powell] would say the same. And suddenly, we just created a new way of saying, 'I'm stuck, can I work with the market in a different way?' and procurement is a core part of that.[73]

Fundamentally, the team helped TfL and London be ready for the future by better understanding and bringing in new technologies, process and culture, and in turn adding millions of pounds' worth of value to the organization.[74]

Leadership and cover

Innovators need the permission and cover of their leadership if they are to flourish and to ensure that other areas across a large organization are not working in the opposite direction. Vernon Everitt encouraged and supported his team, as Shah appreciated.

> 'Keep doing it. If you need any air cover, I'll give it to you.' Whether that was a tech board or a customer board, he was a brilliant advocate. That advocacy obviously came from Peter Hendy and also the GLA, and Boris was an advocate of open data and the Google work stuff that we did, he initiated that with Isabel Dedring so that a lot of those relationships came through there. Innovative partnerships got to be a fundamental pillar of our offering to the organization. People were supportive, because Vernon set the scene, he gave me the licence to operate.[75]

Everitt drove a culture appropriate to a city that now had real-time data in its hands. He would text Shah throughout the day if something had gone wrong. "I knew there was someone who was keeping an eye on whether we've got the information right or not. It was a strike day, and Vernon called me up and said, in his polite way, 'What the heck's going on? This thing is not working.' It drove a culture of having to get the data right to the 30 seconds latency, [instead of] we're working on it, we'll reprint it and get it out tomorrow. This is real time."[76]

Towards the Olympics

"The Games were a triumph for the organization and an extended 'market test' of all the new services that had been invested in – with many people trying TfL for the first time and liking what they found, the ratings of the organization jumped up and have never really gone down."

– Chris Macleod, TfL director of Customer and Revenue until 2021[77]

The London Olympics in 2012 presented TfL with its greatest challenge to date in investment, planning and delivery. Rising to meet the needs of the first Games to be accessed by public transport had already driven major infrastructure investment in and around the Olympic site in East London, on the Channel Tunnel Rail Link (HS1), the DLR and Overground, on roads and services. The challenge of bringing spectators to Stratford without reducing the capital to grinding gridlock was to spread the load across the capacity of the expanded network, managing travel demand and behaviour for weeks at a time during the Olympics and Paralympics in a way that would enable spectators, officials and competitors to travel to the Olympic Park while also supporting the daily working life of Londoners. This would be a key test for the insights and tools developed by Everitt and Macleod since 2007, and for the integration of TfL's operations across all modes and departments.

"I think Vernon would say that he was at it long before the Olympics," conceded then TfL Commissioner Peter Hendy, "but what I do think is that one of the things that the Olympics made us do was to address this issue of travel demand management in a way that actually got us really close to understanding why people do what they do, and what else we could do to persuade them to do something different."[78]

Hendy observed that the Olympics demanded also a closer working relationship between the operating arms of TfL and the planners and marketeers. "That got the operating people very close to Vernon [Everitt] ... and then they realized that this had to be – even within the organization, never mind outside it – a partnership of quite substantial dimensions."[79]

The Olympics really focused the TfL mind for Everitt. "Everyone suddenly said, 'Travel demand management, that's the thing. How do we get people to travel differently? How do we manage the roads differently?'" The work since 2007 then really came to the fore, and for Everitt that "was the thing I think that really saved us. There'd been big investment into Stratford, the Jubilee line still had reliability problems. The sense in the media was that transport might let everyone down and become a national embarrassment. We all pulled together to make sure that never happened. I don't think the Olympics would have worked as well as it did if we hadn't done all that prior work."[80]

How will your travel be affected during the Games?

27 July – 12 Aug and 29 Aug – 9 Sept

Find out which journeys will be busier and how to get around more easily at **GetAheadoftheGames.com** or follow us on Twitter **@GAOTG**

Working together:

MAYOR OF LONDON

MAR 014701.12

National Rail

Department for **Transport**

HIGHWAYS AGENCY

Transport for London

The International Olympic Committee (IOC) had consistently expressed concern that London's already stretched transport networks might not have the capacity to deliver a public transport Games at Stratford. The Evaluation Committee of the IOC visited the Olympic site in February 2005 and repeated this concern, despite being conveyed in Range Rovers onto the site through the newly completed Channel Tunnel Rail Link. But later that year, on 6 July, against the odds with Paris as favourites, the 2012 Olympic Games were awarded to London. (See Chapter 11 for the considerable part played by TfL in this achievement.)

Demonstrating TfL's commitment to deliver a London Games had attracted government investment in infrastructure (Overground, DLR) and attention to the transport demand management techniques being developed in TfL Marketing from 2008. Chris Macleod remembered that "the Games really started to focus everybody's minds quite a long way ahead. From 2009, 2010, already there was a lot of thinking even in the marketing area about what the Games work would look like, and thinking about the positioning of that and getting our suppliers lined up to deal with it. But that was also the time that we developed our customer model, we developed our purpose. We started using Every Journey Matters around the time of the Games."[81]

Chris Macleod recalls the four years "running up to the Games was when a lot of that heavy lifting was done, not because of the Games, but rather the Games were a focus. That's probably when we did very famous campaigns, because our budgets were much, much bigger then than they've ever been since. I think our budget [today] is probably a quarter, a fifth of what it was back in 2010."[82]

Integration had been on Hendy's agenda for some time, but the unmovable deadline of the Games focused the corporate mind as the planning and momentum built. Project Horizon led the line in creating a new integrated organizational structure from early 2012, sweeping away duplication and promoting joined-up thinking and planning. Chris Macleod recalls the creation of the single, centralized marketing team:

> Up until that point, there had been a resistance to the idea of TfL as a brand, and even of monitoring its reputation. LU had been monitoring its brand for about seven years up to that time … I didn't feel a burning deck of the Games coming up, but it was obviously there. I just wanted to do a reputation survey for TfL … What it showed was people didn't really know what we stood for, their experience was inconsistent, and they didn't think we were very good value for money. They thought we were quite innovative, but in terms of trust we were again very mixed. The other thing that drove that reputation piece was also about funding for the

facing: Poster from TfL's innovation travel demand management campaign for the Olympics, 2012

organization – the virtuous cycle of the better that people think us, the more likely we will be to get better funding for projects.[83]

From the external research agency's perspective, Vincent Nolan saw how the customer model swung the organization, slowly but steadily changing its whole culture.

> It was almost like a re-education of the whole organization. 'This is our reputation, this is how it works.' The thing about insight, and I think there was a lot of insight in that model, is that it makes sense to you on a gut level. You just see it and go, 'Yeah, of course, now you mention it, it's obvious. Now you've explained it to me, that's very easy to understand.' It seemed to go through the organization like a dose of salts – suddenly everybody was able to talk about it.[84]

Everitt and Macleod embarked on what they still think of as

> the world's biggest travel demand management campaign, designed to re-engineer the way London worked for the eight to ten weeks of both the Paralympics and London 2012 Games. We had to re-engineer the place, which leveraged very heavily on all of those insights that we'd got from our customer research, plus new insights. We talked about being open and more liberal with our information. We published every single schedule of what the major stations would look like in London, if people didn't change their travel behaviour during the Olympics ... We published the whole lot as a way of saying, 'Look, here's the challenge that we've got for this period. This is therefore the reason why we need you to help us, people of London and employees of London, this is why we need you to help us work differently for this period.'[85]

After the parade – the post-Olympic legacy

TfL and its predecessor LT were accustomed to being the sole authoritative source of information on the transport network and their services; if there was a problem, they knew about it first and advised on what to do in the case of disruption – where to go, which bus to take. The digital revolution and the rise of the smartphone and social media in the years before the Games had begun to offer new channels of communication, alternative voices and sources of real-time information. Customers experiencing delays or stuck outside a station would broadcast their predicament, complain at a lack of information and offer good and poor advice on what to do. TfL recognized that it had to become part of that conversation; it had to learn to use new social media channels as part of its suite of communications, to share information about delays, durations, alternatives, apologies in real time with their customers. The challenge of the Games made the growing email customer database and social media tweets and postings a key part of TfL's advance information on the impacts of Games traffic on Londoners' commute.

Olympic transport director Mark Evers recalled, "For TfL, the North Star customer metric was to ask Londoners, 'Do you think that TfL cares about its customers?' And you take those who either agree or strongly agree with that statement, and you bundle them up and report it as a percentage. We saw the best part of a double-digit shift in that prior to the Games and after." This recognition that TfL could take on perhaps the greatest logistical challenge that a city can face, and do a good job of it, gave people the confidence that "TfL knows what it's doing, and that provided us with this great platform to continue with things like travel demand management afterwards, because the trust that you build then allows you to have better conversations with your customers and to inform them about challenges that might be coming up on the network."[86]

In the years after the Games, travel demand management and tailoring information to customers on particular lines, stations or bus routes became regular practice for major public events and engineering closures. Analysing where in the customer journey the pain points were located led to a range of initiatives to promote better customer awareness and practice in the TfL frontline workforce and in its bus drivers. This was realized from 2015 with the closure of Tube ticket offices and the creation of better station entrance environments, and with Tube, bus driver and contact centre staff customer training.

The ticketing revolution started with Oyster's introduction in 2003 had by 2015 led to only four per cent of all ticket transactions being conducted in person at station ticket offices. During that year, 260 Underground ticket offices were closed and the staff transferred out from behind the security window into the ticket hall and onto the gate line, helping customers with ticket machines and general information. As part of this move, all station staff went through week-long customer service training to give them the confidence to be the friendly face at the gate line. As Evers noted, "Confidence in providing first-class customer service is a real challenge, if you've spent the previous 15 or 20 years sort of sat behind a desk with security glass in front of you."[87] They were equipped with digital tablets to access real-time information when needed. A new uniform designed by Wayne Hemingway was introduced in 2015, using new fabric technology. The uniforms were more comfortable to wear and also looked good, with flashes of colour against the dark blue fabric that made staff more easily seen by customers seeking assistance.

The removal of ticket offices was an opportunity to improve the ambience of the stations, the front doors to the Tube network. The commissioning of a new Station Design Idiom with Studio Egret West was to ensure that future station designs would build upon the network's high-quality design heritage and provide customers with welcoming, comfortable and straightforward journeys. It aimed to provide a welcoming environment, better lit, free of clutter, without graffiti and with clear customer information and signage. This had to work across an estate that included the cathedral-like stations on the Jubilee line, the heritage of the world's first Underground at Baker Street, the Leslie Green tiled bull's-blood façades, the modernism of Charles Holden's Arnos Grove and other modernist stations on the Piccadilly and Northern lines, as well as those stations that "don't exactly fill you with joy".[88] Gareth Powell, LU's director of Strategy and Service Development, said: "Our stations are important public spaces for our customers to enjoy, our staff to work in, and as a defining part of what makes London great. This Design Idiom is about ensuring we put great design at the heart of what we do, now and for the future."[89]

During 2016, TfL celebrated its long design heritage with a series of events created by the London Transport Museum under the banner of 'Transported by Design'. The centenary of Edward Johnston's commission to design the Underground typeface was marked by the typeface being tidied up, some of its original quirks restored and made fit for digital reproduction as Johnston 100.

In 2015, TfL had embarked on its most ambitious ever programme of customer service training for all London bus drivers, 'Hello London'. The customer and complaints data suggested that the customer experience on bus services needed more consistency, especially in terms of identified pain points: buses not always stopping, drivers' lack of helpfulness or acknowledgement of their customers, and the way conflict was managed, as customers sometimes had the perception that the driver had been rude or showed offensive behaviour. Customers could also be better informed about their journey by more driver announcements being made. Over two years, 25,000 drivers and garage managers from 10 companies went through an interactive and varied learning programme to share their experiences and the challenges of supporting 31 million bus journeys, with 8100 buses operating across 675 routes and 19,000 stops. Feedback from drivers and TfL's mystery shopping customer satisfaction surveys following the Hello London work demonstrated that it had an enormous benefit, "but it's also one of those things that's a bit like painting the Forth Bridge", commented Evers. "You need to keep at it, because operational roles are enormously challenging, there's so much for operational colleagues to be thinking about. There's also a reasonably high degree of churn in some of these roles, bus driving in particular."[90]

The reputation rises

The Underground had been measuring its reputation since 2000, based on the difference between those who thought the organization was on its way up or the way down. With the success of the Games and its transport, there was a sharp improvement in people's perception of the transport network seen in TfL surveys.

Everitt expected this to tail off after the Olympics, once the afterglow had gone. However, the change was maintained, and public perception of the transport network has steadily drifted up ever since. "There was a demonstrable step change in public perception of the public transport network, and the importance of the network in sustainability and the environment."[91]

"When we started tracking our reputation based on the original qualitative research, that's when it became clear that doing the Games had [brought] a huge reputational uplift," Ian Pring recalled. "The fact was that we didn't mess it up as many people thought we would. The fact that we really delivered a good service during the time had a huge uplift. What's interesting now is that the 'Waitrose prices for an Aldi service' quote is anachronistic."[92] The customer reputation model continued to inform TfL until the advent of Covid. Knowing how the customer's perceptions are informed by various elements of their experiences is an invaluable tool both for targeting and shaping communications externally with customers and for putting the customers' case internally.

The impact of Covid

"The depth of customer expertise and insights, as well as functional capabilities, enabled TfL to re-boot the business strongly as London returned to a new normal."[93]

– Chris Macleod, 2025

When Covid and the lockdown of London struck in March 2020, TfL's marketing expertise was obliged to go into reverse, exhorting Londoners to keep off the transport network, not to make unnecessary journeys, to leave space for essential workers to get to hospitals, to use masks and to stay two metres apart from other people. TfL's library of customer insights proved invaluable in managing during the pandemic and the two lockdown periods, enabling its full arsenal of communications channels to get the messages across through advertising, emails, social media, signage and staff announcements. (Chapter 15 explores in detail the impact of the pandemic on London in general and on TfL in particular.)

Recovery after the lockdowns identified a new competitor for TfL, the attraction of not travelling at all; working from home, meals from Deliveroo, box set bingeing on high-end Netflix and other content all became well-established habits during lockdown. The subsequent recovery of restaurants, theatre, live music, museums and galleries in the central zone required TfL's insight and demand management tools to be used to entice Londoners back onto public transport from exile in their homes.

In 2025, the campaign to reverse a car-led recovery to Covid, to get people back onto public transport, to take walking and cycling options, continued across all channels to be informed by the full range of research methods, from quantitative to qualitative, ethnographic and behaviour science. The numbers have still not returned to those pre-Covid highs, and it is clear that TfL is operating in a different world since the pandemic. TfL finds itself in competition with working from home. Good customer service is needed to influence whether people will use the network or choose to stay at home, jump into an Uber with three of their mates, use a Lime bike, or get Uber Eats and stay in. "For the first time, the customer is important from a TfL business case perspective," Mark Evers reflected. "We need to be investing in the quality of our customer experience to protect and to seek to grow ridership, and that brings a very different mindset to the organization."[94]

Conclusion

The shift within TfL in its attitude to and understanding of customers over the years since 2007 has been massive. The organization has moved from being primarily concerned with operational reliability to the combination of a series of customer metrics that still include reliability but also emphasize care, trust and innovation, making the transformation from being producer-led to customer-led. Customer Marketing lead Ian Pring remembers the volley of negativity that was once aimed at TfL. "Reading the *Evening Standard*, it was just a detested service virtually. We've done work in [recent] years, where people were actually quite liking it. There's been a definite shift amongst the users towards, 'Yeah, TfL are doing a good job, they're okay.' It may be qualitative, but it's been a massive shift from nothing but negative to suddenly, people going 'I know what's going on, and I feel like they are talking to me'."[95]

"We're getting customer satisfaction scores now that from my analysis 15 years ago I'd said, 'If our numbers move in such a way as this, we'll be round about 85 [percentage satisfaction level], and that is about as good as we're going to get given all sorts of constraints,' and we are now hitting 85 per cent, we're disappointed if we don't hit it."[96]

From 2012, TfL has become recognized as a benchmark customer service organization, which other public services look to for innovation and best practice. Customer attitudes of course change continuously, as Chris Macleod has noted: "The more customer-orientated we become, the more it becomes clear how much work we've got to do. We did some tremendous stuff between 2012 and the present, really important work on customer closeness, and we're bringing frontline staff closer to customers." [97]

In the post-Covid world no-one travels habitually, people choose to travel, and working from home has made commuting a more discretionary activity than before the pandemic. TfL is now competing to attract customers, to increase its market share by demonstrating its competitive advantage over other means of mobility, or

A TfL Covid poster at Westminster station reminding passengers about masks and social distancing, May 2020

even over working from home. 'Let's Do London' was a post-pandemic campaign to encourage Londoners back into the delights – cultural, hospitality, entertainment – of the central zone.

TFL's customers do not stand still and the pace at which new services become baked into the expected norm is rapid. Pring recalled doing sessions with customers just six months after the new Victoria line trains had come in [2010], and "people in the session saying, 'They've been about for ages'. TfL spends all this money on massive improvements and massive leaps forward, and six weeks later customers are like, 'Oh, well, that's just how it's always been'."[98]

The last word goes to Vernon Everitt, who led on promoting the customer mentality within TfL from 2007 to 2022. "We've always had a massive culture of consultation for the Mayor's Transport Strategy, and you have public scrutiny, we do try and listen. The thing we've done in this period is to listen a bit more – really listen to what people are saying out there, listen to what our staff are saying, about what would enable them either to move around the city more effectively, or to do a better job."[99]

10.

THE SECOND MAYOR

"Without a doubt we knew more about what he wanted than he did."

– David Brown, TfL head of Surface Transport 2006–11[1]

The 2008 mayoral election saw Boris Johnson pick up the transport reins from Ken Livingstone. After a chaotic start, Johnson's first term eventually settled to deliver significant innovations with the New Routemaster bus, contactless payment, cycle superhighways and the winding up of the Underground PPP. There was also continuity from the Livingstone years, with the steady improvement of Tube and bus services. Delivering the transport strategy for the Olympics was a huge overarching task, which drove greater integration across TfL's operations and innovation in customer insight and behaviour management. The re-election of Johnson for a second term in May 2012 was immediately followed by the remarkable high point of the 2012 London Olympics.

The Conservative candidate

"The very qualities that gave the Tories palpitations – his comic dilettante reputation – was the one that made Boris so popular with the people."

– Sonia Purnell, 2012[2]

Speaking immediately after the 2008 election count and the declaration of victory, the second London mayor, Boris Johnson, paid generous public tribute to his defeated rival, praising "the very considerable achievements of the last mayor of London" and describing Livingstone as "a very considerable public servant". Johnson went on to say: "You shaped the office of mayor. You gave it national prominence, and when London was attacked on 7 July 2005 you spoke for London." Johnson also spoke of the "courage and the sheer exuberant nerve with which you stuck it to your enemies", and expressed a desire that the new Conservative administration could "discover a way in which the mayoralty can continue to benefit from your transparent love of London".[3]

Johnson was to serve two terms as London mayor; when he stood down at the 2016 mayoral election, 52 per cent of Londoners believed he had done a 'good job' while only 29 per cent thought it a 'bad job'. His subsequent career in Parliament, and as prime minister from 2019 to 2022, undoubtedly thrived on the exposure he had garnered from being London mayor; might his mayoralty have also been a personal high point for Johnson, the time when his socially liberal instincts were most closely in line with the city that had elected him? The challenging task here is to assess the Johnson mayoralty and TfL in isolation from his subsequent political rise and fall.

For whoever contested the 2008 mayoral election, Livingstone was going to be a formidably experienced and politically wily opponent. The search for a Conservative mayoral candidate had once more not found the big name with star quality from outside politics that David Cameron as leader had sought. Remaining in the frame by early 2007 was Nick Boles, former director of right-wing think tank Policy Exchange, and he became Cameron's preferred candidate. Boles had then been obliged by illness to stand down, leaving the nomination "in a pretty desperate state" according to Daniel Moylan, later Johnson's deputy chair of TfL. "Boris was bullied into doing it … The assumption was that Boris would be a chairman-of-the-board-type mayor, and that he'd have people who do everything for him. Well, anyone who knows Boris or worked with Boris knows that chairman of the board he is not. People say Boris doesn't do detail, but he does do detail. He does a lot of detail on the stuff he's interested in."[4]

Johnson was not initially energized by the prospect of the mayoralty, despite this ambitious politician's Westminster career appearing to be on hold. When the editor of the *Evening Standard*, Veronica Wadley, made it clear that London's paper would back him, opinion polls began to suggest Livingstone was not as impregnable as he seemed; chancellor and campaign manager George Osborne had his doubts, but as nomination day approached on 16 July 2007 "it was too late for cold feet – no other viable candidate had come forward, and now they were left with someone who did not actually need their support to win the candidacy, for he had his own power base, popular support and genius for publicity".[5] Johnson, despite his own party's doubts, was the only candidate of any party remotely capable of taking on Livingstone.

His campaign was initially treated as a bit of a joke, not least because that's how the candidate appeared to take it himself, hosting *Have I Got News for You*, in his *Daily Telegraph* column and by his dishevelled appearance. "History books will not recall how laughingly people took Boris Johnson's candidature for mayor in 2008," suggested Tony Travers to this author.

"David Cameron thought Boris was the right candidate, because he thought he was going to lose," recalled Dan Ritterband, later director of marketing and comms for Johnson. "Cameron said to me, 'We just want a good fight, we don't expect you to win.' … We filmed on Primrose Hill for his launch video. He arrived and quite strangely couldn't tell our camera crew why he wanted to be mayor of London."[6] On Primrose Hill, with London laid out behind him, Johnson over several takes had difficulty in remembering to recommend his website, BackBoris.com, and appeared devoid of a manifesto for his campaign.

The Conservatives might not have rated Johnson as a winner, but they were keen for him not to be a disaster that would have reflected badly on the party's leadership. The former Conservative treasurer, Jonathan (Lord) Marland, raised funds to employ Australian election guru Lynton Crosby to lead the campaign. Crosby, workaholic and election addict, had masterminded victories for John Howard in Australia and had worked on the unsuccessful 2005 general election campaign with Marland for the Conservatives. He needed to be sure that Johnson was a serious candidate, and in turn his engagement encouraged Johnson to believe that his campaign had a chance of winning. Crosby and Marland shaped and channelled the candidate with an "unforgiving regime of discipline and preparation", extending to haircuts, new suits, regular hours at campaign HQ and media training.[7]

The Conservative candidate had the benefit of early and sustained support from the *Evening Standard*. Both Wadley and cyclist journalist Andrew Gilligan were to concoct a relentless campaign against Livingstone. "Nobody had seen journalism like the journalism Veronica Wadley and Gilligan had produced, and it went on day after day after day, and he did uncover some stuff that was not complimentary for Ken. But Ken would not change from trusting the people who worked with him."[8] Despite Gilligan winning Journalist of the Year at the British Press Awards for his relentless investigative journalism, even some of his colleagues on the *Standard* thought the paper was straying "dangerously close to becoming the Evening Boris".[9]

The Liberal Democrat candidate Brian (Lord) Paddick's team on the doorsteps of London were commonly met with the response, "I'm voting for Boris because he is a laugh".[10] Crosby ensured that this was supported by simple and emotive populist messages such as a new Routemaster, reducing youth crime and making public transport safer.

The transport agenda again formed the election headlines. The Johnson manifesto proposed not only a new Routemaster but also abolishing the western extension to the congestion charge zone and more provision for cyclists. Above all, Johnson projected himself as being a popular alternative to Livingstone. The incumbent's campaign had, by comparison, been lacklustre, hindered by third-term familiarity and with little sparkle in the face of Johnson's larger-than-life persona. It was also characterized by PR gaffes, which were eagerly exploited by the *Evening Standard*'s

campaign. TfL Commissioner Peter Hendy observed that "Boris was everything by then that Ken wasn't: he was funny, he was different, he adjusted himself to be left-leaning for a multicultural city … alive to the concerns of local people."[11] Johnson won the 2008 election by 53 per cent to Livingstone's 46 per cent of the vote in the second round. This was the first Conservative victory in a London-wide election since the 1977 GLC elections.

A majority of London voters assumed in 2008, as subsequently national voters were to do, that behind the tousle-headed vote winner there was a serious politician with a future vision waiting to step forward into London government. Crosby's discipline had brought election success, but the new administration had no such plan on arrival in office. It was only on polling day itself, Thursday 1 May, that Johnson and his advisors met to outline the key appointments that were announced on the following Saturday.[12] This ushered in several months of chaos as deputy mayors and advisors came and went, occasioned by bogus claims and previous racist comments being exposed. "Boris lacked the vison of Ken's 'cadre', and when he unexpectedly won the mayoralty he was consequently isolated and vulnerable to panicky – and arguably disastrous – appointments such as Lewis and now Parker."[13]

Handover and chaos

For TfL, this was the first transition to a new mayor and political administration; there was no template for how it should work. A change of mayor in the American model, to which the London model had originally looked, typically brings wholesale changes with political appointments to senior positions in the executive. Would Johnson eject senior executives such as Peter Hendy, who had served Livingstone? On their side, the GLA and TfL executives faced the challenge of adapting to a new style of mayoralty, to a mayor who had never managed an executive organization of any size and whose election team had contracts that concluded on election day and in the early months proved to be flaky and transient. The uncertainty was twofold. Would the executive survive, and who would form the mayor's advisory team? Would the new mayor prove to be an amusing figurehead or a visionary leader for London?

Johnson found himself being run by Conservative Central Office and the grandees from the Tory thank tanks who had shaped, funded and managed his ultimately successful campaign. Anthony Mayer was the chief executive of the GLA in 2008 and the returning officer for the mayoral election. He explains: "Transition was very, very difficult indeed because basically Boris didn't have a clue, he'd never done anything like that. He was being run by Tim Parker[14] and a clique from that Tory think tank [Policy Exchange], Lord Marland and Angus Maude. He'd won the election, which they didn't think he was going to, and arrived with this ragbag of complete nonentities, three or four of whom were sacked within weeks ... They didn't trust him at Tory Central Office. They wanted to put in Tim Parker to be the executive mayor."[15]

The chaos of this transition was in stark contrast to the advent of Livingstone and his close-knit team back in 2000. The people around Johnson, being pushed to one side and having Parker imposed upon them by Central Office, asked: "You're the mayor, why are you allowing this to happen?"[16] Anthony Mayer brought these concerns to a head.

> I took Boris, as a service to him ... took him out to lunch at Joe Allen's, and basically said, 'Look Boris, there is a conspiracy against you, they want to make you a ceremonial mayor with Tim Parker running the place'. Undeniably he took my advice and within weeks had sacked Tim Parker and did his master stroke, which was hiring Simon Milton.[17] Milton was not a well man but was a highly competent operator who basically ran the GLA for Boris without ever being a threat to him. The mayoralty was, I think, rescued by Simon Milton and then Eddie Lister, who is a player, where Boris was the front man, the jollifier, leaving his two political aides to do the business.[18]

Hendy believes that Johnson had not expected to win until just before the election.

He was able to win without a clear manifesto except to abandon the western extension of the congestion charge and not to be Ken. I think he had done no preparation about what being the mayor was really like. All this jumble of people rolled in, mostly pushed by somebody else ... Steve Norris went to see Boris, and as he came out of City Hall announced that he was going to be on the board of TfL and the LDA [London Development Agency], regardless of whether he'd agreed that with Boris, and also sent him Kulveer [Ranger] because he was one of his protégés. Boris just sort of took him on board. I think you can say that was a pretty hapless way of doing business. He never actually selected any of those people.[19]

Eventually, the appointment in June 2009 of the former leader of Westminster City Council and chair of the Local Government Association, Simon Milton, as chief of staff brought stability, alongside the TfL executive, which held and articulated a transport vision for the city based on the London Plan. Milton was highly capable, got a grip on City Hall and imposed normality. His experiences within local government had prepared him well. Tony Travers noted in his 2011 obituary: "His key role during the past three years was to oversee the process of revising the London Plan, the mayor's key document in guiding the future of the city. The outer boroughs of London were given new priority in the process. Despite continuing problems with his health, he was able to provide the Johnson regime with stability until his untimely death. He was an intelligent, calm and modest man whose influence on London government will be felt for years to come."[20]

Hendy and the TfL team were treated with mistrust by the incoming administration. "They came in incredibly suspicious, because you must be Ken's person, mustn't you, because you've got on with him. What they don't understand is the mayor comes and goes, but the mayoralty in the long-term future of London is a permanent thing. Boris later said to me once or twice, 'You're not really doing this for me, are you?' I said to him once, feeling a bit arsey about it, I said, 'No, because you'll be gone and we'll still be here and we'll still have to run the place'."[21]

Daniel Moylan, an experienced Kensington and Chelsea borough politician, appointed to the TfL board by Johnson in 2008 and deputy chair of TfL from January 2009, recognized that the new administration's instincts were to replace Hendy as commissioner.

In the course of the 2008 election, some emails had been published in which Peter had been briefing for Ken that could be regarded as political briefing ... it made the Conservatives very suspicious. There were people around Boris who wanted to get rid of Peter ... but most local government officers are capable of working with different political parties, you need to give them their chance to prove it. I wasn't in the camp at all of getting rid of Peter, I was trying to keep him. But Peter went in and on day one – I wasn't around at that stage – he simply told Boris how he was going to implement his manifesto and do everything, and put TfL at his disposal. That didn't work with some of the people around the mayor, they still wanted TfL smashed up.[22]

Hendy put effort into convincing the Johnson team that he was a loyal and trustworthy public servant. Livingstone, in his only post-election conversation with Johnson, recommended that "you should keep Peter [Hendy] and you should keep Tim [O'Toole]".[23] Against the background of the departures from the GLA and from the new administration, and also the high-profile sacking of Sir Ian Blair, the Metropolitan Police commissioner, Hendy and TfL's leadership were right to be nervous about their tenure in the untested dynamics of transition to a new mayoral administration.

As a committed public servant, and recognizing the jeopardy posed by the first change of mayor, Hendy had planned meticulously for transition. Isabel Dedring as TfL's director of policy had been responsible for compiling the TfL 'ring binder', headed by a spreadsheet of all the commitments made by the main candidates during the 2008 election campaign.

> The election is on a Thursday, the count is on a Friday, Saturday is the day the old administration has to clear out, and then Sunday is the day the new administration comes in … Peter was just straight in there. 'We've prepared this spreadsheet with all your things, and here's what we think … Here are 10 things we could announce next week, here are 10 things we can announce in the next month … we've switched gears and we're ready to go.' This showed that the organization had a fully worked-out plan, as it had for all the candidates of course.[24]

Leon Daniels, MD Surface Transport from 2011, believes that "Boris and team were impressed with the plan, they had something to work from".[25]

"Peter was brilliant at transitioning the organization," recalled David Brown, MD of Surface Transport. "We knew more about what was in Boris's manifesto and what commitments he'd made than he did himself, and without a doubt we knew more about what he wanted than he did."[26] Having two politically savvy commissioners in Kiley and Hendy ensured that the London mayoralty did not follow the American precedent of political appointees arriving with the change of mayor. Dedring suggests that "because both Bob and Peter are quite political, it avoids you having that whole need to endlessly put a political appointee in".[27]

"We were prepared to teach, train, educate, listen, do all the right things in a professional way," David Brown recalled, "but in the end we would do what the mayor wants us to do. We would advise accordingly and help set policy and deliver it. Ultimately we're a professional body doing the right things for Londoners and for whom they had voted."[28]

Nevertheless, in those early days, Hendy and the TfL team had their work cut out with the new administration. As David Brown emphasized, transport "is the biggest part of the mayor's portfolio. A lot of people in City Hall just wanted to take control of TfL and saw it as a big lumbering beast. I'm exaggerating perhaps, but Boris would have been influenced by this view … that would have been his view as an MP and as someone who has a libertarian view of the world. We needed to prove the value of the things we did, why we did them and how we could continue to deliver."[29]

David Brown noted that the difference between the Livingstone and Johnson administrations was immediately evident in 2008.

> The people around Boris were not beholden to him in the same way as Ken's people were, neither politically, ideologically, career-wise, nor socially. They all had their own different agendas … you never really knew whether it was something they wanted or whether it was what Boris wanted. The problem was sometimes that Boris didn't even know what he wanted himself, so they were reinterpreting what they thought he wanted with their own political agenda or personal agenda. That created more confusion, not less confusion."[30]

Tony Travers warned after the chaotic summer of 2008 that Johnson would have "to impose his 'settled will' from Hillingdon and Havering to London Bridge" to allay the confusion.[31]

Livingstone had been well protected by his team and had not sought to be friendly with the senior executives. By contrast, David Brown recalled,

> Boris was good fun to work for. When you went into a regular meeting with Boris, you never felt like you were going into the headmaster's office in Tom Brown's school days; you'd inevitably laugh at some point or other. You'd also inevitably have to try and get them to focus on the issues you were presenting. It was all a big sweet shop for Boris, all these amazing goodies that he could play with and things he could do and it was all quite different and exciting, certainly in the early days.[32]

Daniel Moylan believed it was important to have a commissioner "with very strong operational experience and credibility, and in Peter you had that. Now Kiley was different … brought in for a different purpose, more to do with PPP. When you have somebody like Peter, who's quietly forceful, he's not a table banger, but what he's got is confidence in his own operational mastery … basically, he knows how to run trains, he knows how to run buses, he's got the confidence that he knows how it's done. He can talk to Boris and he can also stand up and say, 'Some things you can't do, Mr Mayor, this can't be done, and [with] other things, we'll find a way'. He had the credibility of doing that."[33]

Hendy reflected:

Ken's view of the development of London in the original London Plan is still very substantially what's in the London Plan today. For all his faults he knew exactly what London should be like and how it should work … I think the difference is whether you look at it from a political angle and say, 'Well, that bloke's a philanderer and useless and an opportunist', or whether if you sit, as I did, and Mike [Brown, TfL commissioner from 2015] did, and say, 'We've got to work with this bloke, how can we get the best out of it, and what can we do?' You don't have to agree with his politics, but actually very substantially, latterly [Johnson] left us on our own to do what we thought was the right thing for London – and that's not a bad position to be in.[34]

Johnson himself acknowledges his debt to Hendy and the TfL team. "Peter was and is brilliant, and I was very lucky with him … I was under terrific pressure the whole time to find someone else … if he thought that it was right and a good thing for Londoners, he really sucked his teeth as he got his head around how he could make it happen … you could throw him almost any project, no matter how difficult, and he would get it done."[35]

Change and continuity

The initial changes made by the Johnson administration had been well trailed in the campaign. The oil deal with Venezuela was ended, mayoral newspaper *The Londoner* was dropped, and the western congestion charge zone, created in 2007, was removed at Christmas 2010, with a 3 per cent increase in traffic but no significant increase in congestion. The extension of the zone had attracted criticism when it was introduced, and had played well in Johnson's populist manifesto; "I've always believed that West Londoners never wanted the extension of the congestion charge and had it foisted upon them."[36]

Nevertheless, after he had been elected Johnson actually looked at the numbers for the western extension and discovered that by and large, as Hendy recalls:

A majority of people in the area of the extension, which by then had been in for longer because it had gone in before the election, were actually in favour, and I remember him saying to me, 'What should I do?' And I said, 'Well, you'd better get rid of it because you campaigned to get rid of it. Whether or not people say they like it now, you made such a bloody huge fuss in your election, get rid of it.' I don't think he had any option. I think my advice wasn't good in transport terms, but it was certainly good on electoral honesty.[37]

The new mayor cancelled unfunded Livingstone projects such as the Cross River Tram from Waterloo to Camden and new road crossings over the Thames, and also reduced the funding for accessibility projects. His major first-week announcement was to ban drinking on the Tube, allegedly provoked by Lynton Crosby's experience of drunken behaviour by his compatriots on the London network.[38] Meanwhile, key major projects being continued from the previous regime were given fresh impetus by the Johnson administration. The new mayor was a regular cyclist rather than a Tube user, so there was an early emphasis on cycling, realized in the cycle hire scheme and a programme for more cycle lanes and their segregation from the traffic.

On your bike – cycle hire and cycle lanes

Cycling in London had a long history before its 21st-century revival. While the boneshakers and penny farthings of the Victorian era had originally been the preserve of leisured men, the invention of the safety bicycle and pneumatic tyres popularized and democratized cycling in the 1880s, while the drop frame and absence of a crossbar opened the bicycle up to women from the 1890s. Cycling grew steadily as a means of getting to work as well as becoming a popular and egalitarian leisure pursuit.

Cycles were banned from pavements in 1888 and given the right to use the main carriageway, which was regarded as a triumph by the cycling lobby. When London's first cycle paths opened alongside the Western Avenue from Hanger Lane to Greenford in 1934, cyclists were equivocal, the paths being regarded as a threat to their hard-won right to ride on the main carriageway. After the Second World War the opportunity to integrate dedicated cycle paths into urban planning was lost. With the exception of New Towns such as Stevenage, Harlow and Milton Keynes, cycling's opposition to segregation, post-war austerity, transport budgets focused on the car and the motorway system caused London to miss the chance to develop a system of segregated cycle lanes, as became commonplace in Amsterdam and other Dutch cities.[39] Across the UK, cycle use reached its peak in 1949 and then began a long decline in the face of private car ownership and growing traffic congestion.

A modest recovery of cycling in the 1970s had encouraged the GLC under Livingstone to support the London Cycle Network in the early 1980s, a network of suggested routes, signposted through back streets, which connected borough centres across the capital and avoided main roads. These were not widely welcomed. "It is slower and more dangerous than doing the same journey on main roads because the back streets have so many junctions."[40]

In 2007 Livingstone and Commissioner Hendy were invited by the mayor of Paris, Bertrand Delanoë, to the finish of the Tour de France, the race having started three weeks earlier with the first-ever UK Grand Départ from London. Livingstone recalled seeing "Bertrand's new Vélib bike hire scheme, and I asked TfL to prepare a similar scheme for London. Jenny Jones led a TfL team to Paris to look at the details, and on 31 August 2007 the *Evening Standard* reported, "TfL officials want it up and running in three years".[41] In 2008 Livingstone announced an ambition to increase cycling in London by 400 per cent by 2025, with a budget of £400 million to include bike parking provision at rail and Tube stations and 12 Cycle Superhighways connecting outer and inner London.

In January 2008 David Brown "presented to Ken Cycle Superhighways and bike hire, and then I took virtually the same paper in July 2008 and presented them to Boris ... Ken had thought about a cycle hire but he hadn't actually commissioned it. I gave the same information to Boris, and he did commission it." Johnson had seen it as being free to London, but there was significant cost and it had proved really hard for TfL to find a sponsor.[42] Brown well remembers the day Johnson "cycled with Marcus Agius, the Barclays [first sponsors of the cycle hire scheme] chairman, round the corner of the Shell building on the South Bank, to be confronted by a massed group of press and photographers. It was a great success. Even Boris was taken aback at how much of a big deal this actually was."[43]

Brown understood the political significance of the TfL Cycle Hire scheme to the new administration, and the imperative to deliver on time.

> This was not something that I was prepared to just delegate, and wait for the explosion, it was way too important for that. With the bike hire scheme, we were introducing it a year quicker than would be normal. I went quickly from having two-monthly meetings to daily meetings as we grappled with the issues. There was, for instance, a severe flood in a factory in Mexico that was crucial for parts for another factory in Canada. This was putting the launch date in jeopardy. I remember saying, 'I don't care if you hire a jumbo jet, just get the bikes across here!' Setting up the bike hire scheme was seat of the pants, because of the timescales involved. There was certainly blood, sweat and tears on that project ... I defy anyone who's going to be taking responsibility for something like that to stay a million miles away from it ... There was no choice as far as I was concerned. There was a high risk of it not being delivered, I had to get involved. If you're going to get shot, you might as well have had a good try at getting it right.[44]

The TfL Cycle Hire scheme was launched in 2010 with 6000 bikes and 400 docking stations, which soon grew to 8000 bikes from 570 stations. The London media and public took rapidly to the alliterative 'Boris Bike'. "What we are creating is not just a cycle hire scheme, but a new form of public transport of the greenest and healthiest of kinds," enthused Johnson. "It will become the cornerstone of the cycling revolution in the capital and will, I'm sure, convert legions of people to the pleasures of pedal power."[45]

The launch of the scheme formed part of the growing effort to promote the 'active travel' agenda of public transport, walking and cycling. The first two pilot Cycle Superhighways were ready in 2010, from Barking to Tower Hill (CS3) and from

Collier's Wood to the Bank (CS7). There was some concern that these were simply blue paint and existing bus lanes, but, with cyclist deaths in the headlines, separation of lanes, better arrangements at junctions and traffic light priority were introduced as investment grew and the network spread.

Innovation – a new bus for London

"I want to introduce a 21st-century Routemaster that will once again give London an iconic bus that Londoners can be proud of … I want to see the next generation Routemaster, with conductors, running on the streets of London by the end of my first term as mayor."

– Boris Johnson, mayoral manifesto, *Getting Londoners Moving*, 2008[46]

The design and delivery of a new bus for London is the supreme example of a mayor's influence on transport. The idea of a successor to the venerable and iconic Routemaster had caught the public's eye in Johnson's campaign. This populist pledge played on Londoners' nostalgia for the 1954 Routemaster bus, with its distinct rounded body, its face, hop-on-and-hop-off facility and cheeky conductor calling

Routemaster approaching Vauxhall Bridge in 1973

David Brown, MD Surface Transport, 2006–11, later CEO Go-Ahead Group, 2011–21

out the stops. Johnson tapped into a public unease about the off-the-peg utilitarian buses, and especially the bulk and paucity of seats in the recently introduced Mercedes Citaro articulated buses. "Wouldn't it be wonderful if we could design a beautiful successor to the cyclist-killing bendy bus, a 21st-century Routemaster?" Johnson had suggested at the Conservative mayoral hustings in September 2007.[47]

Johnson presented himself to the London electorate as a man-of-the-people cyclist, denigrating the imagined dangers of the 18-metre Mercedes articulated buses which, since being first trialled on route 207 in October 2001, had been specified in TfL contracts for the limited stop Red Arrow services 507 and 521, then on some of the busiest routes on the network such as the 12, 38, 73 and 149. Articulated buses were available off the peg from Mercedes to meet the need for capacity as demand grew. Three sets of doors could load passengers more quickly than conventional double deckers. They carried 142 as opposed to 77 passengers, albeit with only 49 seats. Their downside proved to be fare evasion, roughly twice that of a double decker, which earned them the soubriquet of the 'free bus'.[48] There was no evidence of their causing more cyclists' deaths than other buses.

Transport had again been the main agenda in the third mayoral election, and now even the design of the humble bus had become a political issue. This was a challenge for TfL's busmen and their contractors, reversing the benefits of the artics' capacity and fast boarding, and potentially reintroducing a costly second crew member, the conductor, to guard the fabled open platform.

Despite an *Evening Standard* campaign for retention, questions in the House, and mayoral candidate Steve Norris pledging in the 2004 mayoral election to retain them, Routemasters last ran in regular service on 9 December 2005, on the 159 route from Marble Arch to Streatham Hill, the streets and stops packed with Christmas shoppers and TV crews. One enthusiast held up a home-made banner reminding people of Livingstone's words from 2001 – "Only some ghastly dehumanized moron would actually want to get rid of the Routemaster"[49] – while disability campaigners carried placards shouting 'Good Riddance to the Routemaster'.

Livingstone and Hendy had bought back and refurbished 49 cast-off Routemasters to increase the capacity of the bus fleet, anticipating a rising demand created by the congestion charge. The first of these, RM1933, had been recovered from working exile in Glasgow and Carlisle, returning to service on route 13 in June 2001 after being refurbished with a new Cummins Euro2 engine, Allison gearbox and retrimmed seats. In 2003 there were still nearly 600 Routemasters in service, all at least 35 years old. There was a pragmatic rationale for refurbishing vintage buses as a stop-gap measure – they cost a third of the price of a new bus, and a conductor made for quicker boarding and fewer delays than one-person operation – with new buses to be provided within the decade by a proper successor to the Routemaster.[50] By 2003 Hendy himself had asserted that making the bus fleet accessible through low-floor vehicles was now more important to TfL than retaining a historic icon.[51]

It was David Brown, as MD of Go-Ahead London from 2003 to 2006, who had introduced the Mercedes Citaro articulated buses, long in use in continental Europe, to increase capacity and shorten boarding times on busy TfL routes. "Many of them did exactly the job they were meant to do, to move large numbers of people. Boris had said that they killed cyclists. One of the first things I remember saying to Boris was, 'You can't say that, it's not factually correct.' They had never killed a cyclist, that was a fact … But the buses had become a political issue, so we had to get rid of the artics."[52]

Brown had sought to hold on to them until the very last, really because the [limited stop] Red Arrows[53] routes were ideally suited to artics, transporting large numbers of commuters from Waterloo into the City and "from a transport perspective should have been retained. The Bus team produced a film which showed the boarding time of artics as being dramatically better than a non-artic, giving quicker journeys. But I'd lost the case. I held them up as long as possible and Boris in the end said, 'No, I've made a commitment so we're going to have to get rid of them', which in my opinion was a complete waste of public money."[54]

The New Bus for London (NBfL)[55] was born out of Johnson's personal animus against artics, after a close shave in 2004 while he was cycling around an artic on Shaftesbury Avenue.[56] He struck a popular and nostalgic chord with Londoners by proposing to replace these generic European buses with a new Routemaster, a real London bus. The financial cost to bus companies such as Arriva and the leasing companies of disposing of bendy buses would be high: £15.3 million was written off by the Dawson Group alone.[57]

TfL bus executives had a design competition ready for Johnson to announce at the London Transport Museum in July 2008. The competition caught the public imagination, raised the profile of the new bus project and harvested a wide range of ideas through school, university and corporate involvement. Brown conceded that "to be honest … we were playing for time to see whether this was going to be serious and to get our brains around how we do this."[58]

"The response was incredible," recalls David Hampson-Ghani, who was taken on to manage the project. "We hadn't done much publicity – just a couple of stories in the *Evening Standard* and *Metro* – but got more than seven hundred entries from all over the world, even India, China, Singapore, the US, Hong Kong."[59] The entries ranged from retrospective to futuristic, from wacky to derivative, especially in the Imagine schools category, buses having play areas, tables and computer games. One eminently practical suggestion was that buses should have handles lower down for children to hold onto. The professional categories attracted some remarkably complete entries, both from the 'one-man-band guy in his bedroom' to major names in vehicle design. The entries were judged by a panel of senior figures from TfL and the mayor's office, and the results announced in December 2008.

The joint winners were established bus and truck designers Capoco – rounded corners with a Routemaster-style grille – and a partnership between Foster & Partners and luxury car manufacture Aston Martin. What characterized many of the entries were strong visual references to the original Routemaster, taking the mayor literally at his word, notably at the front of the bus: a radiator grille and headlights, offset driver's cab, the platform with a pole.

TfL had now grasped this as an opportunity, despite initially despairing at being committed to a return to the open rear platform. Johnson had said to Hendy, "It's a bit romantic, used to travel on them when I was a kid." Hendy was quietly "rather proud of it, because David and I had said, 'We'd better make something of this'. It was Daniel's [Moylan] idea to get a decent designer, and how right he was, it's produced something of elegant substance. What we got out of it was a three-doored bus with a lot of capacity. 'Well, that'll do'," Hendy judged.[60]

The briefing to Hampson-Ghani, who had worked on the Channel Tunnel, HS1 and TfL's Dial-a-Ride, when he was recruited to project manage the new bus initiative, conceded that this was a crazy idea. David Brown had said to him:

> What Boris wants is a modern incarnation of the Routemaster. It's all sepia tone, backward-looking, retrospective, Glory Days-type stuff, but it needs to be the best we can do ... we've got to bite the bullet, make it work for us the best that we could do which basically means whatever Boris wants, retro-looking, conductor, open rear platform, all of which we know is crazy. How could we make that future-proof, make these buses, if they ever get to the streets, to work for us?"[61]

The competition raised the media profile of the workhorse bus, the interest of glamorous design houses such as Aston Martin, and the public esteem for 'their' bus which Johnson had mined in his campaign. The NBfL had now become a serious project with a tight political deadline of May 2012, the next mayoral election. The TfL team under Hampson-Ghani worked up a tender specification for the procurement of a prototype bus to meet the mayoral timetable. "If it never happened, if in the run-up to the competition they'd lost appetite, we could pull it."[62] The tender package included all the competition entries, from whimsy to serious technical work.

The NBfL specification was innovative, being output-based on emissions and passenger numbers and mute on the power source. The team found opposition within TfL and beyond. "Pretty much everyone we spoke to in TfL said, 'You'll never be able to make this work, you'll never do this, or you've got to do it this way'," recalls Hampson-Ghani. "We were challenged all the time ... A lot of the answers that came back were, 'Because we've always done it that way'. Immediately you hear that, you know that's not going to stand up, and I could say that because I'm not from a bus industry background."[63]

Developing a specification to procure new buses was unusual for TfL, which typically procured bus services for its routes rather than the vehicles themselves. The 1950s Routemaster had been the last vehicle type to be built by London Transport to its own specification. Due to the financial haircut the operators had had over dropping the artics, it was decided early in the project that TfL would procure the new buses itself and supply them to the operators. In the event, TfL raised the capital at a lower borrowing rate and did not pay for the buses through the bus contract, which the operators would have loaded by writing off a bus within five years.[64]

As the project gained momentum, TfL's busmen soon picked up on the potential for the new bus to be technically innovative. Reducing emissions, for example, had not been part of the mayor's vision, but would be part of TfL's realization of the mayoral bus. "We also were aware back in 2008 that fuel efficiency and emissions were a big thing," recalls Hampson-Ghani, "Even back then nitrous oxide [NOx] and CO_2 were big factors … TfL was looking forward to a future-proof bus." As he explains:

> The bus has got to be able to do 200 miles a day, it's got to be on the road for 18 days, without any servicing, those parameters that you had to get from the real world, that's what operators want. It has a statutory inspection every 28 days, 56 days. We didn't specify an engine; the engineering team were aghast. 'Surely you've got to say it's a Volvo, Cummins or something?' 'No, anything you like'; we were driving the market towards electrical hybrid as a minimum. We were building the rest of the specification around outputs, not around inputs."[65]

The tender was advertised in April 2009, and six bus manufacturers, all of whom had kept their powder dry by not entering the design competition, were invited to negotiate for the contract to design and build the new bus, with a capacity of at least 87 passengers, two staircases, three doors and an open rear platform capable of being closed off. It would be a hybrid, 11 metres long, 40 per cent more fuel-efficient than a diesel bus, and 15 per cent more efficient than the current hybrids in operation. Critically, the manufacturer would need to be capable of building 600 buses over three years. By November 2009, following tender briefings, the field reduced itself to two bidders, Alexander Dennis and Wrightbus.

The tender scoring was on the basis of the technological and performance submission, as Hampson-Ghani recalled, not wanting to be swayed by imagery or a pretty picture. "Let's get the technology right, let's get the engineering right, and then we're sure to be able to wrap a design onto that." [66] Wrightbus, from Ballymena in Northern Ireland, was appointed in December 2009, judged to be technically superior, more open to suggestions than its rivals, and brave enough to flag up what was unachievable.

When presented, the Wrightbus designs were disappointing, not least to Hampson-Ghani. "At that stage it was clear that try as best they might, we weren't getting the iconic element. Boris wanted an iconic bus for London, a legacy design statement; we weren't getting it. We were getting iterations, incremental flair, but it wasn't step-change flair. I thought they weren't bad – I'm no creative designer – but they weren't 'flair' enough."[67] TfL had flagged to bidders their intention to nominate a design consultant to the project.

Hampson-Ghani and his boss, head of Buses Mike Weston, were called in to see the deputy mayor, Daniel Moylan, at Windsor House, and given the immediate impression that the proposals were all in the bin.

> 'This is never going to meet Boris's requirements, we need something better, go and speak to Thomas Heatherwick' were almost his exact words. 'They'll make this look good.' ... Mike Weston and I looked at one another. We thought, what the hell does Thomas Heatherwick know about buses? Daniel Moylan told us to go and speak to him, so we did. Thomas came into TfL's Palestra offices with his number two Stuart Wood, wide-eyed young designers with quite a reputation. There we were in Palestra, us in suits and ties, and these creative types. We said, 'What do you know about buses?' 'Nothing'. 'Have you ever designed any automotive products?' 'No!' 'What's the nearest you've ever been?' 'We did a boat once, we did a sketch for some yachts.' Then they turned it back on us. 'What do you know about creative design?' 'Not much'.[68]

Daniel Moylan, the mayor's right-hand man not only as deputy chair of TfL from 2009 but also chair of the mayor's Design Advisory Panel, was the key figure in shaping and realizing Johnson's vison for an iconic new bus. Moylan had recognized the need for fresh eyes and creative influence on the project. Heatherwick, already a world-renowned designer, was a fan of Frank Pick's London Transport design legacy and of the original Routemaster design, believing that London buses were not just pieces of industrial design, but "two-storey buildings on wheels that need to be thought of as part of the capital's architecture".[69]

The Heatherwick Studio was contracted by TfL as design consultants, much as Douglas Scott had been involved to design the exterior appearance of the original Routemaster. For Thomas Heatherwick, advances in the industrial design of public transport had left the humble bus behind. As he explained, "Bus interiors had grown increasingly chaotic, with their peculiar seating arrangements, fluorescent yellow handrails, over-bright strip lighting and protruding lumps of machinery encased in mysterious fibreglass housings." He maintained that his aim was to "recalibrate the countless compromises that had accumulated over the years to create an interior that felt as calm, as co-ordinated, as possible".[70] While his brief was the exterior and interior design, inevitably this had to be joined up with the Wrightbus design approach to chassis, power train and batteries. David Brown recalls, "Heatherwick was very good, and I realized that to have any hope of getting the ideas across and a new bus built we needed someone who was not a normal bus designer and who was admired and trusted by City Hall. It was great fun working with his team, though there were a lot of arbitration decisions that I had to make!"[71]

Wrightbus, established bus body builders who had already submitted their own design for the new bus, were now being told that the exterior was going to be designed by these hot-shot young guys who had never designed a vehicle in their short if illustrious careers. As Hampson-Ghani recalled,

> Heatherwick came back very quickly with some incredible sketches that you could see instantly – that's it, that's the sort of thing. We had no idea that it could be productionized, turned into reality. But they had this clean-sheet-of-paper vision that no one else would have had, they knew what iconic meant. They didn't know a thing about buses and how buses work. We had this period of matchmaking: we had to introduce Thomas Heatherwick and his team to the gritty world of manufacturing and bus-making in Northern Ireland.[72]

The relationship was very difficult to start with, observed Hampson-Ghani.

> Wrightbus did not like this at all … Wrights wanted the bus to be built square because it's easier to make, whereas Thomas, of course, was saying, 'Ah, these sweeping curves, just echo the curves of the NS [1920s open-staircase double decker] in the rear, this plunging windscreen just makes this beautiful elevation'. Daniels and the TfL team had to negotiate between the maker, who wanted it as simple as possible, and the designer, who wanted it to look beautiful 'because Thomas wanted to soften the box-like picture of the bus'."[73]

Hampson-Ghani recalls that his project had a tight schedule to meet.

> We'd got to go from a blank piece of paper to a working bus in less than three years; never been done before. We had to stick to the statutory requirements – you can't have a bus heavier than 11 tons on an axle, can't be longer than 12 metres. It became a fascinating exercise with robust conversations. 'That will never work!' 'But you've got to make it work.' 'Do you realize how much that will cost?' 'I don't care about how much it costs.' 'I want the windows to be flush fitting, because it looks good.' 'But that's difficult to maintain'. 'We want this shape for the rear platform.' 'That's never going to happen, you can't make that.' 'How do you think that's going to work?' 'That's your job.' There's me in the middle as project

The New Bus for London, later called the New Routemaster: interior and exterior design by Heatherwick Studio, built by Wrightbus in Ballymena, Northern Ireland

manager, playing referee between the Wrightbus engineers and the Heatherwick design studio. However, over the years, it developed into a very, very strong and collaborative relationship and was very fruitful; we all got on really well with each other.[74]

The first public outing for the design of the NBfL was a mock-up of the bus revealed to the press in November 2010, and then moved to the London Transport Museum in Covent Garden to stand alongside its predecessors. It was indeed different, both in its smooth external appearance and sweeping glazing, and the innovative mechanical engineering beneath the skin. Heatherwick and the team were conscious of the design legacy of London Transport, and early in the project had taken inspiration from the museum's collection of London buses at the Acton Depot; the new bus's swooping back has a strong nod to the curving open staircases of the first motor buses, the seats covered in moquette, the Treadmaster floor covering, a Routemaster feature, is patterned with grooves sweeping around the rear platform and in the cream and warm red colour palette. As on the first Routemaster, the handrails, poles and elegant curving rail across the top deck front window had a metallic finish.

In contrast, the interior lighting above each row of seats was by warm yellow LEDs, the bell pushes were wireless, there were two staircases, three doors and glazing that swept both down across the front and up the staircases. A semicircular rear door secured the open platform. The electric motors were driven by a 75kWh battery, charged by a 4.5-litre Cummins turbo diesel cantilevered under the rear staircase. This drive train and its management software was then at the cutting edge of diesel hybrid technology.

The open platform had from the start attracted a great deal of interest in Johnson's Routemaster reveries about hopping on and off from the back. Moylan was adamant that this was an essential feature of the brief, even though it was already an anachronism. This led to the curved door being designed for the rear platform for times when conductors were not available, let alone affordable. Brown had to work hard to convince the mayor of the need to have a door across his much-trumpeted open platform to future-proof the design. "I knew that an open-platform bus was not sustainable at any level, from the cost of additional crew or on health and safety grounds.[75] If we wanted this bus to stand the test of time it had to have a door that could be closed on the rear."[76]

The popular appeal of the return to hop-on-and-hop-off platformed buses blissfully ignored the cost of employing a conductor. Bus operators had long since opted for one-person operation – the first in London were introduced in the late 1960s – and bus design had responded with rear engines and front entrances, enabling fares to be checked by the driver. Conductors had only persisted in London up to 2005 because of the longevity of the original platformed Routemaster. In the age of the cashless bus and Oyster cards, the conductor had little to do other than guard the platform. TfL never had the money for a return to crew operation, recalled Leon Daniels. "We did the first few routes as crew and then we slipped in the route 9 with just a driver. Over time, we unwound all the crew operation back again. The biggest cost in bus operation is labour."[77] The conductors were phased out in 2016 to save money, and front-door-only boarding to reduce fare evasion was instituted from August 2019, bringing what was eventually renamed the New Routemaster (NRM) into line with other double-deck buses. From June 2015 the rear-door operation was modified to a simple sliding mechanism that only opened with the other doors.

Vanity project or iconic success?

The first prototype was unveiled at the Millbrook testing track in June 2011, with LT1 launched at Wright's Ballymena works in November 2011, driven out of the works past a nervous press and VIP group by Mayor Johnson.

The first prototype entered public service on 27 February 2012 on the 38 route from Clapton Pond to Victoria. Leaning out from the bus's open platform, Johnson was at his most ebullient. "Christmas has arrived early," he boomed, declaring that the red paint and "sinuous curves" of the vehicle would "brighten the day of all who see it humming along our great city's streets".[78] The interior had dark red walls, gold-coloured handles and a creamy ceiling. "If Farrow and Ball did public transportation it might look a bit like this. It comes as something of a surprise that the upper level doesn't have a homely AGA tucked away at the back."[79] The bus was so obviously different from the off-the-peg models. "It is not until you've taken a ride on the new Routemaster that you become fully aware of how unlovely our current fleet of buses is ... the demonstrative return of good design to the capital's infrastructure."[80]

The new bus was well received by passengers. TfL conducted face-to-face interviews with users of the new bus in June 2012, which revealed that a majority found the vehicle quieter and more comfortable than conventional buses and offered a smoother ride; 35 per cent of them "strongly liked the overall design and environment" of the bus, compared to just 11 per cent who felt that way about other types of bus.[81]

Wrightbus's Patrick Chapman was pleased with the result, on which Heatherwick had a significant influence.

> The New Routemaster is very bespoke, but it has certainly given us a great opportunity to show what can be done when you embrace design and materials and the actual feel of the interior. Many operators put their brand at the forefront of what they want the bus to say, rather than thinking about the passenger experience. The passenger's experience was always the drive behind the new Routemaster – new lighting, new materials, a more welcoming environment.[82]

When the prototypes entered service in the warm summer of 2012, however, the high interior temperatures and a lack of opening windows led to major criticism. Heatherwick had thought opening windows would distract from the smooth lines of the vehicle. Wrights convinced him and TfL that their cooling system would be adequate to keep the vehicle cool. Mike Weston recalls,

> Downstairs it probably was adequate, but upstairs it wasn't. We ended up retrofitting opening windows a year or so later. With hindsight you knew it probably wasn't going to work ... one of the challenges [was] because Thomas was friendly with Daniel [Moylan]; you have to think how much you push back, because when all that happened you went back round the loop and you got Daniel on your case ... I still maintain that despite things like the windows, without someone like Thomas pushing the boundaries of design, because the curved back end was quite difficult for the manufacturer to produce ... unless you had somebody pushing those boundaries, you would have ended up with another version of a box-type bus.[83]

The problem was understood only after the run across Salisbury Plain for the Imberbus event in August 2012 revealed that the new bus had negative pressure inside, aerodynamically sucking air in from the outside. The bus sucked in sandy dirt from the roads across the plain, up the stairs and over the engine, warming it further, to the top deck, activating the air cooling system, which pulled power from the batteries and ultimately caused the engine to run more, heating the air even more in a warming cycle. Taken with passengers' perception of cooling from a breeze when windows are open, TfL retrofitted opening windows to the fleet in response to the *Evening Standard*'s front-page headlines about the 'Roastmaster'.

Leon Daniels, MD Surface Transport from 2011, remains bullish today about the new bus:

> To those people who said the new Routemaster is ugly and is overly hot and too expensive, the answers are: it's a Heatherwick production and it is beautiful ... We had three campaigns: ventilation potentially our fault, a supplier that went into liquidation, and a quality-control problem, which is microscopic compared [to the original Routemaster] ... Here we sit, 12 years later, those 1000 vehicles are still running.[84]

Daniels had been concerned at the challenge of taking a new bus from commissioning to prototype in such a compressed period of time. "It took a good 10 to 15 years for the original Routemaster fleet to finally settle down into the icon that they now are. On that scale of progress, competition in 2008, results in 2010, Millbrook test vehicle running up some miles in 2011, deliveries of the first six by the mayoral election ... We cheated a bit. In fact, we only got three into service, but we numbered the third one LT6. It looked like there were six, but there were in fact only three."[85] Producing a new bus in a two-year time schedule from specification to prototype was a heroic act, an incredible feat.

The new bus was eventually formally dubbed the New Routemaster by Moylan, Daniels having made case for the new bus no longer being new and the absence of a workable plural (New Buses for London?). It is an obvious name, the affection for the iconic diesel, open-platform 1950s Routemaster had been played on by Johnson's election manifesto and campaign. The new bus has proved a worthy and innovative successor.

Legacy

"At the time the buses were more expensive than standard double-decker buses, £353,000 to £250,000 [for a London spec hybrid]," recalled Mike Weston, TfL director Buses, in 2024. "The bit you can't quantify is what it did in terms of raising the profile of the bus network in London."[86]

In 2025, 12 years after the New Routemaster was launched, 998 NRMs still carry passengers and decorate London streets.[87] The bus still divides opinion along the lines of it being a great bus but a costly vanity project. It was a success for the mayor who originally proposed it as a popular line in his manifesto, and a triumph for TfL who delivered the bus in just three years. "It's still known as the Boris Bus, isn't it?" Mike Weston reflected. "It met his aspiration but also came with something that was practical for the future … it's still in use."[88]

Johnson's deputy and design advocate Daniel Moylan regrets that the new bus did not fully realize its potential to be a design icon. He wanted an iconic bus running on all double-decker routes with a related single-deck design. "By the time we left office … we put in the order that would bring it up to a thousand … none have been ordered since, and instead you've got these terrible buses going around London again, looking so dowdy and miserable compared to the very grand New Bus for London."[89]

For Wrightbus, however, the new Routemaster left little legacy. The new bus was not sold outside London, despite world tours to promote it and trials in West Yorkshire and Dundee. Its hybrid technology was rapidly overtaken by developments in all-electric technology. The SRM, a variant on the NRM without the open platform and second staircase, was used on route 13 in London from 2016, and criticized by the new mayoral administration for looking like the NRM. With a trough in UK bus orders, Wrightbus went into administration in 2019, was rescued by the JCB group and has since re-established itself in a more buoyant bus market. A contract to supply 1000 zero-emission buses in London to the Go-Ahead group was announced in October 2024.

Twelve years on, the environmental challenge has pushed bus technology towards all-electric. "I used to say they were the greenest, cleanest buses in the country, which they were then, but not any more," reflects Leon Daniels on the move from hybrid to pure electric. "No noise, no vibration, no fluids, no leaks, much more refined … The New Routemaster is easily the most manoeuvrable, its steering lock is just fabulous. None of them have the looks it has and none of them are three-door. Every European city you can name, and many others, have three-door open boarding across the network on trams and on buses."[90]

There was legacy in improved standing on the world stage for UK engineering and design competence. The box-like bus has become more rounded, and windows on stairs and other features of the NRM live on, especially in terms of componentry, which contributed to some of the early work on electric buses. Leon Daniels believes it moved buses forward with much more thought being given to the interior, to passenger ambience. "I'm very sad we didn't sell to anybody else. Then again, how many original Routemasters sold anywhere else? Fifty to Newcastle, 65 to BEA, so the old Routemaster didn't do terribly well in the export market for the same reason. Nobody today would say the original Routemaster was a failure because it didn't sell elsewhere. Was it worth it? Probably it was."[91]

Remarkably, the New Routemaster has remained political. At the 2012 election Livingstone pledged to get rid of the new bus if he was elected, and when Sadiq Khan followed Johnson as mayor in 2016 he instructed TfL that the New Routemaster was not to be used on any TfL posters or imagery. In December 2016 Khan announced no further NRMs would be purchased on grounds of cost. Daniel Moylan was surprised about "how strongly the Labour Party took against it. It had no redeeming features as far as they were concerned; it was entirely a political thing."[92]

The New Routemaster, inevitably the Boris Bus, has certainly left a visible legacy of Johnson's mayoral years. Daniels suggested that

> of all the things you can do as mayor, if you commission a new Tube line, you'll be long since gone before it's open. If you try and build a bridge, it may never get built. We delivered a bus inside a mayoral term, and a thousand within two mayoral terms. On that basis, it was worth it. It shook up the manufacturers as well as making progress towards an even greener fleet ... given that it's taxpayers money, on balance, it was a great project to be involved in, it was a good thing.[93]

A mid-life refurbishment programme was undertaken from 2022 on the moquette and interiors of the new buses in response to wear and tear from 10 years on the road. Approaching its designed life of 14 years, conversion to all-electric to prolong the life of the NRM is now feasible. TfL aims to move to all-electric fleet by 2030 and is currently establishing the viability of conversion for its NRM fleet. The New Routemaster continues to stand out from the crowd and embellish the London street scene.

PPP – the final curtain

"Tube Lines will rob us blind, but they'll do a good job because he had unwavering faith in Bechtel ... Metronet will never work. It's a disaster – and you watch, they'll go bankrupt."

– Bob Kiley to Tim O'Toole, 2002[94]

The Metronet public–private partnership (PPP) had gone into administration in 2007, but the Tube Lines PPP contract remained in place for the Jubilee, Northern and Piccadilly lines. Approaching the first contract review in March 2010, Tube Lines asserted its commitment to improving performance and delivering projects on time, and cited its record to 2008 of cutting delays on the three lines by 50 per cent; the Misery line (the Northern line) was 65 per cent more reliable than in 2003, new cars had added 17 per cent to the capacity of the Jubilee line, and the Piccadilly was 70 per cent more reliable than in 2003. More than seventy stations had been upgraded, 70 out of 93 escalators refurbished, graffiti on trains 'virtually' eliminated, cleanliness improved.[95]

Tube Lines' denouement was brought about by their proposing a huge programme of weekend closures running into 2010 for the upgrade of the Jubilee line signalling. The line had been partly or fully closed every weekend through 2009, a programme due for completion originally by July which had overrun and disrupted, among others, The O2 arena and the Michael Jackson 'This Is It' comeback tour. "Tens of thousands of his fans will be caught up in weekend closures of the Jubilee line at the start of his 50-date residency in London. Senior TfL officials and bosses of O2 have held crisis talks over the closures, which threaten to leave thousands of people with major delays getting to and from the concerts. North Greenwich, on the Jubilee line, is the only Tube link to the venue. Commissioner Peter Hendy said he was 'frustrated' by the situation."[96]

Hendy, O'Toole and TfL were generally frustrated by the remaining PPP contract, being unable to address issues other than through the third-party PPP Arbiter, and by the disruption passengers were experiencing from endless works closures. The application of the vaunted private-sector approach evidently did not improve the work or offer innovation in the contracting partnership. In the summer of 2006, Metronet had not de-stressed the rails for the summer to allow for heat expansion, causing speed buckling and speed restrictions. Tube Lines' ballast train split the Piccadilly line track; uninspected track bolts had sheared, driving the rails apart and derailing the train. Underground MD O'Toole complained in 2009 that "I have still got one of the track bolts in my office and it didn't happen that night, it had been going on for weeks ... those are fundamentally awful things to have happened, and the truth is the shareholders didn't know what they were taking on. It's not a way to run a railway."[97]

"Nobody recognized that track access is not a free issue of no value; after you've had a hundred closures on the Jubilee line at weekends, it's got a huge value." Hendy recalled sitting in a meeting with Johnson to address closures with Riley Bechtel, head of the US project managers, at which Bechtel asserted, 'I'll take this railway whenever I like to do the work that I'm contracted to.' Boris then said, 'Does that include simultaneously suing the client as well as trying to do the work for him?' and Bechtel said, 'Oh yeah, yeah, I don't see anything wrong with that.' At which point it became evident even to Boris that this wasn't the way to run a railway – and it wasn't."[98]

The bold solution to this worsening situation was at the review to buy out the remaining shareholders, Bechtel and Amey (Ferrovial), bringing the PPP formally to an end. This would prove the biggest non-financial nationalization of the century, a bold move, especially for a Conservative mayoral administration. Daniel Moylan claimed the political credit: "Without boasting ... that would never have happened without me, because TfL needed to be absolutely certain. This was a very audacious thing to do … crashing the PPP, which was the big transport triumph of Boris's first term … to buy in the capital of the company in order to subvert the government's intentions … they needed political support, which I gave them."[99]

Moylan had not only to smooth the path of nationalization with the government and convince TfL he could deliver, but also to keep Johnson onside as the mayor was unsure whether it would work and needed to be reassured.

> Boris kept running out on the other side … kept coming up with other ideas which wouldn't have worked at all, like bringing Tim O'Toole back to run Tube Lines … Bringing him back to run the Tube might have been a good idea. Bringing him back to work for the enemy was Boris's great idea … Why would you bring back somebody you rated in order to work for the other side? We had to put a stop to that. Boris was operating under a deadline because Bechtel was about to start work on the Northern line, having failed to deliver the Jubilee line. Boris was understandably very, very anxious to find a way out of this. We had to work very hard to keep him on the right track, because I couldn't say, 'This will definitely work'. What I said was, 'This is the only thing that will work'.[100]

For Moylan, crashing the PPP was the biggest achievement of the first Johnson term. Reclaiming control over the Tube upgrades was a mayoral imperative: "The Jubilee line was causing us huge purgatory, and the Northern line was due to follow." The buyout of Tube Lines landed in a week when government focus was elsewhere after the 2010 general election. "For a week after that general election, they were all locked in a cupboard. The Cabinet Office tried to work out who the government was, and we signed it that week with no one to stop us. Philip Rutnam[101] was furious … the public never noticed it. We just said, 'We're going to buy them out anyway. You can't stop us, who is your secretary of state, by the way? Have you cleared this with your secretary of state?"[102]

Perhaps what was most remarkable was how long the PPPs had actually lasted. This must be put down to the government being so concerned about Livingstone and Kiley that "the system was hard wired to take away meaningful oversight", according to Tube MD Tim O'Toole, with both Metronet and Tube Lines putting in structures that made it much more in their interest to take money out of the system than to complete the job.

> I mean, money flew out so fast – at Metronet you had a lot of very good companies involved, and yet they bought into a structure that they could not even see what was going on and Metronet just became a cheque-writing business. It literally had no records of what it was spending its money on, which we learnt when we took it over … When the Arbiter came in he was overwhelmed by this chorus of 'The Mayor and TfL are up to no good and we are the private sector and we are the ones who are going to save this'.[103]

The Arbiter proved very susceptible to that story, so nothing was done for the first couple of years. For O'Toole, "It wasn't until you got into year four or five that suddenly everyone started to say 'Things are not going well here, things look like they are not being delivered, maybe we ought to get more information' – and it wasn't until the collapse of Metronet itself that information started to flow."[104]

While it cost £310 million to buy out Tube Lines, refinancing the debt repaid all the purchase costs within just two years and Tube Lines' debt of £2 billion was already on TfL's balance sheet. The end of the PPP excursion demonstrated what an expensive and cumbersome method it had been to fund the upgrade of the Tube. Meanwhile, the National Audit Office had ruled in 2006 that the PPP expenditure was not off the government's balance sheet after all. Moylan maintains that "by that stage, very few people in the Labour Party were still willing to defend the PPP, or wanted their reputation tied up with it, so it died".[105]

A cable car for London

"Welcome aboard the Emirates Air Line, we will be reaching a cruising altitude of 295 feet. Thank you and enjoy your flight."

– Announcement as cable car pod doors closed, 2012

The construction of a cable car from the Millennium Dome (now The O2 arena) on the Greenwich Peninsula across the Thames to the Royal Docks was a mayoral project, the response to a multimillion-pound Gulf sponsorship offer. TfL's MD for Planning, Michèle Dix, was asked how best to spend the offer, and among the ideas reviewed a 1998 cable car proposal for this location, the Skyway, was dusted off. Boris Johnson jumped at the idea. TfL planners could justify it as more than a tourist attraction: a stepping stone for pedestrians and cyclists across the river, resilience if the Jubilee line was down, and helping to promote development on the north bank. [106] It had to be high enough to clear cruise liners and low enough to allow take-off from London City Airport. Daniel Moylan was also clear that it had to be beautiful; he had Thomas Heatherwick in mind as designer, but the procurement process did not deliver this.

Johnson revived the project as a novel but, as he maintained, integrated part of the transport network, even though TfL thought it a distraction. TfL's original estimate was £25 million, but by the time it opened in June 2012, delivered by the London Rail DLR team a month before the Games, that sum had risen to £60 million, at the time the most expensive cable way ever built. EU funding of £8 million and sponsorship by Emirates airline offset this by £36 million over 10 years, and gave its operation the branding and allure of an airline with boarding cards; "Cabin crew, doors to manual and cross check," said Johnson on his first flight. "None of my

words can express the excitement and pleasure you are about to have. I felt like the Yuri Gagarin of the cable car." Presaging the Brexit debate, he opined that it was a better use of Brussels' money than bailing out Greek debt.[107] Arnold Schwarzenegger shared a pod with Johnson on his way to the Olympic stadium on 13 August 2012 after watching the US basketball team secure gold in the Dome. The film star and former California governor praised London's cycling provision while the mayor talked about James Bond and development opportunities as they swung across the river. Arriving at Royal Dock, Arnold Schwarzenegger "goes one way, Boris goes the other way, to the bicycle that he's been allowed to chain up nearby. The only time I've ever seen a crowd not follow Boris, but actually follow the person with him. The crowd immediately goes, 'There's Arnie!', starts to film, and Boris gets on his bike to cycle up to Stratford."[108]

Having been foisted with what had been seen as a white elephant – by 2013 only four Oyster card commuters a week were using its service – TfL doughtily promoted the cable car primarily as a visitor attraction. Temporary respite was found as part of the dedicated transport provision for the Nightingale Hospital put up during the Covid pandemic. Afterwards, when the journey was slowed down during post-Covid distancing, the cable car went viral as an ideal location for dates and proposals of marriage in the Instagram age. Suddenly it went from a service that everybody regarded as a marginal thing to having its own following. With 30- to 40-minute queues, "We started putting queue entertainers to keep the kids happy," Gareth Powell, MD Surface Transport, reflected. "We ended up with this situation where [after Covid] one of the fastest-recovering service economic stories was the cable car of all things; it got itself to six or seven in London attractions!"[109]

It was difficult to attract sponsors after the Emirates' lucrative deal of £3.6 million a year expired in 2022. Indeed, *The Guardian*'s correspondent reported that "according to a well-placed source, senior TfL executives messaged last week: 'Storm Eunice was our last hope'." Unfortunately for its critics, while the high winds tore a hole in the nearby Millennium Dome, the cable car was left unscathed.[110] Sponsorship of £420 million a year was eventually concluded with technology firm IFS, and the cable car renamed the IFS Cloud Cable Car. It remains a stand-alone ride, without integration into the TfL ticketing system even though it appears on the Tube map. It is still the only form of transport in London that needs no operating subsidy, and the slower it goes the higher is customer satisfaction. The Royal Docks is an area of significant residential development and now the home of City Hall, so perhaps Johnson's airline will become more than a monument to his mayoralty.

London's cable car, the Emirates Air Line, a TfL project delivered for the Games, offering a novelty ride and cross-river link in the transport network

11.

TO THE GAMES

"You can't have the greatest show on earth without an audience."

– TfL25 digital posters, 2025

The successful bid in 2005 to host the 2012 Olympic Games on brownfield land in the Lower Lea Valley at Stratford, East London, posed a huge multi-dimensional challenge to TfL. An already busy and overstretched transport network had been recognized as the potential weakness in London's case, and consequently attracted the mitigation of £5 billion central government investment in infrastructure. By dint of an unmissable deadline and target, transport planning for the Games drove integration across TfL operations, planning, marketing and communications. The 2012 Olympic and Paralympic Games were the biggest sporting event ever mounted in the UK, and were notable for officials, athletes and spectators successfully accessing them by public transport. The Games shifted London's transport centre of gravity significantly eastwards and were a high point for its status as a world city.

Building a coalition

"It was time for Transport for London and its partners to bring together an ambitious programme of transport investment: one that would not only help the capital produce a sporting spectacular of world-class standard but that would leave a legacy of transport improvements to benefit Londoners for years to come. The cost: £6.5 billion. The time available: seven years."

– TfL, 'The London Games in Motion', 2013, p. 11

London had hosted the Olympics on two previous occasions, both in exceptional circumstances. In 1908 the devastating eruption of Mount Vesuvius caused the Italian government to divert funding previously earmarked for a Games in Rome to Naples instead, and the Games were moved to London. Twenty-two nations and some 2000 individuals participated at the Shepherd's Bush stadium, with the first-ever opening ceremony presided over by George V. In 1939, the International

The exterior of Westminster Tube station decorated for the 1948 London Olympic Games

Olympic Committee (IOC) awarded the 1944 Games to London; in the event, they were delayed by the Second World War until 1948. Germany and Japan were excluded, while the Soviet Union excused itself. Billed as the Austerity Olympics, using existing venues and based at the 1923 Empire Stadium and Empire Pool Wembley, the first Olympics since the Nazis' 1936 Berlin Games welcomed 4104 athletes from 59 nations to a battered post-war London. The male athletes were housed in former RAF camps at West Drayton and Uxbridge and at barracks at Richmond, the women in London colleges. All were subject to food rationing, albeit to twice the normal ration for key workers in coal mines and docks.

A bid to host the Games in London had gained Ken Livingstone's support in 2001. Livingstone had professed little interest in sport before; as he said, "The only sporting event I had ever attended had been a test match at the Oval in 1972 where I'd fallen asleep over the course of a long hot afternoon."[1] "He was to Muscular Christianity what crocodiles are to vegetarianism" suggests Dave Hill.[2] In a Mansion House speech after the Games were secured, Livingstone suggested, "The only sporting event that I've ever got involved in is stabbing someone politically in the back",[3] but he was very much attracted by the potential regenerative legacy for East London of even an unsuccessful bid. "I started reading the sports pages for the first time in my life," Livingstone professed, impressed on a visit to the mayor of Athens by the three new underground lines of the Athens Metro and the tidying up of the city occasioned by the 2004 Olympics held there.[4]

It was clear that it would take an exceptional and multi-dimensional bid to secure the 2012 Games against significant rivals such as Paris, the bookmakers' favourite, bidding for the third time in a row. A strong bid demanded national backing, the unqualified support of the British Olympic Association (BOA), significant investment in infrastructure, centralized transport planning and delivery, and leadership of a high order. A sympathetic New Labour government from 1997 and the creation of the GLA and TfL in 2000 opened a window of opportunity, the stars uniquely aligning for a third London Olympiad. In a rare decade of unity, the challenge and the prize of the Olympics drew together a cross-party approach to a credible and attractive bid by London against the IOC criteria.

The London bid for the 2012 Olympic Games had followed the GLC under Horace Cutler failing to gain national support to make bid for the 1988 Games, and decades of notably unsuccessful bids, by Birmingham and Manchester, to host the 1992, 1996 and 2000 Games. Lukewarm central government support, notably from Margaret Thatcher, undermined the bidding. Britain's poor record in completing major projects, the absence of any strategic leadership for London and the mounting costs of hosting the Games had rendered London a distant Olympic prospect. For 2012 the stars would need to make an unprecedented alignment.

The striking Back the Bid moquette on a Circle line train in 2004

Olympic celebrations in Trafalgar after winning the 2012 Olympic bid

With the need of a demonstrable legacy, the BOA had settled early on the site in Stratford. The scale and complexity of a bid based in the Lower Lea Valley on a brownfield site across four London boroughs was not to be underestimated. The 500-acre (200-hectare) site had previously been home for workers in the London Docks, and included a gas works, a concrete batching plant, a factory manufacturing artificial manure, a car breaker's yard, railway sidings, a power station and three bus depots. The area still had several thousand people working there, in addition to residents, student accommodation and two travellers' sites. Redeveloping the entire site would require heroic levels of demolition, soil and groundwater remediation and an area the size of 10 football pitches of Japanese knotweed to be cleared, before construction could begin on the stadium, eight other venues, landscaping and a new bus garage at West Ham.[5]

The multiple demands of the site required a rare and prolonged coalition between public and private enterprises, national, regional and local government, parks, water, power and transport agencies, its complexity challenged by the IOC's remorseless timetable. Even with the national, mayoral and local authority political stars being dragged into alignment, the challenge of piecing together the Stratford site, managing the rich and conflicting cocktail of tenants and property owners, allotments, waterways and electricity pylons, controlling the costs of site mitigation and the building of eye-catching stadium sports venues, reconciled with the need to score higher than any previous Games in terms of community and sporting legacy, was a wicked challenge that only an immovable deadline and political unanimity could hope to drive to a successful resolution.[6] The often-conflicting parties uniquely coalesced thanks to the strategic potential and convening power of an elected mayor and his transport executive.[7]

Building a bid

Transport was a key factor in the bid for an Olympics accessed by public transport. In the bid document submitted to the IOC in 2003, it was conceded that transport in London at that time was not up to coping with an Olympic Games. This leveraged significant government funding from a sceptical Chancellor Gordon Brown.

Hugh Sumner had worked for London Underground across senior operational roles since 1985, but was 'resting' after setting up the Sub-Surface PPP contract, signed in 2003. Sumner was invited by Jay Walder into TfL to do "a bit of transport planning" after the failure of a previous appointment. As director of Transport for the Olympic Delivery Authority (ODA) Sumner immediately found himself in the midst of the largest and most complex urban planning operation ever undertaken in London:

> I wandered along ... and was told that I was expected to put a team together, live off the land, bit of money from TfL, bit of money from the London Development Agency [LDA] and we were going to try and win the bid. Within the space of about twenty-four hours, I saw Barbara Cassani [who was chairing the bid], who said basically, 'We're going to expect you to do all transport anywhere in the UK. So animal, vegetable, mineral, by air, land or sea, it's down to you lot and by the way, if you cock this up and lose the bid, which is what you are likely to do, I'll haunt you forever!'[8]

The initial prequalification submission was made in July 2003, and the IOC's technical evaluation then reduced nine cities to five by May 2004: Madrid, Moscow, New York, Paris – and London.

When Sebastian Coe was appointed as chair of the London Organizing Committee of the Olympic and Paralympic Games (LOCOG) in May 2004, London was still regarded as lagging far behind Paris. Coe's credibility as an Olympian, central government investment, and TfL's work on the Overground, DLR, Stratford station, transport planning and demand management, were all needed to close the gap.

"Against all the odds, we got through," Sumner recollected, "cut down to five cities from the original nine. Our key rivals at that stage were Paris, who everyone thought would be a shoo-in for the 2012 Games ... We learnt a lot from Athens and the Athenians. We'd been there a couple of times to get inside information about how to approach the bid."[9] The final bid was submitted in November 2004, and the IOC undertook evaluation visits to the five candidate cities in February and March 2005.

Sumner and the Olympic Transport team worked through what the volumes would be, whether the transport systems could cope, doing the big modelling, calculating how much adjustment to background demand would be needed, trying to get as much detail as possible established in advance of the imminent IOC Evaluation Commission visit to London. The IOC was given a clear programme of works about transport: how it would operate, where the bases would be, what park and ride sites there were, how they would make the news work. Sumner explains what happened, six months out from decision day:

> Our pitch to the IOC for the Evaluation Commission visit was, 'We've done this amount of work already. If you wanted to run it in twelve months' time we'd give it a good shot and we'd be there, or thereabouts. Now, that's a slight exaggeration because it's probably more like two years. But we tried to get this so far advanced, we've modelled this day by day during the Games. Here's how the load risk capacity works, this is what happens if one of the Underground lines fails. It's inspiring confidence in the bid team itself and also in the IOC.[10]

In February 2005 the four-day visit by 12 members of the IOC took place, greeted with a fanfare by the London Philharmonic Orchestra at Stratford station. They viewed the site from a 22-floor viewing deck, with stadium, velodrome and other sites marked by coloured blimps, and then visited all the venues, had all the presentations. Sumner and his team planned and timed the delegates' journey patterns around London:

> We pulled out all the stops. They split into three groups. One of the groups we blasted through the High Speed 1 tunnels, the running tunnels, we blagged blacked-out Range Rovers, stuck the delegates in the vehicles, put on videos for them to show how wonderful transport was. Another group we shut on a cab ride on the Jubilee line train, which was the one that happened to be decaled up in London 2012 bid livery ... all their vehicles had lead vehicles and trail vehicles, had a couple of helicopters up in the air all the time, had satellite tracking on everything, and we played with all the traffic lights. We did whatever it took to get them to travel at the speed of light – and it worked. Very discreetly, no blue lights or anything like that, we proved that transport could work.[11]

The IOC delegates met PM Tony Blair at 10 Downing Street and attended a banquet with the Queen at Buckingham Palace.

Hugh Sumner, ODA transport director *(centre)* with mayor Livingstone *(left)* and
IOC delegates at Stratford station during the evaluation visit in February 2005

Understanding the IOC's priorities, getting inside their heads, was the key
for Sumner and his team. The IOC needed to feel confident that the host city
understood their needs and was willing to do whatever it took to meet them.
Sumner continues:

> Without transport, the Games goes bong. If an athlete doesn't turn up – and
> it has happened at previous Games – they don't compete. If half the triathletes
> aren't there when the gun goes and the triathlon starts, it's going to be a bit
> embarrassing. Similarly, the technical officials, the people who officiate the event,
> who start the events, and those judges, if they're not there, you can't hold it. Nor
> can you if your broadcasters aren't there – you're talking a huge global audience,
> so your TV is absolutely critical. In fact, you can run a Games, actually, without
> spectators, they just create the atmosphere. But fundamental are, have you got
> the athletes, have you got the technical officials, have you got the broadcasters?
> If you've got some snappers, that's good, and if you've got some written media
> as well, that's good, and it'd be really nice if you had some spectators as well. That
> hierarchy of need is very clear.[12]

In 2006, Sebastian Coe wrote, "Visitors converging on the Olympic Park for the
opening ceremony by public transport, cycling or walking will enter into a new
landscape of green parkland and clean waterways providing a lush backdrop for

modern, energy-efficient sports stadia just six kilometres [less than four miles] from London. An 80,000-seat stadium, an Aquatics Centre, four Multi-Sport Arenas, a Velodrome, Hockey Centre, training, catering, broadcasting and security facilities. Next door, 4000 units to accommodate 17,000 athletes and officials, transformed from 500 acres on urban wasteland."[13] For everyone to converge on the site, transport infrastructure had to be upgraded and a plan developed to integrate and manage spectators and commuters alike.

Two days in July 2005

On 6 July 2005 the IOC met in Singapore to receive the final bid presentations, and announced its choice of the host city for the Olympic Games of 2012. A hushed crowd in Trafalgar Square heard Jacques Rogge, head of the IOC, announce from Singapore that "the Games of the thirtieth Olympiad are awarded [slight pause] to the city of London." The bid team in Singapore – Coe, Livingstone and Tessa Jowell – and the British Olympians and crowds around Nelson's Column jumped for joy and hugged each other tearfully. The news was relayed simultaneously, and Parisians slumped in disbelief: London, 54 votes; Paris, 50 votes. Livingstone declared it "one of the best days London has ever had ... and it is one of the proudest days for Britain and for British sport".[14] Commuters headed for home feeling good about their city and its future, with a copy of the *Evening Standard* under their arm, its headline proclaiming 'We've Won!'

As the news from Singapore was sinking in, and Trafalgar Square was being cleared of the remains of the Olympics party the following morning, that euphoria was deflated as three terrorist bombs exploded on the Tube and one on a bus, killing 52 passengers and wounding more than seven hundred, some of whom suffered life-changing injuries. These two days in July 2005 provided TfL with its two greatest tests to date: the opportunity to plan and mount the most complex integrated transport strategy and operation ever attempted in the capital, and a monstrous terrorist attack on the London network. This was London's worst terrorist incident and a major test for TfL and London's resilience; if it had taken place a few days earlier it would surely have scuppered the bid. (See Chapter 5 for details of the 7/7 terrorist bombings.)

Planning and building

The draft ODA Transport Plan of October 2006 for the London 2012 Olympic and Paralympic Games stated: "For spectators we want London 2012 to be remembered as a public transport Games. We plan for all spectators to travel to venues by public transport, park and ride or by walking or cycling.[15]

View over Stratford station towards the proposed Olympic site, February 2005

Hugh Sumner recalled the period after the IOC announcement.

> There is elation, but sheer terror at the same time. To most people on the outside
> of the Games, you just see great TV images, and you have no idea what this
> takes. If you spend enough time with people who do this thing permanently, you
> understand the enormity of what you're letting yourself in for. I mean, they say
> there is nothing bigger than this in peacetime that any nation ever faces in terms
> of mobilization. You're moving four times the number of people and materials
> they did in the entire second half of 1944, but you're doing it in 16 days. You get
> it wrong, you will destroy the city's reputation. I mean, Atlanta is only known for
> two things: one, it is the home of Coca-Cola, and two, they made a pig's ear of the
> Games – and it was Games transportation that made the headlines.[16]

The mixed reviews of Atlanta in 1996 had convinced the IOC never again to be
hosted by a city without significant public funding commitment to underwrite
commercial interests, and convincing evidence of commitments to good
communications systems, transport and traffic management and to the overall
financial package.[17]

The ODA's chief executive, David Higgins, said: "Historically, the Lower Lea Valley
has suffered from poor transport links and this has been a major obstacle to its
redevelopment. These transport improvements for the Games will help transform
the Lower Lea Valley to one of the best-connected areas in the capital, bringing
economic and social benefits that go far beyond 2012, and far beyond sport. Early
consultation with a wide range of stakeholders will encourage, challenge and
improve our plans. We are determined that London 2012 will leave a legacy to be
proud of. The draft plan will be out to consultation until February 2007, with a full
plan published in summer 2007."[18]

The plan outlined that "one train every 15 seconds will serve the park, with the
rail system carrying 240,000 people per hour, an increase of 100,000 on the usual
daily rate. The Javelin rail service, the bullet train at the heart of the rail plans, will
speed spectators from Central London to Stratford International Station in the
Olympic Park in just seven minutes; London will use an Olympic Route Network
of major roads to transport the athletes and other members of the 'Olympic
Family' to ensure that they get to their venues on time; Transport plans will be
sustainable, minimising environmental impacts wherever possible. The on-going
renewal of the bus, train and taxi fleets will ensure that London's transport is at the
forefront of low emissions technology and walking and cycling will be encouraged
– with new cycle lanes and walking routes connecting the park into the wider
London networks."[19]

A huge programme of rail infrastructure construction in East London had been
under way for years, galvanized by the prospect of the Games, as Sumner recalls.

In total about £6.5 billions'-worth of infrastructure was being completed or needed to be completed to support the actual Games operation itself, including High Speed 1. We deliberately timed various bits of announcement during the bid process. It happened to be that while the IOC were in town we announced we were going to buy the new high-speed trains for the domestic high-speed rail service. You then announce another time that we're extending the Docklands Light Railway to Woolwich Arsenal. All these things that are necessary for the bid, but necessary too for the future of the UK and of London, were sequenced deliberately to intimate that we're going to deliver.[20]

The Underground benefited from new signalling technology upgrading the Central, Jubilee and Victoria lines to increase their capacity by speeding journeys for more frequent services. Extensions to the DLR to Woolwich and Stratford International, four new stations and longer trains added 50 percent to its capacity and connected it to five Olympic venues. On the Jubilee line, automatic train controls[21] and more trains gave an extra 33 per cent or 12,500 passengers in the peak hours, while new trains from 2009 on the Victoria line were capable of running 33 trains per hour.

Overground services on the East London and North London lines were refurbished and extended, with upgrades also to national rail lines via Stratford into Liverpool Street. The new transport hub next to the Olympic Park at Stratford 's extended station brought together two Tube lines, the DLR, Overground, HS1 from the Channel Tunnel, the new Javelin service offering a seven-minute service to Stratford International station from St Pancras. The jewel of the upgrade programme gave a facelift to King's Cross St Pancras, full access at Green Park and a new bus terminus at London Bridge. On the streets, hybrid buses were cleaner and more efficient, there were more cycle lanes, and the TfL Cycle Hire scheme's network was extended to the Olympic Stadium.

The Olympic Road Network (ORN) was planned and installed to ensure that all athletes, officials and media teams could reach their events on time. Across the 109-mile ORN, temporary markings, variable message boards and signage were introduced over four nights from 1 July, with 1300 traffic lights resequenced. Traffic levels within inner London fell by 16 per cent during the Games. The bid had envisaged that 80 per cent of the athletes would be within 20 minutes' travel time of their events. This was a tough target for the TfL planners to deliver, as David Brown, TfL MD Surface Transport to 2011, reflects:

It was all about achieving certain journey times, predominantly from hotels in the West End to Stratford and the Olympic Stadium. The times had been agreed with the IOC, formed part of our contract, and therefore could not be changed, and they were totally unrealistic and that was it. We were given 42 minutes for vehicles to get from Heathrow to Stratford. We thought this was completely mad, and realized it would involve potentially unacceptable and draconian measures. Not only did it involve looking into the granularity of every single junction and, for instance, banning vehicle access to the ORN, we realized that we needed to be more strategic and look at consolidation centres and reducing the number of deliveries to offices and shops. When we looked at deliveries even to our own building, Palestra, and the repetition and range of deliveries, we realized this was a herculean task. Although this required a lot of co-operation and co-ordination, the reduction in deliveries could have been another legacy of the Games."[22]

Fit for Future staff briefings to transport staff, led in person by Mike Brown (MD Underground and Rail) and Leon Daniels (MD Surface Transport since 2011), engaged some 19,000 TfL colleagues in a briefing and bus tour of the Stratford construction site in the months leading up to the Games. An uneasy and fractious collaboration existed between the three developers of the Stratford City site, the key to public access to the site from a new Stratford station ticket hall and bridge over the road and railway. There were difficulties with Westfield even up to 48 hours before the opening ceremony.

The depth of planning and scenario testing, simulations, tabletop exercises and 'London Prepares' events at the stadium ensured that London was as ready as could be for the arrival of 300,000 international visitors and 5.5 million day visitors. In early 2012, Leon Daniels maintained that his biggest challenge in the run-up to the Olympics was:

> to make the people who were planning it, stop planning it, because there was a danger they would still be planning it now ... Actually, I had to prise their fingers off the plans to let the people who were going to deliver it, deliver it. I can remember in May 2012, I said, 'Please, it's May, we've only got three months to go, we've got to rehearse, do simulations and desktop exercises. Whatever state it's in now, just leave it, we'll fill in the gaps around it.' They got so close to it over such a long period of time, they almost couldn't bear the thought of it actually having to be enacted.[23]

For TfL's director of Games Transport, Mark Evers, it became increasingly clear, 18 months or so out from the Games, that the people that were going to have to manage the transport network through the Games (largely in TfL) were a different set of people from the people who were planning for it. "Peter [Hendy] recognized that ultimately, as Transport commissioner, the buck was going to stop with him, and he was going to be very much on the hook for this."[24] David Brown remembers Hendy saying to the ODA, "We move this number of people on a regular basis in London when events coincide; you need to trust us to deliver and get out of our way."[25]

The overnight installation of the Olympic Road Network lanes was just one demanding component in the complexity of the Olympic transport strategy

The governance of the Games transport was given great strength by the collaboration between at least twelve different agencies involved in its delivery: TfL, Network Rail, the train operating companies, Heathrow, the DfT, the police services, NHS, LOCOG, the ODA. Evers recalled, "There was a huge community that came together ... Peter grasped the figurehead role of being the face of Transport for London, even of those parts of the transport solution that were beyond his direct control ... Peter had a real personal drive and accountability; nobody pushed him into the role. He saw the requirement and stepped forward into it, and did a fantastic job."[26]

"I thought, my neck is on the line," said Hendy, as he took over the chair of the Olympic Transport Board. To make the Olympics delivery work he had to get the right people up and down the organization working in the same place, and create the atmosphere where they could work together. "We got them all together and gave them stirring speeches … you have got to get on with each other. There was a huge amount of meticulous planning, but that is not how you deliver Stratford station every day during the Games. By the time you get there everybody knows what to do and have got all the numbers in their phones to make things happen when they are not … but I am convinced that it was the collaboration that made the Olympic transport work." The remaining leadership job was for him to take all the major political and media stuff on the chin. "By the time I got there I was well fired up because that is what you have to do."[27]

Hendy had suggested that Mike Brown should return from Heathrow to head the Underground through this challenge. Brown recalls that this move was secured by a phone call from Mayor Johnson:

> This was the thing that sold it to me … 'Mike, I need you back to fix the Tube for the Olympics. You don't want to be lying on your deathbed – and Mike, I hope it's a long time away, but you don't want to be lying on your deathbed thinking, "I could have been the guy that came back and fixed the Tube for the best Olympics ever".' I thought, oh, what a **** you are, Boris, because that's exactly the thing that got under my skin. I wanted there not to be a single headline about my Tube, which I still felt was my Tube, letting down London, letting down the Olympics. I came back and got stuck into that … real detailed granular focus on reliability.[28]

Get Ahead of the Games

"A massive trial of your product."

– Chris Macleod, TfL Customer director[29]

The Games were a test not only of the freshly built infrastructure but also of innovative techniques of demand management on the network, for spectators, local businesses and Londoners. TfL pledged to influence travel behaviour like never before by developing the tools to establish a 'marketing relationship' with each customer. 'Get Ahead of the Games' was an integrated communications and marketing campaign to influence the travel behaviours of Londoners, encouraging them to change their normal habits and free up space for the Games crowds. This was to be a public transport Olympics, with every Games ticket having a free travelcard to access and return from venues.

TfL began talking to businesses from 2010 about the impact of the Games, at conferences, through the trade press and on radio. From January 2012 in the run-up to the event, the Get Ahead of the Games campaign warned Londoners of the need to prepare and for the likely impact of the Games on their travel habits. The campaign analysed customer insight and Oyster data to make predictions station by station, route by route, through posters, newspaper adverts, radio adverts, social media and digital to reduce and shift peak demand on the network to free up capacity for traffic to the Games. Try a different line, avoid the hotspots, work from home or try cycling were among the poster slogans encouraging people to adapt their regular routes to work. Some 60,000 emails were sent out during the Games as updates and tailored information to customers. An accessible network was also pledged for all venues to enable everyone with any form of restricted mobility to get to the Games.

Vernon Everitt, MD for Customers, Communication and Technology at TfL recalled:

> Very, very rarely do you get a moment in time when everybody's looking at you. From the moment that London won the Olympic Games, there was talk about how could we possibly move everybody around. The transport system was not at its most robust at the point that we won it. Part of the deal for getting the Olympics was that there was going to be billions of pounds of investment to make sure that London was shown at its best with a safe and efficient transport system … We knew that 2012 was going to be a defining moment for the organization. It was one of the most extraordinary things, as we progressed towards the Olympic Games, everything cleared down and the eyes of the world were on us as the transport authority. We were running the organization in a different way. Peter [Hendy] decided to separate out the Olympics from the day-to-day operations, which was an extraordinarily wise thing to do. TfL took ownership of everything, even though we didn't have direct accountability for absolutely everything to do with the Olympics. He took the view that we were going to be held responsible for it anyway, so you might as well own the lot.[30]

For TfL Customer director Chris Macleod, the Games were:

> One of those things that marketing people dream about; it was a massive trial of your product. There were a lot of people who didn't use public transport at all, or used it very seldom, who now needed to use it, actually had to use it or got free tickets, or it was simply the best thing to do. Their experience was very good, particularly of the Overground and some of the Tube lines. It was almost like a forced sampling exercise.[31]

TfL worked hard with London businesses to promote 'business as unusual', to reduce demand on what would be a stretched transport network: working from home, varying leave, changing hours and opening times, adapting delivery schedules. Oyster data had contributed a clear view of where demand fell at key stations and interchanges, so local posters suggested travelling before or after the anticipated peak of demand and avoiding Games stations such as Bank and London Bridge for equestrian events in Greenwich Park, Wembley for Westminster for the Horse Guards and events such as the marathon on the Mall, and Stratford for the stadium and athletes' village. The information provided to Londoners and to London's businesses describing the anticipated levels of disruption or road change that was likely on any given day during the Olympic and Paralympic period was unprecedented. "The quality and the richness of the data that you could provide through online tools," suggested Evers, "then the way that you could then disseminate that information very quickly to customers and businesses, was something that we hadn't seen previously."[32]

The Olympic flame touched down in Cornwall on 18 May 2012. London at that moment became the host city, its Transport Co-ordination Centre at Southwark opened 24 hours a day until the end of the Paralympics on 14 September. This was the nerve centre for managing the Olympics with, for the first time, 15 transport agencies in the room, keeping London on the move and the athletes, VIPs, officials and spectators on time.

To the Games, July 2012

"People will remember the Games because of the outstanding sporting performances they witnessed. Yet equally memorable was the spirit of friendliness and helpfulness shown both by our volunteers and regular staff: our travel ambassadors; incident customer service assistants; station teams; and Tube, train and bus drivers. Together they represented not just the best of Transport for London, but the best of London as a world city."

– Commissioner Peter Hendy, 2013[33]

"With public transport this good you don't need cars."

– Kobe Bryant, NBA basketball star and USA Olympic gold medallist

A distinctive and engaging feature of the Games were the volunteer travel ambassadors. These 'Games makers' were trained, and equipped with magenta tabards, big foam pointing hands and digital tablets for up-to-date information.

The Olympic Flame is welcomed by DLR director Jonathan Fox and taken by Aneurin Wood on the train as part of the Paralympic torch relay in August 2012

Their direction of the crowds, their endless enthusiastic cheerfulness, made them an upbeat and personable feature of the 'last mile' of Games visitors' experiences. The final piece in the jigsaw was the positioning of 215,000 distinctive magenta signs to guide thousands of spectators from stations to the 12 sporting venues across the city. "When we got to the Games, there was a sea of magenta," recalled Mark Evers."We had a workforce that had been engaged in the importance of the Games to London, felt really part of it and had a uniform they could be proud of." [34]

In its 2012 end-of-year review, the British magazine Q reflected thus:

> It could all have been so different. As the London 2012 Summer Olympics approached, the tide of scepticism seemed almost irreversible. There was the heavy-handed sponsorship, the draconian security, the ticketing problems, the ballooning budget, and the lurking fear that the opening ceremony might be, in director Danny Boyle's pungent description, 'shite'. It took less than four hours on the night of Friday 27 July to turn the whole country around. Not only was the ceremony demonstrably *not* shite, it was the most surprising, moving, spectacular cultural event this country had ever seen ... modern Britain, in all its berserk, multi-faceted glory. [35]

Right up to 48 hours before the Games, the owners of Westfield Shopping Centre, the route to the Olympic Park from the station, were being difficult and negotiating hard. [36]

Volunteer Games Makers offered enthusiastic welcome and clear directions to the Olympic crowds

"A lot of people were predicting that it was going to be a disaster, and of course those predictions of disaster were really quite helpful because expectations were so poor that they weren't hard to beat," mused Chris Macleod.[37]

By the time the Games arrived, TfL had lifted its own game, drawing on expertise from across TfL and lessons gathered from previous host cities. "We had thought in a meticulous way about how we wanted to move people through the network, and not just people who were making their way to an event but also how you were going to keep the rest of London moving, and ensure that people were able to get on with their lives as well," reflected Mark Evers. "It all came together, alongside a very buoyant and positive atmosphere within London at the time, to create this really magical moment."[38]

The opening ceremony took place at 9 p.m. on the evening of Friday 27 July in front of 62,000 people in the Olympic Stadium. Danny Boyle's 'Isles of Wonder' production was an immediate success – Brunel, the Industrial Revolution, dancing NHS workers, praised as 'a love letter to Britain' and broadcast around the world to an estimated 900 million viewers. In China, state commentators galloped their audience through an explanation of the show from the Industrial Revolution to Mary Poppins, Harry Potter, Sir Paul McCartney and James Bond, "but appeared to be stunned to near silence by the parachuting Queen".[39] As the events got under way, Monday 30 July was a normal working day for Londoners, yet central London seemed quieter than on a Sunday; the Get Ahead of the Games campaign had worked.

Leon Daniels recalls:

The government didn't think we'd done enough to suppress demand. Right up to the day of the opening ceremony they'd say, 'You haven't done enough, this is going to be a crisis' because we have to get rid of 30 per cent of the demand to create the space for the Olympics to move. On the Friday they were saying, 'This is terrible, your name's all over this.' On the Monday we might famously remember there were loads of empty seats in the Olympic Stadium and there was tumbleweed blowing down Regent Street. They rang and said, 'You've completely overdone this, the place is a ghost town.' One of the things that none of the previous host cities ever told us was that actually in the first few days of the Olympics, when all the dull heats in the spurious sports are going on, most of the main people are shopping and sightseeing, going to Stonehenge and to Windsor Castle. Only when the medals start to roll in, you move into the higher-level heats and some of the stars compete and some of the records start to get broken, does it start to warm up, which is broadly Thursday of week one. It was fuelled – I remember the press doing this – by all those pictures of empty seats in the stadium. Because the IOC is such a corrupt organization, there are just thousands of seats given out to people who never get to use them on those early days.[40]

The mayor had been deployed to record announcements on the Tube and bus network. "You'd be standing on the platform," Daniels recalls, "and he'd say, 'Hello, it's the mayor here. It's going be awfully busy over the next few weeks. So look, do us a bit of a favour, change your plans, reroute, read, follow the website.' Anyway, we were sat in the mayor's office and Mike [Brown] was doing his report from LU. One of the things he had to report was an increase in suicides. Boris said, 'Oh my god, it's not my announcements, is it?' So you're stood on the platform, and hear the mayor's voice, and decide to throw yourself in front of a train."[41]

Endless planning had been gone through, but would it be all right on the night? Mike Brown had walked every single Olympic venue, every single pathway from where people would get off Overground trains or the Tube or the DLR: "all the last-mile stuff, got involved with all the granular detail of what was going on everywhere, all the contingency plans, all the numbers of spare drivers, all the numbers of station staff". Brown recalls that he was not brave enough to use his invitation to the opening ceremony. "I stood on the DLR platforms at Stratford and watched the Queen jump out of her helicopter – it was extraordinary – and then I went and had fish and chips in the canteen with the Jubilee line train drivers." Settling into his supper, Brown took a call from the Jubilee line Stratford Market depot saying there had been a signal failure. "Thirty-six seconds later, as I was beginning to non-digest my fish and chips, he rang again and said, 'Mike, it was just a false indication, sorry to alarm you, everything's fine.' The phone never rang again, never rang for the entire Olympics."[42]

Peter Hendy went to London Bridge station to see how things were going on the first Monday of the Games, when the earliest events of the Olympics, the equestrian

The magnificent fireworks display formed part of the opening ceremony in July 2012

events, were taking place at Greenwich Park. It was all very orderly, and "I bumped into Dick Murray [transport correspondent of the *Evening Standard*]. He looked even more morose than he usually did. I said 'Dick, why are you looking so miserable?' He said, 'Because I've written a whole story I can't use.' I said, 'What story is that, then?' He said, 'That the transport has all gone wrong, and you've been fired!' Like the rest of the media, they'd been saying for months nothing would work properly, and even after the opening night and the first weekend they were still unconvinced."[43]

Also on that day, now CEO of Go-Ahead David Brown was at London Bridge, being responsible for train services and HS1:

Myself and a colleague from Network Rail were making ourselves available for interviews. The journalists were anticipating disaster, they had 'smelt blood in the water'; this was the newly rebuilt London Bridge station's first major test, and they expected it to go wrong. But it didn't, nothing happened, there was nothing to see, they couldn't even be bothered to interview me in the end. That afternoon we won our first gold medal ... They never came back to worry about the transport issues again. I'd spent so much time on the Olympic Road network. So much grief, because it was pretty harsh and pretty draconian. I remember it as hand-to-hand combat on every single section.[44]

Mike Brown continued to keep his finger on the operational pulse, and went on to spend "as many late shifts as I possibly could on stations, many of them Stratford on the gate line, just working to the station supervisor's instructions as people arrived for the venue and went home afterwards, and it was extraordinary."[45]

By the Wednesday of the first week, such was the smooth operation of transport across the capital that the media had switched its attention to central London, where it alleged shops and restaurants were deserted, claiming that TfL's innovative travel demand management strategy had been just too successful in suggesting that Londoners should vary their commuting patterns to accommodate the Games. "In truth, the media hadn't factored in that so many people would stay at home and watch the events on television, and those who were out were brilliant at following our advice," reflected Peter Hendy.[46]

The big stores in central London started to complain that sales were down. The *Standard* started a different line – 'Ghost Town London'.

> Boris got really agitated. We said to him, 'Why would you go shopping when the most exciting sport you could ever watch was on the TV, even if you hadn't got tickets?' He wasn't placated. So in the end, one afternoon Vernon and I went up to Oxford Street, we looked in the big shops; some were quiet, but Primark was heaving. I took some pictures of the crowded tills and sent them to [Boris]. What we'd found was foreign tourists, oblivious to the Games, taking the opportunity of relative quiet to stock up on cheap clothes! He gave up then, but in fact what really quietened it all down was that the British started winning medals. Everything else got forgotten, and transport went back to being in the background, working mostly perfectly, as we'd hoped.[47]

TfL was also able to show the analysis from Oyster data, "and say 'No, it's quiet here, but it's busier everywhere where the Games are'."[48] The mayor's bus and Tube announcements were switched off on the Wednesday of the first week, having done their job.

Everitt's recollections are similar.

> When London was allegedly deserted, we were rapidly able to demonstrate that we were carrying more people on the network than we had done at any time in our history. They were just going at a different time. But the city felt different, and because people were so focused on the Games they weren't necessarily going shopping in the West End or eating in the West End, because the Olympics was on and people had other things to watch. Very soon after the beginning of the Games, particularly when we started to win gold medals for Great Britain, everyone forgot all of that. It was a great triumph. It didn't go without its problems. There were some operational difficulties, which the operating side of the organization had geared up for and were ready to deal with, whatever was thrown at them, which they did supremely well.[49]

Howard Smith recalls the Games as being "tremendously exciting and tremendously scary, tremendously lucky in the end". Smith was one of the senior executives rostered in the Olympic Control Centre at Palestra in Southwark. "It was emphasized to us that if anything went wrong, we were the ones who would then represent transport – up to Cobra, frankly; we'd be the ones standing in front of the cameras. By luck and judgement, and it's always both, it turned out to be one of the easiest weeks of my entire career."[50] The first hurdle was to get through the opening ceremony, then the cycling on the weekend and then a slightly quieter time for a week until the build-up in the stadium. "But by the end of the first week, you were beginning just to check in and then say, 'Oh, I'll pop over to Stratford, I'll go for a ride on the cable car'."[51] By the closing ceremony, Peter Hendy was confident enough to be handing out invitations to come along and just watch it ... for the Paralympics afterwards, we're in the stadium because by then we actually felt a reasonable degree of confidence that the transport could look after itself."[52]

Both the Olympic and Paralympic Games saw record attendances at events. During the Olympic Games there were 7.4 million ticketed spectators, 6.25 million of whom were in London, including 2.8 million spectators at Olympic Park venues alone. The Paralympics effectively sold out for the first time in their history, with 2.7 million ticket sales. Almost forty thousand disabled spectators attended ticketed events, many of them by public transport. Road events across London also saw an estimated 1.8 million attending. West End Tube station demand during the Olympics was up by an average 7 per cent from the same day in 2011, with the peak being 27 per cent on Saturday 4 August. The TfL Cycle Hire network saw a record number of users. Retail footfall in the West End was up 16 per cent on the previous year, and hotel occupancy up 3 per cent. Tube journeys during the Games were 35 per cent up on normal levels, the DLR 100 per cent, Overground up 47 per cent. A third of Londoners reported a change in their weekday travel, and this precluded severe crowding and traffic congestion. "People did not all stay at home or leave the city – rather, the majority simply changed the time or way they travelled to avoid hot spots. The re-timing of journeys had the effect of broadening travel demand over the morning and evening peak hours, allowing transport networks to carry record numbers but feel less busy." [53]

For transport in London, the legacy of the Games was £6.5 billion invested in new and improved infrastructure, especially on the Overground and in East London. For accessible transport, there was a legacy of step-free access, audio-visual information displays, hearing induction loops, wide-aisle gates, tactile paving and additional help points. The travel demand management tools developed for the Get Ahead of the Games campaign gave TfL a new suite of tools for managing future Tube closures and major national and public events.

For Mark Evers the most valuable legacy of the Games was for TfL's reputation. "It can plan, build and operate a transport network able to support the most challenging logistical exercise any city can undertake … TfL can support anything else that is proposed for the city in the future, and provides further evidence that London is a great place to live, work and invest in."[54]

After the Games

"One of the most successful Olympics ever, and people remember it for the sport, not for the transport system."

– Vernon Everitt, TfL MD for Customers, Communication
  and Technology during the Games[55]

As the world and its athletes departed, the dust settled on what had proved a highly successful Games for TfL, for London and for the UK. Not only had a rich haul of medals been won, but contrary to expectations London had delivered a public transport Games like no Olympic city had previously ever achieved. The city's transport network had flexed and strained at the seams as passenger numbers on the Tube rose up to Tuesday 7 August, when all records were broken as 4.5 million passengers took the Tube.[56]

For TfL, the demands of bringing transport together for the Olympics had accelerated innovation and integration across transport modes and silos. Macleod recalls that after the Games there was a bit of a reversion to silo: "There were quite a few people who said, 'That's fine, but I want to get back now and get on with my own thing'. The openness and the collaboration around the Games was actually quite uncomfortable for some people. … The irony was that post the Games, it felt like the baronial powers [reasserted themselves] – 'I want something to happen because I want it to happen', rather than because there was logic behind it."[57]

Macleod recalls that very soon after the Games there was some big thing going on in East London. "Everybody was saying, 'Where's our TDM [Travel Demand Management] campaign?' We thought that we just did that for the Games, but no, it's what people are wanting, we need to get out there and communicate with people. We can't go back, we've raised the standard. The TDM team that was established for the Games was retained, partly to look at strategic reprogramming of travel, but also to look at special events and disruptions."[58]

"TfL's contribution to the success of the Games during those months was astonishing," recalls Daniel Moylan. TfL's reputation was transformed as a result. "Because, for anyone who was closely involved, the public perception of TfL in Boris's first term and in the second term were like different worlds." He believes it entirely turned on the way in which the staff, the management, everybody did so brilliantly during the Games. "That whole planning, the staff motivation, the volunteers, the people in the pink jackets, the whole atmospherics of it was absolutely brilliant. Nothing that I can remember went wrong. I mean, trains didn't break down, crowds weren't left stranded, people didn't arrive hours after things started, and it worked."[59] For Leon Daniels, "The Olympics were the most fabulous experience of my life. It was magical to be involved in the preparations, everything. I was there every day."

The high point

On reflection, 2012 now feels like a high point for London and the UK, not least in the radical recasting of our history and national identity in Boyle's opening ceremony. The pride in our city's performance and in that of our athletes over those few golden weeks was to be obscured in subsequent years as Brexit, debates about identity and multiculturalism, and an increasingly divided country have revealed the fissures beneath that apparently unified surface.

Howard Smith rued that for TfL, "right up to the Olympics, everything was moving in the right direction. If you wanted Jubilee line trains refurbished – click your fingers, and Jubilee Line trains, like magic, all got the new moquette." Two or three years after the Olympics, "all of a sudden our ability to spend money met or even exceeded our ability to make or borrow it."[60]

As is ever the case, transport innovation and achievements that were realized in the golden summer of 2012 rapidly became baked into public expectations and into TfL's story. "The Olympics in so many ways was a high point for the organization," reflects Smith. "People who came in [to TfL] after the Olympics … there's an air of irritation … and if anybody mentions getting back the Olympic spirit it's slightly, 'We know what our parents did in the war' … there's a group of people around here who just don't remember it and think it's all literally war stories."[61]

12.

JOHNSON'S SECOND TERM

"I liked the sound of the job primarily because it was basically monarchical. You don't have to worry about cabinet mutinies or backbench unrest ... you had your powers and your budgets, and you just got good things done."

– Boris Johnson, *Unleashed* (2024)[1]

Re-elected shortly before the 2012 London Olympics, in his second term as mayor Boris Johnson was largely concerned with the delivery of initiatives committed to in his first term: the production of 600 New Routemaster buses, new trains and signalling upgrades for the Tube, the Mayor's Vision for Cycling and extending cycle infrastructure. It was also marked by two unsuccessful mayoral *grands projets*, the Garden Bridge and the Estuary Airport. The black taxi trade was disrupted by the arrival of Uber and other app-based transport on demand providers. Johnson applied to be the parliamentary candidate for Uxbridge in August 2014, was elected as an MP in 2015 and served as both mayor and MP, his attention on the mayoralty receding. He stood down in 2016 as ambition in Parliament and the Brexit referendum beckoned.

The 2012 election

"If Boris is the victor, I suspect he will have other forms of leadership on his mind before very long."

– Steve Richards, *The Independent*, 3 May 2012[2]

The 2012 mayoral election took place on 4 May, just four months before the challenge of the Olympic and Paralympic Games. For Labour, Livingstone again secured the party's nomination. His manifesto proposed a cut in Tube and bus fares, to be followed by a fares freeze, and London Living Rent as the capital's housing crisis began to rise up the mayoral agenda. After considerable speculation about his national political ambitions, the incumbent mayor announced that he would stand

Mayoral candidates Johnson and Livingstone clashed after
their LBC debate during the 2008 campaign

for a second term, with a manifesto strong on policing in the wake of the 2011
London riots, on the Olympic legacy, and on transport reducing Tube delays by 30
per cent, building Crossrail and orbital rail links, and extending the TfL Cycle Hire
scheme. In a campaign more like a US presidential campaign, light on policy and
heavy on personal animus, the two leading contenders notably clashed over their
respective personal tax affairs. Following an acrimonious LBC radio debate, they
engaged in a "sweary lift rant", Johnson losing his temper and loudly accusing
Livingstone of being "a fucking liar" over and over again.[3]

On 4 May 2012 turnout was down to 38 per cent from 45 per cent in 2008.
Johnson was elected in the second round with 51.5 per cent to Livingstone's 48.5
per cent of the votes cast. This was closer than expected; support had drifted away
from Livingstone despite Labour doing well on the night in taking control of 32
councils nationally. In London Johnson had bucked the national trend, despite being
in difficulty in the run-up to the election, with poor reliability on the Jubilee line,
unease that cycle lanes were not so 'super' at all – blue paint offering little protection
for cyclists – but perhaps helped by the arrival of the first New Routemaster
prototypes. The day after the election Johnson promised he would not stand as an
MP at the 2015 general election.[4]

The second term

The second term proved to be the delivery phase of the Johnson mayoralty. This time he started with a stable and competent team, despite the loss of Simon Milton in 2011, with Daniel Moylan as deputy chair of TfL, Edward Lister as deputy mayor for policy and Isabel Dedring, who had moved across from TfL as environment advisor and then from 2011 as deputy mayor for transport in succession to Kulveer Ranger. "He had the beginnings of a strong and long-lasting team around him," recalled TfL MD Surface Transport Leon Daniels. "He'd been in the job a while ... he knew what levers he could pull."[5] Daniels also recalled that Johnson was starting to get interested in "mainstream politics and all of the other things that went with it".[6]

Daniel Moylan, a Kensington and Chelsea Conservative, was the conduit between the mayor and TfL.[7] Moylan recalled that to his surprise, "Boris from the outset was extremely focused on trying to tick off all his manifesto commitments. He was bitterly disappointed that some of them were just unrealistic and couldn't be delivered. Not that it made any difference, people never commented on it. A good example of that was going back to two-way working in the southbound Blackwall Tunnel," which for safety reasons could not be reversed.[8]

TfL Commissioner Peter Hendy found it was possible to engage with Moylan.

> He read the papers, you could engage with him and change his mind. In the end, I got on with him really rather well. He would say, 'I don't like this proposal to stop the Circle line going round and round'. I'd say, 'Well, you haven't thought about it. Here are some arguments about why we should do it differently' and he would change his mind ... Daniel loved the new bus, because he's interested in design and he's got very good design principles. We engaged him fully in the new bus – why wouldn't you?[9]

London and TfL in 2013 were on a high in the warm afterglow of the Olympics. As Daniels recalls:

> The New Routemasters [were] coming on stream, Cycle Superhighways. He was influenced tremendously by his close team, people he trusted he relied on, very heavily, Andrew Gilligan for the cycling, Isabel Dedring for TfL generally. He was very forgiving ... there was very poor performance on the Underground at the time, headline news on the Jubilee line. Peter, of course, did what he does, which is to grind through and [tell us], 'The worse it gets, the more reporting you're going to give me, and every day you're going to explain to me and I'm going to ring you every morning and find out'."[10]

Leon Daniels recalled that in those years, "We had a free run, because in most projects, we were in the execution phase. Similar projects were going on the

Underground with automation and S7 & S8 stock ... Ridership was buoyant and growing throughout that period, the earliest traces of ridership growth softening was right at the end of his period; 2016, that was the first time he was just started to see it generally on transport ... by 2016 some of those rail franchises that had gambled on 4 per cent growth were getting 1 per cent."[11] The most visible relics of the Johnson mayoralty can still be seen in London today, reflected Moylan: "the [new] bus, the Cycle Superhighways, and although you won't necessarily associate them with Boris, the upgrades to the Tube. For the ordinary person, the most visible part is the S-stock, signalling upgrades on the Jubilee line and the Victoria line."[12]

The Olympic legacy

As mayor, Johnson inherited the Olympic project – construction was well on its way in 2008 (see Chapter 11) – but he did secure its legacy during his second term in the Olympic Park itself, attracting West Ham United into the stadium, backing the London Legacy Development Corporation (LLDC) to build housing in E20, and as the proponent of 'Olympicopolis', the East Bank cultural quarter – the BBC Music Studios, London College of Fashion for the UAL, V&A East and Sadler's Wells East – for which he secured investment from Chancellor George Osborne in the midst of austerity, and as Richard Brown suggests, "Ten years on, if the planning of the Games was Ken Livingstone's, the shape of legacy is Johnson's."[13]

In retrospect, the 2012 Olympics proved to be a high point for London and for the UK. The seamless operation of the Games transport network and the management of its capacity and then the haul of UK gold medals now seems a golden mirage before the divisions of Brexit and the pain of the Covid-19 epidemic. *Time* magazine presciently suggested during the Games that the biggest winner was London's mayor. "London 2012 has given Boris Johnson's signature blend of erudition and slapstick a worldwide platform, and hitched his star to an event hailed globally as a triumph."[14]

Cycle Superhighways

With major initiatives on Tube and buses rolling over from the first term, the delivery of an extended network of cycle infrastructure was a highly visible badge of Johnson's mayoralty. Since his childhood in Brussels, Johnson had been a cyclist. In the same way as Ken Livingstone used the bus and the Tube, Boris had ridden a bike to work at *The Spectator* and to the House of Commons to avoid crowded buses, and arguably other people. Ben Plowden suggests: "The combination of the money, a cyclist mayor signing up to the London Cycle Campaign's 'Love London, Go Dutch',

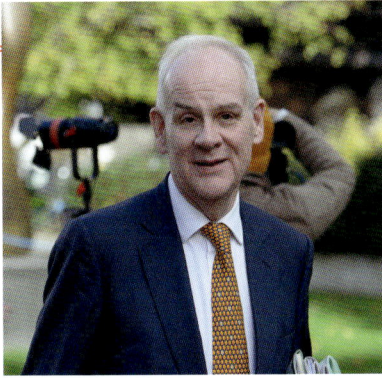

Daniel Moylan, TfL deputy chair 2009–12, and Mayor Johnson's lead on transport, notably the New Routemaster

Leon Daniels, MD Surface Transport 2011–18; he drove the prototype New Routemaster for its press launch in 2011

and the appointment of a Cycling commissioner in City Hall to push this agenda, meant that the level of activity significantly increased."[15]

Following criticism from the cycling lobby on safety grounds of the 'blue paint' approach to the Cycle Superhighways, Johnson appointed cyclist and journalist Andrew Gilligan as Cycling commissioner in January 2013. The Mayor's Vision for Cycling, backed by £1 billion over 10 years, was announced in March 2013. The flagship route proposed in the vision was an east–west cycle route by 2016; "a true Crossrail for the bicycle – will run for at least 15 miles, very substantially segregated, from the western suburbs, through the heart of the capital, to the City, Canary Wharf and Barking in the east. It will, we believe, be the longest substantially segregated continuous cycle route of any city in Europe."[16]

An extensive programme of junction improvements, new cycle infrastructure and segregated cycle lanes was driven remorselessly through both TfL and the boroughs by Gilligan. The extent of the Embankment cycle lanes surprised even Johnson. Leon Daniels related that when "Boris first saw the visuals of the plan for the Embankment, he said, 'Oh, I wasn't expecting all this. I just thought we'd put some more blue paint down.' Boris went mad, as did the businesses disrupted. Gilligan had forced his own agenda. Boris said, 'Who did this?'; we said, 'Gilligan'."[17]

"The Cycle Superhighways were a big imperative, along with the Garden Bridge and the rollout of the new Routemaster programme – all key Boris initiatives of the period."[18] The Embankment scheme remained unpopular with drivers and with Johnson's senior Conservative colleagues, who lobbied to have it removed. In November 2016, Chancellor Philip Hammond, known from his transport minister days as an opponent of cycling, even offered the next mayor, Sadiq Khan, cash to decommission the East–West Cycle Superhighway.[19]

Embankment (*left*) before remodelling for the East–West Cycle Superhighway CS3 and *(right)* with the new cycle lane and junctions installed

Thirteen cyclists were killed in London in 2013, with six deaths in two terrible weeks in November alone, resulting in a 'die-in' being staged outside TfL's HQ by around a thousand demonstrators. HGVs turning left across the cyclists' paths had caused nine deaths alone that year. There were fears that the momentum of cycling growth might be halted by safety fears. The Cycling Vision included new Quietways for the slow or challenged new cyclist, safer junction improvements, building segregation on existing routes and a further extension of the Cycle Hire scheme. Cycling was set to be normalized and doubled over the next 10 years by these measures. This was complemented in June 2013 by TfL's Safe Streets for London road safety plan, which aimed to cut road deaths by 40 percent by 2020 via a range of measures, including redesigning critical major junctions and streets, installing more and upgrading existing traffic enforcement cameras, and working with London boroughs to implement more 20 mph speed limit zones. TfL also worked with HGV owners to fit vehicles with safety equipment to improve the driver's visibility on the offside (the Direct Vision Standard) and offered cycle training to every school pupil in London.[20]

With cycling provision, TfL was exercising its ability to influence travel behaviours and improve the capital through an integrated approach across all modes of transport. "I believe this is about so much more than routes for cyclists," said Peter Hendy. "It is about the huge health and economic benefits that greater cycling can bring. It is about improving London's streets and places for everyone, including those with no intention of getting on a bike. It is about helping the whole transport system meet the enormous demands that will be placed on it."[21]

During these years, road space in London was becoming a scarcer and increasingly contested resource, with the construction of segregated cycle lanes, bus priority measures, increases in the number of white van deliveries and endless closures for services to be dug up. TfL opened the East–West Cycle Superhighway in April 2016 after prolonged and controversial disruption, especially along the Victoria Embankment. This attracted vocal opposition from road users and contributed to bus ridership softening as journey times lengthened and became unpredictable. A London Bus MD expressed what many drivers thought:

> I take my hat off to the cyclists as a lobby. You challenge them at your peril. They are powerful and they will put a good argument together. If I try look at it dispassionately, in the peak travel periods – two hours in the morning and two hours in the evening – I get their argument. At those times it is like the Tour de France 10 times over, all those lanes are being used. If you go at 11 o'clock in the morning, it's an empty space.[22]

For Ben Plowden, TfL director of Surface Transport Strategy and Planning, London had decided – like Berlin, Melbourne, Paris, San Francisco and Sydney – that it needed to be a city with cycling and environmental priorities.

> Cities that rely on internationally mobile, knowledge-based industries, rather than hitting metal in big buildings: tech, medical research, academia, insurance, banking, law – people who work in those industries want to be in those sorts of environments. I had a conversation once with somebody from the Corporation of London. He told me that banks looking to locate in new buildings, or financial institutions or companies looking to locate in the Square Mile, were starting to ask developers how many cycle parking spaces there'd be in the building. Many of their workforce cycle to work on £5000 carbon fibre racing bikes. 'I need 2000 cycle parking spaces,' says bank X to developer Y; that would have been inconceivable a generation ago.[23]

Roads Modernization Plan

"London came to a grinding halt … it was just desperate … if you look back, it felt like the whole of London was a great big building site. All the roads were up."

– Chris Macleod, TfL director of Customer and Revenue 2010–18[24]

The Roads Modernization Plan was announced in 2014 as a response to the traffic congestion caused by population growth and a boom in property investment and development. The plan, enthused Mayor Johnson, was "an integrated response to the way London is changing and growing, looking to create better places, better cycling routes, safer streets and more reliable journeys. It will help London cope with a growing population and create hundreds of thousands of new jobs and homes so we can remain one of the most vibrant, accessible and competitive cities in the world."[25] The plan was a recognition that 26 million trips were made on London's roads each day. With £4 billion up to 2020–21 it represented the biggest investment in the capital's roads for a generation, and included 17 major road scheme and 33 junction improvements, as well as four new Cycle Superhighways, traffic signals technology and maintenance of essential roads, bridges and tunnels such as the Westway and Hammersmith Flyover, key road over rail bridges, the Elephant and Castle roundabout and Highbury Corner. It also included commissioning consultants to look into Johnson's pet projects for a central London road tunnel and putting the North Circular underground.

On the Underground

Major projects to upgrade and increase the capacity of the Underground system, originally part of the PPP contracts, approached delivery. Together new trains and signalling upgrades significantly increased the capacity of the lines and significantly improved the ambience of the passenger's experience.

The opening of the Jubilee line extension on Millennium Night 1999 had been significantly delayed by contractors proving unable to install an innovative moving block signalling system and being obliged to return midway to a conventional fixed block system, which limited the capacity of the extended line to 24 trains per hour. The Tube Lines PPP contract included providing both an extra car on each train, delivered in 2005, and the move to CBTC[26] or automatic train operation. Migration to the new system had caused extended delays and repeated weekend closures on the line in 2007–08, the principal reason for TfL buying out the Tube Lines contract in 2009. When automatic train operation was completed by TfL in 2011, the capacity of the line was increased from 24 to 30 trains per hour.

The new Victoria line 2009 stock at Green Park in May 2013 enabled 36 trains an hour, every 100 seconds in peak service

Replacement of the 1967 trains on the Victoria line began in 2009 and was complete by 2011, with the first introduction of 47 eight-car trains built by Bombardier Transportation. The trains were replaced, and the power supply and signalling upgraded, all without halting the service, an unsung hero project of this period despite the inevitable running-in problems. This was the first time an automatic railway based on fixed block signalling had been upgraded to a cab-based or 'Distance to Go' radio-based system. This enabled capacity to be increased from 27 to 33 trains and then to 36 trains per hour in the peak by 2019. With a train arriving every 100 seconds, the Victoria line is now the most intensively used per mile on the Underground network and is one of the most frequent metro services in the world. The chief limitation on further improvements is no longer the signalling, it is the time taken to clear the platforms by fixed staircases before the next train arrives.

New rolling stock, S-Stock, was ordered from Bombardier at Derby to replace 1960s and 1970s rolling stock on sub-surface lines, the District, Metropolitan and Hammersmith & City lines. The order was originally part of the Metronet PPP, comprising a total of 192 trains (1403 cars), and was then taken on by TfL in 2008. Two configurations were specified: S7 Stock seven-car trains for the Circle, District and Hammersmith & City lines, and S8 Stock with eight cars for the Metropolitan line, with differences in the arrangement of seating. When it was placed, the order was the biggest single rolling-stock order in Britain, at a cost of £1.5 billion. Introduced from 2010, the trains represented a major step forward: the first Underground trains to be fitted with air conditioning, lower floors to ease accessibility for people who have disabilities, and open gangways to allow passengers to move from one car to another while the train is moving. The design offered greater capacity through an extra car on the District line and shorter journey times, and the trains were to prove very reliable. The S-Stock trains were elected by Londoners as one of their 10 favourite transport design icons during London Transport Museum's Year of Design in 2015.[27]

The new trains did much to enhance the Underground's reputation. Tim O'Toole, then MD Underground, never doubted that they would. "I knew, as soon as I went through the specs, this is going to transform everything. We've got to have these trains ... Nothing worse than being stuck on a D-Stock with a lunatic late at night, and that happened to me more than once."[28]

The ticketing revolution that had begun with Oyster in 2003 finally saw cash removed from the bus network in 2014. This was a big step; bus passengers are more numerous and in a lower income bracket than those on the Tube, and more likely to be reliant on cash transactions.

The proposed closure of all 268 Underground ticket offices in 2015 was the revolution's final act on the Underground. Oyster and contactless had reduced the proportion of transactions at the ticket office window to just 4 per cent of all payments. Customer service norms had moved away from the impersonal security-glazed hole in the wall. During 2015, 260 Underground ticket offices were closed, and the staff transferred out into the ticket hall and on the gate line, assisting with ticket machines and information.

In general, the presence and visibility of staff in ticket halls and the enhanced customer service they offered was welcomed, as London Travel Watch reported a year later. "Passengers value visible staff highly, and the quality of service provided by the majority of LU staff is excellent. Subject to being able to access all the information and tickets they need, passengers generally would like to see staff in the ticket hall area rather than exclusively in ticket offices. When staff are more visible and proactively helping passengers, passengers feel safe, secure and satisfied. Overall the satisfaction score remained steady at 85, with staff attention to customers and staff helpfulness higher than before at 96 and 95 respectively."[29]

Steam Underground celebrations

TfL celebrated the 150th anniversary of the world's first Underground railway in January 2013 through a series of events organized with the London Transport Museum. The high point was a steam-hauled recreation of the original 1863 three-mile route underground from Paddington to Faringdon Street. A train of five Victorian teak carriages was hauled by Met No.1, the last steam locomotive built by the Metropolitan Railway at Neasden in 1898, restored to working order for the occasion. Veteran electric locomotive *Sarah Siddons* brought up the rear of the heritage services, packed throughout over both weekends. Steam services were run in between regular Underground service trains, to the amazement of people standing on the platform waiting for their next train. This was very likely the last appearance of a steam train in the central Underground tunnels.

The first train arrived in the bay platform at Moorgate with a precious cargo: Mayor Johnson, TfL leadership, commercial sponsors, the LTM board, staff and guests. As the maroon tank engine pulled its vintage wooden train into the station, whistle blowing, smoke and steam billowing to the roof and down, doors slammed and cameras clicked. The world's media packed the platform and were given the clear message from Boris Johnson, Peter Hendy and Mike Brown that if the last 150 years had taught us anything, it was the need to maintain investment in transport infrastructure if the city was to remain vital and viable.

For Underground MD Mike Brown the extraordinary event brought alive the Tube in people's minds. At the reception at the Renaissance Hotel at St Pancras, after a

The Metropolitan Railway No.1 locomotive was restored for the Tube 150 celebrations in January 2013

short journey back in the latest S-Stock train, he basked in Johnson saying for the first time as mayor, without caveat, how brilliant the Tube and TfL were.[30] That such an event could be contemplated on one of the world's busiest metros confirmed TfL's confidence and competence in the wake of the Olympics. The Underground's reputational score with the public soared to even greater heights than it had during the Olympic Games.

TfL regulates, Uber disrupts

Vehicles have plied for hire on London's streets since the 16th century, and purpose-built horse-drawn 'cabriolets' first appeared from Paris in the 1820s. Regulation through the Public Carriage Office (PCO) began in 1838 under the wing of the Metropolitan Police and passed to TfL in 2000. The requirement for a knowledge test for taxi drivers to obtain a licence was introduced in 1865 and remains today as the world's most demanding training course for taxi drivers. It tests knowledge of 320 standard Blue Book routes through central London and the 25,000 streets within a six-mile radius of Charing Cross, as well as points of interest such as public buildings, stations, courts, places of worship, theatres, parks, sport venues and crematoria. Applicants need to pass a series of 12 'appearances' or oral tests, each progressively more difficult, with an examiner, usually a former taxi driver, which takes on average 34 months to pass. This time is spent at knowledge schools and out bashing the routes on a moped. Training for the Knowledge measurably enlarges the hippocampus, the area of the brain used for spatial memory and navigation.[31]

Black cabs are the only vehicles licensed to be hailed on the street, cab fares being set by TfL as the licensing authority. TfL is obliged to balance the affordability of fares with covering the costs of self-employed taxi drivers. Private hire vehicles or minicabs, by contrast, must be pre-booked at a registered minicab office. Any vehicle that seats up to eight passengers and is available for hire with a driver requires a private hire vehicle (PHV) licence from the PCO. It is the responsibility of the vehicle owner to apply for a licence. The private hire trade had grown since the 1960s, and in 1998 the PCO was empowered to regulate the trade. In response to public safety concerns, TfL tightened progressively the standards applied to private hire drivers and their vehicles from 2001. Vehicles are inspected and MOT tested twice a year, while drivers need to pass a modest 'topographical test', an English language test, a safety, equality and regulatory assessment and an enhanced Disclosure and Barring Service (DBS) check to secure a three-year licence.

Much of the story of TfL since 2000 has focused on harnessing innovation to the cause of keeping London on the move, the engineering, operational and digital remodelling of transport services. The arrival of ride-sharing apps such as Uber disrupted the regulated black cab and private hire trades. As the regulator of these

Uber was an early product of the smartphone age

established trades, TfL found itself attacked from both sides as it sought to respond to digital innovations in the best interests of Londoners.

Uber had originally been launched in San Francisco in 2011 as a service offering limousine rides that cost 50 per cent more than conventional cab fares, a means to monetize spare capacity in private cars. When Uber was launched in London in 2012, it was with a mobile app and regular vehicles. Uber was the child of the smartphone: the potential passenger could see when their ride would arrive, the car's make, colour and registration number and the name of the driver, all paid for in advance and rated afterwards. This was a far better customer experience than looking for a neon-lit cab office or hanging on the phone, let alone waiting on the side of the road on a wet night in the dark for a cab that might never come.

Uber and other ride app operators simply required a self-employed driver, a car and a mobile with a mapping app. This was initially attractive to drivers; there was no need to memorize the A-Z, and they could drive when they wanted – full-time, nights or part-time to fit in with other work or family responsibilities. "It was a dating agency. It put people who wanted rides in touch with people who were prepared to offer them under a common brand, a single app. Uber were not the first to the market with an app. There had been other people with apps before that, they just caught the tide … and they expanded so quickly. They became a household name in many cities, many countries, very quickly."[32]

Uber and its entrepreneurial owners created a new and disruptive service that worked outside or around local regulations drafted to suit the horse-drawn cab and its motorized successors rather than a digital satellite navigation system and a mobile app. Leon Daniels, responsible for taxis and private hire, recalled the advent

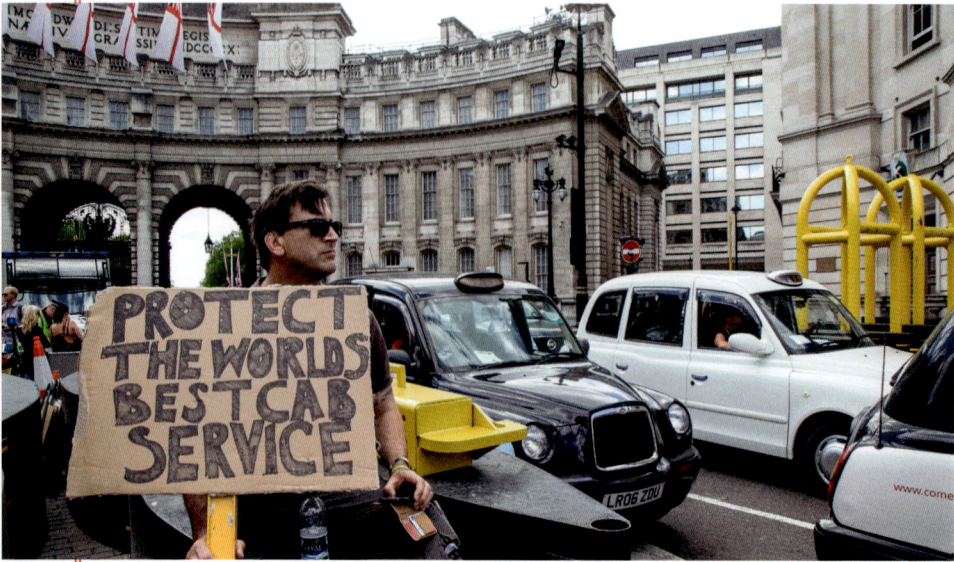

Taxi drivers protesting in June 2014 against
Uber being given a licence to operate

of Uber as "traumatic, that burned through the entire period of Boris's second term because it was revolutionary. We hadn't seen it coming."[33] Daniels reflected:

> London was unprepared, the legislation was of no value. No matter what I thought or the mayor thought, we were compelled to license them because the legislation says 'can', but the interpretation of the High Court means, 'will' be granted a licence, broadly – if you have directors, money, no previous convictions, premises and a phone. Uber had all of those things.[34]

The advent of Uber was a huge threat to the London cab trade and its 24,000 licensed cabbies. The first instincts of the trade were to lobby the mayor as a friend of the cab not to grant a licence, to close down Uber and other ride-sharing apps on the grounds of their being unfair competition. TfL's powers did not extend that far. Daniels found being obliged to grant a licence upset both the private hire market and the taxi drivers and led to angry protests. TfL "didn't have any friends in this at all. We were accused of corruption, bribery, incompetence, malfeasance in public office. We were orally and physically threatened, and attacked at events and walking in the street." For Daniels there were threats on social media, "the whole, 'We know where your children go to school' type thing, a huge level of threats, including physically in the street … I had a police case officer permanently attached to me, not walking with me, but somebody I could call any time, day or night."[35]

"Uber's customers, on the other hand, loved it. It was cheap, plentiful, they went south of the river, and, better than any other taxi or private hire ride, you knew the name of the driver, the registration number, where it was, where you were when you were in it, and you gave the driver scores out of five when you got out, and he gave you scores out of four."[36]

Johnson urged TfL to support the black cab trade by not granting Uber a licence. "If a million Ubers applied for licences tomorrow," Daniels rued, "I'd be granting a million licences, because I don't have powers to control the size of the market … Boris and I had some terse conversations where I'm saying, 'I welcome your views, but it is my decision.' 'Yes, but you will do this, won't you?' 'It's my decision. The law is very clear.'"[37]

Uber itself went through a corporate crisis in 2016–17, when it was revealed that it had a huge data breach of the details of 600,000 drivers and 56 million customers, and paid a ransom to the hackers involved. There were also sexual harassment claims, which led to the departure of 20 senior staff and its combative founder, CEO Travis Kalanick. The disruptor was only brought to heel in London when it became known after investigation in 2017 that Uber's booking process was not as described for the licence or compliant with the regulations. It also became clear that Uber was not reporting drivers accused of sexual assault, who lacked medical certificates, or who were not passing DBS checks. The Metropolitan Police investigated 32 drivers for rape or sexual assault of a passenger between May 2015 and May 2016. In August 2017 Metropolitan Police inspector Neil Billany wrote to TfL about his concern that the company was failing to investigate allegations against its drivers properly.[38]

Moreover, it was also found that Uber was using software to prevent regulatory authorities from gaining full access to the app. Daniels recalls,

> They had a way that they could identify people like me and alter the view of minicab private hire vehicles on my screen. For example, if I was an enforcement officer, they would make the cars invisible to me so I couldn't stop them and inspect them, or I might get a better service than somebody else. 'Greyballing' is basically a way of making vehicles invisible to groups of people, including the enforcement authorities. They never used greyballing in London, but they did use it in other places where the London Uber directors were also directors.[39]

Daniels revoked Uber's licence to operate in London in 2017 on grounds of concern over Uber not being fit and proper to hold an operator's licence.

For TfL and for Daniels, the problem was trying to enforce legislation on private hire that was not designed for the digital world. "The legislation was unhelpful," said Daniels. "Taxi drivers hated it. Private hire traders hated it. Passengers liked it, and the only thing that's really happened now is nobody managed to get rid of them." Over time, Uber were forced to give their drivers employee benefits and holidays, and to pay VAT, which means the price difference with black cabs was seriously eroded. For Daniels "it right-sized the black cab industry, there were 24,000 [black cabs]; it's now 14,000[40] and they're all doing really nicely. On the private hire side, [it's better than] going to some shop front with iron bars and a bloke with a fag and an Alsatian dog and a flashing light outside, which was a feature of every high street."[41]

Uber lost its licence again in 2019 over passenger safety concerns. Inspectors had discovered that at least 14,000 journeys were undertaken by drivers who effectively faked their identity – using another Uber account after exploiting "vulnerabilities" in the company's app. Uber continued to operate on both occasions pending court appeal. After the second appeal, TfL awarded Uber a 30-month licence in March 2022.

There are now only 14,600 black cabs but more than 94,000 licensed minicabs. It is estimated that Uber has 3.5 million users in London each year.[42] In February 2025 a 7.5 per cent rise in black cab fares was proposed by TfL, necessary to cover the increasing cost of running a cab and to "try and ensure that taxi driving remains a viable career". The number of licensed taxi drivers in the capital has fallen to a new low of 16,816, while the number of minicab drivers has increased to 107,998.[43]

Uber continued in its efforts to win over the beleaguered taxi industry; nonetheless, the animosity between black cab drivers and Uber continues. For the black cab drivers, Steve McNamara, general secretary of the Licensed Taxi Driver Association, noted that riders can already hail a ride in a London black cab through numerous apps, including Gett, Taxiapp, FreeNow and ComCab. "We have no interest in sullying the name of London's iconic, world-renowned black cab trade by aligning it with Uber, its poor safety record and everything else that comes with it."[44]

Regardless of competition in the taxi and hire business, for TfL Uber and other ride-sharing apps remain in competition with public transport; they contribute to traffic congestion, reduce public transport use, have no impact on vehicle ownership and increase dependency on the car.[45]

Johnson's 'grands projets'

"A truly beautiful scheme, and every city must keep doing new and interesting things."

– Boris Johnson, *Unleashed*[46]

The mayor's first *grand projet* was the cable car, which was launched over the Thames to the Royal Dock just in time for the 2012 Olympics. It had required a substantial sponsor, the Emirates Airline, to make it fly. For Moylan, the rest of it was easy. "The land you wanted to have the stations on was low-value land, landowners either side were perfectly happy to have it … But it was TfL who unlocked the money."[47]

The cable car was an example of where the mayoral vision was more persuasive than the transport planners or the economic forecasters. The outcome was a tourist attraction that today – rare in the TfL family – makes a positive operating margin. "Many said that they loved living in a city where the mayor delivered weird things and faced off the number-crunchers," Daniels rued.[48]

One *grand projet* that did not fly was the Garden Bridge. This was an idea passionately mooted in the 1990s by actor Joanna Lumley to commemorate Princess Diana. Lumley persisted with her vision for "a pedestrian bridge with a garden upon it ... something almost dreamlike in the centre of a huge vibrant city".[49] Lumley could not persuade Mayor Livingstone in 2002, but did convince engineers Arup to make an outline design, which she successfully proposed in a handwritten letter to Johnson six days after his second election in 2012. "Our cheers and shouts reached the rafters, soared above the Shard," Lumley gushed. "Wonderful news for London." She then outlined her vision for the Garden Bridge as a "green pedestrian bridge, with cycle tracks alongside, with container-grown trees, and beauty and practicality in equal measure". Such a bridge would bring "great loveliness" to the Thames, she wrote, adding, "Please say yes." Lumley referred to Heatherwick as the designer she had in mind, and snared Johnson's interest.[50]

At Johnson's prompting, TfL announced that it was considering a new footbridge to link Temple with the South Bank. Thomas Heatherwick was appointed after a truncated procurement for design advice for a footbridge, with no mention of a garden. Chancellor Osborne pledged £30 million, while TfL contributed £30 million, £20 million of which was on long loan. The rest was to come from private donations, of which £85 million was allegedly pledged. The vision beyond Arup's beautiful visualizations remained vague; even Johnson himself in 2014 "wasn't really sure what it was for", other than making a "wonderful environment for a crafty cigarette or a romantic assignation" – hardly the lofty language suggesting a project with sound vision and purpose. That lack of vision failed to engage with local communities and key stakeholders, and lacked a business case or a sustainable financial model. "Hoping the shortfall could be made up as the project proceeded – the 'jump off the cliff and hope you pass by a parachute as you fall' approach – engineering and design work started. The resulting designs were beautiful, but not beautiful enough to garner the support needed."[51] Unlike the cable car, the bridge would have landed on high-value and crowded banks of the Thames in central London.

In early 2013 Johnson, together with Heatherwick, Edward Lister, the mayoral chief of staff and Isabel Dedring, "jumped on a plane" to San Francisco in an attempt to woo Apple into sponsoring the bridge. In his evidence to the 2017 enquiry, Lister said, "The mayor felt there was a fair chance that Apple might actually sponsor the whole bridge ... We were only there for 24 hours and flew back again. We went, we

Impression by Arup of the Heatherwick Studio design for the unrealized
Garden Bridge between Temple and the South Bank

talked through it all ... It was, 'We do this, we call it the Apple Bridge and you pay for it,
chum'. It was a real sales operation to try and sell it."[52] The mission was unsuccessful.

The vision for an elegant footbridge, a garden bridge across the Thames, was
persuasive, and planning permission was granted in 2014, but as costs rose from
£60 million to £200 million by 2017 (the Millennium Bridge had cost £22 million), as
planning difficulties arose with local residents on its landing points, on the north
bank at Temple over the station and on the south bank in public green space by the
ITV Studios, the tree felling its siting required, and some confusion over whether its
purpose was as a transport link or a cultural attraction, free or paid, cyclists or not,
the project lost momentum. The new mayor, Sadiq Khan, had endorsed it during
his campaign but soon after his election appointed Margaret Hodge MP to review
the project.

Hodge's conclusions were that this was a project born of the political cycle, indeed a *grand projet*, that had been driven forward by the mayor and had "impacted on the actions and behaviour of those around him".[53] It being his urgent priority, the bridge project had not met expected procurement standards nor a business case that offered value for money. Hodge noted, "The mayor was halfway through his second term of office, and it was pressure of time arising from the political cycle that appears to have trumped the need for a robust business justification of the value of the Garden Bridge and a thorough assessment of the risks."[54]

By the time the bridge scheme was abandoned in August 2017, when Sadiq Khan had refused to provide a guarantee for future running costs, a condition of Westminster's planning permission, it had cost £43 million of public money. TfL had done the mayor's bidding, but for this project, unlike the New Routemaster bus or the cable car, had been unable to drag this green elephant over the line.

An even grander vision was to site a new airport for London to the east of the city in the Thames Estuary. This had been proposed at various times since the 1940s, and a site on Maplin Sands had received parliamentary assent in 1973 before being rejected by the incoming Labour government in 1974 in favour of expanding existing airports. An altogether new site in the estuary had the advantage of not being close to the built-up area of London or requiring planes to fly over the capital. It would entail huge cost in terms of road and rail infrastructure, demand an upheaval of heroic proportions of skilled people, services and businesses from West London, and damage the wildlife of the estuary habitats. It would have created 25,000 acres (10,120 hectares) of development land in the vacated Heathrow area.

In 2009 Johnson went out in the Thames Estuary off the North Kent coast in a dredger with Sir Doug Oakervee and other infrastructure experts to look at the site, and provoked next-day headlines about Fantasy Island, which soon became labelled as Boris Island. With the shot in the arm given to big projects by the success of the London Olympics, the idea was revived in the 2012 mayoral elections. TfL's remit did not extend specifically to air transport, but it was responsible for the air quality and health of Londoners and the capital's transport, spatial development and ambient noise strategies. Daniel Moylan recalled the controversy over Heathrow expansion and the Estuary airport:

> I don't know to what extent TfL ever really considered the airport was part of its remit, since there is no TfL air division. But why shouldn't that be? One of the things I will always kick myself over is that we had so much money then, [and] we didn't use a billion pounds to buy Stansted Airport. I thought this would be a wonderful thing to do, but I didn't have the courage to press for it. Then of course, who goes and buys it? The city of Manchester buys it [in 2013 for £1.5 billion] and nobody bats an eyelid. TfL should have bought Stansted when it came up.[55]

As Moylan explained,

> The fact of the matter is that TfL had a slightly distant relationship with the airport, although the money that paid for all the research was on TfL's budget, about £5 million. The staff working on it were working for Michèle [Dix] in charge of Planning. It was a TfL project and that I think was remarkably successful in some ways.[56]

A comprehensive report on the need to look away from expanding at Heathrow and towards Stansted in the short term and the Thames Estuary in the long term was published by TfL in 2016. "If we are to secure the connectivity that meets the UK's long-term economic need, then the only option is a four-runway hub. The Inner Thames Estuary and Stansted, located to the east of London, away from densely populated areas, are each able to deliver that connectivity while absolutely minimizing the local noise and air quality pollution impacts. A mixture of new, planned and existing surface access infrastructure would ensure fast, reliable access and help unlock key development and regeneration sites along the corridor."[57]

The Airports Commission was to report after the 2015 general election, but in September 2014 Sir Howard Davies, chairman of the commission, said the cost, economic disruption and environmental issues made the Thames Estuary airport plan unviable, reflecting the government and Treasury view of this colossal project.[58] In 2015 Johnson repeated his opposition to the third runway at Heathrow, pledging to "lie down in front of those bulldozers and stop the building, stop the construction of that third runway" at Heathrow Airport. His opposition continued when he was in government, though this demanded a trip to Afghanistan in 2019 to avoid the Commons vote that approved the third runway's construction.

Daniel Moylan was proud of the work TfL did on the airport.

> We'll only do it if we can go back and actually start with a proper study of aviation and airport need, and work out a coherent, well-argued plan ... I said, 'Everything we've done until now has to be scrapped, because it's been a disaster. Just forget it ever happened.' ... At every stage, thanks to Michèle and the team, everything we did was regarded with great seriousness. There was no more rubbish about Fantasy Island, and this is just Boris wittering on. There were really solid reports with really solid research. The aviation industry, although it was always sceptical, never thought we were just a joke. They knew they had to take this seriously because of the quality of the research and the arguments.[59]

Perhaps the estuary airport has a lot going for it, but its scale of ambition even in the years of post-Olympic euphoria was always politically and financially too much to swallow for the government and the Treasury. Heathrow has always marshalled strong vested interests behind its cause. At the time of writing, the Labour government has once more proposed to build the third runway at Heathrow.

Was Johnson good for London and for TfL?

"His time at City Hall with the capable and affable Lister at his side was truly the peak of his political career."

– Jack Brown reviewing Johnson's autobiography *Unleashed*[60]

When Johnson stood down after two terms as London mayor in 2016, his record was well regarded by Londoners. A poll commissioned at the end of Johnson's term revealed that 52 per cent of Londoners believed he did a 'good job' while 29 per cent believed he did a 'bad job'.[61]

In judging the two terms, it is difficult but necessary to put to one side what was later revealed by Johnson's Brexit years and his time as prime minister during the Covid 19 pandemic. Even in the mayoral years his none-too-private life was well known, but the mud seemed not to stick, indeed to enhance rather than diminish his reputation as someone who was distinct from other politicians. Tony Travers, London's governance expert, compared the tone of Johnson's mayoralty favourably with that of Ken Livingstone. "The atmosphere has been 'benign and affable', where Mr Livingstone was 'capable of tangling in toxicity'."[62]

Johnson was mayor at a time when the London economy was booming, when TfL's funding position remained strong, when terrorism had failed to strike the city, and when the strategies laid during the Livingstone years in the London Plan, for transport strategy and Oyster and contactless, were rolled forward by an innovative, confident and committed TfL leadership. As Travers has said, "A lot of London's success has not been because of Boris Johnson, but in politics there is a lot to be said for luck."[63]

TfL had not been unduly affected by the government's austerity programme. Insiders believe that their card was marked with the wind-up of the Bombardier contract for automatic train control on the sub-surface railway late in 2013. Mayor Johnson had lost interest in TfL as parliamentary ambition beckoned, and left uncontested the Treasury view that if TfL could afford to settle the contract for £85 million and delay the upgrade for five years, TfL had too much money.[64] In 2015, cuts in the government transport budget were announced by Chancellor George Osborne, including phasing out the £700 million annual subsidy of TfL operations. While capital investment in the NLE extension and for Crossrail was secured, the halcyon days of the multi-year funding agreement had passed, and by 2018 London was to be the only European city without a subsidized transport network. TfL Commissioner Mike Brown, putting a brave face on it, said the settlement would allow TfL to continue to invest in an improved network but added: "It also recognizes the tough decisions we must continue to take to deliver more efficiently for fare- and taxpayers, while protecting and modernizing frontline services."[65]

The 2015 settlement was the start of leaner years for TfL, with significant savings required through reducing management layers, merging functions, renegotiating contracts and delivering transport improvements more efficiently. The aim was to achieve an operating surplus by 2021–22 by progressively reducing the cost of running London's transport network every year. This was on target, but derailed first by the delay to opening the Elizabeth line and the loss of its revenue from 2018, and then by the onset of Covid in 2020.

The two terms of the Johnson mayoralty left a tangible legacy on the city's transport, with signalling and rolling stock upgrades on the Tube, which carried more passengers than ever before, the construction of miles of high-grade cycle infrastructure, the great leap forward of integrated public transport for the Olympics, and the new Routemaster bus. Arguably, without a bicycling mayor the cycle programme would not have moved nearly so far or so fast, nor would TfL have commissioned a new design of London bus without Johnson's animus against the articulated bendy bus.

Peter Hendy was the TfL commissioner during all but the last year of the Johnson mayoralty[66] and reflected:

> He never felt fettered by money because he didn't know how much money he'd got. Some of the things that he did, very good and very bad things, were motivated by just doing something and making it happen, which is, more or less, what the new bus was, certainly what the cable car was and nearly what the Garden Bridge was. I never thought that he understood the real basis of the London Plan. But we at TfL did. So we carried on with a long-term view about what should happen in London, and he added on top of it the things that came into his head that he thought were important. That seems to me to be quite consistent with somebody who's got immense ambition, but not much principle.[67]

TfL's leadership has worked for three different mayors, each with his own approach to the role and to how to use the expertise marshalled by the executive to deliver his manifesto. Working for Johnson was a more personal relationship than the transactional approach favoured by both Ken Livingstone and Sadiq Khan. David Brown was TfL MD of Surface Transport from 2005 to 2011, and considers:

> Boris would naturally bond with you, it's part of his DNA. Ken would answer the questions. I remember coming back on a train journey from Uxbridge Depot, which I used to run, and I was as chuffed as hell because a lot of the people had come out to see Ken, and I knew them all still from 20 years earlier ... I thought this was my opportunity to talk about my upbringing; he wasn't interested in any of that kind of stuff. He kept distant, whereas Boris would have been entirely different.[68]

"Boris was a fabulously intelligent person to work for," says Leon Daniels, who took over from David Brown in 2011, "incredibly nice, incredibly thoughtful, warm. He knew everything about you, he knew about your children's education, he knew about your health, about your holiday."[69] This was not to imply that the relationship was anything more than skin deep. "The key was, he did use people, he used everybody," his friend Peter Guildford suggests. "It was in a charming, buffoonish way. But he used them. The reason people put up with it, by and large, is that at a certain time, when he sensed he had to, he would make time for everybody."[70]

Johnson's own reflections on being London mayor

"I loved the job and certainly improved as I went along … the job in London had changed me, I had become far more serious, more fascinated by the intricacies of policy."

– Boris Johnson in 2022[71]

For the boy who once wanted to be the king of England, Johnson claimed he "liked the sound of the job primarily because it was basically monarchical. You don't have to worry about cabinet mutinies or backbench unrest … you had your powers and your budgets, and you just got good things done".[72] It appeared to be a job that he enjoyed, even if in his autobiography, in which the mayoral years get 10 of the 60 chapters, space on the London years is devoted more to the *grands projets* – the new Routemaster, cycling, the cable car, the Garden Bridge and the Estuary Airport – than to TfL and the bread-and-butter Tube upgrades. "Once I had promised it [the NRM] to Londoners, I had to get it done … Yes, it was a vanity project in which my pride and political future were at stake, but then so is every other great human advance: the Parthenon, the Eiffel Tower, the sewers of Bazalgette."[73] He regrets not being able to build the Garden Bridge, fix aviation capacity in the Thames Gateway, redevelop Heathrow for housing or put road traffic on the North and South Circular roads underground.

The London mayoralty proved to be a springboard for Johnson's national political ambitions. In his last months as mayor, Johnson was also the MP for Uxbridge and Ruislip and a Brexit campaigner. He had cashed in his mayoral chips, and applied his populist message to leaving Europe, which was conclusively voted against by the Londoners who had voted for him as mayor. When Covid struck in March 2020, Londoners and TfL were to find that Prime Minister Johnson had changed radically in his support of the capital from his days as Mayor Johnson.

Elizabeth line
↑ Eastbound platform A

Shenfield
Abbey Wood

Elizabeth line
Westbound platform B ↑

← Heathrow
Maidenhead
Reading

13.

BREAKING
NEW GROUND

"The Elizabeth line is a triumph in architect-led collaboration, offering a flawless, efficient, beautifully choreographed solution to inner-city transport"

– RIBA Stirling Prize, 2024[1]

"The best kind of transport infrastructure facilitates and civilizes the ordinary experience of daily travel. [On the NLE] the judges were impressed by the spatial and material quality of the two new Underground stations as beacons and anchoring points in still-evolving urban landscapes."

– The *Architects' Journal* Awards, 2022[2]

Alongside train and signalling upgrades, new ground was being broken on the Underground from 2009. The first new Tube construction of the 21st century was taking place: the two-station extension of the Northern line, opening in 2021, enabled development around Battersea Power Station, and the Crossrail megaproject opened as the Elizabeth line in 2022. Crossrail would eventually extend to 26 miles of new, full-sized tunnels on a 73-mile route, from Reading in the west deep beneath London to Abbey Wood and Shenfield in the east, at the time the biggest infrastructure project in Europe, and the UK's first digital railway. The delivery of Crossrail through political cycles, an innovative funding method, delay and reprogramming, the challenge of integrating trains, stations and signalling systems, and Covid-19 pushed engineers and operators to their limits. The Elizabeth line represents an outstanding engineering achievement and is today the busiest UK railway line.

Northern line extension

"One of this century's great engineering achievements."

– Mark Wild, Crossrail CEO, March 2022[3]

The first new Tube line constructed in the 21st century was the 2.1-mile extension of the Northern line (NLE) from Kennington to Battersea Power Station. Its purpose was to unlock development in the former industrial strip of London on the south bank of the Thames through Nine Elms and Vauxhall to Battersea Bridge and the chimneys of the power station. Remote from the city yet close to it, the area had been the site of a wide variety of industrial enterprises – candle-making, sulphuric acid, cement, paint, vinegar, lime, white lead and soap – since the late 18th century, intensified by the arrival of railways in the mid-19th century. Two great names of Battersea industry, Price's Candles and Morgan Crucible (manufacturing chemists) employed 2000 workers between them by 1900.[4]

The area went into decline from the 1960s and 1970s with the closure of major employers, the railways, power station and gasworks and the decline of rail and river freight transport. As industry moved to better-connected locations, the area remained shaped by its working past, criss-crossed by railways and viaducts on the approach to Waterloo, Victoria and Clapham Junction, the vacant sites of a 32-acre (13-hectare) GWR railway goods yard and a 45-acre (18-hectare) former waterworks and pumping station, and the remains of riverside factories, engineers and brewers, workshops and wharves. At its western end stood the landmark brick 'temple of power' with its four iconic cream-coloured chimneys, once the generator of a fifth of London's electricity but dark since 1983, its scale and Grade II listed status a stumbling block to redevelopment schemes, from a theme park proposal in the 1980s to demolition for retail, hotels and housing.

By the 1990s industry was being replaced on the waterfront by apartment and office blocks. "In place of the big riverside industries came luxury housing estates … creating a 'millionaires' row' along the riverfront, later described by one critic as a 'private party to which you had not been invited, another London … in which you are not welcome'."[5] The structural state of the power station building and its chimneys gave cause for serious concern. Eventually Malaysian developers SP Setia bought the site in late 2012, and the following year WilkinsonEyre was appointed to restore the power station. Better transport would be needed as a significant catalyst for the development.

Local residents and businesses in north Battersea were poorly served by public transport connections, despite numerous railway lines and major roads criss-crossing the area. Termed the 'Everest of real estate',[6] the long-running power station redevelopment needed better connections to the public transport network to realize its potential. Wandsworth and Lambeth councils made the creation of

The derelict power station, gas holders and industrial decline marked the South Bank at Battersea before regeneration brought by extending the Northern line here in 2021

an enterprise zone and planning permission conditional on a significant developer contribution to the cost of the NLE from Kennington. This was to be the catalyst for up to 25,000 jobs and 20,000 new homes in and around the Vauxhall Nine Elms Battersea Opportunity Area (VNEB), and unlocked section 106 and Community Infrastructure Levy (CIL) developer funding of £259 million of the eventual cost of £1.2 billion for the extension and link to the Tube network. As with the funding case for Crossrail, the NLE was more than a transport argument, being about the wider benefits of jobs and housing that would be enabled by the extended line. As economist Bridget Rosewell recalls, it was "about how you got payback for the cost of building that extension, from the business rates, from the people who would be sited in that place".[7] Collaboration between Wandsworth borough, TfL, central government, the GLA, the neighbouring borough of Lambeth and private sector landowners and developers delivered the extended Tube line within twelve years from inception to completion in 2021.

The Northern line was already the busiest and most complex Tube line, being in effect two lines operated together north and south through central London via Bank and Charing Cross, crossing at Camden Town. The existence of a loop at Kennington to reverse trains made a suitable junction for the departure of the branch to Battersea Power Station, with an intermediate station at Nine Elms. In 2018 the

The crisp, welcoming lines of the Battersea Power Station building
against the mass of the old power station and new housing

work to create a step plate junction at Kennington to join up with the extension to Battersea was as ambitious and innovative as the work to join the two lines at Camden Town had been in 1924. Both were achieved without any disruption to the service; construction at Kennington involved hollowing out the ground around the 1920s tunnel rings to prepare the link to Battersea while service trains continued to rumble through inside. Construction on the extension began in 2015, tunnelling was completed in 2017, and the extension opened on time on 20 September 2021 despite Covid restrictions.

This added two excitingly modern stations to the line, the first in 80 years, delivered for TfL by design and build consortium Ferrovial and Laing O'Rourke (FLO), with station design by Grimshaw. Underground stations have a long history of place-making, helping to establish and define a neighbourhood's identity, gluing communities together and providing a highly visible landmark that helps visitors to navigate. Both Nine Elms and Battersea Power Station have prominent and beckoning ground-level entrances by day and night, giving access by lift and plunging triple escalators to the station box below with their broad and airy

Battersea Power Station at platform level, designed by Grimshaw and opened in 2021

platforms. "Stations to make us proud – classy, understated and luxurious," said *Hidden London* historian Siddy Holloway at the opening, "like Canary Wharf without the platform edge doors."[8]

Within a year, more than five million journeys had been made on the NLE, part of TfL's campaign to attract people back onto the network after Covid. Andy Lord, then TfL's chief operating officer, said in September 2022:

> We opened our new Northern line stations with great pride and excitement a year ago, and it has been fantastic to see how quickly they have become part of the fabric of the city as people have returned in increasing numbers to the Tube network following the pandemic. Since June we've doubled the number of trains serving the extension to give our customers a more frequent service to align with growing demand. Transport plays a critical role in opening up jobs, housing and leisure across the city, with these two new Tube stations clearly demonstrating how faster transport links help neighbourhoods develop and thrive.[9]

The opening of the NLE, with its spacious modern stations, was a shot in the arm for TfL, a demonstration of the power of public transport to bring housing and jobs to regenerate a neglected quarter of the city and to shape the geography of London.

The origins of Crossrail

An east-to-west railway under London in large-diameter tunnels to connect Liverpool Street and Paddington had first been proposed by LNER railwayman George Dow in 1941.[10]

A network of mainline-sized railway tunnels and the removal of bridges over the Thames were a feature of Forshaw & Abercrombie's County of London Plan (1943), the vision for the post-war reconstruction of the capital. This included a Northern Arc railway tunnel from Paddington to Liverpool Street. Post-war austerity caused the plan to be left on a shelf. The name Crossrail was first applied to an east–west line in the 1974 London Rail Study and appeared again in the 1989 Central London Rail Study. This was sponsored by the DfT, Network Rail and London Transport, and has provided the blueprint for rail planning in London ever since. The study recognized the growth in London's economy, more people coming to work in the central area, crowded interchanges where national rail passengers interchanged with the Tube, and the transformation of Docklands occasioned by Canary Wharf. "All this is putting severe strains on London's transport system, which is suffering heavy congestion at peak time, on both road and rail," wrote Paul Channon, then secretary of state for transport, in its introduction.[11]

With government support, Crossrail was developed jointly by London Underground and Network Rail. The project made a start with a draft parliamentary bill, supported by studies, architectural models and a Networker-style mock-up carriage. The bill was rejected in 1994, the victim of recession, Treasury opposition and a reasoned critique of its proposed route and stations by consultants Steer, Davies Gleave for the borough of Tower Hamlets. The project was mothballed, with just four members of staff looking after a warehouse of plans and station models. Significantly, though, the central part of its route from Paddington to Liverpool Street was safeguarded, protecting it from developments that might compromise a future scheme.[12]

As passenger numbers and population in London began to boom once more in the late 1990s, Crossrail's primary purpose of relieving congestion on the network in central London came back into focus, as did the proposals of the 1989 study. In addition to a substantial upgrade of the existing Tube network, it had proposed three cross-city lines: Crossrail East–West (Crossrail 1), Chelsea–Hackney north-east to south-west (Crossrail 2) and the north–south Thameslink. All three offered relief to the central Tube network as well as commuter benefits beyond the M25. Crossrail 1 scored highest on congestion relief in the central zone. When he was elected in 2000, Mayor Livingstone was himself keen on Crossrail 2.

As TfL's new London Rail MD, early in 2001 Ian Brown was asked into the DfT for a 'quiet chat' as the government was keen to pursue Crossrail 1. Brown was asked, "Could you persuade Ken to go with Crossrail 1 rather than 2? If so, we'll put up some seed corn money – £154 million, not a penny more – to set up a joint organization to develop Crossrail." Brown, who had developed the DLR and later would create the Overground, was given the distinct impression that the DfT did not want either Network Rail or London Underground involved. "They [the DfT] wanted to be involved but not to deliver it because their model was the DLR, the concession model. It was agreed that it should be a joint venture project between the government's DfT, two sponsors from the government, two sponsors from TfL– me and the commissioner."[13] Crossrail Limited (CRL) was established in 2001 as the company purposed to define the Crossrail scheme and to win powers from Parliament to implement it, jointly sponsored by the DfT and TfL, a wholly owned subsidiary of TfL.

Funding, costs and route

Concerns over affordability and the demand for funds over time meant that all opportunities to reduce the cost and improve the value for money had to be explored. Central government had offered £5 billion (i.e. one-third of the cost) but sought a significant contribution from TfL and the beneficiaries, the London business community, to fund the project.

Although by 2003 a 'benchmark scheme' had established the basis for the east–west railway under the centre of London, the scale and extent of Crossrail services beyond the central section to the east and west of London was the subject of intense debate. The appraisal of various options gave occasion to question the purpose of the line; was it a cross-London regional railway like Thameslink, or more like the hybrid Paris RER? What routes would the line take beyond the central section, and where were stations to be located? Ultimately a route had to be settled upon to avoid further delay and cost inflation. Crossrail settled into TfL's preferred shape as an urban metro, designed to add significant capacity to the capital's rail network, not an extended regional railway, more of an RER than a Thameslink. Proposed more distant destinations to the east such as Colchester, Chelmsford and Ebbsfleet, a branch to the west into the Chilterns using the Metropolitan line's alignment, and a branch south-west to Richmond and Kingston were not pursued. Branches to the west did embrace Heathrow Airport and Maidenhead, and then Reading. To the east a station at Woolwich was added to support housing development in the area, and the two eastern branches were to terminate at Shenfield and Abbey Wood.

This line was nevertheless a major departure for TfL. The urban metro Crossrail was to run through full-sized railway tunnels at up to 90 mph to Reading, the stations step-free and fully integrated with Network Rail and Underground lines, the fleet of nine-car trains capable of interaction with three different signalling systems along the line, spacious and walk-through with wide aisles and gangways, air-conditioning, audio-visual announcements, comfortable seats, with space for 1500 people on transverse and longitudinal seats covered in a bespoke moquette designed by Wallace Sewell, dedicated spaces for wheelchairs, buggies and luggage, and free Wi-Fi, but without toilets. The stations were designed for future expansion by two extra carriages per train. Intermediate suburban stations in Essex and Berkshire were brought into the TfL network, with roundels, staffing and step-free access.

Innovation in funding

"Crossrail was being proposed to make it easier for people to get into central London which is busy, productive and essential to the economy of the UK, yet has a gridlocked transport system which is harming its competitiveness and the quality of life of its residents and commuters."[14]

– Bridget Rosewell, Chief economic advisor to the GLA, 2002–12

The reputation of large rail infrastructure projects had taken a battering from recent time and cost overruns on the Jubilee line extension, the West Coast Mainline and the Channel Tunnel Rail Link (HS1). Government was reluctant to fund projects on such a scale again, and the chancellor was set on using the PPP

model for the Tube upgrade. The success of the congestion charge and of transport for the 2012 Olympics still lay in the future. Crossrail might be off life support, but a fresh and innovative approach was needed from TfL to secure the £6 to £7 billion of government funding needed.

The initial business case was rejected by Kiley and the TfL board in November 2002, as a benefit–cost ratio of only 1.3 did not offer a strong enough case to take to government. Conventional cost–benefit analysis understated the full benefits of transport investment. At TfL, a Kennedy Business School graduate, Shashi Verma, was tasked – supported by a team from Colin Buchanan consultants, the LSE, Imperial College and economist Bridget Rosewell[15] from the mayor's office – with building "an analysis the Treasury could not challenge",[16] by making a case that was more than just a transport case.[17]

Verma recalled a momentous telephone conversation with Lewis Atter, head of the transport team at the Treasury. "He asked me the very simple question, 'Tell me, what does the government get out of this? Why should we fund it?' I said to Lewis, 'Okay, that's a good challenge to have. I will go and answer that question for you.'"[18] To do this, Verma and the team went back to first principles, being aware that the traditional cost–benefit approach ignored the central purpose of Crossrail: to increase the number of people living and working in London. They sought to draw a direct line between transport investment and GDP. "That was one part of the story, which is agglomeration. The reason you invest in transport is that it improves productivity and results in higher GDP, which results in a higher tax take for the government. That is why the government should invest in this, because they have a direct return from higher taxes."[19]

The second innovation was identifying a mechanism to tap into the benefit that transport brings to property values. The idea of using a supplementary business rate had been proposed by Tony Travers and Stephen Glaister in the 1990s. When Verma started work, "Stephen Glaister said, 'Here's a paper, you should read it.' I will always credit them for the original idea. I made it work and tied it into the agglomeration."[20]

Verma had a seminal meeting with Bob Kiley, TfL commissioner, in spring 2003, four or five months after Jay Walder had tasked him with recasting the Crossrail funding case.

> Jay said to me, you've done all this work, you figured out something interesting, you should go and talk to Bob. On Thursday afternoon we spent three-and-a-half hours in [Kiley's] office; no papers, me explaining to him how I think this will all work, how agglomeration works, how that creates value. What are the value capture mechanisms that we can come up with, how that reduces the burden for the government, and therefore, how this could all be put together. I still remember at the end of it, I had to go pick up my son, I had a 5.45 hard stop. You know, we started at two, still going at half-past five. I'm itching to say, 'Bob, you can stay here as long as you want, but at 5.45 I need to be out of here because I need to pick up my son from nursery.' Half-past five, Bob says to me, 'That's great, kiddo, go get it done.' Wow. I was like, 'What do you mean – go get it done?' He said to me, 'You're the only person who's figured out how to get this project off the ground – so go get him off the ground.' That was typical Bob; I mean, he was very demanding in terms of the quality of ideas, but once he was convinced, he was willing to back it.[21]

Rosewell, economic advisor to the GLA, believed Crossrail finally got permission because of a concerted campaign by a collection of organizations that worked together to articulate a clear and shared vision of the benefits of the railway and the role it would play in delivering more workers to highly productive central London locations. "The size of the project, and its importance to such a range of businesses, communities and stakeholders, meant that time and energy was spent getting across the technical issues to the wider public and politicians in a clear way, so that they all felt they had some skin in the game."[22] It also needed to be accepted by the Treasury and the DfT; their acceptance of non-transport benefits to the London economy was crucial. The government had to be convinced first that this disruption of government business case methodology would work, then that the agglomeration benefit was real, and finally that the business community would be willing to pay a supplementary business rate, a new tax. A year of intense lobbying of business groups followed, creating an unprecedented level of interest in the London business community and making the case to government. Bridget Rosewell saw, step by step, a coalition being built around the "realization that Crossrail created real additional outputs – 'agglomeration benefits'. That gridlock on the system would happen without it was central to this."[23]

For Rosewell, there was a eureka moment for Crossrail in a room at the Treasury, "a big room, a lot of people, big, long table, presentation by the TfL people including the employment benefits, productivity, current transport system unable to cope … You could see the light bulbs going on in people's heads around the room. I thought, 'Right, we've got it' – that was the moment it changed." [24]

The second Crossrail bill went through Parliament and received royal assent in 2008. Crossrail received funding approval for £14.8 billion in the 2010 Comprehensive Spending Review. This was increased to £17.8 billion following the difficulties and delay in 2018, and by a further £1.1 billion in 2020 to complete the railway. The final cost was £18.8 billion, drawn from a combination of central government, TfL and business rates, with £70 million from the owners of Heathrow, £200 million from the City of London, and a European Investment Bank £1 billion loan. By 2022, 40 per cent of the railway's cost had been met by the London business community through direct contributions and the hypothecated Supplementary Business Rate. London First has convincingly argued that with London's net contribution of £42 billion per year to UK plc, the whole of the line has in effect been funded by London.[25]

This was always much more than just another line on the Tube map: it was at the cutting edge of metro innovation. In 2008 Crossrail set out to deliver the UK's first digital railway: three signalling systems on one super-complex train with a digital backbone, a single control centre in Romford capable of drawing together masses of information from train and station systems. In the control room, on one side was the control desk for all the signalling and the overhead line, with an innovative auto switch which meant that maintainers could get on track a lot quicker and get the maintenance done faster. The other side of that control room was all the security and the cameras and monitors for fire alarms and every door. Everything is networked in an enormous comms network that goes back to Romford.[26]

Crossrail trains

A fleet of 70, 200-metre-long, nine-car trains and their maintenance and storage was tendered for in 2011, the contract won in 2014 by Bombardier ahead of Japan's Hitachi and Spain's CAF. Bombardier[27] began to build trains at Derby from 2014. A massive state-of-the-art depot at Old Oak Common was built, and opened in May 2018 on the site of the former GWR steam sheds of 1906, to service, maintain and store 42 of the 70 trains, with automatic inspection systems, ground source heating and rainwater harvested to wash the trains. The Class 345 Aventra trains were extensively tested from the first prototype delivery in 2016, and were introduced on London Rail services (proto-Crossrail) into mainline stations at Liverpool Street from June 2017 and Paddington from May 2018. With the delay to the line's completion, the shiny new trains were delivered, tested on the outer services and piled up in the depot at Old Oak Common. A further 10 trains were ordered in June 2024 due to the line's success, and to mitigate delays at the Derby plant in building trains for HS2.

Crossrail construction

Construction had started in May 2009 with preliminary demolitions and the creation of worksites for access shafts and tunnel portals. In 2011 tunnelling began, with eight tunnel boring machines each 150 metres long worming their way precisely through the city's complex foundations to create 26 miles of new tunnels by 2015. Sub-surface London is notoriously well populated by the deep pile foundations of multi-storeyed buildings, 2000 years of archaeology, the Thames, and sewers, service pipes, cables and the existing Underground lines. Tunnelling needed to thread through the eye of a needle; at Tottenham Court Road, the Elizabeth line tunnel crosses over the Northern line with just 60 cm to spare.

The tunnels of the new line took mainline-sized trains below central London with direct Underground interchange at every station from Paddington to Whitechapel, and with the national rail network at surface stations to west and east of the central tunnel. Station architecture below ground is either in excavated boxes or tunnelled passageways. Tunnelling using sprayed concrete methods rather than cast-iron rings enabled passages to be tall and the corners gently rounded. Lead architects Grimshaw, in consortium with Atkins, GIA Equation and Maynard, created a common look across the line-wide design for the Elizabeth line, an effortless travel environment from wherever the passenger joins that is intuitive, safe, accessible and enjoyable. The design consortium interfaced with different design teams across the 10 central stations and played a unique role developing a line-wide design strategy that conceptually and functionally binds together the distinct stations along the network.[28]

The linings of glass fibre reinforced concrete are part perforated for acoustic absorption, giving a minimalist feel across the line. Lighting is carefully managed to be brighter in busy spaces, warmer elsewhere, typically reflected rather than direct. On the surface, access to each station in the busy London streetscape is different but the overall design palette is consistent. Personality is introduced to the central stations through commissioned artworks incorporated into the stations, such as Spencer Finch's Cloud Index in the glazed canopy above the station box at Paddington and Simon Periton's intricate glazed screen at Farringdon, 'Avalanche', making reference to the nearby Hatton Garden diamond district.[29]

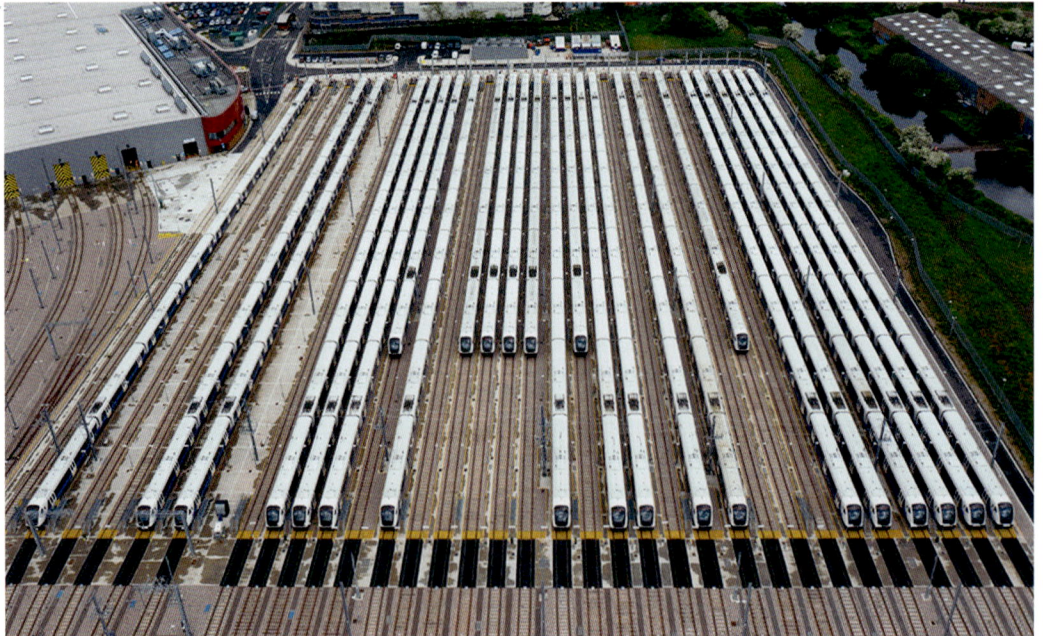

The new Elizabeth line train *(top)*, and *(bottom)*
Elizabeth line trains lined up awaiting service at the
purpose-built Old Oak Common depot, 2018

By the end of 2014 the project was judged to be in good shape, though there were pressures and tensions. Mark Wild, Crossrail CEO, saw the "descent to unreality between 2014 and 2017 … I was on the board, I observed it and we collectively descended in November 2017 to only having a year to go, maximum ambition, only a year to go but we'd lost our sense of reality. By 2018 it was very difficult, because the programme had become discontinuous … the catalysing event that caused this lack of reality was naming a single end date years in advance."[30]

Her Majesty the Queen had visited the Bond Street station construction site in February 2016 when Mayor Johnson announced that the new line would be named the Elizabeth line in her honour. "The Palace was very dubious at first, Her Majesty wanted to be sure that it was going to be popular and successful."[31] At Bond Street, later the last station to complete, the Queen met apprentices, drivers, TfL's Mike Brown and Crossrail chair Terry Morgan, who said, "construction for the new railway is now over 70 per cent complete. The opening of the Elizabeth line in 2018 will be a significant moment for London."[32]

2018: watershed and recovery

**"The courage required to hold up your hand and say 'Stop'
in a megaproject of this type is immense."**

– Tony Meggs, Crossrail chair, in 2019[33]

Unpicking how the project had stumbled and the manner in which it was put back together and triumphantly opened as the Elizabeth line is a heroic story in itself. It illuminates the scale and complexity of a 21st-century megaproject beneath a historic city, and demonstrates the quality of leadership and project skills required to bring this off.

On 26 July 2018, a presentation was made at City Hall by Simon Wright, Crossrail CEO, and Terry Morgan, Crossrail chair, to the mayor, Sadiq Khan, his officials and TfL's commissioner, Mike Brown. The substance was that Crossrail would not be ready to run in December after all. Siemens and Bombardier had not yet been able to start testing the interaction of signals and trains because of the unfinished state of the stations. Throughout 2018 there had been intimations of problems, but this was the point at which a delay of at least a year was formally reported. Crossrail Ltd (CRL) announced late in August 2018 that the line would not be ready for December and would not open until late 2019.

This came as a significant shock to all stakeholders, not least because the CRL team had remained defiantly confident, despite a number of setbacks, that they could fight through and reach the December 2018 opening date. The unexpected announcement at such a late stage created a total breakdown in trust and confidence between the project organization and its sponsors and stakeholders. Simon Wright, in post only from 2018 in succession to Andrew Wolstenholme, CEO since 2011, stood down in November and was replaced by Mark Wild, since 2016 the MD of London Underground. Chair Terry Morgan resigned from Crossrail in December, and was replaced by Tony Meggs in January 2019.

A heroic attitude to opening in December 2018, an end date set as long ago as 2010, had been Crossrail's undoing. Crossrail was a huge and fiendishly complex megaproject that had made 'on time and on budget' its mantra, leading to a pervasive fear of this monumental date being breached and the consequences that would follow. Wild found on arrival as CEO that the increasingly unrealistic opening date had proved to be a catalysing event that had distorted the culture and leadership of the project, had led to opacity in progress and risk reporting, and created a false perception of reality. "The Queen was booked. There was a perception that we could not fail." This had driven the Crossrail project into an organization-wide silent conspiracy in which "we prevented people speaking truth to power in the pursuit of a heroic end date that was probably unachievable; in mid-2017 we were probably done, yet we forged on."[34]

Wild had been a CRL board member as a representative of TfL from 2017 before taking the hot seat as CRL's CEO, and eventually delivered the railway in May 2022. Wild reflected that two project golden rules had been broken.

> First, we thought in 2014 we were halfway there because the civils were finished. We weren't, we were a third of the way there, because we had to do the fit-out, and then we had to do the integration. The railway project was three things: civil engineering, fit-out and integration. For Crossrail, it pretty much took a third, a third, a third to do it. Now Crossrail is uniquely complex but we broke that rule. The other rule we broke is that the last 5 per cent of these projects will take about 20 per cent of the time. And I'd challenge anybody to give me a major programme that's managed to beat that. The last 5 per cent of Crossrail from 2018 took about 26 per cent of the time.[35]

Wild had been involved with project management for 35 years, and Crossrail was by far the biggest thing he had ever seen. One of his first tasks was to bring in people who understood the need to amalgamate all the risks. "In my first two months doing this job, a lot of my effort has gone into getting the right skills base – people with experience and who have done it before. That is not to say that people in the past did not do a fantastic job, but we missed a certain skillset."[36]

Wild and his team had a major task in 2018 unpicking the programme and identifying what still lay outside it. For such a megaproject this took nearly a year to understand. "We interviewed 100 people, and everybody ... said they knew the ball was bust. Typically, they knew their part of the project was behind, 'but I thought his or her bit was worse', or 'if only I could have seen the whole', 'we should have seen Bond Street was behind' … this silent conspiracy as a leader is the thing to really counteract. Have you got transparency and owning the whole, or do you have lip service in a silent conspiracy? I think the art of leadership might be to get that out."[37] "Why do people create an illusion for senior management to feel good?' Wild mused. "The minute you have a false green in a complex world like Crossrail, which is bigger than the ocean [it is fatal]. In Crossrail I had dashboards; in 2018 they were green, they said we were 95 per cent complete. We weren't, we were 60 per cent complete."[38]

Stakeholder scrutiny and anger surfaced at the Public Accounts Committee in March 2019. As witnesses, Wild, three months in post, new CRL chair Tony Meggs, six weeks in post, and DfT permanent secretary Bernadette Kelly faced angry MPs, who were keen to ascribe blame for Crossrail's delay. "Let's start with the obvious one," began Lee Rowley, MP. "We are nearly £3 billion over budget. That is a combination of capital and then revenue loss. And we have no end date. Who is responsible for this screw-up?"[39] They pointed to warning signs, such as an explosion at the Pudding Mill Lane electricity substation in November 2017 and the Jacobs report in April 2018, which identified pressure on programme and sequencing delays across the infrastructure contracts that threatened the start of trial running and operations. "Delivery performance has varied across the rail systems, and concerns remain with general progress at Central Section."[40] "It is incredible – incredible – for senior people, other than Mr Meggs, who was not involved, to sit here and tell me you were not clear that this was going to fall over. It was perfectly clear that it was going to fall over – it is in black and white," continued Rowley, with all the clarity of hindsight.[41]

Tony Meggs sought to demonstrate to the committee that the project had suffered from a degree of compression, by which he meant "it was not properly understood, the final works – the very complex work that is going on right now – had too short a period of time. The extreme commitment within the project … to meeting a particular date – 9 December last year – created an environment in which there was a great deal of over-optimism, and possibly poor reporting upwards of the realities on a day-to-day basis."[42]

Wild maintained that the main cause of delay was the lack of installation of the signalling systems, and that the station works were also a long way behind. "I honestly and objectively believe the aggregation of risk is the key issue." Crucially, the systems' integration across Crossrail's many contracts, the key to a digital railway, had been left to the contractors to address and was simply not on the CRL radar. In his evidence, Wild judged the risk process in Crossrail to be quite well managed, but with the key exception of not properly assessing the amalgamation of system integration.

With hindsight, it is now clear that the management team did not have a good enough grip or understanding of the work still to do – particularly the adjacency of work between stations and trains and the amalgamation of different work streams. We are fixing them now by putting a lot of effort into systematic risk and system engineering risk. I think that is where the gap occurred, because by the time we got to the summer of last year, the amalgamation of systematic risks was not quantified. Hence, we are seeing a large extension of the programme. I do not think the systematic risks were identified at that time.[43]

The other significant reflection from Crossrail's new leadership was that the transition from a civil engineering focus to fit-out and operation had diminished financial and programme control over the project. For Meggs, "a demobilization decision was taken, which was driven again by schedule and, I think, cost pressures, clearly prematurely. The controls on the project – the financial controls and the project controls – and other aspects of the project lost grip in the second half of last year."[44]

The fundamental problem was a compression of the schedule, driven by a ruthless determination to hit a particular date that was set 10 years before. That created an environment in which people were very driven towards that date and not properly seeing all the risks contained in that compression of schedule. Meggs believed "the previous management was excellent in the civil engineering phase of building tunnels and building the core of the stations. For the complex system integration work that is now going on, however – let me put it this way – we have a great deal more expertise in that area now than we had six months ago, led by Mark [Wild]."[45]

Pushed hard on why this had not been identified earlier, Kelly said, "As late as March/April we were still looking at budget overruns of at most £200 million to £300 million. Obviously, we were disappointed and concerned about that, but in a project of this scale it was a warning bell, but it wasn't a sign of problems as major as the ones that we subsequently, over the summer, came to realize were crystallizing … But I also think this reflects in part the fact that the scale of these problems emerged far faster, frankly, than one would have expected."[46]

It was not just the stakeholders who were looking for explanations. The project's staff group was angry, upset and shell-shocked by the emerging story of massive delay. It was important for the new leadership to surface what they called the background conversations. For the operators, these were that the delivery team would do a shoddy job and leave them stranded, that they were cowboys. The delivery team's background conversation was that the operators were creating unnecessary refinements, were 'gold plating'. Neither of these things was actually true or spoken out loud. Wild saw this as a catalytic process: "I would say it took us a good year to flush it out … I think for any leader who wants to change culture, you can't leave dominant things in the background, they must be in the foreground. How you create an environment for somebody to speak in the foreground about what they're really thinking is one of the things you could do to prevent this occurring."[47]

Recovery demanded more people, more expert fire power and capacity to build systems integration. Colin Brown, Crossrail's technical director from 2018, reflected that "we had to pull people in to understand where the software really was, how much complexity we were dealing with, and how we were going to actually carve it into stages. It took us from 2019 through to the middle of 2020 before we really got a grip on it." A year on from the watershed the scale of the remaining task was better understood, and a six-month window for opening the line was outlined for 2021.

The scale of the Elizabeth line build was remarkable: 26 miles of new tunnels, nine central London stations, five shafts, five portals, enormous constructions, with each station a 10-storey building built underground as London worked overhead, 70 new trains that 'talked' to three signalling systems, dedicated communication systems, all joining with existing legacy systems, all integrated into a single control centre at Romford.

A first level of complexity on such a megaproject was having the 10 top tier contractors all working concurrently, all trying to deliver at the same time, all pulling on the same subcontractors, for plant and tier two suppliers, and all wanting access to the railway. "As you get more and more integrated, they're all tripping over themselves, wanting more and more access." Brown recollected that "in 2019 productivity just fell off a cliff because everybody wanted to be the same place at the same time. Normally, that's just standard practice for major railway projects and major infrastructure projects." Crossrail then had to add another layer of complexity on top of its huge scale and concurrent work, "and that's the complexity of system coupling, which, combined with the other two, just pushed the programme into uncharted territory."[48]

Crossrail had sought to pass the risk of integration to the supply chain. But you cannot do that with a complex system. "The first lesson," said Brown, "is you can't outsource systems integration ... an over-reliance on contracts to handle integration, even if they are world-leading in their field, will not give you an integrated system. We didn't have idiots running some of these contracts; Siemens, Bombardier, they are global companies, they really know their stuff, but they needed support."[49]

Design for the more complex parts of the system was needed much earlier. "If you've got something complex to build, let your most complex contracts as soon as you can, otherwise you'll end up just recreating the same path of domino falls that Crossrail fell into. The other issue we had was there was an over-reliance on the individual contracts to actually deliver an integrated system. The programme back then also was going to deliver everything for one big bang commissioning. Obviously, for complex systems you have to deliver in stages."[50]

Crossrail tunnelling machine Elizabeth breaks through at the eastern end of Liverpool Street station in May 2013

BREAKING NEW GROUND   353

"Inevitably, a project carves up the work into contracts and you end up with gaps between those contracts ... contracts force suppliers to become quite silent in their thinking, where people are unprepared to go beyond the bounds of their contracts." For Brown, "integration is primarily a messy, dirty task of making sure that those bridges, those gaps between contracts, are actually sorted."[51] The bringing together of contractors in open dialogue to problem-solve and integrate their works was essential to Crossrail's recovery. Breaking down contractual barriers was facilitated by the dire state of the project by 2018, but demanded the creation of a structured and open approach.

Chris Binns, chief engineer for Crossrail from 2015 to 2022, had been chief engineer of the £7 billion Thameslink upgrade, previously the most complex application of digital technology to a railway which had upgraded the infrastructure and signalling on this busy north–south route through the capital. Even Binns had never worked with such a massive design as Crossrail, then one of Europe's largest and most complex engineering projects. The document control database had over three million designs, documents and drawings. "It is just enormous. It is almost beyond any one person to take in, and took quite some management, but by structuring it, we were able to." [52]

The mammoth task of integration across stations, trains and signals was pursued through open processes and panels, which drew together contractors from around the world to address the challenge of integration. Binns stressed the significance of the 'plateau' process, which was set up in 2019 to resolve and integrate issues across the technical and contractual boundaries. The name had first been attached to the process at a Bombardier aircraft plant in Montreal where, to integrate more effectively the complex interfaces between engine and airframe design, system specialists were physically co-located on a mezzanine area known as the Plateau.[53]

Mark Wild brought the term 'plateau' and the practice into Crossrail, with Bombardier and Siemens specialists co-located at Stratford with Howard Smith's systems teams, "with daily and weekly 'drumbeats', 'sprints', problem-solving and mutual support. This brought signalling and train integration and other systems quickly through to an operational railway."[54] This was headed up by Pradeep Vasudev as head of systems integration:

> It was about all of us working towards a single goal ... Bringing the operator inside the tent made a huge difference, because the operator understood very clearly and felt the pain that the operator would have, even during the test programme ... That trust made a huge difference, but it also gave us the ability then to prioritize how the contractors delivered their software to us, so we could tell them, 'We need these fixed; we can wait on those' ... as long as there was trust between all parties, they would accept some things that didn't work, knowing they're going to come

HM The Queen meets Mike Brown, the mayor and Crossrail staff at Bond Street in 2016 when the new line named in her honour was announced

good later. That kind of relationship in this type of project, with all its complexity, you need that level of trust and transparency to be able to deal with it.[55]

On his arrival to the project in 2018, Colin Brown was interested to know how many bugs there were in the software.

Siemens clearly [knew], but they didn't want to share it. On the train, we did have data, because Howard [Smith] and his team had already got it from Bombardier … You need to build the capability in the organization for you to earn the right to get transparency from the supply chain. Pradeep and I went to Stockholm for ETCS,[56] went to Derby, went to Paris, it was face to face with the engineers to make them realize, 'Oh, hang on, these guys will actually get it if I hand this stuff over'. That was really important – to build that trust.[57]

As the project found its feet once more, it was brought to a grinding halt by Covid-19. All site work stopped at lockdown in March 2020, with site works being recovered only from August. In a curious way, hybrid working from home was a boon to some elements of the project, enabling, for example, the huge task of generating the safety assurance documentation to be worked on away from distraction.

By the spring of 2021, the commissioning of the railway could start, trains test-running to timetable and building reliability in the system by ironing out the bugs in the complex digital architecture. Station works still needed to be completed, especially at Bond Street, which had been revealed as being far behind the programme. Wild described thousands of people being involved in works below London, despite trains running through the platforms to the timetable as stations and systems were being completed and systems integrated.

By the end of 2021 the final stage of testing began: trial operations, with full trial running of the eventual timetable to test the system before opening to passenger service in May 2022. Having taken such a reputational hit in 2018, there was a steely determination on the project's part not to skimp on the testing and trial running; Wild reflected that "we probably waited at least four to five months to cook the railway more", to have it ready for reliable service from opening.[58]

The recovery of the project from the deep hole of 2018 had demanded a fresh project culture enabled by sophisticated and committed leadership; openness where there had been opacity, owning the whole rather than the individual contract, putting in place the right teams at the right stage of the project, everyone focused on the endgame and the steps needed to reach it. The working culture was led and modelled right from the top. As Vasudev recalled:

> There was effectively a plateau at the CEO level in the last year or so. Every week we would have meetings with the CEO, Mark Wild, the CEO of Siemens, the CEO of Alstom, etc. all meeting. So that level of working and commitment was all the way up at the top and all the way down at the working level, it was a complete transparency and ownership of the overall plan.[59]

Collaborative behaviours were modelled from the top down, instigated by Mark Wild in what Brown described as his "Northern-style vocabulary of one-liners – 'owning the whole', 'don't walk past the trash', 'modelling the core behaviours' – which forced us all to role-model him; 'if you haven't got the ball, stay in position', 'keep your foot on the ball' – one-liners that actually we collectively started to exhibit from the top down in the project team, which the supply chain started to pick up on as well."[60]

Andy Byford, an LU graduate trainee at Regent's Park station in the 1980s, had left London to pursue an illustrious career around the world's metros in Sydney, Toronto and New York. Byford was appointed to follow Mike Brown in May 2020 as TfL commissioner 004, as he liked to remark. His commitment from the off was to get the Elizabeth line open and secure a long-term funding agreement from government.

A construction shaft at Essex Wharf, Whitechapel, in October 2018

Byford brought the Crossrail project back in-house to TfL. This freed CEO Wild from answering to the project board every four weeks at GLA meetings and "spending more time on answering committee questions than doing the doing". Byford described his role as like that of the line blocker in American football: "Leave the politics to me, leave all the outward-facing stuff to me, I'll deal with that. I'll buffer you from it. What I want you to do is drive the contractors. If someone called Mark to a hearing, I'd say, 'He's not going, I'll go.' It was a good double act."[61]

Byford was a force of nature, and displayed a highly visible style of leadership, with weekly staff video briefings from all round the TfL family. He was clear from the start that getting the Elizabeth line open was what he was there for. "He was pretty ruthlessly focused, with a relentless interest," Smith recalled, "clearing the way and getting the whole of TfL – everything from fares and ticketing to LU operational readiness – focused on the idea that the thing that mattered was opening the Elizabeth line."[62] For Byford, getting the line open was always much more than a being a cheerleader. "It was specific hard yards, it was hard input with a very good team. Mark had built a fabulous team, it was his success, wonderful people, and right down to the project managers and contract management, wonderful people." Byford believes his contribution was "to show what was possible, to drive the thing and not accept 'Oh, well, another slippage'; [instead] we will find a way to mitigate any slippage such that the end date doesn't slip. Mark and I were a good combo."[63]

As Byford recalled,

> We drove that to the finish line every single day. It was an obsession of mine. I had Mark and his three key direct reports [Howard Smith, Jim Crawford, Richard Schofield][64] report to me every single day for two years, even on the weekend. Mark did me an update every day during the week; we had an 8 a.m. call where I wanted to know, 'In the last 23 hours, 59 minutes, 59 seconds, has anything cropped up that you need to elevate to me? I want to know within 24 hours, so that we can do something about it.' We were fixated on having it ready for the Queen's Jubilee.[65]

This enabled Byford to manage the multiple stakeholders – the mayor's office, DfT, the business community – to win political support, to build confidence in the project's recovery and the funding to get it across the line.

Byford's visible leadership and the project's open plateau method extended into the crucial testing and commissioning phase of the railway. Smith chaired monthly, then eventually weekly, T-Minus meetings "that gauged and agonized over readiness to open something so huge and novel" as Crossrail. The group included at "super senior level" the Crossrail team: London Underground, Network Rail – including CEO Andrew Haines, Alstom, train builders and MTR train operators – and also the TfL commissioner; they worked through one hundred lines to establish red, amber,

The Whitechapel station's crisp architecture emerges between 2018 and 2021

green against the programme as opening approached. "A Wild mantra was 'red is good', the complete opposite of the Crossrail first five or 10 years … where everybody started every meeting saying, 'Everything's green' and then cross-questioned each other, either blatantly or in code. At T-Minus, there was 100 per cent trust, the form wasn't to cross-question each other on should it be red, should it be green, where are you? The discipline was that for all of us, if you're saying green or amber, you're saying you're all right."[66]

Wild had exhibited a quality of leadership that won huge respect from those above and below him, exhibiting a heroic lack of ego in a performative and shouty political and senior executive world. Within days of the line opening, he quietly moved on to the next job – heading the SGN gas distribution network. It will be of great significance that in 2024 he returned to lead the opening of another UK railway troubled by short-term performative politicking and funding issues, HS2.

In 2023, looking back on the recovery of the project, Crossrail chair Tony Meggs reflected on the high order of mature leadership exhibited:

> Mark, personally, I think that he has very strong leadership characteristics, but not a huge ego at all … It is really about mature leadership … real maturity is getting your kicks in different ways, and that is getting your pleasure from helping other people to succeed. The real job of the board and the CEO here is to create the environment where other people can be successful, but that is not an egotistical

Whitechapel station in 2021

job; as Mark says, it requires self-confidence. Indeed, it requires a lot more self-confidence to be that kind of a leader, which is the leader that leads by empowering others. Too often in big projects, we're in a different mode, a kind of military command-and-control mode, and we need to shift into this empowerment, which I think we did, and I think Mark and his team did very successfully.[67]

The Elizabeth line opens

"The first railway in the world … of which it will never be truer to say, if we build it, they will use it."

– Andy Lord, TfL commissioner at Crossrail Legacy seminar, April 2023

The much-anticipated day arrived on 17 May 2022. The Queen's health was failing, and there was uncertainty at Paddington before the royal opening whether she would be able to open 'her' new line in person. Indeed, two plaques were made to cover the contingency of HRH Prince Edward, Earl of Wessex stepping into the breach. Forty-five minutes before the event, there was a call from Buckingham Palace, the plaques were swapped and the Queen's put up, fixed in a lower position. The Queen herself cut a frail figure in her buttercup-yellow coat and hat as she descended into the station's airy brick-walled ticket hall with Lord-Lieutenant Sir Kenneth Olisa. As the lift doors opened to the sounds of 'Morningtown Ride' sung by the TfL choir, she was introduced to TfL Commissioner Andy Byford, who in turn introduced Mayor Sadiq Khan, PM Johnson, Minister of Transport Grant Shapps and key members of station staff. At Byford's invitation, the smiling 96-year-old monarch then pulled the cord to open purple curtains revealing the commemorative plaque. Customer Experience Assistant Kofi Duah then showed the Queen how to top up her Oyster card at the ticket machine. Then Her Majesty rode back up in the lift to be whisked away by limousine to the muffled cheers of guests and the crowds outside. The Earl of Wessex and the VIPs descended to platform level and took a short ride with Howard Smith to Tottenham Court Road, where they were given a tour of the platform level with its cool lighting and acoustic baffling.[68] The prince then rode back to Paddington in the train cab for the forward view down the tunnel. The Elizabeth line opened for public service a week later, on 24 May.

The scale of the achievement is so great that it is worth reiterating what was involved in the building of the Elizabeth line. It is 73 miles long, of which 26 miles were in new tunnels, serving 40 stations, 10 of which were also new. The trains were 200 metres long, with a capacity for 1500 passengers, almost twice that of a Tube train. The line extended east and west beyond London and brought 1.5 million more people to within 45 minutes' journey time of central London. The line added 10 per cent to the capacity of the Underground network, with interchange to all the other

HM The Queen opens the Elizabeth line at Paddington on 18 May 2022

lines on the Tube, the most significant addition to the capital's rail network since the Victoria line in 1968. The first phase opened as three separate railways: Paddington to Abbey Wood, Reading and Heathrow to Paddington mainline, and Shenfield to Liverpool Street mainline. The line ran six days a week to allow for further testing and software updates. The real railway challenge was in November 2022, when trains began to run through the central section from both the east and the west, across three signalling systems. From May 2023 a fully integrated service pattern allowed seamless travel across the whole line, with 600 million journeys made on the line by its third anniversary in May 2025.[69] The line has already made a positive impact throughout its length on job creation, connectivity and development.[70] "The findings from these reports confirm that the railway is powering important regeneration through new jobs and homes," said Andy Lord in January 2025. "As we look ahead to the next 500 million journeys, we will continue to focus on improving things for our customers, to ensure we remain London's most popular railway."[71]

The Elizabeth line set a new standard for an underground railway in terms of ambience, speed and comfort. Passenger numbers on the new line grew rapidly and soon represented up to one in six of all rail journeys in the UK. As with all large infrastructure projects, its gestation and progress had been buffeted by political considerations which prolonged decision-making, made for endless debate over impact models and funding, and ultimately led to a four-year delay due to the

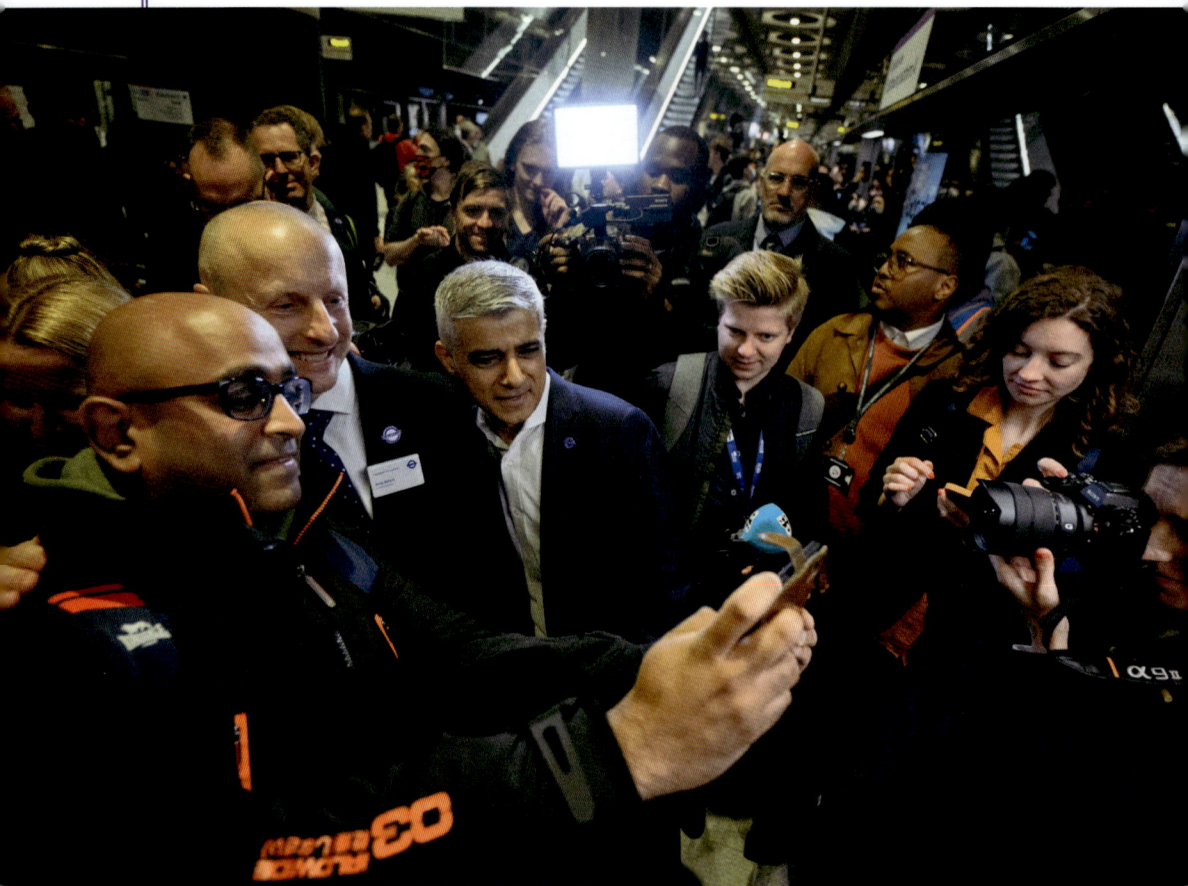

Mayor Khan and Commissioner Andy Byford before boarding
the first public service at Paddington, 25 May 2022

underestimated complexity of integration across the railway's digital architecture and the interruption of the Covid-19 pandemic. This was truly a megaproject in its scale, complexity and innovation. That the line should emerge from adversity in such great shape, winning passenger plaudits and architectural prizes, was a tribute to all who had worked on the project since the 1990s. The result is arguably inconceivable without the convening advocacy of a London mayor, TfL, London First and the London business community.

Denis Tunnicliffe had been chair and chief executive of London Transport from 1998 to 2000 for the opening of the Jubilee line extension, a megaproject from a generation earlier, which had suffered from cost overrun and a fixed opening date of 31 December 1999 for the Millennium celebrations at the Dome. Tunnicliffe remembers saying to his JLE project team: "Remember, delay is only a concept in prospect. It is not a concept in retrospect. When they're using the railway, nobody will remember the delay. It will be irrelevant and frankly, so is overspend."[72]

Elizabeth line – the verdict

"I've spent many hours in front of select committees explaining why Crossrail was late and over budget – I could write a book – but I always believed it would come good in the end, and thanks to a lot of brilliant work, it has."

– Bernadette Kelly, DfT permanent secretary, 2022[73]

In October 2024 the Elizabeth line won the RIBA Stirling Prize for Architecture as the UK's best new building. Speaking on behalf of the prize jury, Muyiwa Oki, RIBA president and jury chair, said: "The Elizabeth line is a triumph in architect-led collaboration, offering a flawless, efficient, beautifully choreographed solution to inner-city transport"[74] that transformed "the typical commuter chaos … into an effortless experience".[75] "This is architecture of the digital age – a vast scheme that utilizes cutting-edge technology to create distinctive spatial characteristics and experiences. It rewrites the rules of accessible public transport, and sets a bold new standard for civic infrastructure, opening up the network – and by extension, London – to everyone.'[76]

"The Elizabeth line is so good it is almost boring," commented the *RIBA Journal*. "The architecture has already been absorbed into the London experience. But it shouldn't be taken for granted. The design makes for frictionless journeys; the enclosed underground spaces feel open and relaxed even when busy, as one tunnel curves seamlessly into the next. The clean clarity of its wall panels, clear grids running through them, the warmth of lighting and integrated systems elevate the travelling experience."[77]

The last word should go to CEO Mark Wild, who is very clear that the principal leadership quality needed for such a megaproject is authenticity.

There is a merit in the humble, kind, authentic leader … the incomplete leader, and in the modern world, it's impossible now for one human being to master every tool; maybe that wasn't the case 30 years ago. Now, in the communication age, the ball is moving so fast that the incomplete leader might be the best one to have. Authenticity, being humble, being able to work from the shopfloor to the top of the organization, able to show your vulnerability, able to sometimes say, 'I don't know, what do you think?' and resilience – in my opinion, they are some of the key elements.[78]

14.

HEADWINDS FOR THE THIRD MAYOR

"I want every single Londoner to get the opportunities that our city gave to me and my family. The opportunities not just to survive but to thrive. The opportunities to build a better future for you and your family, with a decent and affordable home and a comfortable commute you can afford."

– Mayor Sadiq Khan[1]

Improving the quality of the capital's air and the health of its citizens was the overarching objective of Mayor Sadiq Khan's integrated transport strategy, published in 2018. Transport delivered across an increasingly broad urban front as TfL not only upgraded Tube signalling and rolling stock and the bus fleet, but also became the enabler of improving air quality and of housing development and the facilitator of active travel. After a decade, terrorism returned to London's streets in 2016, bringing renewed emphasis on public safety and security. With the decline in the operating grant from central government, TfL's funding situation was weakened just as public demand for transport softened and revenue from the new Elizabeth line was postponed. The advent of Covid-19 from March 2020 saw the capital locked down three times and dependent on its public transport to move essential workers. The pandemic decimated TfL revenue, and the request to government for funding support occasioned political dispute and the effective rollback of London devolution.

The fifth mayoral election

The London mayoral election in May 2016 attracted 12 candidates, all new faces, to the race. After running four times, Ken Livingstone did not stand as a candidate. Labour's London members selected Sadiq Khan, MP for Tooting since 2005 and shadow justice minister, ahead of Tessa Jowell, heroine of the London 2012 Olympics. Boris Johnson had since 2015 turned towards renewed parliamentary ambition and the campaign for the Brexit referendum in June 2016 as a route to power and influence. Zac Goldsmith, the environmentalist MP for Richmond, secured the Conservative nomination. Of the other 10 candidates, all of whom opposed the extension of Heathrow Airport, Sian Berry for the Greens, Caroline Pidgeon for the Liberal Democrats and Peter Whittle for UKIP were leading candidates in the mayoral debate, but the contest from early on was clearly between Khan and Goldsmith. For the first time, housing, the environment and security in the wake of Islamic State terrorism (the attack in Paris took place in November 2015) came to join transport at the top of the mayoral manifestos.

Khan's manifesto had focused on housing, pledging a database of landlords who had been prosecuted for housing-related offences, a mayor-controlled not-for-profit letting agency, and measures to address gender inequality, notably on domestic and sexual violence, the gender pay gap and the high cost of childcare. For transport, he pledged a freeze on rail fares and greener transport. The Greens and Liberal Democrats were focused on the shortage and high cost of housing. Goldsmith's manifesto focused on the economy, promising that his house and infrastructure building policies would help create 500,000 jobs. He also promised a freeze on mayoral taxes and an increase in police numbers. Green issues were a core part of his agenda, with new traffic regulations to encourage cleaner vehicles and the creation of new pocket parks.

Mayoral elections up to 2016 had been dominated by the big personalities of Livingstone and Johnson. The tetchy campaign between Khan and Goldsmith descended into barely concealed racist taunts against Khan, who had become the first Muslim MP when he won Tooting in 2005, and in the other direction accusations of Islamophobia against Goldsmith. Labour had secured seats in London during the 2015 general election against the national trend. In the highest turnout since 2000, at 45 per cent, Khan won the mayoral election with 56.8 per cent of the votes in the second round ahead of Goldsmith's 43.2 per cent, and became London's first Muslim mayor.

The handover – Johnson to Khan

The handover between mayors of differing political hues and contrasting styles was again a challenge for the TfL leadership, led from 2015 by its third commissioner, Mike Brown. Since joining the Underground in 1989, Brown had risen through a series of operational roles to become its chief operating officer, leaving in 2008 to be the MD at Heathrow Airport and returning as MD London Underground in 2010. His team had grown accustomed to what one described as Johnson's "jolly, exciting, humorous, collegiate administration" as opposed to what would be the more sombre regime of Sadiq Khan.[2] As in 2008, with the previous transition from Livingstone to Johnson, it took time to build trust and adjust working relationships with the new mayor and his team. "I don't blame Sadiq for that," Brown reflected. "I was appointed by the previous mayor, I could have been in his eyes a Tory boy ... I've never expressed any political view out loud. Until I left TfL, I'd never voted in a mayoral election."[3] Leon Daniels, MD for Surface Transport, recalled that it was difficult to integrate with Khan's administration when even the deputy mayors had relatively little time with the mayor. "We weren't Boris sympathizers. We were just doing the job, just delivering the goods as we were supposed to do."[4]

During his campaign, Sadiq Khan had made it clear that he thought TfL was good but flabby, and that he was going to move on the fat cats who were running TfL including Mike Brown, whom he mentioned by name. After Vernon Everitt, MD for Customers, Communication and Technology, had rolled the pitch with City Hall, Mike Brown was first in to meet Khan on the Monday after his election on 9 May. "I had a pack in my hand, and I said, 'Mike Brown, TfL. Hi, I will deliver your manifesto." Brown recognized that the Hopper fare was the first real moment "for me from Sadiq to test that I was there for delivery of the things that he wanted to do – that changed the dynamic quite a bit. I remember in those early two or three months sitting beside Ed Lister, who had been Boris's chief of staff, at a dinner in Westminster; Ed Lister said, 'Mike, I feel for you because this first year is just going to be real shit.' I didn't realize he was understating how challenging it would be in that transition."[5]

The introduction of a freeze on general fares and the new Hopper fare – unrestricted bus and tram travel for £1.50 in the first hour – was an early test for TfL set by the new mayor. These were showcase manifesto commitments he wanted introduced quickly, within three months, whereas the TfL technical team said it would take a year. Commissioner Mike Brown pushed the team to do it in six months, "I went back to Sadiq the following week and I said, 'I can do it in four months', which was a real punt actually, but it was an informed punt. I really believed if we put the right resource and energy into it, we could do it."[6] The Hopper fare was introduced in September 2016.

After 15 years of growth in ridership, there had been the first signs in 2016 of a softening in demand across all transport modes, but especially for bus services. No one cause was attributed, but the roads disruption for building Cycle Superhighways, the booming property market and its construction traffic, and the growing numbers of 'white van' deliveries, all contributed to greater road congestion and a less reliable bus service. Plans were made to reduce the service as fares revenue fell. "We were going slower and slower," John Traynor, MD of London General, reflected. "Traffic speeds across London are about nine or nine and a half miles per hour. On some services, such as route 11, which is one of our flagships – Liverpool Street to Fulham Broadway – it was at some times a day down below four miles per hour. You could almost walk quicker. That inevitably led to patronage starting to fall."[7]

Under the TfL bus contracts, operators receive a quality incentive bonus or, if the service falls beneath specification, a penalty. "During that 18-month to two-year period, our quality bonuses went to zero," Traynor rued. "That affected our ability to invest in pay rises and new vehicles, etc. So that wasn't a good period for running our businesses or the quality of the service we were providing. That inevitably led to a sometimes challenging relationship with the regulator [TfL]. I was saying to them, "I didn't dig the roads up, I didn't agree to these schemes or the phasing of them."[8]

Relations between the new mayor and his predecessor Johnson proved politically combative. Khan put the Garden Bridge on review and consequently dropped it, and TfL was instructed not to use the New Routemaster buses (NRMs) on posters and publicity. In late 2016, Sadiq Khan discontinued procurement of the NRMs in favour of off-the-peg buses, and promised a four-year public transport fares freeze.[9]

As Customer and Revenue director, Chris Macleod – and his marketing team – had to adjust to the new mayor's tighter control of the messaging and communications grid, which extended, for example, to intervening on the Tube advertising policy on body image and high-fat foods. "There was just a sense that TfL had somehow been allowed to run wild and needed to be brought under the mayoral whip."[10] Regular London media appearances by the TfL leadership were curtailed by the new regime, replaced by the mayor and his advisors. It took time to get beyond suspicion, beyond what Sadiq Khan did not like – such as the new Routemaster, the Uber licence – to get into the real agenda that emerged, focused on air quality.

'A fairer, greener, healthier and more prosperous city'

"Looking at our transport system as a single, connected whole is the key to addressing London's current and future challenges."

– Sadiq Khan, Mayor's Transport Strategy, 2018[11]

The Mayor's Transport Strategy (MTS) of 2018 had moved a long way in its scope and ambition from the first such strategy in 2001, maturing from its major original task of fixing London's public transport to deploying transport to make a better London. The mayor's vision for the next 20 years was a holistic manifesto for a healthier capital. Beneath the overarching Healthy Streets Approach, which prioritized human health and the transport experience in London, were two principal aims: to reduce Londoners' dependency on cars and to increase the share of active travel – walking, cycling and public transport – to 80 per cent of all trips in London by 2041. Representing the most ambitious transport strategy to date, as Mayor Khan outlined in his foreword, "Transport is a cornerstone of my vision for a fairer, greener, healthier and more prosperous city ... Transport doesn't only shape our daily lives and determine how we get around London – it can create new opportunities for Londoners and shape the character of our city."[12]

The MTS cited continuing car dependency as the cause of poor health in the capital through polluted, congested and dangerous streets. Overcrowded and sometimes unreliable Tube, rail and bus services did not provide an appealing alternative to the private car. "To begin to resolve these problems, London must become a city where walking, cycling and green public transport become the most appealing and practical choices for many more journeys. These active, efficient and sustainable transport choices not only support the health and well-being of Londoners, but also the city as a whole by reducing congestion and enabling the most efficient use of valuable street space."[13] This move to an environmental positioning sharpened during the creation of the strategy, not least because of the new mayor's recent and personal conversion to the centrality of air quality to a better city.

It is significant that when London's third mayor wrote a book it was not a novel, a political autobiography or the life of Churchill or Shakespeare, but a manifesto for greener politics and how to win people around to better air quality. Sadiq Khan's *Breathe – How to Win a Greener World* was published in 2023, a candid account of his journey from "Land Rover driver to electric bike evangelist".[14]

The air we breathe

"Cities are where we will lose or win the climate change battle."

– Christiana Figueres, former executive secretary of the United Nations
   Framework Convention on Climate Change[15]

London's air quality had long been a matter for concern. The city's rapid industrial and population growth in the 19th century was accompanied by choking fogs, the putrefaction of the river Thames and three major cholera epidemics. In response, London's first city-wide infrastructure authority was set up, and from 1859 its chief engineer, Joseph Bazalgette, embarked on a radical renewal and extension of the sewers away from the river to sewage treatment sites to the east of the city, described by *The Observer* as "the most extensive and wonderful work of modern times".[16] The new District Railway opened in 1870 from Westminster east to Blackfriars beneath the new Victoria Embankment, inboard of the sewer.

The question of air quality arose once more in 1952, the year of the Great Smog, when a severe air pollution event affected London for five days from 5 December. Bitterly cold weather and windless conditions led to airborne pollutants, mostly from the use of coal for heating and power generation but also from industry, diesel buses and steam locomotives, to form a thick layer of smog – a dense, greenish-yellow grey fog composed of soot and sulphur dioxide – over the city for five days. This was a far worse 'pea souper' than Londoners had ever experienced,

If you could see London's air, you'd want to clean it too.

The Mayor has introduced a £10 T-Charge for older more polluting vehicles driving in central London. It's part of his bold plan to clean up London's toxic air. Find out what else he's doing at **london.gov.uk/cleanair**

#CleanAir

MAYOR OF LONDON

with visibility reduced to just a few yards. Only the Underground ran; flights were grounded, bus, ambulance and boat services halted, outdoor sports events cancelled, cinemas and theatres closed as the smog crept indoors. Crime rose and people wore smog masks. There may have been as many as 12,000 deaths from respiratory effects, a higher toll than the final cholera epidemic in 1866. The Great Smog proved to be a seminal moment in the public association of poor air quality with ill health.

The Clean Air Act was passed in 1956, restricting the burning of coal in homes and factories in urban areas and authorizing local councils to set up smoke-free zones. The transition away from coal as London's primary heating source towards gas, oil and electricity took years, and during that time deadly fogs periodically occurred, such as one that killed some 750 people in 1962.

London's air pollution remains severe and deadly, less visible but consistently recorded and scientifically analysed. TfL has reported that road vehicles produce nearly half of all nitrogen oxides and emit tiny particles of rubber and metal into the air. "Londoners are developing life-changing illnesses such as cancer, asthma and lung disease. Recent reports show a link between air pollution and an increased risk of developing dementia. More than 500,000 Londoners live with asthma and are more vulnerable to the impact of toxic air … Air pollution contributes to the premature death of thousands of Londoners every year."[17]

A child dies

"London's streets should be for active travel and social interaction, but too often they are places for cars, not people. Most of the main causes of early death in London are linked to inactivity, including the two biggest killers – heart disease and cancer. This inactivity is in part due to an overdependence on cars, even for very short trips. Today's children are the first generation that is expected to live more of their lives in ill health from chronic diseases than their parents."[18]

– Mayor's Transport Strategy, 2018

In 2013, a nine-year-old south Londoner, Ella Adoo-Kissi-Debrah, died from an exceptionally rare and severe form of asthma after 30 hospital visits over three years. The coroner who investigated her premature death following a severe asthma attack and seizure suggested this was "possibly caused by a reaction to something in the air". Her mother learned about the adverse effects of air pollution on health, and began a campaign for clean air and for air pollution to be cited on her daughter's death certificate. Air pollution expert Professor Stephen Holgate re-examined Ella's case, and identified a clear correlation between spikes in air pollution and

facing: The mayor of London's clean air public awareness campaign for the T-charge, 2017

Commuters making their way across London Bridge in April 2014, when London smog and red dust from the Sahara caused high levels of air pollution

Ella's admissions to hospital. At a second inquest, held in 2020, the evidence for air pollution was presented; the finding was that Ella "died of asthma contributed to by excessive air pollution",[19] the first person in the UK for whom air pollution was listed as a cause of death.

Sian Berry, Green Party co-leader, said after the inquest: "History has been made today, and we can finally see a measure of justice for Ella and for her mother Rosamund, who had fought so bravely to bring this case. Now we must see emergency action from all levels of government: the prime minister, the mayor and every local council, to eliminate the sources of deadly air pollution."[20]

Healthy Streets for a healthy city

Each London mayor has had a personal cause that drives innovation in transport. For Livingstone it was the congestion charge, for Johnson cycling, and now for Khan it was air quality – "the biggest public health emergency of a generation"– which emerged in a series of policy measures, starting with a pollution audit for 50 of the most polluted London schools; "It is shameful that children across London are breathing in toxic air simply by going to and from school, and I am determined to do everything in my power to safeguard their health."[21]

The year after Ella's death, Khan, at that time MP for Tooting and shadow secretary of state for justice, was persuaded to run the London Marathon by *Evening Standard* journalist David Cohen, raising money for the Dispossessed Fund supporting vulnerable people across the capital. He finished his first marathon in a respectable time, ahead of parliamentary colleagues Ed Balls and Andy Burnham, and continued to enjoy jogging. During 2015 Khan began to have respiratory symptoms – wheezing, coughing and shortness of breath – that were diagnosed as late-onset asthma, which he has speculated may have been brought on by bad air quality. As he wrote, "Had I known that my Sunday-afternoon runs along Balham High Road were causing permanent and lasting damage to my health, would I have stuck to the gym instead?"[22]

Sadiq Khan learned of Ella's case, which struck a chord for him both as a newly diagnosed asthma sufferer and as a human rights lawyer who might of old have taken on her case. He supported Ella's mother and Holgate in their successful push for a second inquest in 2020. "It gave us concrete evidence that toxicity from transport doesn't just stunt children's lungs – it is a killer."[23]

The key objective of Khan's holistic Healthy Streets Approach was for 80 per cent of trips in London to be made by active travel – by foot, bike or using public transport – by 2041. The strategy set the three areas for the approach to deliver this goal: improving street environments to promote healthier, more efficient and more sustainable transport options; high-quality public transport options to provide an alternative to the car; and new homes and jobs planned around walking and cycling, with public transport for longer trips. Khan's commitment to improving the city's air quality brought a real urgency to the issue, and TfL published the first strategy shortly after his election in May 2016, including a toxicity charge, expanding the Ultra Low Emissions Zone (ULEZ), reducing bus pollution, and diesel scrappage.

The Toxicity or T-charge was launched in October 2017 to rid central London of older, more polluting vehicles. At the time this was an additional £10 on top of the congestion charge of £11.50 in central London. The T-charge had been announced in February after a run of days when weather and atmospheric conditions had led to record levels of nitrogen oxide and particulates across the city.[24] This was later extended into the ULEZ introduced in early 2019, applying an emissions standard-based charge for vehicles within the central London congestion charge zone. This was extended in 2021 to cover the area within the North and South Circular roads, and in 2023 further extended to all Greater London within the M25. This has reduced the number of non-compliant cars on London's roads and averted toxic air pollution equivalent to that emitted by all London's airports combined. Despite widespread acceptance in inner London, ULEZ remains a live political issue in outer London, despite 96.7 per cent of vehicles driving in the expanded zone now being compliant. On an average day in London only 0.2 per cent of vehicles are fined for non-compliance. TfL believes the scheme has taken 80,000 older, more polluting vehicles off the capital's roads since 2017.[25] Net revenue from the ULEZ charge is expected to stop by 2027 as more people switch to cleaner, greener modes of transport.[26]

Against this background, with the need for better air quality driving the aim of reduction on car dependency, a series of initiatives was rolled out that affected every aspect of London's transport provision.

Low-traffic neighbourhoods

By stopping cars, vans and other vehicles from using quiet residential streets as short cuts or 'rat runs', low-traffic neighbourhoods (LTNs) create quieter streets with improved air quality and encourage people to stop using their car and walk or cycle. LTNs use 'modal filters', barriers and signage that allow full use by cyclists and walkers but are access-only for motor vehicles. Such measures had been long been employed in London and other UK cities, "a standard feature in the design of new towns since the 1960s".[27]

Entry gate to the Railton Road low-traffic neighbourhood in Brixton, December 2019

Many more LTNs were introduced in UK cities to boost walking and cycling during the Covid pandemic under Andrew Gilligan's[28] direction from Number Ten. In May 2020 the government offered £250 million for active travel measures, with 141 LTNs implemented in London alone, to counter the potential for a car-led recovery. The evidence from Waltham Forest was that the mini-Holland scheme had since 2014 boosted life expectancy and air quality without pushing up pollution on main roads. Car ownership fell within the scheme, while walking and cycling increased markedly. "We found that people in 'high dose areas' [of traffic interventions], including low-traffic neighbourhoods, were doing 40 to 45 minutes' walking or cycling a week more than people in the control group," says Professor Rachel Aldred, co-author of the study.[29]

A frenzied level of debate arose over LTNs, but their vocal opponents were outnumbered by supporters in TfL's 2024 research: within LTNs, roads are 50 per cent safer, with reduced traffic, and are supported by 58 per cent of the public. In longer-established schemes, such as the mini-Holland scheme in Walthamstow, LTNs enable more active travel, reduce car use and lower crime levels.[30] "[LTNs] have been around for decades," asserted Mary Creagh, then CEO of Living Streets, "supported by the silent majority of people who want healthier, safer streets. It's time for town and city leaders to switch from grey to green and build back better in communities post-Covid."[31]

Bus innovation

With transport responsible for some 20 per cent of London's CO_2 emissions, buses make up just 5 per cent of the transport total. Technical innovation, moving from diesel to hybrid to hydrogen and electric, was applied by TfL to the London bus fleet. Hybrid buses had been pathfinders in London, but extended periods of battery operation followed by a cool diesel engine kicking in to recharge the batteries led to particulates not being burned off nearly so effectively. An induction charging trial demonstrated this on route 69 (Walthamstow Central to Canning Town; Stratford to Canning Town). Induction charging was arranged underneath the bus stands at both ends of the route, so the batteries could be charged back up during the layover and the bus run for longer on battery. "All we managed to do was to move the pollution from one borough in London to another, so that was the death of hybrid, because extended periods of battery operation were only going to result in identical emissions, but redistributed."[32]

The world's first pure electric double-deck bus had been trialled on route 98 in 2015, operated by Metroline from Willesden to Holborn, achieving a range of up to 190 miles over 20 hours' service. Once the technology was proven, at route contract re-tenders TfL could specify buses to address the air quality issue. Between 2016 and 2024 the number of single- and double-deck electric buses grew from just 22 to 1398, while pure diesel to Euro VI emission standards declined from 4804 to 3532. By 2024 the London bus fleet totalled 8776 vehicles, of which 20 were fuel cell buses and 3326 hybrids including 997 New Routemasters. The entire fleet was low-floor and wheelchair accessible.[33] By 2024 all buses operating in London were low or zero emission at the tailpipe. The electric and hydrogen buses are the largest zero emission bus fleet in western Europe.

Fuel cell buses had been trialled since 2001, using a hydrogen fuel cell that combines hydrogen with oxygen to create electricity to drive electric motors on the wheels, the only emission being water. In 2010 eight hydrogen buses were trialled again in London, but they remained high cost to purchase and to fuel. In 2024 there were 20 hydrogen buses in the London fleet. The emissions of other vehicles also came within TfL's view; all new licensed taxis in London must be zero-emission capable. Over half of London's licensed taxis – more than eight thousand vehicles – are already in this category.[34] Low Emission Zone (LEZ) standards for heavy goods vehicles, vans and specialist vehicles over 3.5 tonnes gross vehicle weight (GVW) and buses, minibuses and coaches over 5 tonnes GVW are in place across most of Greater London.

Improving public transport in outer London as an alternative to the private car remains a challenge. Orbital bus services had been trialled in 2008 and again in 2018.[35] Announced in March 2023, over two years 10 Superloop express bus services were added to the network, providing limited stop bus routes circling the capital in outer London. The branded buses connect town centres, railway stations and other transport hubs.

With the mayor's ambition to be a zero carbon city by 2030, TfL now has the largest zero emission bus fleet in Europe, alongside the emissions-based ULEZ and the rollout of charging points for electric vehicles, with London's 21,658 charging points a third of the national total by 2024.[36]

Cycling to Covid and after

"Because active travel, walking and cycling, has not been built into the city historically in terms of the way the city is designed, or the way that this organization works, it does require somebody to champion it."

– Will Norman, Walking and Cycling commissioner, 2024[37]

Will Norman was appointed by Mayor Khan early in 2017. He was following in the footsteps of Andrew Gilligan, who had taken the cycling agenda ruthlessly forward during Johnson's second term. Norman's experience of Gilligan was that of a man determined to succeed whatever the cost, never afraid to upset or anger people

TfL and Chinese manufacturer BYD unveiled the world's first purpose-built electric double-deck bus at City Hall in March 2016

in order to achieve his aims: "The Embankment and Blackfriars, in terms of two bike lanes, were exceptionally bold statements of ambition and intent. I inherited a situation where there was bold intent and there was ambition."[38]

The mini-Hollands scheme had been introduced by Mayor Johnson in March 2014, with three outer London boroughs – Waltham Forest, Enfield and Kingston – winning £30 million each to build Dutch-style cycle infrastructure, including separated cycle lanes, traffic calming measures and blocking residential streets to car traffic. The schemes were initially controversial, with concerns about cycling benefiting at the expense of other modes, traffic displacement and congestion. Research after the first year of implementation suggested that they promoted active travel, more by foot than by cycle, more positive attitudes to cycling, and a new uptake for cycling. For Will Norman, "The fact that more people are choosing to cycle and walk more often brings huge benefits, not only to the health and well-being of individual Londoners but also to the wider community. I'm proud that the programme is giving all boroughs the opportunity to bid for funding to make similar positive changes to their areas."[39]

Active travel was now pursued in the broader context of the Healthy Streets Approach, championed by deputy mayor Val Shawcross, who set a brave, bold direction. Will Norman reflected:

> I'm not sure that would have happened without Val in terms of setting that ambition and ... that embedded the Healthy Streets Approach of designing streets for people rather than for cars, not just in the policy around transport but also in the environment strategy, in the London Plan, in the health strategy. Nick Bowes, in the mayor's office, did a good job of making sure that that was integrated across every policy area and particularly the environment plan, which was really important when you come on to the ULEZ and the air-quality agenda, a sort of a co-ordinated policy piece for changing the city for the better. If you want to dial up the transport outcomes, it's reducing congestion, getting more ridership. If you want to dial up health outcomes, it's less chronic disease, less air pollution – they were a graphic equalizer of outcomes. It flowed through every piece of the policy landscape. It was on everybody's agenda.[40]

Electric bikes and scooters entered the urban transport mix from 2017. The TfL Cycle Hire scheme, which had promoted cycling in central London since its introduction in 2010, was supplemented when independent and unregulated electric bike operators such as Lime arrived, as Uber earlier had, from San Francisco in 2017 and disrupted the market, offering electric bikes by app and without fixed bays. Active in 230 cities worldwide, Lime has come to dominate the dockless cycle market in London. In response, the TfL scheme, sponsored by Santander since 2015 with 20,000 bikes and 1400 stations across inner London, introduced e-bikes to the docked scheme in 2022. The appearance of Lime bikes on pavements, at stations and in huge discarded shoals at major central London events has raised questions about whether this is a convenient and sustainable addition to the transport mix in London or a menace that clogs up pavements.[41]

In response to the potential for electric e-scooters to boost sustainable and active travel, TfL instituted a trial rental scheme in 2021 with Lime and Voi in 11 boroughs, extended to run until September 2025. With 4000 vehicles available and using larger wheels, speed is limited to 12.5 mph and the lights are always on. After fires were caused by defective lithium batteries, e-scooters were banned from TfL stations, premises and services. Since launch, more than five million journeys have been made on rental scooters, replacing 7 per cent of car journeys, TfL reported in May 2025.[42]

In 2010 the Cycling Vision had noted that in London "those most likely to cycle are white men aged 25 to 44. Current cyclists have a higher than average income and are more likely to be resident in inner London".[43] The demographics of cycling have

The distinctive Superloop bus and signage at Broad Street, Teddington, August 2023

not moved significantly in the intervening years, despite the belief that if TfL builds segregated and safer cycle infrastructure, cycling will flourish and grow in numbers and diversity. London has a very different culture from that of the Dutch, where even in 1911 there were more cycles per capita than in any other country in Europe. Despite the rise of the private car in the Netherlands, cycling remained the transport choice for millions and was accommodated in the expansion of cycle lanes and road segregation from the 1970s, with cycle path length nationally doubling in the 1980s to 8600 miles (19,000 km) as part of a national Bicycle Master Plan.[44]

In the years since 2010, cycling infrastructure has seen major investment by TfL in both its quality and extent, being expanded from a 55-mile network in 2016 to 250 miles by 2024. In the years to Covid, the annual growth in cycling from 580,000 daily journeys in 2010 had slackened despite significant investment in infrastructure. The pandemic would once more prompt a net increase in cycling; by 2024, 1.33 million journeys were being made by bike each day, a 26 per cent increase since pre-Covid of 1.05 million in 2019.[45] In April 2025, the City of London Corporation reported that cycling within the City had increased by more than 50 per cent in the past two years. October 2024 saw a record 139,000 people cycling a day across 30 locations – up from 89,000 in 2022. According to the corporation, people cycling now make up 56 per cent of all traffic in the peak commuting hours, and dockless bicycles account for one in six bikes on City streets.[46] Lime bikes – dockless, app-enabled and electric, in 200 cities worldwide, with 16 million journeys in London in 2024 – have broadened the demographics of cycling, as CEO Tom Fyans said when announcing a £20 million investment in London in January 2025: "Lime bikes are changing the face of cycling in London, bringing joy to a huge and diverse audience new to cycling ... With this new investment, Lime is helping ensure new riders cycle and park more responsibly." Nearly half of Londoners aged 18 to 34 now use Lime bikes weekly, and journey numbers rose by 85 per cent in 2024.[47]

Vision Zero and the Direct Vision Standard

"It is neither inevitable nor acceptable that anyone should be killed or seriously injured when travelling in London. When we leave our homes each day, we should feel safe and confident about the journey ahead."[48]

– TfL Vision Zero Plan

Vision Zero is a Swedish approach to road safety, first adopted there in 1997 and then taken up by other cities worldwide. It is based on the principle that no loss of life or serious injury is acceptable. With more than two thousand deaths or serious injuries on London's streets each year, a programme to eliminate these on London's transport network by 2041 was adopted in 2018 under the Vision Zero banner. This brought together a number of initiatives, including the widespread introduction of lower speed limits across the capital, the design of safer streets and junctions, safer travel on buses, and the innovative Direct Vision Standard (DVS) for HGVs.[49]

Mayor Khan tests a five-star-rated Direct Vision Standard truck with Will Norman, Walking and Cycling commissioner, in February 2019

The development and adoption of the DVS is a world-first response to the rise in fatal collisions between HGVs and cyclists. It is a measure of what a driver can see from his cab directly, i.e. without use of mirrors or video cameras. HGVs were understood to be responsible for 63 per cent of fatal collisions with cyclists and as many as 25 per cent of pedestrian deaths. The standard was developed by TfL with the freight and logistics industry, London boroughs and vulnerable road user groups to remedy lethal blind spots in truck drivers' vision around their vehicles, and was rolled out in 2019.[50] After a grace period, from 2021 all HGVs over 12 tonnes entering Greater London were required to hold a valid safety standard permit or risk a penalty notice. By June, 200,000 permits had been issued and the number of serious injuries fell by 64 per cent from 48 in 2017 to 17 in 2021.[51] The standard was tightened further in October 2024, when all trucks over 12 tonnes entering London had either to have a three-star rating or to fit the Progressive Safe System (PSS) kit. This was a world-leading innovation; the principles and standards are being adopted by both the EU and the UN.

Underground and rail

The Northern line extension to Battersea and Crossrail were under construction and fit-out during this period, with the Elizabeth line alone expected to add 10 per cent to the capacity of the Tube network. As chapter 13 describes in detail, in the summer of 2018 it became clear that the opening date of December 2018 for the Elizabeth line was unachievable. This was a blow, not least because the Crossrail team's mantra had long been 'on time and on budget', when in fact it proved to be neither. The delay required additional funding approval from a reluctant government and worsened TfL's financial position, which had anticipated substantial revenue from the new line in its budget and plan. The delay announced in 2018 and the measures taken to open in May 2022 illustrate the challenge of building a megaproject beneath a world city.

The Night Tube, running on selected Tube lines through the night on Fridays and Saturdays to support the nighttime economy and speed late-night journeys home, had been proposed in 2014 and after protracted trade union consultation was eventually introduced on the Victoria, Central, Jubilee, Northern and Piccadilly lines by the end of 2016. The Overground East London line, now the Windrush line, joined the night service in 2018.

The replacement of conventional fixed signals across the Underground network with computerized automatic train control was a vast and complex upgrade, designed to increase the capacity of the Underground network. This was an investment almost invisible to passengers other than the sharp-eyed, who might have seen signals covered in black plastic and then removed from across the network. The first line to benefit was the Hammersmith and City in 2019.

top: Mayor Sadiq Khan on the first Night Tube train on the Victoria line, August 2016
bottom: Night Tube-wrapped train and signage on the Piccadilly line, July 2015

London had lagged behind other world cities in the provision of Wi-Fi connectivity underground. The installation of Wi-Fi began in 2012 in partnership with Virgin Media. In May 2017 infrastructure for 4G connectivity in trains and stations was announced by TfL, and 97 per cent of stations had free connectivity by August. Customers could now access real-time travel information and find alternative routes to manage disruptions. This also enabled TfL to collect Wi-Fi data across the network, depersonalized for data protection but invaluable for better understanding customer paths across the network, managing planning, crowding and safety, especially at busy interchange stations, which Oyster data did not catch. "In the modern, data-driven world, the possibilities are endless."[52]

New trains to replace the Piccadilly line trains were contracted from Siemens in 2018, a £2.9 billion investment for 94 new Tube trains to replace 86 trains in service since 1975. They feature walk-through carriages, air-conditioning, wide doors, better step-free access, digital information screens and on-train CCTV. Built at a new facility at Goole, East Yorkshire, the first new train arrived in London in October 2024 to go through a year-long programme of intensive testing, with the intention of entering passenger service by the end of 2025.

A further section of Victorian rail infrastructure had been brought back to life by incorporation into the Overground network in 2007. The Victorian Gospel Oak to Barking line had been slated for closure in the 1960s, but was handed to TfL as part of the Overground initiative. The protracted electrification of the line by Network Rail was completed in 2018, with an extension to Barking Riverside, a brownfield regeneration site with the potential for 10,000 homes, opened in 2022. New Bombardier Class 710 trains were introduced in 2022, and the line is now enjoying the most successful period in its history since the first section opened in 1868.

In May 2015, the Liverpool Street to Enfield Town, Cheshunt (via Seven Sisters) and Chingford services, as well as the Romford to Upminster service, were transferred from Greater Anglia to TfL to become part of the London Overground network. This brought the Overground network to a total of 113 stations over six lines. The Overground's role as a regenerator of some of the capital's less affluent areas continued to be reflected in its passenger numbers. Forty-five new five-car Bombardier Class 710 trains were introduced on the Overground for the Lea Valley lines out of Liverpool Street to replace the venerable Class 315/317 trains introduced by British Rail in the 1980s. The six lines were renamed in 2024 to make the orange network easier to navigate.[53] Overall the Overground network continues to be a great success and has stimulated regeneration and housing growth: 16 per cent of new homes since 2010 have been within a 10- to 15-minute walk of an Overground station.

The Silvertown Tunnel

The building of a road tunnel beneath the Thames from Silvertown to North Greenwich in 2021 was a controversial initiative alongside the mayor's healthy city agenda.

The original Blackwall Tunnel (and Tower Bridge) had been promoted by the Metropolitan Board of Works to improve horse-drawn communications across the Thames in the East End. A single tunnel opened in 1897, large enough to accommodate two lines of vehicles and foot passengers, its sinuous route dictated by available approaches and pre-existing sewers and structures. At 0.84 miles long, Blackwall was then the world's longest sub-aqueous tunnel. With growing levels of motorized traffic, a second, separate tunnel was proposed in 1938 and opened by the LCC in 1967.[54] Traffic continued to grow, and by the TfL years further Thames crossings in East London had long been proposed to relieve congestion in the tunnels: the need for new river crossings had been supported by the London Infrastructure Plan to 2050, the London Plan and Johnson's 2011 Mayor's Transport Strategy, and focused on a Silvertown Tunnel and bridges further downstream at Gallions Reach and Belvedere.[55]

Major improvements had already taken place in cross-river transport links since 2000, with the extension of the Jubilee line, the Overground between Wapping and Rotherhithe, the extension of the DLR to Greenwich and Woolwich, the Elizabeth line and even the cable car. As population and employment grew in East London, congestion and 20-minute tailbacks as early as 6 a.m. during the morning peak approaching the northbound Blackwall Tunnel became the norm by 2014. When 700 to 1000 incidents a year – over-height vehicles, traffic accidents, emergency repairs – took place that closed the tunnel, there were no alternative routes other than the Rotherhithe Tunnel and distant Dartford crossings, such as the Thames Gateway Bridge (cancelled by Johnson in 2008).

The 'No to the Silvertown Tunnel' campaign believed "planners should continue to invest in crossings for public transport, pedestrians and cyclists; but should also take action to ensure fewer vehicles needlessly enter London in the first place before considering any new road crossings".[56] After a long period of consultation and cross-party protest, largely on grounds of traffic generation and air pollution, and the absence of active travel options, construction began in 2021 and the Silvertown Tunnel opened on 7 April 2025. Built at a cost of £2.2 billion as a public finance initiative (PFI) by the Riverlink consortium, the cost will be met by revenue from tolls on both the Blackwall and Silvertown tunnels over 25 years before ownership reverts to TfL. Cyclists travel through the tunnel on a dedicated zero-emission shuttle bus service.

"Sadiq is doing everything in his power to address the climate emergency we are facing. He's been clear that our recovery after Covid must be a green one and has a clear plan to tackle climate change and improve air quality. Tackling congestion is an important part of cleaning up our air. The new Silvertown Tunnel will radically improve traffic conditions, effectively eliminating the current congestion at the Blackwall Tunnel that causes some of the worst air pollution in London."[57]

Transport and housing

TfL is responsible not only for transport but also for a large estate in and around transport infrastructure. Places for London (PfL), a wholly-owned commercial property subsidiary, was set up in 2022 to bring a new approach to the 5500 acres (2225 hectares) of land in TfL's ownership. PfL was spun out of TfL Property to enable a more commercial approach and funding in pursuit of the housing and income-generating agenda of TfL and the mayor. It is tasked with using TfL's surplus land for the good, for houses and offices. TfL manages 1500 tenancies, many of them in TfL stations or viaducts, and a pipeline of joint ventures with developers that will see some 20,000 homes, many of them affordable, built across London in a decade. This is a tough target; to 2025, 4450 units and starts have been achieved.

London faces financial headwinds

Sadiq Khan's mayoralty and TfL were to face a series of financial challenges. From 2016, demand for public transport, commuter rail and passenger revenue had begun to drop behind its forecast growth as the previously steady increase in people travelling to London showed signs of flattening off.[58] At this point, government support to TfL also began to soften as the glow of the Games dimmed. The 10-year funding agreement secured by TfL in late 2007 now looked extraordinary. Agreed just a few years after the imposition of the PPP, and against the context of national government austerity and the financial crisis of 2008, it was "a remarkable testament to the regard in which TfL had come to be held" suggests Stephen Glaister in a survey of the mayoralty after 20 years.[59] In 2015, as Mayor Johnson's attention moved to the national stage, the government announced that the operating grant to support TfL services would come to an end in 2018, though this was partly mitigated by the retention of business rates in the capital. Together with passenger numbers on the Tube not rising as forecast, bus passenger numbers falling, the mayor's own policy of a fares freeze, the increased cost of Crossrail and the delay in revenue from the Elizabeth line when its opening was postponed in 2018, TfL's financial position had by 2019 become severely constrained. Significant reductions in operating costs were made in these years – by a third between 2016 and 2022 – enabling a surplus on operating costs (including renewals and debt servicing) to be achieved by 2022–23. This was on target to be achieved when, in March 2020, the Covid-19 epidemic blew away the funding model.

In May 2016 the Brexit referendum had seen the country voting by the narrow margin of 51.9 per cent to 48.1 per cent to leave the EU. By contrast, across the 33 London boroughs, 60 per cent voted to remain. The referendum signified a sea change in national politics. The rise of populist arguments for levelling up the regions of the UK and arguing against expenditure in London, despite its net benefit of £42 billion to UK plc, came to the fore as TfL's own financial position weakened. As a prominent Labour politician, Khan's opposition to the Brexiteer Conservative government, rocked endlessly as it was by political division over the subsequent negotiations for withdrawal from the EU, was to put him in a challenging political position up to and then most visibly during the pandemic.

Alongside these financial challenges, the mayor was faced with a succession of unfortunate and terrible events in his first 18 months as London's figurehead at City Hall.

The tragedies of Sandilands and Grenfell

On a dark, wet morning, just after six o'clock on 9 November 2016, a Tramlink two-car tram number 2551, on a service from New Addington to Wimbledon via Croydon, approached the tight curve at Sandilands Junction where the speed limit was 12 mph. The tram, slowing only from 50 to 43 mph, derailed and overturned. In his later evidence, the driver said he was disorientated in the tunnel approaching the junction and failed to slow down. Of the 69 passengers, there were seven fatalities and 62 injuries, 19 of them serious or life-threatening. This was the first fatal accident on a UK tram network since Glasgow in 1959, and the deadliest since an accident at Dover in 1917 had led to 11 deaths.

Leon Daniels went straight to the site – "a terrible scene, very uncomfortable" – and with investigators formed an early view that excessive speed into the sharp curve was the cause. An emergency control facility was set up, and Daniels was on site for several days until the service reopened. "I was very keen that we had to get the service back as quick as possible; the best way to restore confidence in the system is to get the service running immediately. We made a number of changes, including a quite different speed limit arrangement on the approach to that corner. From then on, it was stepped down to negotiate the curve."[60]

The Rail Accident Investigation Board reported that the speed restriction sign was positioned poorly, too close to the curve, so slowing for the sharp curve relied on the driver's route awareness. It was also thought that the driver might have briefly lost awareness through an episode of microsleep. TfL and the tram operators Tramlink Croydon pleaded guilty and were fined in 2022. The driver, Alfred Dorris, was cleared of manslaughter at the Old Bailey in 2023. In his evidence he apologized: "I'm sorry I was not able to do anything to stop myself from becoming disorientated, and I'm deeply sorry I was not able to do anything to reorientate myself and stop the tram from turning over. I'm deeply sorry."[61]

A new Siemens-built Piccadilly line train under test at Wildenrath, Germany

The portal of the Silvertown Tunnel before its opening on 7 April 2025

Before the accident TfL had viewed the risks on the Croydon network as being largely of running trams on-street among road traffic and pedestrians, yet Sandilands was on a stretch of former railway track. For Daniels, the limitations of the 30-year Tramlink PFI contract, concluded in the late 1990s, may have been a contributory factor, as there was no provision for the operators to update the signalling and tram technologies. "We had analogue CCTV, we had line of sight running, we had manual speed limit signs. To some extent, the operational arrangements had been overtaken by technology that might have prevented the incident. Yet you have to add to that other factors – the weather, the rain, whatever the driver's situation was, and so on – meaning that, as is always the case, a combination of factors caused a serious accident."[62]

Immediately after the accident, fatigue monitoring devices were installed on the network's trams, stepped speed restrictions were introduced on the Tramlink and other UK city networks, and in 2019 it was announced that trams were to be fitted with a system that would automatically apply the brakes if the speed limit was exceeded.

Less than a year later, the mayor's role as London's figurehead was again called upon, after an appalling fire in June 2017 in a 24-storey tower block near Latimer Road station in west London had killed 72 and injured 70 residents. "The Grenfell Tower fire was a preventable accident caused by years of neglect by the local council and successive governments," said Sadiq Khan. "The fire was a national disaster requiring a national response."[63] He later described it as his "hardest day" as London

Silvertown Tunnel control centre during commissioning, March 2025

mayor. On the first anniversary of the fire, a Tube driver stopped his train on a bridge near Latimer Road where a community vigil was being held, sounded the whistle and unfurled a green banner in a spontaneous tribute to the victims. Mark Wild, MD London Underground, said: "Our thoughts are with all those affected by the Grenfell tragedy as the local community today remembers the terrible events of a year ago. Yesterday evening one of our Tube drivers gave a moving display of respect for people gathered to remember the tragedy's victims. He has our full support."[64] Wreaths were laid at West London stations and a minute's silence held at midday.

Terror attacks: Westminster Bridge ...

Following the 7/7 attacks in 2005, the security services had been successful in thwarting terrorist threats on London. One of the outcomes of 7/7 had been the setting up of a single control centre, CentreComm, now the Network Management

Control Centre, bringing together road, rail, bus and tunnel operations, the police and other emergency services to co-ordinate the response to routine transport disruptions, major London public events and terrorist incidents. TfL had a good and routine exchange of information with the security services, the police and the military, and briefings with the Home Office. Leon Daniels recalls, "There was a really good relationship with the Metropolitan Police during that period, with periodic tabletop exercises and the use of the camera technology across the whole network."[65]

By 2017, however, after 10 Islamist attacks across mainland Europe in 2016 had killed 135 people, an attack on London was regarded as highly likely. TfL ran campaigns to encourage public vigilance. 'See It, Say It, Sorted' was first launched nationally in November 2016. This now ubiquitous slogan, with its annoying hints of Big Brother, increased calls and texts threefold in its first three years to British Transport Police and 918,000 texts, 96,000 of which were deemed serious, though most were about antisocial or nuisance behaviour on the network.[66]

The first of four attacks between 2017 and 2019 took place on 23 March 2017. A Muslim convert sent a message on WhatsApp revealing his jihadist motivations against Western actions in the Middle East. Seven minutes later he drove his car into the crowded pavement on the south side of Westminster Bridge, causing pedestrians to scatter, killing five people and injuring 50. He then crashed the car into the perimeter fence of the Palace of Westminster and ran into New Palace Yard, where he fatally stabbed an unarmed police officer and was then shot dead by armed police. TfL, working with the security services and Westminster, put in place hostile vehicle mitigation (HVM) measures across all eight of London's bridges, barricades that protected the footpath from the new threat of vehicles as a weapon. "Terrorists just keep probing to find the weakest spots," Daniels reflected.[67]

... and London Bridge

Less than three months later, on the evening of 3 June, three radical Islamist terrorists hired a van and drove north and then southbound over London Bridge. At high speed it mounted the pavement and hit many pedestrians, killing two and throwing another person into the Thames, where he drowned. The van then crashed the central reservation. The men abandoned the vehicle, drew their knives, killed five people outside the Boro Bistro pub and attacked bystanders on Borough High Street. Police and members of the public confronted the attackers. A Romanian baker hit one attacker with a crate and gave shelter to 20 people, while Roy Larner, a diner in the Black & Blue steakhouse, shouting "Fuck you, I'm Millwall", fought the attackers with his fists, giving time for customers in the restaurant to escape. The three attackers were shot dead by armed officers from the City of London and Met Police firearms command, eight minutes after the first emergency call was made.

Leon Daniels was at a dinner party. "I got up, leaving my knife and fork and the half-eaten food on the table, and ran outside, and was taken away in a police car to CentreComm" to oversee TfL's response.[68]

"One of the greatest things about London is our defiant unity in the face of adversity – and that will not change in the aftermath of this horrific attack," announced Mayor Khan. "I'm calling on all Londoners to pull together, and send a clear message around the world that our city will never be divided by these hideous individuals who seek to harm us and destroy our way of life."[69] Days later, Khan said, "I have been overwhelmed by the strength London has shown since Saturday night, from the swift and brave actions of our emergency services to the countless acts of heroism and kindness by ordinary Londoners. This is the best city in the world. We will never be cowed by terrorism."[70] "As a proud and patriotic British Muslim, I say this, you do not commit these disgusting acts in my name."[71]

These two attacks, together with the Manchester Arena suicide bombing in May, were described by Prime Minister Theresa May as "… bound together by the single, evil ideology of Islamist extremism". They were followed by reports of revenge attacks against Muslims, with mosques targeted and a surge in Islamophobic and hate crimes across London.

The worst of these proved to be an Islamophobic attack on the night of 19 June in Finsbury Park. Following the Rochdale child abuse case, the attacker had been recently radicalized by the far right. He hired a van and drove from Cardiff to London intending to attack a pro-Palestinian demonstration attended by Labour leader Jeremy Corbyn in central London. Prevented in his purpose by roadblocks, he drove down Seven Sisters Road shortly after midnight and swerved across the bus lane at speed and intentionally into a group of worshippers who had attended Ramadan prayers at the Finsbury Park Mosque. They were giving first aid to a man who had collapsed in the street when the van rammed into them, killing one and injuring 11 more, before being brought to a halt by bollards. The driver was pulled from the van and beaten until the mosque's young imam, Mohammed Mahmoud, calmed the crowd and appealed for him to be handed over to the police. Witnesses at the scene quoted the terrorist as saying "I want to kill all Muslims" and "This was for London Bridge".[72]

It was an apparent revenge attack by a lone individual against Muslims, the mosque having been temporarily closed in 2003 after it attracted negative attention when its imam, Abu Hamza-Masri, was convicted for terrorist-related offences. The accused was unrepentant at his trial, telling the court it "would have been even better" if Mayor Sadiq Khan had been present, adding: "It would have been like winning the lottery."[73]

After a welcome lull, on 3 December 2019 a British national from Stoke-on-Trent who had been released from jail on licence in 2018, halfway through a 16-year sentence for terrorism offences, was attending a prisoner rehabilitation conference at Fishmonger's Hall on the north end of London Bridge. Regarded as a success story, he was featured as a case study for the programme but instead used the occasion to threaten to detonate a (fake) suicide vest and to attack attendees at the conference with knives, He killed Saskia Jones, a criminology graduate and rehabilitation volunteer, and Jack Merritt, a law graduate who was the course co-ordinator. He was forced out of the hall by staff and attendees, including a convicted murderer on parole, who used chairs, fire extinguishers, a pole and a narwal tusk that had been hanging on the wall. He managed to stab pedestrians on the bridge before being pinned down by members of the public, partially disarmed by a plain clothes police officer and then shot and killed by armed police.

Once more Mayor Khan was called upon to respond on behalf of London, thanking members of the public and the emergency services for their breathtaking heroism, and "calling on all Londoners to pull together and send a clear message around the world that our city will never be divided by these hideous individuals who seek to harm us and destroy our way of life".[74] At the subsequent inquest, the chief coroner concluded that the victims had been unlawfully killed and that "insufficient monitoring of the terrorist, unreasonable belief in his rehabilitation, a lack of information-sharing between agencies, and inadequate security planning at the event were all contributing factors in their deaths".[75]

At the time of this attack, Andy Lord was only a month into his role as MD of the Underground. He was involved in assessing the impact of the attack and adjusting the transport network around London Bridge. Lord observed that, in its response to the attack, beneath senior leadership TfL was still two separate business units, Underground and Surface. "Gareth [Powell][76] and I sought to work much closer ... and then [there were] these reports on the news of this flu virus in China and we needed to start thinking about this more seriously."[77] The changes they made were to equip TfL to face its greatest existential threat.

An election delayed

The sixth mayoral election should have taken place in May 2020, but with the advent of Covid-19 was postponed for a year to May 2021 and became a three-year term. Mayor Sadiq Khan was reselected as the Labour candidate, Shaun Bailey for the Conservatives neither a strong nor a visible candidate; it was reported that the Conservatives had twice sought to deselect him but were unable to find a credible alternative. Bailey, as a London Assembly member, had worked for two and a half years to unseat Khan but despite this a Tory source suggested that they had not worked out their electoral coalition "and they don't know why people should be voting for them".[78]

This was an election in unusual circumstances, with Covid lockdown restrictions prohibiting door-to-door canvassing. Eventually 20 candidates stood for election, but Khan and Bailey led the field. Khan's campaign focused on economic recovery and employment following the pandemic, while on transport he supported 4G connectivity on the Tube, LTNs, a faster move to zero-emission buses and 10,000 homes to be built on TfL land. Bailey's campaign focused on Khan's record, on housing, police and crime, and for transport CCTV at every bus stop, commercial sponsorship of stations, zero-emission buses by 2025 and support for cab drivers to buy electric taxis. Khan recommended giving second preference votes to Sian Berry of the Green Party.

Khan led the opinion polls throughout the campaign, and he won 55 per cent of the second round votes to Bailey's 45 per cent on a 40 per cent turnout, a slight reduction on his 2016 margin, with the Greens' Sian Berry coming third. Khan was to retained his focus on economic recovery following the pandemic that had such a profound impact on London and TfL, and to which chapter 15 is devoted.

As deputy mayor for Transport and deputy chair of TfL, Seb Dance is the link with TfL to continue delivering the mayor's transport strategy. The aim is as ever to promote public transport in London. As he said: "Transport policy should be about encouraging the 'holy trinity' of bus, cycle and walking … Changing people's perception about what freedom is, is really fundamental. We've had 80, 100 years of ingrained belief that the car represents freedom. Now, being able to travel in and out of central London or travelling around outer London *without* your car, and, when you really need your car, having the space to travel on the road – *that* is freedom in the context of a city. That's real freedom."[79]

15.

THE BIGGEST TEST

"Do Not Travel: Stay Home, Protect the NHS, Save Lives"

– TfL's 2020 lockdown mantra

The Covid pandemic arrived in London in March 2020. The capital was locked down from 23 March, and TfL was obliged overnight to turn from promoting the use of public transport to dissuading Londoners from all but essential travel. With just 5 per cent of normal passenger revenue, financial support from central government was soon needed to secure the ongoing operation of trains, buses, trams and the Tube to keep essential workers moving and vital services running in the capital. This placed TfL in the highly charged political firing line between a Conservative central government and a Labour elected mayor. Remarkably, seven separate funding agreements, short-term in nature and with conditions – as much political as financial – that rolled back devolution, were needed to keep the transport network and the capital running through the Covid pandemic. TfL's leadership was obliged repeatedly to expend energy on responding to central government's essentially political agenda. Finally, some certainty was secured in 2022 with a funding agreement lasting 19 months to March 2024.

The approaching storm

In January 2020, Londoners became aware of the rapid spread of a flu-like virus, an acute respiratory disease that had first been recognized among customers at a wholesale food market in Wuhan, China, in December 2019. The first confirmed death in Wuhan was on 9 January. As it spread rapidly through Asia, the World Health Organization first identified Coronavirus 2019, declared Covid-19 to be a public health emergency on 30 January, and raised its threat to pandemic level on 11 March. By 24 January, Covid-19 had spread to Europe with the first confirmed case in Bordeaux, then through two tourists from China to Italy, which caused a major outbreak and the first instance in Europe of a national lockdown from 11 March.

On 3 March, Sadiq Khan launched his campaign for a second term as mayor of London and took questions from journalists about the spread of the virus. Later the same day, PM Boris Johnson gave a press conference to launch his government's Coronavirus Action Plan, convey expert advice about washing your hands, and reassure the nation that it should be "going about its business as usual". Khan and his Conservative predecessor had low opinions of each other, and these would not improve. "But on that day the two men, advised by the same sets of experts, said exactly the same thing to the public: essentially, keep calm and carry on until further notice." [1] This was the last occasion when the mayor and his predecessor demonstrated agreement through the Covid crisis.

TfL celebrated its 20th anniversary on 4 March, marked by the visit of Charles, then the Prince of Wales, and Camilla, Duchess of Cornwall to the London Transport Museum. Arriving by a new electric bus from a temporary bus stop outside Clarence House, they were introduced by the lord-lieutenant to the mayor, to his deputy mayor, Heidi Alexander, and to me as museum director. The new virus was somewhere on the near horizon as Prince Charles shook hands and the mayor welcomed the royal party to the museum, thronged with TfL staff and apprentices arranged to meet the royal couple. The duchess hopped into an air raid shelter and joked that she was self-isolating. The mayor and the TfL commissioner, Mike Brown, made short speeches of welcome to which the future king replied, with praise for how TfL kept London moving: "It is remarkable you manage to make such an immense operation work so well." [2]

On the following weekend, as news from abroad worsened and handshakes were being discouraged, the Premier League was suspended and the England Test team was on the way home from its tour of Sri Lanka. The first Covid case recorded in London and the ninth in the UK, confirmed on 12 February, was a woman who had recently arrived from China carrying the virus. In the five o'clock briefing from 10 Downing Street on 16 March, the prime minister advised people to reduce contact, to stay clear of the pubs, restaurants and theatres that were already going dark around us in Covent Garden. With 500 cases and 23 deaths in London by 17 March, a reduced service began on the Tube. Like others across the city, we closed our workplace from 17 March and began the novel experience of working from home, grappling with Zoom and Teams in our back bedrooms, sheds and kitchens. Social distancing and quarantine measures were introduced on 18 March, and on 20 March all leisure establishments were ordered to close and measures to prevent unemployment promised. A month later, Covid had caused 4697 deaths across the UK.

The storm arrives

"From this evening, I must give the British people a very simple instruction: you must stay at home."

– PM Boris Johnson addresses the nation, 23 May 2020

'Britain Shuts Down' was the headline on Saturday 21 March[3] as we all entered a half-life of uncertainty about the transmission of the disease. We embarked on a routine of daily briefings from Downing Street, mask wearing, social distancing, shielding the medically vulnerable, hand sanitizing, working from home and walks in the park. The full lockdown was announced by Johnson on Monday 23 March: people could leave home only to exercise once a day, shop for essential items, or for medical or care needs. Shops selling non-essential items were closed, and meetings of more than two people who did not live together were forbidden. Non-essential businesses were ordered to close.

Two weeks after the royal celebration of TfL's anniversary, the capital was in an unprecedented lockdown, the most complete shutdown of life in London since the Great Plague and Great Fire of the mid-17th century, and as existential a threat as the Blitz during the Second World War.

We know now that an earlier lockdown, even by a week, would have saved transport lives.[4] London's mayor was not initially invited to attend the COBRA[5] emergency meetings, but after lockdown began, Mayor Khan recalls,

> The decision led to the strangest media round I've ever undertaken, announcing that, until further notice, we were closing down the city. The mood was apocalyptic, some of those filming the interviews were wearing thick face coverings … I had a feeling that things were never going to be same again.[6]

TfL was obliged overnight to turn from promoting the use of public transport to dissuading Londoners from travelling at all. A massive communications campaign – posters, radio and press adverts – was launched to reduce demand, using the email CRM database to tell passengers not to travel unless it was essential and to relay other travel advice. "We developed another award-winning campaign," recalls TfL Customer and Revenue director Chris Macleod, "which was built on all our years of marketing and communications learnings: clear and simple language, an open and honest tone of voice and distinctive and memorable executions."[7] Advice was also provided to businesses, retailers and schools. All construction sites were initially brought to a safe stop in March, including Crossrail, and then brought back on a phased restart and staggered shifts to spread journeys outside the usual peaks to avoid crowding.

The aerosol transmission of the Covid virus was not understood in those first months after the epidemic struck. In response to constantly updated medical and

Piccadilly Circus, looking forlorn and empty in April 2020

government advice, TfL put protocols in place on the transport network to reduce potential transmission through contact, by regular cleaning of Underground cars, surfaces and buses, enforcing social distancing on buses and trains, mandating mask wearing and advocating proper handwashing and sanitizing. The congestion charge and ULEZ were suspended, while services on the Tube and the bus network were maintained, albeit at a reduced level, for key workers to get to work. Masks and advice were handed out at station entrances.[8]

TfL's deputy commissioner, Gareth Powell, recalls:

> At every incident we would just respond to it and then fairly quickly we started to see the impact on services even before lockdown. We were very quickly into, 'How are we going to keep the place moving, how are we going to deal with the volumes, how are we going to keep all our colleagues safe while we do that?'[9]

At that stage Covid transmission was thought to be primarily by contact, so TfL put protocols in place to address that and by so doing to keep the organization calm. TfL's first Covid case was a security guard at Victoria Station House. The first reported Covid death in England was on 6 March 2020. By early May there had been 46,000 deaths in England, 9000 of them in London.[10]

Andy Lord, an engineer and former director of operations at British Airways, had arrived at TfL as MD of London Underground in November 2019. In his first weeks, his greatest concern had been ridership on the Tube dropping and the delay to the Elizabeth line, which his predecessor Mark Wild was busy resetting after the watershed of 2018. Both had a major effect on TfL's financial performance for the year to March 2020. "We had a big target to achieve a billion-pound operating surplus in the Tube," recalls Lord. "We were on track to do it, but our ridership was starting to drop off and the revenue with it, so that was a big focus. Then [Covid] happens; that ensured we didn't hit the target."[11]

From the start, TfL's leadership resolved to do everything necessary to keep the network, the city's lifeblood, running, to enable NHS staff and other essential workers to get to work. During the first lockdown, TfL was carrying just 100,000 people a day, nothing when compared to the usual 5 million on the Tube or 6 or 7 million on the bus network, as Lord recalls, "but those 100,000 people a day were all NHS workers who were going to the various hospitals; if we had not done that the consequences for London and for the NHS would have been unimaginable".[12]

Forty lower-traffic stations and the cable car were closed as well as the Circle and Waterloo & City lines, and a lower frequency of Tube services run, not least because of staff unavailability. Absence rates rose on the Tube and peaked at 35 per cent of drivers unavailable. Many had received letters from the NHS saying they were clinically vulnerable due to existing conditions such as diabetes, and were required to stay at home.

Deep cleaning of a Victoria line train at Northumberland Park depot in May 2020 during the pandemic

Gareth Powell believed:

> The right thing to do was to keep the network running. We did absolutely everything that we could to protect bus drivers and all colleagues as best we could while being worried about the nature of the virus and what it was doing, and at the same time instigating studies on buses from scientists, to try and work it out.[13]

The first step was to bolster staff confidence to come to work by doing all that was known to protect them from exposure to the virus in the workplace. In light of the two-metre social distancing rule, maintenance regimes were re-engineered, vital signallers and control centres were protected, office desks were screened, PPE bought and all but essential staff worked from home.

With 40 transport worker deaths by late May, 27 of whom were bus drivers, there was huge anxiety among drivers about catching the virus at work from their passengers. Heidi Alexander remembers thinking:

> We will never know where people caught this virus; it could be at home, it could be at the supermarket. We had to take decisions to move to middle-door boarding on the buses in order to keep the bus network running. That meant we couldn't collect fares because all the Oyster card readers were right next to the driver. By taking that decision, we were saying, 'It's more important that we keep the bus network running, because the people that are using the bus network at the moment are the people that are going to work in our hospitals and in essential shops, and in other key public services'.[14]

Powell recalled: "We ran the bus network for free to make sure we could protect colleagues ... that was a very difficult set of decisions because of the financial consequences that would flow back to government."[15] Research commissioned by TfL suggested that drivers might have been at increased risk from their age, from living in areas of deprivation, prior medical conditions and being from minority ethnic groups. Edward Martin, a Stagecoach driver from Plymouth, had answered the bus companies' national call for volunteers, came to work at East Ham garage, contracted Covid, and tragically died three weeks after starting.[16]

Despite their fears, frontline staff – bus drivers, Tube and other modes, operational and maintenance staff – stepped up during those first weeks and months to keep the capital's arteries functioning. Alexander describes this as a terrifying time. "There were days when I woke up in the morning wondering whether the Tube was still going to be running because the situation was just so volatile and so dynamic."[17] In the midst of this, TfL people did the most amazing things, as Lord recalled:

> They moved out of their homes into rented accommodation ... to protect their wives or husbands who might be working in the NHS, or to ensure they could come to work because they knew how critical it was for London, but if they caught Covid didn't want to take it back to their families. The number of staff who moved out to live on their own was remarkable, plus the teams in this building who supported us. We couldn't have done it without them.[18]

Early in lockdown, there was concern about the potential transmission of the virus at crowded interchanges in the morning peak, such as Stratford and Canning Town. Construction workers travelling to sites in central London were pictured on social media congregating despite the contrary messaging of posters and platform stickers to maintain social distancing. Lord was obliged to go to Canning Town at five in the morning to take a video on his phone because the transport secretary was giving TfL grief; he was publicly accusing TfL of not adhering to social distancing, using this opportunity to bash the mayor.

> We'd had enough of this, and of a couple of unhelpful colleagues who released their own footage, so I went down there and filmed it myself. It was my first meeting with the secretary of state at the time, Grant Shapps, with him, the mayor, deputy mayor, multiple advisors from all sides, and I did the overview. I remember him saying, 'Well Mr Lord, that's all very interesting, but I just need you to guarantee that this won't happen tomorrow'. I said, 'Secretary of state, all I can guarantee is it *will* happen tomorrow', at which point the meeting came to a fairly abrupt end and that was the end of that. We actually did a really good job of managing crowding, but the problem was that there had been a timetable uplift on national rail ... they brought it forward by a week without telling us.[19]

The day after lockdown the health secretary, Matt Hancock, announced the building of emergency field hospitals, dubbed Nightingale hospitals, using MoD experience to support the NHS in the case of existing hospitals being overwhelmed. The London hospital was built in nine days at the ExCel Conference Centre in East London. TfL was asked to make transport provision to get doctors, nurses and patients to the site at Custom House Quay. With a capacity of 400 beds and 150 admissions, the hospital received its first patients on 7 April, but treated only 54 cases during the first wave of the pandemic, as established London hospitals were unable to release any medical staff.[20] The hospital treated recovering Covid patients and offered vaccinations in the second wave of the pandemic, but it closed in April 2021. It was later revealed that its operating model was based on treating influenza pandemics and did not have the critical care support needed by Covid patients.

TfL worked with bus companies to set up dedicated routes at short notice to service the hospital, while the cable car became a dedicated staff shuttle for Nightingale hospital staff. Powell recalled it was the most worrying of situations setting up a field hospital and thinking about the mechanisms by which people will arrive, "even without having to think about what would happen if people then died there in serious numbers".[21]

London Streetspace

The limited capacity of public transport was protected by encouraging people to take the option of walking or cycling safely. Santander cycle hire had seen record demand, with over 1.1 million hires in May 2020, and hire bikes were offered free to NHS and other key workers. New docking stations and 1700 new bikes were made available.[22] The massive Streetspace programme accelerated the creation of cycle lanes and temporary widened pavements on high-footfall shopping streets. With the former Cycling commissioner, Andrew Gilligan, now PM Johnson's transport advisor, the funding deal conditions included specific amounts for active travel. His successor since 2017, Will Norman, welcomed this opportunity to roll out a comprehensive plan, much of which was in the pipeline even if it was technically temporary. This was rapidly developed with the boroughs to enable social distancing by widening pavements outside busy stations such as Brixton and Liverpool Street, the Safer School Streets initiative, which excluded traffic from outside schools, and rolling out plans for separated cycle ways and LTNs. It had taken four years to treble the cycle highways network, and in 2020 it was doubled again.

Leadership

As the virus came over the horizon, the TfL leadership had found itself continually needing to make key decisions as the picture developed day by day. The executive put into place a crisis management team with the key individuals, and a standard agenda, that could meet as and when needed.

By the tenth day of lockdown, the TfL executive committee, the leadership team, had been in the office continuously, not least because the tech was not yet available to work from home. Andy Lord reflected that they would probably have carried on, but had strong feedback from operational colleagues. "They didn't want people who didn't need to be in the operation coming in, because of the whole uncertainty around how you spread the virus."[23] The crisis management team was soon meeting seven days a week, several times a day, sequenced after key meetings with the mayor or his deputy, the DfT, or another Downing Street briefing. "We actually timed some of the executive meetings to happen at five-thirty or six o'clock because we knew there'd be another statement. This enabled the leadership to be best informed, to translate back if we needed to. The strength needed was its ability to be very flexible, but also to make decisions that you could enact straight away and do so with a quite clear audit trail."[24]

At the height of the lockdown, "We would genuinely start communicating with each other at six thirty in the morning," Lord recalls, "and we'd still be communicating at 10 or 11 at night and weekends. At the height of it we would be meeting the deputy mayor twice a day, the mayor daily on top of all the other things, but it worked."[25]

"We were talking to the mayor on video calls in his home," recalls Powell. "We were talking to Cabinet members at their home addresses. We were dialling into team level meetings at Number Ten … it was something that certainly I'd never anticipated doing in my career."[26] Powell remembers that the early decisions during lockdown were difficult, with the scrutiny of regular calls with central government and City Hall against a background of the disease spreading and vulnerabilities not yet being understood. "One of the most difficult aspects was the fact that we didn't know any more than anybody else about the virus, and none of us are medically qualified. But when you're trying to plan something that affects millions of people and thousands of your colleagues you want to take the best advice possible, but you also are looked to, to have a kind of degree of insight and foresight that frankly we didn't have."[27]

The Covid crisis accelerated integration across TfL. In the seven-day week, ever-changing world of the pandemic Lord and Powell agreed single-point accountability for operational decisions. There had always been two separate structures, the Underground and Surface Transport, even during moments of crisis. Powell noted that "this was the first time that somebody had read across – Andy could make a decision on the bus network, on the road network, I could do something that affected the Tube ...That single point of accountability paved the way to integrate the organization in the recovery phase into a combined operation and a combined customer and strategy function."[28]

While all this was going on, TfL had massive construction programmes both on site and under way, not only Crossrail, at the time the largest engineering project in Europe, but also the Northern line extension, Barking Riverside, the Bank station upgrade and the Four Lines Modernization (4LM) programme, all of which were going at full speed. A decision was made to bring them all to a controlled stop because of the social distancing and spacing issue. Mark Wild took the lead on Crossrail, and Stuart Harvey, chief capital officer, for TfL, "did a great job working with all the suppliers and creating a one-way system through construction sites and Bank station," Lord recalls. "I still, to this day, don't know how they did it because there's only one entrance and one exit."[29]

Like the rest of the country, Lord and his TfL colleagues were working from home to keep London on the move, endlessly responding to the funding agreements with government and planning for eventual recovery. "We very quickly coined the phrase," Lord remembers, that "we weren't working from home, we were living in the office. Our homes had become the office and our daily commute was, in my case, six yards downstairs from the bedroom and then six yards to the kitchen." For Powell, "mine was to a room at the back of the garage".[30]

Streetspace for London on Holloway Road, Islington, making more space for cyclists and shoppers while social distancing, August 2020

Mind the funding gap

"There were days in May of last year when I was really genuinely worried about the existence of TfL."

– Heidi Alexander, TfL deputy mayor for Transport, 2021[31]

In the years before Covid, TfL had been through several rounds of savings and efficiencies, with net costs in 2018–19 being reduced by one-third since 2015–16. The medium-term target was a surplus of income over operating costs. At the time, TfL was spending about £600 million every four weeks. When ridership began dropping in March, TfL reserves stood at £1.8 billion, leaving about three months'-worth of cash available. As lockdown took hold and fares revenue all but disappeared, TfL ran down those reserves to maintain the operation of the network. The question of funding to maintain TfL's solvency, and with it the NHS in London and the capital's whole economy, then came to the fore.

In the two years before Covid, despite political differences, the mayor and TfL had negotiated funding to cover the delay to Crossrail. This was significant in the context of the North–South divide and levelling up, with the government not wanting to be seen to invest in London on Crossrail. "London has essentially picked up the tab for the remaining cost," Alexander observed, "because we're borrowing from government but we're using income from future business rate supplement and the mayoral community infrastructure levy to plug the gap." She described those years as

> rubbing along with government … but in the last year, the government has become increasingly interventionist. The pandemic just destroyed TfL's finances, because the way the government had funded TfL from 2015 onwards removed the direct operating subsidy, which was worth about £700 million a year … when you get to a point in April last year [2020], where only 5 per cent of ridership is happening on the Tube, and 15 per cent of ridership is happening on the buses, you don't have to be a sort of mathematical genius to work out that you've got a massive problem. The discussions with government were very difficult.[32]

Seeking funding from the Johnson government was always going to be fraught for TfL against the political crosscurrents. London, uniquely among world cities, was reliant on fares, which were 75 per cent of TfL's income. The government had removed an annual operating subsidy of £700 million from 2015 onwards. At the onset of the pandemic, as Tube income had fallen to 5 per cent of normal, and in order to keep bus drivers safe passengers were no longer having to pay fares, central government would surely have expected to support the capital's transport and

Pandemic life on the Tube *(top)* in April 2020 and *(bottom)* in February 2020; socially distanced, with compulsory masks and encouragement to stay at home

Reduced space to maintain social distancing and masks required on route 199 at Lewisham in May 2020

enable its emergency and NHS services to function. In truth, it proved to be an opportunity for Johnson's government to punish Mayor Khan for his fares freeze and to roll back devolution.

Gareth Powell remembers that "as soon as the question of funding arose it became a really extreme political issue, not just about the management of the consequences of the virus in day-to-day delivery, but also about why the money needed to be spent on TfL as opposed to anything else".[33] "On the one hand, there's a set of things that we would be obliged to do legally should we run out of money, on the other hand there's all the things that we needed to do, and there was a very large difference between those two aspects."[34]

TfL is a public body covered by local government regulations. Its statutory obligations were remarkably limited, and did not include running the Tube or the bus network. It is obliged to declare, under section 114 of the Local Government Finance Act 1988, if expenditure is expected to exceed income in any financial year. With Covid wiping out most of its income, this was clearly the prospect for TfL unless the government was prepared to step in and fund the shortfall. As TfL's reserves were run down it was necessary to plan for the suspension of all but the limited range of statutory services. "Under the legislation, all TfL is required and obliged to do is operate the Woolwich Ferry, which doesn't earn any revenue because it's a free service, to license taxis and private hire vehicles, which doesn't bring a huge amount of revenue in, and to run certain school buses and the traffic lights on the road network for the little traffic that was around."[35]

TfL found itself in the middle of a political tussle between Johnson's Conservative government and the Labour mayor, Sadiq Khan. TfL found itself on a twin track, Powell and Lord making sure that that London kept moving and that they were making the right decisions for everybody's safety, while Mike Brown and his chief financial officer (CFO) Simon Kilonback were focused on negotiating funding support as the political bullets were fired over their heads.[36]

Powell recalled the challenges he had to endure.

> We will be in exec meetings, very seriously putting together actionable plans to bring the whole organization to a stop and effectively to hand the keys to government because we would be insolvent and not a going concern. On the other hand, we were on 'top hundred executive' calls and 'all staff' calls reassuring everybody that everything was going to be fine, that the discussions with government were progressing, that the main focus was on keeping everything moving. Personally I found that the hardest bit, because I was having to have one complete set of reactions for the wider organization and then a completely different plan B that was sitting alongside it, and talking to our board, talking to the mayor, walking everybody through the serious legal implications of the place that we were heading to with government. What was hardest was dealing with the sheer illogicality, frankly, of the government's position on this. It was just hard because you weren't dealing with something that you could rationally debate your way through.[37]

"The discussions with government were very difficult," as Heidi Alexander also acknowledged.

> It's all being played out while you're in the middle of a global pandemic. The mood music that existed before the pandemic struck was all about levelling up investment in the North and the Midlands, and not investment in London and the south-east. You could tell that was playing into the discussions that were taking place. The first funding deal that was negotiated was concluded on 14 May, a date that will be etched into my memory for ever as incredibly difficult … We did actually think at one point in time that we might have to issue what's called a section 114 notice about not being able to have any realistic prospect of balancing our budget … This is a £10-billion organization that directly employs 28,000 people. There were days in May [2020] when I was really genuinely worried about the existence of TfL going forward.[38]

The politically motivated brinkmanship of the government's response was remarkably cavalier with the sustainability of the capital city. Lord also remembers the tension on the evening of 14 May. "We're all by our phones and our laptops. Finally, we got the message from Simon Kilonback and Mike [Brown] that they'd got the funding letter. It was literally four minutes to midnight. We were five minutes away from instructing our control centres to bring a controlled stop [to the entire network]."[39]

An entirely different approach had been taken on the national rail network. Transport minister Grant Shapps moved quickly in March to grant national rail operators fresh contracts, at a cost of £3.5 billion to the Treasury, and to bail out private bus operators. TfL's funding was not confirmed until two months after most passenger revenue had disappeared.[40] Government funding of National Rail during 2020–21 increased by £10.4 billion to bail out train operators (and by 3.8 per cent to £5.6 billion on rolling stock and infrastructure enhancements) and to maintain a reduced service on the national rail network, as passenger income dropped by 78 per cent.[41] In September, emergency agreements (National Rail Contracts) replaced the rail franchises, with the DfT collecting revenues and paying the operators' costs plus a management fee.

Meanwhile, TfL was obliged to seek a series of no fewer than seven short-term funding settlements over the Covid years. This consumed executive resources in repeated response and recalculation of TfL's finances, endless negotiation, pushing back at political posturing through the conditions that were attached to funding.

In October 2020, with the first six-month funding agreement approaching its end, government rancour with City Hall was again in the news. In a House of Commons debate, Johnson told MPs: "It was the Labour mayor of London who bankrupted TfL's finances,"[42] and Sadiq Khan demanded an apology from the PM "for telling a blatant lie". It was an astonishing statement to make, to declare that the mayor rather than Covid was to blame for TfL's financial predicament. It was reported that ministers had told the mayor they would take direct control of TfL unless he accepted their conditions for funding: enlarging the congestion zone, higher Tube and bus fares, and a council tax increase.[43] Reflecting on this later, Heidi Alexander maintained that, having looked over the edge of the precipice, neither side liked what they saw at the bottom. "The government doesn't want to import all of the difficult decisions that TfL and City Hall have to take about London's transport network into its own sphere of responsibility … it's quite useful for government to have someone else who is politically responsible for that."[44]

The tensions between City Hall, TfL and government reached a climax in October and November of 2020, Alexander recalled. "When we were negotiating the financial package for the last six months of this financial year, everyone talked about H2. There was a very protracted exchange of correspondence between the mayor and the secretary of state. I remember in one letter, the secretary of state suggested that, if we couldn't come to an agreement on various proposals they'd put forward, they would consider taking a power of direction over TfL, which would fundamentally change the devolution settlement."[45]

At his mayoral election in May 2008, Boris Johnson had suggested his victory showed "that the Conservatives have changed into a party that can again be trusted after 30 years with the greatest, most cosmopolitan, multiracial, generous-hearted city on earth, in which there are huge and growing divisions between rich and poor".[46] In 2020 his government's response could not have been more different. The government effectively took over the direction of TfL during the Covid years, placing two observers on the TfL board, held the mayor and commissioner to month after month of short-term funding negotiations, offered no capital funding and conditionally demanded among other things the introduction of driverless trains, a pensions review, the suspension of free travel for under-18s, the extension of the congestion charge zone, RPI+1 per cent fare increases, higher council tax and the achievement of an operating surplus.

Eventually political theatre was put aside and a further £1.8 billion of funding for TfL was agreed for the six months to March 2021, then extended to May 2021 with a further £0.6 billion. In June 2022 a series of short extensions was prolonged to 3 August 2022, which did finally include funding for the replacement of the 1972 Stock trains on the Piccadilly line by 2027, to be built in Goole, East Yorkshire by Siemens Mobility. By August 2022, when a funding deal to March 2024 was finally agreed, government assistance to TfL for the loss of revenue since March 2020 had totalled £5.3 billion.

Amid the politics of funding, there was an intriguing illustration of TfL's influence and value. For the Downing Street briefings by the PM and the chief medical officer (CMO), Chris Whitty, the only way government knew if lockdown was having any real effect or being complied with was through the data that TfL supplied about travel in London. As Andy Lord rued:

> We were the only organization in the country that had, in effect, a closed transport system, and we could demonstrate that ridership had fallen from where it was to where it is. Go back and look at the presentations on a daily, a weekly basis for lockdown one – the data was always from TfL. Shashi Verma's [chief technology officer] team did a brilliant job because they just put this data engine into action, fed it into all the decision makers, and I know that health and policy decisions across the country were based on their data.[47]

A new commissioner: Andy Byford

Before Covid struck, Commissioner Mike Brown had announced his departure from TfL to lead the restoration of the Palace of Westminster. Now, in the pandemic, Heidi Alexander asked Brown, "Is there any way in which you can stay for a bit longer, because I just think we really need you. I remember watching Andy Lord, as the new managing director of the Tube, just absorb so much from Mike Brown during that period, because Mike had previously been managing director. It was such an intense learning period for Andy. I can remember saying to him, 'I think you've learned in six months what you would have learned in six years, or perhaps learned in six weeks what you would have learned in six years'."[48] Alexander recognized how important it was to have Brown's experience. "He was a very, very calming influence on the whole thing ... if anyone ever writes up the story of TfL during Covid, then Mike Brown definitely needs get top billing in that story."[49] Meanwhile, Alexander was interviewing by Zoom candidates attracted by an international search for the next commissioner.

Brown stayed to lead TfL's response to the pandemic, and found himself at the sharp end of the funding negotiation with mayor and government over the first bailout. "Mike is incredibly balanced, measured, calm – he was a huge support," Lord recalled.[50] The TfL team carried a huge burden throughout the pandemic, undoubtedly made heavier by the politically motivated demands and brinkmanship around the seven short-term funding bailouts.

Andy Byford took up his role as TfL's fourth[51] commissioner in late June 2020. Born in Plymouth to a transport family, he had started his career as a graduate trainee with London Underground in 1989, and worked his way up through Tube operational roles to become general manager for Customer Service in the pre-PPP Bakerloo, Central and Victoria lines (BCV) before moving in 2003 to South-Eastern and Southern rail roles, Rail Corp in New South Wales, CEO of Toronto Transit Commission and finally CEO of the New York Transit Authority from 2017 to 2020.

At the time of his appointment, Byford said he was delighted to be taking up the role of commissioner and to have been chosen to lead the organization where he had started his transport career more than thirty years before.

> In the wake of the Covid-19 pandemic, all transport authorities around the world will need to reimagine how their services and projects contribute to the safe and sustainable restart of the social and economic lives of the cities they serve. It is a huge challenge, but I know that Transport for London has some of the best people anywhere in the world, and we will meet these challenges and will together help build an even better city for everyone.[52]

From the start, Byford was very clear that he saw his task essentially as distilled down to "two main immediate priorities. Number one, lead TfL through and out of the Covid

Commissioner Andy Byford with Mayor Sadiq Khan at Paddington for
the first day of public service on the Elizabeth line, 25 May 2022

crisis with all that entailed – the collapse in ridership, their financial hardship, the
financial cliff that we've fallen off, to maintaining the morale of the organization
and effectively rebuilding the organization to succeed ... The second challenge was to
get the Elizabeth line open. And at that point, there were still two and a half years
to go."[53]

He was a prominent figurehead within the embattled TfL, getting around the
operational depots and units, talking to staff, though socially distanced, and
making a weekly video from various outposts of the TfL empire with the latest
position on funding, the Elizabeth line and Covid responses. His empathy with
frontline colleagues derived from his own experience at Regent's Park early in his
Underground career. "I know what it feels like to be the one person on the spot
surrounded by angry customers, when you're probably least able to service what the
customer wants or to effect a solution."[54]

Byford's fresh, media-savvy approach was a shot in the arm for an organization
under stress during both lockdown periods, boosting internal and operational
morale and messaging the key part they were all playing in keeping London moving.

You're not setting out to be some kind of big personality, but you are saying, 'I'm
accountable. I'm the face of your transit organization, and if it goes wrong, I'm

the person that you need to talk to.' I've always passionately believed in customer service. Every week I'd go out and about the system to rally the troops and try to keep the company's morale up. I made a point of sticking up for TfL in public; you know, if we got something wrong, mea culpa, I'll take the hit for that. If it's not our fault we're not wearing it, no way, so I was kind of feisty in that respect. Those weekly videos were fun to make, but it was meant to engender a real Dunkirk spirit.[55]

As soon as Byford arrived in London, he became aware of the toxic relationship between Number Ten and City Hall. In New York in his previous role he had also found himself caught between the mayor and the governor. "It became apparent to me that, once again, I was the man in the middle in dealing with the particularly difficult dynamic of a PM who thought that his successor was ruining his legacy and the incumbent who thought that his predecessor was trying to shaft TfL and wreck what he was currently doing." This was against a background of a Conservative government that was suspicious of big public service bodies such as TfL. "They particularly didn't like TfL under Sadiq's jurisdiction, there was no love lost between them."[56]

Byford and the TfL team knew they had to distance themselves from the political crossfire, however hard done by they felt. He was insistent that "TfL should not be involved in politics. We shouldn't comment on it. We shouldn't get involved in anything political, I would deal with the permanent secretary. I was once asked by the GLA how much time was I spending on finance and funding, and at the time my answer was, north of 60 per cent."[57]

Covid in itself was an existential threat, but for TfL the funding discussions with government felt like a fight for survival as they were repeatedly taken to the brink of insolvency. In taking up the role of commissioner, Byford had relished the prospect of putting forward a thoughtful, well-argued, responsible submission; "just asking for the minimum that we needed to see us through ... there will be no UK recovery without a London recovery. There'd be no London recovery without a TfL to sustain it and to drive that recovery."[58] But it became apparent to him very early on that these were not really negotiations. Myriad questions were asked of TfL's submission, constantly questioning TfL's cost base. "Why do you need to do this, why do you need to do that?" Byford had expected that they would sit opposite each other and thrash out a deal. "On the contrary, you would suddenly be sent – invariably late, because deadlines would come and go – an 'offer letter' that wasn't even an offer. It was take it or leave it, Her Majesty's government is prepared to extend the further funding package of X to last through Y and with the following conditions; in some cases, the conditions ran to 70 items. We would then convene at 10 o'clock on a Saturday night because suddenly the funding letter had come in. We would hold conferences, internal conferences, conference calls, to go through it with lawyers and with smart financial people."[59]

The so-called negotiations were all-consuming and exhausting for everyone involved. TfL would try to influence the typically political conditions attached to funding.

> In some cases, the quantum was just ludicrous and way off what we had very carefully crafted; we weren't just plucking numbers out of thin air, we could justify the numbers that we'd asked for ... Then they would come with conditions that were just unacceptable to us. I had very robust discussions with the permanent secretary, who was the messenger representing the position of the then transport secretary Grant Shapps, but, on a number of occasions, I had to say I effectively rejected the offer, it was unacceptable as tabled, and I did float on one that we would end up having to hand the keys over, a bit of a calculated risk on my part. I was calling their bluff. I knew they wouldn't want to take control ... My job was to stick up for TfL ... there was one offer in particular that was both really short – a two-week deal – and the actual offer of cash was pretty much de minimis. I wrote to the permanent secretary that it was unacceptable and therefore we weren't accepting it, with all the implications that that carried. I think that did not endear me to government, which is not something I would do lightly; I pride myself on being a professional civil servant. But I was crystal clear on what my role was, and that was to protect TfL.[60]

TfL finally obtained a longer deal, even if only for 19 months. Byford was "very proud that we got £6 billion over the course of the various negotiations ... We wanted a really long-term deal, but we got one that was a year and a half. It's no exaggeration to say that saved TfL, because the alternative was hand back the keys."[61] Byford was always publicly appreciative of the financial support from the government. "I was very determined from the start, and to the day I left, to conduct myself professionally and immaculately such that no one could ever accuse us of being political or unprofessional. As a leader you have to set the example; if I had gone out bad-mouthing the government, or disobeying instructions, whatever, what message does that send to the troops? In expecting everyone at TfL to step up during Covid I had to do the same."[62]

For Byford, it was a delicate balancing act. "I felt sometimes like the UN secretary-general, doing shuttle diplomacy between Number Ten, the DfT, the unions, the workforce, and City Hall and the GLA , shuffling, trying to do a quite a difficult balancing act, but it was exhausting and stressful for all of my executive, it was hard graft."[63]

The TfL team recognized how difficult it was for the new commissioner to take up the role with TfL's offices empty, staff furloughed and operating under protective social distancing. "It was quite hard for Andy to come into a new organization with established procedures without having had the experience of living through the lockdowns in the organization," judged Powell, "and to Andy's absolute credit, the one area that he really wants to roll his sleeves up and focus on is getting the Elizabeth line open."[64] Byford confessed to finding it difficult to arrive at the top of a large organization during Covid: "It added to the complexity of the challenge that I didn't meet my executives, my exec team, the people who reported to me, I didn't meet most of them and didn't meet the board members in person until at least a year in."[65]

Recovery – the cleanest Tube ever

As restrictions began to be lifted and the lockdown gradually relaxed in the early summer of 2020, TfL was concerned about a car-led recovery. Communication and social media assets were devoted to encouraging Londoners back onto public transport by emphasizing that its services were cleaner than they had ever been: "An enhanced cleaning regime is also in operation, which uses hospital-grade cleaning substances that kill viruses and bacteria on contact and provide ongoing disinfection."[66] Key interchanges were frequently cleaned during the day, and "all regular 'touch points', such as poles and doors, are regularly wiped down with a strong disinfectant".[67] Continuous UV cleaning of escalator handrails was trialled, and trains were cleaned with a long-lasting antiviral spray. "By using hand sanitizer and wearing facial coverings that cover both the nose and mouth when on public transport, Londoners can increase their commitment against the spread of coronavirus."[68] TfL did a sponsorship deal with the makers of Dettol, with some 800 antiviral hand sanitizer dispensers being placed at 270 stations.

Government restrictions had begun to be lifted from 13 May; in June, primary schools and non-essential retail were allowed to reopen, and 'support bubbles' with other households were permitted. The hospitality industry finally rejoined the party, with pavement licences granted and a 10 p.m. curfew. Tables and chairs full of outdoor revellers appeared in Soho streets, and groups of up to six were permitted from September. Pubs and restaurants could serve alcohol only with a 'substantial meal'. The ensuing debate would have been hilarious had the issue not been so serious. Environment secretary George Eustice told LBC Radio that a Scotch egg would constitute a substantial meal, while Cabinet Office minister Michael Gove caused confusion by then declaring that the sausage-coated egg was probably a starter before telling the media that it did in fact constitute a substantial meal. The debate continued with the PM's official spokesman refusing to spell out the

Mayor Sadiq Khan in 2021 with a repurposed 1931 'Let's Do London' poster to encourage people back into central London venues and attractions post-Covid

The first day of non-essential shopping at Oxford Circus after
lockdown restrictions were partly lifted on 15 June 2020

difference between a bar snack and a meal and not being prepared to discuss the
relative merits of sausage rolls, pork pies or ploughman's lunches![69]

Most restrictions in London were lifted from 19 July, and TfL sought to increase
service levels and recover income. Lord recalled that an early and principled decision
was to focus all decisions on keeping TfL colleagues, suppliers and customers safe.
"They had to have absolute confidence that our decision-making was based around
their health and safety and well-being in a scenario that none of us had ever faced
before."[70] TfL was back in the business of promoting the use of public transport, this
time in the face of public concern about the safety of going out and being in contact
with other passengers. "We were able to roll out a major promotional campaign,
including an engaging TV commercial, which showcased all that London had to offer,
to encourage customers back onto our services and get the city back on its feet."[71]
A historic LT poster was repurposed as part of the 'Welcome Back London' campaign
to support central London businesses and cultural attractions.

By June 2020, as Tube passenger numbers grew, a timetable uplift was planned.
ASLEF maintained that it was not safe, and called their member drivers not to
work. For Andy Lord the question was, would the drivers come to work? "I was up at
four … I was waiting to watch the first trains on TrackerNet pull out of the depots,

and the texts. We got the first refusal ... by five thirty I think we'd had 20 refusals, which is not a lot in the big scheme of things but at that time in the morning is quite significant. By six thirty it had gone up to 22, but we now had trains out across the network. Most refusals had been at one depot, and they were all union reps. It went from a quite comical moment the night before to an 'Oh hell' moment, then to massive relief – and the service ran. The management team did an outstanding job, the drivers who came to work were brilliant. From that day on, we ran a full Tube service across the entire network."[72]

Returning to public transport in London at this time was a surreal experience. Most passengers complied with social distancing and the mandatory requirement to wear face coverings unless they were exempt, and avoided contact, sitting or standing apart as floor and seat graphic signs demanded. Anyone with a cough became highly suspect and to be avoided. TfL sought reassurance about the safety of the system through independent testing by Imperial College London, which was carried out monthly from September 2020, taking swabs of touch points in stations and on buses, and air samples in ticket halls. No traces of coronavirus on TfL's public transport network were found. Only in 2022 was it understood that the virus that causes Covid is *mainly transmitted through droplets* in the air generated when an infected person coughs, sneezes or speaks.

Retreat – the second lockdown

The government's 'Eat Out To Help Out' campaign to support the hospitality industry in August 2020 offered to pay 50 per cent of a meal out, up to £10 per person. It boosted a beleaguered industry but may have contributed to the second wave of the disease, when the new Omicron variant spread rapidly. Restrictive measures were reinstituted by the government in November 2020 as the new variant caused a second and higher peak of cases. Mask wearing was mandatory again until late February 2021. With the surge at the end of that year, London reached Tier 4, the strictest level, Christmas gatherings in London in 2020 were effectively cancelled, and the third national lockdown came into force from 6 January until 8 March, when schools reopened, and 29 March, when the stay-at-home order was lifted and the rule of six reintroduced.

Meanwhile, the race was on to identify and successfully test a Covid vaccine. In 2020, the first Covid vaccines were developed and made available to the public through emergency authorizations and conditional approvals. In Coventry, the very first Pfizer vaccine was administered to a 91-year-old grandmother, Margaret Keenan, on 8 December. The availability of a vaccine developed in such a short time brought an end to the uncertainty of the pandemic, even if case numbers rose again with new variants to an even higher peak in early 2021. The immunity given by the vaccines was found to wane over time, requiring booster doses to maintain protection, but for the first time the disease appeared to be under control. Nevertheless, Covid had a major impact on London and left a legacy still being assimilated today.

Covid's London legacy

London was initially one of the worst-affected regions in England, with more than three million cases and at least 185,000 deaths in the capital to February 2023. For TfL the immediate legacy of Covid was the deaths of 105 transport staff, who made the ultimate sacrifice to keep London's transport moving, the majority of them working in the bus operation.[73] A memorial and small park was created at Braham Street near Aldgate and unveiled by the mayor and by (now commissioner) Andy Lord in April 2023. They met some of the families of the deceased, including the family of the bus driver who had come up from Plymouth. Powell recalls, "unveiling the memorial and meeting the relatives who have lost family members. That was a sobering moment."[74] "Choosing to serve London as a transport worker is an honourable decision ... it's a truly remarkable collective effort that relies on commitment and resilience from every individual involved," reflected Mayor Khan. "When London might have stopped, our transport workers did not, they were there for us ... we only prevailed because they persevered."[75]

TfL was a frontline service in dealing with the consequences of the virus, and for Heidi Alexander it was a strong reminder of the extent to which transport and the public transport network, "which everyone takes for granted, how absolutely integral it is to life in the city ... it played out in the hospitals two or three weeks later, we got used to that lag between the data on infection rates and people being in hospital. But the extent to which London's public transport network was really on the front line of it in that very first wave was pretty astonishing. I just have nothing but admiration for the people that I worked with at that time who kept the show on the road."[76]

For Powell it taught TfL about just how agile the organization could be under pressure. At the press conferences every evening, the TfL leadership watched what was coming out – "we knew something was going to be said or policy made" – then met to agree action and communications. "When Boris announced lockdown, we got wind it was probably coming ... The first thing we had to do is to put a whole comms plan together to clarify that essential people were still allowed to travel to come to work, and we had to get letters produced to show that."[77]

The pandemic revealed otherwise untested aspects of the GLA Act, not least the absence of a public service obligation on TfL. Alexander was reminded of the impact that not having a legal requirement to provide the services that Londoners depend upon had on TfL. "We were faced with this existential question about where the money was coming from, how were we going to pay people's salaries? How are we going to pay our suppliers? How will we pay our lenders? If there was some agreement between government, City Hall and TfL about the basics that had to be provided, that would have potentially given us more certainty around the fact that government would stand behind us. But it just felt very fragile in May last year, and it was hard to get the attention of government. Everyone was firefighting with the pandemic, and we were saying, 'Well, hang on a minute, you've got a £10 billion organization here that is in danger of not being able to pay its staff'."[78] Alexander remembers the TfL board saying to Mike Brown, "'Could you be instructed by government to stop running Tube services?' and Mike saying, 'Well actually, no, that's my decision as commissioner, and my decision will be that we're going to keep it running. Nurses are going to have to get to hospitals, and people are going to have to get into supermarkets'."[79]

Devolution itself was in effect suspended due to the financial crisis accompanying the pandemic. The Johnson government reverted to type in its attitude to both TfL and the London boroughs. "A huge issue for the mayor, and perhaps in particular for the boroughs, when Covid-19 took hold was what they saw as the cavalier, top-down attitude of Johnson's administration towards consulting them and keeping them informed," suggested London commentator Dave Hill. "As the government's effective takeover of Transport for London during the pandemic also showed, its commitment to ending 'Whitehall knows best' attitudes appeared to be both partial and partisan."

Travel patterns in London appear to have been permanently changed by the pandemic, reflected in travel volumes returning unevenly and slowly to pre-Covid levels, and to a different pattern. While the hybrid working week has become a fixture for office-based workers, in 2025 the consequences for productivity, interactive organizational culture and skills development remain a matter for debate. A steady return to the office has been discernible in London since 2022, with the average worker spending 2.7 days a week in the office in 2024, compared to 2.3 days a year earlier and 3.9 days pre-pandemic. Central London employers have set a lower, 2- to 3-day, mandate than in cities such as New York, Paris and Singapore, where up to 3.5 days a week is the average. The cost of commuting is cited as a barrier to the return. From March to May 2024, TfL trialled an off-peak fares offer on Fridays, but it did not have a noticeable impact on Friday travel and resulted in a revenue reduction of 2.5 per cent.

In 2023–24, overall demand for public transport in London was at 93 per cent of pre-pandemic levels. If the impact of the Elizabeth line is removed, the Underground was back to running at 88 per cent, the bus network at 89 per cent of 2019's passenger numbers. In general, the transport recovery has been strongest at the weekend, while Mondays and Fridays remain quieter, especially on the Tube. Only time will tell how prolonged these shifts in travel patterns will be, but for a transport network more dependent on passenger income than in any other comparable city, the return of demand remains crucial to its future. Active travel, cycling and walking, has increased since 2019, cycling by 26 per cent, but the major shift that might have been caused by the pandemic measures did not happen.

For Gareth Powell and Andy Lord, who led TfL's operational response to Covid, those years demonstrated the strength of TfL as an integrated transport authority. "The devolved model worked really well, and showed its real strengths in terms of operational delivery, but the weakness of it was exposed through the inability of the funding to be self-sufficient." For them the future challenge is to create circumstances in which TfL is more resilient financially in the face of shocks – such as, Powell suggests, "having an underpinning set of agreements where TfL is seen as a national asset with a national focus rather than devolved focus at times of national crisis. There is no such mechanism for that, and I think the organization was exposed, looking back, because it didn't have any such mechanisms in place."

Manchester and the other cities with devolved mayoralties, Powell maintains, "all want what London has despite the challenges of operating within it; I think it's a proven model now for the UK. I hope it is replicated." Lord commented that "You can see the model works because other cities in the UK are trying to copy it and are getting funding settlements to enable them to do it, regardless of their political leadership."

Lord maintains that the pandemic has enabled TfL to have more control in some respects.

"This year [2023–24] we're going to achieve financial sustainability from an operating perspective for the first time in the organization's history, which is a remarkable achievement … What would it take to drive that to a billion by 2030? If we could get to a billion-pound operating surplus, we will actually be making a profit … we would be in control of our own capital investment programme. That's a game changer in terms of making sure we can renew everything we want to do and do small enhancements. We're always going to need some form of financing, wherever that comes from, for major line extensions or major new infrastructure. If you can get to a point whereby you are delivering an operating surplus at a billion pounds a year, your cash reserves are strong, you're servicing your debt and you're delivering and you can renew your assets, then actually, you're in a really strong place. The pandemic has potentially enabled us to do that.[80]

CONCLUSION

"[Transport is] the real test of my mayoralty. If I get it wrong I will be a one-term mayor."

– Ken Livingstone, 2000[1]

"If you're chairman of TfL and you have a brilliant commissioner, you have enormous power. I built things with a speed that was simply impossible to replicate as prime minister … it was an absolute honour and privilege to work with those guys at TfL."

– Boris Johnson, 2025[2]

"The level of skill, expertise and innovation demonstrated by the staff at TfL in putting our climate policies into practice shows why our transport system is envied across the world."

– Sadiq Khan, 2023[3]

TfL is the longest continuously operating transport authority for the capital since the founding of London Passenger Transport Board as a public corporation in 1933. Following nationalization as the London Transport Executive from 1948 to 1962, then a nationalized industry run by the Ministry of Transport until devolution to the GLC in 1970, followed by return to direct control from Whitehall in 1984, the devolution of transport to the London mayor and TfL since 2000 has enabled a revolution in the city's transport in terms of its accountability to Londoners, its carrying capacity, response to the customer in the digital age, and the vision for a more sustainable and healthy city.[4]

As London government expert Professor Tony Travers has observed, "This brief history is instructive because it reveals the uncertainty with which the UK government treated what was, by most accounts, the world's most extensive and successful urban transport system."[5] He expands on this in his Afterword.

The gestation of TfL had been thoughtfully envisioned and planned by the architects of the GLA bill. It was not to be the rebirth of the GLC – quite the opposite: it distilled the qualities of the strong executive mayors of American and European cities and framed them for devolved London government, without serious tax-raising powers but with the powers to make a congestion charge and hypothecate the income to transport improvements. While the vision for the new authority being apolitical may have proved unrealistic, in most other respects devolution over the 25 years has relied upon transport as the key enabler of London, supporting long-term strategic planning and urban development.

This history has charted the shaping of what has come to be termed the 'London model' for public transport, a description typically used by other cities and mayors seeking the benefits and leverage of devolution; at the launch of the Bee bus network in Manchester in 2022 elected mayor Andy Burnham called for "London-style public transport for Manchester".[6] Burnham appointed Vernon Everitt as the commissioner of Transport for Greater Manchester in 2022 to bring to the region his experience from London to integrate Manchester's bus and rail services. "In the late 1980s and throughout the 1990s, transport was an impediment to London, not an asset," Everitt reflected. "Through very far-sighted and massively commendable action by government – you can argue about the PPP and the means by which the capital was brought in, but brought in it was – it's paid enormous dividends both for this city and for the country as a whole."[7]

The London model, TfL, was forged early on by the intersection of an independent elected mayor, born and bred in London, with a clear vision for improving his city based on transport, with a chief executive uninhibited by prior experience in the UK and supported by a new leadership team of experienced, committed and visionary public servants: transport operators, planners and financial experts. This combination of a devolved electoral mandate and an executive committed to innovation has delivered for London.

What could not be planned for in TfL's design was the management of the interface between elected politicians and the executive, between the four-year mayoral short term and the long term of transport investment, development and innovation. The foundation moment in 2000, and handovers between administrations in 2008 and 2016, have all been equally difficult for both parties. They have been characterized by periods of intense test between politician and transport executive to establish that the executive has indeed taken on board the new regime's manifesto commitments, despite being loyal to a predecessor of a different political hue for the previous eight years.

In 2001, the appointment of Bob Kiley was crucially formative for the new organization, not least in his close working relationship with Ken Livingstone, in establishing TfL with a city-wide purview and recruiting a talented innovative leadership team. In 2008, Peter Hendy instinctively understood that his job was to demonstrate on day one to Mayor Johnson that, whatever had gone before, TfL would deliver on his election manifesto, understanding better what had been promised than the mayor did himself. Once more, in 2016 Mike Brown and his team strove after eight years of delivering for Johnson to demonstrate their support for Sadiq Khan's fresh agenda. Professor David Begg has drawn the conclusion that TfL is not run by civil servants:

It is run by people who are much more political, not political in a party sense, but political in terms of a loyalty to the mayor in a way that you don't get from civil servants to a secretary of state ... a secretary state may only be for six months, and the mayor is in it for at least four years so they're loyal to that mayor. Their job is to advise that mayor, but to deliver what that mayor wants, even if they know it's not the right thing. The classic examples would be Mike Brown delivering a fares freeze (everyone at TfL was telling me it was going to be disastrous), Boris pulling out of the second congestion charging zone, getting rid of the bendy buses without consulting bus passengers, going for the Emirates cable car over the Thames rather than big infrastructure development of the Thames crossings. They would say, 'No, this is not right, Mr Mayor, but we'll do what you want; we'll deliver all of this'.[8]

The London model's success owes much to the mayoral powers over both the strategic London Plan and the public transport network. For Michelle Dix, the lock-up between the mayor's land use and transport strategies

meant London had a really clear vision on what it wanted to do, by bringing these things together. In government, you have Department for Transport, you have Housing, Environment, they're disjointed, they're not joined together, whereas the mayor and all the functional bodies have a clear view as to what London should be like. That's the bit that makes us stand out from all other authorities, this ownership of so many parts; you can bring them together and make them work together.[9]

TfL also embraced the challenge of creating an integrated transport network for London. Over its 25 years it has developed from being distinctly siloed between Tube, Bus, Streets and central services. Driven by the imperatives of the 2012 Olympics, the unifying force of Oyster, real-time and digital information and a reaffirmed customer mentality, it has delivered on 'Every Journey Matters', the integrated approach across all the modes to offer a joined-up customer experience from home to destination.

For TfL the task has in many ways become more complex and increasingly tough over time. The challenge has moved from making the Tube and bus service work better to addressing air quality, health and the sustainability of the capital city in the post-Covid world. Transport is inevitably political, because of its call on the public purse and its accountability. Boundaries between mayor and executive have moved towards greater mayoral control in the activities of TfL. Being the mayor's primary policy delivery agent, TfL's influence has been steadily extended far beyond transport operations as the enabler for his wider electoral mandate across economic development, housing, the public realm, inclusion and diversity, culture, health and education. The mayor of London brand is now on every press release, poster, website and piece of print; it is important for the mayoralty to be associated and accountable for TfL's success.

Over the life of TfL, London's position within the UK has come under significant political pressure. The levelling-up agenda has been a strong strand in post-Brexit populist politics. The argument for more levelling-up investment in regional infrastructure has often been couched in terms that felt more like levelling down London. "In the light of the perfectly understandably changed politics of this country over the last couple of years, and the levelling-up agenda, it is absolutely vital that we don't lose or fall back from the gains that have been made in London. That it is genuinely levelling up and not London falling back," suggests Vernon Everitt.[10] The politically motivated conditions put on TfL's short-term funding deals during the pandemic, and the dogfight between an ex-mayor PM and his successor, were neither in the spirit nor the letter of devolution.

The truth about levelling up surely is that local economic regeneration demands devolved governance structures, capable of agreeing regional strategy, generating business plans for effective investment funding. After all, the London model started with establishing the GLA. "TfL is already playing a big role in the national picture," maintained Everitt in his time at TfL. "We work very, very closely with transport authorities all around the country, helping them produce business cases for their own investment, helping them think through how they might want to operate their bus networks and their ticketing systems."[11]

The London model has limited revenue-raising powers for the mayor, which has driven innovative approaches to its capital and project funding beyond the fare box and central government, through prudential borrowing and accountability to the rating agencies and the long-term government support from 2005 to 2015. A new approach after the failure of the PPP was also demanded for the funding of major projects. For Crossrail the combination of the agglomeration argument and business rate supplement convinced the Treasury in 2004 to enable Crossrail to start by 2009, and then in 2012 for the Battersea extension of the Northern line to be secured by the creation of an enterprise zone, developer contributions and the community infrastructure levy.

For TfL the essential quality required of its leadership is to hold a vision for the city's future as well as to meet the demands of the day-to-day transport operation of a world city, to be both scanning the horizon for innovation and delivering the mayor's immediate manifesto. Wickedly, innovation very rapidly becomes baked into the everyday experience of Londoners and is taken for granted, while failure brings forth a cacophony of complaint. Front-line operational management is a tough apprenticeship, and urban transport is a seven-day-a-week taskmaster. There is no hiding place if your part of the network is not performing that day for the 8 a.m. leadership call. All TfL's commissioners, with the exception of Kiley, have been through this demanding school. David Brown, MD of London Buses and later CEO of First Group, reflected on the continuing significance of TfL being led by transport operators, not accountants:

> The people that were in TfL running the buses had a long history of running buses in London. They understood the mechanics and the rationale. They were as protective of the London bus network as anyone could be but also understood how it worked. They were not bureaucrats, because they were deliverers. One of the ways I always differentiate TfL from the DfT, bless them, is there was an output and a delivery ... Peter, myself and Leon had all had commercial backgrounds. We understood fully the motivation for the operators, we knew how to keep them straight but interested.[12]

Looking back over TfL's first quarter century, it is remarkable how much has been achieved for London by TfL under all three mayors, without having the fiscal and statutory independence of their counterparts in Europe or the US. The Livingstone years were formative, and set out the shape of the mayoralty, the potential for strategic direction across the capital and the power of simply being London's leader and figurehead. Nick Raynsford reflected in 2016 that "while the argument can always be advanced for more devolution ... in reality the mayors of London ... have proved the ability of the post to influence outcomes far beyond the formal remit of the GLA. Sub-national government has benefited significantly from this process, and the forces of centralization have been notably reversed."[13]

As current TfL commissioner Andy Lord has maintained, "London's transport network – and the thousands of colleagues who keep London moving every day – are part of the fabric of all our lives, and since 2000 we have delivered momentous positive change across the city and on our services."[14]

An intriguing means of assessing TfL's record is to speculate on what might or might not have happened without devolution in 2000, with no elected mayor, GLA or TfL, with a different model of governance for London. I have turned to Professor Tony Travers of the LSE to assess TfL through a counterfactual Afterword.

AFTERWORD

The policy and governance path leading to the creation of the GLA and TfL in 2000 hints at factors that could, had the world been different, have taken the governance of the capital's transport in very different directions; the geographical area to be covered, central or sub-national government control, regional city-wide and borough interests, the service to be provided, direct provision of contracted services, the relationship with national rail and road provision and funding arrangements. In the light of TfL's 25-year operation, it is worth considering what might have happened differently as a way of contrasting several hypothetical governance models with the actual one.

An alternative scenario might have been for the transfer of London Transport from the GLC to central government in 1984 to have led to a subsequent reform in which a far bigger, elected transport authority might have been created across the south-east, the region that generates more than 40 per cent of the UK's GDP. Rail and bus services across an area far larger than London (though centred on it) could have been run by such an institution. In a body of this kind, the representatives of places outside Greater London would almost certainly have been in a majority. Inner and central London would almost certainly have received lower levels of provision, while more rural areas would have seen better services. Rural bus services would have competed for resources with the Tube. This, broadly, is the dynamic of the Metropolitan Transportation Authority (MTA) in New York State. The MTA, a state-wide agency, has to balance the transport needs of beach communities and small townships with those of Manhattan and Brooklyn. Perhaps unsurprisingly, few New York subway lines have been built or extended in recent decades, while London has managed to deliver an array of new transport infrastructure. A city-focused transport authority gives primacy within its boundaries to the needs of densely populated urban areas, leaving national government to worry about the wider region.

London might have gone in the direction of a combined transport authority such as Transport for Greater Manchester, a combined authority of the leaders of the 10 local authorities with a directly elected mayor providing a figurehead and strategic leadership. In this second scenario, TfL would have come into existence, but under the control of a combined authority of the boroughs and the mayor of London. As with the south-east model outlined above, the dynamics of a combined authority would have been rather different from the mayor being, in effect, the key decision-maker. A combined authority would have been likely to give greater weighting to more local needs for bus services and traffic schemes than to railway megaprojects such as Crossrail.

The needs of the City and West End would have been counterbalanced by outer boroughs, where provision is generally thinner and less frequent. In much the same way as individual boroughs have adopted planning policies to regenerate and develop town centres in places such as Brent Cross, Ealing, Ilford and Lewisham, their influence might well have delivered more local tram systems of the kind found between Beckenham, Croydon and Wimbledon. The Overground would doubtless have been popular with many boroughs, though policies such as the congestion charge and the ULEZ might well have been vetoed. In this model, major roads would probably have seen less spending and local ones more.

A third version of transport in London would have seen a significantly more powerful version of TfL. Most obviously, the whole of the commuter rail system could have been made the responsibility of TfL and the mayor. Such a reform was considered in 2015, when Patrick McLoughlin (secretary of state for transport, 2012–16) agreed to deliver a 'metro' version of national rail services in London by transferring them to TfL. A change of minister stopped the reform. Had TfL taken over these services, it would have been responsible for all the capital's railways except intercity lines. The renationalization of Britain's railways that has begun begs the question of whether the government will again consider a super-TfL with far wider rail responsibilities.

A super-TfL could have assumed responsibility for more roads, particularly those 'local' roads run by the boroughs but that carry major bus routes, such as Oxford Street and Kensington High Street. The regulation of bike-hire schemes, given their distribution across many boroughs, might more logically have been made the responsibility of TfL and not the boroughs. Similarly, the regulation of roadworks might have been made a City Hall duty.

Lastly, a more powerful TfL might have been given access to a wider resource base, including the option to levy taxes to subsidize services and/or to underpin borrowing in relation to new infrastructure. Similarly, the capacity independently to implement 'tax increment finance' arrangements to allow developments such as the one that allowed the funding of the Northern Line extension to Battersea/Nine Elms would have allowed significantly greater freedom to act.

The fourth possible scenario is one in which TfL never came into existence. This could have resulted from a prior decision by the incoming Labour government to deliver a far less extensive set of powers for the mayor of London, along the lines of what was offered to the north-east of England in 2004. Alternatively, the Blair government might have opted for a south-east regional transport authority of the kind considered in the first scenario above. If Labour had lost the 1997 general election, a returned Major government might have built on the work done between 1990 and 1997 but stopped short of devolution.

On the assumption that TfL had never existed, what might have been different? In fairness to the Thatcher and Major governments, there had been some investments and improvements to London's transport system in the period of nationalization between 1984 and 2000. Even before the Thatcher government's renationalization of the Tube and buses, it had allowed the London Docklands Development Corporation to build the first part of the Docklands Light Railway. The Jubilee line extension (from Green Park to Stratford) had been approved by Margaret Thatcher's government. The Heathrow Express, a private initiative delivered by Heathrow Airport Ltd, opened in 1998.

Without devolution?

How many of the key initiatives narrated in this account might not have taken place (or would have been materially different) without the creation of TfL and the mayor as its chair?

A number of the key innovations of the period are simply inconceivable without TfL, most notably congestion charging. No national government would have had the bravery to introduce a road charge in this way. Whitehall had extensively reviewed road pricing during the mid-1990s but had never moved towards introducing the policy. Outside London, Durham County Council introduced a road user charge in a small section of Durham in 2002, while Greater Manchester held a referendum in 2008 that rejected a congestion charge. Nottingham initiated a workplace parking levy in 2012.

It has fallen to sub-national authorities to take the step of charging for road use. As mayor, Ken Livingstone used the legitimacy of his mandate to push through congestion charging despite powerful opposition at the time. It is hard to believe that a UK transport secretary would have used political capital in this way.

Similarly, it is much less likely that the 2012 London would have been held in London. When London won its bid to host the 2012 Olympic Games in 2005 the mayor, Ken Livingstone, was with the British team in Singapore. The settled relationship between the Blair government and London's mayor was self-evidently an element in the city's successful bid in 2005. It is impossible to know whether London would have won without the convening power and commitment of the mayor, but virtually all cities competing to hold such spectacles need the active support of their civic leadership. TfL's capacity to deliver millions of spectators to and from venues was a major element of the bid. In the event, the Olympics led to a substantial investment in rail services at Stratford and one of the largest urban regeneration projects ever in London.

The ticketing revolution that started with Oyster in 2003 and developed into contactless payment was driven only by TfL and the mayor. This has been a visionary innovation, facilitating huge societal change well beyond transport transactions. Many other cities in the UK and overseas have adopted similar technology, drawing on London's success. Another wonder of modern London is the fact that the Underground, buses, Elizabeth line, Overground, DLR, trams and virtually all the local rail services still provided by private companies are within a single ticketing system with zonal fares that generally stop only at the Greater London boundary. Successive mayors and TfL (with help from the government) worked to bring all the national rail companies into London's vast (580 square miles) transport area.

Underground, the Elizabeth line had failed to secure government funding in 1991. The existence after 2000 of TfL and the mayor clearly gave Tony Blair's government the confidence to give the project the go-ahead. It is possible that central government might have revived the line and delivered it, but less likely than with the new structures in place following the 2000 London government reforms. The coming of the mayor of London and TfL created renewed impetus to deliver the project, as well as major upgrade projects at Bank station, Victoria and King's Cross/St Pancras. TfL managed these projects, along with general reinvestment in the Underground, through most of the period from 2000 to 2025. Compared with many badly managed UK infrastructure projects, these appear to have been handled relatively well, thus convincing the Treasury and the Department for Transport to fund them, at least in part. Once again, it is possible the government might have done something similar, but equally TfL shaped the projects and lobbied for resources.

Similarly, the extension of the Northern line to Battersea and the regeneration of that area had been stalled for about forty years. With little or no public money forthcoming to pay for redevelopment, it eventually took the creation of a mayoral opportunity area, a master plan involving Wandsworth and Lambeth councils, and a tax increment financing (TIF) deal to deliver an extension to the Underground that would unlock the area's development potential. The mayor and TfL had to work closely with the Treasury to create the TIF deal, which allowed new tax yield to be captured over a 25-year period, plus developer contributions, to pay for a spur off the Northern line. It was completed on time and on budget.

On the buses, the brief revival of the Routemaster would have been unnecessary without a congestion charge to serve, while the creation of the New Routemaster would not have taken place. Without the near-total agreement of successive mayors about the need for low-emission and/or electric vehicles as part of the solution to London's air-quality problems, there would have been a far slower rollout of the low-emission/electric bus fleet. TfL has moved towards its goal of having a full fleet of zero-emission buses by the mid-2030s. London is well ahead of the rest of the country in terms of moving towards zero-emission vehicles. Again, it is impossible to prove that London's swift move to low-emission vehicles would not have taken place if there had been no mayor or TfL, but evidence from the rest of England suggests that the they have made a major difference. In Greater Manchester, the mayor and Transport for Greater Manchester are moving in a similar direction, again suggesting that the city mayor and transport agency model delivers change. Without the political pressure generated by the introduction of ULEZ, it is unlikely that the Superloop orbital bus services would have been initiated. As a policy, this new bus service shows how the accountability of a locally based body leads to outcomes that would not otherwise be possible.

The introduction of the ULEZ, especially the final, large expansion to cover the whole of the city, was immensely controversial, with significant national and local media opposition. Mayor Sadiq Khan stuck to the policy while making the scrappage scheme for older cars more generous. All three stages would have been unlikely candidates for central government politicians. Indeed, the expansion to the whole of London in 2023 was openly opposed by the government of the day. No TfL and mayor, no ULEZ.

Taxi, minicab and private hire regulation would have remained with the Metropolitan Police, responsible to the Home Office and without democratic oversight. As new kinds of private hire vehicles came into existence, notably internet-based point-to-point services such as Uber, the challenge of regulation became more political. The new, challenger providers not only ate into the traditional cabs' market but adopted different management and employment practices. Private hire regulation would have been significantly more political and complex than the Met's former role in overseeing taxis and minicabs. There would almost certainly have been calls for central government or the 32 boroughs to take a more active role if TfL had not existed. The Department of Transport, as the relevant ministry, would have been remote from London's particular needs. It is hard to see how either of these possible alternatives would have been an improvement on TfL.

Traffic control would have remained the responsibility of a quango, the Traffic Control Systems Unit (TCSU). Roads, despite being commonplace strips of tarmac, are intensely political. Which users should have priority? How should pedestrian crossings work? How should fines be used to police rules and regulations? Should there be low-traffic neighbourhoods (LTNs)? In the political environment of 2025, it is hard to imagine a quango being able to deliver accountable and defensible public policy in relation to roads. A chief executive, however skilled and politically acute, would find it difficult to navigate the challenges of accountable decision-making when it came to putting in cycle lanes, delivering LTNs or delivering reforms to major junctions and interchanges. Without TfL's political legitimacy, roads management would be far less likely to deliver reform.

The 60+ London Oyster concessionary travel scheme was introduced by Mayor Johnson after both candidates committed to it in the 2012 mayoral election. This change is a clear-cut example of a policy that would not have existed (or would have been vastly less likely to exist) unless the mayor controlled TfL. Another is the Night Tube, launched in 2016, after London's Underground had long been compared unfavourably with the New York City Subway, which runs a 24-hour service. Although only a two-days-a-week service, the frequency is generally higher than on the NYC Subway overnight. Like the vastly improved Night Bus network, it is most unlikely that the Night Tube would have come into existence without the mayor and TfL.

A benign minister such as John Gummer or former transport minister (and mayoral candidate) Steve Norris might well have seen advantage in delivering a cycle hire scheme via a centrally controlled London transport agency, though it might have arrived later than the mayor's. On cycling all three mayors have shared a common, pro-cycling approach, and results on the city's streets would have been very different (and less effective) without them and TfL. For the original Cycle Superhighways and the sustained investment in cycle infrastructure, let alone the radical Embankment scheme, mayoral and TfL commitment has been essential to delivery.

It is virtually inconceivable that national government would have created the Overground orbital rail network. The vision and lobbying power of TfL and City Hall politicians, applied to the opportunity of orbital rail and the challenge of the Stratford Olympics, delivered the Overground, one of the best-value pieces of new infrastructure of modern times.

On the road network TfL as a highway authority has delivered major junction redesigns such as those at Elephant and Castle and Old Street to restore a more pedestrian-friendly street scene. It is possible that a national roads agency might have undertaken similar schemes, though there were none in the years immediately before TfL came into existence. It is also possible that individual boroughs might have delivered such schemes. TfL was a pioneer authority, along with Kent County Council, in implementing a 'lane rental' scheme to charge utilities for the use of road space when roadworks are undertaken. It is possible that London's major roads might have been included in the initial lane rental schemes, but TfL's expertise at logistics and management almost certainly made it more likely London was chosen.

The new Thames tunnel at Silvertown became part of TfL's planning during Mayor Johnson's second term, with the project receiving government approval under Mayor Khan in 2018. This was a scheme originated and managed by TfL. Again, it is possible that a government agency might have delivered it, though previous experience suggests this would not have happened. Without TfL, river services would not have been brought within the fare system/Oystercard as there had been no such policy moves before TfL came into existence. Without mayoral promotion, the cable car would not have been built and public money would not have been expended on the ultimately unbuilt Garden Bridge. Places for London, created in 2015, is a TfL subsidiary and large landowner that develops residential and commercial property. If TfL did not exist, nor would Places for London.

The pedestrianization of Trafalgar Square is a useful exception to most of the other initiatives considered here. Plans to pedestrianize the square had their origins during the 'interregnum' between the abolition of the GLC and the creation of the GLA. John Gummer, as self-styled 'minister for London', held consultations about improving central London squares. While the Mayor and TfL ultimately delivered this project, it is a rare example of one that might otherwise have been driven through by central government even if TfL had never existed.

There are other policies that could reasonably be added to those above. For example, 20 mph speed restrictions on the TfL road network and free travel for children and young adults might not have been introduced. TfL's online presence, notably real-time bus information, might well have been less effective if the equivalent for services across England are a guide.

Reflections

As we know, in the year 2000 TfL was created, and was to bring a new, co-ordinated approach to the planning and delivery of both infrastructure initiatives and improved services. The mayor of London, as chair of the organization, became a cheerleader for investment. In many ways this was the key purpose behind the introduction of the office of mayor. Subsequently, the same planning and lobbying role has been given to mayors in other English cities such as Greater Manchester.

Several key attributes have contributed to TfL's 25 years of delivery. First is the fact that the institution operates within the single political/geographical unit of Greater London, which is widely understood to be a continuous urban area held together by rail and bus routes, and which has political accountability precisely contained within that area. This is not a 'regional' authority with a patchwork of city and countryside, or a joint committee with complex lines back to constituent authorities. It is not a distant ministry in Whitehall. Everyone in London knows that the mayor and TfL are responsible for the buses and the Underground, a reality reinforced by the ubiquitous roundel motif that tells everyone precisely which authority and which politician is responsible for each journey. With the best will in the world, riding a 'Southern' train from central London to rural Kent provides few clues to who, apart from the driver, is in charge. On the Underground or a bus, it's the mayor.

TfL and its chair, the mayor, are to blame when things go wrong. The media certainly understand this. Basic search engine trends for 'London Tube' or 'mayor of London' show far higher levels of interest than for ministers or train companies. Like or loathe Sadiq Khan, Boris Johnson or Ken Livingstone, Londoners know they have been personally accountable for transport in the city. This understanding generates pressure for improvement and delivers a relatively direct form of accountability.

TfL undertakes local, regional and national-scale projects. Overwhelmingly, these projects have (against the backdrop of falling British trust in politics and political institutions) mostly been delivered as promised, as the sections above attest. Despite the Elizabeth line's late and somewhat over-budget delivery, TfL oversaw a massive project far more effectively than HS2 has been managed by Whitehall. Similarly, Greater Manchester has delivered Metrolink and bus regulation, and the Liverpool City region operates Merseyrail with their particular versions of local accountability.

The London model has proved to be a powerful force for the city's day-to-day operation and long-term sustainability. What has allowed TfL to deliver – and this to make such a difference to a large and complex city – is the direct 'consumer' pressure felt by its managers and political leaders. TfL is by no means perfect, but it is better run than if central government or a quango were in charge. There are lessons for the future of Britain in this observation.

Professor Tony Travers
Director, LSE London

Notes

Chapter 1

1 Tony Travers, interview 27 April 2011
2 John Campbell, *Margaret Thatcher, Volume Two: The Iron Lady*, London 2003
3 Campbell 2003, p. 384
4 Nick Raynsford, *Substance Not Spin: An Insider's View of Success and Failure in Government*, Bristol 2016
5 Annual Tube numbers peaked pre-Covid at 1.39 billion in 2017–18, and recovered to 1.18 billion in 2023–24; TfL Travel in London report, 2024
6 Raynsford 2016, p. 98
7 Genie Turton, interview 10 February 2020
8 Liz Meek, interview 6 April 2020
9 John Gummer MP, secretary of state for the environment, 1993–97
10 Genie Turton, interview 10 February 2020
11 The London Pride Partnership of local authorities and business leaders published a Prospectus in 1995; not to be confused with the later LGBT London Pride campaign founded in 2004, but tracing its origins to Gay Pride's first event in 1972.
12 Liz Meek, interview 6 April 2020
13 London First's (now BusinessLDN) website, 'About Us', 4 April 2020 and 4 March 2024
14 Tony Blair, 28 April 1998, Evening Standard London Debate at the Guildhall, broadcast by BBC Newsnight; http://bit.ly/4lkRold
15 Tony Travers and Stephen Glaister, interview 3 April 2020
16 Raynsford 2016, p. 98
17 Simon Jenkins, interview in 2020, quoted in Jack Brown, Tony Travers and Richard Brown, eds., *London's Mayor at 20: Governing a Global City in the 21st Century*, London 2020, pp. 21–22
18 New Labour manifesto, 1997 general election; http://bit.ly/4krLI04
19 John Prescott with Hunter Davies, *Prezza: My Story: Pulling No Punches*, London 2008, p. 388
20 Tony Travers and Stephen Glaister, interview 3 April 2020
21 Nick Raynsford, interview 9 October 2019
22 Genie Turton, interview 10 February 2020
23 Raynsford 2016, p. 98
24 Ibid., p. 100
25 Genie Turton, interview 10 February 2020
26 Ibid.
27 Liz Meek, interview 6 April 2020
28 Ibid.
29 Ibid.
30 Ibid.
31 Ibid.
32 Ibid.
33 Livingstone, 2011, p. 378
34 Liz Meek, interview 6 April 2020
35 Tony Travers and Stephen Glaister, interview 3 April 2020
36 Genie Turton, interview 10 February 2020
37 Ibid.
38 Ibid.
39 Prescott 2008, p. 279
40 Liz Meek, interview 6 April 2020
41 Genie Turton, interview 10 February 2020
42 Blair's political secretary when MP for Wolverhampton South from 2005; currently chancellor of the Duchy of Lancaster at Kier Starmer's right hand in the post-2024 Labour Cabinet
43 Liz Meek, interview 6 April 2020
44 Tony Travers and Stephen Glaister, interview 3 April 2020
45 Ibid.
46 Stephen Glaister, interview 30 May 2024
47 Genie Turton, interview 10 February 2020
48 Nick Raynsford 2016, p. 102
49 Tony Travers and Stephen Glaister, interview 3 April 2020
50 Stephen Glaister, interview 30 May 2024
51 Extended in 2007 to include limited powers over housing
52 Tony Travers, *The Greater London Authority, 2000 to 2008*, LSE; http://bit.ly/44mNlib
53 Genie Turton, interview 10 February 2020
54 Ibid.
55 Ibid.
56 Quoted in Livingstone 2011, p.381
57 Genie Turton, interview 10 February 2020
58 Ibid.
59 *The Sun*, editorial, 13 October 1981
60 Alastair Campbell, *The Blair Years: Extracts from the Alastair Campbell Diaries*, London 2007, p. 440
61 Campbell 2007, p. 443
62 Peter Hendy and Leon Daniels, interview 24 May 2011
63 Livingstone 2011, p.380
64 Tony Travers in Anthony Seldon, ed. *Blair's Britain 1997–2007*, Cambridge 2007, p. 62
65 Ken Livingstone interview, 20 December 2019
66 *Evening Standard* editorial, 3 May 2000
67 Livingstone 2011, p. 453; Ken Livingstone, interview 20 December 2019
68 Tony Travers, interview 3 April 2020
69 Genie Turton, interview 10 February 2020
70 Raynsford 2016, p.108
71 Simon Carr, *The Independent*, May 2000
72 Genie Turton, interview 10 February 2020
73 Ibid.
74 Stephen Glaister, 'Transport' in Anthony Selsdon, ed., *Blair's Britain,* Cambridge 2007
75 Genie Turton, interview 10 February 2020
76 Livingstone 2011, p.422

Chapter 2

1 Ken Livingstone, *You Can't Say That,* London 2011, p. 243
2 Quoted in Tony Travers, Jack Brown and Richard Brown, *London's Mayor at 20: Governing a Global City in the 21st Century*, London 2020, p. 83
3 Tony Blair on Ken Livingstone, 1998 in Andrew Hosken, *Ken: The Ups and Downs of Ken Livingstone*, London 2008
4 Tony Blair, *A Journey*, London 2010, p. 270
5 Ken Livingstone, interview 20 December 2019
6 Romney House, 47 Marsham Street, built in 1930s to the design of 'Red Vienna' architect Michael Roseauer, requisitioned by government, temporary GLA offices 2000 until Norman Foster's City Hall by Tower Bridge was ready for occupation in 2002.
7 Alexander Jan, interview 24 April 2024
8 *Local Government Chronicle*, 13 October 2000; http://bit.ly/44HzdPf
9 *Local Government Chronicle*, ibid
10 Anthony Mayer, interview 9 April 2020
11 Ibid.
12 Redmond O'Neill, GLA director of transport; Neale Coleman, senior policy advisor; John Ross, GLA director of economics and business; Jude Woodward, senior advisor, cultural industries and tourism; Lee Jasper, senior advisor for equalities

13 Richard Brown, 'Mayors Need Mates – choosing City Hall advisors', *Centre for London* blog, 30 November 2020

14 Peter Hendy, *The Guardian*, 23 October 2009

15 Neale Coleman, interview 17 December 2024

16 John Ross, Livingstone's director of Economic and Business Policy, 2000–2008 , economist and blogger, leader of Trotskyist party Socialist Action, now senior fellow at Chongyang Institute of Fiscal Studies, Renmin University of China

17 Anthony Mayer, interview 9 April 2020

18 Neale Coleman, interview 17 December 2024

19 Stephen Glaister and Tony Travers, interview 3 April 2020

20 Anthony Mayer, interview 9 April 2020

21 Harry Barlow, Livingstone's campaign advisor

22 Harry Barlow, interview 22 April 2020

23 AJ, conversation with the author April 2024

24 Tony Travers, interview 27 April 2011

25 Transport for London, briefing pack, PWC and GLA, 2000. Thanks to Alexander Jan for sharing his copy of the pack, for which he drafted Livingstone's Foreword.

26 Jay Walder, interview 5 March 2021

27 Stephen Glaister and Tony Travers, interview 3 April 2020

28 Ken Livingstone, interview 20 December 2019

29 Derek Turner, interview 31 January 2020

30 Peter Hendy, interview 5 January 2016

31 BBC News, 9 October 2000

32 David Gunn, responsible for the turnaround of the New York Subway's performance in Kiley's time at the MTA. Kiley tried hard to get him to come to take a similar role in London; Gunn came to London for a month but was ultimately put off by the constraints of the PPP.

33 Jay Walder, interview 5 March 2021

34 Maggie Boepple, interview 24 January 2020

35 Ibid.

36 Ibid.

37 Ed Koch, mayor of New York 1978–89

38 Maggie Boepple, interview 24 January 2020

39 Stephen Glaister and Tony Travers, interview 3 April 2020

40 Ken Livingstone, interview 20 December 2019

41 *The New York Times*, 10 October 2000

42 Isabel Dedring, interview 13 November 2019

43 Stephen Glaister, interview 30 May 2024

44 David Begg, interview 17 December 2019

45 Neale Coleman, interview 17 December 2024

46 William Finnegan, 'Letter from London: Underground Man', *The New Yorker*, 9 February 2004

47 Maggie Boepple, interview 24 January 2020

48 Tim O'Toole, interview 6 February 2020

49 Maggie Boepple, interview 24 January 2020

50 Ibid.

51 Liz Meek, interview 6 April 2020

52 Mike Gapes, MP for Ilford South, in transport debate 26 June 2002; http://bit.ly/4n10k3I

53 David Begg, interview, 17 December 2019

54 Jay Walder, interview 5 March 2021

55 Quoted in Livingstone 2011, p. 485

56 Maggie Boepple, interview 24 January 2020

57 Liz Meek, interview 6 April 2020

58 Jay Walder, interview 5 March 2021

59 Ibid.

60 Maggie Boepple, interview 24 January 2020

61 Jeroen Weimar, interview 5 September 2019

62 Ibid.

63 Denis Tunnicliffe, recruited from aviation as MD of London Underground 1988–98, chairman 1998–2000, CEO of London Regional Transport 1998–2000; created a life peer in 2004

64 Tim O'Toole, interview 14 April 2011

65 Tony Travers, interview 27 April 2011

66 Jay Walder, interview 5 March 2021

67 Ibid. Steve Allen, head of Corporate Finance, notably led on prudential borrowing, 2003–15; Tom Amenta, principal, Corporate Finance, 2001–06; Eric Rothman, head of Business Planning, 2001–04; Lauren Sager Weinstein has had a long and distinguished TfL career as a business planner, chief of staff to Jay Walder 2004–07, head of Oyster Development, 2007–12, head of Analytics, 2012–16, chief data officer 2017–present

68 Isabel Dedring, interview 13 November 2019

69 Charles Monheim, interview, 3 December 2019

70 Jay Walder, interview 5 March 2021

71 Tim O'Toole, interview 20 April 2009

72 Tony Travers, interview 27 April 2011

73 Liz Meek, interview 6 April 2020

74 Quoted in *The Independent*, 5 April 2004

75 The definitive work on the LU PPP is Stephen Glaister's book *The London Underground Public Private Partnership 1997–2010: No Way to Run a Railway*, Cambridge 2025, which he generously shared with me in manuscript and upon which my account of the PPP relies.

76 Stephen Byers, secretary of state for transport, 2001–02; David Rowlands, senior civil servant in Department for Transport, permanent secretary from 2003

77 Liz Meek, interview 6 April 2020

78 Tony Travers, interview 27 April 2011

79 Maggie Boepple, interview 24 January 2020

80 Quoted in William Finnegan, 'Letter from London: Underground Man', *The New Yorker*, 9 February 2004

81 Prestige was a public finance initiative (PFI) contract from 1997 held between TfL and TranSys, a consortium whose principal partners were Cubic Transportation Systems and HP Enterprise Services. TranSys was responsible for developing, installing, managing and maintaining London's automated fare collection system, including the Oyster card, on behalf of TfL. TfL terminated the contract in 2010.

82 Charles Monheim, interview 3 December 2019[3]

83 Jay Walder, interview 5 March 2021

84 Stephen Glaister, interview 22 June 2011

85 Ibid.

86 Ibid.

87 Simon Jenkins is quoted in William Finnegan, 'Letter from London: Underground Man', *The New Yorker*, 9 February 2004

88 Jay Walder, interview 5 March 2021

89 Christian Wolmar, transport journalist, quoted in William Finnegan, 'Letter from London: Underground Man', *The New Yorker*, 9 February 2004

90 Stephen Byers, Labour Party politician, MP from 1992 to 2010. He served in the Cabinet from 1998 to 2002, was implicated in the parliamentary expenses scandal and retired from politics in 2010. During Byers' ministerial career, he was chief secretary to the Treasury, secretary of state for trade and industry, and secretary of state for transport, local government and the regions 2001–02.

91 Sir David Rowlands KCB (1947–2014) was a British civil servant who rose to

the rank of permanent secretary to the department for transport.

92 Shriti Vadera was on the Council of Economic Advisers at the Treasury from 1999 to 2007, where she led on policy for business, competition innovation, productivity and international finance and development issues, and the management of the government's shareholdings, asset sales and public–private partnerships for infrastructure; an influential member of Brown's Treasury team.

93 Liz Meek, interview 6 April 2020

94 William Finnegan, 'Letter from London:Underground Man', *The* New Yorker, 9 February 2004

95 Tony Travers, interview 27 April 2011

96 Liz Meek, interview 6 April 2020

97 *A Tale of Two Infracos*, London Assembly Transport Committee (2007), executive summary, p. 3

98 William Finnegan, 'Letter from London: Underground Man', *The New Yorker*, 9 February 2004

99 Bridget Rosewell, interview 29 November 2024

100 Quoted in *A Tale of Two Infracos*, London Assembly Transport Committee 2007

101 William Finnegan, 'Letter from London: Underground Man', *The New Yorker*, 9 February 2004

102 Lauren Sager Weinstein, interview 31 January 2020

103 Anthony King and Ivor Crewe, *The Blunders of our Governments*, London 2013, revised and updated 2014, p. 221

104 *The Guardian*, editorial, 1 April 2005

105 Daniel Moylan, interview 5 May 2020

Chapter 3

1 Ken Livingstone, *You Can't Say That*, London 2011, p. 423

2 Livingstone 2011, p. 423

3 Keith Dovkants, *Evening Standard*, quoted in Livingstone 2011, p. 460–61

4 *Evening Standard*, 2 September 2002

5 Derek Turner, interview 31 January 2020

6 Simon Jenkins, *Evening Standard*, 25 January 2001

7 Ibid.

8 *Daily Mail* and *The Guardian*, 18 November 2003

9 *The Guardian*, 8 February 2001

10 Adam Blenford, *Evening Standard*, 24 July 2002

11 Bob Kiley, TfL Annual Report, 2003, p.5

12 Derek Turner, interview 31 January 2020

13 Ken Livingstone, quoted in *Evening Standard*, 3 July 2003

14 Livingstone 2011, p. 482

15 Martin Whitley, MD London United, quoted in Roger Torode, *Privatising London's Buses*, London 2015, p. 241, at time of sale to Transdev

16 Stephen Glaister, email to author, 18 February 2025

17 Peter Hendy, interview 25 June 2024

18 Ibid.

19 Mayor's Question Time, 20 October 2004; http://bit.ly/4kBR93V

20 Peter Hendy, interview 25 June 2024

21 *The Times*, 19 March 2003

22 TfL press release, 5 June 2002; http://bit.ly/3GLGiX4

23 TfL press release, 5 June 2002

24 Quoted in TfL press release, 23 May 2006; http://bit.ly/3GHOLdR

25 Peter Hendy, interview, 25 June 2024

26 Bob Kiley, *The Guardian*, 12 October 2001

27 Metronet – Atkins, Balfour Beatty, Adtranz (later Bombardier), Seeboard (later EDF Energy), Thames Water

28 InfraCo – infrastructure company contracted out through the PPP

29 Tube Lines – Amey, Bechtel, Jarvis

30 Tim O'Toole, interview 20 April 2009

31 Tim O'Toole, interview 14 April 2011

32 Ibid.

33 Ibid.

34 Tim O'Toole, interview 20 April 2009

35 Tim O'Toole, interview 7 February 2020

36 Tim O'Toole, interview 14 April 2011

37 Tim O'Toole, interview 20 April 2009

38 Tim O'Toole, interview 14 April 2011

39 Tim O'Toole, interview 7 February 2020

40 Tim O'Toole, interview 14 April 2011

41 Ibid.

42 Charles Monheim, interview 3 December 2019

43 Tim O'Toole, interview 14 April 2011

44 Tim O'Toole, interview 7 February 2020

45 Tim O'Toole, interview 14 April 2011

46 Tim O'Toole, interview 14 April 2011 and 7 February 2020

47 Mike Brown, interview 6 July 2011

48 Tim O'Toole, interview 14 April 2011

49 TfL Rail and Underground Panel, Speak Up and People Strategy report, February 2009; http://bit.ly/44slbkw

50 Tim O'Toole, interview 14 April 2011

51 Tim O'Toole, interview 7 February 2020

52 Chris Bolt, quoted in *The Guardian*, 17 November 2006

53 Stephen Glaister, quoted in *The Guardian*, 1 April 2008

54 Under the Local Government Act 2003, a local authority may borrow for any purpose relevant to its functions of for the 'prudential management of its financial affairs'. The borrowing limit will be related to the revenue streams available with which it can service the debt.

55 Jay Walder, interview 5 March 2021

56 Jay Walder, interview 5 March 2021

57 Tony McNulty, under-secretary of state for transport, 2002–04, minister of state for rail and London from 2004, avoided being labelled as either a Blairite or a Brownite.

58 Jay Walder, interview 5 March 2021

59 Malcolm Murray-Clark and Michelle Dix, job share heads of congestion charging

60 Charles Monheim, interview 3 December 2019

61 Steve Allen, interview 4 July 2023

62 Stephen Glaister, email to author 18 February 2025; TfL Archive – Information Memorandum £3.3 billion Medium Term Note Programme, 25 November 2004

63 Michèle Dix, interview 2 March 2020

64 David Begg, interview 17 December 2019

65 Maggie Boepple, email with author, January 2025; Bob Kiley died in 2016.

66 Ken Livingstone, interview 20 December 2019

Chapter 4

1 Michèle Dix, interview 2 March 2020

2 Martin J. H. Mogridge, *Travel in Towns: Jam Yesterday, Jam Today and Jam Tomorrow?* London 1990

3 Later published as Milton Friedman and Daniel J. Boorstin, 'How to Plan and Pay for the Safe and Adequate Highways We Need' in Daniel Roth, *Roads in a Market Economy*, Aldershot 1996, pp. 223–45

4 Deputy director, the Road Research Laboratory, established by government at Crowthorne, Berkshire, in 1933, privatized as the Transport Research Laboratory in 1996, owned as a non-profit distributing organization by the Transport Research Foundation

5 Martin Whittles, *Urban Road Pricing: Public and Political Acceptability*, Farnham 2003, p. 248

6 R. J. Smeed, *Road Pricing: The Economic and Technical Possibilities*, London 1964

7 David Bannister, *Transport Planning in the UK, USA and Europe*, London 2002

8 'Ringways' in www.roads.org.uk

9 Michael Bailey, 'Road Programme cost estimated at £1700m', *The Times*, 19 August 1970

10 Jane Jacobs, *The Death and Life of Great American Cities*, New York 1961

11 Buchanan Report, 'Traffic in Towns' – Report of the Steering Committee, 1963, para. 22

12 Buchanan Report 1963, para. 30

13 Colin Buchanan, *Traffic in Towns: The specially shortened edition of the Buchanan Report*, London 1964, p. 17

14 Ken Livingstone, *You Can't Say That*, London 2011, p. 319

15 Whittles 2003, p. 248

16 Ken Livingstone, 'The challenge of driving through change: Introducing congestion charging in central London', *Planning Theory & Practice* vol. 5, issue 4, pp. 490–98, London 2004, DOI: 10.1080/1464935042000293224

17 Quoted in Jonathan Leape, 'The London Congestion Charge', *Journal of Economic Perspectives*, vol. 20, no. 4, Fall 2006, pp. 157–76

18 ROCOL, *Road Charging Options for London*, London 2000, p. 5

19 ROCOL was a study commissioned by the DfT and GOL, reported in *Road Charging Options for London*, London 2000

20 Derek Turner, interview 31 January 2020

21 Ken Livingstone, interview 20 December 2019, and Stephen Glaister, email to author 18 February 2025

22 Michèle Dix, interview 2 March 2020 and email to author 12 February 2025

23 Genie Turton, interview 10 February 2020

24 Ibid.

25 Ibid.

26 Ibid.

27 Derek Turner, interview 31 January 2020

28 Michèle Dix, interview 2 March 2020

29 Jay Walder, interview 5 March 2021

30 Derek Turner, interview 31 January 2020

31 Ibid.

32 Peter Hendy, interview 26 June 2024

33 Livingstone 2011, p. 440

34 Both Michèle Dix and Malcolm Murray-Clark had worked on ROCOL

35 Derek Turner, interview 31 January 2020

36 Michèle Dix, interview 2 March 2020

37 Malcolm Murray-Clark, email to author 26 February 2025

38 Michèle Dix, interview 2 March 2020

39 Stephen Glaister and Tony Travers, interview 3 April 2020

40 Martin G. Richards, *Congestion Charging in London: The Policy and the Politics*, London 2006, p. 221

41 Michèle Dix, interview 2 March 2020

42 Peter Hendy interview 26 June 2024

43 Michèle Dix, interview 2 March 2020

44 Derek Turner, *Daily Telegraph*, 15 February 2003

45 Derek Turner, interview 31 January 2020

46 Ibid.

47 Ibid., and Michèle Dix, interview 21 February 2025

48 Malcolm Murray-Clark, email to author 26 February 2025

49 Malcolm Murray-Clark, email to author 26 February 2025

50 Derek Turner, interview 31 January 2020

51 *Evening Standard*, 19 March and 31 May 2002

52 *Sunday Telegraph*, 15 July 2001

53 *Daily Telegraph*, 14 February, 2003

54 Michèle Dix, interview 2 March 2020

55 Derek Turner, interview 31 January 2020

56 Michèle Dix, email to author 12 February 2025

57 Neale Coleman, interview 17 December 2024

58 Jay Walder, interview 5 March 2021

59 Isabel Dedring, interview 13 November 2019

60 Kieron McCarthy, 'Finance', *The Guardian*, 26 November 2002

61 'Madonna blasts congestion charge', BBC News, 2 May 2003

62 Andrew Clark, 'Miss Moneypenny leads attack as campaign splits West End actors', *The Guardian*, 10 February 2003

63 Peter Hendy, interview 25 June 2024

64 Ken Livingstone, interview 20 December 2019

65 Isabel Dedring, interview 13 November 2019

66 *Daily Telegraph*, 17 February 2003

67 Sean O'Neill, *Daily Telegraph*, 18 February 2003

68 Michèle Dix, interview 2 March 2020

69 Derek Turner, interview 31 January 2020

70 *Daily Telegraph*, 14 and 17 February 2003, editorial, 18 February 2003

71 *The Guardian*, 18 February 2003

72 *Evening Standard*, 19 February 2024

73 *Evening Standard*, 27 February 2003

74 Ibid.

75 Neale Coleman, interview 17 December 2024

76 Tim O'Toole, interview 6 February 2020

77 Livngstone 2011, p. 477

78 Charles Monheim, interview 3 December 2019

79 Neale Coleman, interview 17 December 2024

80 Ken Livingstone, interview 20 December 2019, and Stephen Glaister, email to author 18 February 2025

81 Isabel Dedring, interview 13 November 2019

82 Michèle Dix, interview 2 March 2020

83 Peter Hendy, interview 25 June 2024

84 Derek Turner, interview 31 January 2020

85 *Good Practices in City Energy Efficiency: London, United Kingdom – Congestion Charges for Urban Transport*, ESMAP 2011, www.esmap.org

Chapter 5

1 *The Economist*, 9 July 2005

2 This chapter enlarges on my earlier account of July 2005, included in David Bownes, Oliver Green and Sam Mullins, *Underground: How the Tube Shaped London*, London 2012

3 The complex story of the London Games of 2012 has been brilliantly articulated in Dave Hill's book, *Olympic Park: When Britain Built Something Big*, London 2022. The author is delighted to acknowledge his debt to Dave Hill in shaping this chapter and for his support.

4 Peter Hendy, notes from conversation 19 February 2025

5 Quoted in Dave Hill 2022, p. 78

6 *Evening Standard*, 6 July 2005

7 Ibid.

8 Mike Brown, interview 11 July 2023

9 Evidence of Andy (Andrew) Barr to the coroner's inquests. The coroner's report was presented on 6 May 2011 as *Coroner's Inquests into the London Bombings of July 2005* by Lady Justice Hallett.

10 Andy Barr, interview 29 July 2011

11 All these activities were described by survivors in their evidence to the coroner's inquests; all first-person accounts are drawn from the coroner's report unless otherwise referenced.

12 Andy Barr, interview 29 July 2011

13 Ibid.

14 Ibid.

15 Timothy Batkin, driver of the bombed eastbound Circle Line train, set number 204, in the coroner's report

16 Ibid.

17 Sergeant Tony Silvestro, BTP, in the coroner's report

18 Jeffrey Porter, train operator driving train past train bombed at Edgware Road

19 Davinia Douglass née Turrell, the 'lady in the mask', featured in Sri Carmichael, *Evening Standard*, 12 April 2012

20 Emily Marton, in the coroner's report

21 Trevor Rodgers, DTM at Edgware Road, in the coroner's report

22 Ibid.

23 Michael Cooney, in the coroner's report

24 Tom Nairn, driver of Piccadilly line train 331, in the coroner's report

25 Raymond Wright in the coroner's report; he was off duty and riding in the cab with Tom Nairn (both train operators) as the Piccadilly train was very crowded.

26 Julie Gruen, survivor of first car on Piccadilly line train, in the coroner's report

27 Paul Mitchell, survivor from first car of Piccadilly line train, in the coroner's report

28 Julie Gruen, survivor of first car on Piccadilly line train, in the coroner's report

29 Michael Henning, survivor on Piccadilly line train, in the coroner's report

30 Tom Nairn and Raymond Wright, quoted in coroner's report

31 David Boyce, Tom Nairn and Gary Stephens, in the coroner's report

32 Gary Stephens, in the coroner's report

33 Simon Cook, in the coroner's report

34 Ibid.

35 George Psaradakis, in the coroner's report

36 Ibid.

37 PC Sims, in the coroner's report

38 Ibid.

39 George Psaradakis, in the coroner's report

40 Peter Hendy, interview 6 September 2011

41 SMOD – security manager on duty, responsible with Gold Control for strategic response to incidents.

42 Code Amber = Halt all trains in next stations and evacuate all passengers to the surface

43 Tim O'Toole, interview 20 April 2009

44 Peter Hendy, interview 6 September 2011

45 The 2025 BBC documentary has moving accounts of 7/7 from survivors, fire officers, policemen and detectives but not from train operators, station staff or controllers, the first responders.

46 Tim O'Toole, interview 20 April 2009

47 Quoted in BBC documentary, 7/7 – The London Bombings, first broadcast in January 2025

48 Mike Brown, interview 6 July 2011

49 Ibid.

50 Andy Barr, interview 29 July 2011

51 Ibid.

52 Ibid.

53 Mike Brown, interview 6 July 2011

54 Tim O'Toole, interview 20 April 2009

55 Andy Barr, notes of conversation, 22 January 2025

56 Tim O'Toole, interview 20 April 2009

57 Andy Barr, notes of conversation, 17 January 2025

58 Tim O'Toole, interview 20 April 2009

59 Ibid.

60 Peter Hendy, interview 6 September 2011

61 Ibid.

62 Tim O'Toole, interview 14 April 2011

63 Andy Barr, notes of conversation, 17 January 2025

64 Tim O'Toole, interview 20 April 2009

65 Tim O'Toole, interview 14 April 2011

66 Peter Hendy, interview 6 September 2011

67 Peter Hendy, email to author 19 February 2025

68 BBC News, 7 July 2005; http://bit.ly/4lsQxyT

69 The copycat attack failed only because the bombmaker had slightly miscalculated the ratio of ingredients for the explosive devices.

70 Andy Barr, interview 29 July 2011

71 Ibid.

72 Tim O'Toole, interview 20 April 2009

73 Ibid.

74 Tim O'Toole, interview 14 April 2011

75 Tim O'Toole, interview 7 February 2020

76 Coroner's report

77 Lady Justice Hallett to Andy (Andrew) Barr at the end of his evidence, in the coroner's report

78 Lady Justice Hallett to train operator David Matthews at the end of his evidence, in the coroner's report

79 Davinia Douglass née Turrell, the 'lady in the mask'

80 Tim O'Toole, interview 14 April 2011

81 Andy Barr, interview 29 July 2011

82 Peter Hendy, interview 14 January 2021

83 Quoted by Christian Wolmar in 2009; http://bit.ly/46ACgLO

84 Ibid.

85 Tim O'Toole, interview 20 April 2009

86 Tim O'Toole, interview 6 February 2020

87 Mike Brown, interview 6 July 2011, 11 July 2023

88 Mike Brown, interview 6 July 2011

89 Ibid.

90 Chair's Foreword, Report of the 7 July Review Committee, London Assembly, June 2006

Chapter 6

1 Steve Norris, LinkedIn, July 2023: http://bit.ly/44P7Z9F

2 Charles Monheim, interview 3 December 2019

3 Roger Torode, 'The Trials of Ticketing', in James Whiting, ed., Working for London's Buses, Crowthorne 2021

4 David Bownes, Oliver Green and Sam Mullins, Underground; How the Tube Shaped London, London 2012, pp. 210–11

5 Steve Shewmaker, interview 26 October 2022

6 Ibid.

7 Rob Easterby, interview 17 June 2020

8 Roger Torode generously shared his experience of this work in London Buses on smartcards, published in Whiting 2021

9 Prestige – Procurement of Revenue Systems, Ticketing, Integration, Gate and Equipment – invented by Luke Howard, according to Roger Torode, who led the Harrow smartcard trial as the LT BEST (Bus Electronic Smartcard Ticketing) manager

10 TfL evidence to the Transport Parliamentary Select Committee, Future of PFI, May 2011

11 John Hill, interview 17 June 2020

12 EDS, a multinational IT services company founded in 1962, acquired by and incorporated into Hewlett-Packard in 2008

13 John Hill, interview 17 June 2020

14 John Hill and Richard Rowlands, interview 17 June 2020

15 Ibid.

16 Ibid.

17 John Hill, LinkedIn, on Oyster's 20th birthday in 2023; http://bit.ly/3InEpAu

18 Charles Monheim, interview 3 December 2019

19 John Hill, interview 17 June 2020

20 ITSO – Integrated Transport Smartcard Organization, DfT national technical standard to ensure interoperability of cards and readers, introduced after TfL's Oyster, with which it is compatible.

21 Charles Monheim, interview 3 December 2019 and email to author, 20 January 2025

22 Charles Monheim, email to author, 20 January 2025

23 Charles Monheim, interview 3 December 2019

24 John Hill and Richard Rowlands, interview 17 June 2020

25 Charles Monheim, interview 3 December 2019

26 John Hill, interview 17 June 2020

27 http://www.appella.net/study_OYSTER.php

28 Richard Parry, interview 1 November 2023

29 Monheim, interview 3 December 2019

30 The Octopus smartcard was introduced in Hong Kong in 1997, the first application of this technology to the transport environment.

31 Charles Monheim, interview 3 December 2019

32   Ibid.

33   Ibid.

34   MIT – Massachusetts Institute of Technology

35   Charles Monheim, interview 3 December 2019

36   Ibid.

37   John Hill and Richard Rowlands, interview 17 June 2020

38   Ibid.

39   Shashi Verma, interview 16 September 2022

40   Ibid.

41   Shashi Verma, email to author, 3 April 2023

42   Near-field communication (NFC) is a set of communication protocols that enables communication between two electronic devices over a distance of 4 cm.

43   Shashi Verma, interview 16 September 2022

44   Ibid.

45   Ibid.

46   Steve Shewmaker, interview 26 October 2022

47   Thales is a French multinational aerospace, defence and transport corporation specializing in electronics.

48   Steve Shewmaker, interview 26 October 2022

49   Ibid.

50   John Hill and Richard Rowlands, interview 17 June 2020

51   Shashi Verma, interview 16 September 2022

52   TfL press release, 18 November 2008; http://bit.ly/4eSBjAF

53   John Hill and Richard Rowlands, interview 17 June 2020

54   Shashi Verma, interview 16 September 2022; Oyster pay as you go began to be accepted at 350 national rail stations in London from January 2010, resisted by the train operating companies since being offered funding by DfT in 2006.

55   Shashi Verma, interview 16 September 2022

56   Ibid.

57   ITSO – IT solution for a national rail ticketing standard, long advocated by DfT

58   Shashi Verma, interview 16 September 2022

59   Ibid.

60   Ibid.

61   Ibid.

62   Ibid.

63   Charles Monheim, interview 3 December 2019

64   Ibid.

65   Cubic, John Hill and Richard Rowlands, interview 17 June 2020

66   In all, 262 LU ticket offices have been closed, with only those on Network Rail stations still in use: Barking, Ealing Broadway, Finsbury Park, Kensington Olympia, Richmond, Uppminster, Willesden Junction and Wimbledon.

67   TfL press release 1 July 2014, quoting Mike Weston, TfL director of Buses; http://bit.ly/4lBLPDM

68   Shashi Verma and Cole quoted in TfL press release, 13 July 2016; http://bit.ly/4OZK5XI

69   Mike Tuckett, quoted in *Railway Technology*, 3 December 2019: http://bit.ly/3In2o4l

70   John Hill, LinkedIn, http://bit.ly/44JCzBm

71   Steve Shewmaker, LinkedIn, http://bit.ly/4kDk5Zg

72   Shashi Verma, 'Contracting for Ticketing Services', prepared for the Rudin Center, New York University, *Leveraging Technology for Transportation*, 16 June 2010

73   Shashi Verma, interview 16 September 2022

Chapter 7

1   Michael Heseltine was environment minister in Margaret Thatcher's government, and set up the London Docklands Development Corporation in 1981. Quoted in Deyan Sudjic, 'Inside London's Docklands: 40 Years of ambition, politics and financial wrangling', *Financial Times*, 11 June 2021

2   Deyan Sudjic, *Financial Times*, 11 June 2021

3   Jon Willis, *Extending the Jubilee line: The planning story*, London 1997, p. 16 and also in his recent book, Jonathan Willis, *The Railways of London Docklands: Their History and Development*, Barnsley 2022, p. 37

4   Docklands Joint Committee, 'A Strategic Plan for Docklands: Setting the Scene' (1975).

5   Quoted in Michael Heseltine's Foreword to Willis 2022

6   Willis 2022, p. 63

7   Canary Wharf itself takes its name from No. 10 Warehouse (30 Shed) of the South Quay Import Dock. This was built in 1952 for Fruit Lines Ltd, a subsidiary of Fred Olsen Lines for the Mediterranean and Canary Island fruit trade. At their request, the quay and warehouse were given the name Canary Wharf.

8   There is a relief sculpture of von Clemm in Cabot Square, Canary Wharf, a low-key memorial to the man who may have kickstarted not only the Canary Wharf development but also the renaissance in quality dining in London.

9   London Wiki, 'History of London', london.fandom.com

10   'The Lunch that launched London', Footprints of London https://footprintsoflondon/home/blog

11   Lord Heseltine, mastermind of the regeneration of London's Docklands, described the Docklands Light Railway as a "toy town railway". The former minister told the Royal Town Planning Institute in 2013 that the system "fitted the penny-pinching approach that characterizes so much of Britain's attitude to long-term competitiveness and infrastructure", TransportXtra, 29 November 2013; http://bit.ly/4lvs9as

12   The Waterloo & City line was technically still part of BR's Network SouthEast until transferred to London Underground in 1994. Network SouthEast logos can still be seen as part of the platform edging at Waterloo.

13   David L. A. Gordon *The Crash and Rebound of Canary Wharf* (PDF); realestate. wharton.upenn.edu.

14   Ian Brown, interview 9 November 2023

15   Quoted in the *Evening Standard*, 20 May 2015

16   Tony Ridley, interview 5 July 2011

17   Department for the Environment, Transport and the Regions, headed by deputy prime minister John Prescott

18   Howard Smith, interview 21 September 2023

19   Ibid.

20   Howard Smith quoting Ian Brown, interview 21 September 2023

21   Ian Brown, interview 9 November 2023

22   Kiley's answer to question on Silver Link franchise transfer, Mayor's Question Time, 10 April 2005; http://bit.ly/3IrL9xr

23   Ian Brown, interview 9 November 2023

24   Ibid.

25   Ibid.

26   Ibid.

27   Howard Smith, interview 21 September 2023

28   Ibid.; the team was later tasked with delivering the cable car project in 2012 before the Olympics

29   Geoff Hobbs, interview 20 January 2023

30   Dennis Lovett, *The North London Railway 1846–2001*, Clophill 2001

31   A major reduction in the national rail network was undertaken after

the BR chair's report *The Reshaping of British Railways*, London 1963, known colloquially as the Beeching Axe.

32 'Orbirail' in the 2001 Mayor's Transport Strategy was what became the Overground: East, West and North London lines, Gospel Oak to Barking, also Chingford, Enfield and Lee Valley lines and parts of Great Northern and Chilterns networks; Mayor's Transport Strategy 2001, 4e p. 164

33 Ibid., 4a p. 106

34 Geoff Hobbs, interview 20 January 2023

35 Ibid.

36 Ian Brown, interview 9 November 2023

37 Howard Smith, interview 21 September 2023

38 Geoff Hobbs, interview 20 January 2023

39 https://www.urbantransportgroup.org/rail-devolution-success-story-london-overground http://bit.ly/44sfMV9

40 Mayor's Rail Vision for London, TfL, February 2012, Introduction

41 Mayor's Rail Vision for London, TfL, February 2012, Boris Johnson's Mayoral Foreword

42 2013 letter to Boris Johnson from Chris Grayling, leaked to the *Evening Standard*, reported in *The Guardian*, 7 December 2016

43 Customer Focus, Rail User Survey 2024, http://bit.ly/44HTx2X

44 Mayor's Rail Vision for London, TfL, February 2012, Introduction

45 Sadiq Khan 2016; http://bit.ly/3GHi7sS, and BBC News, 9 July 2024

46 See Christian Wolmar, *The Story of Crossrail*, London 2018 for the factors that led to the rejection of the preamble to the private members' bill in 1994; updated and expanded edition published as *Crossrail: The Whole Story*, London 2022

47 Ian Brown, interview 9 November 2023

48 Ibid.

Chapter 8

1 Frank Pick's statement is widely quoted without a reference.

2 Damon Rose, 'The wheelchair warriors', BBC News, undated; http://bit.ly/4lPVHEI

3 Quoted in London Regional Transport (LRT) News, 3 October 1986

4 Quoted in 'An Accessible Routemaster', *Transport for All*, 16 March 2009

5 Quoted in LRT News, 3 October 1986

6 The term BAME was used at this time in terms of diversity statistics but is now officially avoided as it implies a singular of homogenous non-white ethnic identity.

7 TfL, *Action on Equality: TfL's commitments to 2020*, TfL March 2016, p. 9; http://bit.ly/46CY1dO

8 TfL 2016, p. 46

9 Valerie Todd, interview 3 March 2025

10 Ibid.

11 Martyn Loukes, interview 31 January 2025

12 Ibid.

13 TfL response to House of Lords Committee on the Equality Act 2010; http://bit.ly/4kBQz6m

14 Interview with Patricia Obinna, TfL director of Diversity and Inclusion; http://bit.ly/4lPwhsU

15 Patricia Obinna, interview 5 February 2025

16 Valerie Todd, interview 3 March 2025

17 TfL, *Equity in Motion* TfL 2024; http://bit.ly/4eYYIAu

18 TfL, *A fairer transport network*, summary of Equity in Motion strategy, TfL 2024, p. 3; http://bit.ly/46TP60q

19 Patricia Obinna, interview 5 February 2025

20 Valerie Todd, interview 3 March 2025

21 Purpose-built gymnasium, built in 1864, and venue for the gymnastic events at the first National Olympian Games in London in 1866 and the London Olympics of 1908. Today it is a German-themed restaurant, but the original rings for the gym ropes can still be seen in the arched roof.

22 Tanni Grey-Thompson, interview 8 April 2020

23 Ibid.

24 'Community Transport – London 2012 success', Transport for All, 5 September 2012; http://bit.ly/44N0fDm

25 Ibid.

26 Quoted in 'Inclusive Journeys: Improving the accessibility of public transport for people with sight loss', RNIB Research Report, 18 April 2023; http://bit.ly/44XJh86

27 Tanni Grey-Thompson, TfL press release 14 March 2014

28 FoI request 23 October 2023, TfL FoI 2327-2324

29 Sadiq Khan, in Mayor's Foreword to *Equity in Motion*, p. 3

30 Ben Plowden, interview 31 January 2020

31 Formerly the National Pedestrians Association

32 Ben Plowden, interview 31 January 2020

33 Ibid.

34 Ibid.

35 Ibid.

36 Ibid.

37 Ibid.

38 Ibid.

39 Ibid.

40 Ibid.

41 Ibid.

42 Ibid.

43 TfL, *The Mayor's Vision for Cycling in London: An Olympic Legacy for all Londoners*, GLA 2013, p. 4; http://bit.ly/3TCZ2uT

44 TfL 2013, , p. 4

45 Ben Plowden, interview 31 January 2020

46 Val Shawcross, Croydon councillor 1994–2000, Labour politician, Assembly member 2000–16, deputy mayor for Transport under Sadiq Khan, 2016–18 and champion of the Healthy Streets approach from 2016

47 Ben Plowden, interview 31 January 2020

48 Ibid.

49 Ibid.

50 Ibid.

51 SCOOT, the Split Cycle Offset Optimization Technique, is a traffic control system used by TfL to optimize traffic flow and reduce delays. It uses sensors and real-time data to adjust traffic signal timings, ensuring that traffic flows more smoothly through the network.

52 Ben Plowden, interview 31 January 2020

53 Ibid.

54 Ibid.

55 Will Norman, interview 30 September 2024

56 Ibid.

57 Ibid.

58 Dave Hill, '*Leadership is required to combat London's selfish cycling culture*', OnLondon, 9 September 2024: http://bit.ly/44F4FxB

59 TfL 2013, p. 46

60 Chris Macleod, interview 5 February 2025

61 Carlton Reid, Roads Were Not Built for Cars blog, 2012; https://roadswerenotbuiltforcars.com/netherlands/

62 TfL press release, 12 May 2025; http://bit.ly/3IyN6YL

63 TfL press release, 28 November 2024; http://bit.ly/4lTfx8x

64 Jess Warren, 'Cycling in City of London rises by more than 50%', BBC News, 28 April 2025; http://bit.ly/4m2jJwp

65 Quoted in 'Meeting London's Cycling Boom: Lime announces £20M Infrastructure and Safety Plan', The Lime Times blog, 29 January 2025; http://bit.ly/3IEkJIy

Chapter 9

1 Vernon Everitt, in conversation with the author, 31 April 2024

2   Max Weston, facilitator to TfL leadership, notes of conversation with the author, 22 May 2019
3   Peter Hendy, interview 6 September 2011
4   Actually stated by a customer in a 2CV focus group, picked up and repeated by Ian Pring in feedback to TfL colleagues, see note 5
5   Ian Pring, interview 21 October 2019
6   Peter Hendy, interview 26 March 2020
7   Vernon Everitt, interview 27 January 2020 and notes of conversation with the author, January 2025
8   Max Weston, facilitator to TfL leadership, notes of interview with the author, 22 May 2019
9   Peter Hendy, interview 26 March 2020
10 Vernon Everitt, interview 27 January 2020
11 Ibid.
12 Vernon Everitt, interview 31 January 2024
13 Vernon Everitt, interview 31 January 2024 and 16 January 2025
14 Vernon Everitt, interview 27 January 2020 and notes of conversation with the author 17 January 2025
15 Vernon Everitt, interview 31 January 2024
16 Vernon Everitt, interview 31 January 2024 and notes 17 January 2025
17 Vernon Everitt, interview 31 January 2024
18 Quoted in Charlie Dawson, Seán Meehan with Tom Connolly, 'A story of customer-led success: Transport for London', in Charlie Dawson and Seán Meehan, *The Customer Copernicus*, IMD/ the Foundation, 2021, p. 3
19 Chris Macleod, interview 15 September, 2021
20 Vernon Everitt, interview 27 January 2020
21 Ibid.
22 Chris MacLeod, interview 15 September, 2021
23 Richard H. Thaler and Cass R. Sunstein, *Nudge: Improving Decisions about Health, Wealth and Happiness*, New Haven 2008
24 Vincent Nolan, quoted in AQR's *InBrief* magazine, June 2000
25 Vincent Nolan, in Jennings, Nolan and Pring, interview 21 October 2019
26 Mark Ritson, influential former professor of marketing, *Marketing Week* columnist, commentator and teacher
27 Ian Pring, in Jennings, Nolan and Pring, interview 21 October 2019
28 Ibid.
29 Ibid.

30 Kat Jennings and Vincent Nolan in Jennings, Nolan and Pring, interview 21 October 2019
31 Ibid.
32 Ibid.
33 Ibid.
34 Vincent Nolan, in Jennings, Nolan and Pring, interview 21 October 2019
35 Vernon Everitt, interview 27 January 2020 and notes 17 January 2025
36 Ibid.
37 Vernon Everitt, interview 27 January 2020
38 Ian Pring, in Jennings, Nolan and Pring, interview 21 October 2019
39 Kat Jennings, Vincent Nolan and Ian Pring, interview 21 October 2019
40 Ibid.
41 Ibid.
42 Ibid.
43 Ibid.
44 Ian Pring, in Kat Jennings, Vincent Nolan and Ian Pring, interview 21 October 2019
45 Chris Macleod, notes 5 February 2025
46 Chris MacLeod, interview 15 September 2021
47 Ibid.
48 Vernon Everitt, interview 27 January 2020 and notes 17 January 2025
49 Ibid.
50 Ian Pring, interview 21 October 2019
51 Ibid.
52 Vernon Everitt, interview 27 January 2020
53 Ibid.
54 Vernon Everitt, interview 27 January 2020 and notes 17 January 2025
55 Vernon Everitt, interview 27 January 2020
56 Chris MacLeod, interview 15 September 2021
57 Chris MacLeod, *Campaign*, 24 August 2021
58 Vernon Everitt, interview 31 January 2024
59 Rikesh Shah, interview 22 February 2024
60 Vernon Everitt, interview 27 January 2020
61 Rikesh Shah, interview 22 February 2024
62 Charles Arthur, 'Another data win: TfL opens up bus and tube timetables for developers', *The Guardian*, 3 September 2010
63 Power of Information Taskforce Report, February 2009
64 Charles Arthur, 'TfL frees first tranche of data for developers' use', *The Guardian*, 15 June 2010
65 An API, or application programming

interface, is a set of rules and specifications that allows different software systems to communicate with each other. It acts as a messenger, enabling applications to request and exchange data such as live train and bus positioning without needing to know the underlying complexities of the other system.
66 Charles Arthur, 'Live Tube map halted as TfL hit by 50-fold growth in web calls,' *The Guardian*, 2 July 2010
67 Jon Card, 'Open Data is at the centre of London's transition into a smart city', *The Guardian*, 3 August 2015
68 Rikesh Shah, LinkedIn, http://bit.ly/3TyTNwn
69 Rikesh Shah, interview 22 February 2024
70 Ibid.
71 Ibid.
72 Ibid.
73 Ibid.
74 Rikesh Shah, LinkedIn, http://bit.ly/3TyTNwn
75 Rikesh Shah, interview 22 February 2024
76 Ibid.
77 Chris Macleod, email to author 10 April 2025
78 Peter Hendy, interview 26 March 2020
79 Ibid.
80 Vernon Everitt, interview 31 January 2024 and notes 17 January 2025
81 Chris MacLeod, interview 15 September 2021
82 Ibid.
83 Ibid.
84 Vincent Nolan, interview 21 October 2019
85 Vernon Everitt, interview 31 January 2024
86 Mark Evers, interview 7 March 2025
87 Ibid.
88 Ibid.
89 Quoted in TfL press release, 2 December 2015; http://bit.ly/4nGuma1
90 Mark Evers, interview 7 March 2025
91 Vernon Everitt, interview 31 January 2024
92 Ian Pring, interview 21 October 2019
93 Chris Macleod, email to author 10 April 2025
94 Mark Evers, interview 7 March 2025
95 Ian Pring, interview 21 October 2019
96 Ibid.
97 Ibid., and Chris Macleod, email to author 10 April 2025
98 Ian Pring, in Jennings, Nolan and Pring, interview 21 October 2019
99 Vernon Everitt, interview 27 January 2020

Chapter 10

1 David Brown, interview 17 April 2020
2 Sonia Purnell, *Just Boris – A Tale of Blond Ambition*, London 2012, p. 312. Purnell is a biographer and journalist who has worked at *The Economist*, *Daily Telegraph* and *Sunday Times*, including alongside Johnson as *Daily Telegraph* correspondent in Brussels in the early 1990s.
3 'Johnson wins London mayoral race', BBC News, 3 May 2008
4 Daniel Moylan, interview 14 January 2020
5 Sonia Purnell 2012, p. 312
6 Dan Ritterband, interviewed on 'The Rise and Fall of Boris Johnson', Channel 4, March 2024, episode 1
7 Sonia Purnell 2012, p. 328
8 Peter Hendy, interview 25 June 2024
9 Purnell 2012, p. 337
10 Quoted in Purnell 2012, p. 327
11 Peter Hendy, interview 26 June 2024, p. 11
12 Purnell 2012, p. 358
13 Ibid., p. 370. Ray Lewis, black youth leader, deputy mayor for young people for two months in 2008, resigned after allegations of financial misconduct and describing himself as a JP; Tim Parker (see below).
14 Tim Parker, businessman and restructuring specialist at KwikFit, the AA, Clark's Shoes, later chair of the National Trust, Post Office Ltd and HM Courts & Tribunals Service. For six weeks in 2008, Parker was Johnson's first deputy mayor of London, chair of TfL and CEO of the GLA
15 Anthony Mayer, interview 9 April 2020
16 Neale Coleman, interview 17 December 2024
17 Sir Simon Milton, 1961–2011, see Biographies for further information.
18 Anthony Mayer, interview 9 April 2020
19 Peter Hendy, interview 26 March 2020
20 Tony Travers, Sir Simon Milton obituary, *The Guardian*, 12 April 2011
21 Peter Hendy, interview 26 March 2020
22 Daniel Moylan, interview 14 January 2020
23 Leon Daniels, interview 9 January 2020
24 Isabel Dedring, interview 13 November 2019
25 Leon Daniels, interview 9 January 2020
26 David Brown, interview 17 April 2020
27 Isabel Dedring, interview 13 November 2019
28 David Brown, interview 17 April 2020
29 Ibid.
30 Ibid.
31 Tony Travers, 'Boris beware the battle of the egos', *Evening Standard*, 5 April, 2012
32 David Brown, interview 17 April 2020
33 Daniel Moylan, interview 14 January 2020
34 Peter Hendy, interview 26 March 2020
35 Boris Johnson, interview 1 May 2025
36 TfL press release 3 June 2011; http://bit.ly/46Ecy9a
37 Peter Hendy, interview 25 June 2024
38 Purnell 2012, p. 365
39 Matt Brown, 'When London's Cyclists Said "No" to Segregated Lanes', Londonist, 27 May 2024
40 Tom Turner, 'The history of cycle network infrastructure planning in London', Landscape Architects Association, 9 May 2018; http://bit.ly/44qZSkE
41 Ken Livingstone, *You Can't Say That*, London 2011, p. 590
42 Peter Hendy, notes of conversation with author, 14 March 2025
43 David Brown, interview 17 April 2020
44 Ibid.
45 Boris Johnson, BBC News, 22 May 2010
46 Quoted in Tony Lewin, *London's New Routemaster*, London 2014, p. 19
47 Boris Johnson, 6 September 2007
48 'Call for crackdown on bendy bus fare dodgers', *The Guardian*, 25 May 2006. On average there is £6333-worth of fare evasion for each bendy bus a year, compared to £3636 for each conventional bus. In retrospect, front boarding only would have mitigated this.
49 Ken Livingstone quoted in *The London Routemaster Bus*, Carlton Television 2001; http://bit.ly/44ymaRA
50 *The London Routemaster Bus*, Carlton Television 2001, includes interview with Ken Livingstone and Dave Wetzel; http://bit.ly/44ymaRA
51 Peter Hendy quoted in Ben Webster, 'Routemasters put on road to retirement', *The Times*, 19 March 2003
52 David Brown, interview 17 April 2020
53 Red Arrows were high-capacity limited stop routes in central London; the 507 Waterloo to Victoria and 521 Waterloo to London Bridge were the first routes to be converted to articulated operation, in June 2002.
54 David Brown, interview 17 April 2020
55 New Bus for London (NBfL): the project title for the new bus was coined by project manager David Hampson-Ghani. There was resistance to Leon Daniels' suggested name, the New Routemaster, which was only applied much later.
56 Boris Johnson, *Unleashed*, London 2024, p. 76
57 Paul Sainthouse, CEO Dawson Group, notes of conversation with the author, 7 May 2025
58 David Brown, interview 17 April 2020
59 Quoted in Lewin 2014, p. 43
60 Peter Hendy interview, 5 January 2016
61 David Hampson-Ghani, interview 5 August 2024
62 Ibid.
63 Ibid.
64 Ibid.
65 Ibid.
66 David Hampson-Ghani, quoted in Lewin 2014, p. 70
67 David Hampson-Ghani, interview 5 August 2024
68 Ibid.
69 Thomas Heatherwick's foreword to Lewin 2014, p. 9
70 Heatherwick Design Studio, press release quoted in James Whiting, Gavin Booth, Stewart J. Brown et al., *Boris's Bus: The Mayor's New Routemaster*, second enlarged edition, London 2015, p. 42
71 David Brown, interview 17 April 2020 and email to author 16 February 2025
72 David Hampson-Ghani, interview 5 August 2024
73 Leon Daniels, interview 9 October 2024
74 David Hampson-Ghani, interview 5 August 2024
75 Neither EU nor UK regulations had supposed anyone would provide a new open-platform bus, so it was possible to design an open platform. Johnson was keen to say that the EU had prevented it, but this was not true.
76 David Brown, email to author 16 February 2025
77 Leon Daniels, interview 9 October 2024
78 Quoted in Dave Hill, 'How the New Routemaster came full circle: back to a regular old London bus', *The Guardian*, 3 August 2015
79 Ibid.
80 Justin McGuirk, 'The Routemaster's triumphant return to London', *The Guardian*, 23 February 2012
81 Quoted in Dave Hill, 'Boris's Bus (A Political Journey) Part 42: No more Conductors?', *The Guardian*, 9 October 2014
82 Patrick Chapman of Wrightbus, quoted in Lewin 2014, p. 86
83 Mike Weston, interview 3 June 2024
84 Leon Daniels, interview 9 October 2024
85 Ibid.
86 Mike Weston interview 3 June 2024

87 After LT045 was involved in an accident and LT174 in a fire, both were written off in 2022; TfL FoI 3786-2425

88 Mike Weston, interview 3 June 2024

89 Daniel Moylan, interview 5 May 2020

90 Leon Daniels, interview 9 October 2024

91 Ibid.

92 Daniel Moylan, interview 5 May 2020

93 Leon Daniels, interview 9 October 2024

94 Tim O'Toole, interview 6 February 2020

95 'Achievements: Tube Lines is committed to improving performance and delivering projects on time', Tube Lines website; http://bit.ly/4nTdlJN

96 Quoted by Katharine Barney & Amar Singh, 'O2 not thrilled as Jubilee line closes for Jackson's comeback', *Evening Standard*, 20 May 2009.

97 Tim O'Toole, interview 6 February 2020

98 Peter Hendy, interview 6 September 2011

99 Daniel Moylan, interview 14 January 2020

100 Daniel Moylan, 5 May 2020

101 Director general, department for business, innovation and skills and board member 2009–12, permanent secretary at DfT, knighted 2018, resigned in 2020 over bullying of civil servants within the Home Office by home secretary Priti Patel

102 Daniel Moylan, interview 12 April 2024

103 Tim O'Toole, interview 14 April 2011

104 Ibid.

105 Daniel Moylan, interview 12 April 2024

106 Michèle Dix, interview 21 February 2025

107 Quoted by Robert Booth in 'Boris Johnson flies in to open Britain's first urban cable car', *The Guardian*, 28 June 2012

108 Howard Smith, interview 19 February 2025

109 Gareth Powell, interview 8 December 2023

110 Gwen Topham, "Storm Eunice was our last hope", in 'Boris Johnson's Emirates Air Line cable car fails to find new sponsor', *The Guardian*, 27 February 2022

Chapter 11

1 Ken Livingstone, *You Can't Say That*, London 2011, p. 497

2 Dave Hill, *Olympic Park: When Britain Built Something Big*, London 2022, p. 27; Dave Hill has picked his way brilliantly through the complex challenge of the assembly and delivery of the Olympic Park and its infrastructure in his excellent book. The author is delighted to acknowledge his debt to Dave Hill in shaping this chapter.

3 David Brown, email to author, 17 February 2025

4 Livingstone 2011, p. 497

5 *Atkins and the London 2012 Games*, 2015, LTM Library, 203/2015

6 Hill 2022

7 Ibid.

8 Hugh Sumner, interview, 9 May.2013

9 Ibid.

10 Ibid.

11 Ibid.

12 Ibid.

13 Sebastian Coe, introduction to *Construction projects of the 2012 London Olympics*, Construct UK 2006, LTM Library 100/2006

14 Quoted by Ross Lydall and Adrian Warner, 'This is the best day London's ever had', *Evening Standard*, 6 July 2005

15 In LTM Library, 263/2006, quoting ODA chair Sebastian Coe and CEO David Higgins

16 Hugh Sumner, interview, 9 May 2013

17 Gavin Poynter and Iain MacRury, eds., *Olympic Cities: 2012 and the Remaking of London*, London 2009, pp. 121–33

18 Launch of the Olympic Transport Strategy, 30 October 2006 at former German Gymnasium in King's Cross, in 1861 the first purpose-built gymnasium in Britain, used by the National Olympian Games in 1866 and London Olympics in 1908; in April 1914, Irish republican Michael Collins drilled there using refurbished rifles in preparation for the upcoming Easter Rising; 'The German Gymnasium: A Look into the "Abandoned Years" and Michael Collins, London 2017: London Field Studies Projects, http://bit.ly/40ohNXc, citing J. B. E. Hittle, *Michael Collins and the Anglo-Irish War: Britain's Counterinsurgency Failure*, Dulles, Virginia 2011

19 Olympic Delivery Authority, *Transport Plan for the London 2012 Olympic and Paralympic Games*, 2nd ed., June 2011

20 Hugh Sumner, interview 9 May 2013

21 TBTC – transmission-based train control

22 David Brown, interview 17 April 2020

23 Leon Daniels, interview 18 May.2020

24 Mark Evers, interview 7 March 2025

25 David Brown, email to author 17 February 2025

26 Mark Evers, interview 7 March 2025

27 Peter Hendy, interview 5 January 2016

28 Mike Brown, interview 11 July 2023

29 Chris MacLeod, interview 5 February 2025

30 Vernon Everitt, interview 31 January 2024

31 Chris Macleod, interview 5 February 2025

32 Mark Evers, 7 March 2025

33 Commissioner Peter Hendy, quoted in TfL, *The London Games in Motion*, TfL 2013, p. 5

34 Mark Evers, interview 7 March 2025

35 Lynskey, Dorian, end-of-year review of 2012; *Q Magazine*, 318, January 2013: pp. 82–88

36 Peter Hendy, notes of conversation 11 January 2025

37 Chris MacLeod, interview 15 September 2021

38 Mark Evers, interview 7 March 2025

39 Alexandra Topping, 'Olympics opening ceremony: the view from abroad', *The Guardian*, 27 July 2012

40 Leon Daniels, interview 18 May 2020

41 Ibid.

42 Mike Brown, interview 11 July 2023

43 Peter Hendy, email to author 20 February 2025

44 David Brown, interview 17 April 2020, and email to author 17 February 2025

45 Mike Brown, interview 11 July 2023

46 Peter Hendy, email to author 20 February 2025

47 Ibid.

48 Lauren Sager Weinstein, interview 31 January 2020

49 Vernon Everitt interview 31 January 2024

50 Howard Smith, interview 21 September, 2023

51 Ibid.

52 Ibid.

53 TfL Report, 'London 2012 Games Transport – Performance, Funding and Legacy, September 2012; http://bit.ly/4lQtde8

54 Mark Evers, contact officer for TfL Board Report, 'London 2012 Games Transport – Performance, Funding and Legacy, September 2012, p. 16; http://bit.ly/4lQtde8

55 Vernon Everitt interview 31 January 2024

56 Quoted in TfL 2013, p. 4

57 Chris Macleod, interview 15 September 2021

58 Ibid.

59 Daniel Moylan, interview 5 May 2020

60 Howard Smith, interview 21 September 2023

61 Ibid.

Chapter 12

1 Boris Johnson, *Unleashed*, London 2024, p. 77

2 Steve Richards, 'Which mayoral candidate will improve life in the city? That's all London need ask', *The Independent*, 3 May 2012

3 Jason Beattie, 'Swear waves: Bojo's sweary rant at Ken at radio station, *Daily Mirror*, 3 April 2012

4 BBC News, 5 May 2012

5 Leon Daniels, interview 9 October 2024

6 Ibid.

7 Daniel Moylan was deputy chair of TfL, Johnson's transport advisor and conduit to TfL, 2009–12

8 Daniel Moylan, interview 5 May 2020

9 Peter Hendy, interview 26 March 2020

10 Leon Daniels, interview 9 January 2020

11 Leon Daniels, interview 9 October 2024

12 Daniel Moylan, interview 5 May 2020

13 Richard Brown, 'What Boris Johnson did for the Olympic Park', OnLondon 7 July 2022

14 Catherine Mayer, 'The London Mayor is the Biggest Winner of the Olympics', *Time* magazine, 13 August 2012

15 Ben Plowden, interview 31 January 2020

16 Foreword by mayor of London, *The Mayor's Vision for Cycling in London: An Olympic Legacy for all Londoners* GLA, March 2013; http://bit.ly/44FXa9H

17 Peter Hendy, email to author 14 March 2025

18 Leon Daniels, interview 9 October 2024

19 Claim by Cllr Julian Bell at Cycling Cities event, reported by BikeBiz, 21 November 2016, '"Rip out Embankment cycleway for cash", Chancellor tells London Mayor'; http://bit.ly/4kCVyDI

20 TfL, *Safe Streets for London: The Road Safety Action Plan for London 2020*, TfL June 2013; http://bit.ly/458U1AC

21 Foreword by Commissioner Peter Hendy in *The Mayor's Vision for Cycling in London: An Olympic Legacy for all Londoners*, GLA, March 2013, p. 7; http://bit.ly/44FXa9H

22 Dave Hill, 'Q&A: John Traynor, boss of bus operator Go-Ahead London on congestion, Boris, bike lanes, Uber and TfL', OnLondon, 2 October 2018; http://bit.ly/4lKTWsk

23 Ben Plowden, interview 31 January 2020

24 Chris Macleod, interview 5 February 2025

25 Boris Johnson, Foreword to *London's Road Modernization Plan*, TfL 2014

26 CBTC stands for communications-based train control. It is a railway signalling system that uses continuous, bidirectional communication between train and wayside equipment for traffic management and control, which enables reduced distance between trains and increased line capacity.

27 London's transport 'Design Icons' announced, LT Museum Year of Design 2015; http://bit.ly/40JYuY0

28 Tim O'Toole, interview 6 February 2020

29 London Travel Watch, *A review of ticket office closures on the London Underground – the passenger perspective*, November 2016; http://bit.ly/4eJ0pB0

30 Mike Brown, interview 11 July 2023

31 Eleanor A. Maguire, David D. Gadian, Ingrid S. Johnsrude, Catriona D. Good, John Ashburner, Richard S. J. Frackowiak, Christopher D. Frith, 'Navigation-related structural change in the hippocampi of taxi drivers', Proc Natl Acad Sci USA. 2000 March 14;97(8):4398-403; https://pmc.ncbi.nlm.nih.gov/articles/PMC18253/

32 Leon Daniels, interview 9 October 2024

33 Ibid.

34 Ibid.

35 Ibid.

36 Ibid.

37 Ibid.

38 Niamh McIntyre, 'The Uber London ban: The scandals that brought down the ride hailing app', *The Independent*, 22 September 2017

39 Leon Daniels, interview 9 October 2024

40 Ibid.; the number of licensed taxi drivers declined to 16,816 with 14,470 licensed taxi cabs, while minicab drivers has grown to 107,998 with 96,788 licensed private hire vehicles; TfL, *Taxi and private hire action plan 2025*; http://bit.ly/4kCWV5k

41 Leon Daniels, interview 9 October 2024

42 Ross Lydall, 'Uber granted fresh operating licence by Transport for London "with conditions"', *The Standard*, 21 September 2024; http://bit.ly/4611PKR

43 Ross Lydall, 'Revealed: Inflation-busting London taxi fares rise in bid to curb driver exodus, *The Standard*, 26 February 2025; http://bit.ly/4eVH0Od

44 Andrew J. Hawkins, 'London's famed black cabs will be listed on Uber's app in big win for the ridehail company', The Verge, 29 November 2023; http://bit.ly/44KVI6a

45 TfL, Travel in London report 12, 2018

46 Johnson 2024, p. 191

47 Daniel Moylan, interview 5 May 2020

48 Leon Daniels, email to author 26 February 2025

49 Joanna Lumley, *Newsnight*, BBC, 26 June 2014

50 Quoted by Harry Cockburn, 'Garden Bridge: how the vision came crashing down', *The Independent*, 3 March 2018

51 Boris Johnson in 2014 interview for *New Civil Engineer* magazine, quoted in 'London City – Garden Bridge' in the University of British Columbia's blog,

'Why Do Projects Fail?', recorded in the Catalogue of Catastrophe; http://bit.ly/40i5V8D

52 Transcripts of evidence for Dame Margaret Hodge's 2017 review, quoted in Harry Cockburn, 'Garden Bridge: how the vision came crashing down', *The Independent*, 3 March 2018

53 Margaret Hodge, *The Garden Bridge* report, GLA April 2017; http://bit.ly/3UhcaBl

54 Hodge 2017

55 Daniel Moylan, interview 5 May 2020

56 Ibid.

57 Boris Johnson's Foreword to *Landing the right airport*, TfL, March 2016; http://bit.ly/4lwhoeQ

58 Quoted by BBC News, 20 March 2016; http://bit.ly/4kDfTsE

59 Daniel Moylan, interview 5 May 2020

60 Jack Brown, review of *Unleashed* by Boris Johnson, OnLondon 1 November 2024

61 Will Dahlgreen, 'Mayor Boris: the public verdict', YouGov, 5 May 2016

62 John Rentoul, 'London mayoral elections 2016: An analysis of Boris Johnson's record after eight years in office', *The Independent*, 4 May 2016

63 Ibid.

64 Shashi Verma, interview 14 March 2025

65 Mike Brown quoted in Gwyn Topham, 'Transport suffers deepest cuts after London subsidy axed', *The Guardian*, 25 November 2015

66 Peter Hendy left TfL in 2015 to chair Network Rail.

67 Peter Hendy, interview 26 March 2020

68 David Brown, interview 17 April 2020

69 Leon Daniels, interview 9 January 2020

70 Quoted in Sonia Purnell, *Just Boris: A Tale of Blond Ambition*, London 2012, p. 138

71 Johnson 2024, p. 172

72 Jack Brown, review of *Unleashed* by Boris Johnson, OnLondon, 1 November 2024

73 Johnson 2024, p. 136

Chapter 13

1 https://www.architecture.com/awards-and-competitions-landing-page/awards/riba-stirling-prize

2 https://www.architectsjournal.co.uk/news/aj-architecture-awards-2022-winners-revealed

3 Quoted in Rowan Moore, 'A megalopolis of engineering: the verdict on London's £18bn new Elizabeth line', *The Guardian*, 13 March 2022

4 The area's industrial history is comprehensively charted in Andrew Saint

and Colin Thom, 'Industry', in *Survey of London, vol. 49 Battersea*, London 2013

5 Saint and Thom 2013

6 Thomas Lane, 'Battersea power station: the remarkable journey from ruin to rejuvenation', *Building Design*, 7 October 2022

7 Bridget Rosewell, interview 29 November 2024

8 Siddy Holloway, in *Hidden London Hangouts* series 4, episode 6, 20 September 2021; https://www.youtube.com

9 TfL press release, 23 September, 2022; http://bit.ly/4oqfGBO

10 Andrew Dow, *Telling the Passenger Where to Get Off: George Dow and the Evolution of the Railway Diagrammatic Map*, London 2005 pp. 52–55

11 Introduction to *Central London Rail Study*, DfT, London 1989

12 See Christian Wolmar, *The Story of Crossrail*, London 2018, for the rejection of the preamble to the private members' bill in 1994.

13 Ian Brown, interview 9 November 2023

14 Bridget Rosewell, *Planning Curses. How to deliver long-term investment in infrastructure*, Policy Exchange, London 2010

15 Bridget Roswell CBE, distinguished economist and chief economic advisor to the GLA 2002–2012

16 The context and creation of a fresh basis for Crossrail funding is well outlined in *Crossrail (A): The Business Case*, CR14-08-1898.3 and *Crossrail (A): The Business Case (Sequel)*, CR14-08-1898.1, Harvard Kennedy School (HKS Case Program) 2008

17 Bridget Rosewell, interview 29 November 2024

18 Shashi Verma, interview 28 February 2025

19 Ibid.

20 Ibid.

21 Ibid.

22 Bridget Rosewell 2010

23 Quoted in Martin Buck, 'Crossrail project: finance, funding and value capture for London's new Elizabeth line', *Civil Engineering*, vol. 170, issue 6, November 2017; Martin Buck was director of Crossrail 2003–17.

24 Bridget Rosewell, interview 29 November 2024

25 John Dickie, 'London has paid for the Elizabeth line, the whole country is benefiting from it', OnLondon, 9 May 2022

26 Colin Brown, presentation at Learning Legacy seminar 5 April 2023, 'Crossrail

Project 2019 to 2023: Completing the Elizabeth line'; https://learninglegacy.crossrail.co.uk

27 Bombardier was acquired by multi-national train builders Alstom in 2021.

28 See 'The Elizabeth line: line-wide design', Grimshaw, 2018; http://bit.ly/44SQ1CZ

29 Andrew Briffett, *Crossrail: the art of the build*, Crossrail 2018

30 Mark Wild, Learning Legacy seminar, 5 April 2023; Wild's presentation is a masterclass in megaproject leadership and the recovery of the Crossrail project; http://bit.ly/3TBFOpz

31 Boris Johnson, interview 1 May 2025

32 Quoted in Robert Jobson, Royal Line: Crossrail named in honour of the Queen', *Evening Standard*, 23 February 2016

33 Evidence to Public Accounts Committee, Crossrail progress review, HC925, 6 March 2019, Q68

34 Mark Wild, Learning Legacy seminar, 5 April 2023

35 Ibid.

36 Mark Wild, evidence to the Public Accounts Committee, 6 March 2019, Q15

37 Mark Wild, Learning Legacy seminar, 5 April 2023

38 Ibid.

39 Lee Rowley, evidence to the Public Accounts Committee (PAC) 6 March 2019, Q1; Rowley was MP for North East Derbyshire 2017–24, and described himself to the PAC as an ex-project manager

40 Jacobs report, p. 4, quoted at PAC 6 March 2019, Q71

41 Lee Rowley, MP evidence to PAC 6 March 2019, Q78

42 Tony Meggs, evidence to PAC 6 March 2019 Q3

43 Mark Wild, evidence to PAC, 6 March 2019, Q13

44 Tony Meggs, evidence to PAC, 6 March 2019 Q4

45 Tony Meggs, evidence to PAC, 6 March 2019, Q9

46 Bernadette Kelly, evidence to PAC, 6 March 2019, Q143

47 Mark Wild, Learning Legacy seminar, 5 April 2023

48 Colin Brown, Learning Legacy seminar, 5 April 2023

49 Ibid.

50 Ibid.

51 Ibid.

52 Chris Binns, Learning Legacy seminar, 5 April 2023

53 Howard Smith, email to the author 12 February 2025

54 Ibid.

55 Pradeep Vasudev, Legacy seminar, 5 April 2023

56 ETCS – the European Train Control System, a unified train control system that uses on-board computers and trackside equipment to monitor and control train movements across Europe

57 Colin Brown, Learning Legacy seminar, 5 April 2023

58 Mark Wild, Learning Legacy seminar, 5 April 2023

59 Pradeep Vasudev, Learning Legacy seminar, 5 April 2023

60 Colin Brown, Learning Legacy seminar, 5 April 2023

61 Andy Byford, interview 8 February 2024

62 Howard Smith, interview 19 February 2025

63 Andy Byford, interview 8 February 2024

64 Howard Smith, COO and Jim Crawford, chief programme officer, Elizabeth line; Richard Schofield, MD of MTR UK

65 Andy Byford, Green Signals podcast interview with Richard Bowker, 8 July 2024

66 Howard Smith, interview 19 February, 2025

67 Tony Meggs, Learning Legacy seminar, 5 April 2023

68 Four trains were readied for this trip, just to be sure – plans A, B, C and D.

69 London Assembly, *London's Elizabeth line at three: data analysis*; http://bit.ly/4kHNaTv

70 'Transformational Elizabeth line reaches 500 million passenger journeys', TfL press release, 10 January 2025; http://bit.ly/4om4hmA

71 Quoted in *Evidencing the value of the Elizabeth line*, TfL/DfT, London 2024

72 Denis Tunnicliffe, interview 25 May 2011

73 Quoted in *Civil Service World*, 19 December 2022

74 https://www.architecture.com/awards-and-competitions-landing-page/awards/riba-stirling-prize

75 Edwin Heathcote, 'Elizabeth line wins UK's Stirling Prize', *Financial Times*, 16 October 2024

76 Quoted by Eleanor Young, *RIBA Journal*, 16 October 2024

77 Young 2024

78 Linda Walmsley, interview with Mark Wild, 'Inspiring Leaders – Mark Wild – CEO Crossrail', Walmsley Wilkinson, 2019; http://bit.ly/3IyIsjx

Chapter 14

1 Sadiq Khan, full mayoral election acceptance speech, 5 May 2016

2 Leon Daniels, interview 9 October 2024

3 Mike Brown, interview 11 July 2023

4 Leon Daniels, interview 9 October 2024

5 Mike Brown, interview 22 September 2023

6 Mike Brown, interview 11 July 2023

7 John Traynor, MD Go-Ahead, London, OnLondon 2 October 2018

8 John Traynor, MD Go-Ahead, London, OnLondon 2 October 2018

9 Daniel Boffey, 'London's "Boris bus" reaches end of road as Sadiq Khan halts purchases', The Guardian, 31 December 2016

10 Chris Macleod, interview 5 February 2025

11 TfL, Mayor's Transport Strategy, March 2018, The Challenge, p. 4

12 Sadiq Khan, Mayor's foreword to TfL, Mayor's Transport Strategy, March 2018

13 Sadiq Khan, Mayor's foreword to TfL, Mayor's Transport Strategy March 2018

14 Quoted in Sadiq Khan, Breathe: Tackling the Climate Emergency (later subtitled How to Win a Greener World and Seven Ways to Win a Greener World), London 2023, p. 16, p. 21

15 Quoted in Khan 2023

16 'The Metropolitan Great Drainage Works', The Observer,15 April 1861

17 TfL, 'Clearing London's air'; http://bit.ly/4eLu3X6

18 TfL, Mayor's Transport Strategy 2018, The Challenge, p. 5

19 Record of Inquest of Ella Roberta Adoo Kissi-Debrah, London Inner South Coroner's Court, 2020-12-11); http://bit.ly/4lYuJen

20 Harry Cockburn, 'Ella Kissi-Debrah inquest', The Independent, 16 December 2020

21 Sadiq Khan quoted in Matthew Taylor, 'London's most polluted schools to be given air-quality audits', The Guardian, 13 September 2017

22 Khan 2023, p. 10

23 Ibid., p. 17

24 Robin McKie, 'Smog in the cities; the truth about Britain's dirty air', The Guardian, 29 January 2017

25 TfL London-Wide ULEZ first month report, 31 October 2023; http://bit.ly/440j4rm

26 London Assembly, ULEZ Facts, May 2025; http://bit.ly/440ScaK

27 Quoted in Peter Walker, 'Critics of UK low-traffic schemes told that 25,000 filters already existed', The Guardian, 16 May 2021

28 Andrew Gilligan worked in PM Boris Johnson's Policy Unit at 10 Downing Street as transport advisor from 2019.

29 Tom Wall, 'The new road rage: bitter rows break out over UK's low-traffic neighbourhoods', The Guardian, 20 September 2020

30 TfL, The impacts of Low Traffic Neighbourhoods in London, February 2024: http://bit.ly/4eQpMBX

31 Mary Creagh, since July 2024 MP for Coventry East and under secretary of state (minister for nature), DEFRA, quoted in Peter Walker, 'Critics of UK low-traffic schemes told that 25,000 filters already existed', The Guardian, 16 May 2021

32 Leon Daniels, interview 9 October 2024

33 TfL, Bus Fleet Audit, March 2024: http://bit.ly/4eMJkXM

34 TfL press release, 6 December 2023; http://bit.ly/46ci8zE

35 X25 route West Croydon to Heathrow, 2008–10, X140 Harrow to Heathrow from 2019

36 TfL, Travel in London, 2024; http://bit.ly/4kFwb4a

37 Will Norman, interview 30 September 2024

38 Ibid.

39 Quoted in Peter Walker, 'Mini-Holland' schemes have proved their worth in outer London boroughs', The Guardian, 26 June 2018

40 Will Norman, interview 30 September 2024

41 Dave Hill, 'Leadership is required to combat London's selfish cycling culture', OnLondon 9 September 2024; http://bit.ly/40SIvxy

42 TfL press release, 12 May, 2025; http://bit.ly/46u4Pe3

43 The Mayor's Vision for Cycling in London: An Olympic Legacy for all Londoners, 2013, p. 46

44 Carlton Reid, Roads Were Not Built for Cars blog, 8 December 2012; http://bit.ly/3Ud1HLX

45 TfL press release, 28 November 2024; http://bit.ly/440ZZp0

46 Jess Warren, 'Cycling in City of London rises by more than 50%', BBC News, 28 April 2025

47 'Meeting London's Cycling Boom: Lime Announces £20M Infrastructure and Safety Plan', The Lime Times blog, 29 January 2025; http://bit.ly/4lYzi8v

48 TfL, Vision Zero for London; http://bit.ly/40OVOIv

49 TfL, Vision Zero for London; http://bit.ly/40OVOIv

50 Ethan Jupp, 'London's Direct Vision Standard for HGVs to tackle truck visibility "crisis"', Motoring Research, 4 March 2019; http://bit.ly/3GIzARR

51 TfL press release, 29 June 2022; http://bit.ly/4eTYF92

52 Lauren Sager Weinstein's Foreword in TfL, Review of the TfL WiFi pilot, August 2017; Lauren Sager Weinstein is TfL's chief data officer; http://bit.ly/44MyrR1

53 The rebrand celebrates stories from the communities through which the Overground runs: Liberty, Lioness, Mildmay, Suffragette, Weaver and Windrush.

54 Hermione Hobhouse, ed., 'Southern Blackwall: The Blackwall Tunnel', in Survey of London: Volumes 43 and 44, Poplar, Blackwall and Isle of Dogs, London, 1994, British History Online; http://bit.ly/4kKtfmX

55 Michèle Dix, River Crossings in East London, stakeholder presentation, 2014; http://bit.ly/46KhwBk

56 No to the Silvertown Tunnel website; https://silvertowntunnel.co.uk

57 Quoted in Rob Horgan, 'DfT urged to sanction emergency review of Silvertown Tunnel', New Civil Engineer, 22 April 2021

58 Leon Daniels, interview 9 October 2024

59 Stephen Glaister in Jack Brown, Tony Travers and Richard Brown, eds., London's Mayor at 20: Governing a Global City in the 21st Century, London 2020, p. 151

60 Leon Daniels, interview 20 February 2025

61 Quoted in Josh Salisbury, 'Croydon tram crash driver cleared of "not taking reasonable care" of passengers', Evening Standard, 19 June 2023

62 Leon Daniels, interview 20 February 2025

63 Sadiq Khan on BBC News, 18 June 2017

64 Quoted in 'Tube driver halts journey and waves to people holding Grenfell vigil – video', The Guardian, 14 June 2018

65 Leon Daniels, interview 20 February 2025

66 Clellan Coe, 'See It, Say It', The American Scholar, 27 March 2024; http://bit.ly/3TMAtMc, and FoI request 30 April 2024, 01/FOI/24/2616

67 Leon Daniels, interview 20 February 2025

68 Leon Daniels, interview 9 October 2024

69 Mayor Khan's statement reported in The Guardian, 7 June 2017

70 'Mayor of London statements – London Bridge attack'; http://bit.ly/44GM1XH

71 Sadiq Khan, speech at London Bridge vigil, 5 June 2017; http://bit.ly/44GM1XH

72 Quoted in Khalid Amin, 'Eyewitness to attack', The Guardian, 19 June 2017

73 'Darren Osborne guilty of Finsbury Park mosque murder', BBC News, 1 February 2018

74 'Mayor of London statements – London Bridge attack'; http://bit.ly/3IuGESz

75 Sarah Harvey, 'London Bridge terror attack victims were "unlawfully killed", inquest finds', Evening Standard, 28 May 2021

76 Gareth Powell was then MD Surface Transport.

77 Andy Lord, interview 8 December 2023
78 Eleni Courea, 'Tories in crisis over race for London Mayor', *The Times*, 27 March 2021
79 Quoted in Dave Hill, 'The OnLondon discussion', OnLondon, 27 October 2022

Chapter 15

1 Dave Hill, 'Covid Ended in 2022, but London is still feeling its effects', OnLondon, 6 January 2025
2 Sam Mullins, LTM Museum Director, Diary 2020–21, unpublished
3 Heather Stewart and Peter Walker, 'Britain Shuts Down', *The Guardian*, 21 March 2020
4 'Earlier lockdown would likely have saved lives of London bus drivers, reports independent review', UCL News, 19 March 2021; http://bit.ly/3IuQunC
5 COBRA – the Cabinet Office Briefing Rooms, a group of meeting rooms in the Cabinet Office at 70 Whitehall used for committees that co-ordinate the actions of government bodies in response to national or regional crises, or during events abroad with major implications for the UK, such as Covid-19.
6 Sadiq Khan, *Breathe: Tackling the Climate Emergency* (later subtitled *How to Win a Greener World* and *Seven Ways to Win a Greener World*),London 2023, p. 93
7 Chris Macleod, '"Creatively excellent and influential": the best TfL campaigns over 15 years of change', *Campaign*, 24 August 2021; http://bit.ly/4nRCKTW
8 By February 2022 some 149,000 customers had been prevented from travelling, with some 2700 receiving a fixed penalty notice for not wearing the mandatory mask.
9 Gareth Powell, interview 8 December 2023
10 Peter Goldblatt and Joanna Morrison, 'Initial Assessment of London bus driver mortality from Covid-19', UCL Institute of Health Equity 2020; http://bit.ly/44GcFyk
11 Andy Lord, interview 8 December 2023
12 Ibid.
13 Gareth Powell, interview 8 December 2023
14 Heidi Alexander, 17 March 2021
15 Gareth Powell, 8 December 2023
16 Plymouth Live, 25 February 2021; http://bit.ly/40WyKaO
17 Heidi Alexander, interview 11 February 2021
18 Andy Lord, interview 8 December 2023
19 Ibid.
20 Sarah Marsh and Denis Campbell, 'Nurse shortage causes Nightingale hospital to turn away patients', *The Guardian*, 21 April 2020

21 Gareth Powell, interview 8 December 2023
22 Mayor's Question Time, 18 June 2020; http://bit.ly/40ii4dN
23 Andy Lord, interview 8 December 2023
24 Gareth Powell, interview 8 December 2023
25 Andy Lord, interview 8 December 2023
26 Gareth Powell, interview 8 December 2023
27 Ibid.
28 Ibid.
29 Andy Lord, interview 8 December 2023
30 Andy Lord and Gareth Powell, interview 8 December 2023
31 Heidi Alexander, interview 11 February 2021
32 Ibid.
33 Gareth Powell, interview 8 December 2023
34 Gareth Powell, 8 December 2023
35 Andy Lord, interview 8 December 2023
36 Andy Lord, interview 8 December 2023
37 Gareth Powell, interview 8 December 2023
38 Heidi Alexander, 11 February 2021
39 Andy Lord, interview 8 December 2023
40 Gwyn Topham, 'Sadiq Khan launches review of TfL in response to official inquiry', *The Guardian*, 22 July 2020
41 ORR press release, 30 November 2021; http://bit.ly/3GNTkU3. During the May 2025 interview with the author, Boris Johnson still maintained that Sadiq Khan and not Covid had wrecked TfL's finances.
42 Lisa O'Carroll, 'Sadiq Khan accuses Boris Johnson of blatant lie over TfL', *The Guardian*, 21 October 2020
43 PA Media, 'Ministers reportedly threaten to take direct control of Transport for London', *The Guardian*, 20 October 2020
44 Heidi Alexander, interview 11 February 2021
45 Ibid.
46 Boris Johnson, post-election speech 2 May 2008; 'Johnson's speech in full', *The Guardian*, 3 May 2008
47 Andy Lord, interview 8 December 2023
48 Heidi Alexander, interview 11 February 2021
49 Ibid.
50 Andy Lord, interview 8 December 2023
51 Andy Byford frequently referred to himself as commissioner 004, Mike Brown as 003, Peter Hendy as 002 and Bob Kiley as 001.
52 TfL press release, 27 May 2020; http://bit.ly/4eVy5wr
53 Andy Byford, interview 8 February 2024
54 Ibid.
55 Ibid.
56 Ibid.
57 Ibid.
58 Andy Byford, interview 13 February 2024
59 Ibid.

60 Andy Byford, interview 8 February 2024
61 Ibid.
62 Ibid.
63 Andy Byford, interview 13 February 2024
64 Gareth Powell, interview 8 December 2023
65 Ibid.
66 TfL press release, 3 September 2020; http://bit.ly/4lWPGpJ
67 Ibid.
68 Ibid.
69 'How Covid-19 changed the hospitality industry', PopplestonAllen, 30 September 2021; http://bit.ly/44R7tb9
70 Andy Lord, interview 8 December 2023
71 Chris Macleod, '"Creatively excellent and influential": the best TfL campaigns over 15 years of change', *Campaign*, 24 August, 2021; http://bit.ly/4nRCKTW
72 Andy Lord, interview 8 December 2023
73 105 TfL colleagues passed away in service due to Coronavirus-19 up to January 2022.
74 Andy Lord, interview 8 December 2023
75 Sadiq Khan at the opening of the opening ceremony of the London Transport Workers Coronavirus Memorial, 26 April 2023; http://bit.ly/40TEus
76 Heidi Alexander, interview 11 February 2021
77 Gareth Powell, interview 8 December 2023
78 Heidi Alexander, interview 11 February 2021
79 Ibid.
80 Andy Lord, interview 8 December 2023

Conclusion

1 Ken Livingstone when sworn in as London mayor, 3 July 2000
2 Boris Johnson, interview 1 May 2025
3 Sadiq Khan, *Breathe: How to Win a Greener World*, London 2023, pp. 201-02
4 The Combine formally operated from 1909 to 1933 (24 years), the LPTB existed from 1933 to 1947 (14 years), the LTE from 1948 to 1962 (14 years), LTB from 1962 to 1970 (8 years), the GLC from 1970 to 1984 (14 years), and LRT from 1984 to 2000 (16 years). The GLA's ownership of TfL has, at 25 years, exceeded all these earlier institutions.
5 Tony Travers to author, 27 June 2025
6 Pat Hurst, *Evening Standard*, 23 December 2022
7 Vernon Everitt, interview 31 January 2024
8 David Begg, interview 17 December 2019
9 Michèle Dix, interview 2 March 2020
10 Vernon Everitt, interview 31 January 2024
11 Ibid.
12 David Brown, interview 17 April 2020
13 Nick Raynsford, interview 9 October 2016
14 Andy Lord, TfL commissioner, at the launch event for TfL25, 27 January 2025

Biographies

These brief biographies concentrate on the individuals' contributions to TfL's story.

Rt. Hon. Heidi Alexander MP
Labour politician, Lewisham councillor and deputy mayor, 2004–10; MP for Lewisham East, 2010–18; Sadiq Khan's deputy mayor for London 2018–21 and deputy chair of TfL during the Covid crisis; MP for Swindon South from 2024 and secretary of state for transport since 2024.

Steve Allen
Previously senior civil servant in DfT, then project finance with Schroders, Abbey National and Citigroup; TfL's director of Corporate Finance, 2003–07, MD Finance, 2007–15; HS2 chief finance officer, 2015–18; currently VP at CPCS.

Andrew (Andy) Barr MBE
Distinguished London Underground operational career, in NCC as network co-ordination manager on 7 June 2005, later heritage vehicle operations manager at LTM, responsible for steam operations for Tube150 in January 2013 and subsequently.

Maggie Boepple
Boepple, born in Liverpool, worked for Bob Kiley for eight years in various capacities at the MTA in New York after working for Mayor Ed Koch, who appointed her the first woman to be director of intergovernmental relations (chief lobbyist). In London she was senior advisor to Bob Kiley during most of his time as TfL commissioner, 2001–06, often as the velvet glove to his iron fist. After leaving TfL she returned to New York and has worked in cultural organizations, culminating in becoming the first president of the Performing Arts Center at the World Trade Center.

Andrew Braddock
Career in provincial and national bus operations, then as first head of LT's Disabled Passenger Unit in 1991 becoming an influential and well-informed advocate for accessibility. He retired from TfL in 2003, becoming access consultant and transport commentator on European buses, trams and accessibility.

Colin Brown
He had 30 years' experience in the systems engineering and project delivery of complex multidisciplinary infrastructure systems before becoming Crossrail technical director, 2018–22.

David Brown
Started his long career in transport as LT graduate trainee in 1983, GM CentreWest Buses during management buyout, MD London General & London Central, 2003–06; TfL MD Surface Transport, 2006–11; CEO Go-Ahead Group, 2011–21; currently has non-executive roles in the transport industry.

Ian Brown CBE
Starting in the industry as a Railtrack graduate trainee, in a career spanning some 40 years Brown has made an outstanding contribution to public transport and the rail industry. CEO of the DLR 1996–2001, then TfL MD London Rail from 2001, extending the DLR, establishing London Overground, extending the East London line, integrating Croydon Tramlink into TfL and the expanding Oyster pay as you go to all National Rail stations in Greater London. TfL London Rail was the joint sponsor with the DfT of the Crossrail project. Brown retired as TfL MD London Rail in 2011 and currently has non-executive transport roles in Manchester and Toronto.

Mike Brown CBE MVO
Joined London Underground in 1989, rising to become COO from 2003 to 2008, then MD Heathrow Airport 2008–10, returning to TfL as MD London Underground and London Rail, 2010–15; TfL's third commissioner, 2015–20. Since 2022 he has been chair of the Rail Safety and Standards Board and chair of the delivery authority for the restoration of the Houses of Parliament; announced as chair of HS2 in June 2025.

Andy Byford
Started as a graduate trainee for London Underground in 1989, rising to general manager in 2003; operational and safety director, South Eastern trains 2003–06; CEO Southern Railway, 2006–09; COO and CEO RailCorp New South Wales, 2009–11; CEO Toronto Transit Commission, 2011–17; President and CEO New York Transit Authority, 2017–20; TfL's fourth commissioner, 2020–22; VP Amtrak for high-speed rail, 2023–25; in May 2025 appointed special advisor to Amtrak board of directors for the redevelopment of New York Penn Station.

Leon Daniels OBE
A long and distinguished career in the bus industry and a leading figure and pioneer in bus preservation, he began by running the Obsolete Fleet for Prince Marshall in the early 1980s; built up Hong Kong CityBus until it was sold to First Group in 1998; group divisional director for London for First Group from

2001, commercial director UK from 2005; TfL's MD Surface Transport 2011–18, currently a worldwide consultant on urban transport, chair of London Bus Museum at Brooklands, and master of the Worshipful Company of Carmen.

Isabel Dedring
New Yorker, lawyer and civil engineer, Harvard graduate, recruited from McKinsey as chief of staff to Bob Kiley, TfL commissioner 2002–05; GLA's director of Policy Unit 2005–08, Environment Adviser 2008–11 and deputy mayor for Transport, 2011–16; global transport lead at Arup since 2016.

Dr Michèle Dix CBE
Dix worked for the GLC through its graduate scheme, then for six years developing traffic policies and planning new road schemes before joining Halcrow Fox for 15 years as an urban transport planner. She joined TfL in 2000 as co-director of congestion charging with Malcolm Murray-Clark, introducing the congestion charge in 2003, the western extension in 2007, and the development of London's Low Emission Zone; joint TfL's MD for Planning in 2007; named one of Top 50 Influential Women in Engineering in 2016; TfL's MD of Crossrail 2 from 2015 to her retirement in 2021. Currently holds non-executive roles, including the National Infrastructure Commission.

Rob Easterby
Long experience in development of the Oyster card as systems engineer, Cubic Transportation, 1978–2010.

Vernon Everitt
Started his career in financial services and retail regulation; TfL's MD for Customers, Communication and Technology from 2007 to January 2022, leading the successful pan-government and transport industry marketing and communications strategy for the London 2012 Olympic Games. Currently Transport for Greater Manchester's commissioner, bringing London-style solutions to Manchester's public transport; has non-executive roles including chair of Transport for Wales.

Mark Evers
TfL's director of Delivery Unit, 2005–10; director of Olympic and Paralympic Games Transport, 2010–13; director of Corporate Strategy, 2013–15; director of Customer Strategy, 2015–17; LU chief customer officer, 2017–19; TfL chief customer officer, 2019–present.

Andrew Gilligan
Journalist considered instrumental in the Evening Standard campaign to topple Ken Livingstone in 2008, winning Journalist of the Year award in 2008; appointed cycling commissioner for London by Boris Johnson, delivered London's first separated Cycle Superhighways; award from London Cycling Campaign for his "outstanding contribution to cycling". Appointed transport advisor in the Downing Street policy unit by PM Johnson in 2019. In July 2020 he was appointed to TfL's board as one of two special representative attendees during the Covid-19 funding crisis. Gilligan was appointed as a special advisor to Prime Minister Rishi Sunak in March 2023; he joined the Policy Exchange in 2024.

Professor Stephen Glaister CBE
Academic specializing in the economics and regulation of transport. Advisor to the Department of Transport on bus deregulation in 1980s; economic advisor to the Gas Regulator and to the Rail Regulator; chair of the Office of Rail and Road, 2015–18. He has also worked on urban transport evaluation for the World Bank. In London he was a board member of London Regional Transport and of TfL, 2000–08, and a member of the steering group of the DfT's Road Pricing Feasibility Study. In 1998 he was awarded a CBE for services to public transport. Currently professor emeritus of Transport and Infrastructure in the Centre for Transport Studies at Imperial College London.

Baroness Tanni Grey-Thompson DBE DL
Paralympic winner of 16 medals, including two gold medals in wheelchair racing at Athens Games in 2004, and six times London Marathon winner, appointed life peer in 2010; advocate for accessibility and TfL board member, 2008–18.

Thomas Heatherwick CBE RA
Founded his design studio in 1994, specializing in architecture, urban infrastructure, sculpture and design, shot to fame with UK Pavilion at the 2010 World Expo in Shanghai and the Olympic Cauldron for the 2012 London Olympics at Stratford. Commissioned by TfL in 2009 to shape the iconic exterior of the New Bus For London in collaboration with Wrightbus in Northern Ireland.

Peter (Lord) Hendy CBE
Joined London Transport as a graduate trainee in 1975 and rose through London Buses to be MD CentreWest in 1989; at its privatization in 1994 he led a management buyout (with employee involvement) and subsequent sale to FirstGroup, where he became deputy director UK Bus. First TfL MD for Bus and River Services (subsequently Bus, Taxi and River Services), 2001–03; MD Surface Transport (including congestion charging and TfL roads) 2003–06; TfL commissioner 2006–15; chair, Network Rail 2015–24; chair, London Legacy Development Corporation 2017–24. Joined the House of Lords in 2022. Appointed as

minister of state for rail at the DfT in the new Labour administration after the 2024 general election. Hendy has always been active in transport heritage, the owner of two London buses, a founder of Imberbus, a trustee of London Transport Museum 2006–24, and president of the London Bus Museum until 2024.

John Hill

Cubic Transportation Systems, senior programme director 2000–04, notably for smart ticketing; senior account director 2016–17 for TfL's £60m+ account.

Geoff Hobbs

Head of Strategic Planning, London Underground, 1999–2003; head of London Rail Strategy, 2005–13; TfL director of Public Transport Service Planning, 2017–present.

Clive Hodson CBE

MD of LT Buses from bus privatization in 1994, retired in 2001.

Bob Kiley

TfL's first commissioner, 2001–06; previously with the CIA from 1963, including as executive assistant to its director, Richard Helms; deputy mayor of Boston 1972–75; CEO Massachusetts Bay Transit Authority 1975–79; VP Management Analysis Center (now part of Cap Gemini) 1979–83; chair and CEO of the MTA board in New York 1983–90; principal at Kohlberg private equity 1994–98; CEO New York City Partnership 1995–2000. Kiley died in 2016.

Ken Livingstone

London Labour politician, Leader of the GLC 1981–86, MP for Brent East 1981–2001; first mayor of London 2000–08, and unsuccessful candidate 2012.

Andy Lord

Engineer who rose from graduate trainee to director of Operations at British Airways, 1989–2015; John Menzies 2016; TfL's MD London Underground and TfL Engineering, 2019–22; TfL's COO, 2022; TfL commissioner since 2022.

Martyn Loukes BEM

LGBT+ diversity champion while working in TfL from 2005 to 2017 in Marketing as change project manager; chair of TfL's LGBT+ staff network group OUTbound from 2012, currently global lead for change and communication for Autoliv.

Chris Macleod

Previous career in commercial marketing; TfL's head of Marketing Communications 2007–10; director of Marketing 2010–18; director of Customer and Revenue 2017–21; fellow of Marketing Society since 2000, currently non-executive and self-employed customer engagement strategist.

Anthony Mayer

Career civil servant with Department of the Environment, including as PPS to secretary of state for transport; moved into the private sector 1986–87 as assistant director, N.M. Rothschild and Sons; MD (finance and admin) Rothschild Asset Management 1987–91; CEO Housing Corporation 1991–2000; interim commissioner TfL 2000; GLA CEO 2000–08.

Liz Meek

Senior civil servant, GOL head of Policy 1993–2001, responsible for drafting the GLA bill, and seconded to LT/TfL for the transition in 2000–01; GOL regional director 2001–08; North West regional director, 2008–11; later deputy chair Birkbeck College London and currently trustee of mental health and housing charities.

Tony Meggs CBE

Engineer and Stanford business graduate, senior BP executive and former civil servant, CEO of Major Project Authority, and of merged Infrastructure and Projects Authority in 2016. Appointed to chair Crossrail after the resignation of his predecessor Terry Morgan in December 2018 when the project had run into difficulty and delay. Later chair of Sellafield Ltd and currently holds non-executive roles.

Simon Milton

Sir Simon Milton, councillor, became leader of Westminster City Council in 2000 and chair of LGA; appointed by Mayor Johnson in May 2008 as senior advisor for Planning, then deputy mayor for Policy and Planning and crucially, in June 2009, chief of staff to the mayor, managing mayoral advisors and GLA budgets and administration. Milton had leukaemia in 1990; he never fully recovered his health and died in 2011 aged just 49.

Charles Monheim

Long career in public transport including at New York City Transit in the 1980s turnaround, Taiwan High-Speed Rail, Infratil (New Zealand), MTA New York, Hong Kong MTR. Non-executive director at Transport for Greater Manchester, Transport for Edinburgh and board chair of Edinburgh Tram Operating Company, 2015–18. In London as TfL's director of Ticketing and Fares 2001–06 he introduced the Oyster card.

Daniel Moylan, Lord Moylan

London Conservative politician, deputy leader of the Royal Borough of Kensington and Chelsea. Appointed to TfL board by Boris Johnson in 2008, he was chair of the mayor's Design Advisory Panel, 2009; TfL's deputy chair 2009–12, when he was the principal conduit between Mayor Johnson and TfL and took a notable and hands-on lead in the New Bus for London project;

later lead for Estuary airport, chair of Frank Pick memorial committee, and joined the House of Lords in 2020.

Malcolm Murray-Clark
Civil engineer in the GLC's graduate scheme, joined Westminster Council and became principal advisor on transport matters. Joint TfL director of congestion charging in 2000 with Michèle Dix, responsible for the highly successful design and implementation of the world-leading central London congestion charging scheme in 2003, the subsequent western extension to the zone in 2007 (awarded joint transport planners of the year) and the strategy, design and procurement of services leading to the implementation of London's Low Emission Zone, the world's largest scheme of its kind in 2008. Joint TfL MD Planning from 2008.

Will Norman
Appointed as GLA's first Walking and Cycling commissioner in 2017, working to deliver the mayor's pledges to make walking and cycling in London safer and easier. He had previously worked with not-for-profits, governments, UN agencies and European Institutions tackling the global inactivity crisis, with a particular focus on children.

Steve Norris
Conservative politician and businessman, MP for Oxford East 1983–87 and Epping Forest 1988–97; under-secretary of state for transport and minister for transport in London 1992–96, when he advocated for the Jubilee line extension and ensured that London buses stayed red after privatization; subsequently Conservative candidate for Mayor of London in 2000 and 2004; TfL board member 2000-01 and again for mayor Johnson; business interests in property and an extensive portfolio in transport technology and professional bodies.

Redmond O'Neill
Lifelong revolutionary and Irish republican socialist, from joining IMG at Sussex University in the 1970s to Socialist Action. Deputy chief of staff to Mayor Ken Livingstone, director of Transport 2000–08 and principal conduit to TfL. Launched St. Patrick's Day Parade in 2002, the congestion charge in 2003, and Venezuelan oil deal. Died of cancer, aged 55, in 2009.

Tim O'Toole CBE
Businessman and lawyer from a US rail transport background in Pittsburgh, joined Conrail freight railroad in 1987, rising to senior VP 1996-2001; as MD London Underground 2002–09, he was awarded CBE for LU's response to the 7/7 bombings, and deployed the story of the Underground's shaping of London to excellent effect in leading and motivating Tube management and operational staff. UK First Group COO from 2009, CEO 2010–18. Currently holds non-executive roles in North American transport.

Patricia Obinna
TfL head of Employment Law, 2012–23, currently TfL's director of Diversity and Inclusion.

Ben Plowden
Leading environmental campaigner, founding CEO of the national charity Living Streets and senior campaigner at CPRE. Worked for TfL 2002–21 holding a series of directorial roles: borough partnerships, 2002–05; communications, 2005–07; smarter travel unit, 2007–09; better routes & places, 2009–12; strategy and planning, Surface Transport, 2012–16; knowledge assets, commercial consulting and international operations, 2019–20; Covid-19 and recovery programme, 2020–21. He is currently a senior associate in LSE Cities and an associate at PA Consulting.

Gareth Powell
Joined TfL as head of Business Performance, 2003–07; director of Business Planning and Performance 2007–10 and of Transformation 2010–11; Strategy and Service Delivery LU and Rail, 2011–16; Strategy and Surface Transport, 2016–17; MD Surface Transport 2017–22; deputy commissioner, chief Customer and Strategy officer, 2022; MD Stansted Airport since 2022.

Ian Pring
Marketeer and customer insight specialist, TfL Research and Insight manager, 2007–19; Customer Marketing and Behaviour Change lead since 2017.

Nick Raynsford
London Labour politician, advocate for social housing provision and building regualtions, MP for Fulham, then Greenwich and Woolwich until standing down in 2015. As Minister for London from 1997 to 1999 and again from 2001 to 2003, Raynsford was responsible for drafting and delivering the GLA Act and restoring democratic citywide government to London, with the creation of GLA and the commissioning of its home at City Hall. As an MP he promoted bringing DLR and Crossrail to Woolwich. He was deputy chair 2019–20 and then strategic advisor to Crossrail.

Dan Ritterband OBE
Communications advisor, campaign director for the Johnson campaign, 2007–08, director of GLA Marketing & Communications, 2008–12.

Bridget Rosewell CBE
Distinguished economist, chief economist 2002–08 and then chief economic advisor to GLA 2009–12; since then her portfolio of non-executive roles has included

Network Rail, DVSA, the National Infrastructure Commission and consultancy on start-ups and business development.

Richard Rowlands
Cubic Transportation veteran, notably on the development of the Oyster card in London and digital payments systems. Software engineer and project manager 1982–97, group engineering co-ordinator 1997–2003, systems engineering manager 2003–06, engineering manager then director 2006–18.

Lauren Sager Weinstein
Graduate of Harvard Kennedy School, recruited to TfL from US in 2002 to work with Jay Walder on business planning, the Crossrail funding case and as chief of staff 2004–07; TfL's head of Oyster development 2007–11, creating the business requirements and customer proposition for contactless payment with academic research partnerships; key work on the data for the Olympic Games 2012; head of analytics 2012–17, providing data tools for TfL to understand customer travel behaviour and analytic tools to operate and plan London's vast transport network; TfL chief data officer since 2017.

Rikesh Shah
Digital and innovation pioneer within TfL Marketing and Communications 2001–13; commercial development manager 2013–14; senior manager for Digital Partnerships and Open Data 2014–17; head of TfL open innovation 2017–23; RCA guest lecturer since 2021 and currently head of the Innovation Procurement Empowerment Centre and consultant.

Howard Smith OBE
LSE economics graduate and British Rail operations graduate trainee; joined DLR as planning director to deliver the London City Airport extension and then, as director 1998–2004, the Woolwich Arsenal and Stratford International extensions. As TfL's COO London Rail 2004–13 he worked with Ian Brown to develop the Overground network, including the North London and East London lines and the new fleet of trains. In 2012 he led the delivery of the cable car (the 'Emirates Airline') and was one of the senior transport officers for the Olympic Games. From 2004 onwards he was involved in the development of Crossrail, later COO Crossrail 2013–23 and then TfL's director of the Elizabeth line from 2023, planning and establishing the operational railway.

Hugh Sumner
Joined LU from Cranfield School of Management as general manager, Bakerloo line 1988–90, GM, LU Company Plan 1990–93; director of LU Passenger Services, 1995–99, MD InfraCo Sub-Surface 1999–2003;

director of Transport, London 2012 Olympic Delivery Authority 2003–13, accountable for all transport elements of London's bid for the 2012 Olympic and Paralympic Games, and subsequently planned and delivered transport for the Games across all UK venues. He is currently operations director of Mace Group.

Mike Swiggs
A 30-year career with London Transport, including HR, facilities and premises management, industrial relations, company secretariat and LRT pension fund trustee, ultimately as interim CEO of TfL until retirement in 2001.

Valerie Todd CBE
TfL's director of Business Services, Surface Transport 2003–04, director of Equality and Social Inclusion 2004–05, MD Group Services 2005–09; Crossrail director for Talent and Resources 2009–18; HR director, Siemens UK 2018–23; currently non-executive and coaching roles.

Roger Torode
Economics graduate and lifelong busman, joined LT in 1970 with experience in bus operations, ticketing innovation including the Harrow Smartcard trial in 1994, general manager at Walthamstow Garage, commercial director London Forest Travel; 1997 LT European Affairs manager in Brussels, transport author notably of Privatizing London's Buses (London 2015).

Professor Tony Travers
British academic and journalist, specializing in local government. Since 1998 he has been director of LSE London, and before that was director of the Greater London Group, a research centre at LSE for the study of the government of London. He contributes a regular column to the Local Government Chronicle and has also written for The Guardian, the Evening Standard, The Independent, the Financial Times and The Times. He has published a number of books on cities and government and was co-author of London's Mayor at 20: Governing a Global City in the 21st Century (London 2020). He has contributed the Afterword to this book.

Denis Tunnicliffe, Lord Tunnicliffe CBE
Recruited from aviation career as MD London Underground 1988–98, chair and CEO London Transport 1998–2000. He arrived at LT in the wake of the 1987 King's Cross fire, and was responsible for a management revolution on the Tube within the limits of annual financial settlements and lack of capital investment, making the Tube safer, better led and carrying a rapidly growing number of passengers

as the 1990s passed. The Jubilee line extension of 1999 expanded the network and created a series of outstanding new stations. He chaired the Atomic Energy Authority 2002–04 and was created a life peer in 2004.

Derek Turner CBE
Engineer, Traffic director for London 1991–2000, when he introduced the red route system and banned parking on main roads; TfL's MD Streets Management, responsible for implementing bus priority and congestion charging, 2000–03, and awarded transport planner of the year and CBE for services to transport in London; deputy chief executive and director of Network Delivery and Development for the Highways Agency (National Highways) 2005–13, and a consultant from 2013.

Eugenie (Genie) Turton
Senior civil servant, director of GOL 1997–2000, during which time she had prime responsibility for drafting the GLA Act, which created the GLA and TfL; director general for Housing, Planning and Regeneration 2000–04; now holds non-executive roles in the private and charity sectors.

Shashi Verma
Graduate of the Indian Institute of Technology; project manager, The Assam Co. 1993–95; Harvard Kennedy Business School, studying and lecturing on public policy, 1995–99; McKinsey & Co, 1999–2002. He joined TfL as senior principal, Corporate Finance, 2002–06, developing the business case for Crossrail; director of Oyster card, 2006–07; director of Fares and Ticketing 2007–11, pioneering contactless payment; director of Customer Experience, 2011–16; chief technology officer and director of Customer Experience 2016–18; chief technology officer since 2016 and director of Strategy 2018–22.

Jay Walder
American transport executive, grew up and worked in New York for the MTA from 1983 to 1995 in leadership positions, including chief financial officer; Harvard Kennedy Business School lecturer in public policy, 1995–2000; joined TfL as MD Finance and Planning 2001–07; partner, McKinsey London, 2007–09; chair & CEO MTA 2009–11; CEO MTR Hong Kong 2012–14, CEO Motivate 2014; CEO Virgin Hyperloop 2018–21; currently McKinsey senior advisor.

Jeroen Weimar
LSE economic and urban planning graduate; joined TfL as chief of staff to first commissioner Bob Kiley 2001–03; director of Transport Policing and Enforcement 2003–08; COO, Policing and Enforcement 2008–10; Serco's MD Transport 2010–12; First Group,

COO UK Bus 2012–14; left UK to work in Victoria, Australia, in a series of public transport leadership roles; currently secretary to Victoria's Department of Transport and Planning.

Mike Weston
Long career in London bus operations, joining London Transport in 1985, leading on bus contract tender evaluation in 1990s, then bus passenger infrastructure; TfL's director of Bus Operations 2005–13, taking the lead for the New Bus for London project 2008–12; director of Buses 2013–16; currently an independent passenger transport consultant.

Dave Wetzel
After working as a bus conductor and official in the 1960s, Wetzel became political organizer of the London Co-operative Society between 1974 and 1981. Elected as Labour member for Hammersmith and Fulham on the GLC in 1981, and served as chair of the Transport Committee fighting the Fares Fair campaign with Ken Livingstone. Vice chair of TfL 2000 –08, chair of London Buses 2000–01. Wetzel remained an unswerving advocate for Land Value taxation until his death in 2024.

Mark Wild OBE
Electrical engineer and business administration MBA, MD Westinghouse Signals; CEO Public Transport Victoria; TfL's MD London Underground, 2016–18; appointed CEO Crossrail in November 2018, having served on its board since 2017, stood down in May 2022 as the Elizabeth line opened for passengers; CEO SGN, UK gas distribution network, 2022–24; in May 2024 appointed CEO of HS2 Ltd to lead the completion of the railway.

Alex Williams
TFL planner since 2007; director of City Planning, 2017–22; chief Customer and Strategy officer since 2022.

Sir William Wright CBE
Local Unionist politician in Ballymena, Northern Ireland; he joined his father's vehicle body building business in the 1950s and transformed it through his technical vision and business acumen. In collaboration with the Heatherwick Design Studio, Wrightbus built all 1000 of the New Routemaster buses between 2009 and 2016. He died in 2022.

Selected further reading

Theo Barker, *Moving Millions: A Pictorial History of London Transport*, London 1990

Theo Barker and Michael Robbins, *A History of London Transport, Vol.1 The Nineteenth Century*,
 London 1973, revised 1974; Vol. 2 *The Twentieth Century to 1970*, London 1974

Christian Barman, *The Man who Built London Transport: A Biography of Frank Pick*, Exeter 1979

Tony Blair, *A Journey*, London 2010

David Bownes and Oliver Green, *A Century of London Transport Posters*, London 2008

David Bownes, Oliver Green and Sam Mullins, *Underground: How the Tube Shaped London*, London 2012

Jack Brown, *The London Problem: What Britain Gets Wrong About its Capital City*, London 2021

Jack Brown, Tony Travers and Richard Brown, eds., *London's Mayor at 20: Governing a Global City in the 21st
 Century*, London 2020

Colin Buchanan, *Traffic in Towns – The specially shortened edition of the Buchanan Report*, London 1964

Alastair Campbell, *The Blair Years – Extracts from the Alastair Campbell Diaries*, London 2007

John Campbell, *Margaret Thatcher, Volume Two: The Iron Lady*, London 2003

Ken Garland, *Mr Beck's Map*, London 1994

Stephen Glaister, *The London Underground Public Private Partnership 1997–2010: No Way to Run a Railway*,
 Cambridge 2025

Oliver Green and Jeremy Rewse-Davies, *Designed for London: 150 Years of Transport Design*, London 1995

Oliver Green, *Frank Pick's London*, London 2013

Oliver Green, *London's Underground: The Story of the Tube*, London 2023

Dave Hill, *Olympic Park: When Britain Built Something Big*, London 2022

Andrew Hosken, *The Ups and Downs of Ken Livingstone*, London 2008

Jane Jacobs, *The Death and Life of Great American Cities*, New York 1961

Boris Johnson, *Unleashed*, London 2024

Sadiq Khan, *Breathe: Tackling the Climate Emergency* (later subtitled *How to Win a Greener World* and *Seven
 Ways to Win a Greener World*), London 2023

Anthony King and Ivor Crewe, *The Blunders of our Governments*, London 2013

David Lawrence, *A Logo for London*, London 2013

David Lawrence, *Bright Underground Spaces: The London Tube Station Architecture of Charles Holden*, London 2008

David Lawrence, ed., *Omnibus: A Social History of the London Bus*, London 2014

Tony Lewin, *London's New Routemaster*, London 2014

Ken Livingstone, *You Can't Say That*, London 2011

London Transport Museum, *London By Design: The Iconic Transport Designs that Shaped Our City*, London 2016

Dennis Lovett, *The North London Railway 1846–2001*, Clophill 2001

Andrew Martin, *Seats of London: A Field Guide to London Transport Moquette Patterns*, London 2019

Martin J. H. Mogridge, *Travel in Towns: Jam Yesterday, Jam Today and Jam Tomorrow?* London 1990

Ray Orton, *Moving People: From Street to Platform*, London 2000

John Prescott with Hunter Davies, *Prezza: My Story: Pulling No Punches*, London 2008

Sonia Purnell, *Just Boris – A Tale of Blond Ambition*, London 2012

Nick Raynsford, *Substance Not Spin: An Insider's View of Success and Failure in Government*, Bristol 2016

Anthony Seldon and Raymond Newell, *Johnson at 10: The Inside Story*, London 2023

Anthony Seldon, ed., *Blair's Britain*, Cambridge 2007

Richard Taylor, *Edward Johnston: A Signature for London*, Lewes 2016

Roger Torode, *Privatising London's Buses*, London 2015

Transport for London, *The London Games in Motion*, 2013

Jerry White, *London in the Twentieth Century: A City and its People*, London 2001

James Whiting, Gavin Booth, Stewart J. Brown et al., *Boris's Bus: The Mayor's New Routemaster*, London 2013

Jon Willis, *Extending the Jubilee line: The Planning Story*, London 1997

Jonathan Willis, *The Railways of London Docklands: Their History and Development*, Barnsley 2022

Christian Wolmar, *The Story of Crossrail*, London 2018; updated and expanded edition retitled as *Crossrail:
 The Whole Story*, London 2022

Index

Images on cover and opening chapters

front cover: The Elizabeth line at Liverpool Street station, designed by Grimshaw

back cover: Heavy traffic on Regent Street, central London

pages 2–3: The Elizabeth line at Farringdon station, designed by Grimshaw

page 8: Traffic in Regent Street, 28 June 2017

page 16: The Central line at Bank station during the morning peak in the 1990s

page 40: Ken Livingstone faces the media pack as London mayor, December 2000

page 68: Poster illustrating TfL's first major project, the transformation of Trafalgar Square, autumn 2002

page 90: Commuters pour over London Bridge past long queues of traffic

page 114: Chair of the London Olympics, Sebastian Coe, and Mayor Livingstone with a sombre crowd at the Trafalgar Square vigil held on 14 July 2005 for the victims of the 7/7 terrorist bombings

page 144: Bus conductor Agatha Claudette Hart in 1962 with her Gibson ticket machine for issuing paper tickets in exchange for a cash bus fare

page 174: A DLR train approaches Canary Wharf across the Thames, 1988

page 196: A TfL staff member accompanying a passenger at Stratford station in 2021

page 218: An explanatory TfL Tube upgrade campaign poster in 2011

page 282: Stratford station as passengers arrive at and depart from the Olympic stadium assisted by Games Makers and magenta signage, September 2012

page 308: Cycle Superhighway CS8, between Wandsworth and Westminster, opened in July 2011

page 332: The Elizabeth line at Farringdon station, designed by Grimshaw

page 366: Sadiq Khan, first elected as London's mayor in May 2016

page 396: TfL kept services running throughout the pandemic, though few could use them

Photo credits

front cover: TfL/Nick Turpin; *back cover:* TfL/Eleanor Bentall; *endpapers:* Courtesy Wallace Sewell/TfL; 2–3, 363, 408 top, 420 TfL/Nick Turpin; 4 Iakov Kalinin/Dreamstime.com; 169 top left, 217, 223, 249, 376, 390, 396, 407, 408, 410 below TfL/Eleanor Bentall; 16, 90 RichardBaker/Alamy Stock Photo; 18, 20, 55, 77, 83, 134 left, 144, 146, 148, 151, 152, 158, 176, 179, 188 below, 193, 202, 262, 284, 319, 342 © TfL from the London Transport Museum collection; 21 Fox Photos/Hulton Archive/Getty Images; 33, 53, 66, 122, 136–137, 265, 310, 352–353, 384 top PA Images/Alamy Stock Photo; 36, 134 right Trinity Mirror/Mirrorpix/Alamy Stock Photo; 39 Martin Godwin/Getty Images; 40, 101 left Independent/Alamy Stock Photo; 43 The Sunday Times/News Licensing; 56 Mark Graham/Dreamstime.com; 65, 107, 254 © Courtesy of the London Communications Agency, Robert Gordon Clark and Martin Rowson; 68 Image from the London Transport Museum collection. Courtesy OTM (UK) Ltd, now part of Definition Group Ltd.; 8, 75, 81,101 right, 162 right, 169 below right, 183, 196, 200, 203, 208, 231, 271, 282, 295, 300 right, 302–303, 305, 313 right, 315, 332, 336–337, 338, 346 top, 360–361, 379, 381, 382, 384 below, 389, 400–401, 419 © TfL; 82 Image from the London Transport Museum collection. Courtesy Oscar Wilson; 93 top The London Archives; 93 below Evening Standard/Hulton Archive/Getty Images; 95 Leonard Burt/Central Press/Hulton Archive/Getty Images; 110, 117 The Standard Ltd; 114 Jeremy Hoare/Alamy Stock Photo; 121 top, 127 Associated Press/Alamy Stock Photo; 121 below Metropolitan Police/Getty Images; 141 Jon Ratcliffe/Alamy Stock Photo; 143 Vehbi Koca/Alamy Stock Photo; 156 © Roger Torode; 162 left James Monroe Adams IV; 169 top right, below left, 270, 317 TfL/Mike Garnett; 174 Patrickwang/Dreamstime.com; 177 Heritage Image Partnership Ltd/Alamy Stock Photo; 181 Christopher Pillitz/In Pictures Ltd./Corbis/Getty Images; 182 Brian Harris/Alamy Stock Photo; 185 Ian Brown; 188 top, 218 Image from the London Transport Museum collection; 198 left G.P.Essex/Alamy Stock Photo; 198 right Marion Bull/Alamy Stock Photo; 206 TfL/Ross Holdstock; 244 TfL/M+C Saatchi; 250 Peter Macdiarmid/Getty Images; 263 Courtesy Go–Ahead; 280 Andrew Walters/Alamy Stock Photo; 285 Avalon/Construction Photography/Alamy Stock Photo; 286 Graeme Robertson/Getty Images; 289 Getty Images for London 2012; 291 Frank Coppi/Popperfoto via Getty Images/Getty Images; 299 TfL/Darren Ruane; 300 left Amanda Waite/Shutterstock; 308 © ConstructionPhotography.com/TfL; 313 left PjrNews/Alamy Stock Photo; 314 petererikforsberg/Alamy Stock Photo; 321 left Chris Mouyiaris/Dreamstime.com; 321 right Petrajz/Dreamstime.com; 322 Mark Thomas/Shutterstock; 326 Courtesy Heatherwick Studio. Render by Arup; 335 Andrew Holt/Alamy Stock Photo; 346 below TfL/Chris BevanLee; 355 TfL/James O Jenkins; 357, 359 TfL/John Zammit; 364 Leon Neal/Getty Images; 366, 415 Greater London Authority/Caroline Teo; 372 Greater London Authority/Four Agency Worldwide; 374 Jeff Gilbert/Alamy Stock Photo; 391, 403 TfL/Luca Marino

Endpapers

The iconic Barman Moquette by Wallace Sewell (Harriet Wallace-Jones and Emma Sewell), originally designed for the Central, Northern, Piccadilly and Jubilee lines and recoloured for use on the Bakerloo line in 2015.